外研社

新GRE写作5.5

最新修订版

李建林 著

外语教学与研究出版社
FOREIGN LANGUAGE TEACHING AND RESEARCH PRESS
北京 BEIJING

图书在版编目 (CIP) 数据

新 GRE 写作 5.5 / 李建林著. — 修订本. — 北京：外语教学与研究出版社，2011.9
（2018.11 重印）
ISBN 978-7-5135-1372-2

Ⅰ. ①新… Ⅱ. ①李… Ⅲ. ①GRE-写作-自学参考资料 Ⅳ. ①H315

中国版本图书馆 CIP 数据核字 (2011) 第 202027 号

出 版 人　蔡剑峰
责任编辑　王　晶　陈嘉宁
装帧设计　赵　欣
出版发行　外语教学与研究出版社
社　　址　北京市西三环北路 19 号（100089）
网　　址　http://www.fltrp.com
印　　刷　北京市鑫霸印务有限公司
开　　本　787×1092　1/16
印　　张　36.5
版　　次　2011 年 10 月第 1 版　2018 年 11 月第 10 次印刷
书　　号　ISBN 978-7-5135-1372-2
定　　价　59.00 元

购书咨询：（010）88819926　电子邮箱：club@fltrp.com
外研书店：https://waiyants.tmall.com
凡印刷、装订质量问题，请联系我社印制部
联系电话：（010）61207896　电子邮箱：zhijian@fltrp.com
凡侵权、盗版书籍线索，请联系我社法律事务部
举报电话：（010）88817519　电子邮箱：banquan@fltrp.com
法律顾问：立方律师事务所　刘旭东律师
　　　　　中咨律师事务所　殷　斌律师
物料号：213720001

目　录

上篇：ISSUE

下篇：ARGUMENT

前 言

（修订版）

　　2011年8月份以后，GRE考试内容和考试方式都出现了较大变化。这使得这本《GRE写作5.5》的修订成为必然。

　　新GRE考试在语文、数学和作文三个方面都有变化，其中语文和作文这两个部分变化较大。语文部分更强调语言的实际应用能力，而作文部分则更侧重考查考生的逻辑思辨和推理论证能力。

　　总体来讲，改革后的新GRE作文考试给人的感觉是：**应试压力大为减轻，但难度略有增加。**

　　具体而言，新GRE作文主要有以下几个方面的变化：

　　第一，题库中的题目数量大大减少。

　　之前的GRE作文题库中，ISSUE有244道题，而ARGUMENT有242道题。现在ISSUE的题目总量减少到149题，而ARGUMENT也缩至174题。而且，在新GRE作文题库中，无论是ISSUE还是ARGUMENT都有大量这样的题目：完全一样或高度类似，区别仅在于每个作文题目后的写作指引（Instructions）有所不同。但有意思的是，按照本书所提供的针对ISSUE和ARGUMENT的分析思路，这些题目完全可以归并为一道题或一组题来准备（这也是本书所提供的题库压缩的方法之一）；如此一来，作文题目总量实际上又进一步减少了。经过本书的**题库压缩**后，ISSUE的题量变为53道左右，减少了60%以上；而ARGUMENT也减少了一半多，变为85道题左右。相比过去，考生复习备考的压力无疑减轻了许多。

　　第二，出题方式发生较大变化。

　　正如上面已经提到的，新GRE作文每道题目后面都有一个写作指引，考生必须按照指引来写。这是旧GRE作文从未出现过的。所有ISSUE题目共计有六种不同的写作指引，ARGUMENT有八个。每个ISSUE和ARGUMENT作文题目的写作指引分别是这六个和八个中的一个。这些指引为作文题目提出了具体的分析方向和写作要求。这对那些复习时间极短或者考试临场一时找不到写作感觉的考生来说，算是一个写作的引导。因此，也可以说，这在一定程度上缓解了考生备考的压力。

　　第三，ISSUE的写作时间和考题数量都有减少。

　　这个变化增加了新GRE作文的难度。之前，考生在考场上可以从两道ISSUE题目中选择自己更有把握的一道，在45分钟之内完成ISSUE作文。现在，考生只有一道ISSUE题目可选，写作时间也缩至30分钟。ARGUMENT没有变化，依然是一道题目，限时30分钟之内完成。

对于中国考生来说，GRE作文之所以难，主要难在ISSUE。ISSUE作文题目二减一，这不是大问题。关键是写作时间减少到30分钟，这是个不小的压力。

根据ETS（美国教育考试服务中心）所提供的新版ISSUE范文以及笔者本人多年的英文写作经验来看，要想在一篇ISSUE作文中把自己的观点阐述清楚并得到不错的分数，正文的字数不应低于450词，其长度大约是标准页面设置的Word文档的一页再加30个词左右。这对相当一部分中国考生都会是一个挑战。这无形中是要求考生：首先，对自己手里的ISSUE题目必须很熟悉，思路要非常清晰、流畅，基本没有多少边写边想的余地；第二，语言表达要求高了。考生要做到下笔流畅、一气呵成才行，因为你很可能没有修改和润色的时间。这实际是对考生的语法、拼写、句式和行文结构等提出了更高的要求。

而且，在加上了写作指引之后，ISSUE和ARGUMENT作文虽然有了明确的分析和写作方向，但这些指引同时也是对考生写作思路的限制。对那些水平较高的考生更是如此。以前，只要做到不跑题，考生完全可以天马行空般挥洒自己的想象力和才情。ISSUE只要言之成理、持之有据，ARGUMENT只要找到两三个逻辑漏洞，就行了。但有了这些写作指引，情况就大不相同了。

例如，针对"建议类ISSUE题目"（这里的"建议类"是笔者对ISSUE题目所做分类的一种，不是ETS的分类），考生必须按照写作指引的要求去分析题目中的建议所可能带来的后果和利弊；针对一些"事实类ISSUE题目"，考生则必须分析题目中对立或矛盾的两个观点。而至于ARGUMENT，这些指引的要求就更加具体了，比如考生要分析题目中的推论哪些地方需要补充进一步的证据，题目中的建议或预测及其推理依据有哪些疑问，对题目中所列举的现象可否有更为合理的解释，题目中的论证过程是否建立在了一系列不可靠的假设之上，等等。

对比旧GRE写作，不难看出这些写作指引强调的是**不同论证条件下的逻辑思辨和推理论证能力**，远不如过去让考生论证一下自己的新颖观点和找出几个逻辑漏洞那么简单了。

所以说，新GRE作文看似压力减轻，实则难度略增。

不过，考生完全没必要因此而恐慌。本书所提供的独具特色的**"1+5"写作模型**（即一个写作套路加上五种题目分析类型）和**十大论证技巧**可以让考生轻松掌握解剖ISSUE和ARGUMENT的路径，并且在整个备考过程中体验ISSUE和ARGUMENT两种不同写作任务之间互联相通的乐趣。

之前的绝大部分GRE考生实际上是把ISSUE和ARGUMENT这两项写作任务分开来准备的。他们普遍将更多的备考精力放在ISSUE上，认为ARGUMENT更简单，只要找几个逻辑漏洞就可以了。但现在有了具体的写作指引之后，这样做就不妥了。对于ISSUE，现在当然还要按照写作指引展开立论和论证；对ARGUMENT，也要依照指引**论证**题目中结论的欠缺和不足，仅仅指出两三个逻辑漏洞显然已不符合要求。ARGUMENT和ISSUE这两者间的攻与守、破与立的相通之处就是**论证法**或者说**推理依据**。读者在阅读本书的具体过程中，对此自然将心领神会。

另外，鉴于ISSUE和ARGUMENT作文在出题方式以及题库方面的变化（其中包括了一些过去不曾出现过的全新ISSUE和ARGUMENT题目），笔者已将ISSUE和ARGUMENT题库中的所有题目重新分析一遍，并为每一道题目附上了更为详细的分析过程和更为完备的写作提纲。相信这些也会大大缓解考生的备考压力。

同本书的第一版一样，这本修订版的构想和撰写也是在许多学生和读者（其中两位是正在准备出国考试的年轻大学教师）的鼓励和督促下开始的。最先提醒我一定要尽快写出修订版的就是其中的两位学生和一位老师。他们本来是本书第一版的读者，但因为必须要在今年8月份以后考GRE，所以迫切需要本书的修订版。我们多数只是通过电子邮件往来沟通，部分读者甚至至今没有告诉我他们的姓名。但他们的关切和鼓励给了我很大的动力，最终促使我下定决心暂时搁下手头的一切，尽快完成修订版。谢谢他们！

当然，我还要感谢外语教学与研究出版社测试工作室主任陈海燕和责任编辑陈嘉宁。她们的年度工作安排中原本没有这本修订版的出版计划，但为满足考生和读者的急切需要，依然克服困难，多方协调，勉力推进。

所有这些努力与付出，只要能对读者有所帮助，则我心甚慰矣。

李建林

2011年5月于北京通州寓所

前 言
（第一版）

要写一本有关GRE写作用书的念头开始在我头脑里转悠已经是一年前的事情了。

去年的1月21日，美国的教育考试服务中心（Educational Testing Service），也就是大家所熟知的ETS，宣布取消64位来自中国和韩国的考生的GRE综合考试成绩，理由是这些人的作文考试有作弊行为。为证明这个结论属实，ETS开列出了他们的三大罪状：

第一，段落及句子中语言近似，文章的结构雷同。

第二，文章中出现了已发表的作品的句子和例证。

第三，这些学生没能给出他们自己的思想及事例以阐释他们的批判性思维（critical thinking）。

这三条罪状至少在一部分GRE考生身上是事实。而且，背诵所谓的文章开头和结尾的套路、多人共用写作模板，在当时曾一度被奉为GRE作文获得高分的捷径。这种风气发展到最后，部分学生上GRE培训班的目的干脆就简化成了从老师那里获得一个一劳永逸的套路或模板。今天看来，真是"成也萧何，败也萧何"。

那么，我们该怎么办呢？

ETS在发布上述取消64位GRE考生成绩决定的同时，对什么是他们所希望看到的作文说得非常明白：

其一，"...test takers must realize that graduate education community in the United States values most highly the ability of students to **develop their own perspectives in analytical essays**."（考生必须清楚，美国的研究生教育机构最看重学生在他们的分析性写作中所显示出的**提出自己观点的能力**。）

其二，"The graduate community also values students who can illustrate through their essays not just how thoroughly they **memorize and recall citations**, but how much **original thinking** they do to show how they differ from their fellow test takers."（研究生教育机构同样看重这些学生：他们在文章中展示的**不是**多么善于**背诵名篇佳句**，而是他们提出了多少**创见**从而显示了其卓尔不群。）

很明显，要想在GRE作文中取得高分，考生必须要将主要精力放在对文章进行自己独到的分析和论证上，也就是说，考生必须要展示自己的"思想"。而且，这个事件也说明，今后所有GRE作文的培训也不得不将重点转移到对学生分析、论证能力的启发和培养上。否则，很可能要么是南辕北辙，徒走弯路；要么是隔靴搔痒，不得要领。

在当时，我非常清楚地觉察到GRE考生需要一本全新的教材。

同年的寒假期间，我开始在北京新东方学校的GRE班上讲授ISSUE写作。当时，我一反几乎所有GRE写作老师的惯常做法，不给学生提供任何所谓的套路，不教他们如何去背诵华盛顿、哥白尼、爱因斯坦等名人的事迹，也不为他们列举什么灵验的句型，我只教他们如何识别ISSUE作文题目中的分析切入点，如何对题目中的价值判断展开自己的分析，以及如何对题目中的关键概念作自己独特的界定。

在当时ETS取消64位GRE考生成绩事件给众多同学带来的疑惑和浮躁中，这种教学思路的效果颇具戏剧性。

一部分同学觉得理解起来有困难，认为这些不是他们所要的；另外一部分同学异常兴奋，觉得自己大有茅塞顿开之感。其中有几位在外地已经上过GRE班的同学说，直到听完我的课之后，才知道该如何驾驭ISSUE写作。

其实，撇开学生的反应不说，根据自己多年从事英文评论写作的经验和对ETS取消64位GRE考生成绩所传达信息的实事求是的解读，我坚信：自己的做法也许是唯一真正有效的办法。

GRE作文的本质是考查我们对复杂问题的分析能力、论证能力和对推理/论证中的逻辑错误和漏洞的识别能力。不谈这些内容的话都是在隔靴搔痒；避开这些核心内容的教学很可能在误人前程，是在拿考生的拼搏以及他们父母的血汗钱当儿戏。 因为，没有这些能力的话，我们就必然感觉到头脑里没有"思想"；没有"思想"，GRE的两篇作文，尤其是ISSUE作文，是根本写不下去的！

所以，任何写作理论，如果不能告诉读者如何展开自己的分析，从而获得自己的写作思路，其实都没用。问题就这么简单。

寒假班结束不久，SARS病毒光顾中国大江南北。不得已，大家都在家中躲避"非典"。对我来说，这恰是一段难得的时间。我开始系统整理寒假班的讲义。8个月后，就有了呈现在大家面前的这本书的初稿。

在动手写这本书的时候，我给自己定的要求是：**以最简单、最系统、最直接的办法，解决GRE作文最核心的难题。**

就ISSUE写作而言，最核心的难题有三个，即拿到题目之后，感觉**没内容可写、写不长、写得不漂亮**。现在大家只要把书翻到目录部分，一眼就可以看出，针对这些难题的解决方法就是本书的核心内容。

去年5月间，在本书写作最为紧张的时候，我收到三位同学发来的电子邮件，告诉我他们去年3月份"考G"的作文成绩：一位5分，两位5.5分。自然，每人少不了说些感激的话。其实他们不必太感谢我。我批改过他们的作文。在给他们作文的评语中，我就说过他们欠缺的其实不是语言能力，而是思考和分析能力。一旦有了自己的分析和写作思路，他们每人的成绩都应该在5分以上。我充其量是交给了他们一些分析和思考的方法而已。

实际上，对于80％以上的GRE考生，情况也大多如此。他们的GRE写作所遇到的难题不在于知识方面的欠缺（所谓理工科学生缺乏文科知识的说法其实是似是而非的），更不在语言表达上。他们欠缺的是针对GRE写作题目，尤其是对ISSUE题目的分析能力。

这套书现在是由ISSUE分册和ARGUMENT分册两部分组成。这样做会使考生购买教材和复习更方便一些。大家可以根据自己的需要选购教材，集中复习ISSUE写作或者ARGUMENT写作。但考生需要注意的是，GRE作文对考生分析和思辨能力的考查在ISSUE和ARGUMENT两篇作文中都有一贯的体现和要求，只是角度不同而已。本套书的撰写也强调了这一点，大家在阅读时对此会有所体会。

在本套书由起初的构思，到后来的撰写，直至最终付印的过程中，许多人都曾给予过我极大的支持与鼓励。

首先，我要感谢北京新东方学校国外考试部的王海波主任。从一开始我到北京新东方学校讲授GRE作文，到后来本书的撰写，海波都给了我无私的帮助，包括对我授课技巧的建议和撰写本书的督促与鼓励。他是我一位难得的朋友。

其次，我想感谢我的学生们。从他们那里，我意识到了本书真正应该写些什么。尤其是部分同学，比如清华大学的赵明同学以及武汉大学、南京大学和浙江大学的几位同学，在我讲课过程中以及课程结束后，不断给我来信，表示对我讲课内容和风格的理解与支持。没有他们的理解与支持，恐怕我会放弃或者至少推迟本书的写作。

在现有的时间和资源条件下撰写本书，我已经付出了最大的努力，但恐本书仍有疏漏之处，企盼各位同学与同行给予批评和指正。希望本书能对所有正跋涉在光荣与梦想之旅上的人们有所帮助。

李建林

2004年3月3日于北京竹茗园

绪 论

新GRE考试分为写作（Analytical Writing）、语文（Verbal）和数学（Quantitative）三部分。其中，写作由两篇作文构成，即ISSUE部分和ARGUMENT部分。前者要求考生在30分钟内，就一个话题（ISSUE）表明自己的观点，并给出充分的论证；后者要求考生在30分钟内，对一段推理/论证作一番评估，指出其推理和论证过程中的缺陷（关于GRE作文评分方式、评分标准及ETS提供的ISSUE和ARGUMENT范文，请参见本书附录7）。

毫无疑问，对于绝大多数国内考生而言，在GRE写作、语文和数学三部分考试中，写作是头等难题。一般而言，利用半年时间复习准备，GRE语文和数学部分都能得到令人满意的成绩。而花费同样长、甚至是更长的时间去准备GRE作文，效果却往往难以预料。多数同学只能拿到满分6分中的4.5分、4分，甚至更差的成绩。这样的作文成绩在欧美院校的奖学金申请者中，是位居中下的，这同中国考生普遍较高的语文和数学成绩相比，实在不协调。这实际上凸显了一个显而易见的疑问：既然语文能得如此高的分数，为什么作文的表现却平平呢？

GRE写作之难，难在ISSUE。

对于所有考生而言，ARGUMENT写作要相对容易些。这是因为ARGUMENT难点在于对题目中的推理/论证错误的识别。考生只要掌握了常见的论证技巧和一般的推理技能，就能很快对题目展开自己的分析；剩下的不过就是文章上下文的起承转合与衔接过渡的问题。相当一部分考生的ARGUMENT作文的成绩可得5分，可是ISSUE作文仅仅得3或4分。而GRE写作的成绩是两者的平均值，所以最后依然是4分或4.5分。

那么，ISSUE之难，难在哪里呢？

具体而言，难在以下几方面：

第一，思路的问题（也就是头脑里没有"思想"的问题）：

拿到ISSUE题目之后，头脑空空没有思路，不知道该想些什么、该写些什么，即**感觉没内容可写。**

第二，展开论证的问题：

总算找到了若干思路要点，可不知道如何展开论述，甚至有了提纲之后仍一筹莫展，即**感觉写不长。**

第三，文章结构和语言的问题：

结构呆板：文章的开头、结尾过于套路化，正文部分的段落没有节奏感。

语言抽象、生涩、枯燥：语言表意僵硬，读起来像是在嚼隔夜的馒头。

句型单一、句子冗长乏味：句子结构很少变化；片面理解了长句的重要性，以至于生搬硬套长句，句子充满了套话、废话以及单调的定语从句、状语从句和名词性从句。

总结起来，考生的ISSUE写作有三大令人头痛的问题：**感觉没内容可写、写不长、写得不漂亮**。其中最最要命的是怎么解决考生脑子空空、没内容可写的问题。

学生面对的另外一个大难题是**题库的问题**。面对ISSUE新题库中的149道题，学生即使是一天写一篇ISSUE作文，那也是近五个月的时间！而许多考生只能拿出半年来准备整个GRE考试。

对于以上这些问题，现有的所有GRE写作教材都没能很好解决。有的教材干脆回避这些问题，只给学生提供些写作提纲了事。但学生的核心问题是：即使有了提纲，仍然不知道该怎么写，因为**他们根本不知道那些提纲是怎么分析出来的**。对此，该怎么办呢？

着力解决上述核心难题正是本书的特点。

首先，考生之所以感觉没有思路，不知道该想些什么、该写些什么，本质上是因为考生不善分析，**找不到分析题目的切入点**。

对此，本书提出的应对策略是："1+5"写作模型，即：**一个写作套路加上五种题目分析类型及每一类型题目各自的分析切入点**。

一个写作套路是指在文章的正文部分，分正、反两方面展开写作的行文思路或结构。所有ISSUE题目中的观点在一定程度上都是可以赞同的，但肯定也有反对的余地。所以，每个ISSUE题目都可从正、反两方面展开分析。

五种题目分析类型是指因果类、建议类、是非类、定义类和事实类五种题目类型。所有的ISSUE题目都可归入这些题目类型。每种题目类型又都有自己的分析切入点。**由这些分析切入点着手，考生能很快发现自己的写作思路，整理出提纲及写作框架**。也就是说，"1+5"写作模型重在帮助考生学会分析，从而发现自己关于ISSUE题目的观点和"思想"。

至于ISSUE作文写不长，其关键症结是考生不会展开有效的论证。试想，如果一篇议论文只有孤零零的几个要点，没有充分的论证，这篇文章是不可能写长的。而本书所提供的**填入式论证法**所涵盖的**十大论证技巧**和**十一个论证角度**，可以使论证像做文字填空游戏一样轻松。而有了充分的论证之后，文章自然就血肉丰满、观点充实。那时，考生所要考虑的将不再是如何写长，而是如何恰到好处地控制文章的长度。

另一个造成考生文章写不长的原因与写作习惯有关。本书将这一点放在第三章重点讲解。

再来看文章的结构和语言的问题。

对于大多数考生而言，造成他们文章写出来之后感觉晦涩、别扭的主要原因不在他们英语表达能力差，而在于他们不良的语言表达习惯。而这些不良语言表达习惯的形成，往往又是因为一些似是而非的流行观念的影响。

比如，有一种颇为流行的观点认为，在GRE作文中要尽量写长句。似乎句子越长，水平就越高，学问也越大，作文就容易得高分。于是，就有学生为了把句子拉长，不惜往里面填充废话、套话，造出稀奇古怪的句子；也有人去费尽心机地搞什么开头、结尾的套路。这些套路甚至细化到了句型和词的选择。

类似这些做法都很容易窒息语言的活力和作者的想象力，产生了大量僵硬、死板、高度雷同化的语言和文章结构。

ETS的确提到过GRE作文语言的规范化和句型/句式的复杂多变的问题。但是，难道规范化的语言和复杂多变的句型就等于酸文假醋的长句子？

笔者可以负责任地说，任何真正领悟了语言（包括各种形式的现代语言）精神实质的人都会排斥那些冗长、套路化的语言。大家如果以为美国的教授们可能会喜欢较长的段落和句子，那就请翻一翻*Science*和*Nature*这两本权威的西方自然科学杂志，看那里面文章的句子和段落是否很长。

而且，这种做法在ETS于2003年1月21日以64位来自中国和韩国的考生作文出现语言和文章结构高度雷同而取消其GRE考试成绩后，实际已走到穷途末路。考生实在没必要再去碰这根高压线。

那么，到底什么是好的语言？

很简单，**好的语言就是写作风格人性化的语言**。一般而言，人性所固有的特点（如喜欢新奇）以及现代生活的快节奏使得人们不愿意花时间、精力去读那些晦涩、枯燥的长句；人们大都偏爱多变化、富有节奏感的段落和句子。那些给你改作文的人，每天都要批改大量的作文。你给他们读那些千篇一律的内容、故作艰深的长句、呆板僵硬的段落，岂不是自寻死路？

请记住：好的段落和句子永远有三个特点：清楚、简洁、多变。

清楚的意思是句子表情达意准确，不引起歧义；简洁的意思是句子简单、明了，能用五个单词表达的意思，决不用六个单词；多变的意思是句子的长度、句型结构、段落的长短要交叉变化。句子以较短的句子为主，但长短句要结合使用，不能要么都是长句，要么都是如同儿童写的短句。各种句型应该交替变换使用，不能要么就一直是简单句，要么就一直是复合句、复杂句。段落的长度、语气也要交替变化。

剩下的一个难题便是如何对付庞大的ISSUE题库。本书所提供的办法是：**题库压缩**。

虽然ISSUE作文题库庞大，但许多题目所涉及的内容、分析思路是完全一样或高度类似的。而且，部分题目之间也有着彼此补充、相互佐证的特点。据此，我们可以将那些彼此有关联的题目归入一组，整理出它们之间要点的一致性和参照性。这样，同一组的三道、五道、甚至十余道题都可被视为一或两道题。解决了这一或两道题，同一组的其他题只要稍加变通，也就迎刃而解了。

ISSUE题库中所有149道题目经过压缩之后，能减少到53道题（或者说组）左右。考生结合自己的情况，还可以将题目总量进一步压缩。这样一来，最后考生手里的ISSUE题目就不应是单个出现的，而是成组出现的。只要将每一组中一两个题的分析思路、论证要点整理出来，这一组其余的题目不过就是删减和拼加的工作而已，从而大大减轻了复习的工作量。

总体说来，本书就是通过四大策略，即**"1+5"写作模型、填入式论证法、人性化写作风格、题库压缩**，来破解ISSUE作文的。

正如前文已经提到过的，相对于ISSUE作文，ARGUMENT作文准备起来相对容易些。而且，ARGUMENT作文本身的特点也使我们完全可以以最简单、最直截了当的办法将其攻克。

ARGUMENT作文写作中的关键问题在于**题目中的推理/论证错误和缺陷难以识别**。然而实际上，这些推理/论证错误都比较简单。我们依靠自己的生活常识就能把它们一一解决。部分同学因为恐惧ARGUMENT作文中逻辑问题的难度，专门找来讲解形式逻辑的教材来加强这方面的知识。其实完全没有必要。

从本质上讲，**每个ARGUMENT题目都是一个论证的过程：其中有观点，有论据。**这个从论据到论点的论证过程中会出现诸多有问题的逻辑链条。我们的任务只有一个：从两到三个方面证明题目在哪些逻辑链条上出了问题，从而导致其论据不足以支持其论点和结论。

为此，本书下篇的ARGUMENT部分系统讲述了：

1．十大论证技巧及反驳切入点；

2．论证过程中常见的逻辑漏洞诊断。

掌握了这些论证的反驳切入点和推理/论证谬误的诊断技巧之后，大家将发现识别ARGUMENT题目中的推理/论证错误实在是件非常轻松的事情。

到此，ARGUMENT的写作实际上分两步即告完成：第一步，识别ARGUMENT题目中的推理/论证缺陷和谬误，每个缺陷和谬误都是正文部分的一个写作要点，而且这个要点要以主题句的形式居于段首；第二步，做好正文各要点的展开分析以及各要点间的起承转合与衔接过渡，然后，在它们的前面和后面分别加上开头段和结尾段。

另外，本书还提供了新版ISSUE题库中所有题目的分析指要和新版ARGUMENT题库中所有题目的分析指要。前者涵盖了新版ISSUE题库中所有题目的归类、分析提示及写作提纲；后者涵盖了新版ARGUMENT题库中所有题目推理/论证缺陷和谬误的分析提示。这两部分不仅仅告诉大家每道题目的分析结果，而且还告诉大家这些分析结果是怎么得来的。作为大家分析ISSUE和ARGUMENT题目的参考，相信会有较大的帮助。

最后，有一个GRE作文复习准备的误区有必要在这里提一下。

部分考生为了应付写的时候脑子里面没有"思想"这一问题，采取了背诵范文/例文/句型的办法。坦率地说，这是一条死胡同。

如果你计划用三四年，甚至更多的时间使自己的英语水平从整体上有一个较大的提高，背诵经典文章或经典段落的做法也许值得一试。但如果你总共只有半年或一年的时间，而集中准备作文仅占用你所有准备时间的三分之一的话，用背诵范文的办法往大脑里填充思想和提高语言水平的方式则是求败之道。

首先，你没有那么多时间去背诵文章。单词和各种GRE真题已经令人几乎无暇顾及，遑论文章？其次，你很难有那么顽强的毅力在短时间内背诵足够多的文章，毕竟机械背诵已不再是成年人的强项。其三，即便背下那些文章，你果真能把它们用到自己的文章中去吗？语言是用来表达思想的。我们把一篇文章中的语句套用到另一篇文章中去，实际在假设这两个地方要表达几乎同样的思想、情绪和语气等。试问，这种可能性有多大？

而且，GRE写作考试过程中，面对时间压力，除非你所遇到的作文题目恰好就是你已经全文写过的，否则，你的写作切入点和思路发展都是在现有的提纲和平时训练的基础上稍加组织后，在上下文环环相扣、一气呵成之中完成的。考场上那种比较紧张的环境很可能会打乱你所背诵的文章中的既定思路，使你的头脑一片茫然。

更何况万一自己背的材料别人也背过，很多人的作文相似，因而被ETS判为作弊，成绩被取消，岂非得不偿失？

真正的取胜之道其实不难做到，就两个字：多写。

先说文章的开头和结尾。

本书分别提供了一些不同风格的ISSUE和ARGUMENT作文开头和结尾的方式。大家可以根据自己的喜好和风格，同时兼顾文章内容的特点，选择若干自己擅长的文章开头和结尾的方式。然后，ISSUE和ARGUMENT各选十道题目，专门练习写它们的开头和结尾段。这样一两遍下来之后，一般就会形成自己特定的文章开头和结尾的写作习惯。进一步熟练之后，对任何题目大家都可以非常轻松地完成文章的开头和结尾。

再说文章的正文部分。

正文部分完全是文章作者思想的集中展现。对于ISSUE作文来说，作者的思想体现在对题目所涉及问题独到的分析和论证上；对于ARGUMENT作文来说，作者的思想体现在对题目中的推理/论证缺陷和谬误的识别与分析。

有一点是显而易见的：人们总是先在头脑中形成思想，然后才能落笔写出文字。我们感觉没内容可写，根源在于头脑中没有思想；感觉表达得不清晰、混乱，是因为头脑中的思想本来就是混沌纷乱的。先有思想、后有语言的顺序是永远无法颠倒的。否则，你就是背上千万篇文章，一旦别人让你表达一下自己的思想，你除了照搬别人的以外，依然是头脑空空，不知所云。

写好 ISSUE 和 ARGUMENT 的第一步是学会分析和思考，这是本书贯穿始终的精神。

　　针对 ISSUE 作文，本书所提供的办法是：利用"1+5"写作模型整理出文章的思路和写作框架，然后利用本书独具特色的**题库压缩技巧**，选择有代表性的题目，开始练笔。

　　但是，多练习写作不等于动笔就是整篇文章。起初，你可以只练习某些关键概念及复杂思想的表达，然后再练写正文若干要点和分要点的展开和论证、上下文的转折过渡、直至整个段落和整篇文章的写作。如此点面结合、有所侧重的练习会使你既感觉轻松，又能很快看到自己写作水平的提高。

　　对于 ARGUMENT 也是一样，而且练习的过程会更简单，取得的效果会更明显。

　　这是因为，尽管 ARGUMENT 题库中有 174 道题，但所有的题目所包含的无非就是对应**十大论证方式的反驳切入点**和本书所列的**十五个典型推理/论证漏洞**。你也许只需选择十道左右代表这些论证方式和典型推理错误的 ARGUMENT 题目，专门练习对不同论证方式的反驳、对典型错误的分析、上下文的转折过渡，直到整个段落和整篇文章的写作。（注意：那些逻辑术语，比如 *Post Hoc, Non Sequitur* 等，可用也可不用，用通俗的语言表达出来即可。比如，你可以不说：The arguer commits a *Post Hoc* fallacy. 而说：This is a false causation/cause-effect reasoning. 不说：The person has made a *Non Sequitur* mistake. 而 说：The person's reasoning does not follow/mean/indicate that...）

　　当然，大家写得越多，也就越能找到挥洒自如之感。这是因为，**只有自己写出来的思想和语言才是自己的思想和语言**。通过背诵来寻找思想和提高语言水平实际上是在时间紧迫的前提下，又绕了个远道。考试当前，我们要做的是对现有分析能力和语言表达能力的熟练和优化，而不是在短时间内，通过背诵来突击上个大台阶。更何况，**由笔者所批改过的学生作文来看，绝大部分同学所缺乏的不是语言表达能力，而是分析和论证能力。**

　　除了有计划、有针对性地多写之外，还有两个帮助我们提高分析和写作能力的辅助性手段：读和说。

　　虽然读和背都是在摄入信息，但在这两个过程之中，人们所关注的重点大不相同。读的过程同时也是一个理解和消化的过程。读完一篇文章，我们就会了解一些思想；如果对这些思想有不同看法，我们自然就会对之作一番评价，这就是所谓的批判性思维（critical thinking）了。所以，读的效果是：我们知道了别人的思想，同时还可能有了自己的思想。

　　而背却不同。尤其是在短时间内突击背诵的时候，不管是儿童的机械性记忆还是成人的理解性记忆，注意力的焦点更多的是在于尽力记住所背的内容，而不大注意去理解它。结果是囫囵吞枣地记住了内容，但却未必非常清楚内容所表达的思想，更不用说什么批判性思维了。

但是，这里的读不是漫无边际、毫无选择的读。本书的附录8"与ISSUE题目相关的泛读材料"是配合ISSUE写作所涉及的主要话题而精挑细选的。这些文章一方面可以帮助我们熟悉他人的观点，进而启发自己的思路；另一方面可以让我们学会关键概念、复杂思想的表达。值得一读，但切勿背诵。

另一个就是说的训练。有条件的同学不妨结成组，彼此用英语交流对GRE写作题目的看法（如果没人对练，也可以自己和自己说）。说的过程本身可以启发思想是毋庸置疑的；但更重要的是，说是写的前奏。说得清楚，证明你想得清楚；而既然说得出来，你就肯定写得出来。我们实际的写作过程只不过就是把自己头脑里正在说的话写到纸上或者输入电脑而已；其本质就是自己和自己说。而且，通过说来加强写的训练形式非常灵活。只要有可能，张口说（或在心中和自己说）就行了。

但说和写毕竟不同。说重在表意；而写除此之外，还要求准确、精练、规范。所以，说可以辅助写，但不可代替写。而且，写出来的文字可以反复修改。这也是保证我们作文得高分的重要环节。

在本书的撰写过程中，曾有部分读者建议我把部分所谓的"难题"拣出来专门讲解。其实没必要这样，所谓的难易都是相对的，很难绝对地说这些题目是"难题"，那些题目"容易"些。在掌握了本书的"1+5"写作模型之后，所有的题目都是有内容可写的。

但是，有一点再强调一下：在阅读本书的ISSUE篇时，读者会感到其理论部分和提纲部分具有很强的分析性，所以切记在做ISSUE作文时，不要只进行分析却忘了提出自己的论点。所有的ISSUE作文中的分析都是为了支持自己的观点的。若只有分析而没有自己的论点，ISSUE写作看起来就有点儿像是ARGUMENT写作了。这个错误有的同学犯过，所以在此提醒。

以上就是本书全部的核心内容及其所体现的撰写思想。

上篇: ISSUE

第一章

第一大问题：
如何做到有内容可写

★ 一个写作套路

★ 五种题目分析类型

★ 两点注意事项

★ 分析范例

没内容可写的主要表现是：没有思路，不知道该想些什么、该写些什么。出现这些问题的原因是考生不善分析，找不到分析题目的切入点。

我提出的应对策略："1+5"写作模型，即一个写作套路加上五种题目分析类型及各自相应的分析切入点。由这些分析切入点着手，考生能很快发现自己的写作思路，再整理出提纲及写作框架。

第一节　一个写作套路

一个写作套路是指在文章的正文部分，分正、反两方面展开写作的行文思路或结构。所有ISSUE题库中的题目在一定角度/程度上都是可以赞同的，但肯定也有反对的余地。这是因为，ETS本来就是这样来设计ISSUE题目的。

试想，如果一个ISSUE题目拿到手里之后，你感觉到自己的思路受到了限制——对于这个题目好像只能赞同或者反对，那么，这个题目本身的设计就是失败的。好的题目就是提出一个问题，这个问题能够给人留下充分的空间展开分析。同学们应该明白，天下所有的所谓的真理，包括各式各样的"主义"、学说、假说、定律，其实都是有待于不断证伪的，因而不存在绝对的真理。它们在一定的条件下是具有解释力的，但不是永恒的真理。

所以，对所有的题目，我们都可以有条件地同时支持和反对，从而两面兼顾，从两方面同时展开分析。这样写的好处是：

■ 两面兼顾，本身即是看到了问题的复杂性（complexities），这是比较理想的写作思路（关于ETS对GRE作文所定的评分标准及其提供的ISSUE范文，请参见本书附录7）

■ 两面写，左右逢源，文章容易展开，有助于解决文章篇幅不足的问题

■ 两面写的文章结构极好控制，若再配合恰当的论证方法，则行文思路清晰，结构一目了然

■ 文章紧紧围绕着题目展开，思路集中，不易跑题（对于这一点，部分同学可能不以为然：这种小儿科的错误，怎么会在GRE考生中出现呢？但如果考生对题目的中心观点、分析的侧重点的把握出现了偏差，就会在不知不觉中离题万里。笔者所批改的学生作文中，少部分同学的确如此。）

更重要的是，这次GRE作文改革之后，从两方面写ISSUE作文的思路几乎是必需的。这个必要性主要表现在每道ISSUE题目的写作指引（instructions）里面。

作为GRE作文改革的一大变化，ETS为所有的ISSUE作文都附上了一个写作指引；结合具体的ISSUE题目类型，每道ISSUE题目后面的写作指引有可能是下面六个中的一个，具体如下：

❶ Write a response in which you discuss the extent to which you agree or disagree with the statement and explain your reasoning for the position you take. In developing and supporting your position, you should consider ways in which the statement might or might not hold true and explain how these considerations shape your position.

❷ Write a response in which you discuss the extent to which you agree or disagree with the recommendation and explain your reasoning for the position you take. In developing and supporting your position, describe specific circumstances in which adopting the recommendation would or would not be advantageous and explain how these examples shape your position.

③ Write a response in which you discuss the extent to which you agree or disagree with the claim. In developing and supporting your position, be sure to address the most compelling reasons and/or examples that could be used to challenge your position.

④ Write a response in which you discuss which view more closely aligns with your own position and explain your reasoning for the position you take. In developing and supporting your position, you should address both of the views presented.

⑤ Write a response in which you discuss the extent to which you agree or disagree with the claim and the reason on which that claim is based.

⑥ Write a response in which you discuss your views on the policy and explain your reasoning for the position you take. In developing and supporting your position, you should consider the possible consequences of implementing the policy and explain how these consequences shape your position.

可以看出，这六种写作指引都是由两句话组成。前一句实质意义都不大，关键的指引在后一句。其中，③④⑥的后半句尤为典型。

指引③的后一句 "be sure to address the most compelling reasons and/or examples that could be used to challenge your position" 是要求考生 "一定要论及自我立场的对立方会用哪些最有力的理由和例证来挑战自己的观点"。这实际是要求考生在作文中一定要论及反方立场，所以，必须从两方面写。

指引⑥一般出现在后面马上就要讲到的建议类ISSUE题目中。这个指引的后一句 "consider the possible consequences of implementing the policy" 是要求考生必须要考虑到题目中一项政策提议或建议的可能后果。常识告诉我们，当提出一项建议，就要求考虑该项建议的可能后果，此时要考虑的内容只能是实施那项建议所可能导致的不良后果。这样，建议本身以及建议可能产生的后果又构成一个问题的两个方面，所以，又必须从两方面来写。

至于指引④的后一句 "you should address both of the views presented"，这已经是直白地要求考生一定要论及题目中两个不同或矛盾的立场。不从两方面写是不可能了。等到读者看到具体带有指引④的ISSUE题目，就会非常清楚这个指引的实质了。

实际上，指引②也几乎总是出现在建议类ISSUE题目中。这个指引的后一句 "describe specific circumstances in which adopting the recommendation would or would not be advantageous" 要求考生在作文中一定要论及题目中的建议 "会导致有利或不利的结果的具体情形"。考虑一个建议的正、反两种结果的思路，体现在作文中只能是从两方面写的思路。

带有指引①和指引⑤的ISSUE题目本身没有明确提示要从两方面写，但大家随后在理解和应用 "1+5" 写作模型的时候会发现，对这两类ISSUE题目采用两方面写的策略的话，会感觉无论切入题目分析还是展开写作思路都非常方便和自然。

所以，我在这里着重强调一下：**对于ISSUE作文，请一定要从两方面来写。**

假设正文部分有三个意群段（注意：不必是三个自然段。有关意群段和自然段的区别与作用，在第三章中有详细的讲解），两面写文章的常见结构包括：

■ 正、反、合（即支持、反对、然后再将前面正、反两方面的分析综合阐述）

■ 正、反、反（即支持、反对、再反对）

■ 正、反、散（即支持、反对、然后从一个更深更广的角度将对问题的阐述加以发散）

关于"正、反、合"，"正、反、反"和"正、反、散"的应用，在随后对具体题目的讲解过程中，大家自然会理解。

以上这三种结构就能解决所有ISSUE题目的结构（或者说思路）问题。当然，你也可以采用其他结构，比如"正、正、反"，"正、正、散"，"反、反、散"，"正、正、正（完全同意）"，"反、反、反（完全反对）"等，这取决于每个人对题目的理解。但一方面，掌握了上面三个分析思路，其余的分析思路自然水到渠成；另一方面，大家会发现可以"一边倒"写支持或反对的题目为数不多，而不可以两面写的题目却很少，或者基本没有。

第二节　五种题目分析类型

这五种题目分析类型及各自相应的分析切入点分别是：

一、因果类题目

此类题目通常提出或者蕴含了某种因果关系。

因果类题目的常见形式是"Because A，B"这样的句式结构。或者，题目中虽没有明显的这种结构，但可以明确判断出题目实际上是列出了一组因果关系。

例如下面这三道题：

❶ The human mind will always be superior to machines because machines are only tools of human minds.

这道题前后两个判断由连词because连接，说明后者是前者的原因。这是显而易见的因果类题目。

❷ Many important discoveries or creations are accidental: it is usually while seeking the answer to one question that we come across the answer to another.

这道题没有出现表示因果关系的连接词，可是冒号前后两个判断显然表现为一种因果关系。我们可以为其加上表示因果关系的连接词：**Because** it is usually while seeking the answer to one question that we come across the answer to another, many important discoveries or creations are accidental. 这样一来，句中的因果逻辑关系就非常清楚了。

❸ Claim: We can usually learn much more from people whose views we share than from those whose views contradict our own.

Reason: Disagreement can cause stress and inhibit learning.

这道题也没有出现表示因果关系的连接词，但它本身明显是个因果推理过程：先给出一个原因/理由（Reason），然后得出一个结果/结论（Claim）。所以，它属于因果类题目。

因果类题目的分析切入点有两点：

❶ 这个因果关系推理中的原因是否成立？

❷ 假设这个原因成立，从它能否推出结果？

二、建议类题目

此类题目通常是提出了某种解决问题的办法或建议。

题型归类的常见形式是"Someone **should/must** do something to have/do something or for a purpose"（即要想达到某个目的，则应该/必须怎样去做。但有时，题目中并不明确说明这个目的）。或者，题目中虽没有明显的"Someone **should/must** do something to have/do something or for a purpose"这一结构，但可以明确判断出题目实际上是给出了一个建议。

例如下面这三道题：

❶ In order to become well-rounded individuals, all college students should be required to take courses in which they read poetry, novels, mythology, and other types of imaginative literature.

这是个典型的建议类题目：为了某个目的，某人应该去做什么（For a certain purpose, someone should do something）。

❷ No field of study can advance significantly unless it incorporates knowledge and experience from outside that field.

这道题没有第一题的典型形式，但如果将它的句式稍加变化，即成了：No field of study can advance significantly, if it does not incorporate knowledge and experience from outside that field. 言下之意就是，In order for a field of study to advance significantly, it should incorporate knowledge and experience from outside that field. 现在，这就是典型的建议类题目了。

❸ Some people believe that government funding of the arts is necessary to ensure that the arts can flourish and be available to all people. Others believe that government funding of the arts threatens the integrity of the arts.

这道题同样不具备第一题的典型形式。但当一个人对你说It's necessary for you to... 时，他显然是在给出一个建议。

建议类题目的分析切入点有三点：

❶ 题目中的建议可行性如何？

❷ 如果实施题目中的建议，是否会导致同初始目的相矛盾或其他荒谬的结果？

❸ 有无替代或折中方案？

三、是非类题目

此类题目通常是提出或者蕴含了某种好坏、是非的价值判断。

是非类题目的常见形式是"Something/someone is good/bad/worthwhile/important/better/more important/effective..."。总之，此类题目都是对事物性质，比如好/坏、有效/无效、重要/不重要/更重要等的比较和评判。从英语语法结构上讲，是非类题目的特点都可以整理为"主语＋系动词＋表语形容词"的形式，意思是：某物/某人怎样。

例如下面这两道题：

---

① Competition is ultimately more beneficial than detrimental to society.

② The human mind will always be superior to machines because machines are only tools of human minds.

这是旧版ISSUE题库中的一道题目。这道题对竞争作了简单的价值判断（more beneficial than detrimental）。这种只是简单给出一个价值判断的题目，我们将之归类为**单纯性是非类题目**。

这道题我们曾将之归类为因果类题目。但这道因果类题目的结果部分是个价值判断：be superior to machines。这种与其他类型的题目结合在一起的价值判断题目，我们将之归类为**结合式是非类题目**。多数是非类题目属于这种类型。

是非类题目的分析切入点有两点：

① 这种价值判断的标准是什么？

② 这种价值判断的标准是否值得修正？

四、定义类题目

此类题目通常是提出或者蕴含了一个或多个定义。

定义类题目的常见形式：定义类题目主要是在给概念下定义。

例如下面这两道题：

---

① Some people believe that in order to be effective, political leaders must yield to public opinion and abandon principle for the sake of compromise. Others believe that the most essential quality of an effective leader is the ability to remain consistently committed to particular principles and objectives.

这道题主要围绕何为称职的政治领袖（effective political leaders）或者政治领袖最重要的素质（the most essential quality）是什么而展开，完全是在讨论一个概念的定义。这种整个都是关于一个概念的定义的题目，我们把它们归类为**单纯性定义类题目**。但这类题目在题库中所占的比例较小。

---

❷ Most people are taught that loyalty is a virtue. But loyalty—whether to one's friends, to one's school or place of employment, or to any institution—is all too often a destructive rather than a positive force.

这道题目也来自旧版ISSUE题库，它本应该归入下面就要谈到的事实类题目。但实际上大家一眼就能看出：命题loyalty—whether to one's friends，to one's school or place of employment，or to any institution—is all too often a destructive rather than a positive force到底是真是假，关键在于如何界定其中的核心概念——忠诚（loyalty）。如果讲不清楚什么是"忠诚"，这个题目根本写不下去。这种形式上归属于其他题目类型，但题目的展开分析几乎完全取决于其中的关键概念的定义的题目，我们将之归类为**结合式定义类题目**。绝大部分定义类题目都属于这种类型。

在此，有一点值得强调：在日常生活中，所有的判断都是由概念构成的。而只要是概念，就都有一个如何对其含义进行界定的问题。这就是说，实际上所有的ISSUE题目，只要你认为有必要，都可以对其中的任何概念按照你所理解的含义加以界定。大家想一想，几乎所有的理论、学说都必然有一套它们自己的概念体系。日常生活中的各种争论，90%以上实际上都是围绕某些定义展开的。所以，**若想使你的ISSUE作文有深度、有你自己的独到见解，请千万记住"下定义"这个十分重要的技巧**。关于这一点，我们在随后的例子中会有所体现。

对于单纯性定义类题目，它的分析切入点有两个：

❶ 题目中的定义是否抓住了问题的本质？

❷ 能否给出我自己的、更为恰当的定义（恰当的定义就是能很好解释自己的论点、论据以及所列举的现象的定义）？

而对于结合式定义类题目，它的分析切入点只有一个，即：能否给出我自己的更为恰当的定义？

五、事实类题目

此类题目通常指出一个或多个事实。但是要注意：这里的事实并非那种公认的、可反复证实或证伪的现象，如地球是圆的；在地球上观察，太阳每天东升西落等。它在题目中实际上指的是一种观察（observation）或者一种感觉（perception），而持有这种意见的人认为它是事实，并希望我们也相信。

事实类题目的常见形式：凡是不能明确归入因果类、是非类、建议类和定义类题目者，都可归入事实类。

例如下面这道题：

> People's attitudes are determined more by their immediate situation or surroundings than by society as a whole.

到底是什么在界定人的思想与行为呢？题目中，论者认为是我们所处的特定情势或者我们周围的环境在界定我们的思想态度和行为方式，而不是作为一个整体的社会。这是论者的一个观察、判断，他认为这是事实，并希望我们也相信。而且，我们好像也无法把这个题目明确归入因果类、是非类、建议类和定义类。

事实类题目的分析切入点有两个：

❶ 能否从公认的原则或事实中推出相反的判断？

❷ 能否举出相反的事例？

第三节　两点注意事项

在 ISSUE 题目的分析过程中，有两点注意事项：

❶ 要留意题目中是否有逻辑陷阱（如偷换概念、以偏概全、有问题的假设等）。

❷ 要注意部分题目可同时归属不同类别，比如，一个建议类题目同时也是事实类和定义类题目，因此，要多角度分析。关于这一点，随后会专门讲解。

第四节　分析范例

下面通过具体的分析范例，看一看"1+5"写作模型的应用。

在运用这个模型的时候，有一个简单的口诀：**先提正，再求反，因人因题合、反、散**。意思是说，拿到 ISSUE 题目并将之归为具体的题目类型之后，首先可以在某种角度/程度上，同意题目中的立场（先提正）；然后，再从各种类型题目各自的分析切入点入手，分析得出反对意见，修正题目所陈述的观点和体现的思路（再求反）；最后，再结合具体题目的特点和考生自己对这个题目的分析、驾驭能力，确定是将上面一正、一反两方面综合起来阐述（合），还是再提出一个对题目所持立场的反对意见来进行修正（反），抑或是从一个相关的角度将问题发散开来阐述（散），即"因人因题合、反、散"。

下面的分析范例中，有个别例子是旧版 ISSUE 题库中的题目，但考虑到这几个题目较为典型，在这里仍沿用它们作为分析范例。

一、因果类题目分析范例

范例一

It is impossible for an effective political leader to tell the truth all the time. Complete honesty is not a useful virtue for a politician.

题型归类

这是道典型的因果类题目，来自旧版ISSUE题库。因为It is impossible for an effective political leader to tell the truth all the time，所以Complete honesty is not a useful virtue for a politician。

题目分析

第一步：先提正

政治家有时不得不避免说出事实。政治家永远是为特定的党派、组织、国家和民族服务的，没有跨组织的政治家。为了组织的利益，政治家有时必须回避事实。所以，在这个意义上，可以同意题目中的立场。

第二步：再求反

从因果类题目的两个分析切入点着手，找到反对、修正题目所持立场的观点和思路。

首先，**第一个分析切入点：这个因果关系推理中的原因是否成立？**

结合我们的常识和经验，题目的原因部分It is impossible for an effective political leader to tell the truth all the time似乎成立，或者至少较难反驳。于是，放过它。看第二个分析切入点。

第二个分析切入点：假设这个原因成立，从它能否推出结果？

能从It is impossible for an effective political leader to tell the truth all the time推出Complete honesty is not a useful virtue for a politician吗？发现不能。因为：

1. 不符合常识。

说完全的诚实对政治家来说不是一种有用的品德，我们普通百姓不会认可。没有任何国家的老百姓会选骗子做政治领袖。根据常识也可推定政治家本人也未必这么认为。

2. 题目中的因果推理有一个偷换概念的错误。

它将"一个称职的政治领袖不可能总讲真话"偷换为"不诚实"的概念，并进一步推论"诚实对政治家来说不是一种有用的品德"。

这一点就是在做ISSUE题目的分析时，两点注意事项的第一点：留意题目中的逻辑陷阱。类似的逻辑陷阱在随后的例子中还会碰到。

3. 题目中的论者犯了用道德个案否定道德原则有效性的错误。

即使这个因果推论的原因部分是成立的，仍然推不出结论部分。因为诚实作为一项道德操守，它是否有用是个一般化的道德原则问题，它同一个人是否总是讲真话不矛盾。不管称职的领袖（effective leader）是否总讲真话，完全的诚实

11

（complete honesty）作为一项基本的道德操守总是有用的（useful）。总不能说个别人不守法，所以遵纪守法是无用的吧。所以，题目中前后两个判断本质上是互不相干的两个问题，根本不能由前者来推论出后者。诚实是任何个人的道德底线，政治家也不例外。这就是诚实对政治家来说是有用的标准之所在。

4．题目中的推理还有一个以偏概全的错误。

用一个称职的政治领袖（an effective political leader）来推论所有的政治家（a politician）；但实际上，前者未必代表后者。

5．如有必要，讨论一下"有用的"这一价值判断的标准。

诚实作为一项道德要求，判断它是否有用的标准应该是：它是否能从伦理上使政治家相信保护其所代表的组织或群体利益的合理性。如果是，诚实作为一项道德规范就是有用的，不管是否有部分政治家背叛了其所代表的组织或群体的利益。

以上的几点分析，随便找出两三点就足够写出 500 多字的 ISSUE 作文了。

第三步：因人因题合、反、散

结合题目特点以及自己对题目内容的驾驭能力，决定采取"合"的办法，将第一、第二步的分析综合起来，展开论述。这个"合"是通过对什么是一个真正称职的政治家的定义来完成的。即：

真正称职的政治家能做到在自己的良知面前保持诚实，同时能在事实面前做到灵活处理。这是因为，真正称职的政治家必须是有着强烈的责任感和使命感、超凡的政治智慧和领袖魅力，同时忠诚于其所服务的选民并被后者高度信赖的政治家。这样的政治家必然既是诚实的，又是灵活而富有智慧的。言下之意：不该讲出事实的时候，当然要回避事实，但未必非得撒谎不可。不是有句非常知名的外交辞令叫"无可奉告"吗？

完成上面的分析过程之后，同学们自然就可以整理出一个中文提纲：

论点 政治家有时不得不避免说出事实，但这并不意味着诚实对政治家来说不是一种有用的品德。

正 政治家有时不得不避免说出事实。
政治家永远是为特定的党派、组织、国家和民族服务的，没有跨组织的政治家。为了组织的利益，政治家有时必须回避事实。

反 但不能据此推出，完全的诚实不是一种有用的品德。

1．不符合事实：

❶ 大多数政治家认可完的诚实是一种有用的品德。
人不能生活在道德交错之中，政治家也不例外。诚实的外表和伪善的内心会让一个人崩溃。

❷ 选民也认可完全的诚实是一种有用的品德。

2．选民不可能明知道某个政治家是骗子，还仍然选举其做政治领导人。

3．推论中偷换概念：将"一个称职的政治领袖不可能总讲真话"偷换为"不诚实"的概念。

4．用个案否定原则的有效性：用部分政治家不讲真话（或者就是不诚实）来否定一般化的道德原则（凡人都必须诚实）的有效性。而实际上，这两个问题可以是毫不相干的。

5. 题目中的推理还有一个以偏概全的错误：用一个称职的政治领袖来推论所有的政治家。

6. 讨论"有用的"这一价值判断的标准。诚实作为一项道德要求，判断它是否有用的标准应该是：它是否能在伦理上使政治家相信保护其所代表的组织或群体利益的合理性。如果是，诚实作为一项道德规范就是有用的，不管是否有部分政治家不诚实并背叛了其所代表的组织或群体的利益。

（合）真正称职的政治家能做到在自己的良知面前保持诚实，同时能在事实面前做到灵活处理。

真正称职的政治家必须是有着强烈的责任感和使命感、超凡的政治智慧和领袖魅力，同时忠诚于其所服务的选民并为后者高度信赖的政治家。这样的政治家必然既是诚实的，又是灵活而富有智慧的。

因此，可列出以下英文提纲：

Outline

Position Politicians may, in some special circumstances, not be telling the truth, but this does not follow that honesty is not a useful virtue for a politician.

❶ （正）Politicians, considering their special career requirements, sometimes have to shun speaking out the truth. For the interest of their party, nation and/or the public, political leaders occasionally are forced not to talk about a matter as it actually is.

❷ （反）However, we can never infer hereby that honesty is useless for a politician. First, we have observed many politicians avoid telling the truth, but this does not deny the fact that they themselves take, others also agree, honesty as a useful virtue for them. Second, "not to tell the truth" doesn't equal "to lie," because a politician can still keep silent, show partially the true color of the matter in question, or choose to tell the fact in a roundabout way rather than lie. Third, when we say honesty is a useful virtue for a politician, we mention it as an ethical bottom line for everybody, including surely all politicians. Such an ethical rule is effective even all politicians under certain pressure choose to lie.

❸ （合）A really effective politician is one who can always say calmly that "Yes, I'm honest before my conscience," but meanwhile skillfully deal with a fact at the call of special conditions.

我们现在假设自己要写的ISSUE作文分为开头段、结尾段和正文段，上述的"正、反、合"便相当于正文段中的三个意群段（意群段就是文章中在内容和逻辑上相对独立的段落。有关意群段和自然段的区别与作用，在第三章有详细的讲解）。由此，文章就有了如下一个五段式的结构：

```
┌─ 开头段  全文第一意群段
│                              ┌─ (正/正/正) 正文第一意群段/全文第二意群段
├─ 正文段  分三个意群段 ────┤─ (反/反/反) 正文第二意群段/全文第三意群段
│                              └─ (合/反/散) 正文第三意群段/全文第四意群段
└─ 结尾段  全文第五意群段
```

那么，实际上，经过"先提正，再求反，因人因题合、反、散"的分析过程，得到分析结果，然后将分析结果放入一种套路（正、反、合，正、反、反，或正、反、散）之后，文章的写作思路、结构、中心观点便自然而得。到此，文章怎么会感觉到没内容可写呢？

在有了思路和写作框架之后，关于如何将文章写长，我们在第二章中会重点讲解。到时大家就会发现，在知道该写什么之后，解决文章篇幅不足的问题实际是个非常轻松的过程。下面我们来看更多的分析范例。

范例二

> Claim: We can usually learn much more from people whose views we share than from those whose views contradict our own.
>
> Reason: Disagreement can cause stress and inhibit learning.

题型归类

Reason-Claim 结构的因果类题目。

题目分析

第一步：先提正

相同的意见会促进人们的学习；相反的意见有时阻碍人们之间的互相学习。别人的赞同是对一个人自我价值、能力的认可，往往会鼓励后者更积极地去努力。这是人的本性使然。所以，在这个意义上，可以同意题目中的立场。

第二步：再求反

从因果类题目的两个分析切入点着手，找到反对、修正题目所持立场的观点和思路。

首先，第一个分析切入点：这个因果关系推理中的原因是否成立？

"disagreement can cause stress and inhibit learning"这个所谓的事实成立吗？不同意见（disagreement）是否也会令人们兴奋起来，头脑变得更清晰、敏锐，进而发现新问题、新角度，从而有利于学习呢？到此，我们有了第一个反对题目所持立场的观点。

第二个分析切入点：假设这个原因成立，从它能否推出结果？

即使这个事实成立，就可推出"We can usually learn much more from people whose views we share than from people whose views contradict our own"这个结果吗？是否有别的原因影响我们向他人学习呢，比如彼此的了解、关系的远近、发生不同

意见时的特定的心态、年龄、性格等？他人的意见、态度之于我们的学习到底是怎样的效果？促进？妨碍？还是毫不相干？实际上二者之间可以说没有直接的因果关系。这是第二个反对题目所持立场的观点。

第三步：因人因题合、反、散

结合题目特点以及自己对题目内容的驾驭能力，决定采取"合"的办法，将第一、第二步的分析综合起来，展开论述。这个"合"是通过发现一个可以将上述正、反两方面同时加以解释的角度来完成的，即到底他人的意见是否妨碍学习实际是因人而异的。学习的效果几乎完全取决于个人情况：禀赋、性格、动机、所处的环境等。

上面的分析过程完成之后，同学们自然就可以整理出一个中文提纲：

论点 人们彼此间持相同意见是否会促进他们的学习完全因人而异。

正 相同的意见会促进人们学习；相反的意见有时会妨碍人们彼此间的学习。

提供原因（cause-effect）：别人的赞同是对一个人自我价值、能力的认可，往往会鼓励后者更积极地去努力。这是人的本性使然。

反 但依据"disagreement can cause stress and inhibit learning"推不出"We can usually learn much more from people whose views we share than from people whose views contradict our own"。

1. 不同意见不一定就会导致压力并妨碍学习。
每个人对批评的态度不同，对压力的反应各异。因此，同样的批评完全可以让有些人积极奋进，眼界思路更为开阔，从而学得更好。

2. 即使不同意见导致了压力并因而妨碍了学习，也推不出"We can usually learn much more from people whose views we share than from people whose views contradict our own"。
影响一个人学习效果的原因有很多（如学习动机、天赋程度、努力程度、兴趣等），他人的批评和赞同及相应的效果只是众多原因中的一种，所以对一个人的学习效果不足以有决定性作用。

合 到底他人的意见是否妨碍学习取决于每个人的不同情况。
学习的效果几乎完全取决于个人情况：禀赋、性格、动机、所处环境等。

同时，还可列出以下英文提纲：

Outline

Position Whether some mutually shared ideas can make people learn more from each other is quite a personal matter.

❶ **正** It is true that disagreement can cause stress and sometimes inhibit our learning, and as a result we might learn more from people whose views we share than from those whose views contradict our own. Anyhow, people are at least easier to understand each other when they find them sharing the same ground in most cases.

❷ ⟨反⟩ However, disagreement can also benefit us greatly. On the one hand, distinct perspectives on an issue may turn out to sharpen our mind, broaden our ken and shed some new light on the issue in question, and therefore enhance our learning. On the other hand, throughout the human intellectual history, it is always the different schools of thought rather than those who share, on any issue, identical ideas with each other that combine to boost scientific and technological progress.

❸ ⟨合⟩ All in all, which one, disagreement or agreement, will promote our learning from others is quite a personal matter which depends on so many factors such as one's age, motivations, psychological maturity, personal understanding with each other and so on.

二、建议类题目分析范例

范例一

No field of study can advance significantly unless it incorporates knowledge and experience from outside that field.

题型归类

在前面讲解如何对题目进行归类的时候就已经提到，这道题没有建议类题目的典型形式，但如果将它的句式稍加变化，即成了：**No** field of study can advance significantly, **if it does not** incorporate knowledge and experience from outside that field. 言下之意即：**In order for** a field of study **to** advance significantly, it **should** incorporate knowledge and experience from outside that field. 这样就是典型的建议类题目了。

题目分析

第一步：先提正

借鉴某一领域以外的知识和经验可以促进某一学科的发展。大量交叉学科的出现和发展，比如生物化学，分子生物学，天体物理学，经济学对社会学、数学的应用等，都能说明这一点。

第二步：再求反

从建议类题目的三个分析切入点着手，找到反对、修正题目所持立场的观点和思路。

首先，**第一个分析切入点**：题目中的建议可行性如何？

当前的确有许多学科的繁荣可以归因于学科交叉的结果，如生物化学、分子生物学，以及统计学、社会学和历史学在经济学中的应用。但这是确定不移的吗？比如，数学要和哪个学科交叉才能有突破性进展？如果没有同其他学科的交叉便没有本学科的突破性进展，那么牛顿力学是同哪个学科交叉的结果？爱因斯坦的相对论又是同哪个学科交叉？所以，题目中的建议对于部分学科，比如理论数学和理论物理，其可行性是很低的。

第二个分析切入点：如果实施题目中的建议，是否会导致同初始目的相矛盾或其他荒谬的结果？

如果题目中的这个逻辑成立，任何学术领域的科研人员都应该放弃本领域的研究，转而坐在家里，等待别的学科的研究给自己带来学术灵感。这岂不荒谬？

第三个分析切入点：有无替代或折中方案？

除了同其他学科的合理交叉以求借鉴外，引发某一学科重大进展的还有许多其他可能，如该学科长期的学术积累、适宜的社会和经济条件、天才人物的适时出现等，而不必非得是 outsiders' knowledge and experience。

第三步：因人因题合、反、散

结合题目特点以及自己对题目内容的驾驭能力，决定采取"反"的办法来完成文章正文部分的第三个意群段。直接将上面由第三个分析切入点分析而得到的结果当作文章正文部分的第三个意群段。

这样，就有了下面这个中文提纲：

论点 别的领域的知识和经验未必是某一学科发展的必要条件。

㊣ 借鉴某一领域以外的知识和经验可以促进某一学科的发展。

大量交叉学科的出现和发展，比如生物化学，分子生物学，天体物理学，经济学对社会学、数学知识的应用等，都能说明这一点。

㊡ 但不能据此推出：某一研究领域要有重大发展，就必须借鉴该领域以外的知识和经验。

1. 部分学科，如数学，很难同其他学科交叉。牛顿的万有引力学说引发的经典物理学的重大发展，爱因斯坦的相对论引发的物理学和天文学的重大发展等都不是同其他学科直接交叉的结果。

2. 如果所有学科的重大突破必须要借鉴其他学科的知识和经验，牛顿和爱因斯坦应该停止思考，坐等与其他学科交叉。那样的话，还不知要等多久他们才能获得学术成果。

㊡ 有许多其他的途径可以促进某一学科的发展，而不必非得借鉴该领域以外的知识和经验。

有许多其他可以引发某学科重大学术突破的途径，比如，该学科长期的学术积累、适宜的社会和经济条件、天才人物的适时出现等。

同时，还可列出以下英文提纲：

Outline

Position Outsiders' knowledge and experience is not the necessary condition for the prosperity of a field of study.

❶ ㊣ Borrowing knowledge and experience from other fields of study has indeed triggered significant breakthroughs in many subjects. Quite a few new scientific subjects, biochemistry, molecular biology, for example, are undoubtedly the hybrids of subjects originally thought far distant from one another.

❷ ⓐ But such a phenomenon by no means indicates that only through sharing academic light of outsiders, can an area of study make its frog-leap. In fact, truly revolutionary advancement in some fields of study, Newton's law of gravity and Einstein's theory of relativity, for instance, are utterly genius' flash of wisdom, little of which is borrowed from other subjects.

❸ ⓐ As for factors contributing to an academic subjects' significant growth, they include many apart from sharing the outsiders' intelligence, such as long-term academic accumulation, appropriate social and economic support, the good-timing birth of geniuses and so on.

范例二

Colleges and universities should require all faculty to spend time working outside the academic world in professions relevant to the courses they teach.

题型归类

典型的建议类题目。

题目分析

第一步：先提正

的确，将书本上的知识同工作实践相结合，既能有效地指导实践，又能促进部分学科教学质量的提高，比如工程学、机械制造、经济学等。

第二步：再求反

从建议类题目的三个分析切入点着手，找到反对、修正题目所持立场的观点和思路。

首先，**第一个分析切入点**：题目中的建议可行性如何？

对于其他一些学科，比如天文学、理论物理、理论数学等，它们该怎么联系工作实践？部分学科课题，比如关于宇宙起源的学说，要想联系工作实践是极困难的。

第二个分析切入点：如果实施题目中的建议，是否会导致同初始目的相矛盾的或其他荒谬的结果？

如果所有的学科及其教职员工都必须将本学科联系工作实践，否则其教学质量便不能提高的话，那些理论思辨和抽象性比较强的学科（比如理论物理、理论数学、哲学等）就很可能会停止发展了。这些学科本身及其教学的发展所需要的更多是思辨与想象，而不是联系工作实践。

第三个分析切入点：有无替代或折中方案？

除了结合相关的工作实践之外，促进某一学科教学的发展还可以有许多其他选择，如该学科长期的学术积累、完备的教学条件、自由的学术氛围、天才人物的适时出现等。

第三步：因人因题合、反、散

结合题目特点以及自己对题目内容的驾驭能力，这个题目同样采取"反"的办法来完成文章正文部分的第三个意群段。直接将上面由第三个分析切入点分析得到的结果当作文章正文部分的第三个意群段。

这样，就有了下面这个中文提纲：

论点 同工作实践相结合未必能促进部分学科教学质量的提高。

正 联系工作实践的确可以促进部分学科的教学水平。

工程学、机械制造、经济学等应用性较强的学科很显然有这样的特点。

反 但不能据此推出：要想提高某学科的教学质量，就必须把该学科同工作实践相结合。

1. 对于其他一些学科，比如天文学、理论物理、理论数学等，要想联系工作实践是极困难的。

2. 如果所有的学科及其教职员工都必须将本学科联系工作实践，否则其教学质量便不能提高的话，那些理论思辨和抽象性比较强的学科（比如理论物理、理论数学、哲学等）就很可能会停止发展了。这些学科本身及其教学的发展所需要的更多是思辨与想象，而不是联系工作实践。

合 有许多其他的途径可以促进某一学科教学质量的提高。

除了结合相关的工作实践之外，促进某一学科教学的发展还可以有许多其他选择，如该学科长期的学术积累、完备的教学条件、自由的学术氛围、天才人物的适时出现等。

同时，还可列出以下英文提纲：

Outline

Position: Connecting the courses on collegiate campus with the actual professional know-how is not always the necessary condition for improving the teaching quality in those courses.

❶ 正 Workshop experience can really enrich subjects in classroom. This is especially true for such subjects as engineering, machinery manufacturing, economics, and so forth.

❷ 反 But such cases by no means indicate that bridging workshops and classrooms can always work magic. In fact, for some subjects, theoretical physics and some mathematical researches, for example, it is neither necessary nor possible for researchers in these areas to directly apply their knowledge to practical work. These sciences seem only to perform well within the brain cells.

❸ 反 As for methods contributing to the teaching quality, they include many apart from sharing workshop experience, such as the long-term academic accumulation, the sufficient teaching facilities, the free and tolerant academic atmosphere, the good-timing birth of geniuses etc.

三、是非类题目分析范例

范例一

> Competition is ultimately more beneficial than detrimental to society.

题型归类

这道题对竞争作了个简单的价值判断，属于单纯性是非类题目。该题来自旧版 ISSUE 题库，极具哲学思辨味道，是很有代表性的 ISSUE 题目。

题目分析

第一步：先提正

竞争当然给人类带来很多好处：人类现在所享受的科技进步和物质财富实际上都有竞争的贡献。

第二步：再求反

从是非类题目的两个分析切入点着手，找到反对、修正题目所持立场的观点和思路。

首先，**第一个分析切入点**：这种价值判断的标准是什么？

判断竞争是更为有益或有害的标准是什么？或者说，这里的有益和有害的内容包括什么？这里，需要明确有益（beneficial）和有害（detrimental）的判断标准。比如说，有益的定义：其一，推动文明（尤其是物质文明）的发展；其二，促进人性的进步。竞争带来的较为丰富的物质财富可以激发和保护人性中善的一面，比如，有了物质条件作保障，人们可以更好地维护自己的人格、尊严和权利并且互相帮助等。有害的定义：其一，激发人性恶的一面——人们，为攫取财富不择手段；其二，使人沦为工具——人们为了金钱、物质、狂热信仰而去竞争，忽略了人本身的发展目的。

第二个分析切入点：这种价值判断的标准是否值得修正？

既然题目说 "Competition is ultimately **more** beneficial **than** detrimental to society"，那么其蕴含的假设就是竞争的益处和害处二者是可以比较的。然而，二者果真可以比较吗？同样的结果因人、因地、因时而异，怎么比较？按照第一个分析切入点所确定的判断竞争有益或有害的标准，竞争所带来的好处和坏处都可列出许多条，怎么比较？（这实际是题目所暗含的又一个逻辑陷阱：有问题的假设。如果我们果真去比较竞争所带来的好处和坏处到底谁大谁小的话，最后会发现很难说得清楚。无论说好处大还是坏处大，都会失之偏颇。如果说竞争的好处和坏处一样大，又变成了无原则、无标准的摇摆。）这样，就必须对前述的判断标准进行修正。

实际上，竞争最终是有益还是有害于社会在很大程度上取决于我们对其内涵的理解，即这里说的竞争到底是一种什么样的竞争。因此，我们就可以对竞争（competition）进行自己的定义。定义不同，结果可能完全不同。

比如，我们可以这样来定义："Competition means to win, sometimes by whatever means and at whatever cost"，或者也可以这样来定义："Competition is an unremitting pursuit for perfection to continually transcend oneself"。前者重在输赢，为之不择手段、不惜代价，结果难免有害；后者重在自我超越，既有竞争，亦有合作，更多地实现利他的社会价值（如公平、自由、社会正义等），其结果是有益的。

这样，判断竞争到底是有益还是有害的标准就由看结果转变为看原因（到底是什么样的竞争），问题就很容易讲清楚了。

第三步：因人因题合、反、散

结合题目特点以及自己对题目内容的驾驭能力，决定采取"合"的办法，将第一、第二步的分析综合起来，展开论述。这个"合"是通过给竞争下一个定义来完成的，即竞争到底是有益还是有害完全取决于这里说的竞争到底是一种什么样的竞争。

上面的分析过程完成之后，同学们自然就可整理出一个中文提纲：

论点 竞争到底是有益还是有害完全取决于人们对竞争的理解。

正 竞争当然给人类带来很多好处：人类现在所享受的科技进步和物质财富实际上都有竞争的贡献。

1. 推动文明，尤其是物质文明的发展。
2. 促进人性的进步。竞争带来的较为丰富的物质财富可以激发和保护人性中善的一面，比如，有了物质条件作保障，人们可以更好地维护自己的人格、尊严和权利等。

反 但不能简单地说"Competition is ultimately more beneficial than detrimental to society"。毕竟，竞争同样给人类带来诸多有害的结果。

1. 激发人性恶的一面——人们为攫取财富不择手段。
2. 使人沦为工具——人们为了金钱、物质、狂热信仰而去竞争，而忽略了人本身的发展目的。

合 竞争到底是有益还是有害完全取决于这里所说的竞争到底是一种什么样的竞争。

我们可以这样来定义："Competition means to win, sometimes by whatever means and at whatever cost"，或者我们可以这样来定义："Competition is an unremitting pursuit for perfection to continually transcend oneself"。前者重在输赢，为之不择手段、不惜代价，结果难免有害；后者重在自我超越，既有竞争，亦有合作，更多地实现利他的社会价值（如公平、自由、社会正义等），其结果多会有益。

同时，还可列出以下英文提纲：

Outline

Position Whether competition is ultimately beneficial to society is hard to judge and finally up to our understanding of the meaning of competition.

❶ 正 Competition has brought us so much. Never have human beings been better equipped with science and technology and enjoyed greater material abundance over the past than in today. All this has to be attributed to competition which has called up unimaginable creativity out of human beings.

❷ 反 Meanwhile, however, human history has also recorded such sad consequences coming with competition: moral depravity, environmental pollution, enlarging disparity between the poor and the rich, war, and nothingness of human values.

❸ 合 Consequently, we have to clarify what we mean by competition: it means to win, sometimes by whatever means and at whatever cost? Or it means an unremitting pursuit for perfection to continually transcend oneself? The former leads to win-lose or even lose-lose, but the latter can bring us win-win.

范例二

The human mind will always be superior to machines because machines are only tools of human minds.

题型归类

这道题前后两个分句由连词because连接，应将之归类为因果类题目。但这道因果类题目的结果部分是个价值判断，所以，我们又把它称为结合式是非类题目，从因果类和是非类两个角度分别展开分析。

题目分析

第一步：先提正

根据机器是人类的工具，从社会学或者伦理学的意义上，可以推出人类比机器高级。牛马低于人类不仅仅在于它们是低等动物，更在于它们是人类的工具，为人类控制和利用。

第二步：再求反

从因果类题目的两个分析切入点着手，找到反对、修正题目所持立场的观点和思路。

首先，**第一个分析切入点**：这个因果关系推理中的原因是否成立？

题目中的原因部分"machines are only tools of human minds"是个基本的事实，显然成立。关键在于第二个分析切入点。

第二个分析切入点：假设这个原因成立，从它能否推出结果？

因为"machines are only tools of human minds"，所以"the human mind will always be superior to machines"？这里关键的问题是：高级（superior）的判断标准是什么？这个判断标准是否值得修正？由此，题目也就转入了是非类题目的分析。

首先，价值判断的标准是什么？

当题目由"machines are only tools of human minds"这个角度来讨论人的能力是否比机器更高级的时候，所说的是社会学或者伦理学意义上的高级和低级。以社会学或者伦理学意义上的价值判断标准，运用工具者当然居于主体、主动的地位，因而比工具高级。

其次，这个价值判断的标准是否值得修正？

当题目的结果部分出现"human mind **will always be superior** to machines"时，这里的"高级"实际已经引入了多种判断标准，所以，必须对"高级"的判断标准进行修正。"高级"可以是伦理学和社会学意义上的高低、上下之分，也可以是指某一特定的功能，比如记忆量，但人脑好像没有计算机记得多；速度，人脑的单项运算速度不及计算机；创造性，人脑目前略胜一筹；可扩展性，人脑好像不必经常像计算机一样需要升级……所有这些，标准不同，判断结果自然不同。

第三步：因人因题合、反、散

结合题目特点以及自己对题目内容的驾驭能力，决定采取"散"的办法，由一个相关的角度将问题发散开来阐述：虽然借助科技的力量人类似乎无所不能，但人类仍然有其固有的缺陷，并不完美。

上面的分析过程完成之后，同学们自然就可以整理出一个中文提纲：

论点　人类是否比机器高级取决于我们如何定义"高级"。

正　根据机器是人类的工具，可以推出人类比机器高级。
运用工具者必在社会学或者伦理学的意义上高于工具。

反　但不能据此推出：人类的意识/思维能力/智能永远高于机器。
当"高级"的判定标准是指具体的记忆量、运算速度、力量等诸方面时，人类的能力未必永远处于优势。

散　人类远非完美。
人类本身有很多缺点，如人性中的懒惰、贪婪、自私等。由于这些缺点，人类常常陷自我于绝境，比如战争、环境污染造成的后果等。

同时，还可列出以下英文提纲：

Outline

Position　The statement that "The human mind will always be superior to machines because machines are only tools of human minds" sounds precarious for failing to clearly define the meaning of "superior."

❶　正　When we say one thing is superior to another because the latter is a tool of the former, we are judging their relative status in a social or ethical sense. As a matter of fact, we human beings sometimes feel quite self-conceited before the nature is right for our assurance that we can, with the aid of science and technology, turn, sooner or later, all the things around us into a tool.

❷　反　But obviously, the term "superior" allows a definition from many perspectives. It can refer to the memory power, speed, creativity, extensibility, flexibility, and so forth. In these senses, can we still say that the human mind always performs better than machines?

❸ 散 The above analysis might remind us human beings of a bare fact: yes, we are sitting on top of the pyramid of creatures on earth; but we are not perfect. Sometimes, it is man who brings himself to the dead mire, just because he is overly confident.

四、定义类题目分析范例

范例一

Some people believe that in order to be effective, political leaders must yield to public opinion and abandon principle for the sake of compromise. Others believe that the most essential quality of an effective leader is the ability to remain consistently committed to particular principles and objectives.

题型归类

这道题在前面的题型分类中已经提到过，它主要围绕着什么是一位称职的领导的核心素质而展开，完全是在讨论一个概念的定义。属于单纯性定义类题目。

题目分析

第一步：先提正

坚持既定的原则和目标是领导的必要素质。人们从领导那里渴望得到的是明确的目标、坚定的信念和对未来的信心。这一方面是因为领导的能力和魅力；另一方面是因为当面临复杂的局势和压力时，人们本能地倾向于动摇。这时，领导的坚定、沉着和执著就显得尤为重要。

第二步：再求反

从定义类题目的两个分析切入点着手，找到反对、修正题目所持立场的观点和思路。

首先，**第一个分析切入点**：题目中的定义是否抓住了问题的本质？

到底一个称职的领导最为本质的素质是什么是个见仁见智的问题。只要大家有自己的定义，都可以认为题目中的定义未能抓住问题的本质。大家完全可以根据自己的理解以及对这个问题的驾驭能力来提出自己的定义。比如，可以将一个称职的领导最为本质的素质定义为富有远见、合作意识、对组织和群体的忠诚等。

第二个分析切入点：能否给出我自己的、更为恰当的定义（对自己的论点、论据以及所列举的现象有很好解释力的定义）？

在这里，结合自己对题目的分析以及对这个题目驾驭的能力，我将一个称职的领导最为本质的素质定义为：除了恪守原则和目标以外，善于见微知著、广纳群言，而不轻言妥协，因时因势而权变的素质同样重要。毕竟，世界不是一个已经设计好的程序，每个人只要按部就班地去做就行了。

第三步：因人因题合、反、散

结合题目特点以及自己对题目内容的驾驭能力，决定采取"合"的办法，将第一、二步的分析综合起来，展开论述。这个"合"是通过给"称职的领导"下一个定义来完成的，即一个真正称职的领导是一个在任何时候都知道该做什么、如何去做，从而领导民众不断胜利的领导，这样的领导必须兼备两种素质。

上面的分析过程完成之后，同学们自然就可以整理出一个中文提纲：

论点 真正称职的领导不仅要善于坚持既定的原则和目标，同时还要善于见微知著、广纳群言、因时因势而权变。

㊣ 坚持既定的原则和目标是领导的必要素质。

人们从领导那里渴望得到的是明确的目标、坚定的信念和对未来的信心。这一方面是因为领导的能力和魅力；另一方面是因为面临复杂局势和压力，人们本能地倾向于动摇，这时，领导的坚定、沉着和执著就显得尤为重要。

㊎ 但不能据此说，坚持既定的原则和目标是领导最为核心的素质。

领导善于见微知著、广纳群言而不轻言妥协、因时因势而权变的素质也同样重要。有时，只有变才能达到目的。卓越的领导其实更要审时度势、因时因事而权变。

㊏ 一个真正称职的领导应当兼备以上两种素质，既能恪守原则和目标，又能因时因势而权变。

一个真正称职的领导是一个在任何时候都知道该做什么、如何去做，因而领导民众不断成功的领导。这样的领导必须兼备两种素质。

同时，还可列出以下英文提纲：

Outline

Position A truly effective leader is the one who has not only the ability to remain consistently committed to particular principles and objectives, but also the prescience and determination to change and embrace others' ideas at the right time.

❶ ㊣ Undoubtedly, the ability to remain consistently committed to particular principles and objectives is indispensable for a leader, from whom people can expect direction and courage of what and how they can perform while facing a decisive conjuncture.

❷ ㊎ However, a leader's prescience and determination to change the present principles and objectives when necessary is at least as, if not more, important as the ability to adhere to them. Anyhow, the world before a leader is not well programmed in advance; and what he/she should do is not just run after the pre-designed steps. Every so often, a party, a business or sometimes a nation running into its undoing is right for a leader's too adamantly sticking to some so-called principles or objectives.

❸ ㊏ A truly effective leader is the one who can combine the above two qualities together harmoniously and naturally.

范例二

Most people are taught that loyalty is a virtue. But loyalty—whether to one's friends, to one's school or place of employment, or to any institution—is all too often a destructive rather than a positive force.

题型归类

从形式上讲，这道题应该归为我们下面就要谈到的事实类题目。但因为题目的展开分析几乎完全取决于其中的关键概念"忠诚"（loyalty）的定义，所以又可将之归为**结合式定义类题目**。绝大部分定义类题目都属于这种类型。

对于结合式定义类题目，我们分析的切入点只有一个：**结合论证需要，给出自己的、更为恰当的定义**。这道题将在事实类题目的分析范例中详细讲解，此处从略。

五、事实类题目分析范例

范例一

People's attitudes are determined more by their immediate situation or surroundings than by society as a whole.

题型归类

到底是什么在界定人的思想与行为呢？题目中，论者认为是我们所处的特定情势或者我们周围的环境在界定我们的思想态度和行为方式，而不是作为一个整体的社会。这是论者的一个观察、判断，他认为这是事实，并希望我们也相信。而且，我们好像也无法把这个题目明确归入因果类、是非类、建议类或定义类。所以，该题属于事实类。

题目分析

第一步：先提正

说一个人是社会的产物（a product of the society）不算错。但相对于某个具体的人来说，这个所谓的社会也是相对的、具体的，总是由他所接触的、有限的人构成，比如家庭、朋友、老师、名人等等。据此，不能大而化之地说是一个整体性的社会（a society as a whole）而不是某个具体的环境（a specific environment）在影响这个人。

而且，一个人的世界观（outlook of the world）和人生价值（human values）的形成有一个所谓的关键阶段，比如说 18—24 岁？在这个阶段，年轻人更多的是从其他具体的个人及其周围的小环境，而非他不知为何物的社会中去寻找世界观和人生价值。

第二步：再求反

从事实类题目的两个分析切入点着手，找到反对、修正题目所持立场的观点和思路。

首先，第一个分析切入点：能否从公认的原则或事实中推出相反的判断？

其一，任何人所处的小环境尽管是相对独立的，但它和社会大环境并不是隔绝的。一个人的思想和行为，如果追根溯源的话，都能找到其周围整个社会的影子。即便一个人的生活和成长离不开家庭、朋友、老师、名人等等，但这些小环境里的人和事都是社会大环境的产物。小环境如同大海中的岛屿，岛上的生物(也包括人)看似是这个岛屿生态的产物，但这个岛屿生态实际是大海缔造的，所以，它终究是海洋生态的一个组成部分。

其二，由一个人的成长和变化来看，尽管这个人的世界观和人生价值是由青少年时期的成长环境决定的，但其整个人生的观念和价值选择不是一次性的行为(a one-off action)，而是持续变化的。这个人后续的生活、工作经历和个人交往的环境越丰富，他就越接近这个大社会，最终，他更是这个大社会的而不是某个小环境的产物。

第二个分析切入点：能否举出相反的事例？

大家可以举出家人、亲戚、同学、朋友以及自己等许多例子，来证明身边的小社会和大社会的各自作用和影响。

第三步：因人因题合、反、散

结合题目特点以及自己对题目内容的驾驭能力，决定采取"合"的办法，来完成文章正文部分的第三个意群段，即一个人的生活和成长是个持续动态的历程，那么其思想态度和行为方式也是不断调整和变化的。在一个人的儿童和青少年时期，他的思想态度和行为方式几乎纯粹是其家庭和具体的个人生活、学习环境的产物；但他到了成年、中年和晚年，他的思想态度和行为方式更多的是受社会大环境的影响。

上面的分析过程完成之后，同学们自然就可整理出一个中文提纲：

论点 一个人的思想态度和行为方式是不断调整和变化的。

正 个别人或社会小环境对人的思想和行为的影响不容忽视。

1. 说一个人是社会的产物(a product of the society)不算错。但对人们来说，这个社会是相对、具体的，总是由他接触的、有限的人构成，比如家庭、朋友、老师、名人等等。据此，不能大而化之地说是一个整体性的社会(a society as a whole)而不是某个具体的环境(a specific environment)在影响这个人。

2. 而且，一个人的世界观(outlook of the world)和人生价值(human values)的形成有一个关键阶段，比如说18—24岁？在这个阶段，年轻人更多的是从周围小环境，而非大社会中去寻找世界观和人生价值。

反 但是，人终归是其所在环境的产物。

1. 任何人所处的社会小环境尽管是相对独立的，但它和社会大环境并不是隔绝的。一个人的思想和行为，如果追根溯源的话，都能找到其周围的整个社会的痕迹。即便一个人的成长离不开家庭、朋友、老师、名人等等，但小环境里的人和事都是社会大环境的产物。小环境如同大海中的岛屿，岛上的生物（也包括人）看似是这个岛屿生态的产物，但这个岛屿生态实际是这个大海缔造的，所以，它终究是海洋生态的一个组成部分。

2. 由一个人的成长和变化来看，尽管这个人的世界观和价值观是由青少年时期的成长环境决定的，但其整个人生的观念和价值选择不是一次性的行为（a one-off action），而是持续变化的。这个人后续的生活、工作经历和个人交往的环境越丰富，他就越接近这个大社会本身，最终，他是这个大社会的而不是某个小环境的产物。

合 一个人的思想态度和行为方式也是不断调整和变化的。

一个人的生活和成长是个持续动态的历程，那么其思想态度和行为方式也是不断调整和变化的。在一个人的儿童和青少年时期，他的思想态度和行为方式几乎纯粹是其家庭和个人生活、学习环境的产物；但到了他的成年、中年和晚年，他的思想态度和行为方式更多的是受社会大环境的影响。

同时，还可列出以下英文提纲：

Outline

Position A man's attitude and behavior are in a process of continual changes.

❶ 正 We certainly cannot underestimate the influence of some individuals and the close surroundings upon the formation of a person's world outlook and personal values. First, the society, however big a role it plays in shaping a person's social attitudes, are surely composed of concrete components, for example, family, friends, teachers, celebrities and so on. Second, in his 20s – widely agreed a critical period for minting one's social identity and temperaments – he most probably tends to follow the footprints of those immediately around him for his own track. In his young days, the society may be too large and blurring to be of any real significance in developing his social values.

❷ 反 On the other hand, however, men are after all products of their environment. Any character or personality is, if traced down to its terminus, simply a projection against the backdrop of society. There is no objection that any child grows up under the influence, direct or not, of his family, friends, teachers or certain celebrities, but all these people themselves are also products of a concrete society. Such a situation can be likened to vegetation and animals living on an island. Superficially, these vegetation and animals seem to live by the ecological system of the island. But the island ecological surroundings are, after all, a component of the bigger ecological sphere of the ocean embracing the island. A reasonable conclusion is that the vegetation and animals on the island are actually nurtured somehow by the ecological system of the ocean. Moreover, although a young man develops his world outlook and personal values mainly during his 20s, such development is by no means a one-off action.

His world outlook and value system may take shape in his puberty, but mature up in his adulthood, and finally ripen after his middle age as he reads broader, experiences more and reflect deeper along the way. Therefore, it is safe to say that the older we become, the closer we are to the society as a whole than to any immediate situation or surroundings.

❸ ⑤ So, we can see that a man's attitude and behavior are in a process of continual changes. In his childhood and puberty, he learns from and within his relatively small world comprised of family, friends and school. But in his adulthood, particularly in his middle age and later years, he will surely merge with and sail along the river of the bigger, complex, sometimes annoying but unavoidable society.

范例二

Most people are taught that loyalty is a virtue. But loyalty whether to one's friends, to one's school or place of employment, or to any institution—is all too often a destructive rather than a positive force.

题型归类

到底忠诚（loyalty）是好是坏，论者有自己的判断。论题的第二句是论者的一个观察和判断，他认为这是事实，并希望我们也相信。所以，我们把它归入事实类。但显然，命题"loyalty—whether to one's friends, to one's school or place of employment, or to any institution—is all too often a destructive rather than a positive force"到底是真是假，关键在于如何界定其中核心概念"忠诚"的定义。讲不清楚什么是"忠诚"，这个题目根本写不下去。我们将这种形式上归属于其他题目类型，但题目的展开分析几乎完全取决于其中的关键概念的定义的题目，归为**结合式定义类**题目。

本题将从事实类和结合式定义类两种题型同时展开分析。

题目分析

第一步：先提正

毫无原则的忠诚经常使一个组织或群体出现集体疯狂。小到帮派团伙、流氓犯罪，大到政党政治中的朋党勾结、拉帮结派，直至法西斯政权对民众的政治"洗脑"，鼓动集权主义和军国主义，"忠诚"的确起了坏的作用。

第二步：再求反

从事实类题目的两个分析切入点着手，找到反对、修正题目所持立场的观点和思路。

首先，**第一个分析切入点**：能否从公认的原则或事实中推出相反的判断？

1. 忠诚也可以增强组织的凝聚力，使组织成员产生强烈的归属感，从而使组织本身更有力量。人毕竟是社会性的动物，总是生活在各种各样的组织中。而组织的一个特性即是要求其成员对该组织的程度不一的忠诚。没有忠诚，就没有组织，可能也就没有了社会。

2. 从个人友谊的维持、民族种族的繁衍生息，到人们对信仰、信念的坚持，忠诚也在发挥着积极的作用。

第二个分析切入点：能否举出相反的事例？

国家、民族的团结御敌，人类对普遍价值（如平等、自由、生命尊严等）的忠诚推动人性的进步，员工对公司的忠诚促进生产效率的提高等。

文章分析至此，我们就有了这样的问题：既然忠诚既能导致破坏性的结果，又能产生积极的作用，那么，忠诚到底是一种什么样的力量呢？

如果写作文到此只是列举两种相反的事实，而不能对这种看似矛盾的现象给予解释，肯定会给人一种不善分析、思想不深刻的印象；而且，文章至此还会有写不下去的感觉。

这时，只要来个恰当的定义，文章立刻会境界全出，你也会文思如涌。所谓恰当的定义就是能对自己的论点、论据以及所列举的现象有很好解释力的定义。比如我们可以将"忠诚"定义为：

A. 忠诚是对个人或组织基于个体价值和信念基础上的归属（Loyalty is an individual's identification, based on his/her own values and faith, with another person or institution and its creed）；

B. 忠诚是对人或组织的高度认同，但同时以不损害第三方利益为边界（Loyalty is the high-degree identification of a person, without injuring the third party's interests, with another person or institution）；

C. 忠诚是对人或组织的高度认同，并且以不损害人类的普遍价值（如自由、平等，对生命和人性尊严的尊重等）为前提（Loyalty is the high-degree identification of a person with another person or institution, on the precondition that it must not damage universal human values such as liberty, equality, respect for life and dignity）。

无论采用哪一个定义，都能对忠诚到底是积极还是破坏性的力量给出一个非常顺畅的解释。而这个给出一个恰当定义的办法，就是结合式定义类题目的分析切入点。

第三步：因人因题合、反、散

结合题目特点以及自己对题目内容的驾驭能力，决定采取"合"的办法，将第一、第二步的分析综合起来，展开论述。这个"合"是通过对概念"忠诚"的界定来完成的，即忠诚是对个人或组织基于个体价值和信念基础上的归属。有了一个健全的个体价值和信念作基础，忠诚很可能就会是积极的力量，反之，则极容易变成破坏性的力量。

上面的分析过程完成之后，同学们自然就可以整理出一个中文提纲：

论点　忠诚是积极的还是破坏性的力量取决于我们对"忠诚"含义的界定。

正　毫无原则的忠诚经常使一个组织或群体出现集体疯狂。

小到帮派团伙、流氓犯罪，大到政党政治中的朋党勾结、拉帮结派，直至法西斯政权对民众的政治"洗脑"，鼓动集权主义和军国主义，"忠诚"的确起了坏的作用。

（反）不能一概而论地说，忠诚仅仅是一种破坏性的力量。

1. 忠诚也可以增强组织的凝聚力，使组织的成员产生强烈的归属感，从而使组织本身更有力量。人毕竟是社会性的动物，总是生活在各种各样的组织中。而组织的一个特性即是要求其成员对该组织的程度不一的忠诚。没有忠诚，就没有组织，可能也就没有了社会。

2. 从个人友谊的维持、民族种族的繁衍生息，到人们对信仰、信念的坚持，忠诚也在发挥着积极的作用。

3. 国家、民族的团结御敌，人类对普遍性价值（如平等、自由、生命尊严等）的忠诚推动人性的进步，员工对公司的忠诚促进生产效率的提高等。

（合）关键在于我们如何理解忠诚。

忠诚是对个人或组织基于个体价值和信念基础上的归属。有了一个健全的个体价值和信念作基础，忠诚很可能就会是积极的力量，反之，则极容易变成破坏性的力量。

同时，还可列出以下英文提纲：

Outline

Position Whether loyalty is destructive or positive is up to how we define it.

❶ （正）It's true that from a gang's vandalism to partisan strife and to the Nazi holocaust, loyalty plays an infamous role.

❷ （反）On the other hand, however, we have also observed the unimaginable power of loyalty behind humanitarian improvement and social progress.

❸ （合）Loyalty is, to the bottom, an individual's identification, based on his own values and faith, with another person or institution and its creed. Loyalty will not lead to any serious devastation as long as the individual values and faith are sound and independent. An institution's outrageousness always works by first using its members' insanity as the step stone.

在结合具体的范例，将各个题目类型的特点及分析方法讲解完毕之后，有两点需要提醒大家特别留意：

第一，要注意那些**套叠式多角度分析题目**的分析。所谓的套叠式多角度分析题目指的是那些一种题目类型中又叠加进了另外一种类型的题目。比如这两道题：

①因果类题目（范例二）：

The human mind will always be superior to machines because machines are only tools of human minds.

这道因果类题目中叠加了是非类题目："The human mind will always be superior to machines"是个价值判断。

②事实类题目（范例二）：

Most people are taught that loyalty is a virtue. But loyalty—whether to one's friends, to one's school or place of employment, or to any institution—is all too often a destructive rather than a positive force.

这道事实类题目中叠加了结合式定义类题目：该题目的展开分析涉及对关键概念"忠诚"的定义。

对此类题目进行分析时，从题目本身的分析切入点展开之后，还要对其中叠加的题目类型进行分析。

这样分析下来，可以得到很丰富的写作内容，文章思路极容易展开。实际上，如果大家对ISSUE题库中的题目分析了40-50道之后会发现：套叠式多角度分析题目其实比那些单一类型的题目要好写，因为在运用"1+5"写作模型对之进行分析后，大家会有足够的要点可写。

第二，要注意那些**平行式多角度分析题目**的分析。大家可以观察以下这两道题：

①事实类题目（范例二）：

Most people are taught that loyalty is a virtue. But loyalty—whether to one's friends, to one's school or place of employment, or to any institution—is all too often a destructive rather than a positive force.

②是非类题目（范例一）：

Competition is ultimately more beneficial than detrimental to society.

下面，我把"Competition is ultimately more beneficial than detrimental to society"作一下变形：

Most people are taught that competition is a virtue. But competition—whether between one's friends, between schools or places of employment, or between any institutions—is all too often a beneficial rather than a detrimental force to society.

怎么样？是否和事实类题目范例二的陈述几乎一样呢？

这样的变化说明：是非类题目和事实类题目多数情况下是可以相互转化的。再看下面这道题：

定义类题目分析（范例一）：

Some people believe that in order to be effective, political leaders must yield to public opinion and abandon principle for the sake of compromise. Others believe that the most essential quality of an effective leader is the ability to remain consistently committed to particular principles and objectives.

我们在分析这道题目时，是把它归入单纯性定义类的。但这道题也可归入建议类，尽管略显勉强。这是因为这道题的前半部分"Some people believe that in order to be effective, political leaders must yield to public opinion and abandon principle for the sake of compromise"听起来似乎也是个建议，所以，归入建议类也说得过去。

以上这些例子说明了这样一个现象：**部分题目可以归入不止一个题目类型，因而可以从不同的切入点展开分析。**这样的题目即属于平行式多角度分析题目。具体平行式多角度分析题目应该归入哪个题目类型，同学们可以按照自己的写作特长来选择。多数情况下，平行式多角度分析题目只是提供了更多的分析切入方法，分析内容并无太大区别。

作为参考，本书已将新版ISSUE题库中的所有题目进行了归类（请参见本书第五章《新版ISSUE题库各题目分析指要》），但大家也可以根据自己的偏好和擅长进行题目类型的划分。

本章内容小结

❶ 大家要注意体会，使用"1+5"写作模型可以使我们同时得出文章的写作思路和结构框架。拿到ISSUE题目之后，首先要做的就是对它进行归类。随后，按照"先提正，再求反，因人因题合、反、散"的顺序分析出文章正文部分的三个意群段。有了这三个意群段之后，文章到底要表达什么中心思想/观点也就非常清楚了。然后，再加上文章的开头和结尾。这样，对于一篇文章到底要写些什么、该如何写也就了然于胸了。文章没内容可写的问题也就基本得到了解决。

❷ 大家要注意：文章的中心思想/论点一定是在有了正文部分的三个意群段之后，自然而然总结而出的。不要一拿到题目，就先想出一个立场，然后再想办法去证明这个立场。这样做就南辕北辙了，证明起来会觉得很吃力。

❸ 要注意部分题目中所暗含的逻辑陷阱（如因果类题目分析范例一和是非类题目分析范例一）。ETS设计的ISSUE和ARGUMENT这两篇作文是用来取代过去GRE考试中的逻辑部分的，所以无论是ISSUE写作还是ARGUMENT写作都要考查我们的逻辑思维能力。不过，同学们没必要因此就去想办法专门补习逻辑方面的课。ISSUE写作和ARGUMENT写作里面所体现的逻辑知识更多是常识性的，多分析一些ISSUE和ARGUMENT作文题，大家就能很快熟悉这些逻辑方面的知识和规律。

❹ 对于套叠式多角度分析题目，同学们要学会分层次切入分析。这样做的效果是，你能比其他人更多地挖掘出ISSUE题目内容的复杂性。这是ISSUE作文得高分的要素之一。对于平行式多角度分析题目，要尽量找到自己所擅长的分析切入点。多数情况下，平行式多角度分析题目只是提供了更多的分析切入方法，分析内容并无太大区别。

❺ 关于正文部分第三个意群段是"合"、是"反"、还是"散"的问题。"合、反、散"的选择完全因人因题而异，取决于题目特点和同学们对题目的驾驭能力。但要注意，"合"不是指转圈说重复的话，即正着说，反着说，然后正、反一起说。在ETS眼里，"转圈说重复的话"是严重缺乏分析能力的表现。在对分析范例的讲解中，大家想必已经发现，我们通常是通过下一个定义（如事实类题目分析范例二），或者找到一个能正、反双向解释的角度（如因果类题目分析范例二）来完成"合"的。"散"要注意不可跑题。比如，在是非类题目分析范例二中，我们从"人类的意识/思维能力/智能未必永远高于机器"这个判断，自然过渡到"人类远非完美"这个判断。后一个判断同前一个判断自然相关。如果我们从"人类的意识/思维能力/智能未必永远高于机器"这个判断，过渡到"人性是卑微的"，给人感觉就太具体、问题扯得太远，相当于提出了一个新话题，就会有跑题之嫌。

❻ 关于如何处理每道ISSUE题目及其后面的写作指引（instruction）的关系问题。很简单：第一，一定要两面写；第二，参看本书的第五章《新版ISSUE题库各题目分析指要》。按照"1+5"写作模型对ISSUE题目展开分析，大家应该可以体会到，我们的分析思路同那些写作指引的要求是不谋而合的。这个特点在建

议类、因果类、事实类和是非类的题目中尤为突出。比如说，ETS 的 ISSUE 写作指引要求考生分析建议类题目中那些建议的后果与利弊，这一点恰恰就是我们针对建议类题目所提出的第二个分析切入点——如果实施题目中的建议，是否会导致同初始目的相矛盾或其他荒谬的结果？再比如，ETS 要求考生分析事实类题目中的判断在哪些情形之下是成立或不成立的。按照"1+5"写作模型，我们在先对题目中的部分判断作出肯定（也就是"先提正"）后，随即从两个角度"能否从公认的原则或事实中推出相反的判断？"和"能否举出相反的事例？"来"再求反"。这样下来，事实类题目中的判断在哪些情形之下是成立的、在哪些情形之下是不成立的自然也就唾手而得了。如果还不清楚，那就请大家翻翻本书第五章《新版 ISSUE 题库各题目分析指要》，那里每道 ISSUE 题目都有详细的分析过程和参考提纲。

第二章

第二大问题：
如何使文章篇幅达到要求

- ★ 十大论证技巧
- ★ 十一个论证角度
- ★ 论证范例
- ★ 论证技巧的应用

将 ISSUE 作文写长的一个关键办法是展开有效的论证。试想，如果一篇议论文只有孤零零的几个要点，没有充分的论证，这篇文章是不可能写长的。而这里所要讲到的**填入式论证法**，可以使论证像做文字填空游戏一样轻松。

另一个让同学们的文章写不长的原因与同学们的写作习惯有关。这一点将在本书第三章《第三大问题：如何写得漂亮》中重点讲解。

第一节 十大论证技巧

常用的论证方法有十种，包括：因果关系论证法（cause-effect）、引用权威论证法（authority）、反证法（reduction to absurdity）、列举特征式论证法（signs）、统计数据论证法（statistics）、归纳推理论证法（induction）、诉诸常识法（common sense）、演绎推理论证法（deduction）、类比论证法（analogy）、定义法（definition）。将各论证方法的首字母缩写组合起来，即为 "CARSSICDAD"。

下面将这十大论证方法一一讲解。首先，有必要将下面讲解所涉及的概念解释一下。每一个论证方法将按照**论点**、**论据**和**推理依据**的顺序讲解。大家都知道，凡是议论文必然有论点、论据和论证三要素。论点和论据好理解，而论证就是用论据支持论点的过程。但用论据支持论点是否有效，关键在于由论点到论据有没有足够的推理依据。推理依据不成立，论证就是无效论证。

这里顺便讲一下 ARGUMENT 的解题思路：每一道 ARGUMENT 题目本身都是一个从论据到论点的论证过程：其中有观点，有论据。这个从论据到论点的论证过程会出现诸多大大小小逻辑链条。只要我们能证明 ARGUMENT 题目中的论者在任何一个逻辑链条上出了问题，那么，其推理/论证就不能成立。所以，对于 ARGUMENT，我们的任务只有一个：从两到三个方面证明题目在哪些逻辑链条上出了问题，以至于其由论据到论点/结论的推理依据不成立。而 ARGUMENT 所有的分析切入点，就是这里将要谈到的十大论证技巧。正是在这十大论证技巧里面，大家完全可以发现 ISSUE 和 ARGUMENT 两种不同写作任务之间互济相通的乐趣。

一、演绎推理论证法

将一个具体的事例运用到一个一般性原则从而得出结论。例如：

论 点 Demand for this product will go up.

论 据 The price of the product is sliding.

推理依据 Whenever prices of a product go down，demand for it rises.

（说明：由论据 "The price of the product is sliding" 推出论点 "Demand for this product will go up"，这个过程是否有效取决于推理依据 "Whenever prices of a product go down，demand for it rises" 是否成立。下面每一种论证方法都是如此。）

二、定义法

界定一个概念的关键内涵；或者认定某个事物符合某个定义，从而得出结论。例如：

论 点 Radical feminists are not good citizens.

论 据 Radical feminists lack family values.

推理依据 Family values characterize the good citizen.

三、因果关系论证法

将一个判断放入一个因果关系中，指出它或者是原因，或者是结果。例如：

论 点 The Internet may be causing depression.

论 据 When a group of people increased their use of the Internet，they felt depressed.

推理依据 There are no other reasons for the group's depression.

四、归纳推理论证法

从若干个具体事例中推出共性的一般结论。例如：

论 点 Everyone likes the movie.

论 据 I know three people who like the movie.

推理依据 Three examples are enough.

五、列举特征式论证法

指出某事物发生或者存在的征候或迹象。例如：

论 点 The child has chickenpox.

论 据 The child has red spots.

推理依据 These spots are signs of chickenpox.

六、类比论证法

用我们已知的、熟悉的事物同未知的、不熟悉的事物加以比较，并用前者的情况解释后者的情况。分为三种：纵向类比（过去的事物同现在的、同一类事物的类比）、横向类比（同一时期、同一类事物之间的类比）、比喻式类比（不同类别事物之间的类比）。例如：

1. 纵向类比（Historical Analogy）

论 点 Many people will die of SARS.

论 据 Many people died of the Black Death.

推理依据 SARS and Black Death are similar.

2. 横向类比（Literal Analogy）

论 点 China should have its fighter carriers.

论 据 A neighboring country has a powerful carrier fleet.

推理依据 The two countries are similar enough to draw such a comparison.

3. 比喻式类比（Metaphorical Analogy）

论 点 Reading a difficult book should take time.

> **论 据** Digesting a large meal takes time.
> **推理依据** Reading and eating are sufficiently alike to be compared.

七、引用权威论证法

引用公认的权威，或者论证自己就是权威从而对自己的观点加以论证。例如：

> **论 点** China's economy will grow 8 percent this year.
> **论 据** Professors and scientists say so.
> **推理依据** These experts are reliable.

八、诉诸常识法

利用人们的常识［包括：普遍性的价值观念（universal values such as freedom，equality，supremacy of life，dignity and pursuit of happiness）、人们的普遍动机（public motives：desire for love，shelter，food，security，wealth，knowledge，etc.）、生活常识（widely-accepted ideas and practices in life）］进行论证。例如：

1. 诉诸普遍性的价值观念（Universal Values）

> **论 点** The university curriculum should be multicultural.
> **论 据** A multicultural curriculum will contribute to equality and acceptance.
> **推理依据** You value equality and acceptance.

2. 诉诸普遍动机（Public Motives）

> **论 点** You should support this candidate premier.
> **论 据** The candidate can help you get job security and safe neighborhoods.
> **推理依据** You want job security and safe neighborhoods.

3. 诉诸生活常识（Widely-accepted Ideas and Practices in Life）

> **论 点** She was very kind to me.
> **论 据** She treated me with the best tea she had.
> **推理依据** A treatment with the best tea is an expression of kindness.

九、反证法

假设一个观点是正确的，然而却推导出荒谬的结论。例如：

> **论 点** An industrious man must also be thrifty.
> **论 据** With only industry but without thrift，the person will end up bankrupt.
> **推理依据** An industrious person ending up bankrupt sounds absurd.

十、统计数据论证法

提供数据，以资论证。例如：

> **论 点** We should end the current poverty-relief program.
> **论 据** It costs $45 million per year.

推理依据 This is too much; it proves we should end it.

在实际的论证过程中，我们可能并不需要给出推理依据，而只是直接拿论据去证明论点。比如，在演绎推理法的例子中，如果我们想证明论点 "Demand for this product will go up" 的正确性，我们通常只需给出论据 "The price of the product is sliding" 就行了。这是因为读者的思想意识一般都已经有了，或者都已经认可了 "Whenever prices of a product go down, demand for it rises" 这个逻辑前提。但有时为了充分说明问题，作者也需要将推理依据及其合理性加以说明，并给出证明。比如，在引用权威法的例子中，为了证明论点 "China's economy will grow 8 percent this year"，我们会首先给出论据 "Professors and scientists say so"。但为了使我们的论证更为可信，我们会进一步说明并证明推理依据 "These experts are reliable"。

第二节　十一个论证角度

我们可以将上述论证方法归纳为十一个问题，它们就是 ISSUE 写作的十一个论证角度。在对你文章中的要点和分要点进行论证的时候，请一一回答这些问题：

1. 列举特征式论证法：能否列举出我所提出的观点的**典型特征**？

2. 归纳推理论证法：能否给出我所提出观点的**典型例证**？

3. 因果关系论证法：能否给出我所提出观点的**原因与理由**？能否给出反映这种因果关系的例子。

4. 演绎推理论证法：我的观点能否从一个**一般的原则**中演绎推出？

5. 类比论证法：能否给出关于我所提出观点的纵向（historical）、横向（literal）和比喻性（metaphorical）类比？

6. 定义法：我的推理是否需要并且我能否给出题目中**关键概念的定义**？

7. 统计数据论证法：我能否提供有利于我的论证的**统计数据**？

8. 诉诸常识法：我能否利用人们的常识（包括：**普遍性的价值观念、人们的普遍动机、生活常识**）支持我的论证？

9. 引用权威论证法：能否引用**权威**的观点支持我的论点？

10. 反证法：可否**反证**？

11. 反驳和辩护：可有别的主流/错误观点需要反驳？我自己的哪些观点需要**解释和辩护**？

为方便记忆，以上这十一个论证角度可以简单概括为 "CARSSICDAD+R&D"，即：十大论证技巧加上作者对自己观点的解释、辩护和对他人观点的反驳。

第三节　论证范例

下面通过三篇范文，我们来看一下上述十一个论证角度，即 "CARSSICDAD+R&D" 的具体应用。三篇文章都是典型的议论文。其中，第一篇和第三篇分别选自美国《纽约时报》（*New York Times*）和美国有线电视新闻网（CNN），第二篇则是著名的美国《独立宣言》。每篇文章中的各个意群段已经被空行隔开，同学们可以体会一下意群段和自然段的区别。

请阅读这三篇文章，并思考文后问题。这些问题的参考答案在本书后面的附录4。

Censorship or Common Sense

A 5-year-old is not ready to confront the world. This should be obvious, but it doesn't seem that way to many free-speech advocates.

The objections are coming from some usual sources: the American Civil Liberties Union, for example, and Web publishers. They are angry that some libraries around the country have installed software on their computers to block out Internet material that's unsuitable for children.

Traditionally, the library has been a safe place for children. And librarians have long been the guardians of public virtue. While they have been firm supporters of the First Amendment, they haven't generally interpreted it to mean that they should acquire large holdings of published pornography and make such materials available to children.

Librarians have always acquired books according to their own discrimination and their sense of what is appropriate to their neighborhoods. They generally refuse to buy, among other things, pornography. This isn't censorship; it's common sense.

If a library were to have a section of pornographic books, would we want these to be printed in large, colorfully illustrated, lightweight volumes, shelved near the floor where they were easily available to children? Probably not. But we have gone to a great deal of trouble to insure that computers are user-friendly, with brightly colored graphics and easily accessible information. Material on the Internet is not only uncensored but also unedited. Adults can be expected to make their own evaluations of what they find. Children, who lack experience and knowledge, cannot.

The debate over the filtering of the Internet is a bit like the debate over grants given out by the National Endowment for the arts. It's all tangled up in false cries of censorship. Censorship is a legal term; it refers to government action prohibiting material from being circulated. This is very different from a situation in which a museum or an arts panel decides not to use public money to finance an exhibition or an artist.

Commendably, our society defends freedom of speech with great vigor. But there is a difference between allowing everything to be said and allowing everyone to hear it. We should know this by now, having seen the effects that exposure to television and movie violence has on children.

The A. C. L. U. and the American Library Association say that the use of filtering software in computers is censorship because it blocks access to constitutionally protected speech. But these cries are baffling and unfounded. The only control libraries are asserting is over a small portion of the audience, not over the material itself. Moreover, this control has a powerful historical precedent: parental guidance is even older than the Constitution.

The protection of children should be instinctive. A man may have the right to stand on the street and spew obscenities at passers-by, but he would be ordered to leave a kindergarten classroom.

It is absurd to pretend that adults and children are the same audience, and it is shameful to protect the child pornographer instead of the child.

New York Times, October 19, 1998

（问题）
❶ 文章中有两个纵向类比、三个横向类比、一处比喻性类比、两处定义法论证、一处反证，请将这些论证方法找出来。
❷ 文章在哪些地方对他人的不同观点进行了反驳？
❸ 全篇的逻辑结构是怎样的？

（Passage Ⅱ）

The Declaration of Independence

The Declaration of Independence was approved by Continental Congress on July 2, 1776, and published two days later.

When in the Course of human Events, it becomes necessary for one People to dissolve the Political Bands which have connected them with another, and to assume among the Powers of the Earth, the separate and equal Station to which the Laws of Nature and of Nature's God entitle them, a decent Respect to the Opinions of Mankind requires that they should declare the causes which impel them to the Separation.

WE hold these Truths to be self-evident, that all Men are created equal, that they are endowed by their Creator with certain unalienable Rights, that among these are Life, Liberty and the Pursuit of Happiness.

That to secure these Rights, Governments are instituted among Men, deriving their just Powers from the Consent of the Governed.

That whenever any Form of Government becomes destructive of these Ends, it is the Right of the People to alter or to abolish it, and to institute new Government, laying its Foundation on such Principles, and organizing its Powers in such Form, as to them shall seem most likely to effect their Safety and Happiness. Prudence, indeed, will dictate that Governments long established should not be changed for light and transient Causes; and accordingly all Experience hath shown, that Mankind are more disposed to suffer, while Evils are sufferable, than to right themselves by abolishing the Forms to which they are accustomed. But when a long Train of Abuses and Usurpations, pursuing invariably the same Object, evinces a Design to reduce them under absolute Despotism, it is their Right, it is their Duty, to throw off such Government, and to provide new Guards for their future Security.

Such has been the patient Sufferance of these Colonies; and such is now the Necessity which constrains them to alter their former Systems of Government . The History of the present King of Great Britain is a History of repeated Injuries and Usurpations, all having in direct Object the

Establishment of an absolute Tyranny over these States. To prove this, let Facts be submitted to a candid World.

HE has refused his Assent to Laws, the most wholesome and necessary for the public Good.

HE has forbidden his Governors to pass Laws of immediate and pressing Importance, unless suspended in their Operation till his Assent should be obtained; and when so suspended, he has utterly neglected to attend to them.

HE has refused to pass other Laws for the Accommodation of large Districts of People, unless those People would relinquish the Right of Representation in the Legislature, a Right inestimable to them, and formidable to Tyrants only.

HE has called together Legislative Bodies at Places unusual, uncomfortable, and distant from the Depository of their public Records, for the sole Purpose of fatiguing them into Compliance with his Measures.

HE has dissolved Representative Houses repeatedly, for opposing with manly Firmness his Invasions on the Rights of the People.

HE has refused for a long Time, after such Dissolutions, to cause others to be elected; whereby the Legislative Powers, incapable of the Annihilation, have returned to the People at large for their exercise; the State remaining in the mean time exposed to all the Dangers of Invasion from without, and the Convulsions within.

HE has endeavored to prevent the Population of these States; for that Purpose obstructing the Laws for Naturalization of Foreigners; refusing to pass others to encourage their Migrations hither, and raising the Conditions of new Appropriations of Lands.

HE has obstructed the Administration of Justice, by refusing his Assent to Laws for establishing Judiciary Powers.

HE has made Judges dependent on his Will alone, for the Tenure of their Offices, and the Amount and Payment of their Salaries.

HE has erected a Multitude of new Offices, and sent hither Swarms of Officers to harass our People, and eat out their Substance.

HE has kept among us, in Times of Peace, Standing Armies, without the consent of our Legislatures.

HE has affected to render the Military independent of and superior to the Civil Power.

HE has combined with others to subject us to a Jurisdiction foreign to our Constitution, and unacknowledged by our Laws; giving his Assent to their Acts of pretended Legislation:

FOR quartering large Bodies of Armed Troops among us:

FOR protecting them, by a mock Trial, from Punishment for any Murders which they should commit on the Inhabitants of these States:

FOR cutting off our Trade with all Parts of the World:

FOR imposing Taxes on us without our Consent:

FOR depriving us, in many Cases, of the Benefits of Trial by Jury:

FOR transporting us beyond Seas to be tried for pretended Offences:

FOR abolishing the free System of English Laws in a neighboring Province, establishing therein an arbitrary Government, and enlarging its Boundaries, so as to render it at once an Example and fit Instrument for introducing the same absolute Rules into these Colonies:

FOR taking away our Charters, abolishing our most valuable Laws, and altering fundamentally the Forms of our Governments:

FOR suspending our own Legislatures, and declaring themselves invested with Power to legislate for us in all Cases whatsoever.

HE has abdicated Government here, by declaring us out of his Protection and waging War against us.

HE has plundered our Seas, ravaged our Coasts, burnt our Towns, and destroyed the Lives of our People.

HE is, at this Time, transporting large Armies of foreign Mercenaries to complete the Works of Death, Desolation, and Tyranny, already begun with circumstances of Cruelty and Perfidy, scarcely paralleled in the most barbarous Ages, and totally unworthy the Head of a civilized Nation.

HE has constrained our fellow Citizens taken Captive on the high Seas to bear Arms against their Country, to become the Executioners of their Friends and Brethren, or to fall themselves by their Hands.

HE has excited domestic Insurrections amongst us, and has endeavored to bring on the Inhabitants of our Frontiers, the merciless Indian Savages, whose known Rule of Warfare, is an undistinguished Destruction, of all Ages, Sexes and Conditions.

IN every stage of these Oppressions we have Petitioned for Redress in the most humble Terms: Our repeated Petitions have been answered only by repeated Injury. A Prince, whose Character is thus marked by every act which may define a Tyrant, is unfit to be the Ruler of a free People.

NOR have we been wanting in Attentions to our British Brethren. We have warned them from Time to Time of Attempts by their Legislature to extend an unwarrantable Jurisdiction over us. We have reminded them of the Circumstances of our Emigration and Settlement here. We have appealed to their native Justice and Magnanimity, and we have conjured them by the Ties of our common Kindred to disavow these Usurpations, which would inevitably interrupt our Connections and Correspondence. They too have been deaf to the Voice of Justice and of Consanguinity. We must, therefore, acquiesce in the Necessity, which denounces our Separation, and hold them, as we hold the rest of Mankind, Enemies in War, in Peace, Friends.

WE, therefore, the Representatives of the UNITED STATES OF AMERICA, in GENERAL CONGRESS, Assembled, appealing to the Supreme Judge of the World for the Rectitude of our Intentions, do, in the Name, and by Authority of the good People of these Colonies, solemnly Publish and Declare, That these United Colonies are, and of Right ought to be, FREE AND INDEPENDENT STATES; that they are absolved from all Allegiance to the British Crown, and that all political Connection between them and the State of Great Britain, is and ought to be totally dissolved; and that as FREE AND INDEPENDENT STATES, they have full Power to levy War, conclude Peace, contract Alliances, establish Commerce, and to do all other Acts and Things which

INDEPENDENT STATES may of right do. And for the support of this Declaration, with a firm Reliance on the Protection of divine Providence, we mutually pledge to each other our Lives, our Fortunes, and our sacred Honor.

问题
❶ 文章的第二自然段至倒数第二自然段的逻辑思路是怎样的？
❷ 文章在哪些地方对北美十三州宣布独立的行为进行了辩护？

Passage Ⅲ

Skeptical View of Russia's Economy

By Mark Medish

It was John Maynard Keynes who observed that Russia's economy provided ample evidence to support contradictory theories. In this respect, things in Russia today are not much different from the 1920s.

Recent business headlines from Russia point to a flourishing scene, with galloping bond issuances, surging equities and big oil mergers. Macroeconomic performance is also strong. The federal budget is in surplus; inflation is in single digits; the current account is surging; and central bank reserves exceed $60 billion. Real annual gross domestic product growth is about 4 percent. Gone are the days of Russia's International Monetary Fund tutelage. The 1998 financial collapse is a distant memory.

Yet President Vladimir Putin's recent address to parliament on the state of the country was downbeat. He told his countrymen that Russia's "economic foundation, although it has become considerably sounder, is nevertheless unreliable and very weak". Mr. Putin's strength is his candour.

What does he know that investors do not? Could Russia be heading towards another crash or a serious slowdown, as some analysts are now suggesting?

A possible answer is that Mr. Putin and his advisers are convinced that real rouble appreciation, caused by capital inflows fuelled mostly by the oil and gas sector, is a potential risk. Left unchecked, it would undermine the economy's new-found dynamism and competitiveness. Over-reliance on oil revenues will also damp the reformist zeal that is the key to long-run growth.

The deeper reason for his gloominess may be that Mr. Putin distinguishes between headline news and what is happening below the surface. Perhaps the impending parliamentary elections in December and the presidential ballot next March have sharpened his sensitivity to the realities facing the vast majority of Russia's people.

As Mr. Putin noted in his speech, a quarter of Russians survive on incomes below subsistence, as officially defined. Clearly, abundant natural resource wealth is not a sufficient condition for durable, equitable national prosperity. Without a strategic approach to reform, Russia's growth spurt will dissipate and windfall profits will once more retreat offshore.

Opinion polls favour Mr. Putin for a second term. But whether he will be able to refocus his economic programme is an open question. Several crucial tests will determine whether Mr. Putin's legacy is that of a moderniser.

The first test is diversification. Russia must master its hydrocarbons, or they will master Russia. It needs to upgrade, diversify and privatise its pipelines to boost export capacity. The emerging government strategy to develop new exit routes to the Barents Sea and the Far East bodes well.

At the same time Russia must diversify its productive base away from energy and defense towards higher value-added civilian manufacturing, services and the "new economy". Another test, therefore, is whether the authorities find the wisdom to promote small and medium-sized enterprises. Some gains have been made in tax reform, but generally the state is overbearing through its regulation.

The third test is banking reform. Here the shadow of 1998 is long. Will Mr. Putin be able to break the liquidity bottleneck by nurturing a network of financial institutions that actually mediate credit to the real economy? Without this, domestic investment in Russia will remain the domain of industrial heavyweight and oligarchs.

Fourth, Russia needs better infrastructure. The new Russian economy is being hampered by the crumbling Soviet legacy. Again, banks and capital markets should be the conduit for investment.

Finally, a second Putin term will be judged by what it does for social services, including education, pensions, and health. Mr. Putin made clear that Russia is undergoing unprecedented demographic woes in terms of morbidity and life expectancy. An economy can only be as strong as its people.

The international community could do much to help, by ensuring speedier accession to the World Trade Organization, predicated on deeper liberalization and market-oriented structural reforms. But ultimately meeting the challenge will require powerful leadership from Mr. Putin—provided the beleaguered Russian population gives him the opportunity in the forthcoming ballot cycle.

（问题）
❶ 文章的第二至第三自然段运用了什么样的论证方法?
❷ 文章的第四至第八自然段运用了什么样的论证方法?

第四节　论证技巧的应用

了解了常用的论证方法有哪些以及议论文高手在文章中如何使用它们之后，我们现在来看一看，该如何在ISSUE写作中运用这些论证方法。

在系统掌握了"CARSSICDAD+R＆D"的论证方法后，同学们将会有这样的感觉：**根本不用去挖空心思背所谓的经典例证（诸如哥白尼、伽利略、牛顿、爱因斯坦、华盛顿、林肯等的故事）以及各种名篇佳句。只需把"CARSSICDAD+R＆D"一一列出，然后填入相应内容**

即可。这就是**填入式论证法**。这种论证思路使文章的论证过程像是在做文字填空游戏。

下面通过例子来说明这一点。

我们在讲到因果类题目分析范例的时候，曾讲过这道题：

Claim: We can usually learn much more from people whose views we share than from people whose views contradict our own;

Reason: disagreement can cause stress and inhibit learning.

并列出一个中文写作提纲，如下：

论点 **人们彼此间持相同意见是否会促进他们的学习完全因人而异。**

正：相同的意见会促进人们的学习；相反的意见有时妨碍人们彼此间的学习。

提供原因：别人的赞同是对一个人自我价值、能力的认可，往往会鼓励后者更积极地去努力。这是人的本性使然。

反：但不能依据"disagreement can cause stress and inhibit learning"推出"We can usually learn much more from people whose views we share than from people whose views contradict our own"。

■ 不同意见不一定就会导致压力并妨碍学习。

每个人对批评的态度不同、对压力的反应各异。因此，同样的批评完全可以让有些人积极奋进、眼界思路更为开阔，从而学得更好。

■ 即使不同意见导致了压力并因而妨碍了学习，也推不出"We can usually learn much more from people whose views we share than from people whose views contradict our own"。

影响一个人学习效果的原因有很多（如学习动机、天赋程度、努力程度、兴趣等）。他人的批评和赞同及相应的效果只是众多原因中的一种，所以，对一个人的学习效果不足以有决定性作用。

合：到底他人的意见是否妨碍学习取决于每个人不同的情况。

学习的效果几乎纯粹取决于个人情况：禀赋、性格、动机、所处环境等。

提纲中的正、反、合的内容分别是文章正文部分三个意群段的中心思想句。但这些中心思想句都没有给出证明。现在，我们运用"CARSSICDAD+R & D"将第一个中心思想句"正：相同的意见会促进人们的学习；相反的意见有时妨碍人们彼此间的学习"和第二个中心思想句中的分论点"不同意见不一定就会导致压力并妨碍学习"分别展开论证。

论点 **相同的意见会促进人们的学习；相反的意见有时妨碍人们彼此间的学习。**

论据及论证：

因果关系论证法：给出一组因果关系。

别人的赞同是对一个人自我价值和能力的认可，往往会鼓励后者更积极地去努力。这是人的本性使然。

类比论证法：提供纵向、横向或比喻式类比。

赞扬似阳光，批评如冰霜。效果自然不同。

归纳推理论证法：举出若干例子。

儿童的学习特点、家庭教育中的事例等，大家可以随便举出许多，此处从略。

列举特征式论证法：描述若干特征。

赞同可以给人带来成就感、精神振奋、自信、面对挑战的积极心态、更大的学习动力。

反对可以给人带来挫折感、精神萎靡、自卑、面对挑战的消极心态、低迷的学习愿望。

引用权威论证法和统计数据论证法：列出（或者杜撰出）专家或权威机构的观点和相关数据。

杜撰一个某著名心理研究机构的实验过程及结果：

将某小学三年级的一个班的同学分为A组和B组：对于A组的同学，一般不批评，即便出现错误也首先肯定其值得赞赏的方面。一旦有积极表现，立即给予表扬。对于B组的同学，有了积极的表现也不给予表扬，而一旦有了错误，立刻给予批评。

三个月后，A组的学习成绩总体提高了20%，那些过去一贯学习较差的同学，成绩平均提高了40%。而B组的学习成绩整体下降了22%，过去成绩较好的同学的成绩也下降了10%左右。

注意：这样的杜撰一定要符合常理。太离谱也就没人信。

定义法：给出一个恰当的定义。

学习是人与其周围的环境互动（interaction）的结果。

注意：你的定义完全不必非常专业。只要符合常理，并且很好地解释了部分现象即可。批改你作文的人知道你不是专家，但会非常欣赏你独到的视角。

演绎推理论证法：给出一个能推出具体结论的一般原则。

一个富有安全感、归属感的环境通常能增进人们与该环境的良性互动。而表示赞同的姿态和语言有助于增强人与人之间的安全感和归属感，从而导致良性互动，促进学习。

诉诸常识法：列出一个你我都认可的常识。

人们用微笑、见面握手这样简单的表示赞同的举动来增进彼此间的交往、理解与学习。

反证法：假定你所反对的观点是对的，能否推出荒谬的结果？

如果赞同和反对人们彼此间的学习不能带来差别的话，从学校到社会中的各种奖惩措施岂不都没任何意义了？

论点 不同意见不一定就会导致压力并妨碍学习。

论据及论证：

因果关系论证法：给出一组因果关系。

每个人对批评的态度不同、对压力的反应各异。因此，同样的批评完全可以让有些人积极奋进、眼界思路更为开阔，从而学得更好。

类比论证法：提供纵向、横向或比喻式类比。

井无压力不出油，人无压力轻飘飘。

列举特征式论证法：描述若干特征。

有的人听不得不同意见，他们会情绪激动、甚至恶言相向；而有的人却能心平气和、善意对待他人的批评，并且积极进行自我调整。

归纳推理论证法：举出若干例子。

可以举出别人、自己的一些例子，此处从略。

定义法：给出一个恰当的定义。

压力是一个人对其周围环境纯粹主观的反应。

诉诸常识法：列出一个你我都认可的常识。

不同的人会因为性格、健康状况、对人生的心态等的不同，而对同样的压力作出截然相反的反应。

演绎推理论证法：给出一个能推出具体结论的一般原则。

当一个人的警觉程度提高时，其对周围环境的学习和反应水平也会提高。而压力能提高一个人的警觉程度，从而刺激其学习和反应水平相应提高。

引用权威论证法和统计数据论证法：列出（或者杜撰出）专家或权威机构的观点和相关数据。

某大学教务处统计表明：90%的学生的80%的课本知识是在考试前的两三周内掌握的。

反证法：假定你所反对的观点是对的，能否推出荒谬的结果？

如果反对意见总是带来压力并妨碍学习，人类就不会有各种各样的创新了。因为凡创新必定要打破旧俗，必然招来反对。但人类的创新是呈加速度发展的。

反驳与辩解：虽然压力有时能激发人更大的学习动力，但过大的压力会抑制人的学习愿望和创新能力。

大家如果把上面这两个论证中的任何一个的内容写成英文，即使用很简练的语言，每个论证都会有 400 个单词左右。而整篇 ISSUE 作文只要 500 个单词的长度就行了。这样一来，你的文章怎么会写不长呢？

事实上，我们在实际的 ISSUE 写作过程中不可能将每一个要点和分要点都从十一个论证角度依次论证一番。我们显然应将论证的重点放在正文部分三大意群段各自的中心思想/观点的论证上，而对它们的论证又是为整个文章的中心思想/观点服务的。

再者，从所有 "CARSSICDAD+R&D" 所涉及的内容和知识结构来看，除了定义法和演绎推理法稍微需要一点想象力以外，其余的论证方法都是可以信手拈来的。所以，可以说，整个论证过程是颇为容易的。同学们，尤其是理工科的同学，对自己可能存在人文社会科学方面知识不足的担心完全是不必要的。不要忘了：《独立宣言》这篇著名的政治学文献不过是从人们的常识展开论证的。我们只要有一些常识就足够了。而这些所谓的常识通过我们日常生活中的积累、同学们之间的讨论以及本书所附的极有针对性的阅读材料，完全可以迅速补充起来。

ISSUE 写作的关键是要掌握对 ISSUE 的分析方法和展开论证的技巧。而我们的 **"1+5" 写作模型和填入式论证方法**就是为了解决这两个问题而设计的。

还有一点值得大家宽慰的是：我们还会讲**题库压缩**。新版 ISSUE 题库中所有 149 道题目经过压缩之后，至少能减少到 53 道题（或组）左右。同学们结合自己的情况，还可以将题目总量进一步压缩。这样一来，最后同学们手里的 ISSUE 题目就不是单个出现的，而是成组出现的。只要将每一组中一两道题的分析思路、论证要点整理出来，这一组其他题目剩下的工作不过就是删减、拼加而已。这一点在讲到第四章时，大家就会有更真切的体会。

现在如果我们将题目 "Claim: We can usually learn much more from people whose views we share than from people whose views contradict our own; Reason: disagreement can cause stress and inhibit learning." 的中文提纲中各大要点的论证按照实际的写作要求补充完整的话，该提纲就会是如下这个样子：

论点 **人们彼此间持相同意见是否会促进他们的学习完全因人而异。**

正：相同的意见会促进人们的学习；相反的意见有时妨碍人们彼此间的学习。

论证：

A. 提供原因：别人的赞同是对一个人自我价值和能力的认可，往往能鼓励后者作出更积极的努力。这是人的本性使然。

B. 提供类比：赞扬似阳光，批评如冰霜。效果自然不同。

C. 举出例证：儿童的学习特点、家庭教育中的事例等。

反：但不能依据"disagreement can cause stress and inhibit learning"推出"We can usually learn much more from people whose views we share than from people whose views contradict our own"。

A. 不同意见不一定就会导致压力并妨碍学习。

- 提供原因：每个人对批评的态度不同、对压力的反应各异。因此，同样的批评完全可以让有些人积极奋进、眼界和思路更为开阔，从而学得更好。

- 归纳论证：可以举出别人的、自己的一些例子。

- 给出定义：压力是一个人对其周围环境纯粹主观的反应。

- 诉诸常识：不同的人会因为性格、健康状况、对人生的心态等的不同，而对同样的压力作出截然相反的反应。

- 演绎推理：当一个人的警觉程度提高时，其对周围环境的学习和反应水平也会提高。而压力能提高一个人的警觉程度，从而刺激其学习和反应水平相应提高。

- 引用权威论证和统计数据：某大学教务处统计表明：90％的学生的80％的课本知识是在考试前的两三周内学完的。

B. 即使不同意见导致了压力并因而妨碍了学习，也推不出"We can usually learn much more from people whose views we share than from people whose views contradict our own"。

- 提供原因：影响一个人学习效果的原因有很多（如学习动机、天赋程度、努力程度、兴趣等），他人的批评和赞同及相应的效果只是众多原因中的一种，所以，对一个人的学习效果不足以有决定性作用。

合：到底他人的意见是否妨碍学习取决于每个人不同的情况。

论证：

A. 诉诸常识：学习的效果几乎纯粹取决于个人情况：禀赋、性格、动机、所处环境等。

B. 提供原因：如有必要，可以解释为什么禀赋、性格、动机、所处环境等会对学习效果有影响。

C. 提供类比：太阳下的生物有的喜光照，有的喜阴凉，但各自都生长得很好。

D. 举出例证：同学、朋友、自己的学习经历等。

有了这样的一个提纲之后，同学们现在需要做的仅仅是把它加上开头段和结尾段，然后再写成英文罢了。而这样的提纲是怎么来的呢？从其内容来看，大家不用去死记硬背任何东西，只要会应用**"1+5"写作模型和填入式论证法**就行了。这两个方法可以使我们有清晰的思路、完整的结构和充分而多变的论证。

ISSUE 作文满分6分之中，**清晰的思路、完整的结构和充分而多变的论证**可以保证我们得到4分—4.5分。剩下的语言方面，只要我们再能赢得1分，我们的作文就是5分—5.5分。而语言方面的这1分，我们完全可以拿到：只要稍微改变一下你的语言习惯就行了。而后面的第三章就是要重点解决这个问题的。

········ **本章内容小结** ········

① 论证过程中，要尽量使论证方法灵活多变。现在一提到论证方法，有些同学马上就只想到举例和引用名人名言，而且一举例就是诸如哥白尼、伽利略、牛顿、爱因斯坦、华盛顿、林肯等。姑且不说你费了很大的力气能否把那些名人故事及名人名言都背下来。即便你果真背了下来，大家可以想一想，如果那些改作文的读一篇是在讲美国总统华盛顿，读两篇、三篇还是在讲华盛顿，他们会有什么感觉？而张口闭口都是所谓的名人名言，在美国人眼里本来就是缺乏创造性的表现。

② 在举例论证的时候，不要只举那些名人的例子。自己的家人、同学、朋友以及本人的亲身经历，只要典型、有趣、有代表性、有说服力，就都是好例子。大家如果经常读外国期刊，比如《读者文摘》(Reader's Digest)，会发现外国人讲的故事其实绝大多数都是平凡人的小故事。但这些故事读起来很真实、很感人、很有说服力。

③ 十一大论证角度中的反驳与辩解运用与否，要视文章及论证需要而定，不是每个论证过程都必须使用。

④ 建议大家在对论点进行论证的时候，随手将"CARSSICDAD+R & D"写下，并标明各个字母所代表的论证方法；然后，从头至尾一一排列下来。这样，你会发现你能轻松地找到多个论证角度。

大家要把按照"CARSSICDAD+R&D"的办法展开论证当成一个生活习惯。无论是在读题目、读题库，还是在阅读本书开列的参考提纲以及尝试自列提纲时，都要在脑海里想象该如何论证自己的每一个论点。当你发现自己有能力轻松展开一个个丰富、饱满的论证过程的时候，GRE作文所带来的压力和忐忑会一扫而光，那种文思如涌的状态会令你信心大增。

第三章

第三大问题：如何写得漂亮

★ 文章的组织结构：
开头、结尾和正文

★ 语言的表达和句子
的组织

掌握了ISSUE题目的分析和论证方法之后，绝大多数同学现在应该有这种感觉：拿到ISSUE题目之后，已经有内容可写了，并且对文章思路的组织、观点的论证有了极为清晰的轮廓。但是，很多同学对自己的语言表达依然信心不足。从我所批改的同学们的GRE作文来看，大约80%的同学语言问题并不大。这里所说的"问题并不大"意思是：没有严重的语法问题、表情达意较为清楚、遣词造句有所变化。满足这些要求之后，可以说，你的作文不至于因为语言的问题而丢分。

但是的确有近五分之一的同学的作文语言问题较为明显。主要表现为：文章的结构呆板，文章的开头、结尾过于套路化，段落安排没有节奏感；语言表达抽象、生涩、枯燥、表意僵硬；句型单一，句子冗长乏味，对长句的理解片面，以至于生搬硬套，乱造长句。

造成上述问题的原因之一是错误观念的误导。比如，就有人让大家在GRE作文中尽量写长句子。似乎句子越长，水平就越高，学问也越大。也有人去费尽心机地搞什么开头、结尾的套路。这些套路甚至于细化到句子和词的选择。

这些做法都很容易抑制语言的活力和作者的想象力，制造出大量僵硬、死板、高度雷同的语言和文章结构。

另一个原因就是大家的语言习惯问题。到底什么是好的语言？

很简单：**好的语言就是写作风格人性化的语言**。一般而言，人性所固有的特点（比如懒惰、贪婪、喜欢新奇等）以及现代生活的快节奏使得人们不愿意花时间、精力去读那些晦涩、枯燥的长句；人们大都偏爱多变化、富有节奏感的段落和句子。更何况那些给你改作文的人，每天都要批改大量的作文，你给他们读那些千篇一律的内容，故作艰深的长句，呆板、僵硬的段落，岂不是自寻死路？

请记住：好的段落和句子有三个特点：清楚、简洁、多变。清楚的意思是句子表情达意准确，不引起歧义；简洁的意思是句子简单、明了，能用五个单词表达的意思，决不用六个单词；多变的意思是句子的长度、句型结构、段落的长短要交叉变化。句子以较短的句子为主，但长、短要结合使用，不能要么都是长句，要么都是如同幼儿园儿童写的短句。各种句型交替变换使用，不能要么一直是简单句，要么一直是复合句和复杂句。段落的长度和语气也要交替变化。

这些问题在下面的讲解中会有清楚的解释。在比较中，大家会明确地感受到该怎样调整自己的语言习惯。

第一节 文章的组织结构：开头、结尾和正文

文章的开头和结尾多起修饰性的作用，文章真正的分量在正文部分。但不等于说修饰性的部分不重要。文章的开头段要令人耳目一新，急欲一读为快；结尾要让人齿有余香，掩卷欲思。

一、开头

文章开头的功能是：**抓住读者的注意力，同时选定文章叙述和论证的切入点**。第一段可以给出一个反映文章中心思想的主题句，以表明作者的立场。但这并不是唯一的做法，真正的高手往往通过对文章叙述和论证的切入点的精心设计，令读者一下子就感觉到文章要向哪里发展，并顺势展开环环相扣的叙述和论证，直到结尾戛然而止。这样的文章会让人看完第一段后便欲罢不能，直到一口气读完文章。

大家可以将书翻到前面讲解论证范例的部分，看一看"Passage I：Censorship or Common Sense"。这篇文章的开头两个自然段（第一个意群段）并没有给出中心思想句。第一自然段简短切题之后，在第二自然段交代了文章所述问题的背景，然后就直接展开论证。直到文章结束，作者所要阐述的立场得到了有力的论证，但文章自始至终没有中心思想句。

文章开头务必要简短。一至三行解决问题，超过四行便是冗长（除了个别例外情况）。切记！切记！

一般常见的文章开头形式有：

1. 睿智式开头。如：

The most suitable candidate for the country's president should someday be a foreigner, because whenever problems pop up, most people habitually ask "What will foreigners say?"

刚才提到的论证范例部分的"Passage I：Censorship or Common Sense"的开头即是这种风格。

2. 戏剧化的开头。如：

I know who killed Mr. Robinson.

假设这位 Mr. Robinson 是知名人物，他的遇害已是沸沸扬扬、满城风雨。这时，某家报纸的头版出现以这样一句话开头或者干脆为标题的文章，想想看该会是怎样的视觉冲击。

3. 开门见山式开头。如：

No country in the world now can afford a nuclear war.

报纸上经常可以看到这种以一句话开头的文章。不感兴趣的人马上会走开，而感兴趣的读者一眼就知道这正是其关注的话题。

4. 场景描述式开头。如：

Johnson, an all-A's graduate from the Riverside High School, killed his girlfriend yesterday after dragging her, head scratching ground, nearly 10 miles. What's wrong with him?

这种开头像是在你眼前播放一段纪录片。

5. 轶闻趣事式开头。如：

Whenever you see a bald man walking past the No. 9 building, hands folded on back and eyes gazing at ground, you should rewind your watch if it is not 8: 30 a.m. This man is professor Mark. He is now taking his walk and thinking over his philosophical issues as he always does year after year.

这种开头同场景描述式开头的效果有类似之处，只不过更为情趣化和富有故事性。

6. 提问式开头。如：

China has been running at an 8 percent economic growth rate for two decades. Economists are betting the same trend for another 30 years. So, will China soon make further efforts into space exploration?

此种开头抓住读者的胃口，所提问题直击他们的兴奋点，让他们不得不关注文章的内容。

7. 罗列文章要点式开头。如：

Legal abortion is necessary. Otherwise we will be back with vast numbers of women getting amateur surgery in bloody abortion mills.

寥寥几笔，交代文章的主要内容。

而下面这个开头是一些同学的最爱，只是太啰唆、太长，因而令人厌倦：

In my article, I would like to talk first about the necessity of legal abortion. Then, we will turn to the ensued social and personal cost if we do not allow the freedom of abortion. After that, I would like to explore possible alternatives for legal abortion.

8. 提供背景信息式的开头。如：

When in the Course of human Events, it becomes necessary for one People to dissolve the Political Bands which have connected them with another, and to assume among the Powers of the Earth, the separate and equal Station to which the Laws of Nature and of Nature's God entitle them, a decent Respect to the Opinions of Mankind requires that they should declare the causes which impel them to the Separation.

这是我们在论证范例部分所讲范文 "Passage II：The Declaration of Independence" 的开头。因为这篇文章要求内容庄重而严肃，文章的开头有点长。但通常情况下，大家的文章第一自然段应控制在三行以内。

9. 引用名人名言。如：

We hold these truths to be self-evident，that all men are created equal.

但要注意：在西方人眼里，频繁地引用名言佳句是缺乏创造力的表现。所以，能不用的话，就别用。

糟糕的开头：

1. 开头即道歉。如：

In my humble opinion, I would like to talk about... But I'm sorry I might...

想想看，这种开头你是否也用过？

2. 说教式的开头。如：

Youngsters should not smoke. It's dangerous to do that.

这种居高临下、以势压人的派头，最常见于某些报纸的社论。这种嘴脸令任何稍有自尊的人都感到厌恶。

3. 套路式、老生常谈式开头。如：

This is a much-debated issue. Some think this way, some others hold that way, and still others maintain their particular perspectives. I, after careful pondering, would prefer that..."

这种开头不是在请人读你的文章，而是在给读者洗胃。可遗憾的是，部分同学对这种极度缺乏创造性和想象力的开头很是钟爱。

二、结尾

结尾段一般呼应开头段，并通常对全文作简单的概括。结尾段就像你扔给家里养的狗的那块骨头：第一，这块骨头必须很有嚼头；第二，要让狗知道，这是最后一块了。常见形式：

1. 简述文章要点。如：

No one favors abortion. But we have to admit that, in many cases, it is the only humane alternative.

十分简练的结尾。

下面这个结尾就太僵硬了：

In this essay, I have discussed first the language of Professor Zhang's new book, then its historical qualities, and finally its sociological significance.

2. 提出希望、建议、号召、警告等。如：

If you agree with my points, now let's move.

No one knows what is standing ahead of the elected president. So, good luck.

History always repeats itself. We just intentionally choose to ignore.

3. 哲理式的总结。如：

Which one, money or life, is weightier? Few know, and fewer have ever tried to know.

即便你不是哲人，有时也不妨作深沉状。

4. 场景描述式。如：

As China adopted effective measures to adjust economic structure, Chinese economy has been growing at a tremendous speed. When a train has been started full-speed, who can stop it?

画面总是更容易给人留下印象。

5. 引用名人名言。如：

Government of the people, by the people, for the people, shall not perish from the earth.

还有许多富有想象力的结尾，大家按照总的原则要求，完全可以写出许多自己的创意。你可以把你的作文想象为跟朋友的一次谈话。一个话题将近谈完所剩下的你最想说的那一两句，就是你的结尾段。

同文章的开头段一样：**结尾段务必要短，一两行最好，三行已有点长了，四行简直无法接受。**

文章开头和结尾的技巧小结：

①好的文章开头三要素：有趣、短、能提领全文。

②好的文章结尾三要素：有趣、短、耐人回味。

③文章的开头、结尾没有什么所谓的套路。符合上述要求的开头、结尾就是好的开头和结尾。要视文章的内容、自己的写作风格来具体决定用什么样的开头和结尾。所谓的套路不过是作茧自缚。

三、正文

1. **正文部分的段落问题**

请注意：正文部分一般有三个意群段，但不必是三个自然段。所谓意群段指的是文章中在内容和逻辑上相对独立的段落；而自然段则指的是写作过程中，一个要点叙述完毕之后另起一行所出现的独立的成段文字。许多同学喜欢中间正文部分分为三段，意群段和自然段合而为一，黑压压地挤在那里，让人透不过气来。

当你一个段落已经写出五六行时，就要考虑要不要另起一段了。

一个原则：永远是一个要点自成一个自然段；而且，当你拿不准要不要另起一段的时候，那就另起一段。

这就像中国画的留白技巧，留出部分不落任何笔墨，反而显得疏落有致、黑白相宜。三五行的段落和一两行的段落相互错落，这就是节奏感。你的文章会因此而显得漂亮。大家不妨将书翻到前面所讲的论证范例部分，看一看那三篇文章（尤其是第一篇和第三篇）：各意群段都是由若干个自然段组成的。而且，这些自然段都比较短，多数长度都在四行以内，一般不超过五行。有的（比如第二篇文章）甚至一句话便是一个自然段。

2. 正文部分的主题句问题

每个意群段一般都有一个主题句或者主题段（topic paragraph）。而自然段往往是根据上下文的逻辑关系而自然连接，所以，有的自然段不必有主题句。建议大家将主题句/段放在段落之首或者显眼位置（虽然段中、段尾也可以放）。

比如前面所讲的论证范例部分的"Passage III：Skeptical View of Russia's Economy"，该文的第二、第三自然段构成正文的第一个意群段；第四至第十三自然段构成正文的第二个意群段。第一个意群段的主题句是"Recent business headlines from Russia point to a flourishing scene"；第二个意群段有一个主题段，即第四自然段。

3. 正文部分的衔接问题

正文部分的衔接问题（transitions and connections）的实现一般有以下三种方式：

（1）运用表示衔接的词或者词组。如下表：

补充（*Addition*）	again, also, and, and then, besides, equally important, finally, first, further, furthermore, in addition, in the first place, last, moreover, next, second, still, too
比较（*Comparison*）	also, in the same way, likewise, similarly
让步（*Concession*）	granted, naturally, of course
对比（*Contrast*）	although, and yet, at the same time, but at the same time, despite that, even so, even though, for all that, however, in contrast, in spite of, instead, nevertheless, notwithstanding, on the contrary, on the other hand, otherwise, regardless, still, though, yet
强调（*Emphasis*）	certainly, indeed, in fact, of course
举例/说明（*Example or Illustration*）	after all, as an illustration, even, for example, for instance, in conclusion, indeed, in fact, in other words, in short, it is true, of course, namely, specifically, that is, to illustrate, thus, truly
总结（*Summary*）	all in all, altogether, as has been said, finally, in brief, in conclusion, in other words, in particular, in short, in simpler terms, in summary, on the whole, that is, therefore, to put it differently, to summarize
时间顺序（*Time Sequence*）	after a while, afterward, again, also, and then, as long as, at last, at length, at that time, before, besides, earlier, eventually, finally, formerly, further, furthermore, in addition, in the first place, in the past, last, lately, meanwhile, next, now, presently, second, shortly, simultaneously, since, so far, soon, still, subsequently, then, thereafter, until, until now, when

注意：以上这些词或者词组要用得自然，只要达到了使你的文章上下文有机地联系在一起的目的即可，不可滥用，不要搞得满篇都是这些转折过渡词。关键在于结合文章的逻辑发展，自然而灵活地应用。因此，你不必将这个表背下。熟悉起来，会用其中的一些即可。

（2）可以利用主题句实现段落之间的过渡衔接。如：

All these measures have not braked the country's economic slide.

假如这是一个意群段的主题句，当我们读到"All these measures..."的时候，你自然就会想起来，文章的前面肯定已经具体谈到了一些措施（measures）。这样，文章的上下文自然就连接起来了。

The President was equally successful in tinkering the deficit-ridden state-owned enterprises of the country.

既然这位总统"was equally successful in tinkering the deficit-ridden state-owned enterprises of the country"，那么，文章肯定已谈到他别的成功之处。

The deeper reason for his gloominess may be that Mr. Putin distinguishes between headline news and what is happening below the surface.

这句话出自前面所讲的论证范例部分的"Passage III：Skeptical View of Russia's Economy"。句中的"The deeper reason for his gloominess..."实际上就是在告诉我们：前面已经谈到过一些表面的原因。

（3）可以利用句子和段落间的平行、对应结构实现句子与段落之间的过渡衔接。如：

But, in a larger sense, we cannot dedicate—we cannot consecrate—we cannot hallow—this ground. The brave men, living and dead, **who struggled here**, have consecrated it far above our poor power to add or detract. The world will little note, nor long remember, **what we say here**, but it can never forget **what they did here**. It is for us the living, rather, to be dedicated here to the unfinished work which they **who fought here** have thus far so nobly advanced.

—Abraham Lincoln, *The Gettysburg Address*, November 19, 1863

注意这段文字中的四个黑体的句子：这种平行、对应的句式使上下文自然地连接在了一起。

Commendably, our society defends freedom of speech with great vigor. But there is a difference between allowing everything to be said and allowing everyone to hear it. We should know this by now, having seen the effects that exposure to television and movie violence has on children.

The A. C. L. U. and the American Library Association say that the use of filtering software in computers is censorship because it blocks access to constitutionally protected speech. But these cries are baffling and unfounded. The only control libraries are asserting is over a small portion of the audience, not over the material itself. Moreover, this control has a powerful historical precedent: parental guidance is even older than the Constitution.

这两段话出自前面所讲的论证范例部分的"Passage I: Censorship or Common Sense"。文中的黑体部分是平行、对应结构。它们将这两个自然段很自然地连接在了一起。

正文部分问题小结：

1. 注意将正文部分各个意群段分为若干个自然段。各自然段长短结合，但单个自然段一般不要超过五行。

2. 各个意群段一般都有一个主题句或者主题段概括该意群段的主要内容。但不必每个自然段都有一个主题句。

3. 正文部分各个段落之间的过渡衔接有三种方式：

（1）利用转折过渡词或词组

（2）利用主题句

（3）利用平行、对应结构

第二节　语言的表达和句子的组织

一、关于长句

如果一句话超过了三行，你应该考虑将它变成两三句话。我们必须承认，写复杂的长句不是我们的强项，不必自揭己短。部分同学为了把句子写长，不惜往句子中加一些废话、套话（例如"I prefer，after a careful balance，that..."），里面充斥了 which 和 that 引导的各种从句。遗憾的是，即使这些同学现在未必意识到，随着他们英语语言水平的提高，终有一天他们会发现：这样的句子是惨不忍睹的。这样的习惯必须立刻改变。否则，这就是在拿自己的求学前程当儿戏。从句和客套话不是不可用，但不能为了写长句而硬拼硬凑。

关于如何写出漂亮的句子，下面我们还会结合具体的例子讲到这个问题，这里暂不多谈。

另外，请记住：为你赢得作文高分的不是几个长句子，而是独到的视角、严密的逻辑和令人信服的论证。所以，忘掉长句，将句子控制在三行以内。

如果你能写出下面这样的句子，那就请用长句。否则，忘掉它。

Now if nature should intermit her course and leave altogether, though it were but for a while, the observation of her own laws; if those principal and mother elements of the world, whereof all things in this lower world are made, should lose the qualities which now they have; if the frame of that heavenly arch erected over our heads should loosen and dissolve itself; if celestial spheres should forget their wonted motions, and by irregular volubility turn themselves any way as it might happen; if the prince of the lights of heaven which now as a giant doth run his unwearied course, should, as it were through a languishing faintness, begin to stand and to rest himself; if the moon should wander from her beaten way, the times and seasons of the year blend themselves by disordered and confused mixture, the winds breathe out their last gasp, the clouds yield no rain, the earth be defeated of heavenly influence, the fruits of the earth pine away as children at the withered breasts of their mother no longer able to yield them relief—what would become of man himself, whom these things now do all serve?

二、关于语言表达抽象、生涩、枯燥的问题

一般来说，以下问题导致了语言表达的抽象、生涩和枯燥：

■ 喜欢用抽象、概括的表述，很少用具体的细节

■ 喜欢说尽人皆知的废话

■ 喜欢用陈词滥调

■ 喜欢堆砌毫无意义的词

■ 喜欢用生僻词、大词

下面就这些问题依次讲解。

1. 喜欢用抽象、概括的表述，很少用具体的细节

大家可以想一想，我们为什么讨厌有些领导讲话。这是因为他们的讲话充满了假、大、空和废话。这些话主要是由满篇的抽象性和概括性的语言构成的。抽象的概念和概括性的语言不仅使语言枯燥乏味，而且会让你觉得几句话就已把意思表达完毕，让你产生无话可说之感。**有些同学感觉到ISSUE作文无话好说的部分原因即在于此。**

下面是一位美国议员在被问及对在学校里实施祷告制度的态度时的回答：

"First, let me put this issue in perspective. My record shows I have always fought for the cause of education and for our children, who are the hope of this great nation. I recognize the profound complexities in this area and the honest differences presently existing between good men. I assure you I will work for a positive, fair, and democratic solution. Trust me."

大家想想，他的态度到底是什么？这位议员实际上除了一大堆废话外，什么都没说。

抽象概念的典型特点是难以名状。比如爱、成功、自由、好、民主以及女权主义等概念。我们有时以为大家对这些概念有相同的理解，但实际不然。我们只是因为对这些概念都比较熟悉，才认为它们对谁都有同样的意思。其实，这只是误解。

如果让大家给"爱"下个定义，相信会有各种各样的界定。对于有的人，"爱"意味着"慈母手中线，游子身上衣"；有些人马上会想起自己苦涩的青春年华；再有一些人会联想到酒吧间里迷离的氛围。这也是为什么在讲到对ISSUE题目的分析时，我强调要对题目中的关键概念给出你自己的恰当定义。否则，首先，你的问题不大容易讲清楚；其次，关键的概念理不清楚，你会觉得无话可说、无字可写。

而具体的语言所表述的东西完全是可以感觉得到的，如spoon, table, blue eye-shadow, earrings, red apple, green, hot, walking 等。它们的形状、大小、颜色、姿态、甚至味道立刻会在读者的头脑中形成具体的形象。这也是为什么人们常说："A good writer shows in picture rather than tells in words"。

对比下列例子：

Women-only schools teach girls the social grace.

Women-only schools teach a girl how to carry on a conversation while pouring tea, without sloshing the tea into saucer.

We all want success.

I want a gold Rolex on my wrist, a Mercedes in my driveway, and a pretty woman by my arm to parties full of celebrities.

Sue Walker was injured.

Sue Walker smashed two bones in her right foot.

The weather was horrible.

Eight inches of snow fell on Beijing yesterday.

每一组里的两个句子有什么区别？前一个句子都是抽象的短句；后一个句子都是具体的、形象的长句。

59

部分同学文章写不长的原因，除了不善于论证外，另一个原因就是句子过于抽象。几句话好像就把意思表达完了，接下来自然也就无话可说了。

概括性的语言和细节性的表现给人的感觉则截然不同，如：

He has excellent furniture.

He has a La-Z-Boy rocker-recliner.

He has a green velvet La-Z-Boy rocker recliner.

He has a lime green velvet La-Z-Boy rocker recliner with a cigarette burn on the left arm and a crushed jelly doughnut pressed into the back edge of the seat cushion.

到最后，是不是在你的头脑里有了一把摇椅的清晰的样子呢？

又如：

She is really smart.

She does well in school.

She gets straight A's.

She always earned straight A's in physics and mathematics.

该女生连大家都很恐惧的物理和数学都能连年拿到全优的成绩，聪明与否还需多说吗？

抽象性、概括性的描述在中心思想句和主题句中是有用的、必要的，但在随后的论证展开中，则要注意具体细节的表述。大家想一想所谓的列举特征的论证方式实际上就是提供细节，它们使你的论述显得真实、可信。

但这并不意味着应该通篇充满细致的描述——从美国前总统比尔·克林顿的长相到张三脸上的一颗痣。当你觉得应该在你文章的某个地方给读者留下深刻印象的时候，或者在你写出了一个概括性的句子之后，那就请提供细节。如：

He loves fine furniture, and one of his favorites is a lime green velvet La-Z-Boy rocker recliner with a cigarette burn on the left arm and a crushed jelly doughnut pressed into the back edge of the seat cushion.

She is really smart, and always earned straight A's in physics and mathematics in school.

细节描述使你的文章具体而有趣，而且文章也在不知不觉中变长了。细节描述不需要很大的词汇量，也不需要太多的想象力，但它需要你对所描述对象的观察和你对细节的挑选与安排，仅此而已。

2. 喜欢说尽人皆知的废话

Smoking can kill you. And if you've been killed, you've lost a very important part of your life.

Every great man has moments of profound sorrow, and William is no exception.

这些路人皆知的肤浅道理你不必重复一遍。

3. 喜欢用陈词滥调（主要是因为不知道它们竟被认为是陈词滥调）

中国人喜欢从传统那里找到权威感，所以张口即"子曰"、"诗云"。西方人注重具体事件的分析和逻辑推理。引经据典在西方人看来是缺乏创造力的表现。

下列表达曾经非常受欢迎，但人们用得太多、太滥，以至于成了陈词滥调，所以最好不用：

acid test	green with envy
avoid like the plague	happy as a lark

babe in the woods	last but not least
beginners luck	laughing like a hyena
better late than never	love at first sight
black as pitch	a needle in a haystack
blind as a bat	point with pride
brought back to reality	proud as a peacock
busy as a bee/beaver	ripe old age
cool as a cucumber	sadder but wiser
crack of dawn	shoot yourself in the foot
cry over spilt milk	sleep like a log
dog-eat-dog world	slowly but surely
don't count your chickens	state-of-the-art
easier said than done	straw that broke the camel's back
few and far between	tender age
first and foremost	under the weather
flash in the pan	white as a sheet/ghost
gentle as a lamb	

4. 喜欢堆砌毫无意义的词（主要是想把文章拉长）

下列将句子写长的方式实在不可取：

A. Fast driving is dangerous.

B. In my opinion, fast driving is dangerous.

C. In my opinion, fast driving would seem to be rather dangerous.

D. In my humble opinion, though I do not claim to be an expert on this complicated subject, fast driving, in most circumstances, would seem to be rather dangerous in many aspects, or at least so it would seem to me.

算上标点符号，第一个句子是5个字；到最后，变成了45个字。句子写长了，你的读者也吐了。以这样的句子，你的作文无论如何也得不到高分。这样的习惯必须马上纠正过来。

注意下列句子，那些画线部分（在同学们的作文中出现的频率都非常高）完全可以删掉或者换个说法。

（1）All things considered, Connecticut's woodlands are in better shape now than ever before.

（2）As a matter of fact, there are more woodlands in Connecticut now than there were in 1898.

（3）As far as I'm concerned, there is no need for further protection of woodlands.

（4）This is because there are fewer farmers at the present time. 改为：

This is because there are fewer farmers now.

（5）Woodlands have grown in area because of the fact that farmers have abandoned their fields. 改为：

Woodlands have grown in area because farmers have abandoned their fields.

（6）Major forest areas are coming back by means of natural processes. 改为：

Major forest areas are coming back through natural processes (or naturally).

（7）Our woodlands are coming back <u>by virtue of the fact that</u> our economy has shifted its emphasis. 改为：

Our woodlands are coming back <u>because</u> our economy has shifted its emphasis.

（8）<u>Due to the fact that</u> their habitats are being restored, forest creatures are also re-establishing their population bases. 改为：

<u>Because</u> their habitats are being restored, forest creatures are also re-establishing their population bases.

（9）The fear <u>that exists</u> among many people that we are losing our woodlands is groundless.

（10）The era in which we must aggressively defend our woodlands has, <u>for all intents and purposes,</u> passed.

（11）<u>For the most part,</u> people's suspicions are based on a misunderstanding of the facts.

（12）Many woodlands, in fact, have been purchased <u>for the purpose of creating</u> as public parks.

（13）This policy <u>has a tendency</u> to isolate some communities. 改为：

This policy <u>tends to</u> isolate some communities.

（14）The policy has, <u>in a manner of speaking,</u> begun to make inroads into the more rural parts of our state.

（15）<u>In a very real sense,</u> this policy works to the detriment of those it is supposed to help.

（16）<u>In my opinion,</u> this wasteful policy ought to be revoked.

（17）<u>In the case of</u> this particular policy, citizens of northeast Connecticut became very upset. 改为：

Citizens of northeast Connecticut became very upset <u>about this policy</u>.

（18）<u>In the final analysis,</u> the state would have been better off without such a policy.

（19）<u>In the event that</u> enough people protest, it will probably be revoked. 改为：

<u>If</u> enough people protest, it will probably be revoked.

（20）Something <u>in the nature of</u> a repeal may soon take place. 改为：

Something <u>like</u> a repeal may soon take place.

（21）Legislators are already <u>in the process of</u> reviewing the statutes.

（22）<u>It seems that</u> they can't wait to get rid of this one.

（23）They have monitored the activities of conservationists <u>in a cautious manner</u>. 改为：

They have <u>cautiously</u> monitored the activities of conservationists.

（24）<u>The point I am trying to make is that</u> sometimes public policy doesn't accomplish what it set out to achieve.

（25）Legislators need to be more careful of the <u>type of</u> policy they propose.

（26）<u>What I mean to say is that</u> well-intentioned lawmakers sometimes make fools of themselves.

5. 喜欢用生僻词、大词（主要是想显示自己有学问）

外来词：如 *bete noir*，*ne plus ultra*

学究气的词：如 penultimate，symbiotic，alumna，iconicity

诗歌化的词：如 repine，oft，betimes，betoken

技术化的词：如 societal

不常见的单、复数形式：如 datum，stadia，syllabi

　　这些单词，包括你所背的GRE单词，一般人都不认识。它们使你的文章看起来矫揉造作、不自然（awkward and artificial）。真正有学问的人有的是思想，而非几个闪亮的辞藻。古今中外这个道理是一样的，大家不必故弄玄虚。

　　在下面这个列表中，左右两边的词或词组表达的意思是相同的。虽然左边的不算错，但建议首选右边的，因为它们更清楚、直接，更没有陈词滥调的感觉。

achieve	do，make
advise	tell
and/or	and，or
approximately	about
attempt	try
benefit	help
commence	start，begin
conclude	end，stop
contribute	give
deem	think
demonstrate	prove，show
depart	leave
desire	want
dialogue with	talk to
disclose	tell，show
discontinue	stop
due to the fact that	because
e.g.	for example
enumerate	count
exhibit	show
expertise	skill，ability
the fact that	（最好略去不用）
failed to	didn't
finalize	complete，finish
for a period of	for
the following	these
has the ability to	can
herein	here
i. e.	that is
in addition	besides，too
in order to	to
in regard to	about
in the event that	if

in the near future	soon，Wednesday
invaluable	valuable
it is noted that	（最好略去不用）
last but not least	last，finally
locate	find
the majority	most
the month of	（最好略去不用）
my intention is	I will
notify	let me know
not later than	by
not only but also	and
numerous	many
observe	see
obtain	get
parameters	limits
perform	do
personnel	people
possess	own，have
prepared	ready
prioritize	rank
prior to	before
probability	chance
provided that	if
purchase	buy
regarding	about
relative to	about
remainder	rest
remuneration	pay，payment，$50
request	ask
secondly	second
share with	tell，talk to
similar to	like
state	say
state-of-the-art	latest
submit	give，send
sufficient	enough
terminate	end，stop
therefore	so
this point in time	today，now

touch base with	talk to
transmit	send
truly	（最好略去不用）
until such time as	until
utilize	use
very	（最好略去不用）
viable	practical，workable
whenever	when
whether or not	whether
with reference to	about
with the exception of	except
the writer	I，me

改句子练习（答案参见附录1）：

下面的句子较为别扭，应怎样改?

（1）This insult was the last straw. I decided to leave Marcia, and I spent the next few hours preparing for the trip.

（2）Sam's new book illustrates the ludicrous intractability of a particular mind-set.

（3）Scott Daniel was a fine basketball player. I believe he was the best to play in the league in the last 20 years. He was really fine.

（4）*Vis-à-vis* our *tête-à-tête*, I must say the rendezvous filled me with ennui.

（5）In the following weeks at school, I worked frantically. Every day I became busier and busier.

（6）As we entered the restaurant, Nick stated that the chicken there was good but the service was bad.

（7）In the final analysis, there are few rugged individualists in this day and age who are really down to earth in expressing nothing but the truth about the seamy side of life.

（8）Perhaps in the near future we will never know everything about the atom, but some of the recent discoveries have been fascinating.

（9）Graduate school can be a procrustean bed.

（10）Pestering on the part of mendicants should be interdicted.

三、如何写出好句子

好的句子是**清楚、简洁、多变**的句子。所谓清楚，指的是表达没有歧义。这是语言最基本的要求。简洁的意思是句子简单、明了，能用五个单词表达的意思，决不用六个单词。多变的意思是句子的长度、句型结构要交叉变化。句子最好以较短的句子为主，但长、短句要结合使用，不能要么都是长句，要么就都是如同儿童写的短句。各种句型要交替变换使用，不能要么就一直是简单句，要么就一直是复合句和复杂句。

这里具体谈一下句型的变化。

要想做到句型多变，简单易行的办法主要有以下这些：

■ 变换句型
■ 利用同位语、插入语、独立主格结构、分词（现在/过去分词）短语、动词不定式短语、介词短语和形容词短语
■ 利用简单的修辞手段
■ 必要时，还可以考虑用倒装、强调句型和疑问句以变换句型

下面依次讲解。

1. 变换句型造成变化

常见的句型有：简单句、并列句、复合句、并列句—复合句。

（1）简单句：独立的单个句子。如：

We drove from Beijing to Shanghai in one day.

（2）并列句：两个及以上的简单句合在一起所构成的句子，一般用连词and，but，for，or，nor，so，yet（记住由这七个连词的首字母缩写而成的人名"A. B. Fonsy"，就能记住这七个连词）或关系副词"however，moreover，nevertheless，still，accordingly"等连接。如：

We were exhausted, *but* we arrived in time for my father's birthday party.

He had never been to China; *however*, it had always been one of his ambitions.

注意以上两个例句中标点符号用法的区别，并请参见本书书后附录2和附录3了解更多的相关要点。

（3）复合句：一个主句加一个或多个从句即复合句。

Although he is now 79 years old, he still claims to be 65.

（4）并列句—复合句：一个并列句加上一个或多个从句。

After it was all over, my dad claimed he knew we were planning something, *but* we think he was really surprised.

在以上四种句式之间，大家可以选择变化。

请看下面这一小段文字：

Someone is always at my elbow reminding me that I am the granddaughter of slaves. It fails to register depression with me. Slavery is sixty years in the past. The operation was successful and the patient is doing well, thank you. The terrible struggle that made me an American out of a potential slave said "On the line!", the Reconstruction said "Get set!", and the generation before said "Go!". I am off to a flying start and I must not halt in the stretch to look behind and weep. Slavery is the price I paid for civilization, and the choice was not with me. It is a bully adventure and worth all that I have paid through my ancestors for it.

—Zora Neale Hurston

在这一小段文字中，作者（一位当代美国知名黑人女作家）交替使用了四种句型：

简单句：

It fails to register depression with me.

Slavery is sixty years in the past.

并列句：

The operation was successful and the patient is doing well, thank you.

I am off to a flying start and I must not halt in the stretch to look behind and weep.

复合句：

Someone is always at my elbow reminding me that I am the granddaughter of slaves.

It is a bully adventure and worth all that I have paid through my ancestors for it.

并列句—复合句：

Slavery is the price that I paid for civilization, and the choice was not with me.

It is a bully adventure and worth all that I have paid through my ancestors for it.

而且，整段中八个句子的长度也呈现出"长—短—短—较长—长—较长—较长—较长"的变化，很富有节奏感。

2. 利用同位语、插入语、独立主格结构、分词（现在/过去分词）短语、动词不定式短语、介词短语、形容词短语，变换句式结构

以上这几种语言形式在句中位置灵活、形式简便，一般能代替各种从句的语言功能，从而使句子呈现出多样的变化。请对比下列各组例句，体会每组例句前后的变化与效果。

（1）同位语

After her father died, the little girl had no choice but to live in countryside with her grandmother, *who was a really kind-hearted woman.*

After her father died, the little girl had no choice but to live in countryside with her grandmother, *a really kind-hearted woman.*

He was so ascetic that he gave away his inheritance. Instead, he had to rely on the generous help of his Cambridge mentors, Russell and Keynes, to secure academic employment for him.

Always an ascetic, he gave away his inheritance, relying on the generosity of his Cambridge mentors, Russell and Keynes, to secure academic employment for him.

（2）插入语

The general atmosphere of the country and temperament of the people, *and also the favorable climate*, will undoubtedly offer many opportunities for an interesting social life.

The general atmosphere of the country and temperament of the people, *let alone the favorable climate*, will undoubtedly offer many opportunities for an interesting social life.

We must open the gate. *If necessary, we will use force to open it.*

We must open the gate, *by force if necessary.*

（3）独立主格结构

He *tucked a big bundle under his arm* and entered the room.

A big bundle tucked under arm, he entered the room.

The tea was warm. The room was cozy and the conversation was light and pleasant.

The tea was warm, the room cozy, and the conversation light and pleasant.

（4）分词（现在/过去分词）短语

During this period, my father made a family *which was closely united and curiously happy*, as it has never been in my memory.

During this period, my father made a family *closely united and curiously happy*, as it has never been in my memory.

Justice theories have a long tradition, *which can date back to Plato and Aristotle.*

Justice theories have a long tradition, *dating back to Plato and Aristotle.*

（5）动词不定式短语

The old parents decided to build a new apartment *so that they can get ready for their youngest son's marriage right away when necessary.*

The old parents decided to build a new apartment *to get ready for their youngest son's marriage right away when necessary.*

（6）介词短语

Not everyone in North America likes the taste of green tea, *whether it contains caffeine or not.*

With or without caffeine, not everyone in North America likes the taste of green tea.

The active ingredient in the mold turned out to be an infection-fighting agent *that was enormously potent.*

The active ingredient in the mold turned out to be an infection-fighting agent *of enormous potency.*

（7）形容词短语

Only those *who are ignorant of the modern life* would doubt the need of vocational education today.

Only a person *ignorant of the modern life* would doubt the need of vocational education today.

Tragedies usually center around great personalities who are defeated by forces *which are too great even for them to match.*

Tragedies usually center around great personalities defeated by forces *too great even for them to match.*

3. 利用简单的修辞手段，如明喻、暗喻、拟人、排比，使句子出现变化

（1）明喻（用 like 和 as 连接起来的比喻关系）

Her curly hair was *like that of the dog behind her.*

The boss shot up from his chair *like being stung by a wasp.*

（2）暗喻（一种比喻关系，但不用 like 和 as）

Life is a stage, we are just *players,* comic or tragic.

His exceptional performance in the film *rocketed him to instant fame.*

（3）拟人

Once the flood drew back, ants began *building their new nest.*

After several bumps, the car *coughed to a halt.*

（4）排比

His long journey completed and *his men in the Corps of Discovery dispersed,* Lewis died a few years later on his way back to Washington, D. C., completely alone.

The Swiss watchmakers' failure to capitalize on the invention of the digital timepiece was both astonishing and alarming—astonishing in that the Swiss had, since the beginnings of the industrial revolution in Europe, been among the first to capitalize on technical *innovations,* **alarming** in that a *tremendous industrial potential had been lost to their chief competitors, the watchmakers of Japan.*

必要时，还可以考虑用倒装、强调句型和疑问句以使句子出现变化（但要注意，这三种句型太抢眼，所以一篇文章里不可多用）

Never have most Chinese considered buying their house using bank's loan.

So lovely was the baby that it drew all eyes in the room.

It was Coach+ Calhoun *who* came up with the program of recruiting players from foreign countries.

What does he know that investors do not? Could Russia be heading towards another crash or a serious slowdown, as some analysts are now suggesting?

第四章

第四大问题：
新版题库的压缩及
备考策略

★ 新版ISSUE题库中题目
  涉及的主要内容
★ 对新版题库进行压缩的
  依据及办法
★ 新版ISSUE题库的压缩
★ 高效的ISSUE备考策略

我们可以利用题库里的题目相互间的联系，对题目总量进行适当压缩，并相应制订最为有效的ISSUE写作准备方案。

第一节　新版ISSUE题库中题目涉及的主要内容

绝大多数ISSUE作文题目所涉及的内容大致包括以下主题：科学研究/人类社会、传统/现代、生命的意义、理智/情感、教育的目的、学习/实践（间接知识/直接经验）、科技发展/人性、技术进步/社会伦理和习俗、人格/行为、竞争/合作、理想主义/现实主义、经济（社会）发展/环境保护、学校教育/家庭教育、做学问/做人。

对于涉及这些主题的主要观点、关键概念的表达方式，同学们可以通过阅读书后"附录8：与ISSUE题目相关的泛读材料"很快熟悉起来，找到驾轻就熟、有话要说的感觉。

第二节　对新版题库进行压缩的依据及办法

虽然ISSUE作文题库庞大，但许多题目所涉及的内容、分析思路是完全一样或高度类似的。而且，部分题目之间也有补充、相互佐证的特点。据此，我们可以将那些彼此有关联的题目归入一组，整理出它们之间要点的一致性和参照性。这样，同一组的三道、五道、甚至十余道题都可被视为一或两道题。解决了这一或两道题，同一组的其他题只要稍加变通，也就迎刃而解了。这就是我们对题库进行压缩的依据。

具体而言，ISSUE题库中的题目有如下特点：

1. 部分题目内容之间可完全或者部分套用

例如，下面这两道题（题目前的数字是该题在本书第五章中的编号）：

---

11. People's behavior is largely determined by forces not of their own making.

Write a response in which you discuss the extent to which you agree or disagree with the statement and explain your reasoning for the position you take. In developing and supporting your position, you should consider ways in which the statement might or might not hold true and explain how these considerations shape your position.

---

99. People's behavior is largely determined by forces not of their own making.

Write a response in which you discuss the extent to which you agree or disagree with the claim. In developing and supporting your position, be sure to address the most compelling reasons and/or examples that could be used to challenge your position.

这两道题的题目本身完全一样，区别只在于写作指引的不同。但是，正如前面我们已经讨论过的，这两个不同的写作指引无非是让我们多考虑同一个问题的正、反两方面的情形。所以，按照"两面写"的思路，这两个题目的分析思路和写作提纲可以完全一样。大家不妨把书翻到第五章，自己仔细体会一下对它们的分析。所以，这两道题当然可以分到一组，视为同一道题目，并且它们的分析和写作提纲可以完全相同。

再比如下面这两道题：

> **44. Claim**：It is no longer possible for a society to regard any living man or woman as a hero.
>
> **Reason**: The reputation of anyone who is subjected to media scrutiny will eventually be diminished.
>
> Write a response in which you discuss the extent to which you agree or disagree with the claim and the reasons on which that claim is based.

> **75.** In this age of intensive media coverage, it is no longer possible for a society to regard any living man or woman as a hero.
>
> Write a response in which you discuss the extent to which you agree or disagree with the statement and explain your reasoning for the position you take. In developing and supporting your position, you should consider ways in which the statement might or might not hold true and explain how these considerations shape your position.

这两道题的题目本身及各自的写作指引都不相同。但是，我们可以对75题进行下列简单的变形：Because of the intensive media coverage, it is no longer possible for a society to regard any living man or woman as a hero。这样一来，这两道题几乎就是完全相同的两个因果类题目了，区别只在于第44题的原因部分表述得更为具体、详细而已。按照"两面写"的分析框架，并从因果类题目的分析切入点展开分析后，我们同样可以得到这两道题目完全一样的写作提纲。显然，这两道题目可以压缩在一起，视为同一道题目。大家可以自己试一试，按照 **"1+5"写作模型**，这两道题目实际上只能有同一个分析结果。

对以上两组题目的分析和比较可以得出一个重要结论：**对ISSUE的分析，要把重点放在题目本身而不是题后的写作指引**。只有对题目本身按照五大题目类型各自的分析切入点进行分析才能使我们获得写作的内容。至于那些写作指引，完全可以用"两面写"这一写作框架把它们具体的要求全部囊括进来。这就是为什么我在本书的第一章就强调**一定要"两面写"**，这也是**"1+5"写作模型**最具可操作性的特点之一。

2. 分析思路完全可以套用

例如，下面这八道题（为了方便分析，下面的题目将只分析题目本身，不再分析它们各自的写作指引）：

> **22. Claim**: **The best way** to understand the character of a society is to examine the character of the men and women that the society chooses as its heroes or its role models.
>
> **Reason**: Heroes and role models reveal a society's highest ideals.

24. **The best way** to teach is to praise positive actions and ignore negative ones.

29. **The best way** to teach—whether as an educator, employer, or parent—is to praise positive actions and ignore negative ones.

52. **The best way** to teach is to praise positive actions and ignore negative ones.

70. **Claim**: Universities should require every student to take a variety of courses outside the student's major field of study.

Reason: Acquiring knowledge of various academic disciplines is **the best way** to become truly educated.

112. Requiring university students to take a variety of courses outside their major fields of study is **the best way** to ensure that students become truly educated.

122. **The best way** to understand the character of a society is to examine the character of the men and women that the society chooses as its heroes or its role models.

123. **The best way** for a society to prepare its young people for leadership in government, industry, or other fields is by instilling in them a sense of cooperation, not competition.

单单从形式上就可明显看出这八道题的一致性：它们所体现的逻辑思路是一样的，即何种方式是解决何种问题的"**最好方式**"。明白了它们这个逻辑上的共性，这八道题的分析、写作就变得轻松多了。

3. 分析要点互为利用，即一个题目的立场可以是另一个题目若干个要点之一

例如，下面这八道题：

8. **Claim**: In any field—business, politics, education, government—those in power should step down after five years.

Reason: The surest path to success for any enterprise is revitalization through new leadership.

16. Some people believe that in order to be effective, political leaders must yield to public opinion and abandon principle for the sake of compromise. Others believe that the most essential quality of an effective leader is the ability to remain consistently committed to particular principles and objectives.

62. Leaders are created by the demands that are placed on them.

69. Some people believe it is often necessary, even desirable, for political leaders to withhold information from the public. Others believe that the public has a right to be fully informed.

94. The effectiveness of a country's leaders is best measured by examining the well-being of that country's citizens.

114. Any leader who is quickly and easily influenced by shifts in popular opinion will accomplish little.

123. The best way for a society to prepare its young people for leadership in government, industry, or other fields is by instilling in them a sense of cooperation, not competition.

128. Some people argue that successful leaders in government, industry, or other fields must be highly competitive. Other people claim that in order to be successful, a leader must be willing and able to cooperate with others.

粗读下来，大家很快就能发现这八道题都是从不同角度讨论领导/领袖的；所以这些题的分析要点自然可以相互参照、互为利用。因此，把它们归为一组也就顺理成章了。

本书主要就是利用上述ISSUE题目的特点对题库进行压缩的。

第三节　新版ISSUE题库的压缩

详见"附录6：新版ISSUE题库的压缩"。

第四节　高效的ISSUE备考策略

经过压缩，我们可以将新版ISSUE题库的149道题中的129道题归并到33组中去。因为每一组的题目之间都有内容、分析角度一致的地方或观点、角度相互补充之处，所以，至少在理论上，我们可以把每一组题当成一道题来对待。这样的话，这33组（也就是理论上的33道题）加上剩余的没有归纳成组的20道题，**新版ISSUE题库总共149道题已经被减少至53道题**。这相当于将ISSUE的**题量减少了64%**，考生的复习压力就能因此大大减轻。

其实，如果善于发现题目间的联系，我们还可以对它们作进一步的压缩。比如，我们完全可以将第7组题目和第32组放到一起，因为它们都是讨论什么样的人才可以成为领导/领袖、怎样才能当好领导和领袖。同样，我们也可以把第66题"People who are the most deeply committed to an idea or policy are also the most critical of it."放进第29组中去，因为第66题是探讨一个人是如何对待自己的观点，这和第29组中的探讨如何对待他人批评的那些题目也是反向相关的。

但是，大家在刚开始不必强求进一步的压缩。因为如果题目间的联系较为间接，进一步压缩就会有难度，只有对题目的内容和分析非常娴熟之后才会纵横自如。而且，把ISSUE题目总量从149题压缩到53题，这已经是相当可观了，不必再去做生拉硬扯的压缩。

到了最后，经过对每一组和每一道题目的分析思考，你应该有这样的感觉：**自己俨然有了一个完整的思想体系；这个思想体系可以使你随便列出任何ISSUE题目的写作要点和提纲**。这个状态说明你的ISSUE作文准备工作已接近大功告成了。

具体而言，ISSUE作文的复习准备应分为以下四大步骤：

第一步，必须熟悉"**1+5**"写作模型的应用。ISSUE作文的核心难点在于找不到各题目的分析切入点，因而无法对题目展开分析、找不到写作思路。大家一定要在本书的第一章中，结合理论讲解和范例分析，将"1+5"写作模型完全搞懂。这个写作模型是ISSUE分析、写作全过程的起点。

第二步，阅读《新版ISSUE题库各题目分析指要》中对各个题目的分析，体会"1+5"写作模型的具体应用。与此同时，考虑自己能否对每个题目作出不同的分析。

第三步，抛开《新版ISSUE题库各题目分析指要》，结合题库压缩，运用"1+5"写作模型去分析每一组和每一个题目，列出提纲。这时的一个重要任务是：对每一组题，要总结出1—2个**具有广泛适用性的提纲**。该提纲的样式可以和第五章中的一样，也可以在各要点之后再加上论证方法（如同我们在讲解论证方式时所做的那样）。这样的一个提纲要体现对每一组中所有题目的概括和总结。要达到的效果是：只需对这个具有广泛适用性的提纲稍加变动，就可得到同一组里的任意一道题目的提纲。这样的一个具有广泛适用性的提纲就是所谓的模板。**如此，对于新版ISSUE题库149道题，我们只要有差不多50个这样的模板就全部搞定了。**

第四步，按照第三章中对文章篇章结构、造句用词的要求开始练笔。为了做到对每一道题的要点和提纲都了然于胸，我强烈建议大家最好写够50篇左右ISSUE作文。想想当年的旧版ISSUE题库可是有**244**道题！那是什么样的复习工作量啊？！现在经过压缩后，大家手里只有区区**53**道题，完全可以精耕细作。

刚开始写的时候，可以不限时间。重点体会文章的结构、思路展开、论证和语言。然后，在距离考试还有20天左右的时候，开始限时写作。ISSUE作文规定完成时间是30分钟，不算充裕。所以，大家就更有必要对每一组、每一道题细加琢磨，做到临考时提笔动念，思如泉涌；运指流畅，一气呵成。

文章写完要修改。不修改的文章等于吃饭不消化。文章可以自己改（重点改结构和语法），也可以同学间相互改（改文章的思路和论证，看是否论证得令人信服）、请内行改（全面诊断）。有关修改文章的注意事项，请参看本书附录5。

第五章

新版ISSUE题库各题目
分析指要

关于新版ISSUE题库所有题目的题型分类和题目分析的说明：

1. 在阅读本部分内容之前，请务必首先阅读、熟悉本书第一章的所有内容，以便更好理解每个题目分析的步骤、格式以及提纲内容。

2. 所有题目的归类和分析都是本着简单、明了、易分析的原则进行的。对于**平行式多角度分析题**，在指出它们一般可归入的类别后，只按照一个题目类型展开分析。对所有的**套叠式多角度分析题**所包括的题目类型进行了说明，并对其中有一定难度的进行了详细的分析。

3. 在将每个题目归入各自类别之后，并不按照"先提正、再求反、因人因题合反散"的顺序展开分析，而是直接从每一类题目的分析切入点入手，分析出写作思路的核心内容，然后再整理出一个简单的写作提纲。"先提正、再求反、因人因题合反散"的顺序适合同学们自己尝试对题目进行分析时，为自己提供一个清楚的分析步骤。

4. 所有这些题目的写作提纲只可用来参考，以帮助大家运用"**1+5**"**写作模型**整理出自己的分析思路和写作提纲。**在复习准备时间特别紧迫，一时间无法对全部的ISSUE题目进行自己的分析和整理的情况下，考生可以参考下面的ISSUE分析思路和写作提纲，但原则上不鼓励完全照搬这些提纲；读者最好给它们加上一点儿自己的东西（比如自己独有的文章开头和结尾段，增减或变更一两个分析和论证要点等），然后再放心应用。**这是因为如果大家都按照本书的ISSUE提纲来写，大量完全一样的观点和分析思路有可能会招来ETS的"特别关注"而被指责为抄袭。尽管由于考试时大家随机抽取的题目以及写作时各自语言表述会有差异，使得完全一致的可能性极低，但为稳妥起见，还是稍作变化为好。这也是我不把这些分析思路和提纲写得过细，并且全部都用中文书写的原因。而且，本书的主要目的不只是为大家提供写作提纲，更是为了启发同学们学会整理、分析自己的写作思路。大家对这一点应该非常清楚。实际上，同学们在对每个ISSUE题目的分析、思想要点都非常熟悉之后，甚至可以抛开本书有关ISSUE题目的分析，完全按照自己的思路来写。这才是本书整个ISSUE部分讲解的最终目的。

The Pool of Issue Topics

This page contains the Issue topics for the analytical writing section of the GRE revised General Test. When you take the test, you will be presented with one Issue topic from this pool.

Each Issue topic consists of an issue statement or statements followed by specific task instructions that tell you how to respond to the issue. The wording of some topics in the test might vary slightly from what is presented here. Also, because there may be multiple versions of some topics with similar or identical wording but with different task instructions, it is very important to read your test topic and its specific task directions carefully and respond to the wording as it appears in the actual test.

1. As people rely more and more on technology to solve problems, the ability of humans to think for themselves will surely deteriorate. (参考第26、64题)

Write a response in which you discuss the extent to which you agree or disagree with the statement and explain your reasoning for the position you take. In developing and supporting your position, you should consider ways in which the statement might or might not hold true and explain how these considerations shape your position.

题型归类 事实类。

题目分析

（1）能否从公认的原则或事实中推出相反的判断?

　　人们的生命和生活质量还是因为科技进步而有了明显的改善和提高。比如，人们的衣食住行条件、受教育水平、平均寿命、医疗保障水平、应付自然灾害的能力等都得到了极大的改善。不仅如此，所有这些也使得人类有可能摆脱为生存而进行的挣扎，转而对自己的内心、对周围所处的世界进行更为冷静的反思。

（2）能否举出相反的事例?

　　（大家可以举出无数身边发生的例子。此处从略。）

提纲提要

论点 **论者的观点失于简单**

正 现代社会的确出现了科技虽然发展了，但人却变得更加短视和愚钝的现象。比如，科技进步和经济全球化带来的种族和文化冲突、核战争威胁、国家间日益扩大的贫富差距、环境污染（如全球变暖、核泄漏）等。人类社会因为科技的发展而变得似乎更不安全了。那么，科技到底是让我们更聪明了还是更愚蠢了呢?

反 但是，人们的生命和生活质量还是因为科技进步而有了明显的改善和提高。比如，人们的衣食住行条件、受教育水平、平均寿命、医疗保障水平、应付自然灾害的能力等都得到了极大的改善。不仅如此，所有这些也使得人类有可能摆脱为生存而进行的挣扎，转而对自己的内心、对周围所处的世界进行更为冷静的反思。

散 科技不能解决人类面临的一切问题。部分问题（比如，种族和文化冲突、战争、国际恐怖主义、环境污染等）的解决并不只取决于科技进步的大小，而是取决于人类是否有足够的宽容、同情心和自我反省意识。

- -

　　2. To understand the most important characteristics of a society, one must study its major cities. （参考第5、117题）

　　Write a response in which you discuss the extent to which you agree or disagree with the statement and explain your reasoning for the position you take. In developing and supporting your position, you should consider ways in which the statement might or might not hold true and explain how these considerations shape your position.

题型归类 建议类。经过整理，题目可以变成：To better understand the most important characteristics of a society, one should study its major cities. 所以，可归入建议类。

题目分析

（1）题目中的建议可行性如何?

　　任何人只要愿意，都可通过研究一个社会主要城市的特点而了解该社会的特点。所以，题目中的建议当然可行。

（2）**如果实施题目中的建议，是否会导致同初始目的相矛盾或其他荒谬的结果？**

当人们试图通过研究城市而了解某个社会的特点的时候，有一个问题：这些城市是这个社会特点的真实体现吗？纽约就是美国吗？中国的大城市能代表中国农村的现状吗？中国的大都市能代表中国吗？

（3）**有无替代或折中方案？**

城市只代表了一个社会的表层状态。中小城镇和农村中普通人的生活状态才是一个社会的真实写照。正如眼下的中国，繁华都市不是中国的真实面目；代表中国的是七亿多农民、上千万的城市和小城镇工人以及知识分子等。

提纲提要

论点 **城市可能只代表了一个社会的表层状态。**

正 一般而言，某一社会主要城市能在一定程度反映社会的面貌。

反 但是，当人们试图通过研究城市而了解某个社会的特点的时候，有一个问题：这些城市是这个社会特点的真实体现吗？纽约就是美国吗？中国的大城市能代表中国农村的现状吗？中国的大都市能代表中国吗？

反 城市可能只代表了一个社会的表层状态。中小城镇和农村中普通人的生活状态才是一个社会的真实写照。正如眼下的中国，繁华都市不是中国的真实面目；代表中国的是七亿多农民、上千万的城市和小城镇工人以及知识分子等。

---

3. Educational institutions have a responsibility to dissuade students from pursuing fields of study in which they are unlikely to succeed. （参考第13、15、20、32、35、39、46、98、129、135、136、137、140题）

Write a response in which you discuss the extent to which you agree or disagree with the claim. In developing and supporting your position, be sure to address the most compelling reasons and/or examples that could be used to challenge your position.

题型归类 建议类。

题目分析

（1）**题目中的建议可行性如何？**

题目中的建议看似简单，但却未必可行。任何教育机构，只要它们对学生的未来抱非常负责任的态度，都不会仅仅因为学生的想法看起来不大可能成功而设法劝阻学生去追寻他们的梦想。这是因为，如果这个劝阻是真正负责任的、真正为学生和社会的利益考虑的话，它势必需要一个前提：那就是，这些教育机构实际上已经非常确信学生的梦想追求是断然不会成功的。但这个前提基本上难以成立。试问，如果不投入所有身心去努力争取，有谁会在一开始就知道自己的理想会不会成功呢？我们人类今天所做的许多司空见惯的事情，在遥远的当初看起来不都是遥不可及、痴人说梦吗？

（2）**如果实施题目中的建议，是否会导致同初始目的相矛盾或其他荒谬的结果？**

如果实施题目中的建议，其结果很简单：泯灭梦想、故步自封，永远不会有发展和进步。这个结果同声称以探索未知、发掘人类理性的一切可能为己任的教育机构放到一起，是多么不协调。

（3）有无替代或折中方案?

正确的做法不是去劝阻，而应当是鼓励；并且，在学生的探索过程中，教育机构还要及时给他们帮助和引导，从而使他们本人和整个社会都能以最小的代价实现或者至少不断接近梦想。

提纲提要

论点 论者的建议看似好意，但却是不可能的，甚至是有害的。

正 一般而言，教育机构对学生的学术和职业梦想可以提供必要的指导，尤其是当学生的探索行为出现偏差，并可能危害他们本人以及社会的时候。

反 但是，无论是哪个教育机构，只要它们对学生的未来抱非常负责任的态度，都不会仅仅因为学生的想法看起来不大可能实现而设法劝阻学生去追寻他们的梦想。这是因为，**首先**，如果这个劝阻行为是真正负责任的、真正为学生和社会的利益考虑的话，它势必需要一个前提：这些教育机构实际上已经非常确信学生的梦想追求是断然不会成功的。但这个前提基本上难以成立。试问，如果不去投入所有身心去努力、去争取，有谁会在一开始就知道自己的理想会不会成功？我们人类今天所做的许多司空见惯的事情，在遥远的当初看起来不都是遥不可及、痴人说梦吗？

其次，如果实施题目中的建议，其结果很简单：泯灭梦想、故步自封，永远不会有发展和进步。这个结果同声称以探索未知、发掘人类理性的一切可能为己任的教育机构放到一起，是多么不协调。

合 正确的做法不是去劝阻，而应当是鼓励；并且，在学生的探索过程中，教育机构还要及时给他们帮助和引导，从而使他们本人和整个社会都能以最小的代价实现或者至少不断接近梦想。从某种意义上讲，人类和飞蛾没有太大的区别。他们都在向着光明和未知摸索，探索过程中注定要付出代价。如果不去探索，则永远不知道光明在哪里，更不用说找到光明了。

4. Scandals are useful because they focus our attention on problems in ways that no speaker or reformer ever could.

Write a response in which you discuss the extent to which you agree or disagree with the claim. In developing and supporting your position, be sure to address the most compelling reasons and/or examples that could be used to challenge your position.

题型归类

套叠式多角度分析题：可同时归入因果类和单纯性是非类。题目整体是个因果关系判断，即，因为 scandals focus our attention on problems in ways that no speaker or reformer ever could，所以 scandals are useful。结果部分是个价值判断，所以又是一个是非类题。

题目分析

首先，按照因果类题目类型展开分析：

（1）这个因果关系推理中的原因是否成立?

丑闻之所以成为丑闻往往是因为它们以超出道德和法律尺度的冲击力来显示事件的原委

曲直，所以单纯从丑闻的社会影响力来看，它们在某些时点的确能以常人难以企及的效果吸引人们对一些问题的关注。事实上，一些重大的社会变革往往是由丑闻来引爆，从而让公众觉得忍无可忍，于是形成社会变革的共识与合力。因此，题目中的原因部分似乎可以成立。

（2）假设这个原因成立，从它能否推出结果？

这个结论是个是非价值判断。所以，我们就从是非类题目的角度来分析。

其次，按照单纯性是非类题目类型展开分析：

①这种价值判断的标准是什么？

题目中论者显然把丑闻能揭示问题当作判断其有用性的标准。这当然有其道理：社会正常的监督机制难免有其盲点。在这个意义上，揭发丑闻有净化社会的作用。

②这种价值判断的标准是否值得修正？

但是，假如对丑闻的揭发变成了纯粹为了满足公众好奇心的需要，变成了对所谓名人私生活的追踪调查、对政府政策失误的舆论炒作、降格为制造奇谈怪论和社会轰动效应来刺激公众的神经，揭发丑闻就有可能动摇人们对社会公平和正义的信心，侵蚀人们彼此间的信任感和安全感，甚至严重削弱政府的公信力、引发社会动荡。这时，判断丑闻揭发价值的标准就变成了：它是真正有利于解决问题呢，还是仅仅增加谈资、制造轰动效应？

提纲提要

论点 健康的社会不能仅仅靠丑闻来揭示问题

正 社会正常的监督机制难免有其盲点。丑闻之所以成为丑闻往往是因为它们以超出道德和法律尺度的冲击力来显示事件的原委曲直，所以单纯从丑闻的社会影响力来看，它们在某些时点的确能以常人难以企及的效果吸引人们对一些问题的关注。事实上，一些重大的社会变革往往是由丑闻来引爆，从而让公众觉得忍无可忍，于是形成社会变革的共识与合力。在这个意义上，揭发丑闻有净化社会的作用。

反 但是，假如对丑闻的揭发变成了纯粹为了满足公众好奇心的需要，变成了对所谓名人私生活的追踪调查、对政府政策失误的舆论炒作、降格为制造奇谈怪论和社会轰动效应来刺激公众的神经，揭发丑闻就有可能动摇人们对社会公平和正义的信心，侵蚀人们彼此间的信任感和安全感，甚至严重削弱政府的公信力、引发社会动荡。这时，判断丑闻揭发价值的标准就变成了：它是真正有利于解决问题呢，还是仅仅增加谈资、制造轰动效应？

散 当一个社会多是在靠揭发丑闻发现问题时，该社会正常的道德价值和社会管理体系，尤其是其司法和公共舆论体系，可能已经严重失灵了；这个社会很可能已经混乱到了要崩溃的边缘。这才是这个社会的普通民众及其精英群体要认真考虑的问题。

5. **Claim**: Governments must ensure that their major cities receive the financial support they need in order to thrive.

Reason: It is primarily in cities that a nation's cultural traditions are preserved and generated. (参考第2、117题)

Write a response in which you discuss the extent to which you agree or disagree with the claim and the reason on which that claim is based.

题型归类 套叠式多角度分析题：可同时归入因果类和建议类。因为It is primarily in cities that a nation's cultural traditions are preserved and generated，所以 Governments must ensure that their major cities receive the financial support they need in order to thrive。结论是个建议。

题目分析

（1）这个因果关系推理中的原因是否成立？

该题目的原因未必成立。无论城市还是农村，对一个国家的文化传统都是有贡献的。毕竟，一国的文化在大城市和中小城市以及城乡之间的分布是个整体，不应仅仅包括城市文化。

（2）假设这个原因成立，从它能否推出结果？

即使上述原因成立，结论也可能是推不出的。仅仅因为城市产生和保存了一国的文化，城市就应该得到财力支持，这个理由充分吗？国家有这个财力吗？支持城市是否会造成农村经济的萧条，并进而导致部分文化传统的遗失和湮灭？难道就没有其他替代方案吗？

提纲提要

论点 题目中的判断过于简单化。

正 城市经济往往是一国经济的核心。城市的繁荣往往能带动城市周边地区、甚至是整体经济的繁荣。

反 但是，无论城市还是农村，对一个国家的文化传统都是有贡献的。毕竟，一国的文化在大城市和中小城市以及城乡之间的分布是个整体，不应仅仅包括城市文化。

反 即使上述原因成立，结论也可能是推不出的。仅仅因为城市产生和保存了一国的文化，城市就应该得到财力支持，这个理由充分吗？国家有这个财力吗？支持城市是否会造成农村经济的萧条，并进而导致部分文化传统的遗失和湮灭？难道就没有其他替代方案吗？

---

6. A nation should require all of its students to study the same national curriculum until they enter college. (参考第14、96、116题)

Write a response in which you discuss the extent to which you agree or disagree with the recommendation and explain your reasoning for the position you take. In developing and supporting your position, describe specific circumstances in which adopting the recommendation would or would not be advantageous and explain how these examples shape your position.

题型归类 建议类。

题目分析

（1）题目中的建议可行性如何？

建议未必可行。对于那些多民族、多种族、语言文字难以统一的国家和民族来说，要求所有学生在上大学之前都学习同样的课程是较难办到的。

（2）如果实施题目中的建议，是否会导致同初始目的相矛盾或其他荒谬的结果？

强行要求所有学生在上大学之前都学习同样的课程，会导致种族、民族间的矛盾和冲突，更加背离通过国民教育促进民族、种族融合，形成共同文化价值认同的初衷。

（3）有无替代或折中方案？

　　文化融合是个自然而渐进的过程。制定并推广全民统一的课程，但同时充分尊重各民族、种族的特性，保护他们相对独立的文化价值和传统。

提纲提要

论点　**文化融合是个自然而渐进的过程。**

正　通过制定并推广全民统一的课程，用以塑造共同的社会价值和行为规范对于单一民族国家既有必要，又容易做到。对于多民族、多种族的国家来说，在基础教育阶段，在各个民族和种族的教育大纲中体现全体国民共同认可的社会价值也有利于促进民族、种族彼此理解与融合，保持社会稳定。

反　但是，在全国盲目推行一体化的基础教育大纲会碰到一些棘手的问题。首先，对于那些多民族、多种族、语言文字难以统一的国家和民族来说，要求所有学生在上大学之前都学习同样的课程是较难办到的。

　　其次，强行要求所有学生在上大学之前都学习同样的课程，不仅会人为加重教育资源的紧张（比如师资的紧缺、教学设施的不足等），而且会导致种族、民族间的矛盾和冲突，更加背离通过国民教育促进民族、种族融合，形成共同文化价值认同的初衷。

合　文化融合是个自然而渐进的过程。制定并推广全民统一的课程，但同时充分尊重各民族、种族的特性，保护他们相对独立的文化价值和传统。

---

　　7. Some people believe that government funding of the arts is necessary to ensure that the arts can flourish and be available to all people. Others believe that government funding of the arts threatens the integrity of the arts. (参考第80、88题)

　　Write a response in which you discuss which view more closely aligns with your own position and explain your reasoning for the position you take. In developing and supporting your position, you should address both of the views presented.

题型归类　建议类。

题目分析

（1）**题目中的建议可行性如何？**

　　题目中的建议未必可行。政府财力有限，不可能向所有的艺术家提供资助。

（2）**如果实施题目中的建议，是否会导致同初始目的相矛盾或其他荒谬的结果？**

　　政府不是万能的。在政府和艺术家之间存在严重的信息不对称现象（information asymmetry）。这种信息的不对称使得政府对艺术的资助难免厚此薄彼。与此同时，艺术家为了获得资助，也会通过向官员行贿或者进行迎合政府喜好的创作向政府寻租（rent-seeking）。这样的话，不仅使那些真正需要政府资助的处于弱势的艺术家和艺术流派得不到机会，而且艺术作为一种对人类真善美的探索功能也会大打折扣，危及 the integrity of the arts。

（3）**有无替代或折中方案？**

　　政府应尽量资助处于弱势的艺术家和艺术流派，使所有的艺术流派都能得到表现和发展的机会。对主流艺术派别的资助应尽量让商业和民间而不是政府来完成。

提纲提要

论点 政府应尽量资助处于弱势的艺术家和艺术流派。

正 公平、公正的政府资助有利于各种艺术流派都得到发展的机会。

反 但是，题目中的建议未必可行。一方面，政府财力有限，不可能向所有的艺术家提供资助。另一方面，政府不是万能的。在政府和艺术家之间存在严重的信息不对称现象。这种信息的不对称使得政府对艺术的资助难免厚此薄彼。与此同时，一些艺术家为了获得资助，会通过向官员行贿或者进行迎合政府喜好的创作向政府寻租。这样的话，不仅使那些真正需要政府资助的处于弱势的艺术家和艺术流派得不到机会，而且艺术作为一种对人类真善美的探索功能也会大打折扣，危及 the integrity of the arts。

合 政府应尽量资助处于弱势的艺术家和艺术流派，使所有的艺术流派都能得到表现和发展的机会。对主流艺术派别的资助应尽量让商业和民间而不是政府来完成。

- -

8. **Claim**: In any field—business, politics, education, government—those in power should step down after five years.

Reason: The surest path to success for any enterprise is revitalization through new leadership. (参考第111、149题；同时还可以参考第16、62、69、94、114、123、128、147题)

Write a response in which you discuss the extent to which you agree or disagree with the claim and the reason on which that claim is based.

题型归类 因果类。因为The surest path to success for any enterprise is revitalization through new leadership，所以In any field—business, politics, education, government—those in power should step down after five years。结论是个建议，所以也是个套叠式多角度分析题。

题目分析

（1）这个因果关系推理中的原因是否成立？

　　该题目的原因未必成立。领导因素充其量是一项事业（enterprise）成功与否的**必要条件**，而非**充分条件**。没有得力的领导，一项事业也许不能成功；但有了好的领导，一项事业未必一定成功。其他因素，比如领导团队的整体素质、领导和下属及其他同事的沟通与协作、一项事业的管理运营等等，都对事业的成功起着关键作用。

（2）假设这个原因成立，从它能否推出结果？

　　即使上述原因成立，结论也是推不出的。领导五年一换对于所有的领域和工作来说都适合吗？频繁更换领导是否会导致政策的大起大落、管理风格前后差异太大等不利结果呢？保持领导层活力的办法难道只有五年一换，而没有别的替代方案，比如，对领导层定期轮训、加强监督与制衡等？

提纲提要

论点 题目中的判断似是而非。

正 领导的管理理念、策略、甚至是经营风格对任何事业的成败都起着重要作用。

反 但是，领导因素充其量是一项事业成功与否的必要条件，而非充分条件。没有得力的领导，一项事业也许不能成功；但有了好的领导，一项事业也未必一定成功。其他因素，比如领导团队的整体素质、领导和下属及其他同事的沟通与协作、一项事业的管理运营等等，都对事业的成功起着关键作用。

反 即使上述原因成立，结论也是推不出的。领导五年一换对于所有的领域和工作来说都适合吗？频繁更换领导是否会导致政策的大起大落、管理风格前后差异太大等不利结果呢？保持领导层活力的办法难道只有五年一换，而没有别的替代方案，比如，对领导层定期轮训、加强监督与制衡等？

9. In any field of endeavor, it is impossible to make a significant contribution without first being strongly influenced by past achievements within that field.

Write a response in which you discuss the extent to which you agree or disagree with the statement and explain your reasoning for the position you take. In developing and supporting your position, you should consider ways in which the statement might or might not hold true and explain how these considerations shape your position.

题型归类 事实类。

题目分析

（1）能否从公认的原则或事实中推出相反的判断？

基于下列两点原则，题目中的判断未必成立：

其一，前人的工作未必就是科学的。有时，后人需要将前人的工作全部推翻，对之进行全新的变革。这时，一味地跟随前人，很可能反受误导。

其二，后人对前人的科学成就应持实事求是、批判继承的态度。

（2）能否举出相反的事例？

（大家可以举出无数身边发生的例子。此处从略。）

提纲提要

论点 **论者的观点失于简单。**

正 知识总是具有某种延续性和继承性的。借鉴前人成果当然是件有益的事情，多数情况下可以节约很多的时间和精力。

反 但是，前人的工作未必就是科学的。有时，后人需要将前人的工作全部推翻，对之作全新的变革。这时，一味地跟随前人，很可能反受误导。

合 后人对前人的科学成就应持实事求是，批判继承的态度。

10. Nations should pass laws to preserve any remaining wilderness areas in their natural state, even if these areas could be developed for economic gain. （参考 第31、63、67、119、125、148题）

Write a response in which you discuss your views on the policy and explain your reasoning for the position you take. In developing and supporting your position, you should consider the possible consequences of implementing the policy and explain how these consequences shape your position.

题型归类　建议类。

题目分析

（1）题目中的建议可行性如何？

　　在公共财政能力有限的情况下，政府将所有荒原地区都保护起来的计划是否可行值得怀疑。

（2）如果实施题目中的建议，是否会导致同初始目的相矛盾或其他荒谬的结果？

　　政府对本来已是人迹罕至的荒原实施保护的做法很可能是一种不必要的浪费。再者，人和自然之间的平衡并不意味着绝对消除人对环境的影响。绝对消除自然环境中人的因素的做法本身就是在否定人本来也是自然环境中的一部分、并且二者之间本来就相互作用这个客观事实。这可能是另外一种形式的环境破坏。

（3）有无替代或折中方案？

　　人应融入环境、与环境共生，但不破坏环境。

提纲提要

论点　**人应融入环境，但不破坏环境。**

正　考虑到人对自然环境的破坏和影响有时是难以准确估计的，对荒原进行预防性保护也是有必要的。

反　在公共财政能力有限的情况下，政府将所有荒原地区都保护起来的计划是否可行值得怀疑。政府对本来已是人迹罕至的荒原实施保护的做法很可能是一种不必要的浪费。再者，人和自然之间的平衡并不意味着绝对消除人对环境的影响。绝对消除自然环境中人的因素的做法本身就是在否定人本来也是自然环境中的一部分、并且二者之间本来就相互作用这个客观事实。这可能是另外一种形式的环境破坏。

合　人应融入环境、与环境共生，但不破坏环境。

- -

11. People's behavior is largely determined by forces not of their own making. (参考第99题)

　　Write a response in which you discuss the extent to which you agree or disagree with the statement and explain your reasoning for the position you take. In developing and supporting your position, you should consider ways in which the statement might or might not hold true and explain how these considerations shape your position.

题型归类　事实类。

题目分析

（1）能否从公认的原则或事实中推出相反的判断？

　　基于下列两点原则，题目中的判断未必成立：

　　其一，人的思想和行为模式来源于社会，并不等于说人在一次性接受了社会的思想和行为模式的灌输和影响之后，其随后所有的思想和行为模式便一成不变了。人与社会是不断交互作用、相互塑造的。根据其所认可的价值，人是不断主动调整其思想和行为，并同时对周围的环境和社会产生影响的。在此过程中，人的思想和行为显然并非完全受不可控力量的制约。

　　其二，经济的全球化、文化价值的多元化以及随之而来的社会开放度和宽容度的增加，更进一步增加了人们选择其思想和行为方式的自由度和自主权。

（2）能否举出相反的事例？

　　（大家可以举出无数身边发生的例子。此处从略。）

提纲提要

论点　**论者的观点过于片面。**

正　人最终是社会的产物。人的思想和行为本质上都是社会塑造的结果。就此而言，人的行为具有某种对其所在环境和社会被动适应的成分。

反　但是，人的思想和行为模式来源于社会，并不等于说人在一次性接受了社会的思想和行为模式的灌输和影响之后，其随后所有的思想和行为模式便一成不变了。人与社会是不断交互作用、相互塑造的。根据其所认可的价值，人是不断主动调整其思想和行为，并同时对周围的环境和社会产生影响的。在此过程中，人的思想和行为显然并非完全受不可控力量的制约。

反　经济的全球化、文化价值的多元化以及随之而来的社会开放度和宽容度的增加，更进一步增加了人们选择其思想和行为方式的自由度和自主权。

---

　　12. Governments should offer a free university education to any student who has been admitted to a university but who cannot afford the tuition. (参考第25题)

　　Write a response in which you discuss your views on the policy and explain your reasoning for the position you take. In developing and supporting your position, you should consider the possible consequences of implementing the policy and explain how these consequences shape your position.

题型归类　建议类。

题目分析

（1）题目中的建议可行性如何？

　　题目中的建议当然可行。中国的高等教育曾一度完全免费。

（2）如果实施题目中的建议，是否会导致同初始目的相矛盾或其他荒谬的结果？

　　教育完全由政府承担至少有四点弊端：其一，巨大的财政压力。其二，政府补贴会引起大学学费的攀升。其三，部分学生可能会作弊以获得免费高等教育的机会。其四，政府将不得不花费大量的人、财、物力去甄别学生经济状况的真实性，这中间会产生大量的寻租机会，腐败贿赂势难避免。如此一来，最终的结果有可能是既不能保证机会的均等和公平，经济上也会难以为继。

（3）有无替代或折中方案？

　　为了保证教育机会的均等，应该有由政府出资、免费的高等教育机会。至少对那些社会弱势群体，如贫困地区、少数民族等，应当如此。但是，应当有可靠的运作机制保证其机会的均等性和经济上的可持续性，比如：首先，全额由政府提供的免费教育机会的数量应该是有限度和竞争性的。其次，应鼓励企业、慈善机构或个人参与资助。他们在甄别困难学生家庭经济状况方面会更有效，从而避免贪腐机会的出现。第三，应鼓励商业银行向困难学生提供长期、低息或免息贷款以解决其学费，学生的还款记录计入其个人信用档案，以此激励其珍惜机会、努力学习、勤奋工作，等等。

提纲提要

论点 应该有政府出资的免费高等教育机会，但同时要有可靠的运作机制来保证。

㊣ 在政府财力可行的情况下，免费的公立教育有利于做到教育面前的机会均等。

㊨ 但是，教育完全由政府承担至少有四点弊端：其一，巨大的财政压力。其二，政府补贴会助涨大学学费的攀升。其三，部分学生可能会作弊以获得免费高等教育的机会。其四，政府将不得不花费大量的人、财、物力去甄别学生经济状况的真实性，这中间会产生大量的寻租机会，腐败贿赂势难避免。如此一来，最终的结果有可能是既不能保证机会的均等和公平，经济上也会难以为继。

㊌ 为了保证教育机会的均等，应该有由政府出资、免费的高等教育机会，至少对那些社会弱势群体，如贫困地区、少数民族等，应当如此。但是，应当有可靠的运作机制保证其机会的均等性和经济上的可持续性，比如：首先，全额由政府提供的免费教育机会的数量应该是有限度和竞争性的。其次，应鼓励企业、慈善机构或个人参与资助。他们在甄别困难学生家庭经济状况方面会更有效，从而避免贪腐机会的出现。第三，应鼓励商业银行向困难学生提供长期、低息或免息贷款以解决其学费，学生的还款记录计入其个人信用档案，以此激励其珍惜机会、努力学习、勤奋工作，等等。

· ·

13. Universities should require every student to take a variety of courses outside the student's field of study. （参考第 3、15、20、32、35、39、46、98、129、135、136、137、140 题；同时还可以参考第 70、102、112 题）

Write a response in which you discuss the extent to which you agree or disagree with the claim. In developing and supporting your position, be sure to address the most compelling reasons and/or examples that could be used to challenge your position.

题型归类 建议类。

题目分析

（1）题目中的建议可行性如何？

题目中的建议未必可行。首先，许多大学、学院未必具备开设大量学科课程的能力。其次，学生很难有时间和精力在三至四年的时间里去学习专业以外的大量课程。第三，相当一部分学生很可能因为对专业以外的学科毫无兴趣而对这种要求产生强烈的抵制情绪。

（2）如果实施题目中的建议，是否会导致同初始目的相矛盾或其他荒谬的结果？

强行推行题目中的建议至少会带来三点弊端：其一，各个大学课程雷同化，失去其传统的学术特色。其二，学生疲于奔命于众多学科之间，所学浮光掠影，难以专深。其三，湮灭学生的个性和创造力。而这些都同包容一切个性、探索无限未知的现代大学精神格格不入。

（3）有无替代或折中方案？

在大学的头两年，学校可以鼓励学生尽量多选修一些专业及兴趣以外的学科，为其将来的学术发展构筑一个较为完整的框架。但到了后两年以及研究生阶段，则应鼓励学业专深。

对于少数在专门领域较早便显示了天分的学生，应该给他们更多的自由以使其潜能得到最大限度的挖掘。

提纲提要

论点 题目中的建议似是而非。

正 各门各科的知识是相互贯通的。宽博的知识面有利于人们多侧面、多角度地思考和解决问题。

反 但是，题目中的建议会有很多问题：首先，许多大学、学院未必具备开设大量学科课程的能力。其次，学生很难有时间和精力在三至四年的时间里去学习专业以外的大量课程。第三，相当一部分学生很可能因为对专业以外的学科毫无兴趣而对这种要求产生强烈的抵制情绪。

而且，强行推行题目中的建议至少会带来三点弊端：其一，各个大学课程雷同化，失去其传统的学术特色。其二，学生疲于奔命于众多学科之间，所学浮光掠影，难以专深。其三，湮灭学生的个性和创造力。而这些都同包容一切个性、探索无限未知的现代大学精神格格不入。

合 在大学的头两年，学校可以鼓励学生尽量多选修一些专业及兴趣以外的学科，为其将来的学术发展构筑一个较为完整的框架。但到了后两年以及研究生阶段，则应鼓励学业专深。对于少数在专门领域较早便显示了天分的学生，应该给他们更多的自由以使其潜能得到最大限度的挖掘。

---

14. A nation should require all of its students to study the same national curriculum until they enter college. (参考第6、96、116题)

Write a response in which you discuss your views on the policy and explain your reasoning for the position you take. In developing and supporting your position, you should consider the possible consequences of implementing the policy and explain how these consequences shape your position.

（建议类。本题目的分析思路和写作提纲可完全借鉴第6题。）

---

15. Educational institutions should actively encourage their students to choose fields of study that will prepare them for lucrative careers. (参考第3、13、20、32、35、39、46、98、129、135、136、137、140题)

Write a response in which you discuss the extent to which you agree or disagree with the claim. In developing and supporting your position, be sure to address the most compelling reasons and/or examples that could be used to challenge your position.

题型归类 建议类。

题目分析

（1）题目中的建议可行性如何？

题目中的建议未必可行。这是因为到底什么样的职业比较赚钱，这无从准确地提前知晓。我们也许可以根据眼下什么行业、什么职业最赚钱来确定未来的工作和职业方向。但是，在社会分工高度精细化、职业调整越来越频繁的今天，谁能准确地预知未来三年或五年的职业前景？既然如此，一个人一生的事业和职业前景又如何能进行精确规划呢？

（2）如果实施题目中的建议，是否会导致同初始目的相矛盾或其他荒谬的结果?

如果施行题目中的建议，其所导致的弊端至少有三点：第一，几乎所有的人都涌向为数不多看似"钱"景无限的职业。基于大家的认知能力大致相同、现有信息的有限性和未来的不可知性，这几乎是一个必然的结果。这一点，我们从一轮又一轮的计算机热、法律热、金融热、房地产热、MBA热，当然还包括当下最具中国特色的公务员热，都看得非常清楚。其结果只能是这些曾经的热门职业和行业很快出现人力资源供给的过剩、整体收入下降、相当一部分人被迫改行。第二，如果上述第一个结果成立，这随后的结果就是，对个人而言，是教育投入的失败；对国家而言，是国民财富的浪费。第三，会使得一个国家新兴的产业所需要的人力资源得不到及时的补充，影响该国产业结构的转移和提升。这是因为一个国家教育机构的人才产出能力在中短期内是基本恒定的。当人才大量涌向几个看似"热门"的行业时，其他行业的人才供给必然相应减少。

（3）有无替代或折中方案?

一个可能的方案如下：第一，教育机构应有所分工。大学及以上的教育将重点放在通才教育（versatile education）、高端教育和学生兴趣的开发培养上面；而大专（three-year colleges）及以下的教育则将重点放在学生的职业技能和短缺、新兴人才的培养上。第二，政府教育部门、高等院校要密切跟踪企业、行业和世界经济的发展趋势乃至国家战略需求；产业、企业要向教育机构提供及时的人才需求信息反馈。理想的结果是，人尽其才，物尽其用。

提纲提要

论点 一个人的职业应是个人兴趣和市场需求结合的产物，而非教育机构指导的结果。

（正）教育是人们对未来进行的时间和金钱的投资。期待最大收益是理所当然。教育机构假如能够在人才和市场之间发挥好桥梁作用，对学生个人及行业都是好事情。

（反）但是，实施题目中的建议有难度。其至少有如下三个可能的弊端：第一，几乎所有的人都涌向为数不多看似"钱"景无限的职业。基于大家的认知能力大致相同、现有信息的有限性和未来的不可知性，这几乎是一个必然的结果。这一点，我们从一轮又一轮的计算机热、法律热、金融热、房地产热、MBA热，当然还包括当下最具中国特色的公务员热，都看得非常清楚。其结果只能是这些曾经的热门职业和行业很快出现人力资源供给的过剩、整体收入下降、相当一部分人被迫改行。第二，如果上述第一个结果成立，这随后的结果就是，对个人而言，是教育投入的失败；对国家而言，是国民财富的浪费。第三，会使得一个国家新兴的产业所需要的人力资源得不到及时的补充，影响该国产业结构的转移和提升。这是因为一个国家教育机构的人才产出能力在中短期内是基本恒定的。当人才大量涌向几个看似"热门"的行业时，其他行业的人才供给必然相应减少。

（合）一个可能的方案如下：第一，教育机构应有所分工。大学及以上的教育将重点放在通才教育、高端教育和学生兴趣的开发培养上面；而大专及以下的教育则将重点放在学生的职业技能和短缺、新兴人才的培养上。第二，政府教育部门、高等院校要密切跟踪企业、行业和世界经济的发展趋势乃至国家战略需求；产业、企业要向教育机构提供及时的人才需求信息反馈。理想的结果是，人尽其才，物尽其用。

16. Some people believe that in order to be effective, political leaders must yield to public opinion and abandon principle for the sake of compromise. Others believe that the most essential quality of an effective leader is the ability to remain consistently committed to particular principles and objectives. (参考第8、62、69、94、114、123、128、147题)

Write a response in which you discuss which view more closely aligns with your own position and explain your reasoning for the position you take. In developing and supporting your position, you should address both of the views presented.

该题目的分析及提纲请参见本书第一章第四节中"定义类题目分析范例"之范例一。

17. Formal education tends to restrain our minds and spirits rather than set them free. (参考第42、48、68、87、92题)

Write a response in which you discuss the extent to which you agree or disagree with the statement and explain your reasoning for the position you take. In developing and supporting your position, you should consider ways in which the statement might or might not hold true and explain how these considerations shape your position.

题型归类 该题是套叠式多角度分析题，可同时归入事实类和结合式定义类，因为要对题目中的表述 restrain our minds and spirits 的含义进行明确界定。本题将从事实类的角度进行分析。

题目分析

（1）能否从公认的原则或事实中推出相反的判断？

基于两个原则，题目中的判断未必成立：

其一，如果我们将题目中所说的 restrain our minds and spirits 界定为教育方法刻板、未能启发学生进行创造性的思维，那么，这个判断显然不符合事实。至少欧美的现代教育不是这样。

其二，如果我们将题目中所说的 restrain our minds and spirits 界定为只向学生灌输现有的概念和事实的话，题目中判断也未必成立。创新未必就等于放弃已有的知识积累。知识毕竟有其连续性和继承性。

（2）能否举出相反的事例？

（大家可以举出无数身边发生的例子。此处从略。）

提纲提要

论点 **窒息学生心智的往往不是教育本身，而是教育背后的意识形态。**

正 部分教育机构或者部分学科的老师（比如教历史和语文的部分老师）的确表现出过向学生强调概念和事实的识记而不注意启发他们自主思考的倾向。这种教学方法很容易将学生变成记忆的机器，从而窒息他们的创造性。

反 但是，断言 Formal education tends to restrain our minds and spirits rather than set them free 有点儿武断。

首先，如果我们将题目中所说的 restrain our minds and spirits 理解为教育刻板、未能启发学生进行创造性的思维，那么，这个判断显然不符合事实。至少欧美的现代教育不是这样。

其次，如果我们将题目中所说的 restrain our minds and spirits 理解为只向学生灌输现有的概念和事实的话，题目中判断也未必成立。创新未必就等于放弃已有的知识积累。知识毕竟有其连续性和继承性。

㈠ 反思人类历史，真正窒息学生心智的往往不是教育本身，而是教育背后的意识形态（ideologies）。人类所有的知识积累不过是人类与其周围的世界（包括自然世界和人类社会）在沟通、交流之后所写下的日记。这些日记所记录的只不过是些观察和感受而已，全都有待于后来者在进一步的观察和感受后去反复补充和验证，因而也无所谓终极结论或者终极真理。但是，当某些特定的意识形态抽取这本日记中的只言片语，并将其神话为终极真理而强制灌输、不容改变的时候，人类的思想才真的被窒息了。

- -

18. The well-being of a society is enhanced when many of its people question authority. (参考第50、86、115题)

Write a response in which you discuss the extent to which you agree or disagree with the statement and explain your reasoning for the position you take. In developing and supporting your position, you should consider ways in which the statement might or might not hold true and explain how these considerations shape your position.

题型归类　事实类。

题目分析

（1）能否从公认的原则或事实中推出相反的判断?

理论上讲，质疑权威，无论这个权威是政府、专家，还是科研机构、社会名流等等，可以维护个体的权益、抑制集体（其常常以权威或权威拥护者的面目出现）对个体的暴力。但是，超越任何法律秩序和道德公义的框架，对权威的随意质疑和挑战容易导致社会陷入无政府状态。这样的话，反而有害于政治民主和社会正义，进而损害整个社会的福利水平。

（2）能否举出相反的事例?

（大家可以举出无数身边发生的例子，详情从略。）

提纲提要

论点　**论者的观点失于简单。**

㊣ 假如我们将这里的 authority 定义为政府权力机关的话，选民对政府的质疑可以强化对政府的监督，实现民主政治，防范政府对民众利益的侵犯。而如果这里的权威是专家学者、科研机构、社会名流的话，对他们的质疑也有利于维护个体的权益，抑制集体（其常常以权威或权威拥护者的面目出现）对个体的暴力。

㊁ 但是，超越任何法律秩序和道德公义的框架，对权威的随意质疑和挑战容易导致社会陷入无政府状态。这样的话，反而有害于政治民主和社会正义，进而损害整个社会的福利水平。

㈠ 一个社会的繁荣、活力和创造力以及民主政治和社会正义的实现有赖于：其一，人们对自由、民主和社会正义含义的共识。其二，对基于社会和人性的共识而制定的实现民主政治和社会正义的程序的遵守。否则，不可能有真正的自由、民主和社会正义，更谈不上所谓的大众福利。

19. Governments should focus on solving the immediate problems of today rather than on trying to solve the anticipated problems of the future.

Write a response in which you discuss the extent to which you agree or disagree with the recommendation and explain your reasoning for the position you take. In developing and supporting your position, describe specific circumstances in which adopting the recommendation would or would not be advantageous and explain how these examples shape your position.

题型归类 建议类。

题目分析

（1）题目中的建议可行性如何？

题目中的建议不可行。人无远虑，必有近忧。政府不可能只顾眼前、不计将来。

（2）如果实施题目中的建议，是否会导致同初始目的相矛盾或其他荒谬的结果？

没有对将来的规划和承诺，选民不知道政府将会做什么、能给自己带来什么，也无法借此对政府进行监督。社会也许会因此丧失向心力和凝聚力。

（3）有无替代或折中方案？

政府必须兼顾眼前和将来。

提纲提要

论点 政府必须兼顾眼前和将来。

正 眼前的问题往往是最为紧迫的问题，当然要给予足够的关注。

反 但是，人无远虑，必有近忧。政府不可能只顾眼前、不计将来。没有对将来的规划和承诺，选民不知道政府将会做什么、能给自己带来什么，也无法借此对政府进行监督。社会也许会因此丧失向心力和凝聚力。

合 政府必须兼顾眼前和将来。

20. Some people believe that college students should consider only their own talents and interests when choosing a field of study. Others believe that college students should base their choice of a field of study on the availability of jobs in that field. (参考第3、13、15、32、35、39、46、98、129、135、136、137、140题)

Write a response in which you discuss which view more closely aligns with your own position and explain your reasoning for the position you take. In developing and supporting your position, you should address both of the views presented.

题型归类 建议类。

题目分析

（1）题目中的建议可行性如何？

题目中两个不同的建议都可行。

（2）如果实施题目中的建议，是否会导致同初始目的相矛盾或其他荒谬的结果？

如果只是考虑个人的学习兴趣和才华而不考虑毕业后的就业前景，毕业后就业有可能会遇到困难。人的所有压力之中，生存的压力当然是最需要优先考虑的。但反过来，如果学生将自己的学习和研究领域仅仅用就业的前景框限起来，就个人而言，人生失去了很多乐趣；就社会而言，则很有可能因为特立独行、才华横溢之才的淹没而损失了创新精神与活力。

（3）有无替代或折中方案？

就个人而言，生活的过程就是在理想与现实间的徘徊，每个人都不得不在二者之中寻求某种折中和平衡；就社会和政府而言，可以由财政出资在大学设立特别项目或者鼓励企业和个人设专项基金，用来资助确有天分的学生发展他们的兴趣和潜能。

提纲提要

论点 生活的过程就是在理想与现实间的徘徊。

正 兴趣是最好的老师。兴趣往往能告诉我们什么是最适合自己的职业和事业。

反 但是，如果只是考虑个人的学习兴趣和个性才华而不考虑毕业后的就业前景，有可能会面临毕业后的就业困难。人的所有压力之中，生存的压力当然是最需要优先考虑的。但反过来，如果学生将自己的学习和研究领域仅仅用就业的前景框限起来，就个人而言，人生失去了很多乐趣；就社会而言，则很有可能因为特立独行、才华横溢之才的淹没而损失了创新精神与活力。

合 就个人而言，生活的过程就是在理想与现实间的徘徊，每个人都不得不在二者之中寻求某种折中和平衡；就社会和政府而言，可以由财政出资在大学设立特别项目或者鼓励企业和个人设专项基金，用来资助确有天分的学生发展他们的兴趣和潜能。

---

21. Laws should be flexible enough to take account of various circumstances, times, and places.

Write a response in which you discuss the extent to which you agree or disagree with the statement and explain your reasoning for the position you take. In developing and supporting your position, you should consider ways in which the statement might or might not hold true and explain how these considerations shape your position.

题型归类 建议类。

题目分析

（1）题目中的建议可行性如何？

建议不可行。因为人类的理性和对未来和未知的预测能力是有限的，所以没有任何法律可以灵活到把各种情形、时代和场所考虑进去。

（2）如果实施题目中的建议，是否会导致同初始目的相矛盾或其他荒谬的结果？

如果非要考虑到各种情形、时代和场所，其结果是：第一，人类将不得不放弃立法，转而实施一事一议的随机处置。其最终结果充其量是发展出一套法律案例汇编，而不会产生完备的法律体系。第二，过于灵活的法律，会丧失其严肃性和权威感；同时，朝令夕改也会令人无所适从。君主制下的皇帝金口玉言，出口即法。但这种灵活得近乎随意的法律，根本不是法治社会所应有和期待的。

（3）有无替代或折中方案？

下列选择也许是不错的折中方案：第一，法律所倡导和维护的社会终极价值（如，自由、民主、公平、正义以及人的生命权、财产权与人格尊严不容侵犯等）是恒定的，所以捍卫这些人类社会基本价值的宪法当然应该是稳定的，而且是越稳定越好。第二，制定和实施法律的公正、公开、公平和严格的程序也应当是稳定的。否则，再好的法律也会给不逞之徒留下玩弄法律的空间。第三，法律原则之下，可以运用最高法院的司法解释或者判例（judicial precedents）来灵活处置现实中的特殊情况；第四，法律不是万能的。法律之外，可以给媒体、公共舆论、传统习俗和道德以及民间组织（non-governmental organizations）留下社会自我管理和自我校正的空间和机会。

提纲提要

论点 **法律该如何满足现实的特殊要求应视具体的法律而定。**

正 理论上讲，一部把各种可能情况都考虑进去的法律当然是好的。这甚至是许多法律在立法之初所尽力追求的。

反 但实际上，因为人类的理性和对未来和未知的预测能力是有限的，所以没有任何法律可以灵活到考虑进去各种情形。如果非要考虑到各种情形、时代和场所，其结果是：第一，人类将不得不放弃立法，转而实施一事一议的随机处置。其最终结果充其量是发展出一套法律案例汇编，而不会产生完备的法律体系。第二，过于灵活的法律，会丧失其严肃性和权威感；同时，朝令夕改也会令人无所适从。君主制下的皇帝金口玉言，出口即法。但这种灵活得近乎随意的法律，根本不是法治社会所应有和期待的。

合 下列选择也许是不错的折中方案：第一，法律所倡导和维护的社会终极价值（如，自由、民主、公平、正义以及人的生命权、财产权与人格尊严不容侵犯等）是恒定的，所以捍卫这些人类社会基本价值的宪法当然应该是稳定的，而且是越稳定越好。第二，制定和实施法律的公正、公开、公平和严格的程序也应当是稳定的。否则，再好的法律也会给不逞之徒留下玩弄法律的空间。第三，法律原则之下，可以运用最高法院的司法解释或者判例来灵活处置现实中的特殊情况。第四，法律不是万能的。法律之外，可以给媒体、公共舆论、传统习俗和道德以及民间组织留下社会自我管理和自我校正的空间和机会。

22. **Claim**: The best way to understand the character of a society is to examine the character of the men and women that the society chooses as its heroes or its role models.

Reason: Heroes and role models reveal a society's highest ideals. （参考第44、75、84、122题；同时还可以参考第24、29、52、70、77、112、122、123题）

Write a response in which you discuss the extent to which you agree or disagree with the claim and the reason on which that claim is based.

题型归类 套叠式多角度分析题。整体是个因果类题目，但它的结果部分是个建议。

题目分析

首先，按照因果类题目类型展开分析：

（1）这个因果关系推理中的原因是否成立？

该题目的原因未必成立。这是因为，一个社会的所谓的"英雄模范"很可能是出于特殊的意识形态的需要而被人为树立起来的。这样的"英雄模范"未必就能真正反映社会和人心的深层次渴望。

（2）假设这个原因成立，从它能否推出结果？

即使上述原因成立，结论也是推不出的。鉴于这个结果部分是个建议，我们在下面就从建议类题目的分析角度切入分析。

其次，按照建议类题目类型展开分析：

（1）题目中的建议可行性如何？

任何人只要愿意，都可通过研究一个社会视为偶像的男男女女的特点而了解该社会的特点。所以，题目中的建议当然可行。

（2）如果实施题目中的建议，是否会导致同初始目的相矛盾或其他荒谬的结果？

当人们试图通过研究一个社会视为偶像的男男女女的特点而了解该社会的特点的时候，有两个问题：第一，如上面已经提到过的，人为树立的所谓"英雄模范"未必能真正反映社会和人心的深层次渴望。第二，消费文化和快餐式娱乐所打造的炫目的时尚先锋、潮流偶像更多地反映的是社会和时代的泡沫，而不是一个社会的主流价值。我们这个时代明星和偶像太多，以至于我们还没来得及记住他们，他们就消失了。

（3）有无替代或折中方案？

偶像可能只代表了一个社会的表层状态。普通人的生活才是一个社会的真实写照。正如眼下的中国，都市偶像不能代表中国；代表中国的是七亿多的农民、上千万的城市工人以及知识分子等。然而这些人大都寂寂无闻。

提纲提要

论点 偶像可能只代表一个社会的表层状态。

㊣ 一般而言，某一社会所认可的英雄和偶像能在一定程度上反映该社会的面貌状态。

㊙ 但是，当人们试图通过研究一个社会视为偶像的男男女女的特点而了解该社会的特点的时候，有两个问题：第一，一个社会的所谓的"英雄模范"很可能是出于特殊的意识形态的需要而被人为树立起来的。这样的"英雄模范"未必就能真正反映社会和人心的深层次渴望。第二，消费文化和快餐式娱乐所打造的炫目的时尚先锋、潮流偶像更多反映的是社会和时代的泡沫，而不是该社会的主流价值。我们这个时代明星和偶像太多，以至于我们还没来得及记住他们，他们就消失了。

㊌ 偶像可能只代表了一个社会的表层状态。普通人的生活才是一个社会的真实写照。正如眼下的中国，都市偶像不能代表中国；代表中国的是七亿多的农民、上千万的城市工人以及知识分子等。然而这些人大都寂寂无闻。

- -

23. Governments should place few, if any, restrictions on scientific research and development. (参考第 36、72 题)

Write a response in which you discuss the extent to which you agree or disagree with the recommendation and explain your reasoning for the position you take. In developing and supporting your position, describe specific circumstances in which adopting the recommendation would or would not be advantageous and explain how these examples shape your position.

题型归类 建议类。

题目分析

（1）题目中的建议可行性如何？

　　题目中的建议可行。

（2）如果实施题目中的建议，是否会导致同初始目的相矛盾或其他荒谬的结果？

　　基于人的理性的有限性，科研人员并不能保证他们的科研活动必定会给社会带来更多的福利。比如，对克隆人技术的研究就有可能打破现有社会伦理的边界；而对核能的滥用（如2011年日本的福岛核电站事故和上世纪80年代前苏联的切尔诺贝利核事故、全球核技术扩散等）则已经让人类品尝到苦果。

（3）有无替代或折中方案？

　　政府作为社会公共利益的代表，理应对科研的不确定风险进行监控。关键在于如何在科学研究的社会收益和社会风险之间找到平衡。

提纲提要

论点 政府理应对科研的不确定风险进行监控。

正 好奇心和个人兴趣是人们进行科学探索的最大动力。所以，对科研活动施加较少的人为干预，也许更有利于人们的科学创新。

反 但是，基于人的理性的有限性，科研人员并不能保证他们的科研活动必定会给社会带来更多的福利。比如，对克隆人技术的研究就有可能打破现有社会伦理的边界；而对核能的滥用（如2011年日本的福岛核电站事故和上世纪80年代前苏联的切尔诺贝利核事故、全球核技术扩散等）则已经让人类品尝到苦果。

反 政府作为社会公共利益的代表，理应对科研的不确定风险进行监控。关键在于如何在科学研究的社会收益和社会风险之间找到平衡。

- -

24. The best way to teach is to praise positive actions and ignore negative ones. （参考第22、29、52、70、77、112、122、123题）

Write a response in which you discuss the extent to which you agree or disagree with the statement and explain your reasoning for the position you take. In developing and supporting your position, you should consider ways in which the statement might or might not hold true and explain how these considerations shape your position.

题型归类 该题目是平行式多角度分析题，既可归入建议类，也可归入是非类和事实类。这里仅以建议类展开分析。

题目分析

（1）题目中的建议可行性如何？

题目中的建议本身是可行的。

（2）如果实施题目中的建议，是否会导致同初始目的相矛盾或其他荒谬的结果？

从错误和失败中汲取经验也是一个人学习的主要途径之一。一味地表扬而对错误和缺点熟视无睹，有可能让一个人在错误的路上越走也远。实际上，人类文明的进步就是在不断的试错（trial-and-error）过程中取得的。

（3）有无替代或折中方案？

批评中有鼓励，指出错误而不损害被批评者的人格与尊严；鼓励中有更高期待，一个人才能获得不断突破自我的动力。人无完人，善意的批评可以使人进步；人无完人，批评切忌苛责。

提纲提要

论点 **人无完人，善意的批评可以使人进步；人无完人，批评切忌苛责**。

正 鼓励和赞赏有利于调动学生学习的自主性，培养健康、完善的人格。

反 但是，从错误和失败中汲取经验也是一个人学习的主要途径之一。一味地表扬而对错误和缺点熟视无睹，有可能让一个人在错误的路上越走也远。实际上，人类文明的进步就是在不断的试错过程中取得的。

合 批评中有鼓励，指出错误而不损害被批评者的人格与尊严；鼓励中有更高期待，一个人才能获得不断突破自我的动力。人无完人，善意的批评可以使人进步；人无完人，批评切忌苛责。

- -

25. Governments should offer college and university education free of charge to all students. (参考第12题)

Write a response in which you discuss the extent to which you agree or disagree with the recommendation and explain your reasoning for the position you take. In developing and supporting your position, describe specific circumstances in which adopting the recommendation would or would not be advantageous and explain how these examples shape your position.

题型归类 建议类。

题目分析

（1）题目中的建议可行性如何？

题目中的建议当然可行。中国的高等教育曾一度完全免费。

（2）如果实施题目中的建议，是否会导致同初始目的相矛盾或其他荒谬的结果？

高等教育完全由政府承担至少有五点弊端：其一，政府背负巨大的财政压力。其二，政府补贴会导致大学开支连年攀升，直至失控。其三，大学之间难以形成竞争，不会有真正一流大学的产生。第四，免费获得的接受高等教育的机会容易让学生不珍惜，不利于激励和培养优秀人才。第五，免费的大学不会吸引民间和社会投资的参与，导致大学教育机会的相对短缺，人为制造学生接受大学教育机会上的不均等。

（3）有无替代或折中方案？

第一，基础类、公益类、极端紧缺类专业可以适当免费；第二，放开高等教育的民间投资，鼓励高校间的竞争，打造一流高等学府。

提纲提要

论点 论者观点失于偏颇。

正 在政府财力可行的情况下，免费的大学教育有利于做到教育面前机会均等。

反 但是，高等教育完全由政府承担至少有五点弊端：其一，政府背负巨大的财政压力。其二，政府补贴会导致大学开支连年攀升，直至失控。其三，大学之间难以形成竞争，不会有真正一流大学的产生。第四，免费获得的接受高等教育的机会容易让学生不珍惜，不利于激励和培养优秀人才。第五，免费的大学不会吸引民间和社会投资的参与，导致大学教育机会的相对短缺，人为制造学生接受大学教育机会上的不均等。

合 可能的折中方案：第一，基础类、公益类、极端紧缺类专业可以适当免费。第二，放开高等教育的民间投资，鼓励高校间的竞争，打造一流高等学府。

- -

26. The luxuries and conveniences of contemporary life prevent people from developing into truly strong and independent individuals. (参考第1、64题)

Write a response in which you discuss the extent to which you agree or disagree with the statement and explain your reasoning for the position you take. In developing and supporting your position, you should consider ways in which the statement might or might not hold true and explain how these considerations shape your position.

题型归类 事实类。

题目分析

（1）能否从公认的原则或事实中推出相反的判断？

基于下列两点原则，题目中的判断未必成立：

其一，真正的强大是思想力量的强大；真正的独立是一个人对自己生命和生活方式的完全掌控，以及拥有自由、独立的思想。现代社会的舒适、便捷使人们更容易得到这些。

其二，人永远是精神意义上的人。人的独立和强大也总是指精神意义上的独立和强大。

（2）能否举出相反的事例？

（大家可以举出无数身边发生的例子。此处从略。）

提纲提要

论点 论者的观点失于简单。

正 现代社会舒适、便捷的生活的确有使现代人变得头脑发达、四肢羸弱、生活上越来越依赖科技所带来的便利的趋势；而强大的传媒和爆炸的信息洪流也时常让人们无法理解现实社会的真实面目。

反 但真正的强大是思想力量的强大；真正的独立是一个人对自己生命和生活方式的完全掌控，以及拥有自由、独立的思想。现代社会充裕的物质生活条件以及随之而来的舒适方便使人们更容易得到这些。

散 人永远是精神意义上的人。人的独立和强大也总是指精神意义上的独立和强大。

---

27. In any field of inquiry, the beginner is more likely than the expert to make important contributions. (参考第108、110、139题)

Write a response in which you discuss the extent to which you agree or disagree with the statement and explain your reasoning for the position you take. In developing and supporting your position, you should consider ways in which the statement might or might not hold true and explain how these considerations shape your position.

题型归类 事实类。

题目分析

（1）能否从公认的原则或事实中推出相反的判断?

基于下列两点原则，题目中的判断未必成立：

其一，知识总是具有某种延续性和继承性的。因为如果没有或只有很少的基础知识，新手，无论其拥有多么丰富的想象力，往往会流入空想，创造力也因此而大打折扣。

其二，部分学术领域，比如天文观测、化学试验、生物物种培植等等，因为需要常年的观察以积累第一手的资料，往往只有专家才会有所发现和突破。

（2）能否举出相反的事例?

（大家还可以举出无数身边发生的例子。此处从略。）

提纲提要

论点 论者的观点失于简单。

正 因为头脑中没有各种既定习惯和观念的约束，新手做事有时反而更有想象力、更容易比专家实现重大突破。

反 但是，知识总是具有某种延续性和继承性的。因为如果没有或只有很少的基础知识，新手，无论其拥有多么丰富的想象力，往往会流入空想，创造力也因此而大打折扣。

反 部分学术领域，比如天文观测、化学试验、生物物种培植等等，因为需要常年的观察以积累第一手的资料，往往只有专家才会有所发现和突破。

---

28. The surest indicator of a great nation is represented not by the achievements of its rulers, artists, or scientists, but by the general welfare of its people. (参考第85、113、120、121、127、145题)

Write a response in which you discuss the extent to which you agree or disagree with the statement and explain your reasoning for the position you take. In developing and supporting your position, you should consider ways in which the statement might or might not hold true and explain how these considerations shape your position.

题型归类 事实类。

题目分析

（1）能否从公认的原则或事实中推出相反的判断?

在现代意义上的国家和政府出现以前，国家和政府与百姓的关系不是现在这种对等、服务型的关系，而是统治和被统治、主宰者和臣民的关系。那时，一个强大的帝国未必能为百姓谋福利，而多表现为君主的武功和战绩以及依附于帝王将相的艺术家和其他文人的成就。他们也都为人类创造了灿烂的文明。

（2）能否举出相反的事例?

（大家可以随便举出自己熟悉的例子。此处从略。）

提纲提要

论点 论者的观点失于简单。

正 一个真正伟大的国家必然有强大的综合国力。而强大的综合国力不仅仅体现在统治者及少数社会精英（如艺术家、科学家等）的成就上，还必须具体体现在百姓的整体福利水平上。如此，这个国家才会有真正的向心力和凝聚力，才是真正的强大。

反 但是，在现代意义上的国家和政府出现以前，国家和政府与百姓的关系不是现在这种对等、服务型的关系；而是统治和被统治、主宰者和臣民的关系。那时，一个强大的帝国未必能为百姓谋福利，而多表现为君主的武功和战绩以及依附于帝王将相的艺术家和其他文人的成就。他们也都为人类创造了灿烂的文明。

散 国家形态从一家一姓的王朝帝国演变成今天的公民社会和民主政体，这体现了国家和社会对个体越来越多的关注。在现代意义上，一个真正伟大的国家应该是人的个性和自由得到最充分发展和保障的国家。

· ·

29. The best way to teach—whether as an educator, employer, or parent—is to praise positive actions and ignore negative ones. (参考第22、24、52、70、77、112、122、123题)

Write a response in which you discuss the extent to which you agree or disagree with the claim. In developing and supporting your position, be sure to address the most compelling reasons and/or examples that could be used to challenge your position.

（平行式多角度分析题。本题的分析思路和写作提纲可完全借鉴第24题。）

· ·

30. Teachers' salaries should be based on their students' academic performance. (参考第83题)

Write a response in which you discuss the extent to which you agree or disagree with the claim. In developing and supporting your position, be sure to address the most compelling reasons and/or examples that could be used to challenge your position.

题型归类 建议类。

题目分析

（1）题目中的建议可行性如何？

　　单就形式而言，题目中的建议当然可行。学校似乎可以用一些直观的指标，比如考试成绩、竞赛排名、升学率等，来考察学生的成绩（academic performance），并据此确定老师的薪资水平。

（2）如果实施题目中的建议，是否会导致同初始目的相矛盾或其他荒谬的结果？

　　但这种做法的弊端至少有四点：其一，老师会将教学的重点放在高分数、高排名和高升学率上，而忽视学生的整体素质（如独立思考能力、实践动手能力、创新思维能力、道德情操的陶冶等）的培养。其二，老师会更关注学生短期的学习表现而忽视其学术潜力的培养以及对有特殊能力学生的关注。其三，会压抑老师的教学创新意识。第四，最终造成一个国家国民素质和创新能力的退化。

（3）有无替代或折中方案？

　　第一，可以对学生的成绩，比如考试成绩、竞赛排名、升学率等，进行跟踪、记录和比较，但这些不直接和老师的工资挂钩。只有当这些指标出现大幅波动的时候，才把这些指标作为老师教学效果是否存在严重问题的预警和提示，从而尽早干预。第二，选用一些大的时间跨度的指标，比如10年或20年内，老师所教的学生中出现的高端优秀人才的数量、学生在成年后对老师的教书育人对其职业和人生影响力的反馈和评价以及这些老师对教学法的创新和突破等，来对老师的教学效果进行评估，并进而给优秀老师高额的奖励。

提纲提要

论点　**论者的建议基本上不是一个很可取的办法。**

正　对学生成绩用一些直观的指标，比如考试成绩、竞赛排名、升学率等，加以考察，以利于发现老师教学过程中可能存在的不足是可行的，也是必要的，但考察结果未必非得和老师的薪酬直接挂钩。

反　简单挂钩的做法至少有四点弊端：其一，老师会将教学的重点放在高分数、高排名和高升学率上，而忽视学生的整体素质（如独立思考能力、实践动手能力、创新思维能力、道德情操的陶冶等）的培养。其二，老师会更关注学生短期的学习表现而忽视其学术潜力的培养以及对有特殊能力学生的关注。其三，会压抑老师的教学创新意识；第四，最终造成一个国家国民素质和创新能力的退化。

合　可能的折中方案：第一，可以对学生的成绩，比如考试成绩、竞赛排名、升学率等，进行跟踪、记录和比较，但这些不直接和老师的工资挂钩。只有当这些指标出现大幅波动的时候，才把这些指标作为老师教学效果是否存在严重问题的预警和提示，从而尽早干预。第二，选用一些大的时间跨度的指标，比如10年或20年内，老师所教的学生中出现的高端优秀人才的数量、学生在成年后对老师的教书育人对其职业和人生影响力的反馈和评价以及这些老师对教学法的创新和突破等，来对老师的教学效果进行评估，并进而给优秀老师高额的奖励。

31. Society should make efforts to save endangered species only if the potential extinction of those species is the result of human activities. （参考第10、63、67、119、125、148题）

Write a response in which you discuss your views on the policy and explain your reasoning for the position you take. In developing and supporting your position, you should consider the possible consequences of implementing the policy and explain how these consequences shape your position.

题型归类　建议类。

题目分析

（1）题目中的建议可行性如何？

　　该建议未必可行。这是因为，论者的建议中有一个假设：即，我们人类有能力区分出哪些生物物种的灭绝是人类活动造成的，哪些不是。但这个假设显然难以成立。科技进步不仅大大改善了人们的生活，同时也大大增强了人类干预和破坏自然环境的能力（如核事故对环境和生物物种的影响）。人类作为地球生物链上的一个环节，多数情况下我们只是不知道自己的行为已经对环境造成了巨大的破坏而已。

（2）如果实施题目中的建议，是否会导致同初始目的相矛盾或其他荒谬的结果？

　　施行题目中的建议的弊端有二：其一，大量的生物物种受人类活动的影响消失了，而人类却带着一种漠然的无辜感作壁上观。其二，一些纯粹是自然过程所引发的生物物种的灭绝由于人类信奉"不干预政策"，其后果最终危及了人类自己的生存。更要命的是，当人类意识到自己的危险时，可能已经为时过晚。

（3）有无替代或折中方案？

　　第一，人类应改变在人与环境关系问题上的理念：人类只不过是环境的一部分，不是环境的主人。在自然环境面前，人应保持一份敬畏，尽量和这个自然世界共生，而不是去征服它、改造它。第二，利用一切科技手段监测自然因素和人为因素所造成的环境的改变，为人类在这个星球上的生息繁衍争取尽可能长的时间。

提纲提要

论点　题目中的判断似是而非。

㊣　自然环境的改变和生态自我平衡机制的确也导致了一些生物物种的灭绝。对此，依据现有的科技水平，人类有时感到很无能为力。

㊀　但是，以"非我所为，我即无为"的态度，施行题目中的建议的弊端有二：其一，大量的生物物种受人类活动的影响消失了，而人类却带着一种漠然的无辜感作壁上观。其二，一些纯粹是自然过程所引发的生物物种的灭绝由于人类信奉"不干预政策"，其后果最终危及了人类自己的生存。更要命的是，当人类意识到自己的危险时，可能已经为时过晚。

㊎　可能的折中方案：第一，人类应改变在人与环境关系问题上的理念：人类只不过是环境的一部分，不是环境的主人。在自然环境面前，人应保持一份敬畏，尽量和这个自然世界共生，而不是去征服它、改变它。第二，利用一切科技手段监测自然因素和人为因素所造成的环境的改变，为人类在这个星球上的生息繁衍争取尽可能长的时间。

・・・

32. College students should base their choice of a field of study on the availability of jobs in that field. (参考第3、13、15、20、35、39、46、98、129、135、136、137、140题)

Write a response in which you discuss the extent to which you agree or disagree with the claim. In developing and supporting your position, be sure to address the most compelling reasons and/or examples that could be used to challenge your position.

题型归类　建议类。

题目分析

（1）题目中的建议可行性如何？

题目中的建议未必可行。这是因为在社会分工高度精细化、职业调整越来越频繁的今天，人们基本无法准确预知某个专业或行业未来三年或五年的职业前景。

（2）如果实施题目中的建议，是否会导致同初始目的相矛盾或其他荒谬的结果？

如果施行题目中的建议，其所导致的弊端至少有四点：第一，几乎所有的人都涌向为数不多看似"钱"景无限的职业。基于大家彼此大致相同的认知能力、现有信息的有限性和未来的不可知性，这几乎是一个必然的结果。这一点，我们从一轮又一轮的计算机热、法律热、金融热、房地产热、MBA 热，当然还包括当下最具中国特色的公务员热，都看得非常清楚。其结果只能是这些曾经的热门职业和行业很快出现人力资源供给的过剩、整体收入下降、相当部分人被迫改行。第二，如果上述第一个结果成立，这随后的结果就是，对个人而言，是教育投入的失败；对国家而言，是国民财富的浪费。第三，会使得一个国家新兴的产业所需要的人力资源得不到及时的补充，影响该国产业结构的转移和提升。这是因为一个国家教育机构的人才产出能力在中短期内是基本恒定的。当人才大量涌向几个看似"热门"的行业时，其他行业的人才供给必然相应减少。第四，如果学生将自己的学习和研究领域仅仅用就业的前景框限起来，就个人而言，人生失去了很多发展自己爱好和天分的乐趣；就社会而言，则很有可能因为特立独行、才华横溢之才的淹没而损失了创新精神与活力。

（3）有无替代或折中方案？

在大学研究生以下的教育阶段，大学生应该更多地将个人兴趣和天分作为自己专业方向的参考。兴趣是最好的老师，它能引导我们找到最适合自己的职业和事业。而且，在四年本科结束后，最好先工作两三年。通过工作，可以发现最适合自己的职业方向。实际上，现代人的寿命普遍较长，其黄金工作年龄可以一直延长到 65 岁甚至更晚些。所以，年轻人在 35 岁之前可以有许多尝试和发现自己职业生涯的机会。过早确立事业方向反而不利于发现自己的潜能。

提纲提要

论点 生活的过程就是在理想与现实间的平衡。

正 教育是人们对未来进行的时间和金钱的投资。通过找到一份自己喜欢同时又有很好收入的工作，是对大学教育投入的收获。所以，在选择学习专业时，考虑该专业未来的职业前景是再自然不过的想法。

反 但是，把大学教育同未来的就业前景进行简单的对接会面临以下问题：

首先，并不是所有专业的职业前景都可以被清晰地勾画出来。这是因为在社会分工高度精细化、职业调整越来越频繁的今天，人们基本无法准确预知某个专业或行业未来三年或五年的职业前景。

其次，如果人人都把大学的专业学习当作未来就业的预备的话，还会出现如下弊病：第一，几乎所有的人都涌向为数不多看似"钱"景无限的职业。基于大家大致相同的认知能力、现有信息的有限性和未来的不可知性，这几乎是一个必然的结果。这一点，我们从一轮又一轮的计算机热、法律热、金融热、房地产热、MBA 热，当然还包括当下最具中国特色的公务员热，都看得非常清楚。其结果只能是这些曾经的热门职业和行业很快出现人力资源供给的过剩、整体收入下降、相当部分人被迫改行。第二，如果上述第一个结果成立，这随后的结果就是，对个人而言，是教育投入的失败；对国家而言，是国民财富的浪费。第三，会使得一个国家新兴的产业所需要的人力资源得不到及时的补充，影响该国产业结构的转移和提升。这是因为一个国家教育机构的人才产出能力在中短期内是基本恒定的。当人才大量涌向几个看似"热门"的行业时,其他行业的人才供给必然相应减少。第四,如果学生将自己的学习和研究领域仅仅用就业的前景框限起来,就个人而言,人生失去了很多发展自己爱好和天分的乐趣;就社会而言,则很有可能因为特立独行、才华横溢之才的淹没而损失了创新精神与活力。

合 可能的折中方案:在大学研究生以下的教育阶段,大学生应该更多地将个人兴趣和天分作为自己专业方向的参考,尽量多学自己感兴趣的学科。兴趣是最好的老师,它能引导我们找到最适合自己的职业和事业。而且,在四年本科结束后,最好先工作两三年。通过工作也可以发现最适合自己的职业方向。实际上,现代人的寿命普遍较长,其黄金工作年龄可以一直延长到65岁甚至更晚些。所以,年轻人在35岁之前可以有许多尝试和发现自己职业生涯的机会。过早确立事业方向反而不利于发现自己的潜能。

33. As we acquire more knowledge, things do not become more comprehensible, but more complex and mysterious. (参考第57、74、109、133、134题)

Write a response in which you discuss the extent to which you agree or disagree with the statement and explain your reasoning for the position you take. In developing and supporting your position, you should consider ways in which the statement might or might not hold true and explain how these considerations shape your position.

题型归类 事实类。

题目分析

(1)能否从公认的原则或事实中推出相反的判断?

基于下列两点原则,题目中的判断未必成立:

其一,这种现象未必能说明知识积累得越多,我们越难以理解周围的事物。事实上,在我们了解了更多的知识和问题之后,旧的知识体系解释不了一些新问题。但这并不能否定我们对周围的事物理解得更深入、更细致、更接近真实这一事实。

其二,没有经过把问题的细枝末节都搞清楚、从而把问题复杂化的过程,就不会有对问题进行简单地概括,使之更易理解的结果。大道至简,往往发生在穷尽细节之后。

(2)能否举出相反的事例?

(大家可以举出无数身边发生的例子。此处从略。)

提纲提要

论点 **论者的观点失于简单。**

正 有时,随着我们对某一事物认识的深入,这一事物的确会有可能变得更难以解释、显得更为复杂。

反 但这种现象未必能说明知识积累得越多,我们越难以理解周围的事物。事实上,在我们了解了更多的知识和问题之后,旧的知识体系解释不了一些新问题。但这并不能否定我们对周围的事物理解得更深入、更细致、更接近真实这一事实。

反 没有经过把问题的细枝末节都搞清楚、因而把问题进一步复杂化的过程,就不会有对问题进行简单地概括,使之更易理解的结果。若想**大道至简**,往往必先穷尽细节。

34. In any situation, progress requires discussion among people who have contrasting points of view. (参考第49、76、118题)

Write a response in which you discuss the extent to which you agree or disagree with the statement and explain your reasoning for the position you take. In developing and supporting your position, you should consider ways in which the statement might or might not hold true and explain how these considerations shape your position.

题型归类　该题经过整理可以是这个形式：To make progress in any situation, one should discuss with those who have contrasting points of view。所以，该题归为建议类。

题目分析

（1）题目中的建议可行性如何？

任何人只要愿意，都可与持不同意见的人讨论，以求进步。所以，题目中的建议当然可行。

（2）如果实施题目中的建议，是否会导致同初始目的相矛盾或其他荒谬的结果？

会有两个问题：第一，与持不同意见的人讨论未必就能实现不同意见间的相互补充、相互促进，我们经常看见不同意见间水火不容的碰撞。第二，太多的意见、太多的选择有时会使问题变得更加复杂，甚至超出了理性判断的能力范围。比如人们在如何对待凯恩斯主义经济学说这个问题上的困惑，就是典型的事例。凯恩斯主义曾被一些政府和学者当作对一国经济实施宏观调控的不二法门；但在当今各种新兴的经济学说的争辩之下，到底该如何发挥政府的宏观经济调控职能变得又莫衷一是了。

（3）有无替代或折中方案？

若要取得进步，除了要有不同的意见以外，更要有不同意见间的宽容和理解，加上足够的耐心，直到真理较为充分地展示在理性面前。

提纲提要

论点　仅仅有不同的意见未必就能导致进步，还要有不同意见间的宽容。

正　不同的意见有时的确可以相互补充、相互促进。

反　但是，不同意见间的讨论也会带来新的问题：第一，与持不同意见的人讨论未必就能实现不同意见间的相互补充、相互促进，我们经常看见不同意见间水火不容的碰撞。第二，太多的意见、太多的选择有时会使问题变得更加复杂，甚至超出了理性判断的能力范围。比如人们在如何对待凯恩斯主义经济学说这个问题上的困惑，就是典型的事例。凯恩斯主义曾被一些政府和学者当作对一国经济实施宏观调控的不二法门；但在当今各种新兴的经济学说争辩之下，到底该如何发挥政府的宏观经济调控职能变得又莫衷一是了。

散　若要取得进步，除了要有不同的意见以外，更要有不同意见间的宽容和理解，加上足够的耐心，直到真理较为充分地展示在理性面前。

35. Educational institutions should dissuade students from pursuing fields of study in which they are unlikely to succeed. (参考第3、13、15、20、32、39、46、98、129、135、136、

137、140题）

Write a response in which you discuss your views on the policy and explain your reasoning for the position you take. In developing and supporting your position, you should consider the possible consequences of implementing the policy and explain how these consequences shape your position.

（建议类。本题的分析思路和写作提纲可完全借鉴第3题。）

36. Governments should not fund any scientific research whose consequences are unclear.（参考第23、72题）

Write a response in which you discuss the extent to which you agree or disagree with the recommendation and explain your reasoning for the position you take. In developing and supporting your position, describe specific circumstances in which adopting the recommendation would or would not be advantageous and explain how these examples shape your position.

题型归类 建议类。

题目分析

（1）题目中的建议可行性如何？

　　一个政府完全可以不资助前景不明朗的科学研究。无所谓可行不可行。

（2）如果实施题目中的建议，是否会导致同初始目的相矛盾或其他荒谬的结果？

　　如果因为科学研究的结果，比如医学及伦理的结果，不甚清楚，所以政府不予支持，那么，这些科研活动可能带来的巨大福利也因此被放弃。另一个值得考虑的问题是有关政府的职能：政府的天然职责就是为公民谋利益。当一项科研有不确定的医学及伦理的后果时，政府不去想办法搞清楚，又能靠谁呢？

（3）有无替代或折中方案？

　　人们探索未知时，总是要冒一定的风险。这似乎是别无选择。当科学研究的医学及伦理的结果不甚清楚，可能有不确定的危险时，政府应当考虑的焦点不应是要不要做的问题，而是如何安全妥善地以最小的代价来做。

提纲提要

论点 人们探索未知时，总是要冒一定的风险。

（正）对可能带来不确定的医学及伦理风险的科研活动采取审慎态度是必要的。

（反）但是，如果因为科学研究的结果，比如医学及伦理的结果，不甚清楚，所以政府不予支持，那么，这些科研活动可能带来的巨大福利也因此被放弃。另一个值得考虑的问题是有关政府的职能：政府的天然职责就是为公民谋利益。当一项科研有不确定的医学及伦理的后果时，政府不去想办法搞清楚，又能靠谁呢？

（合）人们探索未知时，总是要冒一定的风险。这似乎是别无选择。当科学研究的医学及伦理的结果不甚清楚、可能有不确定的危险时，政府应当考虑的焦点不应是要不要做的问题，而是如何安全妥善地以最小的代价来做。

37. Society should identify those children who have special talents and provide training for them at an early age to develop their talents. (参考第40、47、58、90、142题)

Write a response in which you discuss the extent to which you agree or disagree with the recommendation and explain your reasoning for the position you take. In developing and supporting your position, describe specific circumstances in which adopting the recommendation would or would not be advantageous and explain how these examples shape your position.

题型归类　建议类。

题目分析

（1）题目中的建议可行性如何？

　　题目中的建议：identify those children who have special talents and provide training for them at an early age可行性不强。到底一个孩子是不是天才，该怎么判断？所谓的早教、特教是否就顺应儿童的心理、智力发展规律？这些是直到今天都尚无定论的东西。

（2）如果实施题目中的建议，是否会导致同初始目的相矛盾或其他荒谬的结果？

　　天才是人为教育出来的吗？果真如此的话，我们现在应该比过去拥有成倍多的天才。但实际情况并非如此。另外，我们怎能保证那些所谓的早教、特教不是成年人对儿童未来的一厢情愿的期待，甚至是对他们特殊才能的扼杀呢？

（3）有无替代或折中方案？

　　自然的可能是最好的。

提纲提要

论点　**儿童智力、才能的发展应是个自然而然的过程。**

正　正确的教育、引导当然有利于儿童心智（heart and mind）的发展。

反　但是，到底一个孩子是不是天才该怎么判断？所谓的早教、特教是否就顺应儿童的心理、智力发展规律？这些是直到今天都尚无定论的东西。

　　另外，天才是人为教育出来的吗？果真如此的话，我们现在应该比过去拥有成倍多的天才。但实际情况并非如此。

　　还有，我们怎能保证那些所谓的早教、特教不是成年人对儿童未来的一厢情愿的期待，甚至是对他们特殊才能的扼杀呢？

反　自然的可能是最好的。

---

38. It is primarily through our identification with social groups that we define ourselves. (参考第78题)

Write a response in which you discuss the extent to which you agree or disagree with the statement and explain your reasoning for the position you take. In developing and supporting your position, you should consider ways in which the statement might or might not hold true and explain how these considerations shape your position.

题型归类　事实类。

题目分析

（1）能否从公认的原则或事实中推出相反的判断?

基于下列两点原则，题目中的判断未必成立：

其一，人是一种（也许是地球上唯一一种）具备自我反思能力的动物：人可以通过自我反省和对自己所认可的价值的坚持，而实现对组织和群体的认同、反叛或超越。

其二，要看到年龄、心理等因素对人与社会群体关系的影响。年轻人大多渴盼归属感和认同感。但随着年龄的增长，人们会有更强烈而坚定的自我价值意识，因而更倾向于与组织和群体保持距离。

（2）能否举出相反的事例?

（大家可以举出无数身边发生的例子。此处从略。）

提纲提要

论点　论者的观点失于简单。

正　人是社会性的动物。人总是习惯于通过在群体与组织中发现自己的位置而找到对自我的身份认同。

反　人还是一种（也许是地球上唯一的一种）具备自我反思能力的动物：人可以通过自我反省和对自己所认可的价值的坚持，而实现对组织和群体的认同、反叛或超越。

反　要看到年龄、心理等因素对人与社会群体关系的影响。年轻人大多渴盼归属感和认同感。但随着年龄的增长，人们会有更强烈而坚定的自我价值意识，因而更倾向于与组织和群体保持距离。

- -

39. College students should be encouraged to pursue subjects that interest them rather than the courses that seem most likely to lead to jobs. （参考第3、13、15、20、32、35、46、98、129、135、136、137、140题）

Write a response in which you discuss the extent to which you agree or disagree with the recommendation and explain your reasoning for the position you take. In developing and supporting your position, describe specific circumstances in which adopting the recommendation would or would not be advantageous and explain how these examples shape your position.

题型归类　建议类。

题目分析

（1）题目中的建议可行性如何?

题目中的建议当然可行。

（2）如果实施题目中的建议，是否会导致同初始目的相矛盾或其他荒谬的结果?

如果只是考虑个人的学习兴趣和才华而不考虑毕业后的就业前景，毕业后有可能会遇到就业困难。人的所有压力之中，生存压力是最需要优先考虑的。但反过来，如果学生将自己的学习和研究领域仅仅用就业的前景框限起来，就个人而言，人生失去了很多乐趣；就社会而言，则很有可能因为特立独行、才华横溢之才的淹没而损失了创新精神与活力。

（3）有无替代或折中方案？

就个人而言，生活的过程就是在理想与现实间的徘徊，每个人都不得不在二者之中寻求某种折中和平衡；就社会和政府而言，可以由财政出资在大学设立特别项目或者鼓励企业和个人设专项基金，用来资助确有天分的学生发展他们的兴趣和潜能。其次，大学生们可以通过人生规划，在个人兴趣和理想与现实的压力之间求得某种平衡。在大学研究生以下的教育阶段，大学生更多地将个人兴趣和天分作为自己专业方向的参考。兴趣是最好的老师，它能引导我们找到最适合自己的职业和事业。而且，在四年本科结束后，最好先工作两三年。通过工作，可以尝试发现最适合自己的职业方向。实际上，现代人的寿命普遍较长，其黄金工作年龄可以一直延长到65岁甚至更晚些。所以，年轻人在35岁之前可以有许多尝试和发现自己职业生涯的机会。

> **提纲提要**

论点 生活的过程就是在理想与现实间的徘徊。

正 兴趣是最好的老师。兴趣往往能告诉我们什么是最适合自己的职业和事业。

反 但是，如果只是考虑个人的学习兴趣和个性才华而不考虑毕业后的就业前景，有可能会面临毕业后的就业困难。人的所有压力之中，生存的压力当然是最需要优先考虑的。但反过来，如果学生将自己的学习和研究领域仅仅用就业的前景框限起来，就个人而言，人生失去了很多乐趣；就社会而言，则很有可能因为特立独行、才华横溢之才的淹没而损失了创新精神与活力。

合 首先，就个人而言，生活的过程就是在理想与现实间的徘徊，每个人都不得不在二者之中寻求某种折中和平衡；就社会和政府而言，可以由财政出资在大学设立特别项目或者鼓励企业和个人设专项基金，用来资助确有天分的学生发展他们的兴趣和潜能。

其次，大学生们可以通过人生规划在个人兴趣和理想与现实压力之间求得某种平衡。在大学研究生以下的教育阶段，大学生更多的将个人兴趣和天分作为自己专业方向的参考。兴趣是最好的老师，它能引导我们找到最适合自己的职业和事业。而且，在四年本科结束后，最好先工作两三年。通过工作，可以尝试发现最适合自己的职业方向。实际上，现代社会人的寿命普遍较长，其黄金工作年龄可以一直延长到65岁甚至更晚些。所以，年轻人在35岁之前可以有许多尝试和发现自己职业生涯的机会。

---

40. **Claim**: When planning courses, educators should take into account the interests and suggestions of their students.

Reason: Students are more motivated to learn when they are interested in what they are studying. (参考第37、47、58、90、142题)

Write a response in which you discuss the extent to which you agree or disagree with the claim and the reason on which that claim is based.

> **题型归类** 套叠式多角度分析题。整体是个因果类题目，但它的结果部分是个建议。

题目分析

首先，按照因果类题目类型展开分析：

（1）这个因果关系推理中的原因是否成立？

该题目的原因似乎成立。

（2）假设这个原因成立，从它能否推出结果？

即使上述原因成立，结论也是推不出的。鉴于这个结果部分是个建议，我们在下面就从建议类题目的分析角度切入分析。

其次，按照建议类题目类型展开分析：

（1）题目中的建议可行性如何？

题目中的建议不大可行。首先，学生的个人想法和兴趣千差万别。但作为教学，其最基本的目的是将符合绝大多数学生需求的知识和技能传授给他们。一般性的教学任务和千差万别的学生兴趣之间很难简单对接。其次，学生，尤其是基础教育（primary education）阶段的学生，是否能真正表述清楚他们心中的兴趣和爱好，或者这些兴趣和爱好到底能够持续多久，这些都是问题。其三，基于学生在专业知识和人生阅历方面的局限性，老师，尤其是基础教育阶段的老师，应该在教学过程中居于主导地位。如果知识是海洋，学生是知识海洋中的一艘艘小船，那么老师就应该是领航的旗舰。过分强调学生的兴趣和爱好在教学中的地位，很容易混淆教与学的主次关系。

（2）如果实施题目中的建议，是否会导致同初始目的相矛盾或其他荒谬的结果？

结果会有三个：第一，系统的知识教育变成一个个具体的个人化的体验，大大降低了教育的效率。第二，动摇学生对一个社会主流价值（也应该同时是普世价值）的吸收与传承，导致学生人生和思维方式的迷惘。第三，最极端的结果就是，有可能打乱正常的教学秩序，逼迫老师去迎合学生的志趣，使学生在学校这个准社会里的角色定位发生错乱，不利于其未来的成长。目前中国的部分私立学校就是典型的例子。在那里，老师更像是服务员，而学生则像是小姐和少爷。

（3）有无替代或折中方案？

老师，尤其是基础教育阶段的老师，是教学过程中理所当然的主导者。他们引导孩子进入神奇的知识王国，告诉他们一些基本的事实，帮助他们养成正确的思维方式，从而搭建起一个完整的知识框架。这个框架就像是一个滑翔机的跑道，从那里孩子们可以自由地放飞他们的兴趣、爱好和理想。

提纲提要

论点 老师可以帮助孩子飞翔，但一定要让孩子自己飞。

正 在教学过程中调动学生的兴趣和爱好，激发他们自主学习的能力，可以收到非常好的教学效果。

反 但是，一味地迎合学生的兴趣和要求并不可取。

首先，这未必可行。学生的个人想法和兴趣千差万别。但作为教学，其最基本的目的是将符合绝大多数学生需求的知识和技能传授给他们。一般性的教学任务和千差万别的学生兴趣之间很难简单对接。其次，学生，尤其是基础教育阶段的学生，是否能真正表述清楚他们心中的兴趣和爱好，或者这些兴趣和爱好到底能够持续多久，这些都是问题。其三，基于学生在专业知识和人生阅历方面的局限性，老师，尤其是基础教育阶段的老师，应该在教学过程中居主导地位。如果知识是海洋，学生是知识海洋中的一艘艘小船，那么老师就应该是领航的旗舰。过分强调学生的兴趣和爱好在教学中的地位，很容易混淆教与学的主次关系。

如果强制规定学生的兴趣和爱好必须在教学中居主导地位的话，会有如下三个弊端：

第一，系统的知识教育变成一个个具体的个人化的体验，大大降低了教育的效率。第二，动摇学生对一个社会主流价值（也应该同时是普世价值）的吸收与传承，导致学生人生和思维方式的迷惘。第三，最极端的结果就是，有可能打乱正常的教学秩序，逼迫老师去迎合学生的志趣，使学生在学校这个准社会里的角色定位发生错乱，大不利于其未来的成长。目前中国的部分私立学校就是典型的例子。在那里，老师更像是服务员，而学生则像是小姐和少爷。

（合）老师，尤其是基础教育阶段的老师，是教学过程中当然的主导者。他们引导孩子进入神奇的知识王国，告诉他们一些基本的事实，帮助他们养成正确的思维方式，从而搭建起一个完整的知识框架。这个框架就像是一个滑翔机的跑道，从那里孩子们可以自由地放飞他们的兴趣、爱好和理想。

---

41. The greatness of individuals can be decided only by those who live after them, not by their contemporaries.

Write a response in which you discuss the extent to which you agree or disagree with the statement and explain your reasoning for the position you take. In developing and supporting your position, you should consider ways in which the statement might or might not hold true and explain how these considerations shape your position.

题型归类　事实类。

题目分析

（1）能否从公认的原则或事实中推出相反的判断？

基于下列两点原则，题目中的判断未必成立：

其一，后人有时未必能真正做到客观、公正地评价前人。他们很可能会不考虑前人所处的特定历史背景，用自己的价值判断标准作出轻率的判断。

其二，后人对前人评价的依据只能是各种历史记录和文献。但这些记录和文献是否完整、属实也使后人判断的准确性与客观性打了折扣。

（2）能否举出相反的事例？

（大家可以举出无数身边发生的例子。此处从略。）

提纲提要

（论点）　论者的观点失于简单。

（正）　时间可以沉淀、过滤关于一个人的诸多争议，因而后人更容易对这个人的伟大与否作出判断。

（反）　但是，后人有时未必能真正做到客观、公正地评价前人。他们很可能会不考虑前人所处的特定历史背景，用自己的价值判断标准作出轻率的判断。

（反）　后人对前人评价的依据只能是各种历史记录和文献。但这些记录和文献是否完整、属实也使后人判断的准确性与客观性打了折扣。

---

42. Students should always question what they are taught instead of accepting it passively.

（参考第 17、48、68、87、92 题）

Write a response in which you discuss the extent to which you agree or disagree with the statement and explain your reasoning for the position you take. In developing and supporting your position, you should consider ways in which the statement might or might not hold true and explain how these considerations shape your position.

题型归类 建议类。

题目分析

（1）题目中的建议可行性如何？

未必可行。任何思考的起点都是先提出有意义的问题。然而，基于学生，尤其是基础教育阶段的学生，由于专业知识和人生阅历方面的局限性，他们甚至不知道应该在哪里发问、如何发问。如此，还怎能期望他们提出有意义的问题？老师，尤其是基础教育阶段的老师，应该在教学过程中居于主导地位。如果知识是海洋，学生是知识海洋中的一艘艘小船，那么老师就应该是领航的旗舰。给学生质疑一切的权力，就像是给不懂武术的人一把极为锋利的宝剑；有可能剑没舞好，反倒伤了自己。

（2）如果实施题目中的建议，是否会导致同初始目的相矛盾或其他荒谬的结果？

怀疑一切会导致知识和价值的虚无，人类文明也因此丧失了传承和发展的基础。

（3）有无替代或折中方案？

人类知识的积累和文明的传承总是一个接受、批判、发展、再接受、再批判、再发展的过程。怀疑一切和接受一切都有失于极端。

提纲提要

论点 文明的传承总是一个接受、批判、发展、再接受、再批判、再发展的过程。

正 文明的进步从怀疑开始。

反 但是，任何思考的起点都是先提出有意义的问题。然而，基于学生，尤其是基础教育阶段的学生，由于专业知识和人生阅历方面的局限性，他们甚至不知道应该在哪里发问、如何发问。如此，还怎能期望他们提出有意义的问题？老师，尤其是基础教育阶段的老师，应该在教学过程中居于主导地位。如果知识是海洋，学生是知识海洋中的一艘艘小船，那么老师就应该是领航的旗舰。给学生质疑一切的权力，就像是给不懂武术的人一把极为锋利的宝剑；有可能剑没舞好，反倒伤了自己。怀疑一切会导致知识和价值的虚无，人类文明也因此丧失了传承和发展的基础。

合 人类知识的积累和文明的传承总是一个接受、批判、发展、再接受、再批判、再发展的过程。怀疑一切和接受一切都有失于极端。

---

43. The increasingly rapid pace of life today causes more problems than it solves. (参考第91题)

Write a response in which you discuss the extent to which you agree or disagree with the statement and explain your reasoning for the position you take. In developing and supporting your position, you should consider ways in which the statement might or might not hold true and explain how these considerations shape your position.

题型归类　事实类。

题目分析

（1）能否从公认的原则或事实中推出相反的判断？

同过去比起来，现在人们的生活水平和生活质量有了明显的提高：比如，人们的衣食住行条件、平均受教育水平、平均寿命、医疗保障水平、应付自然灾害的能力等都得到了极大的改善。这使得人们有可能摆脱为生存而进行的挣扎，转而关注一下自己的心灵。

（2）能否举出相反的事例？

（大家可以举出无数身边发生的例子。此处从略。）

提纲提要

论点　**论者的观点失于简单。**

正　科技发展了，效率提高了，但不仅人类面临的旧问题没有得到很好的解决，而且还出现了更为严峻的新问题，比如，经济全球化带来的种族和文化冲突、核战争威胁、国家间日益扩大的贫富差距、环境污染等。人类因为科技的发展而变得似乎更不安全了。

反　但是同过去比起来，现在人们的生活水平和生活质量有了明显的提高：比如，人们的衣食住行条件、平均受教育水平、平均寿命、医疗保障水平、应付自然灾害的能力等都得到了极大的改善。这使得人们有可能摆脱为生存而进行的挣扎，转而关注一下自己的心灵。

散　急匆匆的步伐永远跟不上人类欲望膨胀的速度。科技解决不了人类面临的一切问题。有时我们能否获得幸福的关键在于我们是否愿意停下来，关注一下自己心灵的渴求。毕竟，人永远是精神意义上的人。

- - - - - - - - - -

44. **Claim**: It is no longer possible for a society to regard any living man or woman as a hero.

Reason: The reputation of anyone who is subjected to media scrutiny will eventually be diminished. （参考第22、75、84、122题）

Write a response in which you discuss the extent to which you agree or disagree with the claim and the reason on which that claim is based.

题型归类　因果类。必要的话，可以对题目中hero的概念加以界定。所以，题目还可归类为结合式定义类。

题目分析

（1）这个因果关系推理中的原因是否成立？

该题目的原因未必成立。媒体的追踪报道未必就会消减社会名人的声望。货真价实的社会声望不惧媒体的关注。

（2）假设这个原因成立，从它能否推出结果？

即使上述原因成立，结论也是推不出的。社会英雄未必非得有灼人的声望、耀眼的光环。平凡人，比如慈爱而富有牺牲精神的母亲、忠于职守的警察、秉持正义的法官以及众多处逆境而不自弃的人们，都可以是社会英雄。他们普通而又真实，最经得起媒体的挑剔。

提纲提要

论点 题目中的判断似是而非。

正 现代传媒的确威力巨大。他们有时能制造社会英雄，有时又能毁灭英雄。

反 但是，媒体的追踪报道未必就会消减社会名人的声望。货真价实的社会声望不惧媒体的关注。

反 即使上述原因成立，结论也是推不出的。社会英雄未必得有灼人的声望、耀眼的光环。平凡人，比如慈爱而富有牺牲精神的母亲、忠于职守的警察、秉持正义的法官以及众多处逆境而不自弃的人们，都可以是社会英雄。他们普通而又真实，最经得起媒体的挑剔。

----

45. Competition for high grades seriously limits the quality of learning at all levels of education. (参考第138题)

Write a response in which you discuss the extent to which you agree or disagree with the statement and explain your reasoning for the position you take. In developing and supporting your position, you should consider ways in which the statement might or might not hold true and explain how these considerations shape your position.

题型归类 事实类。

题目分析

（1）能否从公认的原则或事实中推出相反的判断?

基于下列两点原则，题目中的判断未必成立：

其一，学生所处的学习阶段不同，是否让学生关注高分应有所不同：小学生自控能力和学习的自主性差，不善于分析问题的复杂性。这时，鼓励他们争取高分也许能调动他们学习的积极性。而在高中以后的学习阶段，为高分而学习就没太大必要了。

其二，为高分而学的不当之处也许并不在这种做法本身，而在于那些用以判定正确答案与错误答案、高分与低分的标准。绝大多数情况下，我们面临的问题并没有所谓的正确与错误的答案，尤其没有什么标准答案。但当所谓的标准答案满天飞的时候，学生的想象力和创造性反而被窒息了。

（2）能否举出相反的事例?

（大家可以举出无数身边发生的例子。此处从略。）

提纲提要

论点 论者的观点失于简单。

正 一味地追求高分容易忽略教育的根本目的：引导学生探索未知、培养和塑造健全的人格。

反 但是，学生所处的学习阶段不同，是否让学生关注高分应有所不同：小学生自控能力和学习的自主性差，不善于分析问题的复杂性。这时，鼓励他们争取高分也许能调动他们学习的积极性。而在高中以后的学习阶段，为高分而学习就没太大必要了。

反 为高分而学的不当之处也许并不在这种做法本身，而在于那些用以判定正确答案与错误答案、高分与低分的标准。绝大多数情况下，我们面临的问题并没有所谓的正确与错误的答案，尤其没有什么标准答案。但当所谓的标准答案满天飞的时候，学生想象力和创造性反而被窒息了。

46. Universities should require every student to take a variety of courses outside the student's field of study. (参考第3、13、15、20、32、35、39、98、129、135、136、137、140题；同时还可以参考第70、102、112题)

Write a response in which you discuss the extent to which you agree or disagree with the recommendation and explain your reasoning for the position you take. In developing and supporting your position, describe specific circumstances in which adopting the recommendation would or would not be advantageous and explain how these examples shape your position.

（建议类。本题的分析思路和写作提纲可完全借鉴第13题。）

47. Educators should find out what students want included in the curriculum and then offer it to them. (参考第37、40、58、90、142题)

Write a response in which you discuss the extent to which you agree or disagree with the recommendation and explain your reasoning for the position you take. In developing and supporting your position, describe specific circumstances in which adopting the recommendation would or would not be advantageous and explain how these examples shape your position.

题型归类 建议类。

题目分析

（1）题目中的建议可行性如何？

题目中的建议不大可行。首先，学生，尤其是基础教育阶段的学生，是否能真正表述清楚他们心中的兴趣和爱好，或者这些兴趣和爱好到底能够持续多久，到底他们自己希望学什么，该如何学，一个基本的知识框架该如何搭建，这些他们未必清楚；其次，基于学生在专业知识和人生阅历方面的局限性，老师，尤其是基础教育阶段的老师，应该在教学过程中居于主导地位。如果知识是海洋，学生是知识海洋中的一艘艘小船，那么老师就应该是领航的旗舰。过分强调学生的兴趣和爱好在教学中的地位，很容易搞混淆教与学的主次关系。

（2）如果实施题目中的建议，是否会导致同初始目的相矛盾或其他荒谬的结果？

可能的结果会有三个：第一，系统的知识教育变成一个个具体的个人化的体验和尝试，大大降低教育的效率；第二，动摇学生对一个社会主流价值（同时也应该是普世价值）的吸收与传承，导致学生人生和思维方式的迷惘；第三，最极端的结果就是，有可能打乱正常的教学秩序，逼迫老师去迎合学生的志趣，使学生在学校这个准社会的角色定位发生错乱，很不利于其未来的成长和对成人社会的适应。目前中国的部分私立学校就是典型的例子，在那里，老师更像是服务员，而学生则像是小姐和少爷。

（3）有无替代或折中方案？

老师，尤其是基础教育阶段的老师，是教学过程中当然的主导者。他们引导孩子进入神奇的知识王国，告诉他们一些基本的事实，帮助他们养成正确的思维方式，从而搭建起一个完整的、可用的知识框架。这个框架就像是一个滑翔机的跑道，从那里孩子们可以自由地放飞他们的兴趣、爱好和理想。

提纲提要

论点 老师可以帮助孩子飞翔，但一定要让孩子自己飞。

正 在教学过程中调动学生的兴趣和爱好，激发他们自己学习的潜能，往往可以收到非常好的教学效果。

反 但是，一味地迎合学生的兴趣和要求并不可取。

首先，这未必可行。学生，尤其是基础教育阶段的学生，是否能真正表述清楚他们心中的兴趣和爱好，或者这些兴趣和爱好到底能够持续多久，到底他们自己希望学什么，该如何学，一个基本的知识框架该如何搭建，这些他们未必清楚；其次，基于学生在专业知识和人生阅历方面的局限性，老师，尤其是基础教育阶段的老师，应该在教学过程中居于主导地位。如果知识是海洋，学生是知识海洋中的一艘艘小船，那么老师就应该是领航的旗舰。过分强调学生的兴趣和爱好在教学中的地位，很容易搞混淆教与学的主次关系。

如果强制规定学生的兴趣和爱好必须在教学中居主导地位的话，会有如下三个弊端：

第一，系统的知识教育变成一个个具体的个人化的体验和尝试，大大降低教育的效率；第二，动摇学生对一个社会主流价值（同时也应该是普世价值）的吸收与传承，导致学生人生和思维方式的迷惘；第三，最极端的结果就是，有可能打乱正常的教学秩序，逼迫老师去迎合学生的志趣，使学生在学校这个准社会的角色定位发生错乱，很不利于其未来的成长和成人社会的适应。目前中国的部分私立学校就是典型的例子，在那里，老师更像是服务员，而学生则像是小姐和少爷。

合 老师，尤其是基础教育阶段的老师，是教学过程中理所当然的主导者。他们引导孩子进入神奇的知识王国，告诉他们一些基本的事实，帮助他们养成正确的思维方式，从而搭建起一个完整可用的知识框架。这个框架就像是一个滑翔机的跑道，从那里孩子们可以自由地放飞他们的兴趣、爱好和理想。

48. Educators should teach facts only after their students have studied the ideas, trends, and concepts that help explain those facts. (参考第17、42、68、87、92题)

Write a response in which you discuss the extent to which you agree or disagree with the recommendation and explain your reasoning for the position you take. In developing and supporting your position, describe specific circumstances in which adopting the recommendation would or would not be advantageous and explain how these examples shape your position.

题型归类 建议类。

题目分析

（1）题目中的建议可行性如何？

题目中的建议可行。任何人都可以在尽可能先了解了与某一事实相关的思想、趋势和概念之后，再去关注这个事实本身，从而对这个事实有较为全面的理解。

（2）如果实施题目中的建议，是否会导致同初始目的相矛盾或其他荒谬的结果？

　　问题是，对于那些新问题和新现象，没有任何与之相关的思想、趋势和概念的事实，我们是记住它们还是置之不理呢？如果置之不理，我们关于这个世界的知识还会增长吗？

（3）有无替代或折中方案？

　　对那些已经有了一些相关的思想、趋势和概念的事实，我们当然要设法先了解这些思想、趋势和概念，以便更好理解那些事实。而对那些没有相关的思想、趋势和概念的事实，我们也要给予高度关注，因为它们可能是将来或其他研究的重要资料。

提纲提要

论点 论者的观点过于表面化。

正 人们所处的世界，因为有了我们人类所赋予的特定解释而有了意义。仅仅是孤立、零碎的事实并不能直接告诉我们这些事实所代表的含义，但在我们了解了与那些事实相关的思想、趋势和概念之后，它们一下子就会变得丰富而有趣了。

反 但是，对于那些新问题和新现象，没有任何与之相关的思想、趋势和概念的事实，我们是记住它们还是置之不理呢？如果置之不理，我们关于这个世界的知识还会增长吗？

合 对那些已经有了一些相关的思想、趋势和概念的事实，我们当然要设法先了解这些思想、趋势和概念，以便更好理解那些事实。而对那些没有相关的思想、趋势和概念的事实，我们也要给予高度关注，因为它们可能是将来或其他研究的重要资料。

---

49. **Claim**: We can usually learn much more from people whose views we share than from those whose views contradict our own.

Reason: Disagreement can cause stress and inhibit learning. (参考第34、76、118题)

Write a response in which you discuss the extent to which you agree or disagree with the claim and the reason on which that claim is based.

该题目的分析及提纲请参见本书第一章第四节中"因果类题目分析范例"之范例二。

---

50. Government officials should rely on their own judgment rather than unquestioningly carry out the will of the people they serve. (参考第18、86、115题)

Write a response in which you discuss the extent to which you agree or disagree with the recommendation and explain your reasoning for the position you take. In developing and supporting your position, describe specific circumstances in which adopting the recommendation would or would not be advantageous and explain how these examples shape your position.

题型归类 建议类。

题目分析

（1）题目中的建议可行性如何？

政府官员当然可以依靠自己的判断，而不是不容置疑地只执行人民的意愿。

（2）如果实施题目中的建议，是否会导致同初始目的相矛盾或其他荒谬的结果？

主张政治家要依靠自己的判断的理由可能会有：天才领袖会给百姓带来福祉，这样处理问题速度快、效率高，政治精英更懂治国之道等等。但题目中的建议极容易导致没有制约的个人意志，而没有制约的个人意志肯定会导致个人专权，甚至是政治灾难。

（3）有无替代或折中方案？

政府官员和老百姓无所谓谁更聪明。一个完善的制度可能比谁都更可靠。

提纲提要

论点 **制度可能比人更可靠。**

正 面临紧急事态，如突发自然灾害、外敌的突然入侵等，政府官员应当依据他们的职业判断和职业操守迅速作出决定。

反 主张政治家要依靠其自己的判断理由可能会有：天才领袖会给百姓带来福祉，这样处理问题速度快、效率高，政治精英更懂治国之道等等。但题目中的建议极容易导致没有制约的个人意志，而没有制约的个人意志肯定会导致个人专权，甚至是政治灾难。

合 政府官员和老百姓无所谓谁更聪明。一个完善的制度可能比谁都更可靠。

---

51. Young people should be encouraged to pursue long-term, realistic goals rather than seek immediate fame and recognition. (参考第71题)

Write a response in which you discuss the extent to which you agree or disagree with the recommendation and explain your reasoning for the position you take. In developing and supporting your position, describe specific circumstances in which adopting the recommendation would or would not be advantageous and explain how these examples shape your position.

题型归类 建议类。

题目分析

（1）题目中的建议可行性如何？

题目中的建议未必可行，因为它实际在假设年轻人已经具备了垂垂老者对人生的彻悟（enlightening）和智慧（wisdom）。但这个假设很难成立。

（2）如果实施题目中的建议，是否会导致同初始目的相矛盾或其他荒谬的结果？

没有经历过富有地位和声望的人生，不曾在追逐地位、声望过程中体会过兴奋与失落，所谓的long-term, realistic goals听起来更像是教条。

（3）有无替代或折中方案？

人生贵在体验，但体验是难以预先设计的。也许走过来的就是自然的，而自然的就是最好的。

119

提纲提要

论点 人生贵在体验，但体验是难以预先设计的。

(正) 一个人若能较早地确立远大而现实的目标当然是好事。

(反) 但是，题目中的建议未必可行，因为它实际在假设年轻人已经具备了垂垂老者对人生的彻悟和智慧。但这个假设很难成立。没有经历过富有地位和声望的人生，不曾在追逐地位、声望过程中体会过兴奋与失落，所谓的 long-term, realistic goals 听起来更像是教条。

(合) 人生贵在体验，但体验是难以预先设计的。也许走过来的就是自然的，而自然的就是最好的。

---

52. The best way to teach is to praise positive actions and ignore negative ones. (参考第 22、24、29、70、77、112、122、123 题)

Write a response in which you discuss the extent to which you agree or disagree with the recommendation and explain your reasoning for the position you take. In developing and supporting your position, describe specific circumstances in which adopting the recommendation would or would not be advantageous and explain how these examples shape your position.

（平行式多角度分析题，既可归入建议类，也可归入是非类和事实类。本题的分析思路和写作提纲可完全借鉴第 24 题。）

---

53. If a goal is worthy, then any means taken to attain it are justifiable. (参考第 144 题)

Write a response in which you discuss the extent to which you agree or disagree with the statement and explain your reasoning for the position you take. In developing and supporting your position, you should consider ways in which the statement might or might not hold true and explain how these considerations shape your position.

题型归类 事实类。

题目分析

（1）能否从公认的原则或事实中推出相反的判断？

基于人类理性的有限性和问题的复杂性，有时人们知道自己想要什么，但他们也许无法知道自己要采取的实现目的的手段到底会导致什么样的后果。因此，就有了这样一种可能：手段最终反而与目的相冲突。

（2）能否举出相反的事例？

旅游业破坏了环境就是很好的例子。当然，大家还可以举出很多其他的例子。

提纲提要

论点 论者的观点失于片面。

(正) 没有明确的目标，难有具体、果断的行动。

⊘ 但是，基于人类理性的有限性和问题的复杂性，有时人们知道自己想要什么，但他们也许无法知道自己所要采取的实现目的的手段到底会导致什么样的后果。如此，就有了这样一种可能：手段最终反而与目的相冲突。旅游业破坏了环境就是很好的例子。

⊘ 人易有盲目的自信，但难有真诚的谦卑。

54. In order to become well-rounded individuals, all college students should be required to take courses in which they read poetry, novels, mythology, and other types of imaginative literature.

Write a response in which you discuss the extent to which you agree or disagree with the recommendation and explain your reasoning for the position you take. In developing and supporting your position, describe specific circumstances in which adopting the recommendation would or would not be advantageous and explain how these examples shape your position.

题型归类 建议类。

题目分析

（1）题目中的建议可行性如何？

任何人只要愿意，都可读诗、小说、神话和其他富有想象力的文学作品。所以，题目中的建议当然可行。

（2）如果实施题目中的建议，是否会导致同初始目的相矛盾或其他荒谬的结果？

但千人千面，人人兴趣各异。让所有的大学生都去读诗、小说、神话和其他富有想象力的文学作品是否显得单调、枯燥？

（3）有无替代或折中方案？

怡情的方式很多，比如绘画、雕刻、舞蹈等等，未必非得读诗、小说、神话和其他富有想象力的文学作品。

提纲提要

论点 怡情的方式多种多样。

正 诗歌、小说、神话等可激发人的想象力，促使人们审视心灵中的自我。

反 但千人千面，人人兴趣各异。让所有的人都去读诗、小说、神话和其他富有想象力的文学作品是否显得单调、枯燥？

反 怡情的方式多样，比如绘画、雕刻、舞蹈等等，未必非得读诗、小说、神话和其他富有想象力的文学作品。

55. In order for any work of art—for example, a film, a novel, a poem, or a song—to have merit, it must be understandable to most people.

Write a response in which you discuss the extent to which you agree or disagree with the statement and explain your reasoning for the position you take. In developing and supporting your position, you should consider ways in which the statement might or might not hold true and explain how these considerations shape your position.

题型归类 建议类。

题目分析

（1）题目中的建议可行性如何？

题目中的建议可行性不强。艺术的本质是人对自我的精神探索，所表达的几乎纯粹是个人对世界和人的理解。再加上艺术语言的特殊性，能真正理解艺术家思想的人不会太多。

（2）如果实施题目中的建议，是否会导致同初始目的相矛盾或其他荒谬的结果？

如果艺术家的首要目标是让更多的人理解自己的思想和艺术，他很可能会偏离艺术精神探索的方向，变成为讨好观众而创作。这样的艺术不能称其为艺术，而是一种宣传。

（3）有无替代或折中方案？

艺术所表达的精神体验可以是独特的，但形式和语言最好是通俗易懂的。毕竟，不为人所理解的思想无异于旷野悲歌。

提纲提要

论点 艺术中的精神体验可以是独特的，但形式和语言最好是通俗易懂的。

㊣ 艺术不过是用来表达思想的一种特殊语言形式。所以，要求艺术能为更多的人所理解不算过分。

㊰ 但是，艺术的本质是人对自我的精神探索，所表达的几乎纯粹是个人对世界和人的理解。再加上艺术语言的特殊性，能真正理解艺术家思想的人不会太多。

其次，如果艺术家的首要目标是让更多的人理解自己的思想和艺术，他很可能会偏离艺术精神探索的方向，变成为讨好观众而创作。这样的艺术不能称其为艺术，而是一种宣传。

㊌ 艺术所表达的精神体验可以是独特的，但形式和语言最好是通俗易懂的。毕竟，不为人所理解的思想无异于旷野悲歌。

......

56. Many important discoveries or creations are accidental: it is usually while seeking the answer to one question that we come across the answer to another. （参考第59、131题）

Write a response in which you discuss the extent to which you agree or disagree with the statement and explain your reasoning for the position you take. In developing and supporting your position, you should consider ways in which the statement might or might not hold true and explain how these considerations shape your position.

题型归类 因果类。因为it is usually while seeking the answer to one question that we come across the answer to another，所以Most important discoveries or creations are accidental。

题目分析

（1）这个因果关系推理中的原因是否成立？

该题目的原因成立。的确有大量的科学研究成果是在不经意中被偶然发现的。

（2）假设这个原因成立，从它能否推出结果？

即使上述原因成立，结论也是推不出的。首先，绝大部分科学发现与创新是有计划、有目的的科研成果。否则，那些属于大学、私人机构和政府的科研组织岂不没用了？其次，人和动物的一大区别是：人总是预期未来，因而人的行为总是有一定计划性和目的性。有些科研成果看起来是在不经意中发现的，但实际上，人们可能对之已经进行过长期的思考、总结过各种经验教训、做过多种尝试。所谓偶然的发现其实是有计划的研究的继续。

提纲提要

论点 题目中的判断过于简单化。

正 的确有大量的科学研究成果是在不经意中被偶然发现的。

反 但是，首先，绝大部分科学发现与创新是有计划、有目的的科研成果。否则，那些属于大学、私人机构和政府的科研组织岂不没用了？

反 人和动物的一大区别是：人总是预期未来的，因而人的行为总是有一定计划性和目的性。有些科研成果看起来是在不经意中发现的，但实际上，人们可能对之已经进行过长期的思考、总结过各种经验教训、做过多种尝试。所谓偶然的发现，其实是有计划的研究的继续。

---

57. The main benefit of the study of history is to dispel the illusion that people living now are significantly different from people who lived in earlier times. （参考第33、74、109、133、134题）

Write a response in which you discuss the extent to which you agree or disagree with the statement and explain your reasoning for the position you take. In developing and supporting your position, you should consider ways in which the statement might or might not hold true and explain how these considerations shape your position.

题型归类
单纯性定义类。整个题目围绕着研究历史的主要益处的定义展开。

题目分析

（1）题目中的定义是否抓住了问题的本质？

表面上看，研究历史能让我们明白过去和现在存在很多相似之处。历史是连续的。现在的许多问题（如平等、社会正义、战争、王朝兴替等等）只不过是过去同样问题不同形式的表现。

（2）能否给出我自己的更为恰当的定义（恰当的定义就是能对自己的论点、论据以及所列举的现象有很好解释力的定义）？

但是，历史有其阶段性。不同的历史阶段，人们的物质生活状态、价值观念、风俗习惯、所面临的问题和挑战等等，都很不一样。即便是同样的问题，如战争，过去和现在的表现形式、结果也大不一样。现在的核战争及其结果恐怕是过去难以想象的。尽管历史也许是复杂、破碎、甚至是虚假的，但贯穿历史的人性是始终一致的。所以，**研究历史最大的好处其实是对人性规律的理解和把握。**

提纲提要

论点 历史是本关于人性的教科书。

正 表面上看，研究历史能让我们明白过去和现在存在很多相似之处。历史是连续的。现在的许多问题（如平等、社会正义、战争、王朝兴替等等）只不过是过去同样问题不同形式的表现。

反 但是，历史有其阶段性。不同的历史阶段，人们的物质生活状态、价值观念、风俗习惯、所面临的问题和挑战等等，都很不一样。即便是同样的问题，如战争，过去和现在的表现形式、结果也大不一样。现在的核战争及其结果恐怕是过去难以想象的。

反 尽管历史也许是复杂、破碎、甚至是虚假的，但贯穿历史的人性是始终一致的。所以，研究历史最大的好处其实是对人性规律的理解和把握。在整个历史过程中，人性的自私与高尚、狭隘与宽容、贪婪与克制通过不同的形式和问题得到展现。在人类目前所有的知识中，关于人性的知识是最难以理解和把握的。历史恰好是关于人性最好的教科书。

---

58. Learning is primarily a matter of personal discipline; students cannot be motivated by school or college alone. (参考第37、40、47、90、142题)

Write a response in which you discuss the extent to which you agree or disagree with the statement and explain your reasoning for the position you take. In developing and supporting your position, you should consider ways in which the statement might or might not hold true and explain how these considerations shape your position.

题型归类 因果类。因为Learning is primarily a matter of personal discipline，所以students cannot be motivated by school or college alone。

题目分析

（1）这个因果关系推理中的原因是否成立？

该题目的原因未必成立。表面上看，一个人是否愿意学习以及学习的效果如何，完全取决于他是否自律。自己不能自律或缺乏动力，别人是爱莫能助的。但是，一个人的自律习惯和学习动力不是凭空而来，是环境熏陶和习惯养成的结果。而环境熏陶和习惯养成就不一定完全是个人的事情了。

（2）假设这个原因成立，从它能否推出结果？

即使上述原因成立，依然推不出结论：students cannot be motivated by school or college alone。首先，学校里面浓厚的学习气氛会感染学习意愿不强、缺乏学习自主性的学生，使其慢慢养成学习的习惯。其次，学校是从事教育的专门机构，聚集了众多教育专家。学校里面系统的教育制度以及老师们专业、负责、有趣的授课，可以帮助点燃学生的学习兴趣，激发其学习的意愿，进而养成主动学习的习惯。

提纲提要

论点 论者的观点过于表面化。

正 表面上看，一个人是否愿意学习以及学习的效果如何，完全取决于他是否自律。自己不能自律或缺乏动力，别人是爱莫能助的。

反 但是，一个人的自律习惯和学习动力不是凭空而来，是环境熏陶和习惯养成的结果。而环境熏陶和习惯养成就不一定完全是个人的事情了。

⟨反⟩ 学校里面浓厚的学习气氛会感染学习意愿不强、缺乏学习自主性的学生，使其慢慢养成学习的习惯。而且，学校是从事教育的专门机构，聚集了众多教育专家。学校里面系统的教育制度以及老师们专业、负责、有趣的授课，可以帮助点燃学生的学习兴趣，激发其学习的意愿，进而养成主动学习的习惯。

---

59. Scientists and other researchers should focus their research on areas that are likely to benefit the greatest number of people. (参考第56、131题)

Write a response in which you discuss the extent to which you agree or disagree with the recommendation and explain your reasoning for the position you take. In developing and supporting your position, describe specific circumstances in which adopting the recommendation would or would not be advantageous and explain how these examples shape your position.

题型归类　建议类。

题目分析

（1）题目中的建议可行性如何?

题目中的建议可行性不强。这是因为该建议有一个假设的前提：即，科研人员必须预先知道自己的研究能够给社会带来多大的收益，具体而言就是题目所说的会惠及多少人。但这显然很难。对于部分冷门的基础学科、纯粹思辨性的学科（如哲学）以及一些前沿学科，这基本做不到。

（2）如果实施题目中的建议，是否会导致同初始目的相矛盾或其他荒谬的结果?

如果实施题目中的建议，至少会有如下弊端：第一，人类探索心内和身外两重世界的范围将被大大缩小。因为大量的研究领域根本无法说清楚它们到底能惠及多少人。第二，会有大量的科研人员放弃其原有的研究项目。人类从事科研的最初原动力是好奇心。而好奇心应该是没有边界或限制的。如果一个科研项目要实施，首先要看它会给多少人带来好处，那么，那些纯粹为了满足好奇心而不在乎其收益的科研活动将不得不停止。其结果只能是大量的科学家放弃其科研活动。第三，人类认知世界的能力下降。没有了好奇心，就没有了询问；没有了询问，也就不再有知识。

（3）有无替代或折中方案?

两方面都要兼顾。首先，一个社会和一国政府要鼓励任何方向和领域的科研活动，除非这些科研活动会明确引发危及人类生命安全（如各种细菌、生化和核武器）和动摇既存伦理道德秩序（如克隆人的技术）的后果。其次，对那些具备惠及多数人的科研项目（如超级水稻杂交技术），政府要给予大量的财力支持，并同时鼓励民间资助。

提纲提要

论点　实用性的科研目的不应该导致对科研方向和领域的简单框定。

⟨正⟩ 科研活动的实用性是判断科研项目价值的一个重要指标。科研活动总是需要人、财、物的持续投入。如果科研活动的成果不能带来较大的经济收益，科研活动将难以为继。

⟨反⟩ 但是，将科研活动的实用性作为其价值的唯一判定标准会产生很多问题。

首先，这个判定标准基本上无法实施。因为题目中的建议有一个假设的前提：即科研人员必须预先知道自己的研究能够给社会带来多大的收益，具体而言就是题目所说的会惠及多少人。但这显然很难。对于部分冷门的基础学科、纯粹思辨性的学科（如哲学）以及一些前沿学科，这基本做不到。

其次，如果强行实施这个标准，会产生至少三个弊端：第一，人类探索心内和身外两重世界的范围将被大大缩小。因为大量的研究领域根本无法说清楚它们到底能惠及多少人。第二，会有大量的科研人员放弃其原有的研究项目。人类从事科研的最初原动力是好奇心。而好奇心应该是没有边界或限制的。如果一个科研项目要实施，首先要看它会给多少人带来好处，那么，那些纯粹为了满足好奇心而不在乎其收益的科研活动将不得不停止。其结果只能是大量的科学家放弃其科研活动。第三，人类认知世界的能力下降。没有了好奇心，就没有了询问；没有了询问，也就不再有知识。

🔰 正确的选择是两方面都要兼顾。首先，一个社会和一国政府要鼓励任何方向和领域的科研活动，除非这些科研活动会明确引发危及人类生命安全（如各种细菌、生化、核武器和太空武器的研制）和动摇既存伦理道德秩序（如克隆人的技术）的后果。其次，对那些具备惠及多数人的科研项目（如超级水稻杂交技术），政府要给予大力的财力支持，并同时鼓励民间资助。

---

60. Politicians should pursue common ground and reasonable consensus rather than elusive ideals.

Write a response in which you discuss the extent to which you agree or disagree with the recommendation and explain your reasoning for the position you take. In developing and supporting your position, describe specific circumstances in which adopting the recommendation would or would not be advantageous and explain how these examples shape your position.

题型归类 建议类。

题目分析

（1）题目中的建议可行性如何？

建议不可行。没有了政治理想，也就没有了政治本身。政治不过就是实现某一群体政治、经济、意识形态等诸方面理想的过程和手段。

（2）如果实施题目中的建议，是否会导致同初始目的相矛盾或其他荒谬的结果？

没有了政治理想，一个政党、团体、社会也就丧失了其凝聚力。而且，所谓的寻求相同意见，达成共识（pursue common ground and reasonable consensus）也就没有了标准和原则。一个政治理想，只要它符合大多数人的内心渴望，并且可以为绝大多数的个体带来更多的公平、正义和福利，就值得政治家去努力争取。不经尝试，我们永远不知道一个political ideal到底是elusive的，还是realistic的。

（3）有无替代或折中方案？

有人的地方就有政治，有政治就必然有政治理想。而正是为了政治理想，人们才有了寻求相同意见，达成共识的愿望。相同意见和共识不过是人们为了实现政治理想/信念而彼此妥协的结果。

提纲提要

论点 正是为了政治理想，人们才有了寻求相同意见，达成共识的愿望。

正 政治基本上可以定义为寻求共识的艺术。

反 但是，没有了政治理想，也就没有了政治本身。政治不过是实现某一群体政治、经济、意识形态等诸方面理想的过程和手段。没有了政治理想，一个政党、团体、社会也就丧失了其凝聚力，而所谓的寻求相同意见，达成共识也就没有了标准和原则。一个政治理想，只要它符合大多数人的内心渴望，并且可以为绝大多数的个体带来更多的公平、正义和福利，就值得政治家去努力争取。不经尝试，我们永远不知道一个political ideal到底是elusive的，还是realistic的。

反 有人的地方就有政治，有政治就必然有政治理想。而正是为了政治理想，人们才有了寻求相同意见，达成共识的愿望。相同意见和共识不过是人们为了实现政治理想/信念而彼此妥协的结果。

---

61. People should undertake risky action only after they have carefully considered its consequences.

Write a response in which you discuss the extent to which you agree or disagree with the recommendation and explain your reasoning for the position you take. In developing and supporting your position, describe specific circumstances in which adopting the recommendation would or would not be advantageous and explain how these examples shape your position.

题型归类 建议类。

题目分析

（1）题目中的建议可行性如何？

建议看似合理，实则不可行。基于人类理性的有限性和可获得信息的不完整性，人们几乎很难百分之百地对一个充满风险的行为的后果进行准确的估计。行为的风险性越高，其后果难以预料的程度越大。

（2）如果实施题目中的建议，是否会导致同初始目的相矛盾或其他荒谬的结果？

如果凡事都要先考虑后果，人类就裹足不前。对个人来说，如果结果不明，要做的事情就一再延宕（procrastinate），那一生也只好碌碌无为了。人生就像玩扑克牌，如果每一把你都很清楚对方手里的牌，这牌玩起来还有什么意思呢？在好奇与期待中不停地冒一些自己承受得起的风险，这就是人生。

（3）有无替代或折中方案？

人类要进步，个人要发展，有时明知前面有风险也必须往前走。但是，首先，我们尽量把所有能够收集到的信息都收集过来，并进行充分的分析和研究，以利决策。其次，可以将大的计划分步、分时段实施，从而将大风险分解为小风险，直到把风险降到我们可以承受的范围之内。

论点 好奇与期待中，冒一些自己承受得起的风险。

(正) 做事之前先预估后果，这是理性之人的本能。人总不能付无谓的代价，无论其多么小。

(反) 但是，基于人类理性的有限性和可获得信息的不完整性，人们几乎很难百分之百地对一个充满风险的行为的后果进行准确的估计。行为的风险度越高，其后果难以预料的程度越大。如果凡事都要先考虑后果，人类就裹足不前。对个人来说，如果结果不明，要做的事情就一再延宕，那一生也只好碌碌无为了。人生就像玩扑克牌，假如每一把你都很清楚对方手里的牌，这牌玩起来还有什么意思呢？在好奇与期待中不停地冒一些自己承受得起的风险，这就是人生。

(合) 人类要进步，个人要发展，有时明知前面有风险，也必须往前走。但是，第一，我们尽量把所有能够收集到的信息都收集过来，并进行充分的分析和研究，以利决策。其次，可以将大的计划分步、分时段实施，从而将大风险分解为小风险，直到把风险降到我们可以承受的范围之内。

⋯⋯⋯⋯⋯⋯⋯⋯⋯⋯⋯⋯⋯⋯⋯⋯⋯⋯⋯⋯⋯⋯⋯⋯⋯⋯⋯⋯⋯⋯⋯⋯⋯

62. Leaders are created by the demands that are placed on them. (参考第8、16、69、94、114、123、128、147题)

Write a response in which you discuss the extent to which you agree or disagree with the statement and explain your reasoning for the position you take. In developing and supporting your position, you should consider ways in which the statement might or might not hold true and explain how these considerations shape your position.

题型归类 事实类。

题目分析

（1）能否从公认的原则或事实中推出相反的判断？

基于下列两点原则，题目中的判断未必成立：

其一，领袖之所以能在特定的历史时期成为领袖是与其内在的禀赋与能力分不开的。正所谓机遇偏爱有准备的人。不是谁都能随随便便成为领袖的。

其二，一些特殊因素所导致的偶然性（比如，一个人的性格、个人爱好、形象与魅力、特殊的个人经历等等）也对一个人能否在合适的时间、合适的地点成为领袖发挥着作用。

（2）能否举出相反的事例？

（大家可以随便举出自己熟悉的例子。此处从略。）

提纲提要

论点 论者的观点过于片面。

(正) 时势造英雄。特定历史时期的特殊要求所创造的特殊机遇可以使领袖们脱颖而出。

(反) 但是，领袖之所以能在特定的历史时期成为领袖是与其内在的禀赋与能力分不开的。正所谓机遇偏爱有准备的人。不是谁都能随随便便成为领袖的。

(反) 一些特殊因素所导致的偶然性（比如，一个人的性格、个人爱好、形象与魅力、特殊的个人经历等等）也对一个人能否在合适的时间、合适的地点成为领袖发挥着作用。

63. There is little justification for society to make extraordinary efforts—especially at a great cost in money and jobs—to save endangered animal or plant species. (参考第10、31、67、119、125、148题)

Write a response in which you discuss the extent to which you agree or disagree with the statement and explain your reasoning for the position you take. In developing and supporting your position, you should consider ways in which the statement might or might not hold true and explain how these considerations shape your position.

题型归类 单纯性是非类。

题目分析

（1）这种价值判断的标准是什么?

单单用成本分析和责任划分的标准来看，人类似乎没必要为拯救濒危物种付出太高的代价。理由是，第一，我们完全可以把用来拯救濒危物种的巨大物力和财力拿去救济更多需要帮助的人，生产更多的产品，创造更多的就业等等。第二，完全可以假设人类出现在这个星球上之前就已经有大量的物种消亡了。也许那些已经消亡物种的数量比新生的物种还要多。第三，即便我们付出巨大的努力，部分物种仍然会灭绝，我们的努力因此显得有点儿徒劳。

（2）这种价值判断的标准是否值得修正?

但是，基于人类对自己的行为负责以及对自身安全的考虑，拯救濒危物种又是必需的。具而言之，第一，把用来拯救濒危物种的巨大物力和财力拿去救济更多需要帮助的人，生产更多的产品，创造更多的就业等等，看起来是节约了资源，但有些拯救是没有必要的，部分生物物种会永远消失。第二，对于这些消失的物种，人类并不像他们自我认为的那样无辜。科技进步不仅改善了人们的生活，同时也增强了人类干预和破坏自然环境的能力。我们或许已经给部分生物物种带来了致命的威胁，我们只是没意识到，或有意忽略了而已。第三，即便部分生物物种的灭绝纯粹是个自然过程，但如果这个过程已经危及了人类自身生存的话，人类采取行动对这个过程进行干预也依然是有意义的。

提纲提要

论点 题目中的判断似是而非。

正 单单用成本分析和责任划分的标准来看，人类似乎没必要为拯救濒危物种付出太高的代价。理由是，第一，我们完全可以把用来拯救濒危物种的巨大物力和财力拿去救济更多需要帮助的人，生产更多的产品，创造更多的就业等等。第二，完全可以假设人类出现在这个星球上之前就已经有大量的物种消亡了。也许那些消亡物种的数量比新生的物种还要多。第三，即便我们付出巨大的努力，部分物种仍然会灭绝，我们的努力因此显得有点儿徒劳。

反 但是，基于人类对自己的行为负责以及对自身安全的考虑，拯救濒危物种又是必需的。具而言之，第一，把用来拯救濒危物种的巨大物力和财力拿去救济更多需要帮助的人，生产更多的产品，创造更多的就业等等，看起来是节约了资源，但有些拯救是没有必要的，部分生物物种会永远消失。第二，对于这些消失的物种，人类并不像他自我认为的那样无辜。科技进步不仅改善了人们的生活，同时也增强了人类干预和破坏自然环境的能力。我们或许已经给部分生物物种带去了致命的威胁，我们只是没意识到，或有意忽略了而已。第三，即便部分生物物种的灭绝纯粹是个自然过程，但如果这个过程已经危及了人类自身生存的话，人类采取行动对这个过程进行干预也依然是有意义的。

（散）从终极意义上讲，拯救濒危物种的理由可以很简单：那就是，人类对生命的敬畏和对自己知识的谦卑。所有地球上的生命都像我们自己一样有生存的权力，并且它们的存在直接或间接地促成了人类的繁荣。而人类却拿着自己有限的进步沾沾自喜，有意无意放弃了对其他生命形式的悲悯、敬畏和责任。人类最终的悲剧也许不在于无知，而在于自负。

---

64. The human mind will always be superior to machines because machines are only tools of human minds.（参考第 1、26 题）

Write a response in which you discuss the extent to which you agree or disagree with the statement and explain your reasoning for the position you take. In developing and supporting your position, you should consider ways in which the statement might or might not hold true and explain how these considerations shape your position.

该题目的分析及提纲请参见本书第一章第四节中的"是非类题目分析范例"之范例二。

---

65. Every individual in a society has a responsibility to obey just laws and to disobey and resist unjust laws.

Write a response in which you discuss the extent to which you agree or disagree with the claim. In developing and supporting your position, be sure to address the most compelling reasons and/or examples that could be used to challenge your position.

题型归类　建议类。

题目分析

（1）题目中的建议可行性如何？

题目中的建议不可行，因为论者已经将问题过于简单化了。在没有搞清楚什么是正义和不正义，以及该采取何种程序来捍卫正义、消除不正义之前，题目中的建议很可能会导致这样的结果：坚持了不正义的法律、破坏了正义的法律。

（2）如果实施题目中的建议，是否会导致同初始目的相矛盾或其他荒谬的结果？

简单地说 Every individual in a society has a responsibility to obey just laws and to disobey and resist unjust laws 只能导致无政府状态（anarchy）。

（3）有无替代或折中方案？

正义的实现以及非正义的消除都有赖于：其一，人们对正义含义的共识。其二，实现正义和消除非正义的程序。否则，不可能有真正的正义。

提纲提要

论点 正义的实现有赖于人们对正义的共识，以及一个可靠的法律程序。

(正) 理论上讲，题目中的建议是合理的。毕竟，行动上的正义开始于理念上的正义（Justice in action starts from justice in conception）。任何行动上的正义和非正义，首先在于人们对观念上的认同。要消除非正义，人们必先在观念上确认其属于非正义；同理，若要人们去施行某种所谓的"正义"，必须先要人们在观念上高度认同其正义性。所以，在观念层面上，人人都有服从正义、抵制和反对非正义的必要和自由。

(反) 但是在操作层面，简单地说Every individual in a society has a responsibility to obey just laws and to disobey and resist unjust laws实际是将问题简单化了。在没有搞清楚什么是正义和不正义，以及该采取何种程序来消除不正义之前，题目中的建议很可能会导致这样的结果：坚持了不正义的法律、破坏了正义的法律。这只能是无政府状态。例如，集体的利益是否永远高于个体的利益？是否任何时候都可以让个体为集体利益作出牺牲？在城市建设中搞强制拆迁都是以公共利益为动因，那么，所有的强制拆迁都是正义的吗？如果不是，该怎样消除非正义呢？暴力抵制，还是诉诸法律或行政程序？该怎样保证那些法律和行政程序是正义的？那些程序又该以怎样合乎正义的方式产生？这些处理不好，当然就是动荡和无政府状态了。

(合) 正义的实现以及非正义的消除，都有赖于：其一，人们对正义含义的共识。其二，实现正义和消除非正义的法律程序。否则，不可能有真正的正义。

· ·

66. People who are the most deeply committed to an idea or policy are also the most critical of it.

Write a response in which you discuss the extent to which you agree or disagree with the statement and explain your reasoning for the position you take. In developing and supporting your position, you should consider ways in which the statement might or might not hold true and explain how these considerations shape your position.

题型归类 事实类。

题目分析

（1）能否从公认的原则或事实中推出相反的判断？

基于下列两点原则，题目中的判断未必成立：

其一，虽然一个人对某个想法或者做法很关注，但如果他是个很容易自我满足的人，他对这个想法或做法未必就很挑剔或者具有批判精神。

其二，如果一个人习惯于追求完美，那么即便他对某个想法或者做法不很关注，他也会很挑剔。

（2）能否举出相反的事例？

（大家可以举出无数身边发生的例子。此处从略。）

提纲提要

论点 论者的观点失于片面。

(正) 对事情的过分投入和关注有时会让人产生挑剔心理。

⑤ 虽然一个人对某个想法或者做法很关注，但如果他是个很容易自我满足的人，他对这个想法或做法未必就很挑剔或者具有批判精神。

⑤ 如果一个人习惯于追求完美，那么即便他对某个想法或者做法不很关注，他也会很挑剔。

67. Some people believe that society should try to save every plant and animal species, despite the expense to humans in effort, time, and financial well-being. Others believe that society need not make extraordinary efforts, especially at a great cost in money and jobs, to save endangered species. (参考第 10、31、63、67、119、125、148 题)

Write a response in which you discuss which view more closely aligns with your own position and explain your reasoning for the position you take. In developing and supporting your position, you should address both of the views presented.

题型归类 建议类。

题目分析

（1）题目中的建议可行性如何？

题目中的建议几乎不可行。考虑到一个国家和政府资源的有限性，他们不可能不惜成本地去拯救任何濒临灭绝的生物物种。

（2）如果实施题目中的建议，是否会导致同初始目的相矛盾或其他荒谬的结果？

再者，自然世界的进化过程本身也会导致许多动植物物种的消失。当人类不惜成本地介入自然界的进化过程中，实际上是对自然界另一种形式的破坏，因为我们无法预知我们现在自认为安全合理的行为在未来会产生什么样的后果。

但是，对自然界中生物物种的消亡采取一种无动于衷的态度也不明智。这是因为，第一，对于有些灭绝的物种，人类是有责任的。科技进步不仅大大改善了人们的生活，同时也大大增强了人类干预和破坏自然环境的能力。我们或许已经给部分生物物种带去了致命的威胁，我们只是没意识到，或有意忽略了而已。第二，即便部分生物物种的灭绝纯粹是个自然过程，但如果这个过程已经危及了人类自身生存的话，人类采取行动对这个过程进行干预是有意义的。

（3）有无替代或折中方案？

首先，在我们力所能及的范围内尽力去保护由于人类的生产和生活而处于灭绝边缘的生物物种。这是人类对自己贪婪与无知的自我救赎。其次，人类要在处理与周围环境的关系问题上彻底洗心革面。我们必须明白，人类只不过是环境的一部分，不是环境的主人。在自然界面前，人应保持一份敬畏和悲悯之心。

提纲提要

论点 人类对自然界应保持一份敬畏和悲悯之心。

⑤ 人类在处理与自然界关系，尤其在该如何面对那些濒临灭绝生物物种的问题上，经常发现自己处于一种矛盾和尴尬的境地。

⑤ 首先，题目中的建议几乎不可行。考虑到一个国家和政府资源的有限性，他们不可能不惜成本地去拯救任何濒临灭绝的生物物种。再者，自然界的进化过程本身也会导致许多动植物物种的

消失。当人类不惜成本地介入自然界的进化过程中，实际上是对自然界另一种形式的破坏，因为我们无法预知我们现在自认为安全合理的行为在未来会产生什么样的后果。

但是，对自然界中生物物种的消亡采取一种无动于衷的态度也不明智。这是因为，第一，对于有些灭绝的物种，人类是有责任的。科技进步不仅大大改善了人们的生活，同时也大大增强了人类干预和破坏自然环境的能力。我们或许已经给部分生物物种带去了致命的威胁，我们只是没意识到，或有意忽略了而已。第二，即便部分生物物种的灭绝纯粹是个自然过程，但如果这个过程已经危及了人类自身生存的话，人类采取行动对这个过程进行干预是有意义的。

合 折中方案：首先，在我们力所能及的范围内尽力去保护由于人类的生产和生活而处于灭绝边缘的生物物种。这是人类对自己贪婪与无知的自我救赎。其次，人类要在处理与周围环境的关系问题上彻底洗心革面。我们必须明白，人类只不过是环境的一部分，不是环境的主人。在自然界面前，人应保持一份敬畏和悲悯之心。

- -

68. Some people believe that the purpose of education is to free the mind and the spirit. Others believe that formal education tends to restrain our minds and spirits rather than set them free. (参考第17、42、48、87、92题)

Write a response in which you discuss which view more closely aligns with your own position and explain your reasoning for the position you take. In developing and supporting your position, you should address both of the views presented.

题型归类 该题可同时归入事实类和结合式定义类，因为要对题目中的the purpose of education和restrain our minds and spirits的含义进行讨论和界定。

题目分析

（1）能否从公认的原则或事实中推出相反的判断？

关于第一个判断：the purpose of education is to free the mind and the spirit，似乎找不出有什么问题。教育的目的的确就是引导学生养成科学的思维方式，通过思考获得精神的自由。问题主要出在第二个判断：formal education tends to restrain our minds and spirits rather than set them free。

基于下列两个原则，题目中的第二个判断未必成立：

其一，如果我们将restrain our minds and spirits理解为教育刻板、未能启发学生进行创造性的思维，那么，这个判断显然不符合事实。至少欧美的高水平现代教育不是这样。

其二，如果我们将restrain our minds and spirits理解为只向学生灌输概念和事实的话，题目中的判断也未必能成立。创新不等于放弃已有的知识积累。知识和文明毕竟有其连续性和继承性。

（2）能否举出相反的事例？

（大家可以举出无数身边发生的例子。此处从略。）

提纲提要

论点 人们走进学校的目的是为了学会思考并发现价值。

正 教育的目的是什么？是要记住许许多多的事实、概念和原理以做到知识渊博吗？是养成良好的学习习惯吗？是提高受教育者的道德水平吗？是掌握专门的职业技能吗？综合各种对教育目的的界定，to free the mind and the spirit 也许是对教育目的的最好定义。

反 现代教育制度下的确出现过强调概念和事实的识记而不注意启发学习者的自主思考能力的学校，尤其是高等院校，有变成职业培训学校的倾向。但断言 formal education tends to restrain our minds and spirits rather than set them free 似乎有夸大事实的嫌疑：

首先，如果我们将 restrain our minds and spirits 理解为教育刻板、未能启发学生进行创造性的思维，那么，这个判断显然不符合事实。至少欧美的高水平现代教育不是这样。

其次，如果我们将 restrain our minds and spirits 理解为只向学生灌输概念和事实的话，题目中的判断也未必能成立。创新不等于放弃已有的知识积累。知识和文明毕竟有其连续性和继承性。

散 最终判断一个社会的教育是否成功也许有两个缺一不可的标准：第一，学生是否掌握了科学的思维方式。有了它，学生才能独立进行理性和批判地思考。第二，学生是否通过独立思考获得了他人生的价值和信仰。有了它们，学生才会发现生命的意义和方向。

---

69. Some people believe it is often necessary, even desirable, for political leaders to withhold information from the public. Others believe that the public has a right to be fully informed. (参考第 8、16、62、94、114、123、128、147 题)

Write a response in which you discuss which view more closely aligns with your own position and explain your reasoning for the position you take. In developing and supporting your position, you should address both of the views presented.

题型归类 单纯性是非类。

题目分析

（1）这种价值判断的标准是什么？

主张政治领袖应该对公众封闭消息/信息的人可能在运用这样的标准：不加选择地向公众透露信息/消息会损害党派利益、妨碍社会稳定甚至危及国家安全。

（2）这种价值判断的标准是否值得修正？

但是，如果从公众对政府的监督角度或标准来看：公众了解政府及其行为越多，国家越安全。一个习惯于蒙蔽公众的政府最终会欺骗国民、挟持国家，其造成的危害其实不亚于外敌入侵。

提纲提要

论点 一个蒙蔽公众的政府对国家造成的危害，其实不亚于外敌入侵。

正 多数情况下，政治领袖会本能地对公众封闭部分消息。他们笃信不加选择地向公众透露信息/消息会损害党派利益、妨碍社会稳定甚至危及国家安全。

反 但是，如果从公众对政府的监督角度或标准来看：公众了解政府及其行为越多，国家越安全。一个习惯于蒙蔽公众的政府最终会欺骗国民、挟持国家，其造成的危害其实不亚于外敌入侵。

合 特定情况下，政治领袖或政府可以适当控制对公众发布的信息。但最终，公众必须了解政治领袖及政府的所作所为。因为这既是公众的权利，也是确保政治民主和社会稳定的需要。

70. **Claim**: Universities should require every student to take a variety of courses outside the student's major field of study.

Reason: Acquiring knowledge of various academic disciplines is the best way to become truly educated. (参考第22、24、29、52、77、112、122、123题；同时还可以参考第13、46、102题)

Write a response in which you discuss the extent to which you agree or disagree with the claim and the reason on which that claim is based.

题型归类 因果类。

题目分析

（1）这个因果关系推理中的原因是否成立？

该题目的原因未必成立。博学就等于拥有良好的教育吗？如果念了很多书，但是独立思考和独立解决问题的能力很差，或者没有任何批判意识和能力呢？

（2）假设这个原因成立，从它能否推出结果？

即使上述原因成立，结论也是站不住脚的。首先，许多大学、学院未必具备提供大量学科课程的能力。其次，学生很难有时间和精力在三至四年的时间里去学其专业以外的大量课程。其结果只能是学生疲于奔命于众多学科之间，而学得浮光掠影，难以专深。第三，湮灭学生的兴趣、个性和创造力。第四，有些学生很可能因为对其专业以外的学科毫无兴趣而对这种要求产生强烈的抵制情绪。

提纲提要

论点 题目中的判断似是而非。

正 各门各科的知识是相互贯通的。广博的知识面有利于人们多角度地思考和解决问题。

反 但是，博学就等于拥有良好的教育吗？如果念了很多书，但是独立思考和独立解决问题的能力很差，或者没有任何批判意识和能力呢？

反 即使上述原因成立，结论也是站不住脚的。首先，许多大学、学院未必具备提供大量学科课程的能力。其次，学生很难有时间和精力在三至四年的时间里去学其专业以外的大量课程。其结果只能是学生疲于奔命于众多学科之间，学得浮光掠影，难以专深。第三，湮灭学生的兴趣、个性和创造力。第四，有些学生很可能因为对其专业以外的学科毫无兴趣而对这种要求产生强烈的抵制情绪。

71. Young people should be encouraged to pursue long-term, realistic goals rather than seek immediate fame and recognition. (参考第51题)

Write a response in which you discuss the extent to which you agree or disagree with the statement and explain your reasoning for the position you take. In developing and supporting your position, you should consider ways in which the statement might or might not hold true and explain how these considerations shape your position.

（建议类。本题的分析思路和写作提纲可完全借鉴第51题。）

72. Governments should not fund any scientific research whose consequences are unclear. （参考第23、36题）

Write a response in which you discuss your views on the policy and explain your reasoning for the position you take. In developing and supporting your position, you should consider the possible consequences of implementing the policy and explain how these consequences shape your position.

（建议类。本题的分析思路和写作提纲可完全借鉴第36题。）

73. Colleges and universities should require all faculty to spend time working outside the academic world in professions relevant to the courses they teach.

Write a response in which you discuss your views on the policy and explain your reasoning for the position you take. In developing and supporting your position, you should consider the possible consequences of implementing the policy and explain how these consequences shape your position.

该题目的分析及提纲请参见本书第一章第四节中的"建议类题目分析范例"之范例二。

74. Knowing about the past cannot help people to make important decisions today. （参考第33、57、109、133、134题）

Write a response in which you discuss the extent to which you agree or disagree with the statement and explain your reasoning for the position you take. In developing and supporting your position, you should consider ways in which the statement might or might not hold true and explain how these considerations shape your position.

题型归类 事实类。

题目分析

（1）能否从公认的原则或事实中推出相反的判断？

历史是连续的。现在的许多问题（如人与人间的平等、社会正义、战争等）只不过是过去问题的延续。

（2）能否举出相反的事例？

（大家可以举出无数身边发生的例子。此处从略。）

提纲提要

论点 论者的观点过于片面。

正 历史未必能帮助人们对当前的重大问题做出决定。这是因为过去和现在的可比性不大。过去发生的事情，今天未必重演。

反 但是历史是连续的。现在的许多问题（如人与人间的平等、社会正义、战争等）只不过是过去问题的延续。

敌 因为人性的一贯性，今天的问题总有过去问题的影子。因为人性中固有的自负，人们不愿过多地考虑历史中的经验与教训。在整个历史过程中，人性的自私与高尚、狭隘与宽容、贪婪与克制通过不同的形式和问题得到展现。在人类目前所有的知识中，关于人性的知识是最难以理解和把握的。历史恰好是关于人性最好的教科书。

- -

75. In this age of intensive media coverage, it is no longer possible for a society to regard any living man or woman as a hero. (参考第22、44、84、122题)

Write a response in which you discuss the extent to which you agree or disagree with the statement and explain your reasoning for the position you take. In developing and supporting your position, you should consider ways in which the statement might or might not hold true and explain how these considerations shape your position.

（本题可以变形为：Because of the intensive media coverage, it is no longer possible for a society to regard any living man or woman as a hero。这样一来，本题就是典型的因果类题目了，其分析思路和写作提纲可完全借鉴第44题。）

- -

76. We can usually learn much more from people whose views we share than from people whose views contradict our own. (参考第34、49、118题)

Write a response in which you discuss the extent to which you agree or disagree with the statement and explain your reasoning for the position you take. In developing and supporting your position, you should consider ways in which the statement might or might not hold true and explain how these considerations shape your position.

题型归类 事实类。

题目分析

（1）能否从公认的原则或事实中推出相反的判断?

　　基于下列两个原因，题目中的判断未必成立：第一，持不同意见不一定就导致压力，阻碍学习。每个人对批评的态度不同、对压力的反应各异。因此，同样的批评完全可以让有些人积极奋进、眼界思路更为开阔，从而学得更好。第二，即使不同意见导致压力并因此阻碍了人们之间的学习，也推不出 We can usually learn much more from people whose views we share than from people whose views contradict our own。影响一个人学习效果的原因有很多（如：学习动机、天赋程度、努力程度、兴趣等），他人的批评和赞同只是众多原因中的一种。所以，对一个人的学习效果不起决定性作用。

（2）能否举出相反的事例？

（大家可以举出无数身边发生的例子。此处从略。）

提纲提要

论点 持相同意见者是否会促进彼此间的学习完全因人而异。

正 相同的意见会促进人们的学习；相反的意见有时妨碍人们彼此间的学习。别人的赞同是对一个人自我价值、能力的认可，往往会鼓励后者作出更积极的努力。这是人的本性使然。

反 但是，基于下列两个原因，题目中的判断未必成立：第一，不同意见不一定就导致压力，妨碍学习。每个人对批评的态度不同、对压力的反应各异。因此，同样的批评完全可以让有些人积极奋进、眼界思路更为开阔，从而学得更好。第二，即使不同意见导致压力，并因而阻碍了学习，也推不出 We can usually learn much more from people whose views we share than from people whose views contradict our own. 影响一个人学习效果的原因有很多（如：学习动机、天赋程度、努力程度、兴趣等），他人的批评和赞同只是众多原因中的一种。所以，对一个人的学习效果不起决定性作用。

合 到底他人的意见是否妨碍学习取决于每个人的情况。学习效果纯粹取决于个人情况：个人禀赋、性格、动机和环境等。

---

77. The most effective way to understand contemporary culture is to analyze the trends of its youth. (参考第22、24、29、52、70、112、122、123题)

Write a response in which you discuss the extent to which you agree or disagree with the statement and explain your reasoning for the position you take. In developing and supporting your position, you should consider ways in which the statement might or might not hold true and explain how these considerations shape your position.

题型归类 建议类。

题目分析

（1）题目中的建议可行性如何？

任何人只要愿意，都可通过研究一个社会年轻人的特点去了解该社会的特点。所以题目中的建议可行。

（2）如果实施题目中的建议，是否会导致同初始目的相矛盾或其他荒谬的结果？

当人们试图通过研究一个社会年轻人的特点去了解该社会的特点时，会产生一个问题：年轻人是这个社会特点的真实体现吗？他们身上所体现的新潮、前卫的思想和行为就是一个社会的主流价值吗？

（3）有无替代或折中方案？

年轻人只代表一个社会的表层状态。正如眼下的中国，年轻人只代表中国最表层的文化。真正反映中国文化的是七亿多的农民、中小城市的市民以及引导社会主流思想和文化的知识分子。

提纲提要

论点 年轻人只代表一个社会的表层状态。

正 通常情况下，社会状态会最直接地体现在年轻人的身上。

反 但是，当人们试图通过研究一个社会年轻人的特点去了解该社会的特点时，会产生一个问题：年轻人是这个社会特点的真实体现吗？他们身上所体现的新潮、前卫的思想和行为就是一个社会的主流价值吗？

反 年轻人只代表一个社会的表层状态。正如眼下的中国，年轻人只代表中国最表层的文化。真正反映中国文化的是七亿多的农民、中小城市的市民以及引导社会主流思想和文化的知识分子。

---

78. People's attitudes are determined more by their immediate situation or surroundings than by society as a whole. (参考第38题)

Write a response in which you discuss the extent to which you agree or disagree with the statement and explain your reasoning for the position you take. In developing and supporting your position, you should consider ways in which the statement might or might not hold true and explain how these considerations shape your position.

该题目的分析及提纲请参见本书第一章第四节中的"事实类题目分析范例"之范例一。

---

79. **Claim**: The best test of an argument is its ability to convince someone with an opposing viewpoint.

Reason: Only by being forced to defend an idea against the doubts and contrasting views of others does one really discover the value of that idea. (参考第146题)

Write a response in which you discuss the extent to which you agree or disagree with the claim and the reason on which that claim is based.

题型归类 因果类。

题目分析

（1）这个因果关系推理中的原因是否成立？

      基于两个原则，题目中的判断未必成立：其一，辩论很可能因为违背初衷、罔顾事实的自我辩解使得最后胜出的思想、观点未必有价值；同样，因为别人的善辩而被放弃的思想、观点未必就没有价值。其二，尚有别的发现某一思想价值的方法，如，查阅资料、自我反思等。

（2）假设这个原因成立，从它能否推出结果？

      即使上述原因成立，结论也是站不住脚的。一个观点和判断的价值在于其在多大程度上接近真实和真理，而判断的标准只能是实践。雄辩之士也许总能在论辩中获胜，但雄辩不等于真理，雄辩的人不是真理批发商。

提纲提要

论点 雄辩的人不是真理批发商。

（正）辩论有利于明确问题、开拓视角、启发新的思想。

（反）但是，论辩并不能有效证实真理，更不能当作检验真理的唯一标准。这是因为：其一，辩论很可能因为违背初衷、罔顾事实的自我辩解使得最后胜出的思想、观点未必有价值；同样，因为别人的善辩而被放弃的思想、观点未必就没有价值。其二，尚有别的发现某一思想价值的方法，如，查阅资料、自我反思、岁月沉淀使真相大白等。

（反）一个观点和判断的价值在于其在多大程度上接近事实和真理，而这个价值判断的标准只能是实践。雄辩之士也许总能在与其对手的论辩中获胜，但雄辩不等于真理，雄辩的人自然也不是真理批发商。

---

80. Nations should suspend government funding for the arts when significant numbers of their citizens are hungry or unemployed. （参考第7、88题）

Write a response in which you discuss the extent to which you agree or disagree with the recommendation and explain your reasoning for the position you take. In developing and supporting your position, describe specific circumstances in which adopting the recommendation would or would not be advantageous and explain how these examples shape your position.

题目分析

（1）题目中的建议可行性如何？

一个政府该如何支配其收入和其他公共资源，完全取决于该政府对各种事情轻重缓急的顺序安排。是否资助艺术可以同一个政府是否财力雄厚没有直接关系。所以，无所谓可行不可行。

（2）如果实施题目中的建议，是否会导致同初始目的相矛盾或其他荒谬的结果？

温饱问题、工作问题、谋生的技能问题都不可谓不重要。但问题是：人可以不要精神吗？艺术的功能恰恰就是让人们从精神上认识自我。金字塔、万里长城、各种为了不朽而竖立的纪念碑、乃至一切的物质财富都可以湮灭，可那些人类为了满足精神追求而创造的艺术（音乐、美术、小说、诗歌、戏剧、舞蹈等）却可以代代传承，永不磨灭。

（3）有无替代或折中方案？

人永远是精神意义上的人。人注定要在精神和肉体之间寻找平衡。

提纲提要

论点 人注定要在精神和肉体之间寻找平衡。

（正）人所理解的一切，都因为人的生命的存在而有了意义。所以，衣食住行、工作谋生的需要自然是一切一切的基础。

（反）但问题是：人可以不要精神吗？艺术的功能恰恰就是让人们从精神上认识自我。金字塔、万里长城、各种为了不朽而竖立的纪念碑、乃至一切的物质财富都可以湮灭，可那些人类为了满足精神追求而创造的艺术（音乐、美术、小说、诗歌、戏剧、舞蹈等）却可以代代传承，永不磨灭。

合 人永远是精神意义上的人。人注定要在精神和肉体之间寻找平衡。如果非要在肉体与灵魂、物质与精神之间作出抉择的话，人类所选择的肯定是灵魂和精神。

---

81. All parents should be required to volunteer time to their children's schools. (参考第95题)

Write a response in which you discuss the extent to which you agree or disagree with the recommendation and explain your reasoning for the position you take. In developing and supporting your position, describe specific circumstances in which adopting the recommendation would or would not be advantageous and explain how these examples shape your position.

题目分析

（1）题目中的建议可行性如何？

该建议不太可行。现代的家庭，父母一般都需要工作，而且工作的压力普遍较大，甚至还要经常加班。每周从周一到周五他们要忙于工作；周末他们自己也要休息，还要陪孩子娱乐、放松和交流。如果还要分出时间到孩子的学习上，很多父母做不到，至少非常不情愿。

（2）如果实施题目中的建议，是否会导致同初始目的相矛盾或其他荒谬的结果？

强制施行题目中的建议，会有如下弊病：第一，家长们会觉得压力过大，抱怨学校推诿教育责任，从而不予配合。第二，部分家长有可能要求更深地介入学校对其孩子的教育，从而影响学校的教学安排，造成学校和学生家长之间的冲突。第三，造成部分老师以孩子家长不配合为理由，为自己教学效果不良和学生成绩不好找借口。

（3）有无替代或折中方案？

学校作为专门的教育机构，对学生的教育（无论学业还是身心健康方面）应该承担绝大部分的责任。孩子父母至多是做一些辅助的工作，比如性格培养、情感教育、道德伦理的养成等。学校本来就是一个相对简单的小社会，那里的孩子们在学习的同时也在进行适应未来成人社会的角色训练。如果学校把家长和家庭过多地牵扯进来，实际上是学校功能的退化。

提纲提要

论点 **学校为主，家长为辅。**

正 学生的学习及受教育的过程不仅仅是在教室完成的，家长及学生所在社区的配合也很有必要。

反 但是现代家庭，父母一般都需要工作，而且工作的压力普遍较大，甚至还要经常加班。每周从周一到周五他们要忙于工作；周末他们自己也要休息，还要陪孩子娱乐、放松和交流。如果还要分出时间到孩子的学习上，很多父母做不到，至少非常不情愿。

其次，如果强制施行题目中的建议，会有如下弊病：第一，家长们会觉得压力过大，抱怨学校推诿教育责任，从而不予配合。第二，部分家长有可能要求更深地介入学校对其孩子的教育，从而影响学校的教学安排，造成学校和学生家长之间的冲突。第三，造成部分老师以孩子家长不配合为理由，为自己教学效果不良和学生成绩不好找借口。

合 学校作为专门的教育机构，对学生的教育（无论学业还是身心健康方面）应该承担绝大部分的责任。孩子父母至多是做一些辅助工作，比如性格培养、情感教育、道德伦理的养成等。学校本来就是一个相对简单的小社会，那里的孩子们在学习的同时也在进行适应未来成人社会的角色训练。如果学校把家长和家庭过多地牵扯进来，实际上是学校功能的退化。

82. Colleges and universities should require their students to spend at least one semester studying in a foreign country. (参考第97、100、124题)

Write a response in which you discuss the extent to which you agree or disagree with the recommendation and explain your reasoning for the position you take. In developing and supporting your position, describe specific circumstances in which adopting the recommendation would or would not be advantageous and explain how these examples shape your position.

题型归类 建议类。

题目分析

（1）题目中的建议可行性如何？

该建议听起来像是个好主意，但施行起来会有很多困难。首先，国外游学的费用谁来出？政府、学校、还是学生家庭？无论谁出，都是一笔极大的负担。其次，到国外学什么？各国教育制度、文化、学生的个人兴趣可谓千差万别。教育制度（如学分、学时）如何对接？不同、甚至彼此冲突的文化价值之间如何相互理解和宽容？学生的个人兴趣和学校要求之间如何协调？第三，该如何组织实施？学校统一组织还是学生个人申请？学生的个人安全如何保障，等等。

（2）如果实施题目中的建议，是否会导致同初始目的相矛盾或其他荒谬的结果？

强制实施题目中的建议，会有如下弊病：第一，鉴于政府和学校不可能全部承担这些游学费用，自费出行的学生往往会选择那些费用低、教育制度趋同、符合个人兴趣的目的国。这样的话，了解不同文化、丰富阅历、增长学术能力的国外游学目的就大打折扣。第二，分散出行的游学不能保证学生的安全。第三，一些价值不大的国外游学实际是对学生正常学习时间的侵占。

（3）有无替代或折中方案？

折中方案是：第一，此类异国游学不应是强制性的，所以没必要专门为此项活动安排一个学期的时间。第二，在校学习期间，对异国文化风情、社会制度、文化等的了解更适合通过专门的学术或政府交流渠道，将别国的学者、专家、政府官员、民间机构等请进来的方式进行。第三，真正的游学最好等到学生走出校门后，当人生阅历、生活经验和经济能力等条件适合时，结合个人兴趣和目的自行安排，这样会更现实一些。

提纲提要

论点 异国游学最好由个人在条件适合时自行安排。

正 读万卷书，行万里路。异国游学对了解不同文化、丰富阅历、增长学术能力都会很有益处。

反 但是，要求所有在读大学生抽出一个学期的时间到国外游学未必可行。首先，国外游学的费用谁来出？政府、学校、还是学生家庭？无论谁出，都是一笔极大的负担。其次，到国外学什么？各国教育制度、文化、学生的个人兴趣可谓千差万别。教育制度（如学分、学时）如何对接？不同、甚至彼此冲突的文化价值之间如何相互理解和宽容？学生的个人兴趣和学校要求之间如何协调？第三，该如何组织实施？学校统一组织还是学生个人申请？学生的个人安全如何保障，等等。

如果强制实施题目中的建议，会有如下弊病：第一，鉴于政府和学校不可能全部承担这些游学费用，自费出行的学生往往会选择那些费用低、教育制度趋同、符合个人兴趣的目的国。这样的话，了解不同文化、丰富阅历、增长学术能力的国外游学的目的就大打折扣了。第二，分散出行的游学不能保证学生的安全。第三，一些价值不大的国外游学实际是对学生正常学习时间的侵占。

合 折中方案是：第一，此类异国游学不应是强制性的，所以没必要专门为此项活动安排一个学期的时间。第二，在校学习期间，对异国文化风情、社会制度、文化等的了解更适合通过专门的学术或政府交流渠道，将别国的学者、专家、政府官员、民间机构等请进来的方式进行。第三，真正的游学最好等到学生走出校门后，当人生阅历、生活经验、经济能力等条件都适合时，结合个人兴趣和目的自行安排，这样会更现实一些。

83. Teachers' salaries should be based on the academic performance of their students. (参考第30题)

Write a response in which you discuss the extent to which you agree or disagree with the recommendation and explain your reasoning for the position you take. In developing and supporting your position, describe specific circumstances in which adopting the recommendation would or would not be advantageous and explain how these examples shape your position.

（建议类。本题的分析思路和写作提纲可完全借鉴第30题。）

84. It is no longer possible for a society to regard any living man or woman as a hero. (参考第22、44、75、122题)

Write a response in which you discuss the extent to which you agree or disagree with the claim. In developing and supporting your position, be sure to address the most compelling reasons and/or examples that could be used to challenge your position.

题型归类 事实类。

题目分析

（1）能否从公认的原则或事实中推出相反的判断?

基于下列三点，题目中的判断未必成立：

其一，任何社会在任何时候都有它最高或是最流行的价值取向，人们同时也在热切地寻找那些代表了这些价值取向的人。于是，我们的社会总不缺乏各式各样的偶像：时尚明星、行业精英、道德楷模等。

其二，我们之所以觉得偶像像天上的流星一样消逝得太快是因为：第一，在开放的社会和多元价值之下，各种偶像争相炫目登场。他们数量太多，以至于人们能够留给每一个偶像的注意力越来越少。第二，我们人性中矛盾（甚至是黑暗）的成分总使我们在期待和制造偶像的同时，也在毁灭他们。当我们突然发现某个符合我们内心渴望的人的时候，我们把他奉为偶像，为之欢呼；但很快我们就开始以万般挑剔的眼光审视他，希望发现他身上或内心的不完美。没有意外，我们发现偶像死去了。

其三，除了各种炫目光环照耀之下的偶像以外，还有一些默默无闻的偶像。他们朴实、平凡、甚至地位卑贱。但他们以其人性的力量震撼着我们的心魄。他们也是偶像，比如慈爱而富有牺牲精神的母亲、忠于职守的警察、秉持正义的法官以及众多处逆境而不自弃的人们。

（2）能否举出相反的事例？

（大家可以举出无数身边发生的例子。此处从略。）

提纲提要

论点 题目中的判断似是而非。

正 现代社会多元的价值取向、快餐式的文化消费，加之人们浮躁的心态，使得偶像像潮水一样向我们涌来，又像潮水一样无声地退去，我们怀疑这个时代是否还能够产生真正的偶像。

反 但断言 It is no longer possible for a society to regard any living man or woman as a hero 似乎不客观。其一，任何社会在任何时候都有它最高或是最流行的价值取向，人们同时也在热切地寻找那些代表了这些价值取向的人。于是，我们的社会总不缺乏各式各样的偶像：时尚明星、行业精英、道德楷模等。

其二，我们之所以觉得偶像像天上的流星一样消逝得太快是因为：第一，在开放的社会和多元价值之下，偶像争相炫目登场。他们数量太多，以至于人们能够留给每一个偶像的注意力越来越少。第二，我们人性中矛盾（甚至是黑暗）的成分总使我们在期待和制造偶像的同时，也在毁灭他们。当我们突然发现某个符合了我们内心渴望的人的时候，我们把他奉为偶像，为之欢呼；但很快我们就开始以万般挑剔的眼神审视他，希望发现他身上或内心的不完美。没有意外，我们发现偶像死去了。

反 除了各种炫目光环照耀之下的偶像以外，还有一些默默无闻的偶像。他们朴实、平凡、甚至地位卑贱。但他们人性的力量震撼着我们的心魄。他们也是偶像，比如慈爱而富有牺牲精神的母亲、忠于职守的警察、秉持正义的法官以及众多处逆境而不自弃的人们。他们普通而真实，最经得起挑剔目光的审视。

85. Some people believe that in order to thrive, a society must put its own overall success before the well-being of its individual citizens. Others believe that the well-being of a society can only be measured by the general welfare of all its people. （参考 第28、113、120、121、127、145题）

Write a response in which you discuss which view more closely aligns with your own position and explain your reasoning for the position you take. In developing and supporting your position, you should address both of the views presented.

题型归类 建议类。

题目分析

（1）题目中的建议可行性如何？

当一个社会决定要 put its own overall success before the well-being of its individual citizens，它完全可以这么做，哪怕做起来很困难，代价很大。

（2）如果实施题目中的建议，是否会导致同初始目的相矛盾或其他荒谬的结果？

　　题目中的建议实际是个假设：世界上存在独立于社会成员之外的社会利益。但事实证明这个假设很难成立。在人类历史上，几乎所有的专制和暴政都是以社会利益为堂皇的借口，而把某个特定集团或者个人利益凌驾于全体社会成员的利益之上。这正是人类历史上反复上演战争、革命和社会动荡的一个主要原因。

（3）有无替代或折中方案？

　　问题的关键不在于区分何处是社会利益、何处是个人利益。本来就不应该有这样误导性的划分。社会永远是为个体而存在的。当人们谈论社会利益的时候，目的永远是如何更好地维护个人利益。一个社会总是先有个体的福利和繁荣，然后才有整体的福利和繁荣。这个先后顺序不能颠倒。

提纲提要

论点 　社会永远是为个体而存在的。

㊣ 一个真正伟大的国家必然有强大的综合国力。而强大的综合国力不仅仅体现在统治者及少数社会精英的财富成就上，还必须具体体现在百姓的整体福利水平上。如此，这个国家才会有真正的向心力和凝聚力，才是真正的强大。

㊫ 但是，一个社会或国家不能根据所谓的群体利益就得出结论：a society must put its own overall success before the well-being of its individual citizens。该结论实际是个假设：世界上存在独立于社会成员之外的社会利益。但事实证明这个假设很难成立。在人类历史上，几乎所有的专制和暴政都是以社会利益为堂皇的借口，而把某个特定集团或者个人利益凌驾于全体社会成员的利益之上。这正是人类历史上反复上演战争、革命和社会动荡的一个主要原因。

㊢ 问题的关键不在于区分何处是社会利益、何处是个人利益。本来就不应该有这样误导性的划分。社会永远是为个体而存在的。当人们谈论社会利益的时候，目的永远是如何更好地维护个人利益。一个社会总是先有了个体的福利和繁荣，然后才有整体的福利和繁荣。这个先后顺序不能颠倒。

· ·

86. Some people believe that government officials must carry out the will of the people they serve. Others believe that officials should base their decisions on their own judgment. (参考第18、50、115题)

Write a response in which you discuss which view more closely aligns with your own position and explain your reasoning for the position you take. In developing and supporting your position, you should address both of the views presented.

题型归类 　建议类。

题目分析

（1）题目中的建议可行性如何？

　　这两个建议都不存在可行性的问题。在专制政体之下，很多政府官员都是base their decisions on their own judgment；在民主政体之下，虽然法律和制度要求官员必须carry out the will of the people they serve，但有些政府官员们总是以各种借口来逃避法律和制度对权力的约束。权力的本性就是突破约束，无限膨胀。

（2）如果实施题目中的建议，是否会导致同初始目的相矛盾或其他荒谬的结果？

上述两个建议在极端情形之下都会导致问题和灾难。主张政治家要依靠自己的判断的理由可能会有：天才领袖会给百姓带来福祉，这样处理问题速度快、效率高等等。但没有制约的个人意志如果泛滥了，会导致专制独裁和社会动荡。相反，要求官员事事都必须carry out the will of the people they serve，虽说能够保障民主权利和社会稳定，但也会带来一国的立法和行政机构之间的扯皮对抗、拖沓低效。

（3）有无替代或折中方案？

按照简单的"两害相权取其轻"的原则，一个保证官员carry out the will of the people they serve的制度无论对社会整体还是对个人都更可靠一些。这好比性格迥异的两个人做瓷器：一个人动作慢一些，效率低一些，但基本不出或者很少出差错。这样，只要多给点时间，他还是可以做出好瓷器来的。另一个人的动作很快，但有点儿毛糙，赶上他心情好，手下就很出活儿。但如果碰上他心情不爽之时，就没有多少完整的瓷器出来。

提纲提要

论点　制度可能比人更可靠。

正　如何在死板的政治制度和能干的政府官员之间把握好一个恰到好处的度，从而在最大程度上发挥两者的效率，至今仍是人类面临的一个挑战。

反　在极端情形之下，题目中的两个建议都会导致问题和灾难。主张政治家要依靠自己的判断的理由可能会有：天才领袖会给百姓带来福祉，这样处理问题速度快、效率高等等。但没有制约的个人意志如果泛滥了，会导致专制独裁和社会动荡。相反，要求官员事事都必须carry out the will of the people they serve，虽说能够保障民主权利和社会稳定，但也会带来一国的立法和行政机构之间的扯皮对抗、拖沓低效。

合　按照简单的"两害相权取其轻"的原则，一个保证官员carry out the will of the people they serve的制度无论对社会整体还是对个人都更可靠一些。这好比性格迥异的两个人做瓷器：一个人动作慢一些，效率低一些，但基本不出或者很少出差错。这样，只要多给点时间，他还是可以做出好瓷器来的。另一个人的动作很快，但有点儿毛糙，赶上他心情好，手下就很出活儿。但如果碰上他心情不爽之时，就没有多少完整的瓷器出来。一句话，一个完善的制度比人更可靠。

87. **Claim**: Any piece of information referred to as a fact should be mistrusted, since it may well be proven false in the future.

Reason: Much of the information that people assume is factual actually turns out to be inaccurate. (参考第17、42、48、68、92题)

Write a response in which you discuss the extent to which you agree or disagree with the claim and the reason on which that claim is based.

题型归类　因果类。

题目分析

（1）这个因果关系推理中的原因是否成立？

该题目的原因成立。的确有许多人起初以为有些信息是事实，但后来却发现这些信息不准确、甚至是错误的。

（2）假设这个原因成立，从它能否推出结果？

即使原因成立，说 Thus, any piece of information referred to as a "fact" should be mistrusted 也是站不住脚的。首先，论者在偷换概念。虽然许多人起初以为有些信息是事实，但后来却发现这些信息不准确、甚至是错误的，但不是所有的信息都如此。肯定还有一些准确的信息。

其次，对于不太准确的信息，人们不应对其报以不信任，而应该先看问题出在哪里，是事实本身的问题，还是其他问题，比如理论假设的问题？观察和实验的手段不足？人的错觉？等等。

其三，许多信息尽管不准确，但也是先行者可贵的积累，如果利用得好，完全可以为后来者提供方便。实际上，科学的进程就是使认识不断接近事实的过程。

提纲提要

论点 题目中的判断过于简单化。

正 现实生活中，人们经常发现曾以为是事实的信息，后来被证明是不准确和错误的。

反 即使原因成立，说 Thus, any piece of information referred to as a "fact" should be mistrusted 也是站不住脚的。首先，论者在偷换概念。虽然有许多人们起初以为是事实的信息，后来却发现是不准确、甚至是错误的，但不是所有的信息都如此。肯定还有一些准确的信息。

其次，对于不太准确的信息，人们不应对其报以不信任，而应该先看问题出在哪里，是事实本身的问题，还是其他问题，比如理论假设的问题？观察和实验的手段不足？人的错觉？等等。

反 许多信息尽管不准确，但也是先行者可贵的积累，如果利用得好，完全可以为后来者提供方便。实际上，科学的进程就是使认识不断接近事实的过程。

- -

88. **Claim**: Nations should suspend government funding for the arts when significant numbers of their citizens are hungry or unemployed.

Reason: It is inappropriate—and, perhaps, even cruel—to use public resources to fund the arts when people's basic needs are not being met. (参考第7、80题)

Write a response in which you discuss the extent to which you agree or disagree with the claim and the reason on which that claim is based.

题型归类

套叠式多角度分析题。整体是个因果类题目，但它的结果部分是个建议。

题目分析

首先，按照因果类题目类型展开分析：

（1）这个因果关系推理中的原因是否成立？

该题目的原因较为复杂，很难一概而论。其正确与否，基本可以从两个角度来看：第一，在短期和紧急事态下，人的生存需要必须优先考虑。比如，面临战争、自然灾害、严重的粮食歉收等等，这时候，公共资源应该向公众的基本生活需求倾斜。在此情况下，题目中的原因成立。第二，从长期和人的全面发展来看，将公共资源用来支持艺术是完全必要的，即便不能排除在任何时候总有一小部分社会群体需要首先满足他们的基本生存需求。就此而言，题目中的判断略显武断。

（2）假设这个原因成立，从它能否推出结果？

即使上述原因成立，结论也是推不出的。鉴于这个结果部分是个建议，我们在下面就从建议类题目的分析角度切入分析。

其次，按照建议类题目类型展开分析：

（1）题目中的建议可行性如何？

一个政府该如何支配其收入或其他公共资源，完全取决于该政府对各种事情轻重缓急的顺序安排。是否资助艺术同一个政府的财力是否雄厚没有直接关系。所以，无所谓可行不可行。

（2）如果实施题目中的建议，是否会导致同初始目的相矛盾或其他荒谬的结果？

温饱、就业和谋生的技能问题都不可谓不重要。但问题是：人可以不要精神吗？艺术的功能恰恰就是让人们从精神上认识自我。金字塔、万里长城、各种为了不朽而竖立的纪念碑、乃至一切的物质财富都可以湮灭，可那些人类为了满足精神追求而创造的艺术（音乐、美术、小说、诗歌、戏剧、舞蹈等）却可以代代传承，永不磨灭。

（3）有无替代或折中方案？

人永远是精神意义上的人。人注定要在精神和肉体之间寻找平衡。

提纲提要

论点　　人注定要在精神和肉体之间寻找平衡。

正　人所理解的一切，都因为人的生命的存在而有了意义。所以，衣食住行、就业和谋生的需要是一切的基础。在短期和紧急事态下，人的生存需要尤其需要优先考虑。比如，面临战争、自然灾害、严重的粮食歉收等等，这时候，公共资源应该向公众的基本生活需求倾斜。

反　但问题是：人可以不要精神吗？艺术的功能恰恰就是让人们从精神上认识自我。金字塔、万里长城、各种为了不朽而竖立的纪念碑、乃至一切的物质财富都可以湮灭，可那些人类为了满足精神追求而创造的艺术（音乐、美术、小说、诗歌、戏剧、舞蹈等）却可以代代传承，永不磨灭。

合　人永远是精神意义上的人。人注定要在精神和肉体之间寻找平衡。从长期和人的全面发展来看，将公共资源用来支持艺术是完全必要的，即便不能排除在任何时候总有一小部分社会群体需要首先满足他们的基本生存需求。而且，如果非要在肉体与灵魂、物质与精神之间作出抉择的话，人类选择的肯定是灵魂和精神。

---

89. **Claim**: Many problems of modern society cannot be solved by laws and the legal system.

Reason: Laws cannot change what is in people's hearts or minds.

Write a response in which you discuss the extent to which you agree or disagree with the claim and the reason on which that claim is based.

题型归类　　因果类。

题目分析

（1）这个因果关系推理中的原因是否成立？

该题目的原因未必成立。因为道德伦理和思想观念往往表现在人们的日常生活习惯中，所以难以通过立法对它们进行调节和规范，而且，执法成本比较高。法律因此会给人留下"无法改变人们的所思所想"（cannot change what is in people's hearts or minds）的印象。但这不等于说，道德伦理和思想观念是不可以通过立法来改变的。比如2003年"非典"病毒传播期间，中国部分地方出台法规禁止随地吐痰。通过对这种不良行为的约束，人们对公共卫生的思想观念发生了改变：不管他人的卫生健康而随地吐痰的习惯是自私的，不仅危害别人，也危害自己。

（2）假设这个原因成立，从它能否推出结果？

即使上述原因成立，结论也是推不出的。立法或许不直接改变/改造人性。但是，假如人们通过立法可以使社会更富有效率，因而人们的生存状态都大为改善的话，人性之恶（比如，自私、懒惰、贪婪、嫉妒，等等）至少可以被大大降低。

提纲提要

论点 题目中的判断似是而非。

正 因为道德伦理和思想观念往往表现在人们的日常生活习惯中，所以难以通过立法对它们进行调节和规范，而且，执法成本比较高。法律因此会给人留下"无法改变人们的所思所想"的印象。

反 但这不等于说，道德伦理和思想观念是不可以通过立法来改变的。比如2003年"非典"病毒传播期间，中国部分地方出台法规禁止随地吐痰。通过对这种不良行为的约束，人们对公共卫生的思想观念发生了改变：不管他人的卫生健康而随地吐痰的习惯是自私的，不仅危害别人，也危害自己。

反 即使上述原因成立，结论也是推不出的。立法或许不直接改变/改造人性。但是，假如人们通过立法可以使社会更富有效率，因而人们的生存状态都大为改善的话，人性之恶（比如，自私、懒惰、贪婪、嫉妒，等等）至少可以被大大降低。

---

90. Educators should take students' interests into account when planning the content of the courses they teach. （参考第37、40、47、58、142题）

Write a response in which you discuss the extent to which you agree or disagree with the recommendation and explain your reasoning for the position you take. In developing and supporting your position, describe specific circumstances in which adopting the recommendation would or would not be advantageous and explain how these examples shape your position.

（建议类。本题的分析思路和写作提纲可完全借鉴第40题。）

---

91. The primary goal of technological advancement should be to increase people's efficiency so that they have more leisure time. （参考第43题）

Write a response in which you discuss the extent to which you agree or disagree with the statement and explain your reasoning for the position you take. In developing and supporting your position, you should consider ways in which the statement might or might not hold true and explain how these considerations shape your position.

题型归类 单纯性定义类。整个题目围绕着技术进步的主要目标的定义展开。

题目分析

（1）题目中的定义是否抓住了问题的本质？

表面上看，科技进步可以提高人们的工作效率，节省出更多的休闲时间。但实际上人们的工作却越忙越多。互联网和移动通讯已经使人们几乎无时无刻不在工作。

（2）能否给出我自己的更为恰当的定义（恰当的定义就是能对自己的论点、论据以及所列举的现象有很好解释力的定义）？

人们追求技术进步的主要目的是为了解决物质的匮乏和精神的空虚，以消除自己在物质保障和精神生活两方面的不安全感。

提纲提要

论点 论者的观点过于表面化。

（正）表面上看，科技进步可以提高人们的工作效率，节省出更多的休闲时间。但实际上人们的工作却越忙越多。互联网和移动通讯已经使人们几乎无时无刻不在工作。

（反）人们追求技术进步的主要目的是为了解决物质的匮乏和精神的空虚，以消除自己在物质保障和精神生活两方面的不安全感。

（散）科技不能解决人类面临的一切问题。一些问题（比如，种族和文化冲突、战争、国际恐怖主义、环境污染、现代人的心态浮躁与精神空虚等）的解决并不只取决于科技进步的大小，而是取决于人类是否有足够的宽容、同情心和自我反省意识。

· ·

92. Educators should base their assessment of students' learning not on students' grasp of facts but on the ability to explain the ideas, trends, and concepts that those facts illustrate. (参考第17、42、48、68、87题)

Write a response in which you discuss the extent to which you agree or disagree with the recommendation and explain your reasoning for the position you take. In developing and supporting your position, describe specific circumstances in which adopting the recommendation would or would not be advantageous and explain how these examples shape your position.

题型归类 建议类。

题目分析

（1）题目中的建议可行性如何？

题目中的建议只是强调老师在评价学生的学习时，应当将考查的重点放在哪里，所以不存在可行与否的问题。

（2）**如果实施题目中的建议，是否会导致同初始目的相矛盾或其他荒谬的结果？**

但如果简单地实施题目中的建议会有两个问题：第一，如果没有掌握学科的基本事实，对这些事实及其相关概念和趋势的解释岂不成了无源之水、无本之木？第二，对于那些纯粹是新问题、新现象，因而没有任何与之相关的思想、趋势和概念的事实，我们是记住它们还是置之不理呢？如果置之不理，我们对于这个世界的知识还会增长吗？

（3）**有无替代或折中方案？**

对于那些已经有了相关的思想、趋势和概念的事实，我们要设法先了解这些思想、趋势和概念，以便更好地去理解那些事实；对于那些没有相关的思想、趋势和概念的事实，我们要给予高度关注，因为它们可能是将来或其他研究的重要资料。

提纲提要

论点 论者的观点过于表面化。

正 人们所处的世界，因为有了我们人类所赋予的特定解释而有了意义。仅仅是孤立、零碎的事实并不能告诉我们这些事实所代表的涵义，但在只要了解了与那些事实相关的思想、趋势和概念之后，它们一下子就会变得丰富而有趣了。

反 但是，如果简单地实施题目中的建议会有两个问题：第一，如果没有掌握学科的基本事实，对这些事实及其相关概念和趋势的解释岂不成了无源之水、无本之木？第二，对于那些纯粹是新问题、新现象，因而没有任何与之相关的思想、趋势和概念的事实，我们是记住它们还是置之不理呢？如果置之不理，我们关于这个世界的知识还会增长吗？

合 对于那些已经有了相关的思想、趋势和概念的事实，我们要设法先了解这些思想、趋势和概念，以便更好地去理解那些事实；对于那些没有相关的思想、趋势和概念的事实，我们也要给予高度关注，因为它们可能是将来或其他研究的重要资料。

---

93. Unfortunately, in contemporary society, creating an appealing image has become more important than the reality or truth behind that image.

Write a response in which you discuss the extent to which you agree or disagree with the statement and explain your reasoning for the position you take. In developing and supporting your position, you should consider ways in which the statement might or might not hold true and explain how these considerations shape your position.

题型归类
单纯性是非类。

题目分析

（1）**这种价值判断的标准是什么？**

当人们说，在当今社会，极富魅力的外在形象比形象背后的真实更为重要时，人们运用的可能是这样的标准：好的形象容易让人接受形象背后的真实。

（2）**这种价值判断的标准是否值得修正？**

但是对于不同的人，好形象所满足的目的其实很不一样：对于诚实的人来说，好形象容易让人接受形象背后同样有价值的现实和真理；而对于骗子和撒谎者来说，好形象只不过有利于掩盖虚假和骗局。所以，如果考虑到运用好的形象所要达到的不同目的，没有人会简单地说，极富魅力的外在形象总是比形象背后的真实更为重要。

提纲提要

论点 外在形象不等于谎言和欺骗。

(正) 极富魅力的外在形象有时的确比形象背后的真实更重要。这是因为，好的形象容易让人接受形象背后的真实。

(反) 但是对于不同的人，好形象所满足的目的其实很不一样：对于诚实的人来说，好形象容易让人接受形象背后同样有价值的真实；而对于骗子和撒谎者来说，好形象只不过有利于掩盖虚假和骗局。所以，如果考虑到运用好的形象所要达到的不同目的，没有人会简单地说，极富魅力的外在形象总是比形象背后的真实更为重要。

(反) 对任何价值体系而言，外在形象不可能比形象背后的真实更为重要。因为，这无异于鼓励谎言和欺骗。

---

94. The effectiveness of a country's leaders is best measured by examining the well-being of that country's citizens. (参考第8、16、62、69、114、123、128题)

Write a response in which you discuss the extent to which you agree or disagree with the claim. In developing and supporting your position, be sure to address the most compelling reasons and/or examples that could be used to challenge your position.

题型归类 单纯性是非类。

题目分析

（1）这种价值判断的标准是什么？

到底是"国富民强"还是"民富国强"？国家和人民在财富分配这个问题上，哪个应该优先？题目中的判断显然倾向于人民优先的标准。说到底，国家和政府存在的意义在于为国民谋福利。如果国家的利益总是居于国民之上，甚至与民争利、损民利国，那么这个国家就异化为国民的对立面。所以，领导国家为民谋福利应当是对领袖的基本要求。

（2）这种价值判断的标准是否值得修正？

但是，将一国领袖的价值和功能仅仅用该国国民的福利来衡量，又有失于偏颇。下列要素对国民来说同样很有价值：足以自卫的国防能力、廉洁高效低成本的政府、国民高度认同的社会价值和伦理规范、高素质的国民和高水平的公共教育、巨大的社会凝聚力和向心力、便利的公共设施等等。真正有效的判断标准应该是上述各要素的综合。

提纲提要

论点 论者的观点略失于简单。

(正) 说到底，国家和政府存在的意义在于为国民谋福利。如果国家的利益总是居于国民之上，甚至与民争利、损民利国，那么，这个国家就异化为国民的对立面，而不是国民所创设的、为国民服务的政治机构了。

(反) 但是，将一国领袖的价值和功能仅仅用该国国民的福利来衡量，又有失于偏颇。下列要素对国民来说同样很有价值：足以自卫的国防能力、廉洁高效低成本的政府、国民高度认同的社会价值和伦理规范、高素质的国民和高水平的公共教育、巨大的社会凝聚力和向心力、便利的公共设施等等。真正有效的判断标准应该是上述各要素的综合。

⊗ 优秀的国家领袖必须是有着强烈的责任感和使命感、超凡的政治智慧和领袖魅力、忠诚于其所服务的选民并为后者高度信赖的政治家。这样的政治家必然既是诚实的，又是灵活和富有智慧的。可惜这样的领袖可遇而不可求。

---

95. All parents should be required to volunteer time to their children's schools. (参考第81题)

Write a response in which you discuss the extent to which you agree or disagree with the claim. In developing and supporting your position, be sure to address the most compelling reasons and/or examples that could be used to challenge your position.

（建议类。本题的分析思路和写作提纲可完全借鉴第81题。）

---

96. A nation should require all of its students to study the same national curriculum until they enter college. (参考第6、14、116题)

Write a response in which you discuss the extent to which you agree or disagree with the claim. In developing and supporting your position, be sure to address the most compelling reasons and/or examples that could be used to challenge your position.

（建议类。本题目的分析思路和写作提纲可完全借鉴第6题。）

---

97. Colleges and universities should require their students to spend at least one semester studying in a foreign country. (参考第82、100、124题)

Write a response in which you discuss the extent to which you agree or disagree with the claim. In developing and supporting your position, be sure to address the most compelling reasons and/or examples that could be used to challenge your position.

（建议类。本题的分析思路和写作提纲可完全借鉴第82题。）

---

98. Educational institutions should actively encourage their students to choose fields of study in which jobs are plentiful. (参考第3、13、15、20、32、35、39、46、129、135、136、137、140题)

Write a response in which you discuss your views on the policy and explain your reasoning for the position you take. In developing and supporting your position, you should consider the possible consequences of implementing the policy and explain how these consequences shape your position.

题型归类 建议类。

题目分析

（1）题目中的建议可行性如何?

题目中的建议未必可行。这是因为在社会分工高度精细化、职业调整越来越频繁的今天，人们基本无法准确预知某个专业或行业未来三年或五年的职业前景。

（2）如果实施题目中的建议，是否会导致同初始目的相矛盾或其他荒谬的结果?

如果施行题目中的建议，其所导致的弊端至少有四点：第一，几乎所有的人都涌向为数不多看似"钱"景无限的职业。基于大家彼此大致相同的认知能力、现有信息的有限性和未来的不可知性，这几乎是一个必然的结果。这一点，我们从一轮又一轮的计算机热、法律热、金融热、房地产热、MBA热，当然还包括当下最具中国特色的公务员热，都看得非常清楚。其结果只能是这些曾经的热门职业和行业很快出现人力资源供给的过剩、整体收入下降、相当部分人被迫改行。第二，如果上述第一个结果成立，这随后的结果就是，对个人而言，是教育投入的失败；对学校而言，学生毕业即失业会影响学校的教育声望；对国家而言，是国民财富的浪费。第三，会使得一个国家新兴的产业所需要的人力资源得不到及时的补充，影响该国产业结构的转移和提升。这是因为一个国家教育机构的人才产出能力在中短期内是基本恒定的。当人才大量涌向几个看似"热门"的行业时，其他行业的人才供给必然相应减少。第四，如果学生将自己的学习和研究领域仅仅用就业的前景框限起来，就个人而言，人生失去了很多发展自己爱好和天分的乐趣；就社会而言，则很有可能因为特立独行、才华横溢之才的淹没而损失了创新精神与活力。

（3）有无替代或折中方案?

在大学研究生以下的教育阶段，大学生应该更多的将个人兴趣和天分作为自己专业方向的参考。兴趣是最好的老师，它往往能引导我们找到最适合自己的职业和事业。而且，在四年本科结束后，最好先工作两三年。通过工作，可以尝试发现最适合自己的职业方向。实际上，现代社会人的寿命普遍较长，其黄金工作年龄可以一直延长到65岁甚至更晚些。所以，年轻人在35岁之前可以有许多尝试和发现自己职业生涯的机会。过早确立事业方向反而不利于发现自己的潜能。

提纲提要

论点 生活的过程就是理想与现实间的平衡。

正 教育是人们对未来进行的时间和金钱的投资。通过找到一份自己喜欢同时又有很好收入的工作，是对大学教育投入的收获。所以，在选择学习专业时，也考虑该专业未来的职业前景是再自然不过的想法。

反 但是，把大学教育同未来的就业前景做简单的对接会面临以下问题：

首先，并不是所有专业的职业前景都可以被清晰地勾画出来。这是因为在社会分工高度精细化、职业调整越来越频繁的今天，人们基本无法准确预知某个专业或行业未来三年或五年的职业前景。

其次，如果人人都把大学的专业学习当作未来就业的预备的话，还会出现如下弊病：第一，几乎所有的人都涌向为数不多看似"钱"景无限的职业。基于大家彼此大致相同的认知能力、现有信息的有限性和未来的不可知性，这几乎是一个必然的结果。这一点，我们从一轮又一轮的计算机热、法律热、金融热、房地产热、MBA热，当然还包括当下最具中国特色的公务员热，都看得非常清楚。其结果只能是这些曾经的热门职业和行业很快出现人力资源供给的过剩、整体收入下降、相当部分人被迫改行。第二，如果上述第一个结果成立，这随后的结果就是，对个人而言，是教育投入的失败；对学校而言，学生毕业即失业会影响学校的教育声望；对国家而言，是国民财富的浪费。第三，会使得一个国家新兴的产业所需要的人力资源得不到及时的补充，影响该国产业结构的转移和提升。这是因为一个国家教育机构的人才产出能力在中短期内是基本恒定的。当人才大量涌向几个看似"热门"的行业时，其他行业的人才供给必然相应减少。第四，如果学生将自己的学习和研究领域仅仅用就业的前景框限起来，就个人而言，人生失去了很多发展自己爱好和天分的乐趣；就社会而言，则很有可能因为特立独行、才华横溢之才的淹没而损失了创新精神与活力。

🔑 可能的折中方案：在大学研究生以下的教育阶段，大学生应该更多的将个人兴趣和天分作为自己专业方向的参考。兴趣是最好的老师，它往往能引导我们找到最适合自己的职业和事业。而且，在四年本科结束后，最好先工作两三年。通过工作，可以尝试发现最适合自己的职业方向。实际上，现代社会人的寿命普遍较长，其黄金工作年龄可以一直延长到65岁甚至更晚些。所以，年轻人在35岁之前可以有许多尝试和发现自己职业生涯的机会。过早确立事业方向反而不利于发现自己的潜能。

---

99. People's behavior is largely determined by forces not of their own making. (参考第11题)

Write a response in which you discuss the extent to which you agree or disagree with the claim. In developing and supporting your position, be sure to address the most compelling reasons and/or examples that could be used to challenge your position.

（事实类。本题的分析思路和写作提纲可完全借鉴第11题。）

---

100. Colleges and universities should require their students to spend at least one semester studying in a foreign country. (参考第82、97、124题)

Write a response in which you discuss your views on the policy and explain your reasoning for the position you take. In developing and supporting your position, you should consider the possible consequences of implementing the policy and explain how these consequences shape your position.

（建议类。本题的分析思路和写作提纲可完全借鉴第82题。）

---

101. Although innovations such as video, computers, and the Internet seem to offer schools improved methods for instructing students, these technologies all too often distract from real learning.

Write a response in which you discuss the extent to which you agree or disagree with the statement and explain your reasoning for the position you take. In developing and supporting your position, you should consider ways in which the statement might or might not hold true and explain how these considerations shape your position.

题型归类 该题可同时归入事实类和结合式定义类，因为要对题目中的关键概念real learning的含义进行明确界定。

题目分析

（1）能否从公认的原则或事实中推出相反的判断？

基于下列两点原则，题目中的判断未必成立：

其一，如果real learning指的是健全人格的培养、知识的传播以及职业技能的培训，那么电脑、互联网等新型科技都能够完成或帮助完成这些目标。据此，上述技术创新all too often distract from real learning的判断没有根据。

其二，计算机的普及、互联网的迅速发展和数字时代的到来，已经并将继续对教育和学习的方式带来全新的变革。而题目中，论者似乎还在用旧的教育模式来看待现在的教育变化。

（2）能否举出相反的事例？

（大家可以举出无数身边发生的例子。此处从略。）

提纲提要

论点 论者似乎还在用旧的教育模式来看待数字时代教育的变化。

正 现代信息技术的确带来了一些负面的结果，比如，大量无用、甚至有害信息的泛滥，青少年沉迷于网络游戏等。

反 但实际上，如果real learning指的是健全人格的培养、知识的传播以及职业技能的培训，电脑、互联网等新型科技都能够完成或帮助完成这些目标。据此，上述技术创新all too often distract from real learning的判断没有根据。

反 计算机的普及、互联网的迅速发展和数字时代的到来，已经并将继续对教育和学习的方式带来全新的变革。而题目中，论者似乎还在用旧的教育模式来看待现在的教育变化。

---

102. Universities should require every student to take a variety of courses outside the student's field of study. （参考第13、46、70、112题）

Write a response in which you discuss your views on the policy and explain your reasoning for the position you take. In developing and supporting your position, you should consider the possible consequences of implementing the policy and explain how these consequences shape your position.

（建议类。本题的分析思路和写作提纲可完全借鉴第13题。）

---

103. The best ideas arise from a passionate interest in commonplace things.

Write a response in which you discuss the extent to which you agree or disagree with the statement and explain your reasoning for the position you take. In developing and supporting your position, you should consider ways in which the statement might or might not hold true and explain how these considerations shape your position.

题型归类 事实类。

题目分析

（1）能否从公认的原则或事实中推出相反的判断?

基于下列三点原则，题目中的判断未必成立:

其一，任何人的浓厚兴趣（passionate interest）持续的时间总是有限的。激情如火（Passion is like a fire），不可能永远燃烧。如果驾驭不当，会伤人，因此说浓厚兴趣有时会有负面结果。每个沉迷于网络游戏的青少年对那些游戏都充满浓厚兴趣，但他们除了在浪费时间外，好像没有其他收获。

其二，当人们强调激情在科学发现中的作用时，只是看到了表象。真正让人类有所发现的是好奇心和求知欲。人类天生具有好奇心，当这种好奇心和求知欲持续不停地推动人类去探索时，我们就会表现出浓厚兴趣。

其三，无论是浓厚兴趣还是好奇心和求知欲都不能让我们获得思想。我们还必须具备敏锐的观察力和正确的思考方式。否则，我们依旧不会获得思想。

（2）能否举出相反的事例?

（大家可以举出无数身边发生的例子。此处从略。）

提纲提要

论点 **论者很可能只看到了问题的表象。**

正 当我们怀着巨大的热情和兴趣去做事情时，往往会有令人意想不到的结果和发现。激情会给艺术家带来创意，为作家找到灵感，为逆境中拼搏的人点亮希望，为平淡的生活增添色彩。

反 但断言思想来自人们对普通事物的浓厚兴趣只看到了问题的表象。这是因为:

其一，任何人的浓厚兴趣持续的时间总是有限的。如火的激情不可能永远燃烧。如果驾驭不当，正如同火会伤人，浓厚兴趣有时会有负面结果。每个沉迷于网络游戏的青少年对那些游戏都充满浓厚兴趣，但他们除了在浪费时间外，好像没有其他收获。

其二，当人们强调激情在科学发现中的作用时，很可能只看到了表象。真正让人类有所发现的是好奇心和求知欲。人类天生具有好奇心，当这种好奇心和求知欲持续不停地推动人类去探索时，我们就会表现出浓厚兴趣。

其三，无论是浓厚兴趣还是好奇心和求知欲都不能让我们获得思想。我们还必须具备敏锐的观察力和正确的思考方式。否则，我们依旧不会获得思想。

合 人是激情和理性的综合体。激情给生命带来色彩和活力，理性为人生标注方向、打造质感。

· ·

104. To be an effective leader, a public official must maintain the highest ethical and moral standards. (参考第107题)

Write a response in which you discuss the extent to which you agree or disagree with the claim. In developing and supporting your position, be sure to address the most compelling reasons and/or examples that could be used to challenge your position.

题型归类 建议类。

题目分析

（1）题目中的建议可行性如何？

建议不可行。建议实际在用对神的标准来要求人，势必造成人性的虚伪和人格的扭曲。

（2）如果实施题目中的建议，是否会导致同初始目的相矛盾或其他荒谬的结果？

用最高的伦理和道德标准（the highest ethical and moral standards）要求政治领袖，除了会扭曲他们的人格以外，还鼓励公众对政治领袖的苛责和不宽容，这反而不利于他们发挥才干。

（3）有无替代或折中方案？

公众应将关注的重点放在考察政治领袖的能力与才干上，而不是苛责他们是否是道德模范。毕竟，人都有其平常的一面。

提纲提要

论点 公众应将关注的重点放在政治领袖的能力与才干上，而不是伦理上的苛责。

正 当然，一个诚实而可信的政治领袖可以增进社会的福利。选民不可能让骗子和伪君子当他们的领袖。

反 用最高的伦理和道德标准要求政治领袖，除了会扭曲他们的人格以外，还鼓励公众对政治领袖的苛责和不宽容，这反而不利于他们发挥才干。

合 公众应将关注的重点放在考察政治领袖的能力与才干上，而不是苛责他们是否是道德模范。毕竟，人都有其平常的一面。

---

105. **Claim**: Imagination is a more valuable asset than experience.

Reason: People who lack experience are free to imagine what is possible without the constraints of established habits and attitudes. （参考第106、126题）

Write a response in which you discuss the extent to which you agree or disagree with the claim and the reason on which that claim is based.

题型归类 因果类（其结果处是个价值判断，有兴趣的读者可以作进一步的分析）。

题目分析

（1）这个因果关系推理中的原因是否成立？

该题目的原因成立。没有经验的人好像也只能依靠自己的想象力了。

（2）假设这个原因成立，从它能否推出结果？

即使上述原因成立，结论也是推不出的。首先，仅有想象力未必就能发现解决问题的办法。其次，当一个人运用想象力的时候，他不可能完全脱离以往的经验。想象力必定以经验为基础，即便有时这些经验未必是直接经验。没有任何经验基础的想象力纯粹是空想。所以相对于想象力，经验仍然起着更为根本的作用。

提纲提要

论点 题目中的判断过于简单化。

正 有时，想象力的确有打破陈规旧俗的作用。

反 但是，首先，仅有想象力未必就能发现解决问题的办法。其次，当一个人运用想象力的时候，他不可能完全脱离以往的经验。想象力必定以经验为基础，即便有时这些经验未必是直接经验。没有任何经验基础的想象力纯粹是空想。所以相对于想象力，经验仍然起着更为根本的作用。

合 经验和想象力都很重要。关键是要立足于经验，但不囿于经验；善于想象，但不流入空想。

---

106. In most professions and academic fields, imagination is more important than knowledge. (参考第105、126题)

Write a response in which you discuss the extent to which you agree or disagree with the statement and explain your reasoning for the position you take. In developing and supporting your position, you should consider ways in which the statement might or might not hold true and explain how these considerations shape your position.

题型归类 单纯性是非类。

题目分析

（1）这种价值判断的标准是什么？

想象力可以打破头脑中既定的习惯和观念的约束，而单纯的书本知识有时反而会禁锢人们的思想。所以想象力有时会比书本知识更容易激发人的创造力。

（2）这种价值判断的标准是否值得修正？

但是，知识具有延续性和继承性。因为没有或只有很少的基础知识，想象力难免流入空想，创造力也因此大打折扣。

提纲提要

论点 **有时相信知识，反倒不如相信我们的直觉和想象力。**

正 想象力可以打破头脑中既定的习惯和观念的约束，而单纯的书本知识有时反而会禁锢人们的思想。所以想象力有时会比书本知识更容易激发人的创造力。

反 但是，知识具有延续性和继承性。因为没有或只有很少的基础知识，想象力难免流入空想，创造力也因此大打折扣。

散 人类已有的知识只不过是关于对我们周围世界的解释。正确与否、有没有用，都值得怀疑，必须留待以后作进一步的证实。所以，有时相信知识，反倒不如相信我们的直觉和想象力。

---

107. To be an effective leader, a public official must maintain the highest ethical and moral standards. (参考第104题)

Write a response in which you discuss the extent to which you agree or disagree with the statement and explain your reasoning for the position you take. In developing and supporting your position, you should consider ways in which the statement might or might not hold true and explain how these considerations shape your position.

（建议类。本题的分析思路和写作提纲可完全借鉴第104题。）

108. Critical judgment of work in any given field has little value unless it comes from someone who is an expert in that field. (参考第 27、110、139 题)

Write a response in which you discuss the extent to which you agree or disagree with the statement and explain your reasoning for the position you take. In developing and supporting your position, you should consider ways in which the statement might or might not hold true and explain how these considerations shape your position.

题型归类 事实类。

题目分析

（1）能否从公认的原则或事实中推出相反的判断？

基于下列三点原则，题目中的判断未必成立：

其一，人类感知能力是有限的。我们的视觉、听觉和触觉提供给我们的世界的面貌只是这个世界极小、极有限的一部分。

其二，人们对世界的感知具有主观选择性。大家可能更愿意知道自己想知道的、更相信自己愿意相信的事情。

其三，专家也是人，理性方面也有不足，所不同的仅在于程度而已。专家未必垄断真理。

（2）能否举出相反的事例？

（大家可以举出无数身边发生的例子。此处从略。）

提纲提要

论点 **专家未必垄断真理。**

正 因为专家对某一领域有深入而全面的研究，所以他们的意见一般具有较高的参考价值。

反 但首先，人类的感知能力是有限的。我们的视觉、听觉和触觉提供给我们的世界的面貌只是这个世界极小、极有限的一部分。其次，人们对世界的感知具有主观选择性。大家可能更愿意知道自己想知道的、更相信自己愿意相信的事情。其三，专家也是人，理性方面也有不足，所不同的仅在于程度而已。专家未必垄断真理。

微 有时，相信专家不如相信常识。

109. Some people believe that scientific discoveries have given us a much better understanding of the world around us. Others believe that science has revealed to us that the world is infinitely more complex than we ever realized. (参考第 33、57、74、133、134 题)

Write a response in which you discuss which view more closely aligns with your own position and explain your reasoning for the position you take. In developing and supporting your position, you should address both of the views presented.

题型归类 事实类。

题目分析

对于该题目的分析，"更好的了解"（better understanding）的判断标准是必须要讨论的，否则，根本无法说清楚何为"更好的了解"。这个标准我们可以自己界定，比如，第一，科学是否为人类提供了关于这个世界的更详细的信息？第二，科学是否为人类提供了征服大自然的更有力的武器？等等。而笔者所给出的判定标准是：科学是否能使人类更接近真实。在这个判定标准明确之后，可有如下的分析：

（1）能否从公认的原则或事实中推出相反的判断？

基于下列两点原则，题目中的判断未必成立：

其一，每一次重大的科学发现在经过反复验证之后，总能使人类更进一步接近事实，从而使得我们对周围的世界有更深的理解。但有时，科学发现所提供的事实又是相互矛盾的，或者一时间无法用既有的科学理论加以解释。这些相互矛盾和无法解释的事实动摇或者打破了我们对某一问题、学科的原有概念，同时新的令人信服的概念又无从得出。这时候，我们会发现，科学发现似乎使我们远离了真相。比如，最近出现的"超级病毒"。这些几乎可以抵抗任何人类已知抗生素的病毒据说正是因为临床对抗生素的滥用所引发的。那么，人类的困惑就是：到底该不该使用抗生素？该如何使用？抗生素使人类更健康了还是更脆弱了？

其二，每当科学发现相互矛盾或者有些事实无法解释时，科学给人们的印象是：它使这个世界更加复杂、无序和混乱。但当所有看似矛盾的现象得到了证实，当又有了新的理论能解释已知现象的时候，人们会用新的视角观察和思考这个世界。还用"超级病毒"作例子。最终人类肯定能找到对付它的办法。因为到目前为止，人类还从来没有被任何病毒彻底消灭过。科学发现带来的破碎感、无序感和复杂感，最终只能由科学进步去修复和简化。

（2）能否举出相反的事例？

（大家可以举出无数身边发生的例子。此处从略。）

提纲提要

论点 **科学和理性有时不可靠，但人类迄今为止还没有更好的替代办法。**

正 每一次重大的科学发现在经过反复验证之后，总能使人类更进一步接近事实，从而使得我们对周围的世界有更深的理解。

反 但有时，科学发现所提供的事实又是相互矛盾的，或者一时间无法用既有的科学理论加以解释。这些相互矛盾和无法解释的事实动摇或者打破了我们对某一问题、学科的原有概念，同时新的令人信服的概念又无从得出。这时候，我们会发现，科学发现似乎使我们远离了真相。比如，最近出现的"超级病毒"。这些几乎可以抵抗任何人类已知抗生素的病毒据说正是因为临床对抗生素的滥用所引发的。那么，人类的困惑就是：到底该不该使用抗生素？该如何使用？抗生素使得人类更健康了还是更脆弱了？

并且，每当科学发现相互矛盾或者有些事实无法解释时，科学给人们的印象是：它使这个世界更加复杂、无序和混乱。但当所有看似矛盾的现象得到了证实，当新的理论又能解释已知现象的时候，人们会用新的视角观察和思考这个世界。还用"超级病毒"作例子。最终人类肯定能找到对付它的办法。因为到目前为止，人类还从来没有被任何病毒彻底消灭过。科学发现带来的破碎感、无序感和复杂感，最终只能由科学进步修复和简化。

散 科学和理性有时都不可靠，但人类迄今为止还没有找到更好的替代办法。相对我们面对的世界，人类其实非常渺小。科学只是人类的理性之手所擎起的一只小小的蜡烛。烛光所及之外，我们还只能小心翼翼地摸索和猜测。带着谦卑和敬畏，我们或许走得更远，而骄傲和自负只会将我们引入黑暗。

....

110. Critical judgment of work in any given field has little value unless it comes from someone who is an expert in that field. (参考第27、108、139题)

Write a response in which you discuss the extent to which you agree or disagree with the claim. In developing and supporting your position, be sure to address the most compelling reasons and/or examples that could be used to challenge your position.

（事实类。本题的分析思路和写作提纲可完全借鉴第108题。）

....

111. In any profession—business, politics, education, government—those in power should step down after five years. (参考第8、149题)

Write a response in which you discuss the extent to which you agree or disagree with the claim. In developing and supporting your position, be sure to address the most compelling reasons and/or examples that could be used to challenge your position.

题型归类 建议类。

题目分析

（1）题目中的建议可行性如何？

题目中的建议只是个固定任期制而已，当然可行。

（2）如果实施题目中的建议，是否会导致同初始目的相矛盾或其他荒谬的结果？

僵化地实施五年任期制会导致如下问题：第一，领导层五年一换并非适合所有的领域和工作。比如，私营企业的老板、家族企业的董事长，企业是他们的私人财产，让他们五年就下台既不合情理，现实生活中也极为罕见。第二，即便是民主国家的政府领导人也未必非得五年一轮换。频繁更换政府首脑会导致政策的大起大落，一些关乎国家重大利益的长期规划无法实施；并且，政府首脑的频繁更换还会给党派斗争、政坛动荡留下空隙。

（3）有无替代或折中方案？

折中方案：首先，不同领域应当区别对待。其次，如果领导层任期较长，可以考虑别的辅助政策以保持领导层的生机与活力，比如，对领导层定期轮训、加强对领导层的监督与制衡等。

提纲提要

论点 题目中的观点失于简单。

正 领导层的固定任期制对保持领导层的生机与活力，提高企业的竞争力，保证政党和政府领导人的廉洁与效率很有益处。

反 但是，僵化地实施五年任期制会导致如下问题：第一，领导层五年一换并非适合所有的领域和工作。比如，私营企业的老板、家族企业的董事长，企业是他们的私人财产。让他们五年就下台既不合情理，现实生活中也极为罕见。第二，即便是民主国家的政府领导人也未必非得五年一轮换。频繁更换政府首脑会导致政策的大起大落，一些关乎国家重大利益的长期规划无法实施；并且，政府首脑的频繁更换还会给党派斗争、政坛动荡留下空隙。

⊜ 折中方案：首先，不同领域应当区别对待。企业和学校的做法应区别于政党和政府的做法。其次，如果领导层任期较长，可以考虑别的辅助政策以保持领导层的生机与活力，比如，对领导层定期轮训、加强对领导层的监督与制衡等。

112. Requiring university students to take a variety of courses outside their major fields of study is the best way to ensure that students become truly educated. (参考第22、24、29、52、70、77、122、123题；同时还可以参考第13、46、102题。)

Write a response in which you discuss the extent to which you agree or disagree with the statement and explain your reasoning for the position you take. In developing and supporting your position, you should consider ways in which the statement might or might not hold true and explain how these considerations shape your position.

题型归类 单纯性是非类。

题目分析

（1）这种价值判断的标准是什么？

题目中论者认为让学生研读专业以外的课程是让学生获得真正的教育的最好办法。这里的判断标准显然是——博学。

（2）这种价值判断的标准是否值得修正？

但是，将博学当作良好教育的标准显然是有问题的。从功能上讲，博学仅仅指吸收知识，在当今电脑科技高度发达的时代，一个人无论多么博闻强记，终究抵不过一台普通的电脑。所以，知识的输出，也就是知识的加工和再创造，远比博闻强记要有价值。

最终判断一个人的教育是否成功只有两个缺一不可的标准：第一，他是否掌握了科学的思维方式。有了它，学生才能够独立进行理性和批判的思考。第二，他是否通过独立的思考获得了他人生的价值和信仰。有了它们，一个人才会发现生命的方向和意义。

提纲提要

论点 题目中的判断似是而非。

正 各门各科的知识是相互贯通的。广博的知识面有利于人们多角度地思考和解决问题。

反 但是，将博学当作良好教育的标准显然是有问题的。从功能上讲，博学仅仅指吸收知识，在当今电脑科技高度发达的时代，一个人无论多么博闻强记，终究抵不过一台普通的电脑。所以，知识的输出，也就是知识的加工和再创造，远比博闻强记要有价值。

最终判断一个人的教育是否成功只有两个缺一不可的标准：第一，他是否掌握了科学的思维方式。有了它，学生才能够独立进行理性和批判的思考。第二，他是否通过独立的思考获得了他人生的价值和信仰。有了它们，一个人才会发现生命的方向和意义。

⊜ 教育的终极目的是对人心智和灵魂的解放（The purpose of education is to free the mind and the spirit）。博览群书、博闻强记都仅仅是手段而已，其本身并非教育的目的。

113. **Claim**: The surest indicator of a great nation is not the achievements of its rulers, artists, or scientists.

Reason: The surest indicator of a great nation is actually the welfare of all its people. (参考第 28、85、120、121、127、145 题)

Write a response in which you discuss the extent to which you agree or disagree with the claim and the reason on which that claim is based.

题型归类 因果类。

题目分析

（1）这个因果关系推理中的原因是否成立?

该题目的原因似乎成立。

（2）假设这个原因成立，从它能否推出结果?

即使上述原因成立，结论也是推不出的。在现代意义上的国家和政府出现以前，国家和政府与百姓的关系不是现在这种对等、服务型的关系，而是统治和被统治、主宰者和臣民的关系。那时，一个强大的帝国未必体现为百姓的福利，而多表现为君主的武功和战绩以及依附于帝王将相的艺术家和文人的成就。他们也都为人类创造了灿烂的文明。

提纲提要

论点 **论者的观点失于简单。**

正 一个真正伟大的国家必然拥有强大的综合国力。而强大的综合国力不仅仅体现在统治者及少数社会精英（如艺术家、科学家等）的成就上，还必须具体体现在百姓的整体福利水平上。如此，这个国家才会有真正的向心力和凝聚力，才是真正的强大。

反 但是，在现代意义上的国家和政府出现以前，国家和政府与百姓的关系不是现在这种对等、服务型的关系；而是统治和被统治、主宰者和臣民的关系。那时，一个强大的帝国未必体现为百姓的福利，而多表现为君主的武功和战绩以及依附于帝王将相的艺术家和文人的成就。他们也都为人类创造了灿烂的文明。

散 国家形态从一家一姓的王朝帝国到今天的公民社会和民主政体体现了国家和社会对个体越来越多的关注。在现代意义上，一个真正伟大的国家应该是人的个性和自由得到最充分发展和保障的国家。

114. Any leader who is quickly and easily influenced by shifts in popular opinion will accomplish little. (参考第 8、16、62、69、94、123、128、147 题)

Write a response in which you discuss the extent to which you agree or disagree with the statement and explain your reasoning for the position you take. In developing and supporting your position, you should consider ways in which the statement might or might not hold true and explain how these considerations shape your position.

题型归类 事实类。

题目分析

（1）能否从公认的原则或事实中推出相反的判断？

基于下列两点原则，题目中的判断未必成立：

其一，世上无人是万能的。领导和领袖也不例外。作为领导或领袖，他们最重要的素质是判断力。当面临多种意见、各种纷乱的信息时，能迅速识别信息，作出正确决断，这种能力才是最重要的。

其二，领导和领袖面对的形势和局面往往非常复杂。所以他们必须要审时度势，因时因事而变。领袖善于见微知著、广纳群言、因时因势而权变的素质也同样重要。

（2）能否举出相反的事例？

（大家可以举出历史上的史料以及无数身边发生的例子。此处从略。）

提纲提要

论点 领袖不仅要善于坚持，还要善于因时因势而权变。

正 坚持既定的原则和目标是领袖的必要素质。

人们从领袖那里渴望得到的是明确的目标、坚定的信念和对未来的信心。这一方面是因为领袖的能力和魅力；另一方面是因为面临复杂的局势和压力，人们本能地会动摇，这时，领袖的坚定、沉着和执著就尤为重要。

反 但不能据此说，Any leader who is quickly and easily influenced by shifts in popular opinion will accomplish little。这是因为：

其一，世上无人是万能的。领导和领袖也不例外。作为领导或领袖，他们最重要的素质是判断力。当面临多种意见、各种纷乱的信息时，能迅速识别信息，作出正确决断，这种能力才是最为重要的。

其二，领导和领袖面对的形势和局面往往非常复杂。所以他们必须要审时度势，因时因事而变。领袖善于见微知著、广纳群言、因时因势而权变的素质也同样重要。

合 一个真正胜任的领袖应当兼备以上两种素质，既能恪守原则和目标，又能因时因势而变。他在任何时候都知道该做什么、如何去做，从而领导民众不断走向成功。

---

115. Government officials should rely on their own judgment rather than unquestioningly carry out the will of the people whom they serve. (参考第18、50、86题)

Write a response in which you discuss the extent to which you agree or disagree with the statement and explain your reasoning for the position you take. In developing and supporting your position, you should consider ways in which the statement might or might not hold true and explain how these considerations shape your position.

（建议类。本题的分析思路和写作提纲可完全借鉴第50题。）

116. A nation should require all of its students to study the same national curriculum until they enter college. (参考第6、14、96题)

Write a response in which you discuss the extent to which you agree or disagree with the statement and explain your reasoning for the position you take. In developing and supporting your position, you should consider ways in which the statement might or might not hold true and explain how these considerations shape your position.

（建议类。本题目的分析思路和写作提纲可完全借鉴第6题。）

117. It is primarily in cities that a nation's cultural traditions are generated and preserved. (参考第2、5题)

Write a response in which you discuss the extent to which you agree or disagree with the statement and explain your reasoning for the position you take. In developing and supporting your position, you should consider ways in which the statement might or might not hold true and explain how these considerations shape your position.

题型归类 事实类。

题目分析

（1）能否从公认的原则或事实中推出相反的判断？

基于下列两点原则，题目中的判断未必成立：

其一，城市和农村对一个国家的文化传统都是有贡献的。毕竟，一国的文化是个整体，不应只包括城市文化。

其二，由于城市是各种文化和价值交汇、冲撞和相互影响的地方，其文化特点更多体现在开放、包容、多元和变迁。而农村，因为其经济结构较为单一，较少变化，人们的价值观念和生活方式相对更为保守和稳定，所以反而会产生并保持一国的文化传统。

（2）能否举出相反的事例？

（大家可以举出历史上的史料以及无数身边发生的例子。此处从略。）

提纲提要

论点 题目中的判断过于简单。

正 城市经济往往是各种经济要素的汇集地和一国经济的核心。城市一般以其繁荣和时尚带动城市周边地区、甚至是一国整体经济的繁荣和发展。

反 但是不能据此就说 It is primarily in cities that a nation's cultural traditions are generated and preserved. 这是因为：

其一，城市和农村对一个国家的文化传统都是有贡献的。毕竟，一国的文化是个整体，不应只包括城市文化。

其二，由于城市是各种文化和价值交汇、冲撞和相互影响的地方，其文化特点更多体现在时尚、开放、包容、多元和变迁。而农村，因为其经济结构较为单一，较少变化，人们的价值观念和生活方式相对更为保守和稳定，反而会产生并保持了一国的文化传统。

⊜ 城市只代表一个社会的表层状态。小镇和农村里普通人的生活状态才是一个社会的真实写照。正如眼下的中国，繁华都市不是中国的真实面目；代表中国的是七亿多的农民、上千万小城镇工人以及知识分子等。

---

118. We can learn much more from people whose views we share than from people whose views contradict our own. (参考第34、49、76题)

Write a response in which you discuss the extent to which you agree or disagree with the statement and explain your reasoning for the position you take. In developing and supporting your position, you should consider ways in which the statement might or might not hold true and explain how these considerations shape your position.

（事实类。本题的分析思路和写作提纲可完全借鉴第76题。）

---

119. When old buildings stand on ground that modern planners feel could be better used for modern purposes, modern development should be given precedence over the preservation of historic buildings. (参考第10、31、63、67、125、148题)

Write a response in which you discuss the extent to which you agree or disagree with the statement and explain your reasoning for the position you take. In developing and supporting your position, you should consider ways in which the statement might or might not hold true and explain how these considerations shape your position.

题型归类 建议类。

题目分析

（1）题目中的建议可行性如何？

该建议是否可行取决于人们对现代社会发展（modern development）和古建筑（historic buildings）价值孰轻孰重的估量。无所谓可行不可行。

（2）如果实施题目中的建议，是否会导致同初始目的相矛盾或其他荒谬的结果？

有两个问题：第一，城市就像一个人一样，怎能只要现在与眼前，而不要过去呢？一座城市应该是漫长历史中的一个节点。这个节点所连接的未必只有现在和将来，还有过去。第二，建筑，尤其是那些有特色、有代表性的古建筑，在某种程度上是人文历史的活化石。它们承载了太多历史的信息，一旦拆毁便永难复原。而今天的建筑却可以有许多备用施工场地，没有必要非得占用古建筑脚下的那块地。

（3）有无替代或折中方案？

城市开发应在历史和现在之间找到折中。

提纲提要

论点 城市开发应在历史和现在之间找到折中。

正 任何城市，无论多么古老，总得适应现代社会发展的要求。所以，城市的扩张和开发是必然的。

反 但是，一味地让城市古建筑为城市开发和现代建筑腾地方，至少会有两个问题：第一，城市就像一个人一样，怎能只要现在与眼前，而不要过去呢？一座城市应该是漫长历史中的一个节点。这个节点所连接的未必只有现在和将来，还有过去。第二，建筑，尤其是那些有特色、有代表性的古建筑，在某种程度上是人文历史的活化石。它们承载了太多历史的信息，一旦拆毁便永难复原。而今天的建筑却可以有许多备用施工场地，没有必要非得占用古建筑脚下的那块地。

合 城市开发应在历史和现在之间找到折中。

··

120. **Claim**: The surest indicator of a great nation must be the achievements of its rulers, artists, or scientists.

Reason: Great achievements by a nation's rulers, artists, or scientists will ensure a good life for the majority of that nation's people. (参考第 28、85、113、121、127、145 题)

Write a response in which you discuss the extent to which you agree or disagree with the claim and the reason on which that claim is based.

题型归类 因果类。

题目分析

（1）这个因果关系推理中的原因是否成立？

该题目的原因难以成立。在现代政治框架下，一国的科学家和艺术家（现代政治范畴内有政党、政府、议会、司法体系、宪政约束下的君主、公民/选民、科学家和艺术家，唯独没有国家统治者）的成就自然会令该国大多数国民受益。这是由现代社会施行民主政治和公民福利的大趋势导致的。而传统的君主制和皇权政体之下，君主和皇权对其臣民和国家的资源拥有绝对的权威和所有权。艺术家和科学家一般由皇室供养，其数量不多的作品和成果一般也由皇室专有，同普通国民关系不大，给普通百姓带来的益处也有限。

（2）假设这个原因成立，从它能否推出结果？

基于上述原因，该题目的结论不能一概而论。在传统的君主制和皇权政体之下，君主与其百姓是统治和被统治、主宰者和臣民的关系。那时，一个强大的帝国未必体现为百姓的福利，而多表现为君主的武功和战绩以及依附于帝王将相的艺术家和文人的成就。但在现代民主和宪政的政治框架下，国家和政府与百姓的关系是对等、服务型的关系；国家是国民自主创建用以解决该国内外事务的，政府及其官员是选民和公民的雇员。国家和政府的支出完全由选民决定。除了必要的公共开支和公共建设以外，社会财富是集中在百姓个人手中的。这时候，衡量一个伟大国度的指标是其国民（包括艺术家和科学家）的福利程度、科教文化水平、民族和社会的凝聚力和向心力、国民的创新和创造能力，但唯独不包括国家统治者的成就。这是因为在现代政治生态里面，本来就没有国家统治者的位置。

提纲提要

论点　论者的观点失于简单。

正　在传统的君主制和皇权政体之下，君主与其百姓是统治和被统治、主宰者和臣民的关系。君主和皇权对其臣民和国家的资源拥有绝对的权威和所有权。艺术家和科学家一般由皇室供养，其数量不多的作品和成果一般也由皇室专有，同普通国民关系不大，给普通百姓带来的益处也很有限。那时，一个强大的帝国未必体现为百姓的福利，而多表现为君主的武功和战绩以及依附于帝王将相的艺术家和文人的成就。

反　但是，在现代民主和宪政的政治框架下，国家和政府与百姓的关系是对等、服务型的关系；国家是国民自主创建用以解决该国内外事务的，政府及其官员是选民和公民的雇员。国家和政府的支出完全由选民和议会决定。除了必要的公共开支和公共建设以外，社会财富是集中在百姓个人手中的。这时候，衡量一个伟大国度的指标是其国民（包括艺术家和科学家）的福利程度、科教文化水平、民族和社会的凝聚力和向心力、国民的创新和创造能力，但唯独不包括国家统治者的成就。这是因为，在现代政治生态里面，我们可以看到政党、政府、议会、司法、宪政约束下的君主、公民/选民、科学家和艺术家等等的存在和功能，但基本没有国家统治者的位置。

散　国家形态从一家一姓的王朝帝国到今天的公民社会和民主政体体现了国家和社会对个体越来越多的关注。在现代意义上，一个真正伟大的国家应该是人的个性和自由得到最充分发展和保障的国家。

・・

> 121. Some people claim that you can tell whether a nation is great by looking at the achievements of its rulers, artists, or scientists. Others argue that the surest indicator of a great nation is, in fact, the general welfare of all its people. （参考第28、85、113、120、127、145题）
>
> Write a response in which you discuss which view more closely aligns with your own position and explain your reasoning for the position you take. In developing and supporting your position, you should address both of the views presented.

题型归类　事实类。

题目分析

（1）能否从公认的原则或事实中推出相反的判断？

题目中的两个判断都有道理，但都失于片面。这是因为在不同的国家形态和政治生态之下，社会财富和资源在政府和国民之间的分配以及两者之间的社会身份和关系是完全不同的。

具体而言：

在传统的君主制和皇权政体之下，君主与其百姓是统治和被统治、主宰者和臣民的关系。君主和皇权对其臣民和国家的资源拥有绝对的权威和所有权。艺术家和科学家一般由皇室供养，其数量不多的作品和成果一般也由皇室专有，同普通国民关系不大，给普通百姓带来的益处也很有限。那时，一个强大的帝国很难体现为百姓的福利，更多表现为君主的武功和战绩以及依附于帝王将相的科学家、艺术家和文人的成就。

但是，在现代民主和宪政的政治框架下，国家和政府与百姓的关系是对等、服务型的关系；国家是国民自主创建用以解决该国内外事务的，政府及其官员是选民和公民的雇员。国家和政府的支出完全由选民和议会决定。除了必要的公共开支和公共建设以外，社会财富是集中在百姓个人手中的。这时候，衡量一个伟大国度的指标是其国民（包括艺术家和科学家）的福利程度、科教文化水平、民族和社会的凝聚力和向心力、国民的创新和创造能力，但唯独不包括国家统治者的成就。这是因为，在现代政治生态里面，我们可以看到政党、政府、议会、司法、宪政约束下的君主、公民/选民、科学家和艺术家等等的存在和功能，但基本没有国家统治者的位置。

所以，you can tell whether a nation is great by looking at the achievements of its rulers, artists, or scientists 这一观点在传统的君主制和皇权政体之下是对的，但在现代民主和宪政的政治框架下却是错的；而观点 the surest indicator of a great nation is, in fact, the general welfare of all its people 在现代民主和宪政的政治框架下是有道理的，而在传统的君主制和皇权政体之下却是错的。

（2）能否举出相反的事例？

（大家可以举出历史上的史料以及无数身边发生的例子。此处从略。）

提纲提要

论点 **论者的观点失于简单。**

㊣ 在传统的君主制和皇权政体之下，君主与其百姓是统治和被统治、主宰者和臣民的关系。君主和皇权对其臣民和资源拥有绝对的权威和所有权。艺术家和科学家一般由皇室供养，其数量不多的作品和成果一般由皇室专有，同普通国民关系不大，给普通百姓带来的益处也很有限。那时，一个强大的帝国未必体现为百姓的福利，而多表现为君主的武功和战绩以及依附于帝王将相的艺术家和文人的成就。

㊒ 但是，在现代民主和宪政的政治框架下，国家和政府与百姓的关系是对等、服务型的关系；国家是国民自主创建用以解决该国内外事务的，政府及其官员是选民和公民的雇员。国家和政府的支出完全由选民和议会决定。除了必要的公共开支和公共建设以外，社会财富是集中在百姓个人手中的。这时候，衡量一个伟大国度的指标是其国民（包括艺术家和科学家）的福利程度、科教文化水平、民族和社会的凝聚力和向心力、国民的创新和创造能力，但唯独不包括国家统治者的成就。这是因为，在现代政治生态里面，我们可以看到政党、政府、议会、司法、宪政约束下的君主、公民/选民、科学家和艺术家等等的存在和功能，但基本没有国家统治者的位置。

㊍ 国家形态从一家一姓的王朝帝国到今天的公民社会和民主政体体现了国家和社会对个体越来越多的关注。在现代意义上，一个真正伟大的国家应该是人的个性和自由得到最充分发展和保障的国家。

· ·

122. The best way to understand the character of a society is to examine the character of the men and women that the society chooses as its heroes or its role models. （参考第22、44、75、84题；同时还可以参考第24、29、52、70、77、112、123题。）

Write a response in which you discuss the extent to which you agree or disagree with the claim. In developing and supporting your position, be sure to address the most compelling reasons and/or examples that could be used to challenge your position.

题型归类 建议类。

题目分析

（1）题目中的建议可行性如何？

任何人只要愿意，都可通过研究社会偶像的特点来了解该社会的特点。所以，题目中的建议当然可行。

（2）如果实施题目中的建议，是否会导致同初始目的相矛盾或其他荒谬的结果？

当人们试图通过研究社会偶像的特点了解该社会的特点时，会产生两个问题：第一，一个社会的所谓"英雄模范"很可能是出于服务特殊的意识形态的需要而被人为树立起来的。这样的"英雄模范"未必能真正反映社会和人心的深层次的渴望。第二，消费文化和快餐式娱乐打造的炫目的时尚先锋、潮流偶像更多反映的是社会和时代的泡沫，而不是该社会的主流价值。我们这个时代明星和偶像太多，以至于有时我们还没来得及记住他们，他们就消失了。

（3）有无替代或折中方案？

偶像只代表一个社会的表层状态。普通人的生活才是一个社会的真实写照。正如眼下的中国，都市偶像不能代表中国，代表中国的是七亿多的农民、上千万的城市工人以及知识分子等。然而这些人大都寂寂无闻。

提纲提要

论点 偶像可能只代表一个社会的表象，普通人才是该社会的真实写照。

正 一般而言，某一社会所认可的英雄和偶像能在一定程度反映该社会的面貌。

反 但是，当人们试图通过研究社会偶像的特点来了解该社会的特点时，会产生两个问题：第一，一个社会的"英雄模范"很可能是出于特殊的意识形态的需要而被人为树立起来的。这样的"英雄模范"未必能真正反映社会和人心的深层次的渴望。第二，消费文化和快餐式娱乐打造的炫目的时尚先锋、潮流偶像更多反映的是社会和时代的泡沫，而不是该社会的主流价值。我们这个时代明星和偶像太多，以至于有时我们还没来得及记住他们，他们就消失了。

合 偶像可能只代表一个社会的表层状态。普通人的生活才是一个社会的真实写照。正如眼下的中国，都市偶像不能代表中国，代表中国的是七亿多的农民、上千万的城市工人以及知识分子。然而这些人大都寂寂无闻。

123. The best way for a society to prepare its young people for leadership in government, industry, or other fields is by instilling in them a sense of cooperation, not competition. (参考第8、16、62、69、94、114、128、147题；同时还可以参考第22、24、29、52、70、77、112、122题。)

Write a response in which you discuss the extent to which you agree or disagree with the claim. In developing and supporting your position, be sure to address the most compelling reasons and/or examples that could be used to challenge your position.

题型归类　建议类。

题目分析

（1）题目中的建议的可行性如何？

    prepare its young people for leadership in government, industry, or other fields is by instilling in them a sense of cooperation 这一建议的可行性没什么问题。故分析从略。

（2）如果实施题目中的建议，是否会导致同初始目的相矛盾或其他荒谬的结果？

    强调合作意识未必就能培养出年轻人的领导能力并使他们成功。真正的成功不仅仅只是合作意识、竞争意识的问题。真正的成功是人格的成功。如果一味地关注成功本身，不注意健全人格的培养可能会导致人格的扭曲。

（3）有无替代或折中方案？

    成功是人对自我人格缺陷的超越和个人修养的完善。这个超越的过程既要竞争，又要合作，最终目的是不断接近自我完善。

提纲提要

论点　**成功是人对自我人格缺陷的超越。**

正　合作意识对一个人的成功很重要。

反　强调合作意识未必就能培养出年轻人的领导能力并使他们成功。真正的成功不仅仅只是合作意识、竞争意识的问题。真正的成功是人格的成功。如果一味地关注成功本身，不注意健全人格的培养可能会导致人格的扭曲。

合　成功是人对自我人格缺陷的超越和个人修养的完善。这个超越的过程既要竞争，又要合作，最终目的是不断接近自我完善。

- -

124. All college and university students would benefit from spending at least one semester studying in a foreign country. （参考第82、97、100题）

Write a response in which you discuss the extent to which you agree or disagree with the statement and explain your reasoning for the position you take. In developing and supporting your position, you should consider ways in which the statement might or might not hold true and explain how these considerations shape your position.

题型归类　事实类。

题目分析

（1）能否从公认的原则或事实中推出相反的判断？

    下列的几种情形可以说明，题目中论者的判断也许过于乐观。

    首先，国外游学的费用谁来出？政府、学校、还是学生家长？考虑到学生数量的庞大，政府和学校不可能全部承担这些游学费用。自费出行的学生往往会选择那些费用低、教育制度与自己所在学校趋同、符合个人兴趣的目的国。这样的话，了解不同文化价值、丰富阅历、增长学术能力的海外游学目的就大打折扣。

    其次，到国外学什么？各国教育制度、文化、学生的个人兴趣可谓千差万别。教育制度

（如学分、学时、学习内容）如何对接？不同、甚至彼此冲突的文化价值之间如何相互理解和宽容？学生的个人兴趣和学校要求之间如何协调？将这些因素全部考虑进去之后，一个用意良好的海外游学计划，很可能会变成一次非常随意的异国自费游。

第三，该如何组织实施？学校统一组织还是学生个人申请？学生数目庞大，兴趣各异，目的国的文化、教育制度和留学政策千差万别，学校统一组织似乎不大可能。最终只能由学生自己分散安排出行，那么，学生的个人安全如何保障是个很现实的问题。

第四，实际价值不大的国外游学是对学生正常学习时间的侵占。

（2）能否举出相反的事例？

（大家可以举出自己经历的或者身边发生的例子。此处从略。）

提纲提要

论点 异国游学最好由个人在条件适合时自行安排。

正 读万卷书，行万里路。异国游学对了解不同文化、丰富阅历、增长学术能力都会很有益处。

反 但是，要求所有在读大学生抽出一个学期时间到国外游学未必可行。这是因为：
首先，国外游学的费用谁来出？政府、学校、还是学生家长？考虑到学生数量庞大，政府和学校不可能全部承担这些游学费用。自费出行的学生往往会选择那些费用低、教育制度与自己所在学校趋同、符合个人兴趣的目的国。这样的话，了解不同文化、丰富阅历、增长学术能力的海外游学目的就大打折扣。
其次，到国外学什么？各国教育制度、文化、学生的个人兴趣可谓千差万别。教育制度（如学分、学时、学习内容）如何对接？不同、甚至彼此冲突的文化价值之间如何相互理解和宽容？学生的个人兴趣和学校要求之间如何协调？将这些因素全部考虑进去之后，一个用意良好的海外游学计划，很可能会变成一次非常随意的异国自费游。
第三，该如何组织实施？学校统一组织还是学生个人申请？学生数目庞大，兴趣各异，目的国的文化、教育制度和留学政策的千差万别，学校统一组织似乎不大可能。最终只能由学生自己分散安排出行，那么，学生的个人安全如何保障是个很现实的问题。
第四，实际价值不大的国外游学是对学生正常学习时间的侵占。

合 折中方案：第一，异国游学不应是强制性的，所以也没必要为此项活动安排一个学期的时间。第二，在校学习其间，对异国文化、社会制度专门等等的了解更适合通过专门的学术或政府交流渠道，将别国的学者、专家、政府官员、民间机构等请进来的方式进行。第三，真正的游学最好等到学生走出校门后，当人生阅历、生活经验和经济能力等条件成熟时，结合个人兴趣和目的自行安排，这样会更现实一些。

---

125. Some people claim that a nation's government should preserve its wilderness areas in their natural state. Others argue that these areas should be developed for potential economic gain. （参考第10、31、63、67、119、148题）

Write a response in which you discuss which view more closely aligns with your own position and explain your reasoning for the position you take. In developing and supporting your position, you should address both of the views presented.

题型归类 建议类。

题目分析

（1）题目中的建议可行性如何？

在公共财政能力有限的情况下，政府将所有荒原都保护起来的计划的可行性值得怀疑。而严格规划管理下的经济开发，比如发展旅游业，是完全可行的。

（2）如果实施题目中的建议，是否会导致同初始目的相矛盾或其他荒谬的结果？

首先，人和自然的平衡并不意味着要绝对消除人对环境的影响。绝对消除自然环境中人的因素的做法本身就是在否定人本来也是自然环境的一部分这个客观事实。这可能是另外一种形式的环境破坏。其次，政府对本来已是人迹罕至的荒原实施保护的做法是一种不必要的浪费。即便没有人类活动的影响，自然环境也会在自然力量的作用下上演着沧海桑田、沙漠绿洲的变迁。只要人们约束自己的行为和活动，不超出环境生态的承载力，人和自然的和谐相处是完全可以实现的。

（3）有无替代或折中方案？

人应融入环境、与环境共生，但不破坏环境。

提纲提要

论点 人应融入环境，但不破坏环境。

正 考虑到人对自然环境的破坏和影响有时是难以准确估计的，对荒原进行预防性保护也是有必要的。

反 但是，将所有荒原都保护起来的建议似乎不大可行。

首先，在公共财政能力有限的情况下，该建议的可行性值得怀疑。

其次，人和自然的平衡并不意味着要绝对消除人对环境的影响。绝对消除自然环境中人的因素的做法本身就是在否定人本来也是自然环境的一部分这个客观事实。这可能是另外一种形式的环境破坏。

第三，政府对本来已是人迹罕至的荒原实施保护的做法是一种不必要的浪费。即便没有人类活动的影响，自然环境也会在自然力量的作用下上演着沧海桑田、沙漠绿洲的变迁。只要人们约束自己的行为和活动，不超出环境生态的承载力，人和自然的和谐相处完全可能。所以，严格规划管理下的适度经济开发，比如发展旅游业，是完全可以尝试的。

合 人类应该学会的是：要融入环境、与环境共生，但不破坏环境。

---

126. In most professions and academic fields, imagination is more important than knowledge.（参考第105、106题）

Write a response in which you discuss the extent to which you agree or disagree with the claim. In developing and supporting your position, be sure to address the most compelling reasons and/or examples that could be used to challenge your position.

（是非类。本题的分析思路和写作提纲可完全借鉴第106题。）

---

127. The surest indicator of a great nation is not the achievements of its rulers, artists, or scientists, but the general well-being of all its people.（参考第28、85、113、120、121、145题）

Write a response in which you discuss the extent to which you agree or disagree with the claim. In developing and supporting your position, be sure to address the most compelling reasons and/or examples that could be used to challenge your position.

（事实类。本题的分析思路和写作提纲可完全借鉴第28题。）

128. Some people argue that successful leaders in government, industry, or other fields must be highly competitive. Other people claim that in order to be successful, a leader must be willing and able to cooperate with others. (参考第8、16、62、69、94、114、123、147题)

Write a response in which you discuss which view more closely aligns with your own position and explain your reasoning for the position you take. In developing and supporting your position, you should address both of the views presented.

题型归类 建议类。

题目分析

（1）题目中的建议的可行性如何？

到底领袖们是该善于竞争还是善于合作，这仅仅是个人选择的问题，都是可行的。

（2）如果实施题目中的建议，是否会导致同初始目的相矛盾或其他荒谬的结果？

题目中的两个建议各执一端，将竞争与合作这两种素质对领导/领袖的意义割裂开来。真正的成功不仅仅只是合作意识、竞争意识的问题。真正的成功是人格的成功，而一味地关注成功本身，不注意培养健全的人格可能会导致人格的扭曲。

（3）有无替代或折中方案？

成功是人对自我人格缺陷的超越和个人修养的完善。这个超越的过程既要竞争又要合作，最终目的是不断接近自我完善。

提纲提要

论点 **成功是人对自我人格缺陷的超越。**

正 竞争意识与合作意识对一个人的成功都很重要。

反 但帮助领导/领袖走向成功的不仅仅只是合作意识、竞争意识的问题。真正的成功是人格的成功，而一味地关注成功本身，不注意培养健全的人格可能会导致人格的扭曲。

合 成功是人对自我人格缺陷的超越和个人修养的完善。这个超越的过程既要竞争又要合作，最终目的是不断接近自我完善。

129. College students should base their choice of a field of study on the availability of jobs in that field. (参考第3、13、15、20、32、35、39、46、98、135、136、137、140题)

Write a response in which you discuss the extent to which you agree or disagree with the recommendation and explain your reasoning for the position you take. In developing and supporting your position, describe specific circumstances in which adopting the recommendation would or would not be advantageous and explain how these examples shape your position.

（建议类。本题的分析思路和写作提纲可完全借鉴第32题。）

- -

130. Some people believe that corporations have a responsibility to promote the well-being of the societies and environments in which they operate. Others believe that the only responsibility of corporations, provided they operate within the law, is to make as much money as possible.

Write a response in which you discuss which view more closely aligns with your own position and explain your reasoning for the position you take. In developing and supporting your position, you should address both of the views presented.

题型归类　建议类。

题目分析

（1）题目中的建议的可行性如何?

企业无论选择挣钱，还是选择推进社会福利，都是可行的。

（2）如果实施题目中的建议，是否会导致同初始目的相矛盾或其他荒谬的结果?

题目中的两个建议显然各执一端，将企业的两个社会功能割裂开来。简单施行任一个建议，都会带来问题：只讲社会责任和公共福利，而不讲盈利，企业俨然充当了政府的角色。长此以往，企业必定存活不下去。我们中国过去的国有企业之所以经营困难，原因之一便是承担了过重的社会责任，从职工生老病死、孩子上学就业，到职工住房分配、冬季采暖夏季降温，几乎无所不包。相反，企业只讲挣钱，不顾其他，也行之不远。不仅其社会形象差，会令消费者拒绝购买其商品和服务，还有违法违纪的可能。

（3）有无替代或折中方案?

正确的选择是两者的结合。企业既要赚钱，也要顾及必要的社会责任。资本的天性是要赚钱，但赚钱不能以牺牲人性为代价。这是企业要坚守的底线。

提纲提要

论点　资本的天性是要赚钱，但不能以牺牲人性为代价。

㊣　表面上看，企业守法经营、赚取利润是天经地义的事情。

㊃　但是，企业只讲挣钱，不顾其他，也行之不远。不仅其社会形象差，会令消费者拒绝购买其商品和服务，还有违法违纪的可能。同样道理，如果企业只讲社会责任和公共福利，而不讲盈利，则企业俨然充当了政府的角色。长此以往，企业必定存活不下去。我们中国过去的国有企业之所以经营困难，原因之一便是承担了过重的社会责任，从职工生老病死、孩子上学就业，到职工住房分配、冬季采暖夏季降温，几乎无所不包。结果只能是大批国企难以为继。

㊌　正确的选择是两者的结合。企业既要赚钱，也要顾及必要的社会责任。资本的天性是要赚钱，但赚钱不能以牺牲人性为代价。这是企业要坚守的底线。

131. **Claim**: Researchers should not limit their investigations to only those areas in which they expect to discover something that has an immediate, practical application.

Reason: It is impossible to predict the outcome of a line of research with any certainty. (参考第56、59题)

Write a response in which you discuss the extent to which you agree or disagree with the claim and the reason on which that claim is based.

题型归类 套叠式多角度分析题。整体是个因果类题目，但它的结果部分是个建议。

题目分析

首先，按照因果类题目类型展开分析：

（1）这个因果关系推理中的原因是否成立？

该题目的原因似乎可以成立。的确有很多科研活动的结果无法预料。

（2）假设这个原因成立，从它能否推出结果？

即使上述原因成立，结论也是推不出的。鉴于这个结果部分是个建议，我们在下面就从建议类题目的分析角度切入分析。

其次，按照建议类题目类型展开分析：

（1）题目中的建议可行性如何？

在题目中，论者建议研究人员不必将他们的研究局限于那些结果可预料、能够很快见到实际应用效果的领域。言下之意，这是让科研人员都去从事那些异想天开的发现。这当然可行，尽管听起来有点儿荒谬。

（2）如果实施题目中的建议，是否会导致同初始目的相矛盾或其他荒谬的结果？

如果实施题目中的建议，会有两个问题：第一，会导致科研经费的巨大浪费。当大量的科研工作不能很快产生实际效益的时候，之前的投入多半也就打水漂了。第二，人们的科学发现会减少，人类科技进步的节奏会慢下来。虽然有一些科学发现是在偶然中实现的，但不能反过来说，偶然总能带来科学发现。

（3）有无替代或折中方案？

折中方案：科研设计要尽量扎实、科学，并且要做长期连续的追踪和研究。但是，对研究过程中偶然出现的一些意外发现和科研设计未考虑到的情况，也要给予关注。这些意外和特殊情况经常会提醒众人调整科研设计的思路，甚至会导致重大的科学发现。

提纲提要

论点 偶然能带来科学发现，但科学发现不能依赖偶然。

正 的确有一些科研活动，科研人员无法预先知道其结果，也无法预测它们能够给社会带来多大的收益。这对于部分冷门的基础学科、纯粹思辨性的学科（如哲学）以及一些前沿学科，更是如此。

反 但是，如果研究人员仅仅将他们的研究局限于那些结果可预料、能够很快见到实际效果的领域，会有两个问题：第一，会导致科研经费的巨大浪费。当大量的科研工作不能很快产生实际效益的时候，之前的投入多半也就打水漂了。第二，人们的科学发现会减少，人类科技进步的节奏会慢下来。虽然有一些科学发现是在偶然中实现的，但不能反过来说，偶然总能带来科学发现。

⊜ **折中方案**：科研设计要尽量扎实、科学，并且要做长期连续的追踪和研究。但是，对研究过程中偶然出现的一些意外发现和科研设计未考虑到的情况，也要给予关注。这些意外和特殊情况经常会提醒众人调整科研设计的思路，有时甚至会导致重大的科学发现。

⋯⋯⋯

132. Some people believe that our ever-increasing use of technology significantly reduces our opportunities for human interaction. Other people believe that technology provides us with new and better ways to communicate and connect with one another.

Write a response in which you discuss which view more closely aligns with your own position and explain your reasoning for the position you take. In developing and supporting your position, you should address both of the views presented.

题型归类 事实类。

题目分析

（1）能否从公认的原则或事实中推出相反的判断？

基于下列两个事实，题目中的两个观察都有些道理，但又都不全面：

首先，现代科技的确给人类提供了更新、更好的沟通和联系方式：有线电话、无线电话、音频通话、视频对话、即时通讯（诸如MSN、QQ等即时聊天软件）、光缆传输数据、卫星通讯等等，这些都带给人类前所未有的快捷和方便。

其次，这些经济、快捷的沟通方式极大提高了人们沟通和交流的效率，人们生活和工作的节奏于是变得更快、再快，最终到了近乎疯狂的地步，以至于我们一旦稍微慢下来一点，反倒浑身不自在了。于是悖论出现了：科技进步提高了我们的效率，本应留给我们更充裕的时间来彼此交流，但在这种令人目眩的快节奏生活和工作氛围中，我们却发现根本做不到。电话越来越短，短信寥寥片语，逢年过节的问候看似热情，但大多是相互复制和转发的手机短信。我们缺乏真诚，缺乏心与心的沟通，缺乏彼此目光凝视的信赖与温暖；有时，我们甚至害怕与多年不聚的好友见面，因为即便在短信和MSN上聊得很开心，但见面后却不知道该说些什么。现代科技带来的沟通效果，甚至比不上过去一年只是一封的纸笔长信。一句话，科技进步使我们交流的深度和热度降低了。

（2）能否举出相反的事例？

（大家可以举出无数身边发生的例子。此处从略。）

提纲提要

论点 论者的观点失于片面。

正 现代科技的确给人类提供了更新、更好的沟通和联系方式：有线电话、无线电话、音频通话、视频对话、即时通讯（诸如MSN、QQ等即时聊天软件）、光缆传输数据、卫星通讯等等，这些都带给人类前所未有的快捷和方便。

反 但是，这些经济、快捷的沟通方式极大地提高了人们沟通和交流的效率，人们生活和工作的节奏于是变得更快、再快，最终到了近乎疯狂的地步，以至于我们一旦稍微慢下来一点，反倒浑身不自在了。于是悖论出现了：科技进步提高了我们的效率，本应留给我们更充裕的时间来彼此交流，但在这种令人目眩的快节奏生活和工作氛围中，我们却发现根本做不到。电话越来越短，短信寥寥片语，逢年过节的问候看似热情，但大多是相互复制和转发的手机短信。我们缺乏真诚，缺乏心与心的沟通，缺乏彼此目光凝视的信赖与温暖；有时，我们甚至害怕与多年不聚的好友见面，因为即便在短信和MSN上聊得很开心，但见面后却不知道该说些什么。现代科技所带来的沟通效果，甚至比不上过去一年只是一封的纸笔长信。一句话，科技进步使我们交流的深度和热度降低了。

散 现代科技无论多么发达，似乎都永远满足不了我们的各种欲望。我们的步伐无论多么快，都无法缓释内心的焦虑与疲惫。我们很可能被现代科技绑架了：它挟持了我们的身体和感官（body and senses），令我们冷落了自己的心智和灵魂。

---

133. **Claim**: Knowing about the past cannot help people to make important decisions today.

Reason: The world today is significantly more complex than it was even in the relatively recent past. (参考第33、57、74、109、134题)

Write a response in which you discuss the extent to which you agree or disagree with the claim and the reason on which that claim is based.

题型归类 因果类。

题目分析

（1）这个因果关系推理中的原因是否成立？

该题目的原因成立。过去和现在的确很难有可比性。过去发生的事情，今天未必重演。不同的历史阶段，人们的物质生活状态、价值观念、风俗习惯、面临的问题和挑战等等，都不一样。即便是同样的问题，如战争，过去和现在的表现形式、结果也大不一样。现在的核战争及其结果恐怕是过去难以想象的。

（2）假设这个原因成立，从它能否推出结果？

即使上述原因成立，结论也是推不出的。历史是连续的。现在的许多问题（如人与人间的平等、社会正义、战争等）只不过是过去同样问题的延续。

提纲提要

论点 **历史是本关于人性的教科书。**

正 过去和现在的确很难有可比性。过去发生的事情，今天未必重演。不同的历史阶段，人们的物质生活状态、价值观念、风俗习惯、面临的问题和挑战等等，都不一样。即便是同样的问题，如战争，过去和现在的表现形式、结果也大不一样。现在的核战争及其结果恐怕是过去难以想象的。

反 但是，历史是连续的。现在的许多问题（如人与人间的平等、社会正义、战争等）只不过是过去问题的延续。

散 因为人性的一贯性（consistency in human nature），今天的问题总有过去类似问题的影子。只是因为人性中固有的自负，今天的人们不愿过多地考虑历史中的经验与教训罢了。

134. **Claim**: Knowing about the past cannot help people to make important decisions today.

Reason: We are not able to make connections between current events and past events until we have some distance from both. (参考第33、57、74、109、133题)

Write a response in which you discuss the extent to which you agree or disagree with the claim and the reason on which that claim is based.

题型归类 因果类。

题目分析

（1）这个因果关系推理中的原因是否成立?

该题目的原因成立。一方面，过去和现在的确很难有可比性。过去发生的事情，今天未必重演。不同的历史阶段，人们的物质生活状态、价值观念、风俗习惯、面临的问题和挑战等等，都不一样。即便是同样的问题，如战争，过去和现在的表现形式、结果也大不一样。现在的核战争及其结果恐怕是过去难以想象的。另一方面，现代社会的纷乱细节有时会干扰我们对当代事件和历史事件之间相似性的把握。找到过去和现在之间的一致性，需要的不仅仅是穿越历史的睿智，还需要时间的沉淀。

（2）假设这个原因成立，从它能否推出结果?

即使上述原因成立，结论也是推不出的。历史总是连续的。现在的许多问题（如人与人间的平等、社会正义、战争等）只不过是过去同样问题的延续。

提纲提要

论点 历史是本关于人性的教科书。

正 有时，我们的确很难用历史来简单地指导现实。

一方面，过去和现在的确很难有可比性。过去发生的事情，今天未必重演。不同的历史阶段，人们的物质生活状态、价值观念、风俗习惯、面临的问题和挑战等等，都不一样。即便是同样的问题，如战争，过去和现在的表现形式、结果也大不一样。现在的核战争及其结果恐怕是过去难以想象的。

另一方面，现代社会的纷乱细节有时会干扰我们对当代事件和历史事件之间相似性的把握。找到过去和现在之间的一致性，需要的不仅仅是穿越历史的睿智，还需要时间的沉淀。

反 但是，历史是连续的。现在的许多问题（如人与人间的平等、社会正义、战争等）只不过是过去问题的延续。

敌 因为人性的一贯性（consistency in human nature），今天的问题总有过去类似问题的影子。只是因为人性中固有的自负，今天的人们不愿过多地考虑历史中的经验与教训罢了。在整个历史过程中，人性的自私与高尚、狭隘与宽容、贪婪与克制通过不同的形式和问题得到连续展现。在人类目前所有的知识中，关于人性的知识是最难以理解和把握的。历史恰好是关于人性最好的教科书。

135. Educational institutions should actively encourage their students to choose fields of study that will prepare them for lucrative careers. (参考第3、13、15、20、32、35、39、46、98、129、136、137、140题)

Write a response in which you discuss your views on the policy and explain your reasoning for the position you take. In developing and supporting your position, you should consider the possible consequences of implementing the policy and explain how these consequences shape your position.

（建议类。本题的分析思路和写作提纲可完全借鉴第15题。）

136. Educational institutions should actively encourage their students to choose fields of study in which jobs are plentiful. (参考第3、13、15、20、32、35、39、46、98、129、135、137、140题)

Write a response in which you discuss the extent to which you agree or disagree with the claim. In developing and supporting your position, be sure to address the most compelling reasons and/or examples that could be used to challenge your position.

（建议类。本题的分析思路和写作提纲可完全借鉴第98题。）

137. Educational institutions have a responsibility to dissuade students from pursuing fields of study in which they are unlikely to succeed. (参考第3、13、15、20、32、35、39、46、98、129、135、136、140题)

Write a response in which you discuss the extent to which you agree or disagree with the statement and explain your reasoning for the position you take. In developing and supporting your position, you should consider ways in which the statement might or might not hold true and explain how these considerations shape your position.

（建议类。本题的分析思路和写作提纲可完全借鉴第3题。）

138. Some people believe that competition for high grades motivates students to excel in the classroom. Others believe that such competition seriously limits the quality of real learning. (参考第45题)

Write a response in which you discuss which view more closely aligns with your own position and explain your reasoning for the position you take. In developing and supporting your position, you should address both of the views presented.

题型归类 事实类。

题目分析

（1）能否从公认的原则或事实中推出相反的判断？

基于下列两个事实，题目中的两个观察都有些道理，但又都不全面：

其一，学生所处的学习阶段的不同，是否应该让学生关注高分也应有所不同：小学生自控能力和学习的自主性差、不善于分析问题的复杂性。这时，鼓励他们争取高分也许能调动他们学习的积极性。而在高中以后的学习阶段，学生的自主性提高，学习的目的性和方向性非常明确，这时候再让他们为高分而学习就没太大必要了。

其二，为高分而学这种做法的不当之处也许并不在这种做法本身，而在于那些用以判定正确答案与错误答案、高分与低分的标准。绝大多数情况下，我们面临的问题并没有正确答案与错误答案，更不会有标准答案。但当所谓的标准答案满天飞的时候，被教育者的想象力和创造性反而被窒息了。

（2）能否举出相反的事例？

（大家可以举出无数身边发生的例子。此处从略。）

提纲提要

论点 **论者的观点失于简单。**

（正）小学生自控能力和学习的自主性差、不善于分析问题的复杂性。这时，鼓励他们争取高分也许能调动他们学习的积极性。

（反）但是，在高中以后的学习阶段，学生的自主性提高，学习的目的性和方向性非常明确，这时候再让他们为高分而学习就没太大必要了。

为高分而学这种做法的不当之处也许并不在这种做法本身，而在于那些用以判定正确答案与错误答案、高分与低分的标准。绝大多数情况下，我们面临的问题并没有正确答案与错误答案，更没有标准答案。但当所谓的标准答案满天飞的时候，被教育者的想象力和创造性反而被窒息了。

（散）最终判断一个社会的教育是否成功有两个缺一不可的标准：第一，学生是否掌握了科学的思维方式。有了它，学生才能够独立进行理性和批判的思考。第二，学生是否通过独立的思考获得了他人生的价值和信仰。有了它们，学生才会发现生命的方向和意义。

··

139. **Claim**: Major policy decisions should always be left to politicians and other government experts.

Reason: Politicians and other government experts are more informed and thus have better judgment and perspective than do members of the general public. (参考第27、108、110题)

Write a response in which you discuss the extent to which you agree or disagree with the claim and the reason on which that claim is based.

题型归类 套叠式多角度分析题。整体是个因果类题目，但它的结果部分是个建议。

题目分析

首先，按照因果类题目类型展开分析：

（1）这个因果关系推理中的原因是否成立？

该题目的原因未必成立。政治家和专家对各方面情况未必就比普通大众更了解，也未必有更多独到的见解和判断力。假如他们整天人浮于事、无所事事，闲呆在办公室，根本不做研究、不下基层，他们实际上是耳目闭塞的。所以，没有有效的官员和专家选拔、聘任/任命、监督机制，庸才照样能混到政客和专家队伍里去。即便是优秀的专家和官员，也会因为一个劣胜优汰的机制和制度而堕入平庸。

（2）假设这个原因成立，从它能否推出结果？

即使上述原因成立，结论也是推不出的。鉴于这个结果部分是个建议，我们下面就从建议类题目的分析角度切入分析。

其次，按照建议类题目类型展开分析：

（1）题目中的建议可行性如何？

重大决策应该交给谁来做，这是个权力分配的问题。无所谓是否可行。

（2）如果实施题目中的建议，是否会导致同初始目的相矛盾或其他荒谬的结果？

即便政府官员和专家有才有德，我们就能保证他们永远不徇私舞弊、贪污腐化吗？就能保证他们自始至终都站在公众利益的立场，不为既得利益集团所挟持吗？即便他们一心为公，他们能保证在任何时候都完全占有充分的信息和资料，并做出正确决策吗？

（3）有无替代或折中方案？

为避免这些情况的出现，对政府官员和政府所属的专家进行监督、制衡就很有必要了。

提纲提要

论点 制度比人更可靠。

正 现代政治提倡专家治国。政府官员和专家理应对其从事的工作非常精通。

反 但是，政治家和专家对各方面情况未必就比普通大众更了解，也未必有更多独到的见解和判断力。假如他们整天人浮于事、无所事事，闲呆在办公室，既不做研究又不下基层，他们实际上是耳目闭塞的。所以，没有有效的官员和专家选拔、聘任/任命、监督机制，庸才照样能混到政客和专家队伍里去。即便是优秀的专家和官员，也会因为一个劣胜优汰的机制和制度而堕入平庸。

而且，即便政府官员和专家有才有德，我们就能保证他们永远不徇私舞弊、贪污腐化吗？就能保证他们自始至终都站在公共利益的立场，不为既得利益集团所挟持吗？即便他们一心为公，他们能保证在任何时候都完全占有充分的信息和资料，并做出正确决策吗？

合 政府官员和老百姓无所谓谁更聪明。一个完善的制度比谁都可靠。

140. Some people believe that universities should require every student to take a variety of courses outside the student's field of study. Others believe that universities should not force students to take any courses other than those that will help prepare them for jobs in their chosen fields. (参考第3、13、15、20、32、35、39、46、98、129、135、136、137题)

Write a response in which you discuss which view more closely aligns with your own position and explain your reasoning for the position you take. In developing and supporting your position, you should address both of the views presented.

题型归类　建议类。

题目分析

（1）题目中的建议可行性如何？

题目中的两个建议都未必可行。

首先，许多大学、学院未必具备开设大量学科课程的能力。其次，学生很难有时间和精力在三至四年的时间里去学专业以外的课程。第三，有些学生很可能会因为对专业以外的学科毫无兴趣而对这种要求产生强烈的抵制情绪。

至于仅仅为将来的一份工作而学习的建议，实行起来同样困难：这是因为在社会分工高度精细化、职业调整越来越频繁的今天，人们基本无法准确预知某个专业或行业未来三年或五年的职业前景。

（2）如果实施题目中的建议，是否会导致同初始目的相矛盾或其他荒谬的结果？

强行推行universities should require every student to take a variety of courses outside the student's field of study这一建议将带来的弊端至少有三点：其一，各个大学课程雷同，失去其传统的学术特色。其二，学生疲于奔命于众多学科之间，学得浮光掠影，难以专深。其三，湮灭学生的个性和创造力。而这同包容一切个性、探索未知的现代大学精神格格不入。

而如果施行题目中"为工作而学习"的建议，其导致的弊端至少有四点：第一，几乎所有的人都涌向为数不多看似"钱"景无限的职业。基于大家彼此大致相同的认知能力、现有信息的有限性和未来的不可知性，这几乎是一个必然的结果。这一点，我们从一轮又一轮的计算机热、法律热、金融热、房地产热、MBA热，当然还包括当下最具中国特色的公务员热，都看得非常清楚。其结果只能是这些曾经的热门职业和行业很快出现人力资源供给的过剩、整体收入下降、部分人被迫改行。第二，如果上述第一个结果成立，这随后的结果就是，对个人而言，是教育投入的失败；对国家而言，是国民财富的浪费。第三，会使得一个国家新兴的产业所需要的人力资源得不到及时的补充，影响该国产业结构的转移和提升。这是因为一个国家教育机构的人才产出能力在中短期内是基本恒定的。当人才大量涌向几个看似"热门"的行业时，其他行业的人才供给必然减少。第四，如果学生将自己的学习和研究领域仅仅用就业的前景框限起来，人生就失去了很多发展自己爱好和天分的乐趣；就社会而言，则很有可能因为特立独行、才华横溢之才的淹没而损失了创新精神与活力。

（3）有无替代或折中方案？

在大学研究生以下的教育阶段，大学生应该更多地将个人兴趣和天分作为自己专业方向的参考，尽量多学自己感兴趣的学科。兴趣是最好的老师，它能引导我们找到最适合自己的职业和事业。而且，在四年本科结束后，最好先工作两三年。通过工作也可以发现最适合自己的职业方向。实际上，现代人的寿命普遍较长，其黄金工作年龄可以一直延长到65岁甚至更晚些。所以，年轻人在35岁之前可以有许多尝试和发现自己职业生涯的机会。过早确立事业方向反而不利于发现自己的潜能。

提纲提要

论点　题目中的建议都略显片面。

正　接受大学教育到底是为了学习渊博的知识，还是仅仅为了毕业后找到一份满意的工作？强调任何一面都似乎有其道理。毕竟，上大学是为了求知，而所有的学习最终只能落实到一个具体的职业上面。

反 但是，题目中的两个建议施行起来，又有其各自的难度。

首先，许多大学、学院未必具备开设大量学科课程的能力。其次，学生很难有时间和精力在三至四年的时间里去学专业以外的课程。第三，有些学生很可能会因为对专业以外的学科毫无兴趣而对这种要求产生强烈的抵制情绪。

至于仅仅为将来的一份工作而学习的建议，实行起来同样困难：这是因为在社会分工高度精细化、职业调整越来越频繁的今天，人们基本无法准确预知某个专业或行业未来三年或五年的职业前景。

而且，如果简单地按照题目中的两个建议做下去，势必会导致一些违背初衷的问题。

首先，强行推行universities should require every student to take a variety of courses outside the student's field of study这一建议将带来的弊端至少有三点：其一，各个大学课程雷同，失去其传统的学术特色。其二，学生疲于奔命于众多学科之间，学得浮光掠影，难以专深。其三，湮灭学生的个性和创造力。而这同包容一切个性、探索未知的现代大学精神格格不入。

而如果施行题目中"为工作而学习"的建议，其所导致的弊端至少有四点：第一，几乎所有的人都涌向为数不多看似"钱"景无限的职业。基于大家彼此大致相同的认知能力、现有信息的有限性和未来的不可知性，这几乎是一个必然的结果。这一点，我们从一轮又一轮的计算机热、法律热、金融热、房地产热、MBA热，当然还包括当下最具中国特色的公务员热，都看得非常清楚。其结果只能是这些曾经的热门职业和行业很快出现人力资源供给的过剩、整体收入下降、部分人被迫改行。第二，如果上述第一个结果成立，这随后的结果就是，对个人而言，是教育投入的失败；对国家而言，是国民财富的浪费。第三，会使得一个国家新兴的产业所需要的人力资源得不到及时的补充，影响该国产业结构的转移和提升。这是因为一个国家教育机构的人才产出能力在中短期内是基本恒定的。当人才大量涌向几个看似"热门"的行业时，其他行业的人才供给必然减少。第四，如果学生将自己的学习和研究领域仅仅用就业的前景框限起来，人生就失去了很多发展自己爱好和天分的乐趣；就社会而言，则很有可能因为特立独行、才华横溢之才的淹没而损失了创新精神与活力。

合 折中方案：在大学研究生以下的教育阶段，大学生应该更多的将个人兴趣和天分作为自己专业方向的参考，尽量多学自己感兴趣的学科。兴趣是最好的老师，它能引导我们找到最适合自己的职业和事业。而且，在四年本科结束后，最好先工作两三年。通过工作也可以发现最适合自己的职业方向。实际上，现代人的寿命普遍较长，其黄金工作年龄可以一直延长到65岁甚至更晚些。所以，年轻人在35岁之前可以有许多尝试和发现自己职业生涯的机会。过早确立事业方向反而不利于发现自己的潜能。

---

141. It is more harmful to compromise one's own beliefs than to adhere to them.

Write a response in which you discuss the extent to which you agree or disagree with the statement and explain your reasoning for the position you take. In developing and supporting your position, you should consider ways in which the statement might or might not hold true and explain how these considerations shape your position.

题型归类 单纯性是非类。

题目分析

（1）这种价值判断的标准是什么？

当论者说，在信念问题上的妥协会比坚持该信念更有害时，他的标准可能是这样的：人总是通过信仰来解释自己周围的世界。没有了信仰，人们会惶惑不安、内心缺失价值等。严重的情况下，信仰的混乱和缺失会导致社会动荡。

（2）这种价值判断的标准是否值得修正？

坚持信仰的结果会如何？我们同样能看到狂热、残忍（如宗教战争）和社会动荡的一幕幕。信仰只不过是人们对未知世界（unknown world around us）的自认为合理的解释，它本身是非理性的。为信仰而信仰有时会把人贬低为工具（tool or implement）。

提纲提要

论点 信仰本身是中性的，既可带来益处，也可带来破坏。

（正）当论者说，在信念问题上的妥协会比坚持该信念更有害时，他的标准可能是这样的：人总是通过信仰来解释自己周围的世界。没有了信仰，人们会惶惑不安、内心缺乏价值。严重的情况下，信仰的混乱和缺失会导致社会动荡。

（反）那么，坚持信仰的结果会如何？我们同样能看到狂热、残忍（如宗教战争）、社会动荡的一幕幕。信仰只不过是人们对未知世界的自认为合理的解释，它本身是非理性的。为信仰而信仰有时会把人贬低为工具。

（合）信仰可以带来益处，也可以带来破坏。关键在于：是人把信仰当作对世界的一种理解，还是信仰把人当作了工具。

· ·

142. **Claim**: Colleges and universities should specify all required courses and eliminate elective courses in order to provide clear guidance for students.

Reason: College students—like people in general—prefer to follow directions rather than make their own decisions. (参考第 37、40、47、58、90 题)

Write a response in which you discuss the extent to which you agree or disagree with the claim and the reason on which that claim is based.

题型归类 套叠式多角度分析题。整体是个因果类题目，但它的结果部分是个建议。

题目分析

首先，按照因果类题目类型展开分析：

（1）这个因果关系推理中的原因是否成立？

该题目的原因未必成立。首先，这不符合人的本性。在人所有的本性中，自由和自主为其最爱。常听人说"食色，性也"；但很少有人说"自由，性也"。但是，若没有最起码的自由，所谓"食色"本性也就无从谈起。

另外，题目中说大学生及普通大众喜欢听从指示（directions）而非自己去做决定。这里的关键问题是：这个指示指的到底是什么？假设一个国家、学校的管理真正是民主化的，那么，所有这些指示（大到国家的法律法规，小到校规校纪）应是民意的反应，是公民和学生自主参与制定的结果。因此，公众和大学生遵从这些指示是心甘情愿、完全自主的行为。题目实际上是在将人们**行为上**对指示的依从偷换为**本性偏好**依从指示，偷换了概念。

至于在不民主或者假民主的环境下，人们表现出来的对指示的依从，那是因为人们的自主选择权被剥夺了，那完全是另外一个问题。

（2）假设这个原因成立，从它能否推出结果？

即使上述原因成立，结论也是推不出的。鉴于这个结果部分是个建议，我们在下面就从建议类题目的分析角度切入分析。

其次，按照建议类题目类型展开分析：

（1）题目中的建议可行性如何？

大学有足够的权力调整或者取消选修课。所以，题目中的建议无所谓是否可行。

（2）如果实施题目中的建议，是否会导致同初始目的相矛盾或其他荒谬的结果？

大学教育的目的是培养人格健全的人。而具备健全人格的人有一个特点，即思想和行为的自主性。如果大学明确所有必修课并取消选修课，显然是对大学精神的放弃。而且，大学以其百家争鸣、兼收并蓄的学术态度，像一片茂盛的森林一样涵养着一个国家和民族的理性和智慧。如果大学的课程都像小学一样被刻板地规定，等于无形中取消了大学自由探索、自由诘问的权利，那么，这个国家和民族也就失去了理性和智慧的源泉。

（3）有无替代或折中方案？

在大学的前两年，学校可以鼓励学生选修其专业及兴趣以外的学科，为其将来的学术发展构筑一个完整的框架。但到了后两年以及研究生阶段，则应鼓励学业专深。对于少数在专门领域较早便显示了天分的学生，应该给他们更多的自由以使其潜能得到最大限度的挖掘。

提纲提要

论点　题目中的判断似是而非。

正　从行为上看，人们有时更喜欢别人清楚明了地告诉他们该做什么、如何做，而不愿费心费力去自己做决定。

反　但是，建议 Colleges and universities should specify all required courses and eliminate elective courses in order to provide clear guidance for students 显得非常不妥。

首先，这不符合人的本性。在人所有的本性中，自由和自主为其最爱。常听人说"食色，性也"；但很少有人说"自由，性也"。但是，若没有最起码的自由，所谓"食色"本性也就无从谈起。

另外，题目中说大学生及普通大众喜欢听从指示而非自己去做决定。这里的关键问题是：这个指示指的到底是什么？假设一个国家、学校的管理真正是民主化的，那么，所有这些指示（大到国家的法律法规，小到校规校纪）应是民意的反应，是公民和学生自主参与制定的结果。因此，公众和大学生遵从这些指示是心甘情愿、完全自主的行为。题目实际上是在将人们**行为上**对指示的依从偷换为**本性偏好**依从指示，犯了偷换概念的错误。

至于在不民主或者假民主的环境下，人们所表现出来的对指示的依从，那是因为人们的自主选择权被剥夺了，那完全是另外一个问题。

果真实施题目中的建议的话，其破坏性后果是可想而知的：

大学教育的目的是培养格健全的人。而具备健全人格的人有一个特点，即思想和行为的自主性。如果大学明确所有必修课并取消选修课，显然是对大学精神的放弃。而且，大学以其百家争鸣、兼收并蓄的学术态度，像一片茂盛的森林一样涵养着一个国家和民族的理性和智慧。如果大学的课程都像小学一样被刻板地规定，等于无形中取消了大学自由探索、自由诘问的权利，那么，这个国家和民族也就失去了理性和智慧的源泉。

⊜ 折中方案：在大学的前两年，学校可以鼓励学生尽量多选修一些其专业及兴趣以外的学科，为其将来的学术发展构筑一个完整的框架。但到了后两年以及研究生阶段，则应鼓励学业专深。对于少数在专门领域较早便显示了天分的学生，应该给他们更多的自由以使其潜能得到最大限度的挖掘。

---

143. No field of study can advance significantly unless it incorporates knowledge and experience from outside that field.

该题目的分析及提纲请参见本书第一章第四节中的"建议类题目分析范例"之范例一。

Write a response in which you discuss the extent to which you agree or disagree with the statement and explain your reasoning for the position you take. In developing and supporting your position, you should consider ways in which the statement might or might not hold true and explain how these considerations shape your position.

---

144. True success can be measured primarily in terms of the goals one sets for oneself. (参考第53题)

Write a response in which you discuss the extent to which you agree or disagree with the statement and explain your reasoning for the position you take. In developing and supporting your position, you should consider ways in which the statement might or might not hold true and explain how these considerations shape your position.

题型归类 事实类。

题目分析

（1）能否从公认的原则或事实中推出相反的判断？

基于下列两点原则，题目中的判断未必成立：

其一，人是社会的人。人是通过获得社会的认可来发现自我价值的。所以，人很难摆脱社会定义的成功对其的影响。

其二，人们对成功的理解因年龄而异。一般而言，年轻人更急于获得社会的认可，因此总是去追求社会定义的成功。而成年人在历经了人世沧桑之后，对成功的界定更具个人色彩。

（2）能否举出相反的事例？

（大家可以举出无数身边发生的例子。此处从略。）

提纲提要

论点 **论者的观点过于简单化。**

㊣ 成功是一个人对自我的超越。所以真正的成功应该用自我设定的标准来衡量。

㊫ 但是人是社会的人。人是通过获得社会的认可来发现自我价值的。所以，人很难摆脱社会定义的成功对其的影响。

反 人们对成功的理解因年龄而异。一般而言，年轻人更急于获得社会的认可，因此总是去追求社会定义的成功。而成年人在历经了人世沧桑之后，对成功的界定更具个人色彩。

···

145. The general welfare of a nation's people is a better indication of that nation's greatness than are the achievements of its rulers, artists, or scientists. (参考第28、85、113、120、121、127题)

Write a response in which you discuss the extent to which you agree or disagree with the claim. In developing and supporting your position, be sure to address the most compelling reasons and/or examples that could be used to challenge your position.

题型归类 是非类。

题目分析

（1）这种价值判断的标准是什么？

到底该用什么来衡量一个国家的伟大？是该国国民的福利水平，还是该国统治者、艺术家和科学家的成就？这要看哪个尺度更接近于事实了。题目中，论者认为The general welfare of a nation's people is a better indication of that nation's greatness than are the achievements of its rulers, artists, or scientists。这在现代社会无疑是有道理的。

在现代民主和宪政的政治框架下，国家和政府与百姓的关系是对等、服务型的关系；国家是国民自主创建用以解决该国内外事务的，政府及其官员是选民和公民的雇员。国家和政府的支出完全由选民和议会决定。除了必要的公共开支和公共建设以外，社会财富是集中在百姓个人手中的。这时候，衡量一个伟大大国度的指标是其国民（包括艺术家和科学家）的福利程度、科教文化水平、民族和社会的凝聚力和向心力、国民的创新和创造能力，但唯独不包括国家统治者的成就。因为在现代政治生态里面，我们可以看到政党、政府、议会、司法、宪政约束下的君主、公民/选民、科学家和艺术家等等的存在和功能，但基本没有国家统治者的位置。

（2）这种价值判断的标准是否值得修正？

把论者的判断放到传统的君主制和皇权政体之下也未必符合事实。在君主制和皇权政体之下，君主与其百姓是统治和被统治、主宰者和臣民的关系。君主和皇权对其臣民和资源拥有绝对的权威和所有权。艺术家和科学家一般由皇室供养，其数量不多的作品和成果一般由皇室专有，同普通国民关系不大，给普通百姓带来的益处也很有限。那时，一个强大的帝国很难体现为百姓的福利，更多表现为君主的武功和战绩以及依附于帝王将相的科学家、艺术家和文人的成就。

提纲提要

论点 **论者的观点失于简单。**

正 论者的判断在现代社会无疑是有道理的。

在现代民主和宪政的政治框架下，国家和政府与百姓的关系是对等、服务型的关系；国家是国民自主创建用以解决该国内外事务的，政府及其官员是选民和公民的雇员。国家和政府的支出完全由选民和议会决定。除了必要的公共开支和公共建设以外，社会财富是集中在百姓个人手中的。这时候，衡量一个伟大国度的指标是其国民（包括艺术家和科学家）的福利程度、科教文化水平、民族和社会的凝聚力和向心力、国民的创新和创造能力，但唯独不包括国家统治者的成就。因为在现代政治生态里面，我们可以看到政党、政府、议会、司法、宪政约束下的君主、公民/选民、科学家和艺术家等等的存在和功能，但基本没有国家统治者的位置。

反 把论者的判断放到传统的君主制和皇权政体之下也未必符合事实。君主制和皇权政体之下，君主与其百姓是统治和被统治、主宰者和臣民的关系。君主和皇权对其臣民和资源拥有绝对的权威和所有权。艺术家和科学家一般由皇室供养，其数量不多的作品和成果一般由皇室专有，同普通国民关系不大，给普通百姓带来的益处也很有限。那时，一个强大的帝国很难体现为百姓的福利，更多表现为君主的武功和战绩以及依附于帝王将相的科学家、艺术家和文人的成就。

散 国家形态从一家一姓的王朝帝国到今天的公民社会和民主政体体现了国家和社会对个体越来越多的关注。在现代意义上，一个真正伟大的国家应该是人的个性和自由得到最充分发展和保障的国家。

---

146. The best test of an argument is the argument's ability to convince someone with an opposing viewpoint. (参考第79题)

Write a response in which you discuss the extent to which you agree or disagree with the statement and explain your reasoning for the position you take. In developing and supporting your position, you should consider ways in which the statement might or might not hold true and explain how these considerations shape your position.

题型归类 是非类。

题目分析

（1）这种价值判断的标准是什么？

题目中的论者显然在用说服力来衡量一个观点和立论真伪的标准。说服力强、能在争辩中击败不同意见，就说明一个观点和立论的真实性或者价值。但这个标准很不可靠。这是因为：其一，辩论很可能因为违背初衷、罔顾事实的自我辩解，从而使得最后胜出的思想、观点未必有价值；同样，因为别人的善辩而被放弃的思想、观点未必就没有价值。其二，尚有别的发现某一思想价值的方法，如：查阅资料、自我反思等。

（2）这种价值判断的标准是否值得修正？

一个观点和立论的价值只能看其在多大程度上接近事实和真理，而这个衡量的标准是实践。雄辩之士也许总能在辩论中获胜，但雄辩不等于真理，雄辩的人不是真理批发商。

提纲提要

论点 雄辩的人不是真理批发商。

正 辩论有利于明确问题、开拓视角、启发新的思想。

反 但是，辩论或者观点的说服力并不能有效证实真理。这是因为：其一，辩论很可能因为违背初衷、罔顾事实的自我辩解，从而使得最后胜出的思想、观点未必有价值；同样，因为别人的善辩而被放弃的思想、观点未必就没有价值。其二，尚有别的发现某一思想价值的方法，如：查阅资料、自我反思等。

反 一个观点和立论的价值在于其在多大程度上接近事实和真理，而这个衡量的标准是实践。雄辩之士也许总能在辩论中获胜，但雄辩不等于真理，雄辩的人不是真理批发商。

147. The effectiveness of a country's leaders is best measured by examining the well-being of that country's citizens. (参考第8、16、62、69、94、114、123、128题)

Write a response in which you discuss the extent to which you agree or disagree with the statement and explain your reasoning for the position you take. In developing and supporting your position, you should consider ways in which the statement might or might not hold true and explain how these considerations shape your position.

（单纯性是非类。本题的分析思路和写作提纲可完全借鉴第94题。）

148, Nations should pass laws to preserve any remaining wilderness areas in their natural state. (参考第10、31、63、67、119、125题)

Write a response in which you discuss the extent to which you agree or disagree with the claim. In developing and supporting your position, be sure to address the most compelling reasons and/or examples that could be used to challenge your position.

（建议类。本题的分析思路和写作提纲可完全借鉴第10题。）

149, In any field—business, politics, education, government—those in power should be required to step down after five years. (参考第8、111题)

Write a response in which you discuss your views on the policy and explain your reasoning for the position you take. In developing and supporting your position, you should consider the possible consequences of implementing the policy and explain how these consequences shape your position.

（建议类。本题的分析思路和写作提纲可完全借鉴第111题。）

下篇: ARGUMENT

第一章

ARGUMENT题目中推理/论证缺陷和谬误的识别与分析

★ 十大论证技巧及反驳切入点

★ 论证过程中常见的逻辑漏洞诊断

ARGUMENT作文写作中的关键问题在于**题目中的推理/论证缺陷和谬误难以识别**。而实际上，这些推理/论证谬误都比较简单。我们仅仅依靠生活和逻辑常识就能把它们一一解决。有些同学因为惧怕ARGUMENT中逻辑问题的难度，甚至找来专门讲解形式逻辑的教材来加强这方面的知识。这实在是有点小题大做了。

本质上讲，每个ARGUMENT题目都包含一个论证的过程：其中有观点，有论据。这个从论据到论点的论证过程会出现诸多逻辑链条。我们的任务只有一个：从两到三个方面证明题目在哪些逻辑链条上出了问题，导致从论据到论点/结论的推理依据不成立。

同ISSUE题目一样，新版的ARGUMENT题目后面都有一个写作指引。每一道ARGUMENT题目的后面很可能是以下八个指引中的一个（括号内的中文是每个指引的主要含义）：

A: Write a response in which you discuss what specific evidence is needed to evaluate the argument and explain how the evidence would weaken or strengthen the argument.

（题目中的哪些地方需要提供进一步的证据？）

B: Write a response in which you examine the stated and/or unstated assumptions of the argument. Be sure to explain how the argument depends on these assumptions, and what the implications are for the argument if the assumptions prove unwarranted.

（题目中的哪些假设有问题？）

C: Write a response in which you discuss what questions would need to be answered in order to decide whether the recommendation and the argument on which it is based are reasonable. Be sure to explain how the answers to these questions would help to evaluate the recommendation.

（题目中的提议及其立论有哪些问题？）

D: Write a response in which you discuss what questions would need to be answered in order to decide whether the advice and the argument on which it is based are reasonable. Be sure to explain how the answers to these questions would help to evaluate the advice.

（题目中的建议及其立论有哪些问题？）

E: Write a response in which you discuss what questions would need to be answered in order to decide whether the recommendation is likely to have the predicted result. Be sure to explain how the answers to these questions would help to evaluate the recommendation.

（题目中的提议及预测有哪些问题？）

F: Write a response in which you discuss what questions would need to be answered in order to decide whether the prediction and the argument on which it is based are reasonable. Be sure to explain how the answers to these questions would help to evaluate the prediction.

（题目中的预测及其立论有哪些问题？）

G: Write a response in which you discuss one or more alternative explanations that could rival the proposed explanation and explain how your explanation(s) can plausibly account for the facts presented in the argument.

（能否对题目中的逻辑和现象给出一个或多个不同的解释？）

H: Write a response in which you discuss what questions would need to be addressed in order to decide whether the conclusion and the argument on which it is based are reasonable. Be sure to explain how the answers to the questions would help to evaluate the conclusion.

（题目中的结论及其立论有哪些问题？）

应该说，这些写作指引使得ARGUMENT的分析方式同过去有很大的不同。之前的ARGUMENT没有写作指引，因此，对其分析可以是很随意的。通常只要找到题目中的两三个逻辑漏洞就行了。现在这些写作指引实际上规定了考生对ARGUMENT题目展开分析的具体方向，更加强调对ARGUMENT题目中论证过程各个环节的分析。

这就是说：GRE改版后，**ARGUMENT的分析从过去对一个个独立的逻辑漏洞的寻找变成了对推理/论证过程中各个逻辑链条的可靠性与合理性的系统梳理。一系列逻辑链条中的任何一个环节出了问题，ARGUMENT题目中的推论结果就不能成立。相应地，考生对每个ARGUMENT题目的分析也必须由过去主要从逻辑漏洞切入，变成从题目中论者运用的推理/论证方法的切入，以求发现其论证过程各个环节的缺陷和谬误。**

一般来讲，ARGUMENT的分析和写作需要三个步骤：

第一步，识别ARGUMENT题目中论者所采用的论证方法。每个ARGUMENT都是一个简短的推理/论证过程，而这个推理/论证过程必然要有论证方式。如同在ISSUE作文中，我们首先要对所有的ISSUE题目进行归类以便找到分析切入点一样，我们对ARGUMENT的分析也要先识别每个ARGUMENT题目中运用的论证方法（也就是下面马上要谈到的十大论证技巧），以便找到用来理清ARGUMENT推理/论证过程的逻辑起点（或者说反驳切入点）。

第二步，由每个ARGUMENT论证法的逻辑起点入手，发现每个推理/论证过程在诸个逻辑链条上出现的推理/论证缺陷和谬误。

第三步，对每个推理/论证缺陷和谬误展开具体的分析和论证，说明为什么可以认定它们是推理/论证的缺陷和谬误，以及它们是如何影响ARGUMENT题目中论点和结论的有效性。这其实也是每个ARGUMENT题目后面的写作指引的具体要求。如果我们观察ARGUMENT题目后面的那八个写作指引，会发现它们由两句话组成：前一句提示考生展开分析的方向；而后一句则是提示考生要对其发现的推理/论证缺陷和谬误进行解释和论证（至于如何进行解释和论证会在下文中专门探讨）。

具体如何完成上述三大步骤的核心技巧就体现在下面要阐述的**十大论证技巧及相应的反驳切入点以及十五个常见推理论证谬误诊断**之中。掌握了这些论证的反驳切入点和推理论证谬误的诊断技巧之后，大家会发现识别ARGUMENT题目中的推理/论证谬误其实是件非常轻松的事情。

第一节　十大论证技巧及反驳切入点

在讲解ISSUE写作的论证方法时，我们提到了常用的十种论证方法，包括：因果关系论证法、引用权威论证法、反证法、列举特征论证法、统计数据论证法、归纳推理论证法、诉诸常识法、演绎推理论证法、类比论证法和定义法。这些论证方法，除了反证法以外，在ARGUMENT题目中都有涉及。

我们知道，任何论证过程都有论点和论据。而能否用论据有效地支持论点，关键在于从论点到论据有没有足够的推理依据。如果推理依据不成立，论证就是无效论证。所以我们从论证方法入手，反驳ARGUMENT论证的有效切入点就是它的推理依据。下面，我们一一讲解如何运用十大论证方法找到对ARGUMENT的分析切入点：

1. 演绎推理论证法

将一个具体的事例运用到一个一般性原则从而得出结论。例如：

论　点 Demand for this product will go up.

论　据 The price of the product is sliding.

推理依据 Whenever prices of a product go down, the demand for it rises.

反驳切入点 其一，该演绎推理的总原则（即大前提）是否成立。其二，该演绎推理的论据（即小前提）是否成立。显然，二者只要有一个不成立，该演绎推理就无效。

本例中，如果根本不存在某一商品价格下降，其销量上升的规律，或者虽然这个规律存在，但某一商品的价格根本没有下降（比如只是有一个价格下降的假象），那么，依据The price of the product is sliding就推不出 Demand for this product will go up。

2. 定义法

界定一个概念的关键内涵，或者认定某个事物符合某个定义，从而得出结论。例如：

论　点 Radical feminists are not good citizens.

论　据 Radical feminists lack family values.

推理依据 Family values characterize the good citizen.

反驳切入点 这个定义反映了问题的本质吗？有没有例外情况？

本例中，好公民就必然有家庭价值吗？二者有必然联系吗？有没有例外呢？

3. 因果关系论证法

将一个判断放入一个因果关系中，指出它是原因还是结果。例如：

论　点 The Internet may be causing depression.

论　据 When a group of people increased its use of the Internet, they felt depressed.

推理依据 There are no other reasons for the group's depression.

反驳切入点 是否有其他原因导致了这一结果？是否有其他更重要的原因与所讨论的原因共同导致了这一结果？

本例中，是否有其他原因，比如电脑辐射致使因特网使用者情绪抑郁？是否有其他更重要的原因，比如长时间上网导致的饮食和睡眠的紊乱，与网上杂乱、无序的信息共同导致了因特网使用者情绪抑郁？

4. 归纳推理论证法

从若干个具体事例中推出具有共性的一般结论。例如：

论　点 Everyone likes the movie.

论　据 I know three people who like the movie.

推理依据 Three examples are enough.

反驳切入点 归纳所依据的数量足够多吗？具有代表性吗？有没有特殊情况？

本例中，仅仅依据三个人的看法就进行归纳，是否显得过于仓促？这三个人是否因为特殊原因（比如喜欢电影中的某位演员）而对这部电影评价较高，因此他们的看法很难代表大多数人的态度？有多少人不喜欢这部电影？

5. 列举特征式论证法

指出某事物发生或者存在的征候或迹象。例如：

论 点 The child has chickenpox.

论 据 The child has red spots.

推理依据 These spots are signs of chickenpox.

反驳切入点 有没有其他原因导致同样的症候或迹象？

本例中，这个孩子身上的红色斑点就一定是水痘的症状吗？是不是其他疾病（比如花粉过敏）的症状？

6. 类比论证法

用我们已知、熟悉的事物同未知、不熟悉的事物进行比较，并用前者的情况解释后者的情况。类比论证分为三种：纵向类比（过去的事物同现在的同一类事物的类比）、横向类比（同一时期、同一类事物之间的类比）、比喻式类比（不同类别事物之间的类比）。例如：

A. 纵向类比

论 点 Many people will die of SARS.

论 据 Many people died of the Black Death.

推理依据 SARS and Black Death are similar and comparable.

反驳切入点 历史会重演吗？

本例中，过去黑死病导致大量人口死亡的结果会通过今天的"非典"重演吗？

B. 横向类比

论 点 China should have its fighter carriers.

论 据 A neighboring country has a powerful carrier fleet.

推理依据 The two countries are similar enough to draw such a comparison.

反驳切入点 比较的对象之间有足够的可比性吗？

本例中，中国和这个邻国的国情可以完全相提并论吗？

C. 比喻式类比

论 点 Reading a difficult book should take time.

论 据 Digesting a large meal takes time.

推理依据 Reading and eating are sufficiently alike that they can be mutually compared.

反驳切入点 一事物和它被比喻成的事物之间有足够的相似性吗？

本例中，看书和吃饭之间是否很相似？（提示：比喻式类比在 ARGUMENT 题目中极少出现。）

7. 引用权威论证法

引用公认的权威，或者论证自己就是权威从而对自己的观点加以论证。例如：

论 点 China's economy will grow 8 per cent this year.

论 据 Professors and scientists say so.

推理依据 These experts are reliable.

反驳切入点 所引用的权威可信吗？

本例中，这些专家是货真价实的专家吗？他们有足够的公信力吗？

8. 诉诸常识法

利用人们的常识（包括普遍性的价值观念、人们的普遍动机、生活常识）进行论证。例如：

A. 诉诸普遍性的价值观念

论　点 The university curriculum should be multicultural.

论　据 A multicultural curriculum will contribute to equality and acceptance.

推理依据 People widely value equality and acceptance.

反驳切入点 论者强调的价值果真那么重要吗？有没有其他更重要的价值？论者强调的价值的含义明确吗？

本例中，不同文化间的相互平等和彼此接受是一所大学最关注的价值吗？一个国家的特殊文化传统是否应是大学教育的核心价值呢？这里所说的equality and acceptance是什么意思？是指所有文化、宗教都应在一所大学里传播吗？

B. 诉诸普遍动机

论　点 You should support this candidate premier.

论　据 The candidate can help you get job security and safe neighborhoods.

推理依据 People want job security and safe neighborhoods.

反驳切入点 论者强调的动机果真是大家最需要的吗？这些动机果真能像论者所说的那样得到实现？

本例中，大家现在关注的是就业和社区安全吗？论者关于就业和社区安全的承诺能兑现吗？

C. 诉诸生活常识

论　点 She was very kind to me.

论　据 She treated me with the best tea she had.

推理依据 A treatment with the best tea is an expression of kindness.

反驳切入点 论者依据的生活常识成立吗？有没有例外？

本例中，来客敬茶总表示善意吗？是否用咖啡招待客人才是对贵客的礼遇？来客敬茶是否是送客的含蓄表示？

9. 反证法

假设一个观点是正确的，然而却推导出荒谬的结论。例如：

论　点 An industrious man must also be thrifty.

论　据 With only industry but without thrift, the person will end up bankrupt.

推理依据 An industrious person ends up bankrupt sounds absurd.

反驳切入点 推导出的这个结论果真荒谬吗？

本例中，一个人终生勤劳，到老所剩无几就是荒谬？假如这个花光了一生积蓄的人把钱花在了慈善事业上呢，或者他把钱花光了，却过得很幸福呢？（提示：反证法在ARGUMENT题目中极少出现，几乎没有。）

10. 统计数据论证法

提供数据，以资论证。例如：

论　点 We should end the current poverty-relief program.

论　据 It costs $45 million per year.

推理依据 That spending is too high to be sustainable.

反驳切入点 这些数据是由谁调查的？这些调查的方案设计（如调查样本的选择、调查问卷的设计、调查数据的处理、调查结果的核实和验证等等）和实施过程是严格按照科学程序进行的吗？其结论是客观、中立、可信的吗？调查的实施者没有受行业及其他利益相关方的影响吗？独立第三方的相关数据是否支持相同／相似的结论？

本例中，现有的扶贫项目每年花掉4,500万美元，这个数据是谁公布的？这些数据是由谁统计的？怎么统计的？数据是如何处理的？数据的权威性和可信度如何？

ARGUMENT题目经常在两个地方引用数据论证，值得注意的问题有：

其一，调查统计。

对于一般的调查统计，如果是随机抽样调查（random sampling），要注意挑选的样本是否足够多、样本间是否有很大的误差、样本是否具备代表性。

比如，要调查公众对某一执政党上一年产业政策效果的反应，三五个人的意见显然不能说明问题。该执政党党员的态度很可能会有意偏向积极的评价，因而过多反映该党党员意见的问卷统计就可能出现选样误差。只选择某一产业的人群，比如说制造业工人，也可能不具备足够的代表性，因为很可能该执政党的政策特别优惠或者特别损害了该产业工人的利益，等等。

其二，试验对比。

ARGUMENT题目中经常出现诸如要确定某一种药物的疗效的内容。显然，要确定该药物的疗效，需要设置试验组（即test group，使用了该药物的一组）和对照组（即control group，没有使用该药物的一组。该组的人经常被要求服用和试验药物外观一样、但不含任何药物成分的糖丸或镇静剂之类的东西，以消除心理暗示对实验结果的影响）。没有对照组的数据进行比较，单单试验组的数据很难说明实质问题。

另外，试验组和对照组的人群应是同质的。也就是说，要防止这两组人群因其本身的差异而导致实验结果的不同。比如，要确定一种药物降低血压的效果，对照组是中老年人，试验组就不能是青少年。因为青少年的血压一般都没有问题，即便不用药，他们的血压也正常。这样，选青少年做试验组就没意义了，或者至少会影响实验结果的可信度。

这里，还有必要简单总结一下ARGUMENT题目中常见的**数据陷阱**：

A. 绝对数量陷阱

在应该用比率（如百分比）来表明事物变动趋势的时候，题目中却用绝对数量来掩饰。例如：

A recent survey of 2,000 people who had had a heart attack revealed that 158 of them said they had eaten a heavy meal within 24 hours before their heart attack, and 25 of them said they had eaten a heavy meal within 2 hours before their heart attack.

论者说，在2,000名被调查对象中，有183人（158人加上25人）在其心脏病发作前的2—24小时内吃了heavy meals。但问题是，这个比率并不高，仅仅是9%。这么低的比率，很难说明在心脏病和heavy meals之间有很大的相关性。论者在题目中有用看起来较高的绝对数量来掩盖较低的比率的意图。

B. 百分比陷阱

同绝对数量陷阱相反，百分比陷阱是企图用比率的变化来掩饰绝对量的变化。例如：

The City Council should fund the Reader's Club, whose membership increased by 100 percent last year.

一倍的增长似乎非常可观。但如果去年的读者基数是30名，一倍的增长又能说明什么问题呢？

C. 平均值陷阱

在ARGUMENT题目中，平均值经常被用来掩盖个体间的差异。例如：

For the third year in a row, the average household income in our country has risen significantly, 25 percent year on year actually. That prosperity means that families are likely to be spending more time and money on leisure activities.

年平均25%的收入增长率似乎很高，但如果这个国家贫富差距极大的话，只能有极少数富裕家庭才可以享受休闲活动，多数家庭是支付不起休闲费用的。

D. 用整体的数据说明局部情况的陷阱

关于某一区域或群体的整体统计未必代表这一区域或群体内个别地域或个别群体的情况。例如：

The majority of families in Bay City are two-income families, and a nationwide study has shown that such families eat significantly fewer home-cooked meals than they did a decade ago but at the same time express more concern about eating healthily.

题目中的那项对全国范围内双职工家庭饮食习惯的调查对Bay City的双职工家庭来说可能毫无意义——由于地方经济的特点，Bay City的双职工家庭的饮食习惯可能与全国的一般情况截然相反。

E. 模糊数据陷阱

论者用一些模糊的量词，比如most，majority，significantly等来描述数量。这使得人们很难估计实际数量到底是多少。例如：

In an attempt to improve highway safety, Prunty County recently lowered its speed limit from 55 miles per hour to 45 on all major county roads. But the 55 mph limit should be restored, because this safety effort has failed. **Most** drivers are exceeding the new speed limit and the accident rate throughout Prunty County has decreased **only slightly**.

有谁能准确说出most drivers和only slightly的确切比例吗？ 55%和95%都可称为大多数（most），但这两个比率显然有本质不同。3%和13%都可称为略微地（slightly），但实际效果显然不一样。

实际上，有了上述十大论证技巧及相应的反驳切入点，我们已经可以应对所有的ARGUMENT题目了，因为所有的ARGUMENT题目无非都是一些论证，而且所使用的论证方法也都包含在这十大论证技巧的范围内。所以，运用上述反驳切入点，我们可以轻松地把题目论证中的不足和漏洞找出来。关于这一点，大家随后在本书第五章中会有更清晰的体会。

但是，人们习惯于把一些常见的推理论证错误单列为论证过程中的逻辑漏洞。为了便于大家识别，本书会将频繁出现在ARGUMENT题目中的逻辑漏洞（fallacies in reasoning）列出来。但实际上，所有这些逻辑漏洞在本质上都是论证过程中的错误。比如，下面要谈到的逻辑漏洞**"仓促概括"**实际是一个归纳推理的错误；而**"利用从众心理"**这一逻辑漏洞不过是类比不当的推理谬误而已。大家随后在具体的ARGUMENT分析与写作过程中也会发现，这些逻辑漏洞用到的其实并不多，关键还是ARGUMENT中的论证方法。

第二节　论证过程中常见的逻辑漏洞诊断

1. 强词夺理（Begging the Question）

简单提出论点，而不给出任何必要的论据和论证的错误，都是在"强词夺理"。这种逻辑错误一般有三种表现形式：

其一，简单重复型。这种形式的"强词夺理"非常直白，就是一味地强调自己是正确的，却没有给出任何证明。比如：

Question Can you prove why this is true?

Answer Why is this true? It's true because I know it's true.

像这种"因为我正确，所以我正确"的逻辑，是最霸道的"强词夺理"。

其二，夹带问题型。这种强词夺理把一个未经证明的陈述以一个问题的形式说出来，好像这个未经证明的陈述已经是真的似的。比如：

Have you stopped beating your wife yet?

这句话问的是，你是否不再打老婆了。听起来，好像被问的人过去一贯打老婆似的。但实际上，被问的人过去是否打老婆未经证实，问话的人根本没有提供任何证明。

其三，反问型。这种"强词夺理"把一个未经证明的陈述以一个反问的形式说出来，其所隐含的逻辑是：既然你不能证明我错误，那我就是对的。比如：

How do you know that flying saucers haven't been visiting the earth over the past centuries?

If Tom Smith doesn't have magic powers, how could he predict many disastrous happenings so well?

显然，我们不能证明飞碟未曾造访地球和Tom Smith没有神秘力量，但这不等于说过去飞碟曾到过地球，Tom Smith有神秘力量。这两件事情是真是假，应由提出问题的人给出证明。

2. 无关问题（Red Herring）

这种逻辑推理错误的表现形式是：用一个和论点无关或者有误导性的论据来支持论点。比如：

We shouldn't convict John Jefferson, because he is a very talented musician.

实际上，John Jefferson是否是天才音乐家同他是否有罪是两个毫不相干的问题。不相关的事实没有丝毫的说服力。

3. 推不出（Non Sequitur）

这几乎是一个放之四海而皆准的逻辑错误名称。任何推理和论证，只要不能从前提/论据推出结论/论点，它的逻辑错误都叫Non Sequitur。Non Sequitur是拉丁语，意思是it doesn't follow，译成中文是"推不出"或"未必"。比如：

He must be a computer expert, because he has got a very expensive lap-top computer.

显然，一个人拥有一台昂贵的笔记本电脑并不意味着他就对计算机很内行。很多公司的老总随身携带着价格不菲的笔记本电脑，但那可能是用来装点门面的。

4. 一面之词（Stacked Evidence）

犯这种逻辑错误的人习惯强调某一问题中对自己有利的一面，而忽略其他方面。比如：

Television is so important for our everyday life: It offers us educational programs, informs people happenings around the world, brings all family members together after work and therefore strengthens the family values.

但是，论者唯独不提电视传播的色情和暴力对青少年的影响以及电视的强大宣传效应对人们独立思考能力的钝化。

5. 虚假困境（False Either-or Dilemma）

犯这种逻辑错误的人喜欢制造一个非此即彼的困境，让人在二者中择其一。比如：

A woman can either be a mother or have a career.

A university student can either go to graduate school or become a company man.

问题是，果真只有两种可能吗？

6. 在此之后，因此之故（Post Hoc）

这种逻辑错误实际是一种错误的因果关系。它的表现形式是：因为事件A发生在事件B之后，所以事件B是事件A的原因，即 After this, therefore for this。比如：

I found my love after having a haircut of special style, so the haircut must make the thing.

理了个很特别的发型之后就找到了中意的恋人，前者是后者的原因。这可信吗？

除了"在此之后，因此之故"外，还有两种错误的因果关系值得注意：

其一，**将相关性当作因果关系**（Correlation Mistaken for Causation）。当变量A变化，变量B也相应地变化时，A和B之间被认为存在某种相关性，但二者之间未必就存在因果关系。比如：

In the last several years, whenever sales of personal computers went up, sales of athletic shoes also rose strongly; therefore, buyers of personal computers must have bought athletic shoes as well.

凭直觉就可判断上述推理是荒谬的。很可能是良好的经济形势使各种商品的销售量上升。

其二，**将同时发生的两件事情当作因果关系**（Concurrence Mistaken for Causation）。两件事情同时发生很可能是纯粹的巧合，二者间没有任何因果关系。比如：

It is known that in recent years, industrial pollution has caused the earth's ozone layer to thin, allowing an increase in the amount of ultraviolet radiation that reaches the earth's surface. At the same time, scientists have discovered the population of a species of salamander that lays its eggs in mountain lakes has declined. So, the increased ultraviolet radiation must have caused the decreased salamander population.

实际上，很可能不是 the increased ultraviolet radiation，而是农民在田间使用的一种杀虫剂导致了 the decreased salamander population。

7. 仓促概括（Hasty Generalization）

这实际是一个归纳推理的错误。其表现形式是：依据有限数量的事实进行一般性的概括。比如：

Most students in Riverside school must have participated in gang activities in the street yesterday, because six students from this school were found involved in the gang crimes.

这是典型的抓住个别，打倒一片的错误。六个学生怎能代表全校学生的情况？

8. 人身攻击（Ad Hominem）

犯这种逻辑错误的人习惯避开正在讨论的问题不谈，专门攻击他人隐私、道德等问题。比如：

Peter is not fit for this position, because he has just abandoned his girlfriend.

Peter是否适合这个职位关键取决于他的工作能力和职业道德，而他的个人情感问题与正在讨论的问题无关。

但是，避免人身攻击不等于避开所有道德操守问题。假如道德操守问题本身就是讨论的对象，实事求是地讨论一个人的品性不算人身攻击。比如，在中小学教师的选拔聘用过程中，就应当考虑应聘者的道德品行。

9. 道德连坐（Guilt by Association）

"道德连坐"本质上是人身攻击的一种变体。它通常表现为：某一个人和另外一个名声不佳的个人或者组织、团体有关系，因此就否定这个人的品行和能力。比如：

We had better not re-elect Janson Kuan, because the Town Council of which Kuan is a member had not carried out a successful environmental protection policy last year.

实际上，仅仅作为Town Council的一员，Janson Kuan对去年Town Council环保政策的不成功可能根本不负什么责任。但论者认为，因为他是Town Council的一员，所以他必定有错。这显然不正确。

10. 搭斜坡（Slippery Slope）

犯这种逻辑错误的人喜欢设想一连串可怕的后果，用以威胁别人一定要去做什么，而不要做什么。但是，除了威胁之外，他没有给出任何其他有效支持其论点的证明。比如：

We must move immediately to start our environmental protection plans. Otherwise, we will soon see badly polluted air, soil, and water. The countryside will be flooded and the city will be ruined. We will find nowhere to escape.

问题是，环境恶化得会这么快吗？

11. 转移话题（Extension）

这种逻辑错误的表现形式是：抛开正在讨论的话题不谈，转而讨论一个新话题。比如：

The development of an extensive computer-based long-distance learning program will enhance the reputation of Xanadu College. This program would allow more students to enroll in our courses, thereby increasing our income from student tuition.

这段话来自一道旧版ARGUMENT题目。论者由一个关于Xanadu College声望的问题转移到另外一个不相干的增加学校招生和收入的问题，犯了"转移话题"的错误。

12. 偷换概念（Inconsistent Connotation & Denotation）

这种推理错误的表现是：使用概念时，概念的内涵（Connotation）和外延（Denotation）不一致，因而所表达的意思发生了改变。比如：

This medicine contains an element impressively effective for bettering vision of distant objects; therefore, people who develop vision problems should take it.

在这个句子中，一种对治疗远视问题有效的药物被说成对所有的视力问题都有效。但是显然，视力问题不仅仅是远视问题。概念的外延被扩大了。

13. 制造虚假需求（Create False Needs）

这是一个在广告词中大行其道的现象。这种逻辑错误的本质是不提供有效证明，而是利用人们的普遍价值观念和心理动机对人们进行心理操纵。比如：

All parents who are concerned about their children's educational success should buy this new edition of encyclopedia.

为人父母者当然关心子女的教育问题，但这就意味着他们要买这本新版的百科全书吗？对这本新版的百科全书为什么值得购买，论者没有给出任何证明。

14. 利用从众心理（Bandwagon Appeal）

这种逻辑错误的表现在于：它不提供任何逻辑证明，但只强调一点：别人这样做了，所以你也要这样做。比如：

Everyone in the company is learning the new-fashion of line dancing. You should do it too.

因为别人都在学习这种新舞蹈，你也不应例外。为什么？论者没提。

15. 待定假设（Problematic Assumption）

这种推理错误的表现是：推理中蕴含一个假设，只有当这个假设成立时，整个推理才成立。但这个假设到底能否成立尚令人置疑。比如：

Nowadays, more and more people prefer to work at home. We should take advantage of this work-at-home trend by increasing our firm's stock of home office machines such as printers, small copy machines, paper shredders, and fax machines.

这个推理认为，为了充分利用渐成风潮的在家工作的生活方式带来的商机，这家公司应增加打印机、小型复印机、碎纸机和传真机的存货。这个推理必然假设人们在家工作的习惯会导致对这些机器的需求。但是，果真会有这样的需求吗？如果有的话，量会有多大呢？这些都尚待证明。

这种逻辑错误十分常见，以至于新版的ARGUMENT八大写作指引的其中一条就是要求考生专门分析ARGUMENT题目中在各个逻辑环节所出现的问题假设。

以上就是常见的逻辑漏洞。当然，类似的逻辑谬误我们还可列出更多。但以上这些已经足够我们应对ARGUMENT题目了。

在了解了**十大论证技巧及相应的反驳切入点以及常见逻辑漏洞诊断方法**之后，这里有必要回过头去，补充讲解一下对ISSUE作文中因果类题目分析的一个小技巧。

我们已经讲过，因果类题目的分析切入点有两点：(1)这个因果关系推理中的原因是否成立？(2)假设这个原因成立，从它能否推出结果？

我们从第二个分析切入点展开分析时，会产生一个问题：**该如何证明从题目中的原因推不出结果**？答案就是：运用上面所讲的**十大论证技巧及相应的反驳切入点和常见逻辑漏洞诊断方法**。

这是因为从**原因**到**结果**的推理过程，本身就是一个从**前提/论据**到**结论/论点**的推理/论证过程。原因和结果、前提和结论、论点和论据实质上是三组相同的概念。在日常生活中，我们本来就在不自觉地把一个推理的前提当作原因，把结论当作结果；相应地，我们也把论证过程中的论据当作原因，而把论点当作结果。这三组概念的关系如下图所示：

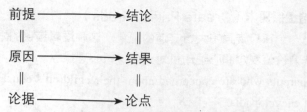

正因为如此，我们可以运用十大论证技巧及相应的反驳切入点和常见逻辑漏洞诊断方法，来对因果类题目中的因果关系推理展开分析。

因果类题目的这一特点鲜明而典型地体现了考生的分析和思辨能力在ISSUE和ARGUMENT两篇作文中的相通之处。

第二章

ARGUMENT
的写作技巧

- ★ ARGUMENT的开头写作技巧
- ★ ARGUMENT的结尾写作技巧
- ★ ARGUMENT正文部分的文章
  结构与写作技巧

ARGUMENT作文从内容到写作要求都与ISSUE作文差别较大。二者最为明显的差别是：ISSUE写作要求作者有自己的观点，并对自己的观点进行令人信服的论证；而ARGUMENT写作则只要求作者对别人的推理和论证是否可信作评论，无需对文章中涉及的问题提出自己的观点。因此，ARGUMENT作文的开头、结尾和正文部分也就不同于ISSUE作文。

第一节　ARGUMENT的开头写作技巧

ARGUMENT作文的开头要比ISSUE作文的开头简单、直接。一般有下列三种最为常见的形式。

一、客套式

这种开头由两部分组成。其一，对要评估的推理论证作出纯粹礼节式的肯定。其二，指出该论证存在的推理问题。比如下面一篇ETS提供的6分ARGUMENT范文的开头（全文请参见本书附录7）：

The notion that protective gear reduces the injuries suffered in accidents seems at first glance to be an obvious conclusion. After all, it is the intent of these products to either prevent accidents from occurring in the first place or to reduce the injuries suffered by the wearer should an accident occur. **However**, the conclusion that investing in high quality protective gear greatly reduces the risk of being severely injured in an accident may mask other (and potentially more significant) causes of injuries and may inspire people to over invest financially and psychologically in protective gear.

很显然，However前面的若干行文字都是客套话；而However之后的内容才是作者对题目中推理的评价，即题目中的推理忽视了真实的原因，导致人们对保护器具的盲目投资和依赖。

这种开头是ETS提供的范文中最为常见的开头方式。

二、开门见山式

这种开头直截了当、直奔主题。请看下面一篇ETS提供的5分ARGUMENT范文的开头。原题目如下：

The following appeared as a letter to the editor of a local newspaper.

Five years ago, we residents of Morganton voted to keep the publicly owned piece of land known as Scott Woods in a natural, undeveloped state. Our thinking was that, if no shopping centers or houses were built there, Scott Woods would continue to benefit our community as a natural parkland. But now that our town planning committee wants to purchase the land and build a school there, we should reconsider this issue. If the land becomes a school site, no shopping centers or houses can be built there, and substantial acreage would probably be devoted to athletic fields. There would be no better use of land in our community than this, since a large majority of our children participate in sports, and Scott Woods would continue to benefit our community as natural parkland.

文章的开头段是这样的：

The author's argument is weak. Though he believes Scott Woods benefits the community as an undeveloped park, he also thinks a school should be built on it. Obviously the author is not aware of the development that comes with building a school besides the facilities devoted to learning or sports.

这种开头干脆利落，直接给出对题目中推理的评价。

三、罗列要点式

这种开头一般先将题目中推理/论证的主要论点和论据总结一下，然后再说出作者对该推理/论证的评价。请看下面这篇ETS提供的6分ARGUMENT范文的开头（这篇文章的题目同上面刚刚谈过的开门见山式开头中所举例子的题目是一样的）：

This letter to the editor begins by stating the reasons the residents of Morganton voted to keep Scott Woods in an undeveloped state. The letter states that the entire community could benefit from an undeveloped parkland. The residents of the town wanted to ensure that no shopping centers or houses would be built there. This, in turn, would provide everyone in the community with a valuable resource, a natural park.

The letter then continues by addressing the issue of building a school on the land. The author reasons that this would also benefit the entire community as a natural parkland since much of the land would be devoted to athletic fields. The author of the letter comes to the conclusion that building a school on the land would be the best thing for everyone in the community.

This letter is a one-sided argument about the best use of the land known as Scott Woods. The author may be a parent whose child would benefit from a new school, a teacher who thinks a school would boost the community, or just a resident of Morganton. Regardless of who the author is, there are many aspects of this plan that he or she has overlooked or chosen to ignore.

该文作者用了两个段落来陈述题目中的推理，然后在第三自然段评价了题目中的推理。

好文章开头有三要素：**有趣、短、能提领全文**。因为ARGUMENT写作的主要任务是对别人的推理和论证是否可信作一番评估，所以写作风格应平实、稳健。由于受文章语气的限制，开头三要素中的"有趣"较难做到；而"短"和"能提领全文"是很容易做到的。

上面所举的三个开头段的例子都能做到"能提领全文"。但是，除了第二个例子还算比较简洁外，例一和例三都显得比较拖沓。尤其是例三，可以算是一个失败的开头段——它好像是账房先生的明细账，有点儿过于琐碎了。

在给定的30分钟时间内写一篇400词—500词的ARGUMENT作文是一件较有挑战性的工作。但例三的长度至少是全文长度的三分之一，这样的比例显然不合适。

因此，我们的结论是：

其一，ETS的作文批改人员不太关注文章的形式，比如文章到底该怎样开头。他们更关注文章所显示的考生的分析能力、对问题复杂性的识别和解释能力以及论证能力。

其二，我们完全可以在某些方面做得更专业，比如写出简短、精炼的文章开头段。简短、精炼的开头必然比拖沓、冗长的开头更有利于拿高分。如果例三这样写的话，效果会更好一些：

According to the letter, residents of Morganton first wanted to keep Scott Woods as a natural undeveloped parkland.

But when the town planning committee proposed to set up a school on the land, the letter writer called on Morganton residents to embrace the idea, arguing this might be the best use of the land.

This letter is a one-sided argument, because there are many aspects that the letter-writer has overlooked or chosen to ignore.

所以，对于本书所附的ETS提供的5分和6分范文，大家要重点参考它们的分析和论证技巧，而不要去模仿开头和结尾的形式。

永远要牢记文章开头三要素：**有趣、短、能提领全文**；文章结尾三要素：**有趣、短、耐人寻味**。即使我们不能完全达到这些要求，也应尽量去做。

第二节　ARGUMENT的结尾写作技巧

同样是受ARGUMENT作文平实、稳健风格的限制，ARGUMENT的结尾样式也应简单。一般也有三种形式：

一、客套式

同客套式开头一样，客套式结尾也由两部分组成。首先，礼节性地肯定题目中的推理；然后指出该论证推理中的问题。请看下面这篇ETS提供的6分ARGUMENT范文的结尾（全文请参见本书附录七）：

The argument for safety gear based on emergency room statistics could provide important information and potentially saves lives. Before conclusions about the amount and kinds of investments that should be made in gear are reached, however, a more complete understanding of the benefits are needed. After all, a false confidence in ineffective gear could be just as dangerous as no gear at all.

本段中的第一句完全是客套，随后的几句则概括了题目中的推理存在的主要问题。

二、提出希望、建议式

这样的结尾只是简单地指出题目中推理/论证的问题，并给出如何改进的希望和建议。请看下面这篇ETS提供的6分ARGUMENT范文的结尾（全文请参见本书附录7）：

The paragraph given merely scratches the surface of what must be said about this University in order to entice students and to convince them that this is the best place to obtain a quality education. Much more work is needed by the public relations department before this can be made into a four-color brochure and handed out to prospective students.

这种形式的结尾还可以更简单（一句话就行了），比如：

Only after evaluating all the facts might students strongly agree that the University of Claria is one of the best universities in the world.

三、没有结尾段

ARGUMENT 作文可以没有结尾段。在将题目中的推理/论证的缺陷和谬误一一陈述清楚之后，文章也就戛然而止。大家可参看本书附录7中ARGUMENT部分的范例一，其中的那篇5分作文就没有任何结尾段。

第三节　ARGUMENT 正文部分的文章结构与写作技巧

ARGUMENT 作文的正文部分主要是对题目中推理/论证的缺陷和谬误的分析，所以，假如正文有三个意群段，这三个意群段是并列或层层递进的关系，而 ISSUE 作文的各意群段之间则是正、反、合，正、反、反，正、反、散的关系。

因此，ARGUMENT 作文的结构应该是这样的：

开头段 全文第一意群段

正文段 分三个意群段
- 推理/论证的谬误之一：正文第一意群段/全文第二意群段
- 推理/论证的谬误之二：正文第二意群段/全文第三意群段
- 推理/论证的谬误之三：正文第三意群段/全文第四意群段

结尾段 全文第五意群段

全文共计五个意群段。当然，不是说所有的 ARGUMENT 作文都必须是这样的结构。正文段也可以有超过三个或者只有两个意群段（即只对题目中的两个推理/论证缺陷和谬误进行充分分析）。有些同学也可能比较喜欢文章戛然而止的感觉，因而不愿再给文章加上个结尾段。这也是可以的。

这里有两个问题需要提醒大家特别注意：

其一，ARGUMENT 文章不可太短。字数最好能在400以上。从统计上看，个别长度不足400词的 ARGUMENT 作文有得5分的，但6分 ARGUMENT 作文的长度一般都会超过400词。不过，ARGUMENT 作文也没必要超过500词，450词也就足够了。

其二，在 ARGUMENT 正文的写作过程中，对题目包含的推理/论证缺陷和谬误的识别固然重要，但**更为关键的是对这些推理/论证缺陷和谬误的分析和论证**，即为什么它们是推理/论证过程中的谬误？这实际上是关于如何展开正文段的写作的问题。

前文已经提到过，ARGUMENT 的写作指引一般由两句话组成。前一句提示考生展开分析的方向，后一句提示考生要对其发现的推理/论证缺陷和谬误进行解释和论证。而这个解释和论证的过程就是 ARGUMENT 正文段分析和写作的展开。

一般而言，有三种对正文段展开分析和写作的办法：

第一，讲明推理/论证的缺陷和谬误。也就是说，作者要明确指出为什么某个地方是推理/论证谬误？它错在哪里？应如何修正？

第二，给出另外一种或多种解释。例如，题目中说事件 A 是事件 B 的原因。如果作者认为 A 不是 B 的原因，他就应该指出真正的原因可能是什么，并论证这个真正原因成立的可能性。

第三，举出例证。同样，假如题目说事件 A 是事件 B 的原因。如果作者认为 A 不是 B 的原因，他只需举出若干相反的例证就行了。

我们不妨看一看下面这篇 ETS 提供的 6 分新版 ARGUMENT 范文是如何展开正文部分的分析的。题目如下：

> In surveys Mason City residents rank water sports (swimming, boating and fishing) among their favorite recreational activities. The Mason River flowing through the city is rarely used for these pursuits, however, and the city park department devotes little of its budget to maintaining riverside recreational facilities. For years there have been complaints from residents about the quality of the river's water and the river's smell. In response, the state has recently announced plans to clean up Mason River. Use of the river for water sports is therefore sure to increase. The city government should for that reason devote more money in this year's budget to riverside recreational facilities.
>
> Write a response in which you examine the stated and/or unstated assumptions of the argument. Be sure to explain how the argument depends on the assumptions and what the implications are if the assumptions prove unwarranted.

首先我们可以将该题目的推论过程简单整理一下。

论点 论者的论点有两个，包括一项预测和一个建议。

(1) Use of the river for water sports is therefore sure to increase.

(2) The city government should for that reason devote more money in this year's budget to riverside recreational facilities.

论据 (1) In surveys Mason City residents rank water sports (swimming, boating and fishing) among their favorite recreational activities.

(2) The Mason River flowing through the city is rarely used for these pursuits, however, and the city park department devotes little of its budget to maintaining riverside recreational facilities.

(3) For years there have been complaints from residents about the quality of the river's water and the river's smell.

(4) The state has recently announced plans to clean up Mason River.

论证方法：题目中论者运用了两种论证法。论据 (1) 是统计数据论证法，论据 (2)、(3)、(4) 都是列举特征式论证法。

文章的全文如下（文中有一些拼写和语法错误，但 ETS 提供的原文如此，故予保留）：

While it may be true that the Mason City government ought to devote more money to riverside recreational facilities, this author's argument does not make a cogent case for increased resources based on river use. It is easy to understand why city residents would want a cleaner river, but this argument is rife with holes and assumptions, and thus, not strong enough to lead to increased funding.

Citing surveys of city residents, the author reports city resident's love of water sports. It is not clear, however, the scope and validity of that survey. For example, the survey could have asked residents if they prefer using the river for water sports or would like to see a hydroelectric dam built, which may have swayed residents toward river sports. The sample may not have been representative of city residents, asking only those residents who live upon the river. The survey may have been 10 pages long, with 2 questions dedicated to river sports. We just do not know. Unless the survey is fully representative, valid, and reliable, it can not be used to effectively back the author's argument.

Additionally, the author implies that residents do not use the river for swimming, boating, and fishing, despite their professed interest, because the water is polluted and smelly. While a polluted, smelly river would likely cut down on river sports, a concrete connection between the resident's lack of river use and the river's current state is not effectively made. Though there have been complaints, we do not know if there have been numerous complaints from a wide range of people, or perhaps from one or two individuals who made numerous complaints. To strengthen his/her argument, the author would benefit from implementing a normed survey asking a wide range of residents why they do not currently use the river.

Building upon the implication that residents do not use the river due to the quality of the river's water and the smell, the author suggests that a river clean up will result in increased river usage. If the river's water quality and smell result from problems which can be cleaned, this may be true. For example, if the decreased water quality and aroma is caused by pollution by factories along the river, this conceivably could be remedied. But if the quality and aroma results from the natural mineral deposits in the water or surrounding rock, this may not be true. There are some bodies of water which emit a strong smell of sulphur due to the geography of the area. This is not something likely to be affected by a clean-up. Consequently, a river clean up may have no impact upon river usage. Regardless of whether the river's quality is able to be improved or not, the author does not effectively show a connection between water quality and river usage.

A clean, beautiful, safe river often adds to a city's property values, leads to increased tourism and revenue from those who come to take advantage of the river, and a better overall quality of life for residents. For these reasons, city government may decide to invest in improving riverside recreational facilities. However, this author's argument is not likely significantly persuade the city government to allocate increased funding.

这篇作文大概有500多词，其行文结构是典型的"五大意群段"，即：开头段、结尾段和中间三个正文意群段。其中，每个正文意群段都分别指出了题目中的一个推理/论证缺陷和谬误，并展开了有效的分析论证。下面我们来看看这三个正文段的分析和写作是如何展开的：

首先，我们来看第二意群段（同时也是第二自然段，作者没有将意群段划分为多个自然段）。

针对论者在论据(1)中使用的统计数据论证法，作者直接对其调查数据的真实性、客观性和可靠性提出了质疑：It is not clear, however, (whether) the scope and validity of that survey (is reliable). 这是论者推理/论证过程中的第一个重大缺陷和谬误。

那么，作者又是如何对这个缺陷和谬误展开分析的呢？他选择了分析论者的统计数据论证法中的各个逻辑链条，即：

其一，The survey could have asked residents if they prefer using the river for water sports or would like to see a hydroelectric dam built, which may have swayed residents toward river sports.

其二，The sample may not have been representative of city residents, asking only those residents who live upon the river.

其三，The survey may have been 10 pages long, with 2 questions dedicated to river sports.

这三个与调查统计相关的逻辑错误依次是：其一，误导性的调查问题设计；其二，调查样本的代表性不足；其三，论者的调查和数据不够充分（或者说是断章取义）。到此，作者不仅点明了论者统计数据论证法中的缺陷和谬误，而且解释了它错在哪里、为什么是错的。

随后，作者又指出了论者应当如何对他的统计数据论证法中的谬误和缺陷进行修正：Unless the survey is fully representative, valid, and reliable, it cannot be used to effectively back the author's argument.

这是一个完整而漂亮的对推理/论证缺陷和谬误的分析和展开。这种分析和展开同样体现在第三和第四意群段。在这两个意群段里，作者重点分析论证了论据(2)、(3)、(4)提到的若干现象都未必能证明the complaints of the Mason River's water quality and its smell 是 the river's being rarely used for water sports 的原因。

在第三意群段，作者指出论者的一大推理/论证缺陷是a concrete connection between the resident's lack of river use and the river's current state is not effectively made，原因是Though there have been complaints, we do not know if there have been numerous complaints from a wide range of people, or perhaps from one or two individuals who made numerous complaints。那么，论者该如何修正其逻辑缺陷呢？办法如下：To strengthen his/her argument, the author would benefit from implementing a normed survey asking a wide range of residents why they do not currently use the river.

整个分析和展开过程清晰而充分。

再看第四意群段。作者首先对论者的假设：a river clean up will result in increased river usage 表示了怀疑。这个怀疑先是通过一个例证来证明：If the river's water quality and smell result from problems which can be cleaned, this may be true. For example, if the decreased water quality and aroma is caused by pollution by factories along the river, this conceivably could be remedied。随后，作者又通过对Mason River水质差这一现象提供另外一种解释，来证明论者的所谓通过清理河道可以净化河流水质的假设不成立：But if the quality and aroma results from the natural mineral deposits in the water or surrounding rock, this may not be true. There are some bodies of water which emit a strong smell of sulphur due to the geography of the area. This is not something likely to be affected by a clean-up. Consequently, a river clean up may have no impact upon river usage.

　　这三个意群段的分析和展开使得作者的ARGUMENT非常充实、饱满，得6分应该是实至名归。

　　所以说，在准确找出题目中的推理/论证错误和漏洞之后，对这些错误和漏洞——剖析就是得高分的关键所在。**切不可简单摆出题目中的推理/论证缺陷和谬误，却不对它们作进一步的分析和论证。**

第三章

ARGUMENT上下文的
起承转合、过渡衔接技巧

鉴于ARGUMENT作文正文部分的三个意群段一般是并列或层层递进的关系，同学们会很自然地运用诸如First, Second, Third, Last but not least这样的转折过渡词或短语。这样的做法当然可以。但是如果所有人都这样做，你不妨对这种账本式的罗列略微作一些变化。

比如，你可以不写First, Second, Third, Last but not least，而写The first point, Then, Moreover, Finally或者For one thing, For another, In addition, Last等。在众多千篇一律的作文之中，只要你的作文看起来有些与众不同，你必然要比别人多一些优势。

ARGUMENT作文上下文的起承转合、过渡衔接技巧与ISSUE作文的要求完全一样，包括三大手段，即利用转折过渡词、利用段落主题句、利用段落或句式的对应结构。

建议大家将书翻到ISSUE篇的理论部分，找到第三章的第一节，其中就有关于文章上下文过渡衔接技巧的详细讲解。

而且，其中关于ISSUE作文的开头、结尾、段落安排与节奏的要求也都同样适用于ARGUMENT作文（当然，关于ARGUMENT作文的特殊要求除外）。

现在，我们可以总结一下ARGUMENT写作复习准备的步骤了。

第一步，掌握ARGUMENT题目中推理/论证缺陷和谬误的识别技巧。只要弄明白前面讲述的十大论证技巧及相应的反驳切入点，以及15个常见推理论证谬误诊断法，这第一步的任务就算轻松完成了。

第二步，阅读后面第五章《新版ARGUMENT题库各题目分析指要》，体会其中对ARGUMENT题库中所有题目的推理/论证缺陷和谬误的分析提示。

第三步，抛开《新版ARGUMENT题库各题目分析指要》中的讲解，自己尝试分析各个ARGUMENT题目中的推理/论证谬误。假如你能轻松识别ARGUMENT每道题目中论者采用的论证方法，并且能从每个ARGUMENT论证法的逻辑起点（反驳切入点）入手，发现每个推理/论证过程在若干逻辑链条上出现的推理/论证缺陷和谬误，然后对每个缺陷和谬误展开充分的分析和论证，那么你的ARGUMENT复习准备工作即将大功告成。

第四步，开始练笔。按照ISSUE篇第三章中对文章篇章结构、造句用词的要求，以及本部分所讲的ARGUMENT的开头、结尾和正文部分的写作技巧与结构问题，大家便可以开始实际写作训练。

新版ARGUMENT题库中有174道题，但经过压缩（具体压缩办法见本篇第四章），题目总量可减少至85题。建议大家借助对《新版ARGUMENT题库各题目分析指要》的阅读，做到对每一道题的主要推理/论证缺陷和谬误都了然于胸。然后你最好挑出一些典型题目，动笔写出50篇文章。

同过去242道ARGUMENT题目比较起来，单就题量而言，现在的174道题目可谓轻松多了。尤其是经过题库压缩之后，同学们实际只需练习85道/组题目，这更是一个令人振奋的数字。所以，我建议考生尽量抽出时间，结合下一章中谈到的新版ARGUMENT题库的压缩方法，把这85道/组题目全部仔细阅读一两遍，并至少把其中的30道/组题目写上一遍。这样才能找到胜券在握的感觉。

刚开始写的时候，可以不限时间，重点体会文章的结构、推理/论证错误和漏洞的识别、表述和分析的展开以及语言的训练。然后在距离考试还有20天左右的时候，开始限时写作。ARGUMENT作文规定时间是30分钟。大家最好在27分钟内写完，留出两三分钟时间来修改。

　　同 ISSUE 作文一样，每写完一篇 ARGUMENT 作文都要修改。文章可以自己改（重点改结构和语法），也可以同学间相互改（重点考查对题目中的推理/论证缺陷和谬误的识别、分析与展开），还可以请内行改（全面诊断）。有关修改文章的注意事项，请参看本书附录5。

第四章

新版ARGUMENT
题库的压缩

改版后的 ARGUMENT 题库有大量这样的题目：题目本身相同或高度类似，但题后的写作指引不同。

例如，下面这两道题（题目前的数字是该题在本书的《新版 ARGUMENT 题库各题目分析指要》一章中的编号）：

14. The following appeared as part of an article in a business magazine.

A recent study rating 300 male and female advertising executives according to the average number of hours they sleep per night showed an association between the amount of sleep the executives need and the success of their firms. Of the advertising firms studied, those whose executives reported needing no more than 6 hours of sleep per night had higher profit margins and faster growth. These results suggest that if a business wants to prosper, it should hire only people who need less than 6 hours of sleep per night.

Write a response in which you examine the stated and/or unstated assumptions of the argument. Be sure to explain how the argument depends on these assumptions and what the implications are for the argument if the assumptions prove unwarranted.

118. The following appeared as part of an article in a business magazine.

A recent study rating 300 male and female advertising executives according to the average number of hours they sleep per night showed an association between the amount of sleep the executives need and the success of their firms. Of the advertising firms studied, those whose executives reported needing no more than six hours of sleep per night had higher profit margins and faster growth. On the basis of this study, we recommend that businesses hire only people who need less than six hours of sleep per night.

Write a response in which you discuss what questions would need to be answered in order to decide whether the recommendation and the argument on which it is based are reasonable. Be sure to explain how the answers to these questions would help to evaluate the recommendation.

可以看出，这两道题的写作指引完全不同，但除了个别措词外，题目内容基本一致。尤其重要的是，这两道题目中的论证方法完全相同。考虑到我们对 ARGUMENT 的分析是从题目中的论证法切入，所以，基本相同的题目内容加上完全相同的论证方法完全可以让我们把这两道题放到一组来考虑，视作一道题目。这也是 ARGUMENT 题库压缩的依据。

当然，这两道题不同的写作指引使得对它们的分析方向和角度有所不同，但这些不同的分析方向和角度其实是指向相同的推理／论证缺陷和谬误的。所以，这些归并到同一组 ARGUMENT 题目的分析要点和写作提纲即便不完全相同，也可以是高度类似的。对于这一点，**大家随后在阅读《新版 ARGUMENT 题库各题目分析指要》一章时会有切身体会**。

新版 ARGUMENT 题库中共有 174 道题，其中的 133 道题可以归并为 44 组。理论上讲，同一组内的若干 ARGUMENT 题目因其内容和论证法的相同或相似可以被视为同一道题目。这样一来，这 44 组题加上其他无法并入一组的 41 道题，就是 85 组／道题。这就是我们进行新版

ARGUMENT题库压缩之后的题量，比原来的题量减少了50%左右。

ARGUMENT题目的分组情况没有像ISSUE那样单列出来。但在所有可以归并到同一组中的ARGUMENT题目的后面，都会有特别标注，以提示它们的分组情况。比如，上面提到的第14题和第118题可以并至一组，那么在第14题的后面会有"参考第118题"的字样；同理，在第118题的后面，也会有"参考第14题"的字样，以方便读者翻阅参考。

第五章

新版ARGUMENT
题库各题目的分析指要

以下是对ARGUMENT题库中所有题目的推理/论证缺陷和谬误的分析提示。

建议大家先把本书《下篇：ARGUMENT》的第一章所讲的**十大论证技巧及反驳切入点，以及15个常见推理/论证谬误诊断办法**阅读一两遍。否则，你可能无法充分体会到这些分析方法和技巧在ARGUMENT题目分析中的应用。

本书分析的这些推理/论证谬误只是每道题中出现的较为明显的几个。如果愿意，大家还可以在每道题目里面找到更多的推理/论证缺陷和谬误。你的分析越独到，文章越容易拿高分。毕竟，对所有ARGUMENT题目的分析作以下演示讲解的根本目的在于启发大家形成自己的分析思路。

以下分析和提纲除一些关键词外都是用中文书写，目的在于避免语言上的雷同。但那些逻辑要点，大家尽可以大胆使用。ETS不会说ARGUMENT作文中逻辑上的相似也算抄袭作弊。

每个题目分析提示的编排是按照这样的顺序进行的：首先把每个题目中的**论据、论点**整理出来，指出论者运用的主要**论证方法**，然后，再逐一分析各论据是否支持论点以及**能否有效推出论点**。

下面就是ARGUMENT题库的内容和分析。

The Pool of Argument Topics

This part contains the Argument topics for the Analytical Writing section of the GRE revised General Test. When you take the test, you will be presented with one Argument topic from this pool.

Each Argument topic consists of a passage that presents an argument followed by specific task instructions that tell you how to analyze the argument. The wording of some topics in the test might vary slightly from what is presented here. Also, because there may be multiple versions of some topics with similar or identical wording but with different task instructions, it is very important to read your test topic and its specific task directions carefully and respond to the wording as it appears in the actual test.

....

1. Woven baskets characterized by a particular distinctive pattern have previously been found only in the immediate vicinity of the prehistoric village of Palea and therefore were believed to have been made only by the Palean people. Recently, however, archaeologists discovered such a "Palean" basket in Lithos, an ancient village across the Brim River from Palea. The Brim River is very deep and broad, and so the ancient Paleans could have crossed it only by boat, and no Palean boats have been found. Thus it follows that the so-called Palean baskets were not uniquely Palean.

Write a response in which you discuss what specific evidence is needed to evaluate the argument and explain how the evidence would weaken or strengthen the argument.

题目整理

论点 The so-called Palean baskets were not uniquely Palean.

223

论据 (1) The Brim River is very deep and broad.

(2) The ancient Paleans could have crossed it only by boat.

(3) No Palean boats have been found.

论证方法

题目中论者主要运用了因果关系论证法。

分析提示

● 首先，论据(3)需要进一步的证据支持。仅仅说迄今没发现Palean人的船，并不等于这些能过Brim River的船就不存在。这是个有待于考古工作进一步证实的问题。再者，是否已经有了可以证明Palean人具备造船技术的其他发现，比如，石斧、石凿等切凿工具、巨大的被凿空的树干等等？这些发现也许不能直接证明Palean人能造船，但可以说明他们的造船技术潜力或者有能力造出其他的过河工具，比如用粗大的树干做独木舟等。

● 其次，论据(1)提到Brim River又深又宽，但并没讲明史前时期这条河是什么样子的。假如Palean人兴盛期并没有这条河，两个村子之间是畅通的陆地呢？或者当时这条河浅且窄，不需要过河工具呢？这样的话，论据(2)就不合理了。

● 第三，论者总假设那些篮子只能被Palean人渡河带到对面的Lithos村。难道Palean人不可以将这些篮子放到河面上，让它漂到对岸？或者一场大洪水将Palean人做的篮子冲到了Lithos村？因此此处需要更多的关于这种篮子的制作材料、质地等资料。

● 第四，论者只是说Palean人没有造船能力，因此过不了河，但并没有提供Lithos村的造船能力的证据。假如Lithos村的人能造出用来渡河的船呢？那样的话，Palean人的篮子同样可以被Lithos村的船运回去。

● 第五，Palean人的篮子还有可能是被远古的商人以物物交换的古老贸易方式辗转带到Lithos村。这方面的证据没有提供，但同样关键。

2. The following appeared as part of a letter to the editor of a scientific journal.

"A recent study of eighteen rhesus monkeys provides clues as to the effects of birth order on an individual's levels of stimulation. The study showed that in stimulating situations (such as an encounter with an unfamiliar monkey), firstborn infant monkeys produce up to twice as much of the hormone cortisol, which primes the body for increased activity levels, as do their younger siblings. Firstborn humans also produce relatively high levels of cortisol in stimulating situations (such as the return of a parent after an absence). The study also found that during pregnancy, first-time mother monkeys had higher levels of cortisol than did those who had had several offspring."

Write a response in which you discuss one or more alternative explanations that could rival the proposed explanation and explain how your explanation(s) can plausibly account for the facts presented in the argument.

题目整理

论点 The birth order can affect an individual's levels of stimulation.

论据 (1) In stimulating situations (such as an encounter with an unfamiliar monkey), firstborn infant monkeys produce up to twice as much of the hormone cortisol, which primes the body for increased activity levels, as do their younger siblings.

(2) Firstborn humans also produce relatively high levels of cortisol in stimulating situations (such as the return of a parent after an absence).

(3) The study also found that during pregnancy, first-time mother monkeys had higher levels of cortisol than did those who had had several offspring.

论证方法

题目中论者主要运用了归纳推理论证法。

分析提示

● 首先，很可能不是 birth order，而是 first born infant monkeys，first-time mother monkeys 和 firstborn humans 这三个生命形态的共同特点影响了 hormone cortisol 的分泌水平。因为它们都属于灵长类（primates）。作为一种较为高级的生命形态，受到外界的刺激后，它们为了迅捷作出反应而分泌较多的 hormone cortisol 是很正常的现象。并且生命安全越是面临威胁（比如 to encounter with unfamiliar circumstances, strangers or preyers），hormone cortisol 的分泌水平越高；反之，就较低。如果是这样的话，题目中论者的推论就未必成立了。

● 第二，hormone cortisol 的分泌水平是否与特定的年龄阶段有关？因为我们看到，first born infant monkeys、firstborn humans 和 first-time mother monkeys 都是在同较年幼的 siblings 和生育过多胎的 mother monkeys 比较，在相同的刺激环境下才分泌出较多的 cortisol。如果较幼小的 rhesus monkeys 和人类，以及生过多胎的 mother monkeys 总体上都不分泌或者分泌较少的 hormone cortisol，那么题目中论者的推论也不成立。

● 第三，是否是某种情绪或者情感影响了 hormone cortisol 的分泌水平？因为 first born infant monkeys、firstborn humans 和 first-time mother monkeys 都是在强烈情绪和情感的刺激下（比如 meeting an unfamiliar monkey, reunion with a parent after an absence, and first-time birth of baby monkey 这些恐惧、愉悦和焦虑等）才分泌较高的 hormone cortisol。如此的话，hormone cortisol 的分泌水平同 birth order 也无关。

3. The following appeared as a letter to the editor from a Central Plaza store owner.

"Over the past two years, the number of shoppers in Central Plaza has been steadily decreasing while the popularity of skateboarding has increased dramatically. Many Central Plaza store owners believe that the decrease in their business is due to the number of skateboard users in the plaza. There has also been a dramatic increase in the amount of litter and vandalism throughout the plaza. Thus, we recommend that the city prohibit skateboarding in Central Plaza. If skateboarding is prohibited here, we predict that business in Central Plaza will return to its previously high levels."

（参考第 171 题）

Write a response in which you discuss what questions would need to be answered in order to decide whether the recommendation is likely to have the predicted result. Be sure to explain how the answers to these questions would help to evaluate the recommendation.

题目整理

论点 题目中的论点分别是一个建议和一项预测。

(1) The city should prohibit skateboarding in Central Plaza.

(2) If skateboarding is prohibited, the business in Central Plaza will return to its previous high levels.

论据 (1) Over the past two years, the number of shoppers in Central Plaza has been steadily decreasing while the popularity of skateboarding has increased dramatically.

(2) Many Central Plaza store owners believe that the decrease in their business is due to the number of skateboard users in the plaza.

(3) There has also been a dramatic increase in the amount of litter and vandalism throughout the plaza.

论证方法

题目中论者运用了因果关系论证法和统计数据论证法。

分析提示

- 首先，针对论据(1)，需要回答的问题是：the popularity of skateboarding has increased dramatically 到底是不是 the number of shoppers in Central Plaza has been steadily decreasing 的原因。论者提供的论据不过是同时发生的两件事情，但不能据此说其中的一件事情是另一件事情的原因。很可能有其他的原因，比如经济萧条、人口数量与结构的改变、人们收入水平的降低等导致了 Central Plaza 客流的降低。

- 同理，针对论据(3)，值得探讨的问题依然是哪个才是真正原因。"大厦乱扔垃圾和破坏公物现象上升"和"滑板运动大为流行"两个事件同时发生，但后者未必是前者的原因。论者怎么不说大厦的管理不善才是真正导致大厦乱扔垃圾和破坏公物现象上升以及来大厦购物的顾客人数大降的问题之所在呢？

- 论据(2)引用了统计数据进行论证。我们要问：这里的 Many Central Plaza store owners 中的 many 到底是多少？占了所有 Central Plaza 商家的多大比例？被调查的人是否认真回答了问题？他们是否有代表性？另外，论者本人也是 Central Plaza 的商家。他在收集这些调查数据时是否做到了客观公正？这些问题都值得考虑。

- 第四，论证建议禁止在 Central Plaza 玩滑板，是否考虑到了后果？假如正是因为许多年轻人喜欢到 Central Plaza 去玩滑板，并因此给大厦带去了旺盛的人气、客流和潜在的购物人群，那么限制玩滑板，其结果岂不违背了初衷？

4. The following appeared in a letter from a homeowner to a friend.

"Of the two leading real estate firms in our town—Adams Realty and Fitch Realty—Adams Realty is clearly superior. Adams has 40 real estate agents; in contrast, Fitch has 25, many of whom work only part-time. Moreover, Adams' revenue last year was twice as high as that of Fitch and included home sales that averaged $168,000, compared to Fitch's $144,000. Homes listed with Adams sell faster as well: ten years ago I listed my home with Fitch, and it took more than four months to sell; last year, when I sold another home, I listed it with Adams, and it took only one month. Thus, if you want to sell your home quickly and at a good price, you should use Adams Realty."

Write a response in which you examine the stated and/or unstated assumptions of the argument. Be sure to explain how the argument depends on these assumptions and what the implications are for the argument if the assumptions prove unwarranted.

题目整理

论点 Adams Realty can help sell homes quickly and at good prices, therefore clearly superior to Fitch Realty.

论据 (1) Adams has 40 real estate agents; in contrast, Fitch has 25, many of whom work only part-time.

(2) Adams' revenue last year was twice as high as that of Fitch and included home sales that averaged $168,000, compared to Fitch's $144,000.

(3) Homes listed with Adams sell faster as well: ten years ago I listed my home with Fitch, and it took more than four months to sell; last year, when I sold another home, I listed it with Adams, and it took only one month.

论证方法

题目中论者运用了列举特征式论证法、统计数据论证法和类比论证法。

分析提示

● 论据(1)运用了列举特征式论证法。论者的假设是：房地产经纪人（estate agents）多，表示其服务质量和效率必然高。这显然很成问题。"Fitch has 25, many of whom work only part-time"完全可以是因为该公司管理高效；而"Adams has 40 real estate agents"很可能说明它的低效率。

● 论据(2)的数据论证也充满了问题假设。首先，那些数据是由谁调查的、怎么调查的、数据是如何处理的都没有明确说明。其次，revenue的意思是销售收入。论者说去年Adams的销售收入是Fitch的两倍，实际是在假设Adams的利润水平也高于Fitch。这未必。假如Adams的运营成本(operating cost)高出Fitch，其利润水平(profit margins)可能要低于Fitch，甚至亏损(make losses or deficit)。第三，论者说"Adams' home sales averaged $168,000, compared to Fitch's $144,000"，并进而假设Adams的房子都能卖出高价。这同样漏洞百出。假如

Adams 和 Fitch 这两家公司的市场定位 (market positioning) 不同, 前者主要销售高端房产, 而 Fitch 主要经营中低端市场的话, Adams 所售房屋的均价高于 Fitch 是再正常不过的事情。这就意味着, 房屋可否卖出高价是取决于房屋本身的质量和相应的市场价位, 而并非任由 Adams 公司人为地卖出个好价钱。

- 论据 (3) 是个类比论证, 但它有个要命的假设: 十年间一切都没变。十年前, Fitch 卖房卖得慢, 现在还是如此吗? 去年, Adams 卖房卖得快, 那么十年前它也一样卖得快? 而且论者还假设, 十年前 Fitch 卖房慢和去年 Adams 卖房快都是因为公司本身而不是其他原因。假如, 十年前, 因为经济不景气, 所有的房地产公司卖房都卖得慢呢? 或者, 去年因为经济回暖, 任何一家房地产公司的房子都卖得快呢?

5. The following appeared in a letter to the editor of the Balmer Island Gazette.

"On Balmer Island, where mopeds serve as a popular form of transportation, the population increases to 100,000 during the summer months. To reduce the number of accidents involving mopeds and pedestrians, the town council of Balmer Island should limit the number of mopeds rented by the island's moped rental companies from 50 per day to 25 per day during the summer season. By limiting the number of rentals, the town council will attain the 50 percent annual reduction in moped accidents that was achieved last year on the neighboring island of Seaville, when Seaville's town council enforced similar limits on moped rentals."

(参考第 159、173 题)

Write a response in which you discuss what questions would need to be answered in order to decide whether the recommendation is likely to have the predicted result. Be sure to explain how the answers to these questions would help to evaluate the recommendation.

题目整理

论点 题目中的论点是一个建议和一项预测。

(1) The town council of Balmer Island should limit the number of mopeds rented by the island's moped rental companies from 50 per day to 25 per day during the summer season to reduce the number of accidents involving mopeds and pedestrians.

(2) By limiting the number of rentals, the town council will attain the 50 percent annual reduction in moped accidents.

论据 (1) On Balmer Island, where mopeds serve as a popular form of transportation, the population increases to 100,000 during the summer months.

(2) Neighboring island Seaville last year realized a 50 percent annual reduction in moped accidents when Seaville's town council enforced similar limits on moped rentals.

论证方法

题目中论者主要运用了纵向和横向的类比论证法。

分析提示

● 首先在论据(2)中，论者把去年发生在邻岛Seaville的事情同本岛今年的情形进行简单类比。那么问题是：去年的事情今年是否同样可行？别的地方的做法，本地是否行得通？两个岛屿的具体情况，比如人口密度、交通工具、交通设施、道路状况、交通警察的力量配备、交通执法水平、人口素质等是否都有可比性？

● 其次，论者只是说"Seaville's town council last year enforced **similar limits** on moped rentals and realized a 50 percent annual reduction in moped accidents"，但并没有提供关于这个"similar limits"的细节。那么，我们要问的问题是：去年Seaville岛的政策是如何实施的？是简单地限制moped的数量，还是同时实施了配套措施，比如对moped驾驶员进行交通法规的教育、对行人的教育和管理、改善交通标志、加强天气预报及路况预警等等？对这些，论者都语焉不详。

● 论者在整个论证过程中，始终暗含的意思是：moped驾驶员以及过多的moped引发了频繁的交通事故。但这一点论者并未证明。于是我们不得不问：难道没别的原因：比如如同论据(1)表明的，夏季该岛上骤然增加的人口？本地交通标志不足、交警配备不够？交通管理低效？

● 再有，论者建议的限制moped的措施仅限于夏季的几个月，但其要达到的目标却是a 50 percent annual reduction in moped accidents。我们要问：夏季Balmer岛上涉及moped的交通事故占该岛全年涉及moped的交通事故多大比例？如果该岛上发生涉及moped的交通事故绝大部分都发生在冬、春、秋三季，那么即便是对岛上的moped实施更大比例的限制，恐怕也很难实现全年降低50%的目标。

● 最后，论者限制moped的建议是否会导致岛上因为交通工具的不足而引发进一步的拥堵以及交通混乱，进而带来更多的交通事故？岛上现有的公共交通设施能否满足限制moped之后可能增加的交通需求？等等这些都是关键的疑问。

6. Arctic deer live on islands in Canada's arctic regions. They search for food by moving over ice from island to island during the course of the year. Their habitat is limited to areas warm enough to sustain the plants on which they feed and cold enough, at least some of the year, for the ice to cover the sea separating the islands, allowing the deer to travel over it. Unfortunately, according to reports from local hunters, the deer populations are declining. Since these reports coincide with recent global warming trends that have caused the sea ice to melt, we can conclude that the purported decline in deer populations is the result of the deer's being unable to follow their age-old migration patterns across the frozen sea.

Write a response in which you discuss what specific evidence is needed to evaluate the argument and explain how the evidence would weaken or strengthen the argument.

题目整理

论点 The purported decline in deer populations is the result of the deer's being unable to follow their age-old migration patterns across the frozen sea allegedly melting away due to the global warming.

论据 (1) Arctic deer live on islands in Canada's arctic regions. They search for food by moving over ice from island to island during the course of the year. Their habitat is limited to areas warm enough to sustain the plants on which they feed and cold enough, at least some of the year, for the ice to cover the sea separating the islands, allowing the deer to travel over it.

(2) Local hunters say the deer populations are declining.

(3) The reported decline of the deer population coincides with recent global warming trends that have caused the sea ice to melt.

论证方法

题目中论者主要运用了因果关系论证法和引用权威论证法。

分析提示

● 首先，论据(2)在引用权威进行论证。那么这些被认为是权威的猎人们的判断是可信的吗？他们判断的依据是什么？可否通过其他手段进行更准确的验证？是否正是这些猎人的猎杀或盗猎行为(poaching)造成了鹿群数量的下降？还有，这次Arctic deer数量的下降是否在正常的范围之内？以往是否也发生过类似的或者规模更大的鹿群数量下降的事件？如果发生过，后来其数量是否又能够恢复到正常水平？这些都需要具体证据的支持。

● 其次，论据(3)力图用鹿群数量的下降和近年来全球气候变暖这两件同时发生的事，来证明是全球气候变暖致使鹿群多年来的迁徙路线上冰层的融化，进而造成了鹿群数量的下降。但这是一种错误的因果关系推理：同时发生的两件事情未必就存在因果关系。全球气候变暖并非是突发事件，而是持续了数十年或上百年的过程。但为什么单单现在发生了鹿群数量下降的情况？这个因果关系需要更多的证据支持。另外，有无可能对鹿群迁徙的路线做一次详细的调查，以探明到底该路线上的冰层出现了何种变化？这样的调查结果对题目中讨论的问题至关重要。

● 第三，论据(1)的描述是Arctic deer多年来的迁徙以及生活习性。但这些观察权威、可信吗？这些鹿群的生活习性、迁徙路线有没有发生变化？这些也有待进一步证实。

● 最后，是否是全球气候变暖导致的其他后果，比如Arctic deer喜欢吃的某种植被的面积的萎缩、新的细菌和病毒的滋生、北极地区空气成分的变化、Arctic deer繁殖能力的下降等因素致使鹿群数量的下降？

7. The following is a recommendation from the Board of Directors of Monarch Books.

"We recommend that Monarch Books open a café in its store. Monarch, having been in business at the same location for more than twenty years, has a large customer base because it is known for its wide selection of books on all subjects. Clearly, opening the café would attract more customers. Space could be made for the café by discontinuing the children's book section, which will probably become less popular given that the most recent national census indicated a significant decline in the percentage of the population under age ten. Opening a café will allow Monarch to attract more customers and better compete with Regal Books, which recently opened its own café."

（参考第98、99题）

Write a response in which you discuss what questions would need to be answered in order to decide whether the recommendation is likely to have the predicted result. Be sure to explain how the answers to these questions would help to evaluate the recommendation.

题目整理

论点 题目中的论点是一个建议和一项预测。

(1) Monarch Books should open a café in its store.

(2) Opening the café would attract more customers.

论据 (1) Monarch, having been in business at the same location for more than twenty years, has a large customer base because it is known for its wide selection of books on all subjects.

(2) Space could be made for the café by discontinuing the children's book section, which will probably become less popular given that the most recent national census indicated a significant decline in the percentage of the population under age ten.

(3) Opening a café will allow Monarch to attract more customers and better compete with Regal Books, which recently opened its own café.

论证方法

题目中论者主要运用了因果关系论证法和类比论证法。

分析提示

● 首先，论据(3)通过一个类比论证力图说明，既然竞争对手Regal Books开了咖啡馆，那么Monarch也应该效仿。但问题是：二者之间是否有可比性？Regal开咖啡馆也许是因为其售书的收入过低，不得不靠开小咖啡馆来增加收入以维持其图书经营。Regal这种不得已而为之的举措值得Monarch效仿吗？再者，Regal开了咖啡馆后，果真带来了更多的购书顾客了吗？这一点论者并未提供证据。

● 论据(2)说可以通过撤掉书店里的儿童图书区来为咖啡馆腾地方，并且依据the last national census indicated a significant decline in **the percentage of the population under age ten**，推出the children's book section will likely become less popular。但这个因果推理很成问题。首先，总人口中十岁以下儿童所占百分比的缩小，就等于十岁以下儿童的绝对数量减少吗？很可能这个年龄段儿童的绝对数量仍在持续增加，而其他年龄段的人口，比如30至40岁之间或者60岁以上的人口增加过快才造成十岁以下儿童在总人口中的比例下降呢？其次，即便十岁以下儿童的比例和绝对数量在减少，我们也推不出儿童读物不再受人欢迎这一趋势。较少的儿童顾客完全可以购买更多的儿童图书。而且，如果因为儿童在总人口中的比例或者绝对数量的减少，他们的父母也许更有财力增加他们的教育投入，因而乐意为他们购买更多的图书呢？更何况，如论者所言，Monarch 的一个传统优势是 its wide selection of books on all subjects。如果撤掉了儿童图书区，是否会因此削弱了自己的优势，从而影响了读者来购书的整体愿望了呢？

● 论据 (1) 依据自己是多年老店，并且因为 "its wide selection of books on all subjects" 而知名，就断定自己有广泛的顾客群 (a large customer base)。这似乎是想当然。这些潜在的顾客会成为真正的购买人群吗？假如 Monarch 在书店里开了咖啡馆，随之而来的各种饮料和食品的气味、可能的纷乱嘈杂是否会令部分购书顾客不喜欢，或者破坏了 Monarch 书店原有的宁静的气氛，并赶跑一部分当前的和潜在的顾客？

8. The following appeared in a memo from the director of student housing at Buckingham College.

"To serve the housing needs of our students, Buckingham College should build a number of new dormitories. Buckingham's enrollment is growing and, based on current trends, will double over the next 50 years, thus making existing dormitory space inadequate. Moreover, the average rent for an apartment in our town has risen in recent years. Consequently, students will find it increasingly difficult to afford off-campus housing. Finally, attractive new dormitories would make prospective students more likely to enroll at Buckingham."

Write a response in which you discuss what specific evidence is needed to evaluate the argument and explain how the evidence would weaken or strengthen the argument.

题目整理

论点 Buckingham College should build a number of new dormitories to serve students' housing needs.

论据 (1) Buckingham's enrollment is growing and, based on current trends, will double over the next 50 years, thus making existing dormitory space inadequate.

(2) The average rent for an apartment in our town has risen in recent years.

(3) Students will find it increasingly difficult to afford off-campus housing.

(4) Finally, attractive new dormitories would make prospective students more likely to enroll at Buckingham.

论证方法

题目中论者主要运用了因果关系论证法和统计数据论证法。

分析提示

● 首先，论据 (1) 提到，照目前的招生速度，50 年后 Buckingham College 的招生量会增加一倍，现有的宿舍将不够用。但论者必须提供进一步的证据来证明 50 年增长一倍是一个非常快的增速。因为从常识来分析，50 年增加一倍实际上是很慢的速度。按照复合增长率来计算，只要保持 **15%** 的年增长率，五年就可实现数量的翻番。论者需要提供具备可比性的其他大学，或者 Buckingham College 过去数年间的招生增长速度，用来作参照和比较。或者，论者假如能提供在未来几十年该地区需要接受大学教育的人口数据，也会有利于我们的判断。否则，我们无法判断论者所说的增长速度究竟是快是慢，他据以做出的推测也没有说服力。

- 论据 (2) 提到，该大学所在镇上的公寓的平均租金水平近年来在上升。这组数据也同样非常模糊。首先，论者说的是 average rent。而平均价格是将高端公寓和中低端公寓的价格水平总体拉平的结果。很可能是，高端公寓的价格涨了很多，而备受大学生青睐的中低端公寓价格基本没变，甚至是下降了。如此的话，平均价格上升对学生实际没有影响。再者，论者只是说公寓的价格涨了 (has risen)。但具体涨了多少？同过去相比是正常波动，还是大幅度上涨？都没有说明。第三，论者说最近几年价格上涨了。这也很模糊。是过去三年、五年还是八年？有可能是，起初几年价格上涨了，但最近却又稳定或者走低了。这样的话，就不能判断未来的价格趋势。

- 依据论据 (1)(2)，论者得出结论说 "Students will find it increasingly difficult to afford off-campus housing"。这也需要进一步的证据来证明。假如在学生公寓的价格水平上涨的同时，学生以及他们的家庭收入水平、消费水平也同步或者更快上升呢？那样的话，他们的支付能力就不会受到影响。再者，政府对这些大学生租住校外公寓有没有补贴？对这些学生公寓有没有税收优惠？有没有贴息贷款支持等等。这些也都可以直接影响学生的支付能力，但论者没有提及。

- 论据 (4) 认为漂亮的学生宿舍会吸引更多的学生来 Buckingham College 就读，这有点儿想当然了。有证据表明宿舍状况是学生选择学校的重要考虑因素吗？即便是，会占多大分量？再者，谁说校园里那些古朴、带有旧时代气息的建筑，包括学生宿舍，不会吸引学生呢？如果都建成崭新的现代学生公寓，学生也许不喜欢了呢？但论者并没提供这方面的资料。

---

9. Nature's Way, a chain of stores selling health food and other health-related products, is opening its next franchise in the town of Plainsville. The store should prove to be very successful: Nature's Way franchises tend to be most profitable in areas where residents lead healthy lives, and clearly Plainsville is such an area. Plainsville merchants report that sales of running shoes and exercise clothing are at all-time highs. The local health club has more members than ever, and the weight training and aerobics classes are always full. Finally, Plainsville's schoolchildren represent a new generation of potential customers: these schoolchildren are required to participate in a fitness-for-life program, which emphasizes the benefits of regular exercise at an early age.

（参考第88、90题）

Write a response in which you examine the stated and/or unstated assumptions of the argument. Be sure to explain how the argument depends on these assumptions and what the implications are for the argument if the assumptions prove unwarranted.

题目整理

论点 Nature's Way next franchise store in the town of Plainsville should prove to be very successful.

论据 (1) Nature's Way franchises tend to be most profitable in areas where residents lead healthy lives, and clearly Plainsville is such an area.

(2) Plainsville merchants report that sales of running shoes and exercise clothing are at all-time highs.

(3) The local health club has more members than ever, and the weight training and aerobics classes are always full.

(4) Finally, Plainsville's schoolchildren represent a new generation of potential customers: these schoolchildren are required to participate in a fitness-for-life program, which emphasizes the benefits of regular exercise at an early age.

论证方法

题目中论者主要运用了归纳推理论证法、引用权威论证法和列举特征式论证法。

分析提示

● 论据(1)运用了归纳推理论证法：即Nature's Way在那些居民注重健康生活的地区都赚到了钱，Plainsville的居民看起来很注重健康，所以该公司在Plainsville开店也会赚到钱。这里面的假设是：第一，论据(2)(3)(4)列举的特征/现象(Signs)都确实能说明Plainsville镇的居民注重健康生活。其次，没有其他因素会令该镇居民(即便他们果真都注重健康生活)不购买Nature's Way销售的健康食品以及相关产品。我们在下面的分析中会看到，这些假设都是很成问题的。

● 论据(2)是引用权威论证。论者引用Plainsville当地商人的说法，该地区的跑鞋以及运动服的销量达到了最高水平(all-time highs)，并认为这说明当地居民很注重健康生活。这个判断首先要假设这些商人的观察是客观、可信的。其次，还要假设没有其他原因促使跑鞋和运动服销量的上升，比如，因为婴儿潮(baby boom)时期出生的孩子已进入青少年时期，他们普遍喜好运动，所以会购买体育运动服饰。或者因为一项全国或全球体育赛事(the Olympic games or the World Cup soccer for instance)的举行引发了该镇居民的体育运动热和购买运动服饰热等等。这些特定的人口特征或者暂时的现象都不能说明该镇居民具有健康的生活习惯。再次，论据(2)还要假设销量的all-time highs是一种显著的上升。假如该镇上的跑鞋和运动服的销量一向很低，比如每年也就是100多件，现在上升两倍，到了300件，这的确是个all-time high，但依然是个非常低的水平，不足以信。

● 论据(3)提到健康俱乐部会员的增加以及举重和健美操训练班的爆满，并据此认为Plainsville镇居民都注重健康生活，这里面也有问题。首先，这些健康俱乐部以及举重和健美操训练班到底能接收多少会员和学员？假如这些都是VIP俱乐部或者规模很小的班，那么所谓的会员增加以及人员爆满就不能说明什么问题了。其次，论者还要假设，参加这些俱乐部以及健美操训练班的人不是特定的人群，比如体重超常的人群。如果他们仅仅是些急于减肥的人，就不能说明所有Plainsville的居民都在积极锻炼。

● 至于论据(4)，其假设的成分就更大了。镇上的学龄儿童要参加一个fitness-for-life项目，并且这个项目强调了 the benefits of regular exercise at an early age。如果这些孩子如论者所说是 Nature's Way 潜在消费人群的话，论者实际在假设：第一，这些孩子在总人口中占较大比例。其次，参加 fitness-for-life 项目会产生对 Nature's Way 产品的需求。第三，这些孩子对 Nature's Way 所售产品的需求不会随着他们年龄的增长而改变。

● 最后，即便论据(2)(3)(4)列举的现象都说明 Plainsville 镇居民的确注重健康生活，论者结论的成立依然还要基于以下两个假设：第一，体育锻炼还不足以满足人们对健康的需求，人们为了健康还必须购买各种健康食品和相关产品。第二，没有其他竞争对手，镇上的人们需要健康食品时，只能去买 Nature's Way 的产品。但这个假设好像不很靠谱(very precarious)。

---

10. Twenty years ago, Dr. Field, a noted anthropologist, visited the island of Tertia. Using an observation-centered approach to studying Tertian culture, he concluded from his observations that children in Tertia were reared by an entire village rather than by their own biological parents. Recently another anthropologist, Dr. Karp, visited the group of islands that includes Tertia and used the interview-centered method to study child-rearing practices. In the interviews that Dr. Karp conducted with children living in this group of islands, the children spent much more time talking about their biological parents than about other adults in the village. Dr. Karp decided that Dr. Field's conclusion about Tertian village culture must be invalid. Some anthropologists recommend that to obtain accurate information on Tertian child-rearing practices, future research on the subject should be conducted via the interview-centered method.

(参考第21、23题)

Write a response in which you discuss what questions would need to be answered in order to decide whether the recommendation and the argument on which it is based are reasonable. Be sure to explain how the answers to these questions would help to evaluate the recommendation.

题目整理

论点 Future research on the subject should be conducted via the interview-centered method to obtain accurate information on Tertian child-rearing practices.

论据 (1) Twenty years ago, Dr. Field, a noted anthropologist, visited the island of Tertia. Using an observation-centered approach to studying Tertian culture, he concluded from his observations that children in Tertia were reared by an entire village rather than by their own biological parents. Recently another anthropologist, Dr. Karp, visited the group of islands that includes Tertia and used the interview-centered method to study child-rearing practices.

(2) In the interviews that Dr. Karp conducted with children living in this group of islands, the children spent much more time talking about their biological parents than about other adults in the village.

(3) Dr. Karp decided that Dr. Field's conclusion about Tertian village culture must be invalid.

论证方法

题目中论者主要运用了类比论证法和引用权威论证法。

分析提示

● 论据(1)用到了纵向类比论证。对论据(1)，我们的问题是：20年来，Tertia岛上居民的生活方式、文化传统有没有发生根本性的改变？ 20年是一个相当长的时间跨度，在此期间，该岛屿与外界是封闭的，还是与外界有频繁的交往和相互影响？ 其次，20年间，包括Tertia岛的那一组岛屿(也就是Dr. Karp最近去访问的那些岛屿)之间是否相互影响，并最终形成了共同的文化和生活习俗？

● 论者在论据(2)中实际上有一个假设：即，如果孩子是被村里人集体抚养的话，那么这些孩子谈话中不会老提及亲生父母。但这个假设有科学依据吗？ 其次，题目中提到，Dr. Karp访谈的孩子不只是来自Tertia岛，还包括其他岛上的孩子。那么问题就来了：在Dr. Karp访问的孩子中，来自Tertia岛的孩子占多大比例？ 如果这个比例很小，这位博士很有可能是在用其他岛的岛民的生活习俗来推测Tertia岛上的生活习俗。这显然有问题。第三，Dr. Karp在访谈中是如何设计问题的？ 如果这些问题具有很强的倾向性（biased）和诱导性(inductive)，那么他的结论也就很可疑了。第四，即便这位博士的问题设计得很客观、科学，这些孩子有没有可能在回答问题时受到情绪的干扰？ 他们的回答是否客观、可信？ 他们有无可能因为特别想知道自己的亲生父母而不自觉地讲了很多关于亲生父母的事情？

● 在论据(3)中，Dr. Karp断言Dr. Field的研究结论失实。但问题是：即便Dr. Karp是权威的专家，他的判断就是可信的吗？ 是否更应该由合格的独立第三方(independent third-party)来做谁是谁非的判断？

● 最后，在结论中，一些人类学家依然建议采用Dr. Karp的interview-centered method来做进一步的研究，以便Tertian岛上孩子们的领养问题获得准确信息。这是假设interview-centered method要比Dr. Field的observation-centered method更有利于获得精确信息。但这是个未经证实的假设。而且，难道没有更好的研究方法，比如"浸入式(immersion method)"研究法？ 这个方法要求研究者完全同研究对象的生活融合在一起，因而也许是更好的办法呢？

11. The council of Maple County, concerned about the county's becoming overdeveloped, is debating a proposed measure that would prevent the development of existing farmland in the county. But the council is also concerned that such a restriction, by limiting the supply of new housing, could lead to significant increases in the price of housing in the county. Proponents of the measure note that Chestnut County established a similar measure ten years ago, and its housing prices have increased only modestly since. However, opponents of the measure note that Pine County adopted restrictions on the development of new residential housing fifteen years ago, and its housing prices have since more than doubled. The council currently predicts that the proposed measure, if passed, will

result in a significant increase in housing prices in Maple County.

Write a response in which you discuss what questions would need to be answered in order to decide whether the prediction and the argument on which it is based are reasonable. Be sure to explain how the answers to these questions would help to evaluate the prediction.

题目整理

论点 The proposed measure, if passed, will result in a significant increase in housing prices in Maple County.

论据 (1) Chestnut County established a similar measure ten years ago, and its housing prices have increased only modestly since.

(2) Pine County adopted restrictions on the development of new residential housing fifteen years ago, and its housing prices have since more than doubled.

论证方法

题目中论者主要运用了类比论证法，包括纵向、横向两种类比。

分析提示

● 论据(1)和(2)各自用一个县和Maple县进行类比，但得出的结论却大相径庭。针对类比论证，我们的问题永远是可比性。于是问题就是：10到15年前，Chestnut县和Pine县所处的整体经济环境(macro-economic environment)、两个县当时的房屋市场供求状况(supply and demand)、人口结构(demographic structure)、土地供应(land supply)、居民的生活水平(living conditions)和购买力(purchase power)等是否相似？当时两个县的这些指标在今天的Maple县是什么一种情形？有无可比性？

● 其次，这三个县要限制开发的房地产项目是否类似？从题目中可以看到，Maple县和Chestnut县要限制的地产项目类似，都是the supply of new housing，就是说这些房屋既可能是住宅(residential houses)，也可能是商业地产(commercial property)；而Pine县限制开发的是new residential housing。那么，问题来了：是否因为具体限制的地产项目的不同而导致了不同的结果？Maple县该考虑何种房地产开发的品种结构？

● 第三，从题目中可知，Maple县之所以要限制房地产项目，其目的在于prevent the development of existing farmland in the county，从而避免the county's becoming overdeveloped。那么，问题是：难道解决问题的办法只有限制和不限制房地产项目这一种？发展旅游经济，搞金融、电子、信息化技术或者教育、设计等产业是不是一种既发展了地方经济，同时又能避免占用耕地，避开过度开发土地资源的办法？

12. Fifteen years ago, Omega University implemented a new procedure that encouraged students to evaluate the teaching effectiveness of all their professors. Since that time, Omega professors have begun to assign higher grades in their classes, and overall student grade averages at Omega have risen by 30 percent. Potential employers, looking at this dramatic rise in grades, believe that grades at Omega are inflated and do not accurately reflect student achievement; as

a result, Omega graduates have not been as successful at getting jobs as have graduates from nearby Alpha University. To enable its graduates to secure better jobs, Omega University should terminate student evaluation of professors.

Write a response in which you discuss what specific evidence is needed to evaluate the argument and explain how the evidence would weaken or strengthen the argument.

题目整理

论点 Omega University should terminate student evaluation of professors to enable its graduates to secure better jobs.

论据 (1) Fifteen years ago, Omega University implemented a new procedure that encouraged students to evaluate the teaching effectiveness of all their professors. Since that time, Omega professors have begun to assign higher grades in their classes, and overall student grade averages at Omega have risen by 30 percent.

(2) Potential employers, looking at this dramatic rise in grades, believe that grades at Omega are inflated and do not accurately reflect student achievement; as a result, Omega graduates have not been as successful at getting jobs as have graduates from nearby Alpha University.

论证方法

题目中论者主要运用了因果关系论证法、引用权威论证法和类比论证法。

分析提示

● 论据 (1) 力图运用因果关系论证法来证明学生成绩的提高是老师为了讨好学生而故意打高的结果，这是犯了"在此之后，因此之故"的错误。我们需提供证据来证明不是其他原因引起了相同的结果，比如，面对学生评估教学效果的压力，教授们纷纷改进了教学方法、加强课题研究、下工夫备课、注意把握学生的学习心理等；或者是随着老师教学水平的改进，学生们的学习积极性提高了，学习效果也大大改善等。

● 论据 (2) 引用了一些雇主 (employers) 对该校学生成绩提高的看法，他们觉得该校学生成绩有水分，被人为地打高了。这是引用权威的论证法。但是否有证据表明这些雇主的看法是客观公正的？他们掌握真实情况，做过认真调查吗？对这些，我们需要更具体的资料佐证。

● 论据 (2) 里论者总结说，是因为雇主怀疑 Omega 学校毕业生的成绩使得这些学生在找工作时竞争不过 Alpha 大学的毕业生。这又是一个"在此之后，因此之故"的错误。我们需要证据来证明不是其他的原因在起作用，比如 Alpha 大学是否对他们的毕业生进行了全面的就业辅导 (employment tutoring)？他们大学的专业和课程设置是否更符合就业市场的需求？

● 最后，还有一个重要的信息论者没有提供：Alpha 大学是否也采取了让学生评估老师教学效果的措施？如果该校没有采取类似措施，论者在两个学校之间的类比实际上缺乏可比性。两个学校之间的任何差异（比如说 Alpha 大学更为可口的饭菜和更平滑的操场跑道）都被随便拿来解释两校毕业生就业率的不同，这显然十分荒谬。

13. In an attempt to improve highway safety, Prunty County last year lowered its speed limit from 55 to 45 miles per hour on all county highways. But this effort has failed: the number of accidents has not decreased, and, based on reports by the highway patrol, many drivers are exceeding the speed limit. Prunty County should instead undertake the same kind of road improvement project that Butler County completed five years ago: increasing lane widths, resurfacing rough highways, and improving visibility at dangerous intersections. Today, major Butler County roads still have a 55 mph speed limit, yet there were 25 percent fewer reported accidents in Butler County this past year than there were five years ago.

Write a response in which you discuss what specific evidence is needed to evaluate the argument and explain how the evidence would weaken or strengthen the argument.

题目整理

论点 Prunty County should undertake the same kind of road improvement project that Butler County completed five years ago.

论据 (1) Prunty County last year lowered its speed limit from 55 to 45 miles per hour to improve highway safety on all county highways. But this effort has failed: the number of accidents has not decreased, and, based on reports by the highway patrol, many drivers are exceeding the speed limit.

(2) The road improvement project that Butler County completed five years ago by increasing lane widths, resurfacing rough highways, and improving visibility at dangerous intersections succeeded: Today, major Butler County roads still have a 55 mph speed limit, yet there were 25 percent fewer reported accidents in Butler County this past year than there were five years ago.

论证方法

题目中论者主要运用了列举特征式论证法、引用权威论证法以及类比论证法。

分析提示

● 在论据(1)中，论者用两个突出现象来证明去年Prunty县限速的失败：交通事故数量未降，很多司机依然超速。但我们需要证据来表明，这一切都是限速而不是其他原因造成的。比如，自去年限速以来，是否该县汽车数量大大增加？是否出现了超过正常年份的雨雪大雾等恶劣天气？是否该县流动人口大增而公共交通没能跟上？至于交通巡逻人员汇报的很多司机超速的问题，更需要有证据来支持：比如，有没有证据表明这些交通巡逻人员的汇报是真实可信的？他们说的many drivers中的many到底是多少？是纯粹的主观感觉，还是同历史数据进行过比照？是否有特殊原因导致诸多司机超速，比如交通标识不明、路上行人车辆少从而司机不自觉地加速？或者，因为交通巡逻经常出现在路面上，司机害怕被他们盘查，因而不自主地躲避这些巡逻人员从而出现超速？这些都需要更多的证据支持。

● 同理，对于证据(2)列举的若干用以证明Butler县五年前采取的有效措施这一现象，同样需要证据来表明，所有的那些积极效果不是来自其他原因，比如：是否五年来，该县的公共交通状况得到极大改善，人们都不愿开车而选择乘坐公交？是否该县因为人口老龄化加剧或者人口外迁，从而导致路上的机动车数量急剧减少？是否五年间该县政府对机动车征收了过高的财产税和过路费，从而使人们不得不放弃开车了呢？等等。

● 最后，论者建议Prunty县效法Butler县五年前的措施，这实际上是在作类比论证。但这两个县有可比性吗？不同的城市地理环境、交通设施状况、人口数量等是否会使Butler县的措施无法在Prunty县施行呢？况且，一项五年前的措施今天还管用吗？这些都需要更多的证据支持。

---

14. The following appeared as part of an article in a business magazine.

"A recent study rating 300 male and female advertising executives according to the average number of hours they sleep per night showed an association between the amount of sleep the executives need and the success of their firms. Of the advertising firms studied, those whose executives reported needing no more than 6 hours of sleep per night had higher profit margins and faster growth. These results suggest that if a business wants to prosper, it should hire only people who need less than 6 hours of sleep per night."

(参考第118题)

Write a response in which you examine the stated and/or unstated assumptions of the argument. Be sure to explain how the argument depends on these assumptions and what the implications are for the argument if the assumptions prove unwarranted.

题目整理

论点 If a business wants to prosper, it should hire only people who need less than 6 hours of sleep per night.

论据 (1) A recent study rating 300 male and female Mentian advertising executives according to the average number of hours they sleep per night showed an association between the amount of sleep the executives need and the success of their firms.

(2) Of the advertising firms studied, those whose executives reported needing no more than 6 hours of sleep per night had higher profit margins and faster growth.

论证方法

题目中论者主要运用了统计数据论证法、因果关系论证法和归纳论证法。

分析提示

● 首先，论据(1)引用了一项涉及300名观察对象的研究。这项研究是论者所有推论的基础。那么，针对这项研究，保证论者推论正确的前提是：这300名参加研究的人员具有足够的代表性，对他们的遴选（selection）是严格按照抽样调查的操作程序进行的，其中的男女比例的设计也是科学合理的，能反映行业整体男女比例的实际情况；并且，实施这项研究的机构的中立性、客观性也是有保证的，没有受到有关的行业、产业及其他利益相关方的干扰和影响。如果这些假设不能保证，论者的整个结论就很值得怀疑了。

● 论据(2)是一个因果关系的论证。论者认为那些广告公司的管理人员每晚不足6个小时的睡眠是他们所在的公司 had higher profit margins and faster growth 的原因。在这个推论中，论者实际在假设没有其他的原因导致了该结果，比如：是否是这些睡眠较少的经理人所服务的行业普遍出现了繁荣气象，因此业务繁多，使得他们不得不加班加点做业务。而公司的盈利水平因为整个行业的繁荣而迅速增长？也就是说，不是他们睡眠较少而是行业的普遍景气给他们公司带来了盈利？再比如，是否是因为这些高盈利的广告公司的管理严格？在管理的高压下，这些经理人不得不拼命工作，一再压缩自己的睡眠时间？这样的话，这些广告公司的高盈利实际上不是这些经理人睡眠少的结果，而是严格的管理带来的。最后，论者的推论要成立还必须有一个假设：在任何时候，只要那些经理人减少睡眠时间，总能使公司的利润增长。如果这个假设听起来较为滑稽，那么，合理的结论只能是：应该还有其他原因在影响那些公司的盈利水平。

● 在结论中，论者断定任何公司想要盈利，都应该聘请睡眠时间少的人员。这实际上是把一个行业内部尚存疑问的结论简单归纳、推广到其他行业，这不太可取。

---

15. The following memorandum is from the business manager of Happy Pancake House restaurants.

"Recently, butter has been replaced by margarine in Happy Pancake House restaurants throughout the southwestern United States. This change, however, has had little impact on our customers. In fact, only about 2 percent of customers have complained, indicating that an average of 98 people out of 100 are happy with the change. Furthermore, many servers have reported that a number of customers who ask for butter do not complain when they are given margarine instead. Clearly, either these customers do not distinguish butter from margarine or they use the term 'butter' to refer to either butter or margarine."

(参考第51、130、131、133题)

Write a response in which you discuss one or more alternative explanations that could rival the proposed explanation and explain how your explanation(s) can plausibly account for the facts presented in the argument.

题目整理

论点 The change of replacing butter with margarine in the southwestern United States has had little impact on our customers.

论据 (1) Only about 2 percent of customers have complained, indicating that an average of 98 people out of 100 are happy with the change.

(2) Furthermore, many servers have reported that a number of customers who ask for butter do not complain when they are given margarine instead.

(3) Clearly, either these customers do not distinguish butter from margarine or they use the term 'butter' to refer to either butter or margarine.

论证方法

题目中论者主要运用了统计数据论证法和引用权威论证法。

分析提示

● 论据(1)试图在告诉我们一项调查。但这项调查是由谁做的？是怎么做的？数据是如何处理的？其客观公正性是否可以保证等等，论者都没有说明。其次，论者说仅有2%的顾客投诉，其余98%的顾客都满意。这显然很成问题。另外一种完全可能的解释是：几乎绝大部分客人都非常不满意，但许多人不愿向店家投诉，只是心里暗自决定下次不再来这里消费了。这样的话，虽说表面上只有2%的顾客投诉，但实际上顾客已经怨声载道。再者，即便这些没有投诉的98%顾客心里没有不满，一部分人也许不太在意butter和margarine（人造黄油）的区别，但至少不能如论者说的是happy with the change。论者的这种"非此即彼的逻辑"（either-or logic）很难自圆其说。

● 为证明自己的推断正确，论者在论据(2)中引用服务员的反馈：a number of customers who ask for butter do not complain when they are given margarine instead。这同样很难站住脚。这里的服务员也许没有汇报真实情况。如果每位顾客的要求都必须满足的话，这意味着他们的工作量将会增加很多。因此，这些服务员很可能掩盖事实说顾客对butter还是margarine抱无所谓态度。其次，即便服务员反映的情况属实，但很可能顾客们没有表达他们的真实想法。他们没投诉并不表示他们内心没有不满（That they did not voice it does not mean they did not hate it!）

● 至于论据(3)则完全是论者一厢情愿的想当然，用一个自我编造的两难困境来麻痹自己。没有人会连butter和margarine都区别不开，而顾客用butter来随便指称butter或margarine的说法更是牵强。更为合理的解释是这些顾客不愿为了一点儿黄油而去破坏就餐时的心情。

16. In surveys Mason City residents rank water sports (swimming, boating, and fishing) among their favorite recreational activities. The Mason River flowing through the city is rarely used for these pursuits, however, and the city park department devotes little of its budget to maintaining riverside recreational facilities. For years there have been complaints from residents about the quality of the river's water and the river's smell. In response, the state has recently announced plans to clean up Mason River. Use of the river for water sports is, therefore, sure to increase. The city government should for that reason devote more money in this year's budget to riverside recreational facilities.

Write a response in which you examine the stated and/or unstated assumptions of the argument. Be sure to explain how the argument depends on these assumptions and what the implications are for the argument if the assumptions prove unwarranted.

题目整理

论点 题目中的论点有两点，分别是一项预测和一个建议。

(1) Use of the river for water sports is, therefore, sure to increase.

(2) The city government should for that reason devote more money in this year's budget to riverside recreational facilities.

论据 (1) In surveys Mason City residents rank water sports (swimming, boating, and fishing) among their favorite recreational activities. The Mason River flowing through the city is rarely used for these pursuits, however, and the city park department devotes little of its budget to maintaining riverside recreational facilities.

(2) For years there have been complaints from residents about the quality of the river's water and the river's smell.

(3) The state has recently announced plans to clean up Mason River.

论证方法

题目中论者主要运用了统计数据论证法和引用权威论证法。

分析提示

- 首先，在论据(1)中，论者引用了一项统计调查，声称Mason City residents rank water sports (swimming, boating, and fishing) among their favorite recreational activities。这里面有待证实的假设是：参与调查的居民具有普遍的代表性，能代表该市绝大部分的居民；调查方案设计的问题是科学、没有误导性的；参与调查的居民在回答问题时，如实地表达了他们内心的想法；实施调查的机构客观、资质完备，没有受到任何其他利益相关方的影响和干扰，等等。

- 同理，在论据(2)中，论者在引用这些抱怨Mason River水质和气味的居民时，也必须假设：第一，这些居民反映了大多数市民的心声。第二，正是这条河流的水质和气味使他们不愿到这条河里做他们喜欢的水上运动。第三，没有其他原因，比如这条河流湍急的水流、湿滑的河岸、多岩石的河床等等，会使得即便该河的水质得到改善，Mason 市的居民也不会到那里进行水上运动。第四，没有其他水上运动场馆吸引这些居民前去游玩，从而令他们放弃Mason River上的水上运动项目，等等。

- 论据(3)说州政府最近已经宣布了要清理Mason River的计划。我们同样需要知道以下假设是否属实：首先，这一计划能如期实施。其次，河道清理计划能彻底解决河流的水质和气味问题。第三，没有其他原因，比如别的运动项目（室内健身、篮球、跑步、自行车运动等等）的流行，会使Mason 市的居民对水上运动不再有兴趣。

- 最后，论者建议市政府在今年的预算中加大对河边娱乐设施的投入。这里面也需要以下假设：第一，清理后的河流以及水上运动的兴起会使河边娱乐设施成为必要。第二，清理河道的工作很快能完成，能引起居民对这些河边娱乐设施的兴趣。第三，没有其他的投资渠道，比如私人投资、政府和民间的合作开发、公众捐资等来筹措这笔资金。

17. The following appeared in a memorandum from the manager of WWAC radio station.

"To reverse a decline in listener numbers, our owners have decided that WWAC must change from its current rock-music format. The decline has occurred despite population growth in our listening area, but that growth has resulted mainly from people moving here after their retirement. We must make listeners of these new residents. We could switch to a music format tailored to their tastes, but a continuing decline in local sales of recorded music suggests limited interest in music. Instead we should change to a news and talk format, a form of radio that is increasingly popular in our area."

(参考第93、109、110题)

Write a response in which you discuss what specific evidence is needed to evaluate the argument and explain how the evidence would weaken or strengthen the argument.

题目整理

论点 WWAC radio station should change to a news and talk format.

论据 (1) To reverse a decline in listener numbers, our owners have decided that WWAC must change from its current rock-music format. The decline has occurred despite population growth in our listening area, but that growth has resulted mainly from people moving here after their retirement.

(2) We could switch to a music format tailored to their tastes, but a continuing decline in local sales of recorded music suggests limited interest in music.

(3) News and talk format is a form of radio that is increasingly popular in our area.

论证方法

题目中论者主要运用了统计数据论证法、列举特征式论证法和类比论证法。

分析提示

● 首先，论据(1)提到，为了扭转听众人数下降的趋势，WWAC电台必须要改变其现行摇滚乐的模式。这显然是假设现行摇滚乐的模式是其听众数量下降的原因。那么，需要的进一步的证据是：到底是什么原因导致该广播电台听众人数的下降？论者有没有进行客观、翔实、可信的调查研究？论者仅仅是在主观猜测？另外，论者还提到该广播电台覆盖的区域人口数量在增加，并说增加的人群主要是从外地搬迁来的离退休人员。这实际上是在引用统计数据进行论证。我们同样需要更多的证据来显示：这些增加的人口到底有多少？分别是什么职业和教育背景？他们的收入、经济状况和消费水平如何？这些对判断这部分增加人口的广播收听倾向至关重要。

● 论据(2)说该电台本来要推出适合这部分新增人群趣味的音乐，但该地区录音制品销量的下降说明这些人对音乐的兴趣不大。对这些模糊而又充满疑问的推论，我们需要具体的材料来证明：第一，到底是什么导致该地区录音制品销量的下降？是这些新来的离退休人员不感兴趣，还是其他人群导致了销量的下降，比如说年轻人，有了其他获得音乐的方式，比如网上下载MP3？或者其他原因，比如不景气的经济使得当地人的总体收入水平和消费能力下降，他们不得不削减了一些不必要的开支，因而使录音制品销量下滑？更重要的是，论者还要提供证据表明：即便该电台推出了适合这些新增人口趣味的音乐，新音乐不会因为不受其他听众的欢迎，从而导致这部分观众的流失。那样的话，该电台的听众同样不会增加。

● 在论据(3)中，论者说新闻和访谈的节目形式在该地区越来越受欢迎，并建议采用这种形式。这是在把自己和本地区的其他电台作类比，或者是在利用人们的从众心理（bandwagon appeal）进行推理。但是，到底WWAC电台和其他电台是否具有可比性？其他电台覆盖听众的人口结构、听众趣味、运营模式是否和WWAC不同？一旦采用了新闻和访谈的节目形式，是否会流失一部分现有的观众呢？这些都需要更多的证据。

···

18. The following is a memorandum from the business manager of a television station.

"Over the past year, our late-night news program has devoted increased time to national news and less time to weather and local news. During this period, most of the complaints received from viewers were concerned with our station's coverage of weather and local news. In addition, local businesses that used to advertise during our late-night news program have canceled their advertising contracts with us. Therefore, in order to attract more viewers to our news programs and to avoid losing any further advertising revenues, we should expand our coverage of weather and local news on all our news programs."

（参考第20题）

Write a response in which you examine the stated and/or unstated assumptions of the argument. Be sure to explain how the argument depends on these assumptions and what the implications are for the argument if the assumptions prove unwarranted.

题目整理

论点 We should expand our coverage of weather and local news on all our news programs to attract more viewers to our news programs and to avoid losing any further advertising revenues.

论据 (1) Over the past year, our late-night news program has devoted increased time to national news and less time to weather and local news. During this period, most of the complaints received from viewers were concerned with our station's coverage of weather and local news.

(2) Local businesses that used to advertise during our late-night news program have canceled their advertising contracts with us.

论证方法

题目中论者主要运用了因果关系论证法和统计数据论证法。

分析提示

● 首先，结合论者的论点，论据(1)陈述的现象必定要基于三个假设：其一，电视观众的绝大多数抱怨都是天气和地方新闻变少了这一事实，而不是其他，比如，节目制作粗糙了、报道不深入细致了、时效性太差了等等。否则，就很难说观众的不满仅仅是因为天气和地方新闻的节目时间被减少了。其二，论者提到的 **most of the complaints** received from viewers 必须有足够的数量，并且具备代表性。如果在一年内，仅仅有十来个投诉电话，而且是三五个人不断打过来的，即便这些投诉中的90%都是反映天气和地方新闻被减少这一变化，也很难有说服力。其三，所有这些关于天气和地方新闻的投诉基本上都是指向夜间新闻（late-night news program）那个时间段的，因为过去的一年中，只有这个时间段的天气和地方新闻减少了。否则，就有可能是其他时间段的天气和地方新闻的报道出了问题，结果账却给算到了晚间新闻的天气和地方新闻节目的头上。

● 同样，针对论据(2)，论者也需要类似假设：第一，这些取消了合同的地方公司数量有多大？占多少比例？如果仅仅是数百家公司里的三五家这么做，就不足为虑。其次，他们取消合同的原因正是因为天气和地方新闻报道时间的减少。如果是别的情况，比如当地经济萧条、他们公司的资金运转出现压力、出现了更有效的广告投放渠道、公司的广告目的已经实现、公司销售战略的调整等等，论者的推论就很不可靠了。

● 最后，在结论中论者建议为了吸引观众、避免广告收入的流失，应 expand the coverage of weather and local news on **all our news programs**。这同样需要以下假设：这样做会让夜间新闻节目以外的所有其他节目的观众都欢迎这种变化。否则，他们很可能拒绝继续看那些节目，致使无法实现 to attract more viewers to our news programs and to avoid losing any further advertising revenues 的目的。

....

19. Two years ago, radio station WCQP in Rockville decided to increase the number of call-in advice programs that it broadcast; since that time, its share of the radio audience in the Rockville listening area has increased significantly. Given WCQP's recent success with call-in advice programming, and citing a nationwide survey indicating that many radio listeners are quite interested in such programs, the station manager of KICK in Medway recommends that KICK include more call-in advice programs in an attempt to gain a larger audience share in its listening area.

Write a response in which you discuss what questions would need to be answered in order to decide whether the recommendation and the argument on which it is based are reasonable. Be sure to explain how the answers to these questions would help to evaluate the recommendation.

题目整理

论点 KICK in Medway should include more call-in advice programs in an attempt to gain a larger audience share in its listening area.

论据 (1) Two years ago, radio station WCQP in Rockville decided to increase the number of call-in advice programs that it broadcast; since that time, its share of the radio audience in the Rockville listening area has increased significantly.

(2) A nationwide survey indicates that many radio listeners are quite interested in such programs.

论证方法

题目中论者主要运用了因果关系论证法、统计数据论证法和类比论证法。

分析提示

● 在论据(1)中，电台WCQP增加了call-in advice programs的数量，随后就有了its share of the radio audience in the Rockville listening area has increased significantly这样的效果。我们要问：二者前后之间必然有因果关系吗？是否有别的原因导致了同样的结果，比如：当地人口结构的变化，老年人口增加，他们更喜欢听广播？一些WCQP的竞争对手们转而经营别的媒体（电视、互联网等）而退出了广播电台媒体，从而使得WCQP的听众增长很多？或者是因为WCQP同时还推出了其他的节目，正是这些节目吸引了大量的听众？另外，论者还提到了一个表示增长程度的副词significantly。然而，这是一个较为模糊的数量概念。到底增加多少才可说成是significantly？30%，50%，还是200%?该电台原来的市场份额是多少？如果两年前的份额仅仅是1%，那么即便是增加了两倍达到了3%，也依然是个微不足道的份额。

● 论据(2)引用了一个全国性的调查。问题是：这项调查是谁做的？可否保证其独立性、公正性和代表性？而且，这里面同样有一个模糊数据many。在调查中表示对call-in advice programs很大兴趣的听众到底有多少？占受访对象的多大比例？他们是否准确表达了他们的意见？他们声称的和他们实际的收听广播的行为、选择是否一致？

● 整个论证链条中，论者是在将KICK in Medway将要做出的选择同两年前的WCQP in Rockville做过的事情作类比。那么，二者之间是否具备足够的可比性？两地的经济发展水平、听众的兴趣、人口结构、报道倾向等等是否具有参照性？即便两年前二者之间可以比较，但两年来是否发生了新的变化？这些都是必须回答的问题。

20. The following is a memorandum from the business manager of a television station.

"Over the past year, our late-night news program has devoted increased time to national news and less time to weather and local news. During this time period, most of the complaints received from viewers were concerned with our station's coverage of weather and local news. In addition, local businesses that used to advertise during our late-night news program have just canceled their advertising contracts with us. Therefore, in order to attract more viewers to the program and to avoid losing any further advertising revenues, we should restore the time devoted to weather and local news to its former level."

(参考第18题)

Write a response in which you discuss what specific evidence is needed to evaluate the argument and explain how the evidence would weaken or strengthen the argument.

题目整理

论点 We should restore the time devoted to weather and local news to its former level to attract more viewers to the programs and to avoid losing any further advertising revenues.

论据 (1) Over the past year, our late-night news program has devoted increased time to national news and less time to weather and local news. During this time period, most of the complaints received from viewers were concerned with our station's coverage of weather and local news.

(2) Local businesses that used to advertise during our late-night news program have just canceled their advertising contracts with us.

论证方法

题目中论者主要运用了因果关系论证法和统计数据论证法。

分析提示

● 首先，结合论者的论点，判断论据(1)可否成立需要下面三方面的证据：其一，绝大多数电视观众都是投诉天气和地方新闻变少了这一事实，而不是其他，比如，节目制作粗糙了、报道不深入细致了、时效性太差了等等。否则，就很难说明观众的不满只是因为天气和地方新闻的节目时间减少了。其二，论者提到的 **most of the complaints** received from viewers 是否有足够的数量和代表性。如果在一年内，仅仅有十来个投诉电话，并且这些电话就是三五个人不断打过来的，即便这些投诉中的90%都是反映天气和地方新闻被减少这一事实，也很难有说服力。其三，所有投诉针对天气和地方新闻的投诉是否都是指向夜间新闻那个时间段的，这是因为过去的一年中，只有这个时间段的天气和地方新闻减少了。否则，就有可能是其他时间段的天气和地方新闻的报道出了问题，结果账却给算到了晚间新闻的天气和地方新闻节目的头上。

● 同样，针对论据(2)，论者也需提供更多的证据：第一，这些取消了合同的地方公司数量有多少？占多大比例？如果仅仅是数百家公司里面的三五家公司，根本不足为虑。其次，他们取消合同的原因是否是因为天气和地方新闻报道的减少。如果是别的情况，比如当地经济萧条、他们公司的资金运转出现压力、出现了更有效的广告投放渠道、公司的广告目的已经实现、他们销售战略的调整等等，论者的推论就很不可靠了。

● 最后，在结论中论者建议 "restore the time devoted to weather and local news **to its former level**" 以便吸引观众、避免广告收入的流失。那么，这样做是否有以下可能：有关天气和地方新闻的节目时间恢复到过去的长度，这势必会减少其他节目时间，比如全国新闻节目的时间，从而会流失喜欢看全国新闻的观众，to attract more viewers to our news programs and to avoid losing any further advertising revenues 这样的目的也就无法实现。论者也必须提供这方面的佐证。

- -

21, The following appeared in an article written by Dr. Karp, an anthropologist.

"Twenty years ago, Dr. Field, a noted anthropologist, visited the island of Tertia and concluded from his observations that children in Tertia were reared by an entire village rather than by their own biological parents. However, my recent interviews with children living in the group of islands that includes Tertia show that these children spend much more time talking about their biological parents than about other adults in the village. This research of mine proves that Dr. Field's conclusion about Tertian village culture is invalid and thus that the observation-centered approach to studying cultures is invalid as well. The interview-centered method that my team of graduate students is currently using in Tertia will establish a much more accurate understanding of child-rearing traditions there and in other island cultures."

（参考第10、23题）

Write a response in which you discuss what specific evidence is needed to evaluate the argument and explain how the evidence would weaken or strengthen the argument.

题目整理

论点 论者的论点包括对别人的否定和对自己的肯定。

(1) My research proves that Dr. Field's conclusion about Tertian village culture is invalid and thus that the observation-centered approach to studying cultures is invalid as well.

(2) The interview-centered method that my team of graduate students is currently using in Tertia will establish a much more accurate understanding of child-rearing traditions there and in other island cultures.

论据 (1) Twenty years ago, Dr. Field, a noted anthropologist, visited the island of Tertia and concluded from his observations that children in Tertia wcrc rcared by an entire village rather than by their own biological parents.

(2) However, my recent interviews with children living in the group of islands that includes Tertia show that these children spend much more time talking about their biological parents than about other adults in the village.

论证方法

题目中论者主要运用了演绎推理论证法。论者有以下的推理过程：

<u>大前提</u>：如果Tertia岛上的孩子是被村里人集体养大的，他们的言谈中应该有很多内容涉及抚养他们长大的村里人。

<u>小前提</u>：这些孩子在Dr. Karp主持的访谈中谈的更多的是他们自己的亲生父母而不是抚养他们长大的村里人。（这个小前提实际上是大前提的逆否命题）

<u>结论</u>：Dr. Field得出的结论：Tertia岛上的孩子是被村里人集体养大，而非他们的亲生父母，该结论是错误的，因而他的研究方法也是错误的。

分析提示

● 首先，论据(1)提到，这两位专家的研究前后相距20年。那么，我们需要证据来表明：20年来，Tertia岛上居民的生活方式、文化传统有没有发生根本性的变化？ 20年是一个相当长的时间跨度，在此期间，该岛屿同外界（比如大陆居民）是封闭的，还是有频繁的交往？其次，20年间，包括Tertia岛的那一组岛屿（也就是Dr. Karp最近去访问的那些岛屿）之间是否有相互影响，并最终形成了不同以往的、共同的文化和生活习俗？

● 论者在论据(2)中实际上有一个假设：即，如果孩子是被村里人集体抚养的话，这些孩子不应该经常谈及他们的亲生父母。但有证据表明这个预设的假设有科学的吗？是经得起理论和实地考察反复检验的吗？其次，题目中提到，Dr. Karp访谈的孩子不只是来自Tertia岛，还包括其他岛上的孩子。那么我们需要更多的资料来证明：在Dr. Karp访问的孩子中，来自Tertia岛的孩子的比例是否过小？如果比例过小，他很有可能是在用Tertia岛以外的岛民的生活习俗来推测Tertia岛上的生活习俗。这显然是大有问题的。第三，Dr. Karp是如何设计他的访谈问题的？如果这些问题具有很强的倾向行、诱导性，那么他的结论也就很可疑了。第四，即便他的问题设计得很客观、科学，那么这些孩子有没有可能在回答问题时受到情绪的干扰？他们的回答是否客观、可信？他们有无可能因为特别想知道自己的亲生父母而不自觉地讲了很多关于亲生父母的事情？

● 在结论中，Dr. Karp断言Dr. Field的研究结论是失实的、其研究方法是错误的，而自己的研究方法会得出更为准确的结论。但问题是：即便Dr. Karp是权威专家，他的判断就是可信的吗？他的中立性、客观性是否值得怀疑？两位专家的结论仅仅是不同而已，这就必然意味着其中一个人肯定是错误的吗？即便二者之中有一个是错误的，谁能保证肯定是Dr. Field错了呢？所以，我们依然需要等待更深入的研究、收集更多的证据来检验两位专家的结论。

---

22. According to a recent report, cheating among college and university students is on the rise. However, Groveton College has successfully reduced student cheating by adopting an honor code, which calls for students to agree not to cheat in their academic endeavors and to notify a faculty member if they suspect that others have cheated. Groveton's honor code replaced a system in which teachers closely monitored students; under that system, teachers reported an average of thirty cases of cheating per year. In the first year the honor code was in place, students reported twenty-one cases of cheating; five years later, this figure had dropped to fourteen. Moreover, in a recent survey, a majority of Groveton students said that they would be less likely to cheat with an honor code in place than without. Thus, all colleges and universities should adopt honor codes similar to Groveton's in order to decrease cheating among students.

（参考第119、120、138题）

Write a response in which you discuss what questions would need to be answered in order to decide whether the recommendation and the argument on which it is based are reasonable. Be sure to explain how the answers to these questions would help to evaluate the recommendation.

题目整理

论点 (1) Groveton College has successfully reduced student cheating by adopting an honor code, which calls for students to agree not to cheat in their academic endeavors and to notify a faculty member if they suspect that others have cheated.

(2) All colleges and universities should adopt honor codes similar to Groveton's in order to decrease cheating among students.

论据 (1) Groveton's honor code replaced a system in which teachers closely monitored students; under that system, teachers reported an average of thirty cases of cheating per year. In the first year the honor code was in place, students reported twenty-one cases of cheating; five years later, this figure had dropped to fourteen.

(2) Moreover, in a recent survey, a majority of Groveton students said that they would be less likely to cheat with an honor code in place than without.

论证方法

题目中论者主要运用了统计数据论证法和类比论证法。

分析提示

● 首先，在论据(1)中，论者提到在过去由老师来监督学生作弊行为的制度中，每年老师报告的学生作弊事件大概有30起；而在新的honor code制度之下，第一年学生们仅报告了21次的作弊事件，五年后，该数字降为14。那么，我们要问：以前学生作弊较多，是否同老师监管较严、逢弊必抓必报有关？而新制度下呈下降趋势的学生作弊事件是否同学生自我监督较松、甚至隐瞒不报有关？而且，论者并没有提到过去和现在该校的学生数量。假如过去的学生数量较多，30个作弊事件仅占学生的较低比例；而现在虽然学生作弊的绝对数量下降了，但由于学生总人数的下降故学生作弊的比例上升了呢？更何况，论者只是告诉了我们新的honor code实施后第一年和第五年的情形，并没有涉及第二年至第四年学生作弊的情况。假如这中间几年学生作弊的事件数量又重新上升了呢？我们还能说这个新政是有效的吗？还能预测未来它会依然有效？

● 在论据(2)的调查中，论者说多数的Groveton students said that they would be less likely to cheat with an honor code in place than without。针对调查我们永远要问：这里的majority到底是多少被调查学生中的majority？如果仅仅只有20个学生参与了抽样调查，即便他们中的18个人都表示新的honor code让他们不再作弊了，但相对该校可能几万的学生来说，样本过小，说明不了什么问题。而且，这些学生说了他们的真实想法了吗？有没有可能因为新政对他们有利而故意隐瞒自己的态度？这项调查是由谁来做的？其客观、中立、可靠性有保证吗？等等都是很重要的问题。

● 在结论(2)中，论者建议All colleges and universities should adopt honor codes similar to Groveton's in order to decrease cheating among students。这实际是类比论证：在一地有效的办法，在其他地方也会有效。但论者并没有提供其他高校的学生作弊情况。假如其他学校学生作弊现象不多，还有效仿这个honor code的必要吗？即便其他学校也有严重的学生作弊现象，但那里学生作弊的原因和Groveton College的是一样的吗？这个尚存疑问的honor code在那里是否必然有效？这些都没答案。

23. The following appeared in an article written by Dr. Karp, an anthropologist.

"Twenty years ago, Dr. Field, a noted anthropologist, visited the island of Tertia and concluded from his observations that children in Tertia were reared by an entire village rather than by their own biological parents. However, my recent interviews with children living in the group of islands that includes Tertia show that these children spend much more time talking about their biological parents than about other adults in the village. This research of mine proves that Dr. Field's conclusion about Tertian village culture is invalid and thus that the observation-centered approach to studying cultures is invalid as well. The interview-centered method that my team of graduate students is currently using in Tertia will establish a much more accurate understanding of child-rearing traditions there and in other island cultures."

(参考第 10、21 题)

Write a response in which you examine the stated and/or unstated assumptions of the argument. Be sure to explain how the argument depends on these assumptions and what the implications are for the argument if the assumptions prove unwarranted.

题目整理

论点 论者有两个论点，包括对别人的否定和对自己的肯定。

(1) My research proves that Dr. Field's conclusion about Tertian village culture is invalid and thus that the observation-centered approach to studying cultures is invalid as well.

(2) The interview-centered method that my team of graduate students is currently using in Tertia will establish a much more accurate understanding of child-rearing traditions there and in other island cultures.

论据 (1) Twenty years ago, Dr. Field, a noted anthropologist, visited the island of Tertia and concluded from his observations that children in Tertia were reared by an entire village rather than by their own biological parents.

(2) However, my recent interviews with children living in the group of islands that includes Tertia show that these children spend much more time talking about their biological parents than about other adults in the village.

论证方法

题目中论者主要运用了一个演绎推理论证法。论者 Dr. Karp 有以下的推理过程：

大前提：如果 Tertia 岛上的孩子是被村里人集体养大的，他们在言谈中应该经常谈及抚养他们长大的村里人。

小前提：这些孩子在 Dr. Karp 主持的访谈中谈的更多的是亲生父母而不是其他人。(这个小前提实际上是大前提的逆否命题）

结论：Dr. Field 得出的 Tertia 岛上的孩子是被村里人而非亲生父母养大的判断是错误的，因而他的研究方法也是错误的。

分析提示

● 首先，论据(1)(2)提到，这两位专家的研究前后相距20年，对同一课题的研究结论差异较大。若要论据(1)(2)有效，论者势必要假设：首先，20年来，Tertia岛上居民的生活方式、文化传统没有发生根本性的变化。在此期间，该岛屿同外界（比如大陆居民）没有频繁的交往和相互影响。其次，20年间，包括Tertia岛的那一组岛屿（也就是Dr. Karp最近去访问的那些岛屿）彼此间没有相互影响，文化和生活习俗都不一致。

● 论者在论据(2)中的推论实际蕴含了一个假设：即，如果孩子是被村里人集体抚养的话，那么这些孩子谈话中不会老提及亲生父母。但这个假设是否科学、是否经得起推敲尚不得而知。其次，题目中提到，Dr. Karp访谈的孩子不只是来自Tertia岛，还包括其他岛上的孩子。那么，Dr. Karp要假设：在他访问的孩子中，来自Tertia岛的孩子的比例不至于过小。否则，他很有可能是在用其他岛的岛民的生活习俗来推测Tertia岛上的生活习俗。这显然有问题。第三，Dr. Karp的推论还要假设，其访谈题目的设计是科学、可靠的。如果设计的问题具有很强的倾向性和诱导性，那么他的结论就很可疑。最后，这些孩子有没有可能在回答问题时受到情绪的干扰？他们的回答是否客观、可信？他们有无可能因为特别想知道自己的亲生父母而不自觉地讲了很多关于亲生父母的事情？这些都是待定的假设。

● 在结论中，Dr. Karp断言Dr. Field的研究结论失实、其研究方法是错误的，而自己的研究方法会得出更准确的结论。这里同样有一连串的假设：比如，Dr. Karp作为一位权威专家，他的判断就是中立、客观的。两位专家不同的结论中，必定有一个是错误的。未来的研究和更多的证据不会证明Dr. Karp是错的，或者俩人都有正确的地方等等。

---

24. A recently issued twenty-year study on headaches suffered by the residents of Mentia investigated the possible therapeutic effect of consuming salicylates. Salicylates are members of the same chemical family as aspirin, a medicine used to treat headaches. Although many foods are naturally rich in salicylates, food-processing companies also add salicylates to foods as preservatives. The twenty-year study found a correlation between the rise in the commercial use of salicylates and a steady decline in the average number of headaches reported by study participants. At the time when the study concluded, food-processing companies had just discovered that salicylates can also be used as flavor additives for foods, and, as a result, many companies plan to do so. Based on these study results, some health experts predict that residents of Mentia will suffer even fewer headaches in the future.

（参考第26、28题）

Write a response in which you discuss what questions would need to be answered in order to decide whether the prediction and the argument on which it is based are reasonable. Be sure to explain how the answers to these questions would help to evaluate the prediction.

题目整理

论点 Based on these study results, some health experts predict that residents of Mentia will suffer even fewer headaches in the future.

论据 (1) A recently issued twenty-year study on headaches suffered by the residents of Mentia investigated the possible therapeutic effect of consuming salicylates. Although many foods are naturally rich in salicylates, food-processing companies also add salicylates to foods as preservatives.

(2) The twenty-year study found a correlation between the rise in the commercial use of salicylates and a steady decline in the average number of headaches reported by study participants.

(3) At the time when the study concluded, food-processing companies had just discovered that salicylates can also be used as flavor additives for foods, and, as a result, many companies plan to do so.

论证方法

题目中论者主要运用了统计数据论证法、因果关系论证法和引用权威论证法。

分析提示

● 首先，论据(1)提到了一项为时20年的研究。那么我们的问题是：有多少人参与了这项调查？这些调查对象有足够的代表性吗？调查对象的选择是否考虑到了其年龄、职业、饮食习惯、自身体质等等方面的差异？这项调查是由谁来做的？其客观、中立、可靠性有保证吗，等等。

● 其次，论据(2)提到了这项研究揭示的在the commercial use of salicylates与steady decline in the average number of headaches reported by study participants之间的相关性。但相关性不等于是因果关系。我们的问题是：有没有其他原因导致了20年间the steady decline in the average number of headaches reported by study participants这一结果？比如，期间人们生活水平的改善？居住条件的提高？卫生保健设施和医疗水平的加强？甚至是Mentia地区环境和气候的变化等等？而且，论者提供的只是参与调查的人员报告的头疼病例的平均数。是否有部分参与调查的人员在这20年间头疼的发病次数上升了？这部分人群占参加调查的总人数多大比例？最后，论者并没有提供那些没有食用食品中含有salicylates防腐剂的人群的头疼病发病情况。假如这部分人根本就没有头疼病或者出现的极少，是否可推测说，根本无需使用这种防腐剂，人们的头疼病也会消失？

● 论据(3)提到了食品加工公司关于salicylates可以用作调味添加剂的发现。但食品加工公司的中立性、客观性很值得怀疑。他们有没有可能为了行业利益而故意作出对自己有利的结论？他们的研究是否经过了独立的第三方的确定和认可？而且，一旦salicylates被用作调味剂，被许多食品类公司采用（如题中所述many companies plan to do so），加上食品中天然含有的这种元素的含量以及它作为食品防腐剂被食用者摄入体内的含量，是否会导致消费者摄入过量而经常引发头疼或者别的疾病？论者都必须给出回答。

25. The following was written as a part of an application for a small-business loan by a group of developers in the city of Monroe.

"A jazz music club in Monroe would be a tremendously profitable enterprise. Currently, the nearest jazz club is 65 miles away; thus, the proposed new jazz club in Monroe, the C-Note, would have the local market all to itself. Plus, jazz is extremely popular in Monroe: over 100,000 people attended Monroe's annual jazz festival last summer; several well-known jazz musicians live in Monroe; and the highest-rated radio program in Monroe is 'Jazz Nightly,' which airs every weeknight at 7 P.M. Finally, a nationwide study indicates that the typical jazz fan spends close to $1,000 per year on jazz entertainment."

（参考第100、102、164题）

Write a response in which you discuss what specific evidence is needed to evaluate the argument and explain how the evidence would weaken or strengthen the argument.

题目整理

论点 A jazz music club in Monroe would be a tremendously profitable enterprise.

论据 (1) Currently, the nearest jazz club is 65 miles away; thus, the proposed new jazz club in Monroe, the C-Note, would have the local market all to itself.

(2) Jazz is extremely popular in Monroe: over 100,000 people attended Monroe's annual jazz festival last summer; several well-known jazz musicians live in Monroe; and the highest-rated radio program in Monroe is 'Jazz Nightly,' which airs every weeknight at 7 P.M. Finally.

(3) A nationwide study indicates that the typical jazz fan spends close to $1,000 per year on jazz entertainment.

论证方法

题目中论者运用了诉诸常识法、列举特征式论证法和统计数据论证法。

分析提示

● 论据(1)运用常识展开论证：其他条件相同的情况下，有谁会舍近求远呢？但我们需要明确的证据表明，这家计划中的爵士俱乐部会吸引本地的Jazz fans。否则，那些热爱爵士乐的人，是不会在乎跑到65英里之外的俱乐部。

● 论据(2)运用列举特征式的论证方式，力图说明Jazz is extremely popular in Monroe。但是，论者提到的现象都需要进一步的佐证：首先，虽然over 100,000 people attended Monroe's jazz festival last summer，但有多少人是Monroe本地人？占其中多大比例？而several well-known jazz musicians live in Monroe完全可以是因为这个地方风景怡人，同是否Jazz is extremely popular in Monroe没任何关系。至于the highest-rated radio program in Monroe is 'Jazz Nightly,' which airs every weeknight同样说明不了什么：如果所有其他节目都很差，即便Jazz Nightly在人们的评价中名列第一，也未必说明当地人真正喜欢它。其实，即使上

面这三点都的确说明了Jazz is extremely popular in Monroe，仍然推不出A jazz music club in Monroe would be a tremendously profitable enterprise。有证据表明凡是做流行的行当就必定能赚到钱吗？要开这家俱乐部的话，其经营者的管理能力如何？资金是问题吗？有没有竞争对手？其他的娱乐项目会分流爵士爱好者吗？等等都是要考虑的因素。

- 论据(3)是统计数据论证。首先，论者需要提供进一步的证据表明：这项研究的方案设计（如调查样本的选择、调查问卷的设计、调查数据的处理、调查结果的核实和验证等等）和实施过程是严格按照科学程序进行的；其结论是客观、中立、可信的；调查的实施者没有受行业及其他利益相关方的影响。其次，还要证明没有影响Monroe爵士乐爱好者的消费习惯的特殊因素。论者说的调查是全国范围的。一个全国的典型指标对一个具体的地方来说，可能没有意义。Monroe当地的消费水平如何、该地区的爵士迷是否愿意为这项娱乐花钱、他们是习惯自我娱乐还是去俱乐部消费，这些都会左右他们在爵士乐方面的消费支出。

---

26. The following appeared in the summary of a study on headaches suffered by the residents of Mentia.

"Salicylates are members of the same chemical family as aspirin, a medicine used to treat headaches. Although many foods are naturally rich in salicylates, for the past several decades, food-processing companies have also been adding salicylates to foods as preservatives. This rise in the commercial use of salicylates has been found to correlate with a steady decline in the average number of headaches reported by participants in our twenty-year study. Recently, food-processing companies have found that salicylates can also be used as flavor additives for foods. With this new use for salicylates, we can expect a continued steady decline in the number of headaches suffered by the average citizen of Mentia."

（参考第24、28题）

Write a response in which you discuss what specific evidence is needed to evaluate the argument and explain how the evidence would weaken or strengthen the argument.

题目整理

论点 With this new use for salicylates, we can expect a continued steady decline in the number of headaches suffered by the average citizen of Mentia.

论据 (1) The following appeared in the summary of a study on headaches suffered by the residents of Mentia. Salicylates are members of the same chemical family as aspirin, a medicine used to treat headaches. Although many foods are naturally rich in salicylates, for the past several decades, food-processing companies have also been adding salicylates to foods as preservatives.

(2) This rise in the commercial use of salicylates has been found to correlate with a steady decline in the average number of headaches reported by participants in our twenty-year study.

(3) Recently, food-processing companies have found that salicylates can also be used as flavor additives for foods.

论证方法

题目中论者主要运用了统计数据论证法、因果关系论证法和引用权威论证法。

分析提示

● 首先，论据(1)提到了一项为时20年的研究，这是论者全部立论的基础。那么需要的进一步的证据包括：有多少人参与了这项调查？这些调查对象有足够的代表性吗？调查对象的选择是否考虑到了其年龄、职业、饮食习惯、自身体质等等方面的差异？这项调查是由谁来做的？其客观、中立、可靠性有保证吗，等等。

● 其次，论据(2)提到了这项研究所揭示的在 the commercial use of salicylates 与 steady decline in the average number of headaches reported by study participants 之间的相关性。但相关性不等于是因果关系。我们需要进一步的证据来表明：有没有其他原因导致了20年间 the steady decline in the average number of headaches reported by study participants 这一结果？比如，期间人们生活水平的改善？居住条件的提高？卫生保健设施和医疗水平的加强？甚至是 Mentia 地区环境和气候的变化等等？而且，论者提供的只是参与调查的人员报告的头疼病例的平均数。是否有证据显示部分参与调查的人员在这20年间头疼的发病次数上升了？这部分人群占参加调查的总人数多大比例？最后，论者并没有提供那些没有食用食品中含有 salicylates 防腐剂的人群的头疼病发病情况。假如这部分人根本就没有头疼病或者出现的极少，是否可推测说，根本无需使用这种防腐剂，人们的头疼病也会消失呢？

● 论据(3)提到了食品加工公司关于 salicylates 可以用作调味剂的发现。但食品加工公司的中立性、客观性很值得怀疑。有没有证据表明他们没有出于行业利益而故意作出对自己有利的结论？他们的研究是否经过了独立的第三方的确定和认可呢？而且，一旦 salicylates 被用作调味剂，加上食品中天然含有的这种元素的丰富含量以及它作为食品防腐剂被食用者摄入体内的含量，是否会导致消费者摄入过量而经常引发头疼或者别的疾病？论者都必须给出进一步的证据以利于对其预测的评估。

27. The following appeared in a letter to the editor of a local newspaper.

"Commuters complain that increased rush-hour traffic on Blue Highway between the suburbs and the city center has doubled their commuting time. The favored proposal of the motorists' lobby is to widen the highway, adding an additional lane of traffic. But last year's addition of a lane to the nearby Green Highway was followed by a worsening of traffic jams on it. A better alternative is to add a bicycle lane to Blue Highway. Many area residents are keen bicyclists. A bicycle lane would encourage them to use bicycles to commute, and so would reduce rush-hour traffic rather than fostering an increase."

(参考第29题)

Write a response in which you discuss what specific evidence is needed to evaluate the argument and explain how the evidence would weaken or strengthen the argument.

题目整理

论点 A bicycle lane would encourage local people to use bicycles to commute, and so would reduce rush-hour traffic rather than fostering an increase.

论据 (1) Commuters complain that increased rush-hour traffic on Blue Highway between the suburbs and the city center has doubled their commuting time. The favored proposal of the motorists' lobby is to widen the highway, adding an additional lane of traffic.

(2) But last year's addition of a lane to the nearby Green Highway was followed by a worsening of traffic jams on it.

(3) A better alternative is to add a bicycle lane to Blue Highway. Many area residents are keen bicyclists.

论证方法

题目中论者主要运用了引用权威论证法、类比论证法和列举特征式论证法。

分析提示

● 论据(1)实际是个引用权威论证法，提到了乘车上下班者（commuters）的抱怨和开车族（motorists）的建议，他们和论者都提出了解决上下班高峰期（rush-hour）交通拥堵的问题。但首先我们需要进一步的证据来说明，讨论中的交通改革方案到底是要解决谁的问题。因为commuters包括的不仅仅是开车的人，还包括乘公交车的人以及使用其他交通工具（比如自行车）的人。开车的人当然希望路更宽、行车道更多，但乘坐公交车以及骑自行车的人却很可能抱怨开车的人抢道、占道而引发交通拥堵。所以，论者需要提供Blue Highway上行驶的公交车、私家车和自行车的各自比例，以及他们对交通拥堵的实际影响，否则关于解决交通拥堵的办法实际上无从讨论。

● 论据(2)是个类比论证。Green Highway去年采取的办法效果不好，现在在本地实施效果未必也不好。我们需要证据表明这两条公路的相互可比性，比如：两条公路的等级一样吗？附近的人口数量一样吗？路上行驶的交通工具相似吗？在过去的一年间，两条公路周边的人口、车辆等状况又有了什么新的变化？是什么原因导致Green Highway在增加了一条行车道之后反而更拥堵了？等等。

● 论据(3)是列举特征式论证法。依据many area residents are keen bicyclists这一地方特征，推论出当地人在多出一条自行车道后，会骑自行车上下班，从而减缓交通压力。这似乎太想当然了。我们需要的进一步的信息包括：是不是Blue Highway连接的郊区和市中心距离过远，骑车上下班不大现实？当地人会愿意长途骑车吗？当地的天气、气候适合人们一年四季骑自行车上下班吗？骑自行车的人多了以后，Blue Highway上的交通管理难度是否会进一步加大，从而导致更大的混乱和拥堵？

28. The following appeared in the summary of a study on headaches suffered by the residents of Mentia.

"Salicylates are members of the same chemical family as aspirin, a medicine used to treat headaches. Although many foods are naturally rich in salicylates, for the past several decades, food-processing companies have also been adding salicylates to foods as preservatives. This rise in the commercial use of salicylates has been found to correlate with a steady decline in the average number of headaches reported by participants in our twenty-year study. Recently, food-processing companies have found that salicylates can also be used as flavor additives for foods. With this new use for salicylates, we can expect a continued steady decline in the number of headaches suffered by the average citizen of Mentia."

(参考第24、26题)

Write a response in which you examine the stated and/or unstated assumptions of the argument. Be sure to explain how the argument depends on these assumptions and what the implications are for the argument if the assumptions prove unwarranted.

题目整理

论据 With this new use for salicylates, we can expect a continued steady decline in the number of headaches suffered by the average citizen of Mentia.

论据 (1) The following appeared in the summary of a study on headaches suffered by the residents of Mentia. Salicylates are members of the same chemical family as aspirin, a medicine used to treat headaches. Although many foods are naturally rich in salicylates, for the past several decades, food-processing companies have also been adding salicylates to foods as preservatives.

(2) This rise in the commercial use of salicylates has been found to correlate with a steady decline in the average number of headaches reported by participants in our twenty-year study.

(3) Recently, food-processing companies have found that salicylates can also be used as flavor additives for foods.

论证方法

题目中论者主要运用了统计数据论证法、因果关系论证法和引用权威论证法。

分析提示

● 首先，论据(1)提到了一项为时20年的研究，这是论者全部立论的基础。如果论者的预测成立，他必须首先假设这项研究本身是可信的，这些假设包括：该项调查的样本选择是科学、合乎规范的；调查对象有足够的代表性；有可能对调查结果产生干扰的调查对象的年龄、职业、饮食习惯、自身体质等等方面的因素已经被排除；调查实施方的客观、中立性有保证，他们没有受到相关利益方的影响等等。

● 其次，论据(2)提到了这项研究揭示的在 the commercial use of salicylates 与 steady decline in the average number of headaches reported by study participants 之间的相关性。但相关性并不等于是因果关系。若要论据可信，论者实际在假设：没有其他原因导致了20年间 the steady decline in the average number of headaches reported by study participants 这一结果，比如，期间人们生活水平的改善、居住条件的提高、卫生保健设施和医疗水平的完善、甚至是 Mentia 地区环境和气候的变化等等。而且，论者提供的只是参与调查的人员报告的头疼病例的平均数。这意味着他还要假设参与调查的人员在这20年间头疼的发病次数显著上升这一现象没有出现。最后，论者并没有提供那些没有食用食品中含有salicylates防腐剂的人群的头疼病发病情况。假如这部分人根本就没有头疼病或偶尔发病，那就等于说，根本无须使用这种防腐剂，人们的头疼病也会消失。这对论者的推论是个很大的削弱。

- 论据(3)提到了食品加工公司关于salicylates可以用作调味添加剂的发现。但论者首先要假设：食品加工公司的中立性、客观性很可信，比如他们没有出于行业利益而故意作出对自己有利的结论，他们的研究是否经过了独立的第三方的确定和认可等等。并且，论者还要假设，salicylates被用作调味剂后，加上食品中天然含有的这种元素的含量以及它作为食品防腐剂被食用者摄入体内的含量，不会导致消费者因为摄入过量的salicylates而引发经常性的头疼或者别的疾病。

---

29. The following appeared in an editorial in a local newspaper.

"Commuters complain that increased rush-hour traffic on Blue Highway between the suburbs and the city center has doubled their commuting time. The favored proposal of the motorists' lobby is to widen the highway, adding an additional lane of traffic. Opponents note that last year's addition of a lane to the nearby Green Highway was followed by a worsening of traffic jams on it. Their suggested alternative proposal is adding a bicycle lane to Blue Highway. Many area residents are keen bicyclists. A bicycle lane would encourage them to use bicycles to commute, it is argued, thereby reducing rush-hour traffic."

（参考第27题）

Write a response in which you discuss what questions would need to be answered in order to decide whether the recommendation and the argument on which it is based are reasonable. Be sure to explain how the answers to these questions would help to evaluate the recommendation.

题目整理

论点 A bicycle lane should be added to the Blue Highway to encourage local people to use bicycles to commute and reduce rush-hour traffic.

论据 (1) Commuters complain that increased rush-hour traffic on Blue Highway between the suburbs and the city center has doubled their commuting time. The favored proposal of the motorists' lobby is to widen the highway, adding an additional lane of traffic.

(2) Opponents note that last year's addition of a lane to the nearby Green Highway was followed by a worsening of traffic jams on it.

(3) These opponents suggested alternative proposal is adding a bicycle lane to Blue Highway. Many area residents are keen bicyclists. A bicycle lane would encourage them to use bicycles to commute, it is argued, thereby reducing rush-hour traffic.

论证方法

题目中论者主要运用了引用权威论证法、类比论证法和列举特征式论证法。

分析提示

- 论据(1)实际是在引用权威展开论证，提到了乘车上下班者的抱怨和开车族的建议，他们和论者都提出了解决上下班高峰期交通拥堵的问题。但首先我们要问：讨论中的交通改革方案到底是要解决谁的问题？这是因为commuters包括的不仅仅是开车的人，还包括乘公交车的人以及使用其他交通工具（比如自行车）的人。开车的人当然希望路更宽、行车道更多，但乘坐公交车以及骑自行车的人却很可能抱怨开车的人抢道、占道而引发交通拥堵。所以，论者需要提供Blue Highway上行驶的公交车、私家车和自行车的各自比例，以及他们对交通拥堵的实际影响，否则关于解决交通拥堵的办法实际上无从讨论。

- 论据(2)是个类比论证。但Green Highway去年采取的办法效果不好，现在在本地实施效果未必也不好。于是，我们的问题是：这两条公路的相互可比性到底如何？比如说，两条公路的等级一样吗？附近的人口数量一样吗？路上行驶的交通工具相似吗？在过去的一年间，两条公路周边的人口、车辆等状况又有了什么新的变化？是什么原因导致Green Highway在增加了一条行车道之后反而更拥堵了呢？等等。

- 论据(3)是列举特征式论证法。依据many area residents are keen bicyclists这一地方特征，推论当地人在多出一条自行车道后，会骑自行车上下班，从而减缓交通压力。这似乎太想当然了。显而易见的问题是：Blue Highway连接的郊区和市中心是否距离过远从而使得骑车上下班不大现实？当地人会愿意长途骑车吗？当地的天气、气候适合人们一年四季骑自行车上下班吗？骑自行车的人多了以后，Blue Highway上的交通管理的难度是否会进一步加大，从而导致更大的混乱和拥堵？

30, The following appeared as a recommendation by a committee planning a ten-year budget for the city of Calatrava.

"The birthrate in our city is declining: in fact, last year's birthrate was only one-half that of five years ago. Thus the number of students enrolled in our public schools will soon decrease dramatically, and we can safely reduce the funds budgeted for education during the next decade. At the same time, we can reduce funding for athletic playing fields and other recreational facilities. As a result, we will have sufficient money to fund city facilities and programs used primarily by adults, since we can expect the adult population of the city to increase."

Write a response in which you discuss what specific evidence is needed to evaluate the argument and explain how the evidence would weaken or strengthen the argument.

题目整理

论点 We will have sufficient money to fund city facilities and programs used primarily by adults, since we can expect the adult population of the city to increase.

论据 (1) The birthrate in our city is declining: in fact, last year's birthrate was only one-half that of five years ago. Thus the number of students enrolled in our public schools will soon decrease dramatically, and the adult population of the city will increase.

(2) We can safely reduce the funds budgeted for education during the next decade, and at the same time, we can reduce funding for athletic playing fields and other recreational facilities.

论证方法

题目中论者主要运用了统计数据论证法和因果关系论证法。

分析提示

● 论据(1)引用了一组数据，即 The birthrate in our city is declining: in fact, last year's birthrate was only one-half that of five years ago，然后据此作出的因果关系推论。对于这组至关重要的数据，我们首先需要进一步的证据表明：这组数据的出处是哪里？是地方政府机构？中央政府机构？还是官方研究机构？民间研究机构？抑或是自我猜测？出处不同，其权威性和可信性也大为不同，当然也会影响随后的所有推论。其次，论者只是说 last year's birthrate was only one-half that of five years ago，这看起来是很大的下降（是五年前的一半）；但论者并未提供这五年间生育率的连续变化数据。假如仅仅是去年一年比五年前降低一半，而中间的年份同五年前相比变化不大，甚至略有上升的话，那么，去年的下降只是个别年份的特殊情况，并不必然导致出生率的整体下降，也不能说明未来几年就会下降的趋势。如此，论者的整体推论就大成问题了。

● 依据 The birthrate in our city is declining: in fact, last year's birthrate was only one-half that of five years ago，论者随即有两个推论：其一，the number of students enrolled in our public schools will soon decrease dramatically；其二，he adult population of the city will increase。这两个推论里有很多"数据陷阱"。其实，即便 Calatrava 市出生率在下降的数据可信，他的上述两个推论依然未必成立。首先，孩子的入学年龄一般是 6 岁。那就是说，应该在六年后，Calatrava 市公立学校的入学儿童数量会下降，而不是论者说的 soon decrease dramatically。其次，如果未来有其他情况发生，比如大量的外地居民迁入 Calatrava 市或者当地年轻人生育观念的改变等等，论者的结论就更不可靠了。至于论者的第二个推论 the adult population of the city will increase，就更漏洞百出了。首先，即便如论者所说，未来 Calatrava 市的人口出生率会下降，其正常的结果应该是成年人和老年人占总人口比例（而不是人口的绝对数量）的逐步上升、儿童和青少年占总人口比例（同样不是其绝对数量）的逐年下降。但论者这里所指的恰恰是人口的绝对数量（the adult population）。假如未来出现其他情况，比如当地居民移居别处、老龄人口的离世、当地人口自我更新能力下降（新生人口少而死亡的老龄人口慢慢增加）等等，成年人的人口数量完全有可能大量减少。对这些情况，论者都要提供进一步的资料。

● 在论据(2)中的两个推论 We can safely reduce the funds budgeted for education during the next decade 和 we can reduce funding for athletic playing fields and other recreational facilities 同样需要进一步的证据支持。首先，Calatrava 市只是刚刚出现出生率下降的趋势，而论者断言可以在未来十年中减少教育预算，完全没有充分考虑今后人口出生率的趋势以及其他可能导致该地学龄儿童和青少年人口增加的情况。而且，假如该城市的成年人对教育的需求增加了呢？难道就不需要增加教育预算吗？至于第二个推论 we can reduce funding for athletic playing fields and other recreational facilities，论者完全是在假设那些运动场地和娱乐设施都是为孩子和青少年准备的。难道成年人就不需要运动和娱乐了？

31. The following appeared in a letter to the editor of Parson City's local newspaper.

"In our region of Trillura, the majority of money spent on the schools that most students attend—the city-run public schools—comes from taxes that each city government collects. The region's cities differ, however, in the budgetary priority they give to public education. For example, both as a proportion of its overall tax revenues and in absolute terms, Parson City has recently spent almost twice as much per year as Blue City has for its public schools—even though both cities have about the same number of residents. Clearly, Parson City residents place a higher value on providing a good education in public schools than Blue City residents do."

Write a response in which you discuss what specific evidence is needed to evaluate the argument and explain how the evidence would weaken or strengthen the argument.

题目整理

论点 Clearly, Parson City residents place a higher value on providing a good education in public schools than Blue City residents do.

论据 (1) In our region of Trillura, the majority of money spent on the schools that most students attend—the city-run public schools—comes from taxes that each city government collects.

(2) The region's cities differ, however, in the budgetary priority they give to public education. For example, both as a proportion of its overall tax revenues and in absolute terms, Parson City has recently spent almost twice as much per year as Blue City has for its public schools—even though both cities have about the same number of residents.

论证方法

题目中论者主要运用了统计数据论证法和列举特征式论证法。

分析提示

● 论据(1)引用了一个数据：In our region of Trillura, the majority of money spent on ... public schools comes from taxes that each city government collects. 对于这个数据，我们首先需要进一步的证据表明：该数据的出处是哪里？是地方政府机构？中央政府机构？还是官方研究机构？民间研究机构？抑或是论者的自我猜测？出处不同，其权威性和可信性也大为不同，当然也会影响随后的所有推论。其次，对这个重要数据，论者的表述是非常模糊的。这个majority到底指绝对数量还是百分比？有没有一个较为准确的数据区间，比如800万到1000万美元或者各个公立学校总支出的80%—95%等等。否则，对这个模糊数据的解释有可能过于随意而影响其论证的可信度。

● 论据(2)是个列举特征式论证：利用近年Parson City对公立学校较Blue City每年几乎高出一倍的预算投入来证明前者对公立教育的重视。但这里我们至少需要如下证据：第一，论者提供的是最近年份的预算投入。那么在以前，两个城市的公立教育投入有多少？假如在过去几十年来，Blue City每年的公立教育投入都要高出Parson City五倍、十倍甚至更多，以至于该市的公立教育完全满足了当地居民的需要，那么论者的数据还能说明什么问题？第二，论者只是用教育预算的总量及其占当地税收的比重来进行比较。有没有其他没有反映在财政支出上、但同样重要的指标，比如公立教育的开放度、教育大纲设计的科学性、对学生创造性的开发和培养、学校教职员工的生活条件等等？这些方面的差别未必直接反映在地方财政支出上，但显然也很能说明地方政府对教育的重视。第三，论者说两个城市的居民数量大体相当。这同样是非常模糊的表述。两地具体的人口结构如何？未来会有什么样的变化？假如，现在Parson City的学龄儿童和青少年人数比Blue City多出两倍，并且未来这部分人口的数量还会以每年高出Blue City 50%的速度增加？

● 论者在结论中说：Parson City residents place a higher value on providing a good education in public schools than Blue City residents do. 这有偷换概念的嫌疑。之前，论者始终在谈论政府的教育开支，这同两个城市的居民谁更重视公立学校几乎没什么联系。如果说是两地居民通过民主选举或其他手段影响了地方政府的财政支出，这似乎可以解释得过去，但论者需提供这两个城市居民对其所在地政府财政支出行为具有影响力的证据。

・・

32. The following appeared in a memo from a vice president of Quiot Manufacturing.

"During the past year, Quiot Manufacturing had 30 percent more on-the-job accidents than at the nearby Panoply Industries plant, where the work shifts are one hour shorter than ours. Experts say that significant contributing factors in many on-the-job accidents are fatigue and sleep deprivation among workers. Therefore, to reduce the number of on-the-job accidents at Quiot and thereby increase productivity, we should shorten each of our three work shifts by one hour so that employees will get adequate amounts of sleep."

（参考第104、105、106、167题）

Write a response in which you examine the stated and/or unstated assumptions of the argument. Be sure to explain how the argument depends on these assumptions and what the implications are for the argument if the assumptions prove unwarranted.

题目整理

论点 We should shorten each of our three work shifts by one hour so that employees will get adequate amounts of sleep to reduce the number of on-the-job accidents at Quiot and thereby increase productivity.

论据 (1) During the past year, Quiot Manufacturing had 30 percent more on-the-job accidents than at the nearby Panoply Industries plant, where the work shifts are one hour shorter than ours.

(2) Experts say that significant contributing factors in many on-the-job accidents are fatigue and sleep deprivation among workers.

论证方法

题目中论者主要运用了类比论证法和引用权威论证法。

分析提示

- 论据(1)在两家公司间作了个类比论证。论者显然把Panoply Industries公司上班总时间比Quiot公司少一个小时解释为During the past year, Quiot Manufacturing had 30 percent more on-the-job accidents than nearby Panoply Industries的原因。论者犯了个将同时发生的两件事情解释为因果关系的错误。工作时间的长短未必就是导致企业事故发生率差别的原因，其他因素，比如员工工作时有没有安全保护措施、员工是否严格遵守车间工作流程要求、工厂安全巡检是否严格、员工的工作情绪、工作压力的大小等等都能导致这个差异。

- 论据(2)引用权威进行论证。但论者立论成立的前提是：这些专家的学术、职业、专业背景同这两家公司所在的行业、生产环境、员工工作特点等都高度吻合，因而是合格的专家。并且，他们关于员工疲劳和缺少睡眠同工作中事故发生率的研究完全适用于这两家公司。

- 在结论中，论者建议Quiot公司要走得比Panoply公司更远：每天三个班次各减少一个小时的上班时间，让员工得到充分的休息，减少班上事故，提高工作效率。但这个建议若要实现，必须假设：首先，员工会将这减少的一个小时的上班时间用来休息，而不干别的。其次，其他有可能引起班上事故的因素都能得以消除。再次，该公司员工上班总时间的减少不会降低这家公司的生产效率，影响其竞争力。否则，采取的那些措施对Quiot公司没意义。

33. The following appeared in a memorandum from the planning department of an electric power company.

"Several recent surveys indicate that home owners are increasingly eager to conserve energy. At the same time, manufacturers are now marketing many home appliances, such as refrigerators and air conditioners, that are almost twice as energy efficient as those sold a decade ago. Also, new technologies for better home insulation and passive solar heating are readily available to reduce the energy needed for home heating. Therefore, the total demand for electricity in our area will not increase—and may decline slightly. Since our three electric generating plants in operation for the past twenty years have always met our needs, construction of new generating plants will not be necessary."

Write a response in which you examine the stated and/or unstated assumptions of the argument. Be sure to explain how the argument depends on these assumptions and what the implications are for the argument if the assumptions prove unwarranted.

题目整理

论点 本题的论点包括一个预测和一项建议。

(1) The total demand for electricity in our area will not increase—and may decline slightly.

(2) Construction of new generating plants will not be necessary.

论据 (1) Several recent surveys indicate that home owners are increasingly eager to conserve energy.

(2) At the same time, manufacturers are now marketing many home appliances, such as refrigerators and air conditioners, that are almost twice as energy efficient as those sold a decade ago.

(3) Also, new technologies for better home insulation and passive solar heating are readily available to reduce the energy needed for home heating.

(4) The electric power company's three electric generating plants in operation for the past twenty years have always met local needs.

论证方法

题目中论者主要运用了统计数据论证法、因果关系论证法和类比论证法。

分析提示

● 论据(1)举出了几项最近的调查。但论者的立论要成立，必须要假设：首先，这些调查的方案设计（如调查样本的选择、调查数据的处理、调查结果的核实和验证等等）和实施过程是严格按照科学程序进行的；其结论是客观、中立、可信的；调查的实施者没有受行业及其他利益相关方影响。

● 论据(2)至少需要两个假设：其一，消费者愿意淘汰旧家电，购买节能电器。其二，消费者对节能电器的需求不会大幅度增加。如果居民现在家用电器的数量是过去的两倍甚至更多的话，即便用这些节能电器，他们的总用电量很可能也是上升的。

● 论据(3)至少需要假设：这些新技术不至于因成本过高而很难在房屋建筑中大规模采用；或者这些新技术没有安全隐患，比如高电磁辐射、光污染、防火阻燃效果差等等。

● 论据(4)要假设：其一，居民使用家电的范围扩大，比如用电做饭、采暖、制冷等，不会造成更多的电力需求。其二，中短期内，当地的经济发展水平、人口结构、居民的用电方式同过去20年相比不会发生大的变化，比如大量移民的到来、石油和天然气的短缺、工业用电需求增加等等。

34. The vice president of human resources at Climpson Industries sent the following recommendation to the company's president.

"In an effort to improve our employees' productivity, we should implement electronic monitoring of employees' Internet use from their workstations. Employees who use the Internet from their workstations need to be identified and punished if we are to reduce the number of work hours spent on personal or recreational activities, such as shopping or playing games. By installing software to detect employees' Internet use on company computers, we can prevent employees from wasting time, foster a better work ethic at Climpson, and improve our overall profits."

（参考第58、94题）

Write a response in which you examine the stated and/or unstated assumptions of the argument. Be sure to explain how the argument depends on these assumptions and what the implications are for the argument if the assumptions prove unwarranted.

题目整理

论点 We should implement electronic monitoring of employees' Internet use from their workstations to improve our employees' productivity.

论据 (1) Employees who use the Internet from their workstations need to be identified and punished if we are to reduce the number of work hours spent on personal or recreational activities, such as shopping or playing games.

(2) By installing software to detect employees' Internet use on company computers, we can prevent employees from wasting time, foster a better work ethic at Climpson, and improve our overall profits.

论证方法

题目中论者主要运用了因果关系论证法。

分析提示

- 论据(1)中，论者至少有两个假设：首先，他假设公司存在员工上班期间上网购物和玩游戏现象，否则，他所有的论证都只不过是在捕风捉影（boxing with the shadow），没有任何意义。其次，他要假设分清员工在上班期间使用互联网到底是在工作还是在做个人私事是很容易的事情，也许对一些小公司来说，做到这一点其实很难。

- 论据(2)的成立需要的假设：首先，论者要假设在公司电脑上安装软件监控员工的上网活动这个做法是合法的，不侵犯员工的个人隐私。其次，他假设员工没有有效的技术手段去反监控，从而使这种监控措施完全无效。第三，他还要假设在员工的电脑上安装监控软件不会在公司与员工之间制造不信任感，削弱员工对公司的归属感与忠诚度，从而出现人浮于事、消极怠工、降低工作效率现象（这实际会浪费更多的工作时间）。这样一个人人自危、每天像贼一样被监督的员工怎么会有职业道德（work ethics），关心公司利润?

- 在结论中，论者说监控员工上网行为是为了 to improve our employees' productivity。他这样讲实际上还需要这样的假设：除了电子监控外，没有别的更好的办法了。但实际肯定不是这样：教育员工提高时间管理能力，改善业绩考核、增强员工的荣誉感、在公司内部开展更丰富有趣的娱乐活动等等都是不错的办法。

35. The following appeared in a letter from the owner of the Sunnyside Towers apartment complex to its manager.

"One month ago, all the showerheads in the first three buildings of the Sunnyside Towers complex were modified to restrict maximum water flow to one-third of what it used to be. Although actual readings of water usage before and after the adjustment are not yet available, the change will obviously result in a considerable savings for Sunnyside Corporation, since the corporation must pay for water each month. Except for a few complaints about low water pressure, no problems with showers have been reported since the adjustment. I predict that modifying showerheads to restrict water flow throughout all twelve buildings in the Sunnyside Towers complex will increase our profits even more dramatically."

（参考第52、128、129题）

Write a response in which you discuss what questions would need to be answered in order to decide whether the prediction and the argument on which it is based are reasonable. Be sure to explain how the answers to these questions would help to evaluate the prediction.

题目整理

论点 Modifying showerheads to restrict water flow throughout all twelve buildings in the Sunnyside Towers complex will increase our profits even more dramatically.

论据 (1) One month ago, all the showerheads in the first three buildings of the Sunnyside Towers complex were modified to restrict maximum water flow to one-third of what it used to be.

(2) Although actual readings of water usage before and after the adjustment are not yet available, the change will obviously result in a considerable savings for Sunnyside Corporation, since the corporation must pay for water each month.

(3) Except for a few complaints about low water pressure, no problems with showers have been reported since the adjustment.

论证方法

题目中论者主要运用了归纳推理论证法、因果关系论证法和列举特征式论证法。

分析提示

● 论据(1)实际是个归纳推理。论者认为如果在这三座公寓楼采用的节水省钱的办法有效的话，那么，将其推广到其他楼里会同样有效。但问题是：这三座楼有足够的代表性吗？里面住户的人数、居住习惯、对洗浴水流的要求能代表所有12座公寓楼的情况吗？再者，这项试验是在一个月前实施的，那么，一个月期间公寓住户的情况是否能代表全年的情况？这一个月是不是一年中的淡季？这些问题必须回答。

● 论据(2)运用了因果关系推理：因为the corporation must pay for water each month，所以the change will obviously result in a considerable savings for Sunnyside Corporation。但这个推论非常不可靠。首先，如论者所说actual readings of water usage before and after the adjustment are not yet available，所以我们并不知道减小洗浴龙头的水流是否真的节水了。假如用户在洗浴时，是否因为水流变小了而洗更长的时间？当地的水价是多少？如果该公寓所在的城市靠近河流，取水非常方便，因而水价极低呢？最后，水费开支占该公司的总开支中多大比例？如果水费只占该公司总开支中的较小比例，所谓的a considerable savings for Sunnyside Corporation也就很难成立了。

● 论据(3)是列举特征式论证。论者认为住户很少投诉，因此问题也就基本不存在。但没有人反映问题不等于没问题。这个推论太想当然了。

● 最后，在结论中论者认为如果将这项节水措施推而广之的话，the Sunnyside Towers complex will increase our profits even more dramatically。但问题是：其他公寓的住户会像这三座公寓里的住户一样接受水流小的龙头吗？他们会因为不适应而搬走吗？或者因为龙头出水小，他们在使用过程中频繁地调整水龙头阀门，导致水龙头损坏而增加了成本呢？所有这些，都使得论者的结论the Sunnyside Towers complex will increase our profits even more dramatically很难成立。

··

36. The following report appeared in the newsletter of the West Meria Public Health Council.

"An innovative treatment has come to our attention that promises to significantly reduce absenteeism in our schools and workplaces. A study reports that in nearby East Meria, where fish consumption is very high, people visit the doctor only once or twice per year for the treatment of colds. Clearly, eating a substantial amount of fish can prevent colds. Since colds represent the most frequently given reason for absences from school and work, we recommend the daily use of Ichthaid—a nutritional supplement derived from fish oil—as a good way to prevent colds and lower absenteeism."

(参考第163、166题)

Write a response in which you discuss what specific evidence is needed to evaluate the argument and explain how the evidence would weaken or strengthen the argument.

题目整理

论点 An innovative treatment has come to our attention that promises to significantly reduce absenteeism in our schools and workplaces.

论据 (1) A study reports that in nearby East Meria, where fish consumption is very high, people visit the doctor only once or twice per year for the treatment of colds. Clearly, eating a substantial amount of fish can prevent colds.

(2) Since colds represent the most frequently given reason for absences from school and work, we recommend the daily use of Ichthaid—a nutritional supplement derived from fish oil—as a good way to prevent colds and lower absenteeism.

论证方法

题目中论者主要运用了统计数据论证法、类比论证法和因果关系论证法。

分析提示

● 论据(1)提到了一项研究报告，对此，我们需要进一步的证据来说明：这些调查的方案设计（如调查样本的选择、调查数据的处理、调查结果的核实和验证等等）和实施过程是否是严格按照科学程序进行的；其结论是否客观、中立、可信的；调查的实施者有没有受行业及其他利益相关方影响等等。其次，论者提到East Meria的居民吃鱼多，因此那里的人感冒少。前者不一定是后者的原因。论者提到East Meria，实际是想把它和West Meria进行类比。我们需要进一步的信息表明二者之间是否有可比性，比如：有没有其他原因导致East Meria的居民感冒少，比如他们更注意锻炼？那里的环境更健康？或者特殊的人口结构（比如青壮年人口所占比例高，老人和儿童占比例少）？等等。再次，即便吃鱼可以减少感冒，论者所说的eating a substantial amount of fish到底指吃多少？天天吃？顿顿吃？怎么吃？这些都需要更多的资料佐证。

- 对于论据(2)中的因果关系论证，论者需提供证据表明：首先，West Meria的人旷工旷课的理由是否是因为感冒？假如仅仅是个借口呢？其次，即便吃鱼可以减少感冒，论者推荐食用的Ichthaid（一种从鱼油提炼而来的营养添加剂）会和新鲜的鱼一样管用吗？其推荐的使用剂量（daily use）合适吗？会不会有副作用？这些也都需进一步的佐证。

....

37. The following appeared in a recommendation from the planning department of the city of Transopolis.

"Ten years ago, as part of a comprehensive urban renewal program, the city of Transopolis adapted for industrial use a large area of severely substandard housing near the freeway. Subsequently, several factories were constructed there, crime rates in the area declined, and property tax revenues for the entire city increased. To further revitalize the city, we should now take similar action in a declining residential area on the opposite side of the city. Since some houses and apartments in existing nearby neighborhoods are currently unoccupied, alternate housing for those displaced by this action will be readily available."

Write a response in which you discuss what specific evidence is needed to evaluate the argument and explain how the evidence would weaken or strengthen the argument.

题目整理

论点 To further revitalize the city, we should now take similar action in a declining residential area on the opposite side of the city.

论据 (1) Ten years ago, as part of a comprehensive urban renewal program, the city of Transopolis adapted for industrial use a large area of severely substandard housing near the freeway. Subsequently, several factories were constructed there, crime rates in the area declined, and property tax revenues for the entire city increased.

(2) Since some houses and apartments in existing nearby neighborhoods are currently unoccupied, alternate housing for those displaced by this action will be readily available.

论证方法

题目中论者主要运用了类比论证法和因果关系论证法。

分析提示

- 首先，论据(1)列举的改造土地、建造工厂与随后出现的crime rates in the area declined, and property tax revenues for the entire city increased这两个现象之间未必是因果关系。我们需要

进一步的证据表明不是其他的原因导致该结果：比如整个国家和地区的经济处于上升周期，经济一片繁荣，社会就业充分，那么犯罪率降低和房地产税收增多是很正常的事情。

● 论据(2)中，论者必须提供更多的材料来说明：邻近地区的房子足够多而不是一个模糊的数量（some）来安置要迁来的居民；这些目前空置的房屋和公寓是否适合居住；更重要的是，那些需要搬迁的居民是否愿意住在这里，这个地区的居民是否愿意接纳这些新迁来的住户等等。而且，一些新的问题不会因为这些新迁来的居民而产生，比如，学校、医院、养老机构、购物中心、道路交通、生活垃圾处理中心等等公共资源是否够用？新迁来的居民是否能够就近找到工作，从而妥善地安顿下来？等等。

● 论者的结论是建立在一个类比推理之上的：十年前，该城市实施的一项土地开发项目收到了良好的效果；现在如法炮制，效果也应一样。但论者必须有足够的证据表明：十年前后，这两个要开发的地方完全具有可比性。一些显而易见的问题需要回答：这期间，这个城市所处的经济周期相类似吗？十年前，要开发的区域是个severely substandard housing area，而现在要开发的是个declining residential area，二者有可比性吗？再者，开发这个新项目的目的是要to further revitalize the city，但要达到这一目的，只有论者提到的这一种办法吗？是否有其他更好的办法？

38. The following appeared in a memo from the new vice president of Sartorian, a company that manufactures men's clothing.

"Five years ago, at a time when we had difficulties in obtaining reliable supplies of high quality wool fabric, we discontinued production of our alpaca overcoat. Now that we have a new fabric supplier, we should resume production. This coat should sell very well: since we have not offered an alpaca overcoat for five years and since our major competitor no longer makes an alpaca overcoat, there will be pent-up customer demand. Also, since the price of most types of clothing has increased in each of the past five years, customers should be willing to pay significantly higher prices for alpaca overcoats than they did five years ago, and our company profits will increase."

（参考第95、96题）

Write a response in which you discuss what specific evidence is needed to evaluate the argument and explain how the evidence would weaken or strengthen the argument.

题目整理

论点 论者的论点包括一个建议和一项推测。

(1) We should resume production of our alpaca overcoat.

(2) This coat should sell very well.

论据 (1) Five years ago, at a time when we had difficulties in obtaining reliable supplies of high quality wool fabric, we discontinued production of our alpaca overcoat. Now, we have a new fabric supplier.

(2) Since we have not offered an alpaca overcoat for five years and since our major

competitor no longer makes an alpaca overcoat, there will be pent-up customer demand.

(3) Also, since the price of most types of clothing has increased in each of the past five years, customers should be willing to pay significantly higher prices for alpaca overcoats than they did five years ago, and our company profits will increase.

论证方法

题目中论者主要运用了因果关系论证法和归纳推理论证法。

分析提示

● 论据(1)是个因果关系论证。论者提到，五年前Sartorian公司因为没有高质量羊毛布料的供应而不得不停产alpaca overcoat。现在有了一种新布料的供应，所以建议恢复生产。但首先，论者并未讲明现在供应的新布料就是过去的high quality wool fabric，也没有说明它是否完全可以替代过去的high quality wool fabric。那么，用这种新布料是否能生产出当年的alpaca overcoat尚存疑问。其次，即便用这种新布料完全可以生产出可与当年的alpaca overcoat相媲美的产品，有了这种布料是否就是恢复生产alpaca overcoat的唯一决定因素呢？五年间市场情况是否已经全然不同？生产这种新布料做成的alpaca overcoat是否需要购进新机器？员工是否需要重新培训？这些都需要进一步的证据支持。

● 论据(2)也是个因果关系论证，但论者所列的两个原因都未必支持This coat should sell very well。原因很简单，消费者很可能不再喜欢alpaca overcoat了。五年了，流行风尚不知道已经转了多少个轮回，当年的时尚也许早就被今天的消费者淡忘了。论者至少应该提供现在的消费者对当年的alpaca overcoat的印象表述以及消费倾向的调研报告。

● 论据(3)是个典型的归纳推理：因为五年来很多品种的服装价格都上涨了，所以alpaca overcoat肯定也能卖个高价。但论者要先证明，今天的消费者还像五年前一样喜欢alpaca overcoat。其次，消费者即便仍像过去一样喜欢alpaca overcoat，没有其他因素（比如品种繁多的服装款式、品位、时尚风格等等）致使消费者的分流，因而根本无法带来论者期望的高利润。再次，即使现在alpaca overcoat在市场上依旧抢手，但如果Sartorian公司的竞争对手迅速跟进，并造成市场供应的饱和，论者所期望的高利润同样不会实现。

---

39. A recent sales study indicates that consumption of seafood dishes in Bay City restaurants has increased by 30 percent during the past five years. Yet there are no currently operating city restaurants whose specialty is seafood. Moreover, the majority of families in Bay City are two-income families, and a nationwide study has shown that such families eat significantly fewer home-cooked meals than they did a decade ago but at the same time express more concern about healthful eating. Therefore, the new Captain Seafood restaurant that specializes in seafood should be quite popular and profitable.

（参考第174题）

Write a response in which you discuss what specific evidence is needed to evaluate the argument and explain how the evidence would weaken or strengthen the argument.

题目整理

论点 The new Captain Seafood restaurant that specializes in seafood should be quite popular and profitable.

论据 (1) A recent sales study indicates that consumption of seafood dishes in Bay City restaurants has increased by 30 percent during the past five years.

(2) Yet there are no currently operating city restaurants whose specialty is seafood.

(3) Moreover, the majority of families in Bay City are two-income families, and a nationwide study has shown that such families eat significantly fewer home-cooked meals than they did a decade ago but at the same time express more concern about healthful eating.

论证方法

题目中论者主要运用了统计数据论证法和因果关系论证法。

分析提示

● 论据(1)利用统计数据进行论证。但首先，我们需要进一步的证据来表明：这些调查的方案设计（如调查样本的选择、调查数据的处理、调查结果的核实和验证等等）和实施过程是严格按照科学程序进行的；其结论是客观、中立、可信的；调查的实施者没有受行业及其他利益相关方的影响。其次，即使这些数据可信，但假如五年前consumption of seafood dishes in Bay City restaurants是个很低的水平，30%的上升能说明什么问题？再者，五年来，当地餐馆提供的其他菜品的销量如何？假如海鲜以外的其他菜品的销量五年间都至少增长了150%，那么30%的增长实际上是个微不足道的变化。

● 在论据(2)中，论者作了个因果关系论证：因为Bay City存在海鲜菜肴专营的市场空白，所以开一家海鲜餐馆肯定赚钱。但是，我们需要搞明白为什么会出现这个市场空白。如果是一些不可控的原因，比如新鲜海产品的及时供应非常困难、运输和储存海产品的成本非常高、加工海鲜食品所需要的佐料奇缺、当地的气候条件不适合经常食用海鲜等等，所谓的市场空白也就不存在了。

● 论据(3)同样利用统计数据进行论证。但首先，普遍情况未必可以代表具体个案，一个全国范围内的调查对Bay City来说毫无意义。其次，即使那些双职工家庭eat significantly fewer home-cooked meals than they did a decade ago，论者有证据证明他们会去餐馆吃海鲜吗？而且，当论者说，那些双职工家庭eat significantly fewer home-cooked meals than they did a decade ago but **at the same time express more concern about healthful eating**时，他实际上是在假设未来Captain Seafood restaurant提供的海鲜食品在这些双职工家庭眼里会是healthy food，但这一点论者并未证明。

40. Milk and dairy products are rich in vitamin D and calcium—substances essential for building and maintaining bones. Many people therefore say that a diet rich in dairy products can help prevent osteoporosis, a disease that is linked to both environmental and genetic factors and that causes the bones to weaken significantly with age. But a long-term study of a large number of people found that those who consistently consumed dairy products

throughout the years of the study have a higher rate of bone fractures than any other participants in the study. Since bone fractures are symptomatic of osteoporosis, this study result shows that a diet rich in dairy products may actually increase, rather than decrease, the risk of osteoporosis.

Write a response in which you discuss what specific evidence is needed to evaluate the argument and explain how the evidence would weaken or strengthen the argument.

题目整理

论点 This study result shows that a diet rich in dairy products may actually increase, rather than decrease, the risk of osteoporosis.

论据 (1) A long-term study of a large number of people found that those who consistently consumed dairy products throughout the years of the study have a higher rate of bone fractures than any other participants in the study.

(2) Bone fractures are symptomatic of osteoporosis.

论证方法

题目中论者主要运用了统计数据论证法和列举特征式论证法。

分析提示

● 论据(1)中提到了一项调查对象范围很广的长期研究，是典型的统计数据论证法。但首先，我们需要进一步的证据来表明：这些调查的方案设计（如调查样本的选择、调查数据的处理、调查结果的核实和验证等等）和实施过程是严格按照科学程序进行的；其结论是客观、中立、可信的；调查的实施者没有受行业及其他利益相关方的影响。另外，论者对一些关键数据的表述非常模糊，比如，a long-term 是多长，3年、5年，还是8年、10年？ a large number of people 到底是多少人？调查对象是否有足够的代表性？他们的年龄、饮食习惯、生活环境有什么特点？等等这些都需要更多的信息佐证。

● 而且，论者在论据(1)中列举的仅仅是一种相关性，并不是因果关系。我们需要进一步的证据来显示：不是其他原因导致了那些长期食用奶制品的人骨折发生率偏高，比如：这些骨折的人整体年龄是否偏大？他们的饮食结构和习惯是否类似？他们是否来自相同的地区，是他们所在地区特殊的地理环境（土壤、水质、各种微量元素的摄入等等）导致骨折的高发病率呢？是否因为某种特殊的基因使得他们的身体很难吸收奶制品中的维生素和钙？等等。

● 论据(2)是典型的列举特征式论证法。论者依据 those who have consistently consumed dairy products throughout the years of the study have a higher rate of bone fractures than any other participants in the study 和 bone fractures are symptomatic of osteoporosis，得出结论 a diet rich in dairy products may actually increase, rather than decrease, the risk of osteoporosis。但是，是否有证据表明只有 osteoporosis 这种病的症状是骨折？如果有其他一种未知的疾病，在人们大量食用维生素和钙后被诱发出来，其早期症状就是骨折呢？

41. The following appeared in a health newsletter.

"A ten-year nationwide study of the effectiveness of wearing a helmet while bicycling indicates that ten years ago, approximately 35 percent of all bicyclists reported wearing helmets, whereas today that number is nearly 80 percent. Another study, however, suggests that during the same ten-year period, the number of bicycle-related accidents has increased 200 percent. These results demonstrate that bicyclists feel safer because they are wearing helmets, and they take more risks as a result. Thus, to reduce the number of serious injuries from bicycle accidents, the government should concentrate more on educating people about bicycle safety and less on encouraging or requiring bicyclists to wear helmets."

（参考第123、125题）

Write a response in which you examine the stated and/or unstated assumptions of the argument. Be sure to explain how the argument depends on these assumptions and what the implications are for the argument if the assumptions prove unwarranted.

题目整理

论点　论者的论点包括一个解释和一项建议。

(1) These results demonstrate that bicyclists feel safer because they are wearing helmets, and they take more risks as a result.

(2) To reduce the number of serious injuries from bicycle accidents, the government should concentrate more on educating people about bicycle safety and less on encouraging or requiring bicyclists to wear helmets.

论据　(1) A ten-year nationwide study of the effectiveness of wearing a helmet while bicycling indicates that ten years ago, approximately 35 percent of all bicyclists reported wearing helmets, whereas today that number is nearly 80 percent.

(2) Another study, however, suggests that during the same ten-year period, the number of bicycle-related accidents has increased 200 percent.

论证方法

题目中论者主要运用了统计数据论证法。

分析提示

● 论据(1)(2)举了两项研究。但论者的立论要成立，必须要假设：这些调查的方案设计（如调查样本的选择、调查数据的处理、调查结果的核实和验证等）和实施过程是严格按照科学程序进行的；其结论是客观、中立、可信的；调查的实施者没有受行业及其他利益相关方的影响，等等。

● 论据(1)(2)这两项研究揭示了一个违背常理的结果：骑自行车戴安全帽的人增多了，然而自行车事故却增长了两倍。论者的解释是，因为骑自行车的人戴了安全帽，感觉安全了，所以就会骑车冒险。这个结论需要一系列的假设：首先，现在的安全帽和过去的安全帽一样安全可靠。其次，戴安全帽足以避免绝大多数事故。第三，没有其他的因素导致了同样的结果，比如：现在的自行车设计的行车速度较快、自行车数量的急剧增加、没有足够的自行车专用车道、机动车数量的急剧增加、行人和机动车不守交规、交通管理力量严重欠缺、人口的大量增加以及道路拥堵程度的上升等。

● 论者在结论中建议加强自行车安全教育而不是强调骑车人佩戴安全帽以减少自行车事故。这个建议同样要假设：自行车安全教育会引起大家的重视，政府会常年坚持实施这种教育，未来自行车还会是人们的主要交通工具，如果人们注意行车安全就可以避免大部分的交通事故等。另外，论者认为不必强调安全帽的重要性，这一点似乎也与人们的常识相悖。

42. The following is a letter to the head of the Tourism Bureau on the island of Tria.

"Erosion of beach sand along the shores of Tria Island is a serious threat to our island and our tourist industry. In order to stop the erosion, we should charge people for using the beaches. Although this solution may annoy a few tourists in the short term, it will raise money for replenishing the sand. Replenishing the sand, as was done to protect buildings on the nearby island of Batia, will help protect buildings along our shores, thereby reducing these buildings' risk of additional damage from severe storms. And since beaches and buildings in the area will be preserved, Tria's tourist industry will improve over the long term."

Write a response in which you discuss what specific evidence is needed to evaluate the argument and explain how the evidence would weaken or strengthen the argument.

题目整理

论点 In order to stop the erosion, we should charge people for using the beaches.

论据 (1) Erosion of beach sand along the shores of Tria Island is a serious threat to our island and our tourist industry.

(2) Although this solution may annoy a few tourists in the short term, it will raise money for replenishing the sand.

(3) Replenishing the sand, as was done to protect buildings on the nearby island of Batia, will help protect buildings along our shores, thereby reducing these buildings' risk of additional damage from severe storms.

(4) And since beaches and buildings in the area will be preserved, Tria's tourist industry will improve over the long term.

论证方法

题目中论者主要运用了因果关系论证法和类比论证法。

分析提示

● 论据(1)提到，Tria岛沙滩上的沙子流失严重，会影响该岛的旅游业，该判断是论者所有推论的大前提。但关于这个判断的真实性我们无从证实。论者应提供证据来说明：这个判断是如何得到的？如果有具体的调查过程，这些调查的方案设计（如被调查海滨区域的选择、调查数据的处理、调查结果的核实和验证等等）和实施过程是否是严格按照科学程序进行的？其结论是客观、中立、可信的吗？调查的实施者有没有受行业及其他利益相关方的影响？

● 论据(2)是个因果推理。论者显然已经预见到向游客收取沙滩使用费会令游客不满，但依然认为这项措施会带来收入，用来补充沙滩流失的沙子。但我们需要更多的资料来证明，大部分游客不会因为该项收费过高便不再去沙滩游玩了。如果是那样的话，论者设想的收费收入实际上会很少。

● 论据(3)是个类比论证。论者认为既然Batia岛通过补充海滩上流失的沙子避免了滨海楼群遭受严重风暴的损害，那么Tria岛如法效仿也应收到类似效果。但问题是两地的可比性如何？ Tria岛海滩所处的位置、面对的海潮的冲刷力度、海滨的岩层结构等是否会使补充流失沙子的计划无法在Tria实施？或者即便补充了，但很快又流失了？另外，Batia和Tria两地滨海楼群的建筑质量是否相差不大？如果Tria的滨海楼群的建筑质量过差的话，即便海滩的问题解决了，这些滨海楼群是否能够顶得住咸湿海风和雨水的自然侵蚀、海边频繁的地壳变动（比如地震和地震引发的海啸等）依然是个疑问。这些，论者需提供更多的佐证。

● 论者在论据(4)中认为，海滩和滨海楼群一旦得到保护，长远看Tria岛的旅游业肯定好，这也是个因果关系论证。但论者需提供证据表明，没有其他不利因素会影响Tria岛的未来发展，比如：整体经济走向萧条，因此游客数量急剧萎缩；附近其他岛屿和旅游地不会构成竞争；Tria岛的旅游设施、旅游项目的开发和管理能够保持良好的状态，能持续吸引游客等。

43. The following appeared in a memorandum written by the chairperson of the West Egg Town Council.

"Two years ago, consultants predicted that West Egg's landfill, which is used for garbage disposal, would be completely filled within five years. During the past two years, however, the town's residents have been recycling twice as much material as they did in previous years. Next month the amount of recycled material—which includes paper, plastic, and metal—should further increase, since charges for pickup of other household garbage will double. Furthermore, over 90 percent of the respondents to a recent survey said that they would do more recycling in the future. Because of our town's strong commitment to recycling, the available space in our landfill should last for considerably longer than predicted."

Write a response in which you discuss what specific evidence is needed to evaluate the argument and explain how the evidence would weaken or strengthen the argument.

题目整理

论点 The available space in our landfill should last for considerably longer than predicted.

论据 (1) Two years ago, consultants predicted that West Egg's landfill, which is used for garbage disposal, would be completely filled within five years. During the past two years, however, the town's residents have been recycling twice as much material as they did in previous years.

(2) Next month the amount of recycled material—which includes paper, plastic, and metal—should further increase, since charges for pickup of other household garbage will double.

(3) Furthermore, over 90 percent of the respondents to a recent survey said that they would do more recycling in the future.

(4) The town government and the residents there make strong commitment to recycling.

论证方法

题目中论者主要运用了统计数据论证法和因果关系论证法。

分析提示

● 论据(1)是个统计数据论证。首先，论者的立论要成立，必须要提供进一步的证据表明：这些调查的方案设计（如调查样本的选择、调查数据的处理、调查结果的核实和验证等等）和实施过程是否是严格按照科学程序进行的；其结论的客观性、中立性和可信度是否有保证；调查的实施者有没有受行业及其他利益相关方的影响，等等。其次，即使这些数据是可靠的，依然可能说明不了问题：假如两年前居民回收废品的数量很低的话（比如平均每家回收半斤），一倍的增长其实没什么意义。

● 论据(2)是个因果关系论证，引用的原因是一个常识性观念：因为环保部门上门收垃圾的收费要提高一倍，人们势必会更积极回收垃圾废品的以减少垃圾数量，降低生活成本。但和论据(1)谈到的问题一样：如果之前的收费本来就极低的话，a double garbage pickup charge会有多高？能刺激居民积极回收废品吗？另外要格外重视的是：论据(2)提到的可回收的废品是paper, plastic, and metal，然而未来要提高一倍的上门收取垃圾的费用指的是pickup of **other household garbage**。就是说，是除paper, plastic, and metal以外的其他生活垃圾的分拣费用才会提高一倍。但问题是这些除paper, plastic, and metal以外的其他生活垃圾在居民的生活垃圾中占多大比例？从生活常识来看，其实不多。所以，如果不能补充更有力的证据，论者的论证就会大打折扣。最后，论者在论据(2)中谈到下个月可回收垃圾的数量增加的趋势。问题是：这个趋势会持续多久？假如半年以后，因为种种原因，居民送来的可回收垃圾数量又下降了呢？对此，我们同样需要更多的佐证。

● 论据(3)依然在利用统计数据展开论证。我们同样想知道：这些调查的方案设计（如调查样本的选择、调查数据的处理、调查结果的核实和验证等等）和实施过程是否是严格按照科学程序进行的；其结论的客观性、中立性和可信度是否有保证；调查的实施者有没有受行业及其他利益相关方的影响；被调查者是否回答了他们的真实想法；他们是否有参与垃圾废品回收再利用的条件，等等。

● 论据(4)还是一个因果关系论证：因为The town government and the residents there make strong commitment to recycling，所以The available space in our landfill should last for considerably longer than predicted。但我们需要证据表明：这个原因推测得出论者说的结果吗？有没有其他干扰因素，比如：the West Egg Town的外来移民突然急剧增加，导致生活垃圾暴增？那个垃圾填埋坑（landfill）坍塌或被掩埋，其容量迅速变小，很快被填满了？或者，因为经济步入萧条期，人们不再通过回收垃圾及废品的办法获得原材料，从而导致需要填埋的垃圾迅速增加？等等这些都需要更多的佐证。

44. The following appeared in a letter to the editor of a journal on environmental issues.

"Over the past year, the Crust Copper Company (CCC) has purchased over 10,000 square miles of land in the tropical nation of West Fredonia. Mining copper on this land will inevitably result in pollution and, since West Fredonia is the home of several endangered animal species, in environmental disaster. But such disasters can be prevented if consumers simply refuse to purchase products that are made with CCC's copper unless the company abandons its mining plans."

Write a response in which you examine the stated and/or unstated assumptions of the argument. Be sure to explain how the argument depends on these assumptions and what the implications are for the argument if the assumptions prove unwarranted.

题目整理

论点 Such disasters can be prevented.

论据 (1) Over the past year, the Crust Copper Company (CCC) has purchased over 10,000 square miles of land in the tropical nation of West Fredonia.

(2) Mining copper on this land will inevitably result in pollution and, since West Fredonia is the home of several endangered animal species, in environmental disaster.

(3) But such disasters can be prevented if consumers simply refuse to purchase products that are made with CCC's copper unless the company abandons its mining plans.

论证方法

题目中论者主要运用了因果关系论证法和演绎推理论证法。

分析提示

● 论据(1)举了CCC公司在热带岛国West Fredonia买地的事，论者随后就在论据(2)中说在岛上开采铜矿会带来污染以及生态灾难，似乎在作一个因果关系的论证。但论者在这里面首先就假设：CCC公司的买地行为是为了开采铜矿。但这不一定就是事实。假如CCC买了这块地恰恰是为了保护该岛的生态环境呢？实际上许多跨国公司为了提高自己的公共形象，都做一些公益事业，而环保是从事公益事业的一个主要方式。或者，即便CCC公司购买这块地是为了将来开采铜矿，但假如这是一项远期战略储备计划，真正的开采要等到很长一段时间以后呢？那样的话，买地其实不一定立即就导致污染和生态灾难。

● 论据(2)运用了一个因果关系论证，而且该因果推论中的原因是运用人们的常识。但这个因果关系推论极其勉强。开矿的确会破坏环境，加之West Fredonia岛上有若干濒危动物，如果处置不当，可能会带来不良的生态后果。但这不是必然会发生。假如CCC公司采取了全面、有效的环保措施？

● 论者的结论 Such disaster can be prevented是建立在一个前提之下，即 consumers simply refuse to purchase products that are made with CCC's copper unless the company abandons its mining plans，也就是集体的市场抵制（boycott）。这里面实际上是个演绎推理：

- **大前提**：集体的市场抵制会迫使所有的公司放弃其不利于环保的生产计划；
- **小前提**：消费者不买CCC公司的产品是有效的市场抵制行为；
- **结论**：CCC公司最终会放弃West Fredonia的铜开采计划。
- 但这个推论显然需要一系列的假设：首先，消费者能够轻易识别出CCC公司生产的产品。其次，所有的或者绝大多数消费者都愿意加入这个抵制行动。第三，该项抵制行动不会造成大量失业以及经济动荡等后果，以至于人们发现抵制的代价过高，甚至高过环保和生态保护的收益。最后，即便CCC公司放弃了West Fredonia的铜开采计划，其他公司不会取而代之前去开采。否则，预期的环保和生态保护目的依然无法实现。

45. The following is part of a memorandum from the president of Humana University.

"Last year the number of students who enrolled in online degree programs offered by nearby Omni University increased by 50 percent. During the same year, Omni showed a significant decrease from prior years in expenditures for dormitory and classroom space, most likely because instruction in the online programs takes place via the Internet. In contrast, over the past three years, enrollment at Humana University has failed to grow, and the cost of maintaining buildings has increased along with our budget deficit. To address these problems, Humana University will begin immediately to create and actively promote online degree programs like those at Omni. We predict that instituting these online degree programs will help Humana both increase its total enrollment and solve its budget problems."

（参考第49题）

Write a response in which you discuss what questions would need to be answered in order to decide whether the prediction and the argument on which it is based are reasonable. Be sure to explain how the answers to these questions would help to evaluate the prediction.

题目整理

论点 论者的论点包括一项建议和一个预测。

(1) Humana University will begin immediately to create and actively promote online degree programs like those at Omni to address these problems.

(2) Instituting these online degree programs will help Humana both increase its total enrollment and solve its budget problems.

论据 (1) Last year the number of students who enrolled in online degree programs offered by nearby Omni University increased by 50 percent. During the same year, Omni showed a significant decrease from prior years in expenditures for dormitory and classroom space, most likely because instruction in the online programs takes place via the Internet.

(2) In contrast, over the past three years, enrollment at Humana University has failed to grow, and the cost of maintaining buildings has increased along with our budget deficit.

论证方法

题目中论者主要运用了统计数据论证法和类比论证法。

分析提示

● 首先论据(1)(2)都引用了调查数据。针对这些数据我们要问：这些调查数据是如何得来的？其客观性、中立性和可信度是否有保证？收集这些数据的人有没有因为自己的既得利益而歪曲了这些数据或者有选择地使用数据？论者有没有参考独立的第三方提供的有关网上教育对传统教学影响的研究结论以及相关数据？

● 论据(1)说，去年the number of students who enrolled in online degree programs offered by nearby Omni University increased by 50 percent。那么，下列问题需要回答：之前Omni大学网上学位项目的招生人数是多少？如果当时的人数很低的话，增长50%并不能说明什么问题。还有，其他也推出了网上学位项目的大学的招生增长情况如何？如果其他大学类似项目的招生增长幅度至少都是150%，那么50%的增长就不值一提。

● 另外，论据(1)还说，去年Omni showed a significant decrease from prior years in expenditures for dormitory and classroom space，并猜测这个结果是因为instruction in the online programs takes place via the Internet。这个猜测似乎有理：网上授课当然不需要宿舍和教室。但问题是，就没有其他原因导致同样的结果吗？比如，Omni大学传统教育的住校生招生人数大幅度下滑，因此该校可以放弃传统教育住校项目，而不得不通过这些网上学位项目来维持运营了呢？

● 论据(2)列举Humana大学的情况同Omni大学完全相反。通过两校之间的类比，论者显然得出结论：这个差别是因为Humana没有推出类似Omni大学的网上学位项目。对此，我们要问：这两个学校完全可比吗？他们所在地区的那些处于大学教育年龄段的青少年的人口数量是否有巨大的差异？两地的经济发展水平是否有很大差异？两校提供的教育项目所针对的目标人群是否差别很大？等等。还有，其他大学传统住校项目的招生情况如何？至于论者所说的Humana大学过去三年中the cost of maintaining buildings has increased along with our budget deficit，这个结果是否同建筑材料、建筑工人工资的普遍上涨有关，而不是因为没有推出网上学位项目？再者，到底Humana大学用于宿舍和教学楼的维护费用增加的数目和速度是多少？如果绝对数目占该校总支出的比重较低，并且其增速不高于其他支出，论者的推论就没有说服力。

46. The following appeared in a health magazine published in Corpora.

"Medical experts say that only one-quarter of Corpora's citizens meet the current standards for adequate physical fitness, even though twenty years ago, one-half of all of Corpora's citizens met the standards as then defined. But these experts are mistaken when they suggest that spending too much time using computers has caused a decline in fitness. Since overall fitness levels are highest in regions of Corpora where levels of computer ownership are also highest, it is clear that using computers has not made citizens less physically fit. Instead, as shown by this year's unusually low expenditures on fitness-related products and services, the recent decline in the economy is most likely the cause, and fitness levels will improve when the economy does."

Write a response in which you examine the stated and/or unstated assumptions of the argument. Be sure to explain how the argument depends on these assumptions and what the implications are for the argument if the assumptions prove unwarranted.

题目整理

论点 Experts are mistaken when they suggest that spending too much time using computers has caused a decline in fitness. The recent decline in the economy is most likely the cause, and fitness levels will improve when the economy does.

论据 (1) Since overall fitness levels are highest in regions of Corpora where levels of computer ownership are also highest, it is clear that using computers has not made citizens less physically fit.

(2) The economy of Corpora is declining this year and people's expenditures on fitness-related products and services are unusually low.

论证方法

题目中论者主要运用了列举特征式论证法和因果关系论证法。

分析提示

● 论据(1)是列举特征式的论证过程。论者的推论中有一个假设：如果专家所说spending too much time using computers has caused a decline in fitness是对的，就不应该出现Overall fitness levels are highest in regions of Corpora where levels of computer ownership are also highest这种现象。反过来说（也就是原命题的逆否命题），现在，居然出现了这样的现象，于是专家的判断是错的。但论者的推论若要成立，至少要假设两种情况不存在：其一，不存在某个地区有higher levels of computer ownership，但那里的人却没有spending too much time using computers。但这个假设未必成立。我们身边很多人拥有的电脑不止一台，但他们用电脑的时间却不多。如此一来，论者提到的有些Corpora地区电脑拥有率很高，但人们的健康水平也很高这两种现象并存就丝毫不矛盾了。其二，Corpora地区这样的居民不存在：拥有多台计算机，同时健康水平也很高。这个假设同样很难成立。因为我们的确发现过有些人每天使用电脑的时间很长，同时也很注意锻炼。在他们身上也会出现论者认为"用电脑很多，但身体健康未受损害"这样看似矛盾的现象。但由于这部分人在总人群中占的比例小，不能代表使用电脑人群的总体情况，因此专家的关于spending too much time using computers has caused a decline in fitness的判断未必受到削弱。

● 论据(2)是个因果关系论证。论者有这样的一个推论过程：经济下滑导致this year's unusually low expenditures on fitness-related products and services，致使only one-quarter of Corpora's citizens meet the current standards for adequate physical fitness。所以经济下滑是最终的原因。这个推论若要成立，论者必须假设不存在其他原因。但这个假设同样很难成立：很多情况，比如Corpora的居民生活节奏加快，人们没有时间从事体育锻炼；对保健产品和服务质量和效果的怀疑；人口结构的改变（老年人口的减少和青壮年人口的增加）等等都会导致人们不再投资于保健产品和服务。退一步讲，即便经济下滑导致了 this year's unusually low expenditures on fitness-related products and services，依然不能肯定地说是 this year's unusually low expenditures on fitness-related products and services 导致了 Corpora citizens 健康水平的整体下降。因为很可能有其他原因，比如：环境恶化、青壮年大量向外移民、该地区居民长期的饮食习惯等等。

47. The following appeared in a memorandum from the owner of Movies Galore, a chain of movie-rental stores.

"Because of declining profits, we must reduce operating expenses at Movies Galore's ten movie-rental stores. Raising prices is not a good option, since we are famous for our low prices. Instead, we should reduce our operating hours. Last month our store in downtown Marston reduced its hours by closing at 6:00 p.m. rather than 9:00 p.m. and reduced its overall inventory by no longer stocking any DVD released more than five years ago. Since we have received very few customer complaints about these new policies, we should now adopt them at all other Movies Galore stores as our best strategies for improving profits."

（参考第111、112题）

Write a response in which you discuss what specific evidence is needed to evaluate the argument and explain how the evidence would weaken or strengthen the argument.

题目整理

论点 To reduce operating expenses, Movies Galore should reduce its operating hours and decrease its stocks of old DVDs and adopt the new policies at all its stores as the best strategies for improving profits.

论据 (1) Raising prices is not a good option, since we are famous for our low prices.

(2) Last month our store in downtown Marston reduced its hours by closing at 6:00 p.m. rather than 9:00 p.m. and reduced its overall inventory by no longer stocking any DVD released more than five years ago. So far, customers only voiced very few complaints about these new policies.

论证方法

题目中论者主要运用了因果关系论证法和归纳推理论证法。

分析提示

● 论据(1)是个因果关系论证：因为Movies Galore一向以价廉出名，所以提高价格不可取，应缩短营业时间来降低运营成本。我们需要以下证据以判断上述推论的合理性：首先，缩短三个小时的营业时间可以减少多少运营成本？就常识而论，充其量也就节省水费、电费以及其他很少的办公费用（如订书钉、胶水等等）。所以，这个措施未必能起到有效降低Movies Galore运营成本的作用。其次，Movies Galore的竞争对手是否提高音像租金？假如其他音像出租店都提价或者其出租价格本来就比Movies Galore高，那么即使Movies Galore

的出租价格略涨些，其价格也依然很有竞争力。再次，当论者说因为不能提价，所以就必须缩短营业时间时，他犯了人为设置两难困境的错误。难道就没有其他办法，比如，调低员工工资、降低进货价格、注意随手关灯关水龙头以及复印纸重复利用等等以厉行节约举措？

● 论据(2)是个归纳推理论证法：论者认为在downtown Marston店实施的措施在其他店也可以实施。但下列几点关键点需要更多的材料佐证：首先，在downtown Marston店采取的措施是否有效降低了其运营成本？降了多少？如果这些措施的实际效果不明显，其他店没必要仿效该措施。其次，论者说downtown Marston店的做法几乎没有遭到顾客的投诉。但是，有证据表明那些没有投诉的顾客心里没有不满吗？第三，论者建议将downtown Marston的做法推广到所有的店铺。但问题是downtown Marston店的做法到底是否具备标本意义？其他店是否有一些特殊情况难以仿效？

● 最后，论者在结论中认为缩短营业时间、减少旧DVD的库存是降低运营费用、提高利润的最好措施。但这样做是否会导致与初衷相悖的后果，比如DVD库存减少了顾客会不会认为可选择的品种不多，渐渐就不再光顾了？或者，因为Movies Galore缩短了营业时间，一些顾客发现他们在最方便的时间（比如晚上6点以后至8点之前）无法租到DVD？对这些会直接影响Movies Galore盈利状况的因素，论者需提供更多资料加以说明。

---

48. The following appeared in a magazine article about planning for retirement.

"Clearview should be a top choice for anyone seeking a place to retire, because it has spectacular natural beauty and a consistent climate. Another advantage is that housing costs in Clearview have fallen significantly during the past year, and taxes remain lower than those in neighboring towns. Moreover, Clearview's mayor promises many new programs to improve schools, streets, and public services. And best of all, retirees in Clearview can also expect excellent health care as they grow older, since the number of physicians in the area is far greater than the national average."

Write a response in which you discuss what specific evidence is needed to evaluate the argument and explain how the evidence would weaken or strengthen the argument.

题目整理

论点 Clearview should be a top choice for anyone seeking a place to retire.

论据 (1) It has spectacular natural beauty and a consistent climate.

(2) Housing costs in Clearview have fallen significantly during the past year, and taxes remain lower than those in neighboring towns.

(3) Moreover, Clearview's mayor promises many new programs to improve schools, streets, and public services.

(4) And best of all, retirees in Clearview can also expect excellent health care as they grow older, since the number of physicians in the area is far greater than the national average.

论证方法

题目中论者主要运用了因果关系论证法和诉诸常识法。

分析提示

● 论据(1)提到Clearview壮美的（spectacular）自然景色、稳定的（consistent）气候，但这里的spectacular和consistent都是很模糊的描述。到底spectacular是什么样子？是像沙漠戈壁一样苍凉恢弘，还是像热带海滨一般风光旖旎？不同的人有不同的想象。consistent又是什么样的气候？一年四季都冰天雪地，还是四季都骄阳似火，抑或全年都温暖如春？这需要详细说明。再者，到底这些spectacular natural beauty and consistent climate是否利于退休者的健康生活？依然没有说明。

● 论据(2)说去年当地住房成本大幅下降，那里的税收也比邻近的城镇低。但问题是：现在的房价已经降到了什么水平？如果之前都是高的吓人的房价，即便如论者说的显著降低（have fallen significantly）了，也可能依然高不可攀。关于税负水平也是一样：虽然那里的税收比周围地区低，但是否依然居于较高的水平？论者只是说那里的税同周边比要低，但并未提及其他政府征收的费用，比如道路交通费、教育附加费、卫生防疫费、治安管理费等等。最后，论者只谈到了房价和税负水平，并未涉及其他方面，比如医疗、娱乐、食品和服务等等。这些成本是否也很高？

● 论据(3)只是说市长承诺要改善schools, streets, and public services，但它们的现状如何？何时才会有改观？会改善多少？我们无从得知。

● 论据(4)说Retirees in Clearview can also expect excellent health care as they grow older, **since the number of physicians in the area is far greater than the national average**。注意论者说的只是内科大夫（physician）的数量。单单一个科别的大夫的数量能说明该地区的整体医疗水平吗？其他非常关键的指标，比如每千人所拥有的病床数和医生和护士的平均数量、这些医护人员的教育背景、该地区人口的平均寿命及其变化趋势、婴儿出生率和死亡率、产妇生产死亡率、重大卫生防疫事故发生率以及其导致的病患和死亡人数等等都必须提供才行。

---

49. The following is part of a memorandum from the president of Humana University.

"Last year the number of students who enrolled in online degree programs offered by nearby Omni University increased by 50 percent. During the same year, Omni showed a significant decrease from prior years in expenditures for dormitory and classroom space, most likely because online instruction takes place via the Internet. In contrast, over the past three years, enrollment at Humana University has failed to grow and the cost of maintaining buildings has increased. Thus, to increase enrollment and solve the problem of budget deficits at Humana University, we should initiate and actively promote online degree programs like those at Omni."

（参考第45题）

Write a response in which you examine the stated and/or unstated assumptions of the argument. Be sure to explain how the argument depends on these assumptions and what the implications are for the argument if the assumptions prove unwarranted.

题目整理

论点 To increase enrollment and solve the problem of budget deficits at Humana University, we should initiate and actively promote online degree programs like those at Omni.

论据 (1) Last year the number of students who enrolled in online degree programs offered by nearby Omni University increased by 50 percent. During the same year, Omni showed a significant decrease from prior years in expenditures for dormitory and classroom space, most likely because online instruction takes place via the Internet.

(2) In contrast, over the past three years, enrollment at Humana University has failed to grow and the cost of maintaining buildings has increased.

论证方法

题目中论者主要运用了统计数据论证法和类比论证法。

分析提示

● 首先论据(1)(2)都引用了调查数据，它们是论者所有推论的基础。但论者必须假设：这些数据的客观性、中立性和可信度是有保证的，收集这些数据的人没有因为自己既得利益而歪曲了这些数据或者有选择地使用数据等。

● 论据(1)提到去年the number of students who enrolled in online degree programs offered by nearby Omni University increased by 50 percent。那么，至少下列问题需要回答：以前Omni大学网上学位项目的招生人数是多少？假设人数很低，增长50%其实并不能说明什么问题。还有，其他也推出了网上学位项目的大学的招生增长情况如何？如果这些大学招生增长幅度都至少150%，那么50%的增长就不值一提。

● 另外，论据(1)还提到去年Omni showed a significant decrease from prior years in expenditures for dormitory and classroom space，猜测这个结果是因为instruction in the online programs takes place via the Internet。这个猜测似乎有理：网上授课当然不需要宿舍和教室。但问题是，假如有其他原因呢？比如，Omni大学传统教育的住校生招生人数出现了大幅度的下滑，因而该校可以放弃传统教育住校项目，而不得不通过这些网上学位项目来维持运营了呢？

● 论据(2)列举Humana大学的情况同Omni大学完全相反。通过两校之间的类比，论者得出结论：这个差别是因为Humana没有推出类似Omni大学的网上学位项目。这个推论是假设这两个学校完全可比，并且没有其他原因导致这种差别。但问题是：他们所在地区处于大学学龄段的人口数量是否不同？两地的经济发展水平有很大差异？两校提供的教育项目所针对的目标人群是否差别很大？等等。还有，其他大学传统住校项目的招生情况如何？至于论者说的Humana大学过去三年中the cost of maintaining buildings has increased along with our budget deficit，这个结果是否同建筑材料、建筑工人工资的上涨有关，而不是因为没有推出网上学位项目呢？再者，到底Humana大学用于宿舍和教学楼的维护费用增加的数目和速度是多少？如果绝对数目占该校总支出的比重较低，并且其增速不高于其他支出，论者的推论就没有说服力。

50. An ancient, traditional remedy for insomnia—the scent of lavender flowers—has now been proved effective. In a recent study, 30 volunteers with chronic insomnia slept each night for three weeks on lavender-scented pillows in a controlled room where their sleep was monitored electronically. During the first week, volunteers continued to take their usual sleeping medication. They slept soundly but wakened feeling tired. At the beginning of the second week, the volunteers discontinued their sleeping medication. During that week, they slept less soundly than the previous week and felt even more tired. During the third week, the volunteers slept longer and more soundly than in the previous two weeks. Therefore, the study proves that lavender cures insomnia within a short period of time.

Write a response in which you discuss what specific evidence is needed to evaluate the argument and explain how the evidence would weaken or strengthen the argument.

题目整理

论点 The study proves that lavender cures insomnia within a short period of time.

论据 (1) In a recent study, 30 volunteers with chronic insomnia slept each night for three weeks on lavender-scented pillows in a controlled room where their sleep was monitored electronically. During the first week, volunteers continued to take their usual sleeping medication. They slept soundly but wakened feeling tired.

(2) At the beginning of the second week, the volunteers discontinued their sleeping medication. During that week, they slept less soundly than the previous week and felt even more tired.

(3) During the third week, the volunteers slept longer and more soundly than in the previous two weeks.

论证方法

题目中论者主要运用了统计数据论证法。

分析提示

● 论据(1)力图证明服用睡眠药物的效果。但问题是："They slept soundly but wakened feeling tired"这个效果是否与被测试者在新环境中（a controlled room）睡眠不适应或者那些电子监控仪器的干扰有关？论者没有提供证据加以说明。

● 论据(2)力图证明停用睡眠药物的效果。但问题是："they slept less soundly than the previous week and felt even more tired"这个效果是否与被测试者停用睡眠药物之后的心理自我暗示有关？论者仍然没有说明。

● 论据(3)提到"During the third week, the volunteers slept longer and more soundly than in the previous two weeks"。但问题是：the volunteers slept longer and more soundly than in the previous two weeks有具体指标吗？怎么才算slept longer and more soundly？多了几个小时？睡眠中的电子监控结果如何？受试者醒后的精神状态如何？等等。没有较为精确的数据，我们无从判断第一周、

第二周和第三周过后的显著差别。而且，论者能肯定没有其他原因，比如心理作用、环境的影响、前两周的过于疲劳等导致这一结果？

- 当论者依据论据(3)作出判断 the lavender cures insomnia within a short period of time 时，他实际上在假设 During the third week, the volunteers slept longer and more soundly than in the previous two weeks 就足以支持他的判断。但是，要注意：论者在论据(3)中只是说受试者 slept longer and more soundly **than in the previous two weeks**。这是在同前两周作比较，而不是同正常人作比较。论据(3)的结果只能说明受试者的睡眠比前两周有改善，而不能说明他们的失眠症被治愈了。

- 论者的整个推论过程中最大的问题是：整个研究没有设置另外一组没有使用或者使用了假的 lavender-scented pillows 的受试者作比较。如果没有使用或者使用了假的 lavender-scented pillows 的受试者的情况和论据中的那30人的情况相反，将是对题目中结论的有力支持；如果两组情况一样，则论者的结论大有问题。

---

51. The following memorandum is from the business manager of Happy Pancake House restaurants.

"Butter has now been replaced by margarine in Happy Pancake House restaurants throughout the southwestern United States. Only about 2 percent of customers have complained, indicating that 98 people out of 100 are happy with the change. Furthermore, many servers have reported that a number of customers who ask for butter do not complain when they are given margarine instead. Clearly, either these customers cannot distinguish butter from margarine or they use the term 'butter' to refer to either butter or margarine. Thus, to avoid the expense of purchasing butter and to increase profitability, the Happy Pancake House should extend this cost-saving change to its restaurants in the southeast and northeast as well."

(参考第15、130、131、133题)

Write a response in which you discuss what questions would need to be answered in order to decide whether the recommendation is likely to have the predicted result. Be sure to explain how the answers to these questions would help to evaluate the recommendation.

题目整理

论点 To avoid the expense of purchasing butter and to increase profitability, the Happy Pancake House should extend this cost-saving change to its restaurants in the southeast and northeast as well.

论据 (1) Butter has now been replaced by margarine in Happy Pancake House restaurants throughout the southwestern United States. Only about 2 percent of customers have complained, indicating that 98 people out of 100 are happy with the change.

(2) Furthermore, many servers have reported that a number of customers who ask for butter do not complain when they are given margarine instead.

(3) Clearly, either these customers cannot distinguish butter from margarine or they use the

term 'butter' to refer to either butter or margarine.

论证方法

题目中论者主要运用了统计数据论证法和引用权威论证法。

分析提示

● 论据(1)试图在告诉我们一项调查。针对这项调查，我们的问题是：这些调查的方案设计（如调查样本的选择、调查数据的处理、调查结果的核实和验证等）和实施过程是否是严格按照科学程序进行的？其结论的客观性、中立性、可信度是否有保证？调查的实施者没有受行业及其他利益相关方的影响？有没有参考独立的第三方提供的相关数据？等等。其次，论者说只有2%的顾客投诉，剩下98%顾客的反应都被他解释成满意。这显然有问题，论者的逻辑是"非此即彼"，是一个"虚假困境"。论者实际上否认了这种可能，即绝大部分客人都非常不满意，但许多人不愿向店家投诉，只是心里决定下次不再来这里消费了。这样的话，虽说表面上只有2%的顾客投诉，但实际上大部分顾客已经怨声载道。再者，即便这些没有投诉的98%顾客并非心里都很不满，其中的一部分人也许不太在意butter和margarine的区别，但论者不能把他们都说成是happy with the change。这种"非此即彼的逻辑"很难自圆其说。

● 论据(2)是个引用权威的论证手法。论者引用服务员的话：a number of customers who ask for butter do not complain when they are given margarine instead. 对此，我们同样要问：首先，这里的服务员有没有汇报真实情况？如果每位顾客的任何合情合理的要求都必须满足的话，这意味着他们的工作量将会增加很多。因此，这些服务员因为劳累或者工作态度的问题，很可能对顾客的要求推脱延迟，并且掩盖事实说顾客对得到是butter还是margarine抱无所谓态度。其次，即便服务员反映的情况属实，但顾客到底有没有表达他们的真实想法呢？顾客没投诉并不表示他们没有不满。

● 论据(3)是论者编造的又一个"虚假困境"。很少有人会连butter和margarine都区分不开，而顾客用butter来随便指称butter或margarine更是牵强。更大的可能是这些顾客不愿为了一点儿butter而破坏了就餐时的心情。论者需要进一步的调查以弄清楚顾客的真实心态。

● 在结论中，论者建议把人造黄油代替天然黄油的办法推广到东南部和东北部的连锁店。这里隐含着一个归纳推理：在一地看似有效的做法，在另外一地也会有效。但问题是，别的地方的顾客也会那么温和地表达他们的不满吗？那些地方的竞争是否激烈，顾客们稍有不满就会选择其他餐馆？或者，那里的消费者因为传统习惯，根本就不能接受人造黄油呢？这些问题论者都要回答。

52. The following appeared in a letter from the owner of the Sunnyside Towers apartment building to its manager.

"One month ago, all the showerheads on the first five floors of Sunnyside Towers were modified to restrict the water flow to approximately one-third of its original flow. Although actual readings of water usage before and after the adjustment are not yet available, the change will obviously result in a considerable savings for Sunnyside Corporation, since the corporation must pay for water each month. Except for a few complaints about low water pressure, no problems with showers have been reported since the adjustment. Clearly, restricting water flow throughout all the twenty floors of Sunnyside Towers will increase our profits further."

(参考第 35、128、129 题)

Write a response in which you discuss what questions would need to be answered in order to decide whether the recommendation is likely to have the predicted result. Be sure to explain how the answers to these questions would help to evaluate the recommendation.

题目整理

论点 Restricting water flow throughout all the twenty floors of Sunnyside Towers will increase our profits further.

论据 (1) One month ago, all the showerheads on the first five floors of Sunnyside Towers were modified to restrict the water flow to approximately one-third of its original flow.

(2) Although actual readings of water usage before and after the adjustment are not yet available, the change will obviously result in a considerable savings for Sunnyside Corporation, since the corporation must pay for water each month.

(3) Except for a few complaints about low water pressure, no problems with showers have been reported since the adjustment.

论证方法

题目中论者主要运用了归纳推理论证法、因果关系论证法和列举特征式论证法。

分析提示

● 论据(1)是归纳推理。论者认为如果在 Sunnyside Towers 公寓楼的头五层采用节水省钱的办法有效的话，那么，将其推广到其他楼层会同样有效。但问题是：这五层楼有足够的代表性吗？里面居住的人数、居住习惯、对洗浴水流的要求能代表所有楼层的情况吗？再者，这项试验是在一个月前实施的，那么，这一个月期间公寓住户的情况是否能代表全年的情况？这一个月是不是一年中的淡季或者旺季？这些问题必须回答。

● 论据(2)进行了因果推理：因为 the corporation must pay for water each month，所以 the change will obviously result in a considerable savings for Sunnyside Corporation。但这个推论非常不可靠。首先，如论者所说 actual readings of water usage before and after the adjustment are not yet available，所以我们并不知道减小洗浴龙头的水流是否真的节水了。假如住户在洗浴时，因为水流小而洗更长的时间呢？用水岂不一样多甚至更多？再者，当地的水价是多少？如果该公寓所在的城市靠近河流，取水非常方便，因而水价极低呢？最后，到底水费开支占该公司总开支的多大比例？如果水费只占较小比例，a considerable savings for Sunnyside Corporation 就很难成立了。

● 论据(3)是列举特征式论证。论者认为住户很少投诉，因此不存在问题。但住户没有反映问题不等于没问题。

● 最后，在结论中论者认为如果将这项节水措施推而广之的话，会获得更多的利润。但问题是：其他楼层的住户会接受这个水流小的龙头吗？他们会因为不适应这样的水流而搬走？

或者，因为龙头出水小，他们在使用过程中就频繁地调整水龙头阀门，致使水龙头破损，从而增加了 Sunnyside Towers 的运营成本？因此论者的结论 Restricting water flow throughout all the twenty floors of Sunnyside Towers will increase our profits further 很难成立。

53. The following appeared in a health magazine.

"The citizens of Forsythe have adopted more healthful lifestyles. Their responses to a recent survey show that in their eating habits they conform more closely to government nutritional recommendations than they did ten years ago. Furthermore, there has been a fourfold increase in sales of food products containing kiran, a substance that a scientific study has shown reduces cholesterol. This trend is also evident in reduced sales of sulia, a food that few of the most healthy citizens regularly eat."

（参考第144、151题）

Write a response in which you discuss what specific evidence is needed to evaluate the argument and explain how the evidence would weaken or strengthen the argument.

题目整理

论点 The citizens of Forsythe have adopted more healthful lifestyles.

论据 (1) Their responses to a recent survey show that in their eating habits they conform more closely to government nutritional recommendations than they did ten years ago.

(2) Furthermore, there has been a fourfold increase in sales of food products containing kiran, a substance that a scientific study has shown reduces cholesterol.

(3) This trend is also evident in reduced sales of sulia, a food that few of the most healthy citizens regularly eat.

论证方法

题目中论者主要运用了统计数据论证法、列举特征式论证法和归纳推理论证法。

分析提示

● 论据(1)引用一项调查展开论证。但这个调查的方案设计（如调查样本的选择、调查数据的处理、调查结果的核实和验证等等）和实施过程是严格按照科学程序进行的吗？那些调查对象有没有因为从众心理或者担心别人的嘲笑而故意夸大他们的"健康生活习惯"？其结论的客观性、中立性和可信度都有保证吗？调查的实施者没有受行业及其他利益相关方的影响？这些，论者都未加说明。

● 论据(2)是个列举特征式论证。但论者说的这些现象是该地居民意识到kiran是一种利于健康的物质，因而主动调整生活习惯的结果吗？假如因为生活水平下降，他们不得不消费某些特定食品，如玉米、大豆、荞麦，而这些食品中含较多的kiran呢？或者这些居民偏爱的某些食品含有较高的kiran含量？再者，论者说含kiran的食品销量上涨了四倍（fourfold increase）是源于大部分的Forsythe居民还是小部分人？如果是后者，那么实际上只是一部分人的特殊行为，缺乏代表性。还有，从上下文来看，含kiran的食品销量上涨了四倍是在

10年间实现的。那么，其他含有较高营养成分（比如 Vitamin、Calcium、Unsaturated fatty acid 等）的食品在这10年间的销量增长情况如何？如果普遍都高，那么，含有 kiran 的食品销量上涨了四倍并不能说明问题。最后，kiran 对身体有益只是科学研究的一个说法。这个说法是否可信、是否被科学家反复验证过依然是个未知数。所有这些，论者都要加以说明。

● 论据(3)也是列举特征式论证，也有同样问题：论者说 sulia 是"最健康的市民"不怎么吃的一种食品。但问题是"最健康的市民"不怎么吃的食品就是不利于健康的食品吗？首先，青壮年一般都是最健康的群体。但假如青壮年普遍喜欢吃肉而不喜欢吃蔬菜，那么，蔬菜就是不利于健康的食品吗？另外，是否有其他原因导致 Forsythe 居民的 sulia 消费量减少，比如当地气候的变化、耕地的减少等使得 sulia 的种植（假如它是一种作物的话）变得越来越困难，或者因为进口和运输的问题，这种 sulia 运不进来，因此 sulia 在当地的消费量自然减少了？这些都需要更多的佐证。

● 最后，论者的全部推论实际是个归纳推理：论者用 Forsythe 居民的饮食习惯的变化这一事实来说明他们的生活习惯（lifestyles）更健康（healthful）了。但健康的生活习惯仅仅就是食用健康食品吗？该地居民的运动习惯如何？文艺娱乐习惯怎样？他们的生活节奏是否很快、压力是否很大？他们对生活环境的要求如何？居民间的关系是否融洽、社会心态是否宽容？等等这些内容论者并未提及。

---

54. Humans arrived in the Kaliko Islands about 7,000 years ago, and within 3,000 years most of the large mammal species that had lived in the forests of the Kaliko Islands had become extinct. Yet humans cannot have been a factor in the species' extinctions, because there is no evidence that the humans had any significant contact with the mammals. Further, archaeologists have discovered numerous sites where the bones of fish had been discarded, but they found no such areas containing the bones of large mammals, so the humans cannot have hunted the mammals. Therefore, some climate change or other environmental factor must have caused the species' extinctions.

（参考第165题）

Write a response in which you examine the stated and/or unstated assumptions of the argument. Be sure to explain how the argument depends on these assumptions and what the implications are for the argument if the assumptions prove unwarranted.

题目整理

论点 Humans cannot have been a factor in the species' extinctions. Therefore, some climate change or other environmental factor must have caused the species' extinctions.

论据 (1) There is no evidence that the humans had any significant contact with the mammals.

(2) Further, archaeologists have discovered numerous sites where the bones of fish had been discarded, but they found no such areas containing the bones of large mammals, so the humans cannot have hunted the mammals.

论证方法

题目中论者主要运用了演绎推理论证法。

分析提示

● 论据(1)是个演绎推理。具体过程如下：

● 大前提：如果人类是那些哺乳动物绝迹的原因，那么相关的证据应该能够被发现；

● 小前提：没有任何相关的证据出现；

● 结论：Humans cannot have been a factor in the species' extinctions。

● 但这个推理的一个重大缺陷是：那个大前提是论者自我假设的。这个假设未经证实。难道说人类做了某件事，就非得留下证据不可吗？没有发现证据就意味着证据不存在？即便目前没有发现相关证据，那么今后也不可能发现这些证据吗？目前有限的考古手段是否很难发现证据？

● 论据(2)还是一个演绎推理，其过程如下：

● 大前提：如果是人类猎杀了那些哺乳动物，那么这些动物的骨头应该能够被发现；

● 小前提：没有在任何地方发现这些骨头；

● 结论：The humans cannot have hunted the mammals。

● 在这个推理中，大前提同样是论者自我假设的。我们的疑问是：难道人类猎杀了这些哺乳动物，就非得留下它们的骨头不可？没有发现那些骨头就意味着那些骨头不存在？即便目前没有发现那些骨头，难道今后也不可能发现？目前有限的考古手段是否很难发现证据？

● 随即论者得出结论：Some climate change or other environmental factor must have caused the species' extinctions.在此，论者犯了"非此即彼"的错误。难道人类只有和那些哺乳动物密切接触、猎杀它们才灭绝它们？没有其他原因吗，比如，人类砍伐了那些哺乳动物栖息的森林、争夺了它们赖以生活的食物、带给了它们一些致命的传染病菌、驯养了一些专门猎杀那些哺乳动物的家畜？等等。

55. The following appeared in an editorial in a business magazine.

"Although the sales of Whirlwind video games have declined over the past two years, a recent survey of video-game players suggests that this sales trend is about to be reversed. The survey asked video-game players what features they thought were most important in a video game. According to the survey, players prefer games that provide lifelike graphics, which require the most up-to-date computers. Whirlwind has just introduced several such games with an extensive advertising campaign directed at people ten to twenty-five years old, the age-group most likely to play video games. It follows, then, that the sales of Whirlwind video games are likely to increase dramatically in the next few months."

Write a response in which you examine the stated and/or unstated assumptions of the argument. Be sure to explain how the argument depends on these assumptions and what the implications are for the argument if the assumptions prove unwarranted.

题目整理

论点 The sales of Whirlwind video games are likely to increase dramatically in the next few months.

论据 (1) Although the sales of Whirlwind video games have declined over the past two years, a recent survey of video-game players suggests that this sales trend is about to be reversed.

(2) The survey asked video-game players what features they thought were most important in a video game. According to the survey, players prefer games that provide lifelike graphics, which require the most up-to-date computers.

(3) Whirlwind has just introduced several such games with an extensive advertising campaign directed at people ten to twenty-five years old, the age-group most likely to play video games.

论证方法

题目中论者主要运用了统计数据论证法和因果关系论证法。

分析提示

● 论据(1)提到了一项最近的调查。但论者的立论要成立，必须要假设：首先，这些调查的方案设计（如调查样本的选择、调查数据的处理、调查结果的核实和验证等等）和实施过程是严格按照科学程序进行的；其结论是客观、中立、可信的；调查的实施者没有受行业及其他利益相关方的影响。其次，论者引用这个以电子游戏玩家为对象的调查意在说明Whirlwind公司未来电子游戏（video games）的销量，实际上是在假设电子游戏玩家的态度和评价对一款游戏的销售前景很有指示意义。但到底是游戏玩家、经销商、游戏的设计人员还是运营商（比如网吧老板、大型服务器供应商等）和业内专家在一款游戏的未来销量这个问题上更有发言权？仅仅参照是游戏玩家的态度和评价来预测未来市场走势似乎过于局限。

● 论据(2)列举了上述调查的具体内容，结果发现players prefer games that provide lifelike graphics。如果这个调查结果可信，论者必须假设：这些被调查的游戏玩家说的是他们的真实想法，并且具有代表性。但这些假设很可能有问题：是否游戏的故事性和趣味性、逼真的音响效果、同网络及电脑的硬件性能相匹配程度等特性也同样重要？

● 论据(3)是个因果关系论证过程。论者指出该公司生产了games that provide lifelike graphics，也做了广告，并据此得出结论：the sales of Whirlwind video games are likely to increase dramatically in the next few months。但这个结论需要一系列的假设：画面逼真的游戏必然能被市场接受吗？这些游戏未来的市场价位如何？其故事性和趣味性、逼真的音响效果、同网络及电脑的硬件性能相匹配程度等特性如何？如论据(2)所言，这些游戏需要配置the most up-to-date computers。那么，游戏玩家和网吧的商家愿意投资去升级电脑吗？Whirlwind公司针对10到25岁的人群还做了大量的广告。但这个人群的总体消费能力如何？该公司的竞争对手如果推出了性价比更为优越的游戏了呢？

56. The following appeared in a memo from the vice president of marketing at Dura-Sock, Inc.

"A recent study of our customers suggests that our company is wasting the money it spends on its patented Endure manufacturing process, which ensures that our socks are strong enough to last for two years. We have always advertised our use of the Endure process, but the new study shows that despite our socks' durability, our average customer actually purchases new Dura-Socks every three months. Furthermore, our customers surveyed in our largest market, northeastern United States cities, say that they most value Dura-Socks' stylish appearance and availability in many colors. These findings suggest that we can increase our profits by discontinuing use of the Endure manufacturing process."

（参考第57、82题）

Write a response in which you examine the stated and/or unstated assumptions of the argument. Be sure to explain how the argument depends on these assumptions and what the implications are for the argument if the assumptions prove unwarranted.

题目整理

论点 The company is wasting the money it spends on its patented Endure manufacturing process. Instead，it can increase its profits by discontinuing use of the Endure manufacturing process.

论据 (1) A recent study of our customers suggests that our company is wasting the money it spends on its patented Endure manufacturing process, which ensures that our socks are strong enough to last for two years.

(2) We have always advertised our use of the Endure process, but the new study shows that despite our socks' durability, our average customer actually purchases new Dura-Socks every three months.

(3) Furthermore, our customers surveyed in our largest market, northeastern United States cities, say that they most value Dura-Socks' stylish appearance and availability in many colors.

论证方法

题目中论者主要运用了统计数据论证法和归纳推理论证法。

分析提示

- 论据(1)举出了一项研究，该研究是论者整个推论的起点。但论者的立论要成立，必须要假设：这项研究的方案设计（如调查样本的选择、调查数据的处理、调查结果的核实和验证等等）和实施过程是严格按照科学程序进行的；其结论是客观、中立、可信的；调查的实施者没有受行业及其他利益相关方的影响。

- 在论据(2)中，论者：Dura-Sock has always advertised its use of the 'Endure' process, but the new study shows that **the average Dura-Sock customer actually purchases new Dura-Socks every three months**.论者想说顾客并不看重该公司袜子的耐穿度。但假如Dura-Sock的消费者每三个月购买一次新的Dura-Socks并非是因为他们讨厌这种袜子耐穿，而是因为他们喜

欢每三个月更新一次的Dura-Socks的颜色和款式呢？或者因为Dura-Sock的袜子广受欢迎，人们经常拿它来馈赠亲友呢？

● 论据(3)是个归纳推理：论者以美国东北部城市的消费者喜欢Dura-Socks款式和颜色的事实来说明其他地方的顾客也有一样的消费偏爱。但论者能证明的消费者具有代表性吗？其次，假如顾客喜欢Dura-Socks的样式和多种颜色，并不讨厌这种袜子耐穿呢？难道，顾客看重那些袜子的外观和颜色就必须放弃其耐用性？

● 结论是：Dura-Sock can increase its profits by discontinuing its use of the 'Endure' manufacturing process. 论者实际是在假设：Dura-Socks的经磨耐穿的工艺妨碍了该公司利润的增长。但这一点论者并未证实。而且，从常识来讲，假如袜子不耐穿，即便它们花色新颖、款式时尚，也未必受顾客欢迎。因此论者的结论很难成立。

---

57. The following appeared in a memo from the vice president of marketing at Dura-Sock, Inc.

"A recent study of our customers suggests that our company is wasting the money it spends on its patented Endure manufacturing process, which ensures that our socks are strong enough to last for two years. We have always advertised our use of the Endure process, but the new study shows that despite our socks' durability, our average customer actually purchases new Dura-Socks every three months. Furthermore, our customers surveyed in our largest market, northeastern United States cities, say that they most value Dura-Socks' stylish appearance and availability in many colors. These findings suggest that we can increase our profits by discontinuing use of the Endure manufacturing process."

（参考第56、82题）

Write a response in which you discuss what specific evidence is needed to evaluate the argument and explain how the evidence would weaken or strengthen the argument.

题目整理

论点 The company is wasting the money it spends on its patented Endure manufacturing process. Instead，it can increase its profits by discontinuing use of the Endure manufacturing process.

论据 (1) A recent study of our customers suggests that our company is wasting the money it spends on its patented Endure manufacturing process, which ensures that our socks are strong enough to last for two years.

(2) We have always advertised our use of the Endure process, but the new study shows that despite our socks' durability, our average customer actually purchases new Dura-Socks every three months.

(3) Furthermore, our customers surveyed in our largest market, northeastern United States cities, say that they most value Dura-Socks' stylish appearance and availability in many colors.

论证方法

题目中论者主要运用了统计数据论证法和归纳推理论证法。

分析提示

● 论据(1)举出了一项研究，该研究是论者整个推论的起点。但论者的立论想成立，还需要下列相关信息：这项研究的方案设计（如调查样本的选择、调查数据的处理、调查结果的核实和验证等等）和实施过程是否是严格按照科学程序进行的；其结论是否客观、中立、可信；调查的实施者有否受行业及其他利益相关方的影响。

● 在论据(2)中，论者说：Dura-Sock has always advertised its use of the 'Endure' process, but the new study shows that **the average Dura-Sock customer actually purchases new Dura-Socks every three months**.论者想说顾客并不看重该公司袜子的耐穿度。但我们需要证据表明，Dura-Sock 的消费者每三个月购买一次新的 Dura-Socks 是因为他们讨厌这种袜子耐穿吗？有没有别的原因，比如因为他们喜欢 Dura-Socks 的颜色和款式？或者是因为 Dura-Sock 的袜子广受欢迎，人们经常拿它来馈赠亲友呢？

● 论据(3)是个归纳推理：论者以美国东北部城市的消费者喜欢 Dura-Socks 款式和颜色的事实来说明其他地方的顾客也有一样的消费偏爱。但美国东北部城市的消费者具有代表性吗？其次，假如顾客喜欢 Dura-Socks 的样式和多种颜色，并不讨厌这种袜子耐穿呢？难道，顾客看重那些袜子的外观和颜色就必须放弃其耐用性？这些都需要进一步的佐证。

● 结论：Dura-Sock can increase its profits by discontinuing its use of the 'Endure' manufacturing process.论者实际是在假设：Dura-Socks 的经磨耐穿的工艺妨碍了该公司利润的增长。但这一点论者并未证实。而且，从常识来讲，假如袜子不耐穿，即便它们花色新颖、款式时尚，也未必受顾客欢迎。因此论者的结论很难成立。

----

58. The vice president of human resources at Climpson Industries sent the following recommendation to the company's president.

"In an effort to improve our employees' productivity, we should implement electronic monitoring of employees' Internet use from their workstations. Employees who use the Internet inappropriately from their workstations need to be identified and punished if we arc to reduce the number of work hours spent on personal or recreational activities, such as shopping or playing games. Installing software on company computers to detect employees' Internet use is the best way to prevent employees from wasting time on the job. It will foster a better work ethic at Climpson and improve our overall profits."

（参考第 34、94 题）

Write a response in which you discuss what specific evidence is needed to evaluate the argument and explain how the evidence would weaken or strengthen the argument.

题目整理

论点 We should implement electronic monitoring of employees' Internet use from their workstations to improve our employees' productivity.

论据 (1) Employees who use the Internet inappropriately from their workstations need to be identified and punished if we are to reduce the number of work hours spent on personal or recreational activities, such as shopping or playing games.

(2) Installing software on company computers to detect employees' Internet use is the best way to prevent employees from wasting time on the job. It will foster a better work ethic at Climpson and improve our overall profits.

论证方法

题目中论者主要运用了因果关系论证法。

分析提示

● 论据(1)中，论者的建议Employees who use the Internet inappropriately from their workstations need to be identified and punished是有前提条件的，即，如果we are to reduce the number of work hours spent on personal or recreational activities, such as shopping or playing games。那么，至少有两个事实需要确认：首先，是否该公司已经存在员工上班期间上网做个人私事或娱乐，影响工作效率这个事实？如果不是的话，论者所有余下的推理、论证都只不过是在捕风捉影，没有任何意义。其次，是否有办法弄清员工在上班期间使用互联网到底是在工作还是在做个人私事或者娱乐（对小公司来说，做到这一点其实很难）？若做不到这一点，则论者的建议根本无法实施，仅是空谈而已。

● 论据(2)中，论者在没有提供任何有效证据的情况下，断言Installing software on company computers to detect employees' Internet use是防止员工浪费工作时间的最好办法。这个判断若要成立，下面几种情形需要进一步的资料加以说明：首先，论者要确认在公司电脑上安装软件监控员工的上网活动这个做法是合法的，不会侵犯员工的个人隐私。其次，他要确认员工没有有效的技术手段去反监控，从而使这种监控措施完全无效。第三，他还要确认在员工的电脑上安装监控软件不会在公司与员工之间制造不信任感，削弱员工对公司的归属感与忠诚度，从而使他们消极怠工、降低工作效率（这会浪费更多的工作时间）。这样一个人人自危、每天像贼一样被监控的员工还会有职业道德，关心公司利润吗？第四，论者还要确认是否有别的更好的办法防止员工浪费工作时间，比如：教育员工改进时间管理形式、优化对他们的业绩考核、增强他们工作的荣誉感、在公司内部开展更丰富有趣的娱乐活动等都是不错的办法。

● 在结论中，论者说对员工上网行为的监控是为了to improve our employees' productivity，那么论者至少要证明：购买和安装这些监控软件以及随后的监督和维护费用不高，不会增加公司的运营成本。

59. The following appeared in a memo from the president of Bower Builders, a company that constructs new homes.

"A nationwide survey reveals that the two most-desired home features are a large family room and a large, well-appointed kitchen. A number of homes in our area built by our competitor

Domus Construction have such features and have sold much faster and at significantly higher prices than the national average. To boost sales and profits, we should increase the size of the family rooms and kitchens in all the homes we build and should make state-of-the-art kitchens a standard feature. Moreover, our larger family rooms and kitchens can come at the expense of the dining room, since many of our recent buyers say they do not need a separate dining room for family meals."

Write a response in which you examine the stated and/or unstated assumptions of the argument. Be sure to explain how the argument depends on these assumptions and what the implications are for the argument if the assumptions prove unwarranted.

题目整理

论点 To boost sales and profits, we should increase the size of the family rooms and kitchens in all the homes we build and should make state-of-the-art kitchens a standard feature.

论据 (1) A nationwide survey reveals that the two most-desired home features are a large family room and a large, well-appointed kitchen.

(2) A number of homes in our area built by our competitor Domus Construction have such features and have sold much faster and at significantly higher prices than the national average.

(3) Our larger family rooms and kitchens can come at the expense of the dining room, since many of our recent buyers say they do not need a separate dining room for family meals.

论证方法

题目中论者主要运用了统计数据论证法、类比论证法和因果关系论证法。

分析提示

● 论据(1)提到一项全国的调查。但论者的立论要成立，必须要假设：这些调查的方案设计（如调查样本的选择、调查问卷的设计、调查数据的处理、调查结果的核实和验证等等）和实施过程是严格按照科学程序进行的；其结论是客观、中立、可信的；调查的实施者没有受行业及其他利益相关方的影响。

● 论据(2)是个类比论证。论者的推论过程是：既然Domus Construction所建的带有大起居室（family room）和设备齐全的厨房的房子畅销，Bower Builders公司如果效仿，结果也会同样好。但论者要假设，不是其他原因，比如：一流的建筑质量、空间设计、室内外装修以及新颖的市场营销手段、良好的物业管理、绝佳的地理位置等等，促使Domus Construction的房子卖得既快价格又高。

● 论据(3)是个因果关系论证。但其中的原因部分实际上是个简单的市场调查。论者需要假设：接受调查的购房者的数量足够多；他们的家庭人口结构、对房屋的兴趣要求、居住习惯等等具有足够的代表性；他们的回答是他们的真实想法，等等。

● 在结论中，论者建议公司建造的所有房屋中都加大起居室和厨房的面积，并且厨房的建造标准要最好的（state-of-the-art）。论者要假设这样做不会使Bower Builders建造的房屋成本过高，很多人根本买不起。那样的话，boost sales and profits 的目的就无法实现了。

60. The following appeared in a letter from a firm providing investment advice for a client.

"Most homes in the northeastern United States, where winters are typically cold, have traditionally used oil as their major fuel for heating. Last heating season that region experienced 90 days with below-normal temperatures, and climate forecasters predict that this weather pattern will continue for several more years. Furthermore, many new homes are being built in the region in response to recent population growth. Because of these trends, we predict an increased demand for heating oil and recommend investment in Consolidated Industries, one of whose major business operations is the retail sale of home heating oil."

（参考第145、146、150、154、155题）

Write a response in which you examine the stated and/or unstated assumptions of the argument. Be sure to explain how the argument depends on these assumptions and what the implications are for the argument if the assumptions prove unwarranted.

题目整理

论点 该题目的论点包括一项预测和一个建议。

We predict an increased demand for heating oil and recommend investment in Consolidated Industries, one of whose major business operations is the retail sale of home heating oil.

论据 (1) Most homes in the northeastern United States, where winters are typically cold, have traditionally used oil as their major fuel for heating.

(2) Last heating season that region experienced 90 days with below-normal temperatures, and climate forecasters predict that this weather pattern will continue for several more years.

(3) Furthermore, many new homes are being built in the region in response to recent population growth.

论证方法

题目中论者主要运用了统计数据论证法、类比论证法、引用权威论证法和列举特征式论证法。

分析提示

● 论据(1)是个类比论证，其中的推理过程是：既然美国东北部的家庭传统上都用燃油采暖，那么他们现在和将来也会如此。但这个推论需要一系列的假设：传统的习惯不会改变吗？油价的频繁波动是否会迫使这些家庭调整采暖习惯以降低生活成本呢？电采暖是否会以其清洁、成本低廉的优势慢慢取代传统的燃油采暖？在其他地区和城市生活的年轻人是否会把那里不同的采暖方式（如电采暖、地热采暖、管道采暖等）带到这个地区，从而改变本地居民的采暖习惯？等等。

● 论据(2)引用统计数据进行论证，同样需要以下假设：首先，论者要假设90天的低温期（below-normal temperatures）是个较长的时间段。如果常年的低温期都高于90天，那么上个采暖季90天的低温期也就不算什么了。其次，论者说的低温期应该是一个低于平均值较多的温度。否则，如果模糊地说 below-normal temperatures，很难有说服力。第三，论者引用了权威，也就是 climate forecasters，来支持其观点。但论者要假设：这些天气预报员是真正的专家，他们的预测比较可靠。

● 论据(3)运用了列举特征式论证法：既然人口增加了、建的房子多了，对燃油的需求自然就会上升。但这里要假设：第一，这些增加的人口多数都要买房。假如他们都租房住呢？或者，他们是流动人口，冬季的时候都要离开此地区呢？第二，那些新建的房屋都会采用燃油采暖，而不是其他的采暖方式。

● 即便上述论据都有道理，论者的预测（there will be an increased demand for heating oil）和投资 Consolidated Industries 公司的建议若要成立依然要假设：第一，该地区燃油的使用效率不会大幅度提高，即便他们依旧使用燃油采暖，但对燃油的需求量却下降了。第二，Consolidated Industries 公司会因该地区居民的燃油采暖而受益，直接带来销售和利润的上升。否则，对其的投资建议似乎没什么有力的依据。

---

61. The following appeared in an article in the Grandview Beacon.

"For many years the city of Grandview has provided annual funding for the Grandview Symphony. Last year, however, private contributions to the symphony increased by 200 percent and attendance at the symphony's concerts-in-the-park series doubled. The symphony has also announced an increase in ticket prices for next year. Given such developments, some city commissioners argue that the symphony can now be fully self-supporting, and they recommend that funding for the symphony be eliminated from next year's budget."

（参考第139、141、143、162题）

Write a response in which you discuss what questions would need to be answered in order to decide whether the recommendation and the argument on which it is based are reasonable. Be sure to explain how the answers to these questions would help to evaluate the recommendation.

题目整理

论点 The symphony can now be fully self-supporting, and some city commissioners recommend that funding for the symphony be eliminated from next year's budget.

论据 (1) Last year, private contributions to the symphony increased by 200 percent and attendance at the symphony's concerts-in-the-park series doubled.

(2) The symphony has also announced an increase in ticket prices for next year.

论证方法

题目中论者主要运用了统计数据论证法、类比论证法和因果关系论证法。

分析提示

● 论据(1)列举了两个重要数据。但下列问题需要说明：第一，论者说：Last year, private contributions to the Symphony increased by 200 percent. 那么一年前，这个交响乐团得到了多少私人赞助？如果数量很少（比如仅仅两三万美元），那么200 percent 的增长基本上就没什么意义。其二，公园音乐会的上座率也存在类似问题：如果之前的基数很低，提高一倍说明不了什么问题。再者，这些公园音乐会是收费的吗？收多少？这些公园音乐会是否能有效带动这个交响乐团在音乐厅里演出的上座率？这些通常具有音乐普及和教育性质的公园音乐会能否使公众对交响乐产生兴趣并成为实际的消费者？等等这些都是疑问。其三，论者说的那些数据是去年的情况。去年的情况能说明今年和未来的状况吗？假如今后境况变得更差了呢？论者犯有纵向类比的错误。

● 论据(2)是个因果关系论证。论者认为既然The Symphony has also announced an increase in ticket prices for next year，那么他们的收入就不成问题了。但是，其一，乐团只是宣布下一年的票价上浮计划而已。这个计划对今年的票房收入没影响。其二，即便下一年提了票价，能提多少？其三，提高票价之后，音乐会的上座率会下降吗？可否维持现状或者稳定上升？第四，乐团运营的其他费用，比如：付给乐团成员的工资、设备和道具的成本、演出场地的租金、宣传和交通费用等等，会上升吗？如果这些费用上涨较多，提高票价并不能带来多少净收入。第五，其他交响乐团是否会对该乐团构成很强的竞争？其他的音乐形态，比如摇滚、戏剧、电影是否会分流一部分观众和听众？等等。

● 题目中的结论只是some city commissioners的判断。问题是：这些city commissioners是否能够代表其他commissioners的意见？他们的立场有没有受行业及其他利益相关方的影响？Grandview市公众是什么态度？既然是公共财政的预算，公众的意见才是最重要的。

62. The following appeared in a memo from the director of a large group of hospitals.

"In a laboratory study of liquid antibacterial hand soaps, a concentrated solution of UltraClean produced a 40 percent greater reduction in the bacteria population than did the liquid hand soaps currently used in our hospitals. During a subsequent test of UltraClean at our hospital in Workby, that hospital reported significantly fewer cases of patient infection than did any of the other hospitals in our group. Therefore, to prevent serious patient infections, we should supply UltraClean at all hand-washing stations throughout our hospital system."

（参考第121、122、124题）

Write a response in which you examine the stated and/or unstated assumptions of the argument. Be sure to explain how the argument depends on these assumptions and what the implications are for the argument if the assumptions prove unwarranted.

题目整理

论点 To prevent serious patient infections, we should supply UltraClean at all hand-washing stations throughout our hospital system.

论据 (1) In a laboratory study of liquid antibacterial hand soaps, a concentrated solution of UltraClean produced a 40 percent greater reduction in the bacteria population than did the liquid hand soaps currently used in our hospitals.

(2) During a subsequent test of UltraClean at our hospital in Workby, that hospital reported significantly fewer cases of patient infection than did any of the other hospitals in our group.

论证方法

题目中论者主要运用了统计数据论证法和归纳推理论证法。

分析提示

● 论据(1)(2)运用的都是统计数据论证法。针对论据(1)，论者需要假设：这个实验室研究的方案设计（如试验样本的选择、数据的处理、研究结果的核实和验证等等）和实施过程是严格按照科学程序进行的；其结论是客观、中立的；试验的实施者没有受行业及其他利益相关方的影响，等等。其次，要注意，这次实验室研究用的是浓缩的UltraClean溶液（a concentrated solution of UltraClean）。一般而言，即使这种溶液的杀菌、消毒效果一般，其高浓缩液体的使用效果会比相同成分普通浓度的溶液要好。问题是：其他品牌的浓缩洗手液同相同品牌的普通浓度的洗手液比，其杀菌效果如何？假如浓缩型洗手液至少比普通洗手液的效果要好70%以上的话，论者说的UltraClean浓缩型洗手液除菌效果比其他溶液强40%的优势也就不稀奇了。

● 论据(2)说的是UltraClean浓缩型洗手液在Workby医院使用效果较好。但论者必须假设不是其他原因导致了that hospital reported significantly fewer cases of patient infection than did any of the other hospitals in our group这一结果，比如：是否是Workby特殊的气候使试验期间感染的病例较少？是否是Workby地区的公共卫生状况较好、人们比较健康？是否Workby那家医院严格的卫生管理降低了病人的感染率？是否是Workby地区独特的人口结构（比如青壮年居多，老人和儿童所占比较小）使那里的病例感染率不到一半？等等。

● 结论中，论者主要依据UltraClean洗手液在Workby医院的良好表现，建议将UltraClean推广到所有医院。这里论者运用归纳推理：既然同样的东西在一地有效，在其他地方也应有效。但论者必须假设：其他地方以及那里的医院没有一些特殊的情况会使这种推广收不到预期效果，比如：医院的卫生管理水平、公共卫生状况、地理环境和气候、人们的生活习惯以及对洗手液的消费偏好、各地不同的人口结构，等等。

---

63. The following appeared in a letter to the editor of the Parkville Daily newspaper.

"Throughout the country last year, as more and more children below the age of nine participated in youth-league sports, over 40,000 of these young players suffered injuries. When interviewed for a recent study, youth-league soccer players in several major cities also reported psychological pressure exerted by coaches and parents to win games. Furthermore, education experts say that long practice sessions for these sports take away time that could be used for academic activities. Since the disadvantages outweigh any advantages, we in Parkville should discontinue organized athletic competition for children under nine."

Write a response in which you examine the stated and/or unstated assumptions of the argument. Be sure to explain how the argument depends on these assumptions and what the implications are for the argument if the assumptions prove unwarranted.

题目整理

论点 Since the disadvantages outweigh any advantages, we in Parkville should discontinue organized athletic competition for children under nine.

论据 (1) Throughout the country last year, as more and more children below the age of nine participated in youth-league sports, over 40,000 of these young players suffered injuries.

(2) When interviewed for a recent study, youth-league soccer players in several major cities also reported psychological pressure exerted by coaches and parents to win games.

(3) Furthermore, education experts say that long practice sessions for these sports take away time that could be used for academic activities.

论证方法

题目中论者主要运用了统计数据论证法和引用权威论证法。

分析提示

● 论据(1)提到有四万多名小运动员受伤。这个数字让人觉得问题好像很严重。但我们要问：首先，这些受伤的孩子占所有小运动员的多大比例？这个比例高吗？假设这个比例同孩子们在正常的玩耍嬉戏活动中受伤比例差不多，或者是略高一点，那么，论者所提的问题就不是个大问题，属于正常现象。其次，在这些四万多名受伤的孩子中，9岁以下的孩子占多大比例？假如这个年龄段受伤孩子的比例是所有年龄段受伤孩子中占比例最低的，那么，论者暗示的"因为more and more children below the age of nine participated in youth-league sports，所以越来越多的孩子运动中受伤"的逻辑就很难成立。第三，这些孩子的伤势如何？如果仅仅是擦伤、轻微扭伤，恐怕也说明不了什么问题。

● 同论据(1)一样，论据(2)也是个统计数据论证法。但论者要做以下假设：其一，那些youth-league soccer players in several major cities 能代表所有参加各种体育运动项目的孩子。如果别的城市或者其他运动项目中的孩子并没有感受到压力呢？第二，这些孩子所称的压力不是别的因素（比如学习压力、各个运动队之间的竞争等）引起的。第三，在访问中，这些孩子说的都是他们的真实感受。以他们的年龄和心理承受能力，难道他们没有夸大心理压力的可能？

● 论据(3)在引用权威进行论证。但论者需要假设这些权威（education experts）从专业技术上讲是合格的，能做到中立、客观。

● 结论的原因部分说Since the disadvantages outweigh any advantages。在此，论者假设自己说的disadvantages和advantages是可精确衡量的。但在整个论证过程中，只字未提体育运动有哪些好处。这有一面之词（stacked evidence）的嫌疑。至于结论"we in Parkville should discontinue **organized athletic competition** for children under nine"，有"仓促概括"之嫌。整个论证过程中，论者只谈到youth-league sports，尤其是其中的soccer players，但结论却是要停止所有的organized athletic competition。论者在此实际假设soccer players具有充分的代表性，但这显然有问题。那些在运动中身体冲撞和接触较少的体育项目（比如羽毛球和乒乓球）也很容易致伤吗？

64. Collectors prize the ancient life-size clay statues of human figures made on Kali Island but have long wondered how Kalinese artists were able to depict bodies with such realistic precision. Since archaeologists have recently discovered molds of human heads and hands on Kali, we can now conclude that the ancient Kalinese artists used molds of actual bodies, not sculpting tools and techniques, to create these statues. This discovery explains why Kalinese miniature statues were abstract and entirely different in style: molds could be used only for life-size sculptures. It also explains why few ancient Kalinese sculpting tools have been found. In light of this discovery, collectors predict that the life-size sculptures will decrease in value while the miniatures increase in value.

Write a response in which you discuss what questions would need to be answered in order to decide whether the prediction and the argument on which it is based are reasonable. Be sure to explain how the answers to these questions would help to evaluate the prediction.

题目整理

论点 In light of this discovery, collectors predict that the life-size sculptures will decrease in value while the miniatures increase in value.

论据 (1) Collectors prize the ancient life-size clay statues of human figures made on Kali Island but have long wondered how Kalinese artists were able to depict bodies with such realistic precision. Since archaeologists have recently discovered molds of human heads and hands on Kali, we can now conclude that the ancient Kalinese artists used molds of actual bodies, not sculpting tools and techniques, to create these statues.

(2) This discovery explains why Kalinese miniature statues were abstract and entirely different in style: molds could be used only for life-size sculptures.

(3) It also explains why few ancient Kalinese sculpting tools have been found.

论证方法

题目中论者主要运用了因果关系论证法。

分析提示

● 论据(1)根据在Kali岛上发现的人的头颅和手的模具，得出结论：岛上那些真人大小、形象逼真的泥塑不是雕刻而成的，而是用这些模具铸成的。但问题是：如果这些模具是供雕刻临摹用的仿真模型呢？也许正是比照这些逼真的模型，那些古代的雕刻家才得以雕刻出栩栩如生的雕像呢？

● 论据(2)：因为这些模具只能制造真人大小的塑像，所以，那些不是真人比例的小塑像就只能做得较为抽象，风格也就不同于那些真人比例的泥塑。这也未必。难道那些小泥塑不可以是Kali岛上古代艺术家们在雕刻真人大小的泥塑前，用来构思的草稿？

● 论据(3)中有这么一个假设：如果那些泥塑是雕刻而成的，岛上应该会出土雕刻工具之类的东西。因为没有发现这雕刻工具，所以那些泥塑不是雕刻而是铸造出来的。而新发现的模具恰好提供了泥铸塑像这一判断的很好佐证。但问题是：是否那些雕刻工具因时间久远、遭风化侵蚀而不复存在了？目前没有发现这些雕刻工具，难道将来也不会发现？

● 结论 "In light of this development, collectors should expect the life-size sculptures to decrease in value and the miniatures to increase in value" 中有这样的假设：铸造的塑像没有收藏价值，而雕刻的作品收藏价值较高。这个假设未经证实。从常识上讲，文物的价值取决于其稀缺性及其工艺水平，和文物本身的制作手段的关系似乎不是那么密切。而且，题目中的结论是部分collectors的观点。但这些人的专业水准可靠吗？他们的立场中立吗？这些都是很关键的问题。

· ·

65. When Stanley Park first opened, it was the largest, most heavily used public park in town. It is still the largest park, but it is no longer heavily used. Video cameras mounted in the park's parking lots last month revealed the park's drop in popularity: the recordings showed an average of only 50 cars per day. In contrast, tiny Carlton Park in the heart of the business district is visited by more than 150 people on a typical weekday. An obvious difference is that Carlton Park, unlike Stanley Park, provides ample seating. Thus, if Stanley Park is ever to be as popular with our citizens as Carlton Park, the town will obviously need to provide more benches, thereby converting some of the unused open areas into spaces suitable for socializing.

Write a response in which you examine the stated and/or unstated assumptions of the argument. Be sure to explain how the argument depends on these assumptions and what the implications are for the argument if the assumptions prove unwarranted.

题目整理

论点 (1) Stanley Park is no longer the most heavily used public park.

(2) If Stanley Park is ever to be as popular with our citizens as Carlton Park, the town will obviously need to provide more benches, thereby converting some of the unused open areas into spaces suitable for socializing.

论据 (1) Video cameras mounted in the park's parking lots last month revealed the park's drop in popularity: the recordings showed an average of only 50 cars per day. In contrast, tiny Carlton Park in the heart of the business district is visited by more than 150 people on a typical weekday.

(2) An obvious difference is that Carlton Park, unlike Stanley Park, provides ample seating.

论证方法

题目中论者主要运用了统计数据论证法和类比论证法。

分析提示

● 论据(1)是引用统计数据论证。论者将上个月Stanley公园停车场平均每天只有50辆车同Carlton公园工作日平均每天150多人的客流进行比较，以证明后者更受游人欢迎。但这个推论需要以下的假设：其一，Stanley公园停车场里小汽车的数量可以说明游人的数量。但这个假设很难成立。难道所有的游客到 Stanley 公园来都必须开车，并且必须将车停到公园里的停车场？假如很多人不开车去呢？或者即便开车去但将车停在别处呢？其二，为了说明两个公园游人的数量，可以将一个公园里所停小汽车的数量同另一个公园里的游客人数比较。但这种比较显然不恰当。因为根本无法把去了 Stanley 公园但没有开车，或者虽然开车去了但没把车停在该公园停车场的游客统计在内。第三，大家要注意：即便是拿两个公园的日均客流量来比较，这种比较依然不恰当。因为论者说起 Stanley 公园时，用的是"上个月平均每天"的游客人数；然而当他说起 Carlton Park 时，用的是"除去周末的工作日（也就是周一到周五）平均每天"的游客人数。这种比较对 Stanley 公园很不公平。因为 Carlton 公园地处繁华的商业区（in the heart of the business district）。一般而言，商业区的人流在工作日会比较大，周末则较少；而处在非商业区的 Stanley 公园情况很可能相反，那里的人流周末较多，而工作日较少。这样就会出现 Stanley 公园日平均游客较少，而 Carlton 公园日平均游客较多的情况。

● 论据(2)将两个公园进行类比，用 Stanley 公园里的凳子少来解释两者人流量差异的原因。这里，论者是在假设没有其他原因造成这种人流的差异，比如：两个公园在城市里不同的位置、周围居民不同的工作和生活习惯、两个公园不同的功能（比如一个主要是展示园林绿化，而另一个则是主题公园供人们娱乐）以及其他偶然性的因素等等。

● 在结论中，论者认为 Stanley 公园应增加长凳，并且 converting some of the unused open areas into spaces suitable for socializing，以使它能够同 Carlton 公园一比高低。这里，论者是在假设这样做不会带来相反的效果。假如 Stanley 公园的传统优势就是其精致的园林设计和空旷宜人的绿地，那么，往空地（unused open areas）上放太多的凳子岂不破坏了它原有的景致，致使游人进一步减少？

66. The following appeared in a memo from the owner of a chain of cheese stores located throughout the Unitcd States.

"For many years all the stores in our chain have stocked a wide variety of both domestic and imported cheeses. Last year, however, all of the five best-selling cheeses at our newest store were domestic cheddar cheeses from Wisconsin. Furthermore, a recent survey by Cheeses of the World magazine indicates an increasing preference for domestic cheeses among its subscribers. Since our company can reduce expenses by limiting inventory, the best way to improve profits in all of our stores is to discontinue stocking many of our varieties of imported cheese and concentrate primarily on domestic cheeses."

（参考第 107、108 题）

Write a response in which you discuss what questions would need to be answered in order to decide whether the recommendation is likely to have the predicted result. Be sure to explain how the answers to these questions would help to evaluate the recommendation.

题目整理

论点 The best way to improve profits in all of our stores is to discontinue stocking many of our varieties of imported cheese and concentrate primarily on domestic cheeses.

论据 (1) For many years all the stores in our chain have stocked a wide variety of both domestic and imported cheeses. Last year, however, all of the five best-selling cheeses at our newest store were domestic cheddar cheeses from Wisconsin.

(2) Furthermore, a recent survey by Cheeses of the World magazine indicates an increasing preference for domestic cheeses among its subscribers.

(3) Our company can reduce expenses by limiting inventory.

论证方法

题目中论者主要运用了归纳推理论证法、统计数据论证法和因果关系论证法。

分析提示

- 论据(1)是个归纳推理。论者认为这家新开奶酪店的销售情况能说明其他所有店的销售趋势。问题是：这家新开的店具有足够的代表性吗？该店的地理位置、周边居民的生活喜好、该店采用的一些促销活动、去年国际国内市场奶酪的价格变动导致的居民对奶酪的消费选择等等，这些是否是去年该店销售特点的原因呢？再者，论者所说的这家新店的销售特点是去年的情况。那么，今年还会和去年一样吗？未来几年又将如何？这些都是很大的疑问。

- 论据(2)引用了一项市场调查。首先，我们的问题是：该调查的方案设计（如调查样本的选择、调查问卷的设计、调查数据的处理、调查结果的核实和验证等等）和实施过程是严格按照科学程序进行的吗？其结论是客观、中立、可信的吗？调查的实施者没有受行业及其他利益相关方的影响？其次，此次调查中的被调查人员是Cheeses of the World的订户，他们能代表所有的消费者吗？这些订户的消费偏好、收入水平、消费习惯的稳定性等等是否因为过于特别而很难具有市场指示意义呢？

- 论据(3)举出了限制库存的一个理由：降低成本。但问题是：减少进口奶酪的库存虽说可能在一定程度上降低这家连锁店的运营成本，但是否会导致其销售的奶酪品种的大幅度减少？这家连锁店的传统是储备各式各样的国内外奶酪品种，所以选择的多样性很可能是顾客喜欢这家连锁店的一个重要原因。假如没有了选择的多样性，顾客的数量大幅度减少，论者所期望的to improve profits in all of our stores还会出现吗？

- 结论说 **the best way** to improve profits in all of our stores is to discontinue stocking many of our varieties of imported cheese and concentrate primarily on domestic cheeses。难道没有别的更好的提高利润的办法了？提高员工效率、调整营业时间以迎合顾客的特殊需要、调整店面的空间布局、加大广告宣传等都是可以尝试的办法。

67. The following appeared as part of a business plan developed by the manager of the Rialto Movie Theater.

"Despite its downtown location, the Rialto Movie Theater, a local institution for five decades, must make big changes or close its doors forever. It should follow the example of the new Apex Theater in the mall outside of town. When the Apex opened last year, it featured a video arcade, plush carpeting and seats, and a state-of-the-art sound system. Furthermore, in a recent survey, over 85 percent of respondents reported that the high price of newly released movies prevents them from going to the movies more than five times per year. Thus, if the Rialto intends to hold on to its share of a decreasing pool of moviegoers, it must offer the same features as Apex."

Write a response in which you discuss what questions would need to be answered in order to decide whether the recommendation is likely to have the predicted result. Be sure to explain how the answers to these questions would help to evaluate the recommendation.

题目整理

论点 The Rialto Movie Theater must make big changes or close its doors forever, and it should follow the example of the new Apex Theater in the mall outside of town.

论据 (1) When the Apex opened last year, it featured a video arcade, plush carpeting and seats, and a state-of-the-art sound system.

(2) Furthermore, in a recent survey, over 85 percent of respondents reported that the high price of newly released movies prevents them from going to the movies more than five times per year.

(3) If the Rialto intends to hold on to its share of a decreasing pool of moviegoers, it must offer the same features as Apex.

论证方法

题目中论者主要运用了类比论证法和统计数据论证法。

分析提示

● 论据(1)是个类比论证。论者列举了Apex剧院去年开业时的一些做法，认为Rialto影院应该效仿。但问题是：Apex剧院在配备了电玩室（video arcade）、豪华地毯和座椅以及一流的音响设备后，其票房收入出现了什么变化？市场份额持续增长了吗？那个电玩室为其带来了多少收入、多少潜在的电影观众？有多少人是因为该剧院的豪华地毯和座椅以及一流的音响设备而放弃其他影院到这里来看电影呢？再者，论者所说的情况是Apex剧院去年的做法。那么，今年还会和去年一样吗？未来几年又将如何？这些论者都没说，所以也无从比较和判断。

● 论据(2)提到了一项最近的调查。首先，我们的问题是：该调查的方案设计（如调查样本的选择、调查问卷的设计、调查数据的处理、调查结果的核实和验证等等）和实施过程是严格按照科学程序进行的吗？其结论是客观、中立、可信的吗？调查的实施者没有受行业及其他利益相关方的影响？其次，论者通过这项调查试图说明，观众因为现在新上演的电影票价太贵，所以他们不愿去看电影。但是，假如观众每年平均看七八次电影，减少到五次其实并没有降低太多。再者，电影观众少了未必就等于票房收入也少了。票房收入完全可能因为票价的提高而上升。

● 论据(3)说"If the Rialto intends to hold on to its share of a decreasing pool of moviegoers, it must offer the same features as Apex."首先，正如我们对论据(1)的分析，到底Apex去年的经营

业绩如何，论者并没有提供令人信服的证据。那怎能让Rialto去贸然模仿呢？其次，即便Apex去年的经营业绩不错，但Rialto就必须亦步亦趋地模仿吗？二者的可比性如何？别忘了，题目中已经把两家剧院地理位置的差异讲得很明白：Rialto地处市中心（downtown area），而Apex地处市区外的一家购物中心（mall）里面。不同的地理位置可以采取相同的营销策略吗？更何况两者可能还有其他的差异，比如目标观众、电影档次、经营理念等等呢？再者，即便Rialto需要hold on to its share of a decreasing pool of moviegoers，但办法应该远不止Apex所采用的那一种吧？

68. A recent study reported that pet owners have longer, healthier lives on average than do people who own no pets. Specifically, dog owners tend to have a lower incidence of heart disease. In light of these findings, Sherwood Hospital should form a partnership with Sherwood Animal Shelter to institute an adopt-a-dog program. The program would encourage dog ownership for patients recovering from heart disease, which should reduce these patients' chance of experiencing continuing heart problems and also reduce their need for ongoing treatment. As a further benefit, the publicity about the program would encourage more people to adopt pets from the shelter. And that will reduce the incidence of heart disease in the general population.

Write a response in which you examine the stated and/or unstated assumptions of the argument. Be sure to explain how the argument depends on these assumptions and what the implications are for the argument if the assumptions prove unwarranted.

题目整理

论点 Sherwood Hospital should form a partnership with Sherwood Animal Shelter to institute an adopt-a-dog program.

论据 (1) A recent study reported that pet owners have longer, healthier lives on average than do people who own no pets. Specifically, dog owners tend to have a lower incidence of heart disease.

(2) The adopt-a-dog program would encourage dog ownership for patients recovering from heart disease, which should reduce these patients' chance of experiencing continuing heart problems and also reduce their need for ongoing treatment.

(3) As a further benefit, the publicity about the program would encourage more people to adopt pets from the shelter. And that will reduce the incidence of heart disease in the general population.

论证方法

题目中论者主要运用了统计数据论证法和演绎推理论证法。

分析提示

● 论据(1)列举了一项最近的研究，该研究是论者所有推论的起点。这项研究显示了pet owners与longer, healthier lives以及dog owners与lower incidence of heart disease之间的联系

（注意：不是因果关系）。但论者的立论要成立，必须要假设：这项研究的方案设计（如调查样本的选择、调查问卷的设计、调查数据的处理、调查结果的核实和验证等等）和实施过程是严格按照科学程序进行的；其结论是客观、中立、可信的；调查的实施者没有受行业及其他利益相关方的影响，等等。

- 论据(2)有两个推论：第一，The adopt-a-dog program would encourage dog ownership for patients recovering from heart disease；第二，心脏病康复病人拥有狗会reduce these patients' chance of experiencing continuing heart problems and also reduce their need for ongoing treatment。就第一个推论而言，论者至少需要两个假设。首先，他要假设那些康复中的心脏病患者乐意去Sherwood Animal Shelter领养狗。其次，Sherwood Animal Shelter提供的狗的品种、脾气特点等符合这些心脏病患者的要求。

- 论据(2)的第二个推论，论者需要以下假设：首先，当论者说，心脏病康复病人拥有狗会reduce these patients' chance of experiencing continuing heart problems and also reduce their need for ongoing treatment时，显然已经把论据(1)中提到的相关关系假设成了因果关系。但这个假设不可靠，因为很可能是其他原因导致了论据(1)所说的"拥有宠物狗的人普遍寿命长且健康、得心脏病几率低"这一现象，比如：养狗的人心态平和、愿意付出爱等。其次，还要假设拥有宠物狗不会带来其他不利于心脏病人康复和治疗的问题，比如，繁琐的日常清洗和喂养、卫生防疫、经常出门遛狗等等不会影响病人的康复。

- 论据(3)也有两个推论：第一，the publicity about the program would encourage more people to adopt pets from the shelter；第二，更多的人去领养狗will reduce the incidence of heart disease in the general population。这两个推论分别需要两个假设：其一，实施adopt-a-dog program会带来较大的宣传效果，从而令公众知晓这个项目，并愿意到Sherwood Animal Shelter去领养狗。其二，普通人群都有潜在的心脏病危险。但这两个假设都很成问题。

69. The following appeared in a memo from a vice president of a large, highly diversified company.

"Ten years ago our company had two new office buildings constructed as regional headquarters for two regions. The buildings were erected by different construction companies—Alpha and Zeta. Although the two buildings had identical floor plans, the building constructed by Zeta cost 30 percent more to build. However, that building's expenses for maintenance last year were only half those of Alpha's. In addition, the energy consumption of the Zeta building has been lower than that of the Alpha building every year since its construction. Given these data, plus the fact that Zeta has a stable workforce with little employee turnover, we recommend using Zeta rather than Alpha for our new building project, even though Alpha's bid promises lower construction costs."

（参考第70、115题）

Write a response in which you discuss what questions would need to be answered in order to decide whether the recommendation and the argument on which it is based are reasonable. Be sure to explain how the answers to these questions would help to evaluate the recommendation.

题目整理

论点 We recommend using Zeta rather than Alpha for our new building project, even though Alpha's bid promises lower construction costs.

论据 (1) Ten years ago our company had two new office buildings constructed as regional headquarters for two regions. The buildings were erected by different construction companies—Alpha and Zeta. Although the two buildings had identical floor plans, the building constructed by Zeta cost 30 percent more to build. However, that building's expenses for maintenance last year were only half those of Alpha's.

(2) In addition, the energy consumption of the Zeta building has been lower than that of the Alpha building every year since its construction.

(3) Zeta has a stable workforce with little employee turnover.

论证方法

题目中论者主要运用了归纳推理论证法。

分析提示

● 论据(1)说Zeta公司十年前建的大楼的维护成本较低。去年，Zeta所建这幢大楼的维护成本仅是Alpha公司所建的相同大楼的一半。但问题是：是否是其他一些与Zeta公司及其所建工程无关的因素导致这幢大楼的维护成本较低？比如，大楼所在地区较低的人工成本、该地区良好的环境条件（比如没有工业污染、没有沙尘暴、天气不是太潮湿、四季气候稳定等）、这幢大楼的使用者爱护这幢楼的内外设施、良好的物业管理等。其次，论者只提到去年一年两幢大楼维护成本的差异。那么，在过去十年间，这两幢大楼的维护成本差异如何？如果十年平均下来，Alpha大楼的年维护费用反而比Zeta大楼更低呢？论者仅选取一年的数据进行比较，有歪曲数据的嫌疑。

● 论据(2)提到，Zeta大楼的能耗自建成以来就比Alpha大楼低。同样的问题是：是否是其他一些与Zeta公司及其所建工程无关的因素导致这幢大楼能耗较低？比如，大楼所在地区一年四季天气晴朗、日照充足、温度适宜，这样的话，Zeta大楼根本不需要制冷或制热的空调系统，能耗自然就低。而Alpha大楼所在城市因为四季以及早晚温差大、天气经常剧烈变化，必须高度依赖空调，其能耗自然就高。另外，其他的因素，诸如两个大楼不同的物业管理水平、人们的节能意识、两个大楼不同的使用率（比如Zeta大楼的使用面积只有一半，而Alpha大楼全部面积常年投入使用）、两地不同的用电成本等。

● 论据(3)提到Zeta公司的员工队伍稳定，基本没有人员流动。论者意在说明Zeta公司较好的人事管理和员工队伍素质。但很可能是其他的原因，比如Zeta公司缺乏良好的个人绩效考评机制、平均主义的分配方式或者员工年龄偏大等，使那里的员工不愿离去。或者因为Zeta公司养了一大批懒散的员工，这些员工难找工作，所以不愿离开这家能偷懒的公司。如此的话，Zeta公司稳定的员工队伍同其人事管理水平和员工队伍素质实际上没什么关系。

● 最后，即便论者所说的论据都有道理，用十年前的事情来说明当前也不合适。这十年间，两家公司没有发生变化？

70. The following appeared in a memo from a vice president of a large, highly diversified company.

"Ten years ago our company had two new office buildings constructed as regional headquarters for two regions. The buildings were erected by different construction companies—Alpha and Zeta. Although the two buildings had identical floor plans, the building constructed by Zeta cost 30 percent more to build. However, that building's expenses for maintenance last year were only half those of Alpha's. Furthermore, the energy consumption of the Zeta building has been lower than that of the Alpha building every year since its construction. Such data indicate that we should use Zeta rather than Alpha for our contemplated new building project, even though Alpha's bid promises lower construction costs."

(参考第69、115题)

Write a response in which you discuss what specific evidence is needed to evaluate the argument and explain how the evidence would weaken or strengthen the argument.

题目整理

论点 We should use Zeta rather than Alpha for our contemplated new building project, even though Alpha's bid promises lower construction costs.

论据 (1) Ten years ago our company had two new office buildings constructed as regional headquarters for two regions. The buildings were erected by different construction companies—Alpha and Zeta. Although the two buildings had identical floor plans, the building constructed by Zeta cost 30 percent more to build. However, that building's expenses for maintenance last year were only half those of Alpha's.

(2) Furthermore, the energy consumption of the Zeta building has been lower than that of the Alpha building every year since its construction.

论证方法

题目中论者主要运用了归纳推理论证法。论者认为既然Zeta公司10年前的一个建筑项目做得好，新的建筑项目也应该可以做得好。

分析提示

● 论据(1)指出Zeta公司十年前建的大楼的维护成本较低。去年，Zeta所建这幢大楼的维护成本仅是Alpha公司所建的相同大楼的一半。但论者需要进一步的证据表明：是否是其他一些与Zeta公司及其所建工程无关的因素导致这幢大楼的维护成本较低？比如，大楼所在地区较低的人工成本、该地区良好的环境条件（比如没有工业污染、没有沙尘暴、天气不是太潮湿、四季气候稳定等）、这幢大楼使用者爱护这幢楼的内外设施、良好的物业管理，等等。其次，论者只提到去年一年两幢大楼维护成本的差异。那么，在过去十年间，这两幢大楼的维护成本差异如何？如果十年平均下来，Alpha大楼的年维护费用反而比Zeta大楼更低呢？论者仅选取一年的数据进行比较，有歪曲数据的嫌疑。

- 论据(2)提到，Zeta大楼的能耗自建成一来每年都比Alpha大楼低。论者同样要证明：是否是其他一些与Zeta公司及其所建工程无关的因素导致这幢大楼的能耗较低呢？比如，Zeta大楼所在地区一年四季天气晴朗、日照充足、温度适宜，这样的话，Zeta大楼不需要特别的制冷或制热的空调系统，能耗自然就低。而Alpha大楼所在城市因为四季以及早晚温差大、天气经常剧烈变化，必须高度依赖空调，其能耗自然就高。另外，其他的因素，诸如两个大楼不同的物业管理水平、人们的节能意识、两个大楼不同的使用率（比如Zeta大楼的使用面积仅有一半，而Alpha大楼全部面积常年投入使用）、两地不同的用电成本等等。
- 最后，即便论者所说的论据都有道理，但用十年前的事情来说明当前恐怕也不合适。这十年间，两家公司难道没有发生变化？是否现在Alpha公司在各方面都比Zeta公司做得更好了呢？这些也需要更多的佐证。

71. The following is a letter to the editor of the Waymarsh Times.

"Traffic here in Waymarsh is becoming a problem. Although just three years ago a state traffic survey showed that the typical driving commuter took 20 minutes to get to work, the commute now takes closer to 40 minutes, according to the survey just completed. Members of the town council already have suggested more road building to address the problem, but as well as being expensive, the new construction will surely disrupt some of our residential neighborhoods. It would be better to follow the example of the nearby city of Garville. Last year Garville implemented a policy that rewards people who share rides to work, giving them coupons for free gas. Pollution levels in Garville have dropped since the policy was implemented, and people from Garville tell me that commuting times have fallen considerably. There is no reason why a policy like Garville's shouldn't work equally well in Waymarsh."

Write a response in which you discuss what specific evidence is needed to evaluate the argument and explain how the evidence would weaken or strengthen the argument.

题目整理

论点 Traffic here in Waymarsh is becoming a problem, and it would be better to follow the example of the nearby city of Garville.

论据 (1) Although just three years ago a state traffic survey showed that the typical driving commuter took 20 minutes to get to work, the commute now takes closer to 40 minutes, according to the survey just completed.

(2) Last year Garville implemented a policy that rewards people who share rides to work, giving them coupons for free gas. Pollution levels in Garville have dropped since the policy was implemented, and people from Garville tell me that commuting times have fallen considerably.

(3) There is no reason why a policy like Garville's shouldn't work equally well in Waymarsh.

论证方法

题目中论者主要运用了统计数据论证法、类比论证法和引用权威论证法。

分析提示

● 论据(1)提到了相隔三年的两个调查。关于这两个调查，我们需要知道：这些调查的方案设计（如调查样本的选择、调查问卷的设计、调查数据的处理、调查结果的核实和验证等等）和实施过程是否是严格按照科学程序进行的；其结论是否是客观、中立的；调查的实施者没有受行业及其他利益相关方的影响，等等。没有这些资料，我们无从判断Waymarsh的交通现状。

● 论据(2)提到去年相邻的Garville采取鼓励人们"拼车"（to share rides to work）以降低交通拥堵的办法，并举出两个积极的结果：第一，Pollution levels in Garville have dropped since the policy was implemented。第二，people from Garville tell me that commuting times have fallen considerably。针对污染下降的结果，我们需要证据表明：不是其他的原因导致了同样的结果。比如，去年Garville的天气如何？如果去年较常年多风多雨的话，空气污染自然会降低。再如，去年Garville是否发生过相当规模的工业迁移？这个城市的主体经济结构是否从高污染的工业和制造业变成了以低污染或无污染的服务业、电子和文化创意？去年该城市是否施行了严厉的污染控制措施？

● 在谈到第二个积极结果时，论者运用了引用权威论证法，即：people from Garville tell me that commuting times have fallen considerably。但论者需要提供证据来解释下列疑问：这些people的数目是多少（人数太少，则不足立信）？他们对Garville去年的污染状况的观察是否客观、公正、可信？论者对这些人说法的观察的转述是否客观、公正、可信（信息在传递过程中往往会失真、扭曲）？等等。

● 基于对Waymarsh和Garville这两个城市的类比，论者断言：There is no reason why a policy like Garville's shouldn't work equally well in Waymarsh. 但两个城市的可比性如何？二者之间的人口数量、交通基础设施的状况、城市管理水平、汽车保有总量、人们对"拼车"的接受程度等等都会影响论者判断的可信度，因而需要更多资料佐证。

---

72. The following appeared as a letter to the editor of a national newspaper.

"Your recent article on corporate downsizing* in Elthyria maintains that the majority of competent workers who have lost jobs as a result of downsizing face serious economic hardship, often for years, before finding other suitable employment. But this claim is undermined by a recent report on the Elthyrian economy, which found that since 1999 far more jobs have been created than have been eliminated, bringing the unemployment rate in Elthyria to its lowest level in decades. Moreover, two-thirds of these newly created jobs have been in industries that tend to pay above-average wages, and the vast majority of these jobs are full-time."

*Downsizing is the process whereby corporations deliberately make themselves smaller, reducing the number of their employees.

Write a response in which you discuss what specific evidence is needed to evaluate the argument and explain how the evidence would weaken or strengthen the argument.

题目整理

论点 The claim that the majority of competent workers who have lost jobs as a result of downsizing face serious economic hardship, often for years, before finding other suitable employment is undermined by a recent report.

论据 (1) A recent report on the Elthyrian economy found that since 1999 far more jobs have been created than have been eliminated, bringing the unemployment rate in Elthyria to its lowest level in decades.

(2) Moreover, two-thirds of these newly created jobs have been in industries that tend to pay above-average wages, and the vast majority of these jobs are full-time.

论证方法

题目中论者主要运用了统计数据论证法。

分析提示

● 论据(1)(2)举了一项研究报告中的数据。关于这项报告，我们需要知道：获取那些数据和结论的调查方案的设计（如调查样本的选择、调查问卷的设计、调查数据的处理、调查结果的核实和验证等等）和实施过程是否是严格按照科学程序进行的；其结论是否客观、中立；调查的实施者没有受行业及其他利益相关方的影响，等等。没有这些资料，我们无从判断Elthyria的经济和就业现状。

● 针对论据(1)，我们需要关注两种可能：第一，论者说的since 1999 far more jobs have been created than have been eliminated是Elthyria总体的就业市场情况，而那些正在减小规模（downsizing）的公司可能属于个别不景气的行业。所以，整个经济形势不错，市场中提供的就业机会较多这一现象同个别行业处于萧条状态、员工大量失业这些事实之间并不矛盾。第二，论者说当前Elthyria的失业率是几十年来的最低。但论者在这里只是把Elthyria自1999年以来的就业状况同过去的几十年比较，这个时间跨度过大，时间点过于模糊。所以，1999年以来相对几十年前较好的就业状况，并不能排除最近一两年、两三年里，Elthyria的就业形势不好这一现实。这两点论者需作进一步的说明。

● 论据(2)也存在类似问题。虽说Two-thirds of the newly created jobs have been in industries that tend to pay above-average wages, and the vast majority of these jobs are full-time，但此种情形很可能完全只是那些新兴行业，如电子、互联网、物流、创意设计等等，而那些正在减小规模的公司恰恰不在这些行业之列。如此的话，论据(2)还有说服力吗？况且，那另外三分之一的新增就业岗位出现在哪些行业？其工资水平如何？如果这些工作岗位普遍都由过去的固定工作变成了短期、临时的工作，并且日平均工资比过去低，论者还能说Elthyria的总体经济以及就业形势一片大好吗？这些都需要更多资料来佐证。

....

73. The following appeared on the Mozart School of Music Website.

"The Mozart School of Music should be the first choice for parents considering enrolling their child in music lessons. First of all, the Mozart School welcomes youngsters at all ability and age levels; there is no audition to attend the school. Second, the school offers instruction in nearly all musical instruments as well a wide range of styles and genres from classical to rock. Third, the faculty includes some of the most distinguished musicians in the area. Finally, many Mozart graduates have gone on to become well-known and highly paid professional musicians."

Write a response in which you examine the stated and/or unstated assumptions of the argument. Be sure to explain how the argument depends on these assumptions and what the implications are for the argument if the assumptions prove unwarranted.

题目整理

论点 The Mozart School of Music should be the first choice for parents considering enrolling their child in music lessons.

论据 (1) First of all, the Mozart School welcomes youngsters at all ability and age levels; there is no audition to attend the school.

(2) Second, the school offers instruction in nearly all musical instruments as well a wide range of styles and genres from classical to rock.

(3) Third, the faculty includes some of the most distinguished musicians in the area.

(4) Finally, many Mozart graduates have gone on to become well-known and highly paid professional musicians.

论证方法

题目中论者主要运用了因果关系论证法。

分析提示

● 论据(1)听起来像是一句非常熟悉的广告词：莫扎特音乐学校欢迎任何年龄、任何起点的儿童，入学无需任何考试（audition，一种类似于考试的试听或试唱）。如此承诺至少需要以下假设：首先，论者假设该校有办法让年龄很小、没有任何音乐基础、甚至对音乐不感兴趣的孩子认知音乐并喜欢上音乐。其次，任何进了这所学校的孩子，无论入学时的基础如何，都能在该校取得进步。再次，这些诱人的承诺不会让一部分家长觉得不切实际，从而不选择这所学校。

● 论据(2)这个理由同样听起来很好：该校可以教授任何乐器和任何风格的音乐。论者实际是在假设：首先，任何乐器和风格的音乐，不管它们如何冷门，都有孩子愿意学。其次，任何乐器和风格的音乐，该校都能找到称职的老师。再次，该校老师的指导和教学都能被孩子们接受，所有教学都能收到明显的效果。

● 论据(3)说该校的音乐老师中，有一部分是当地最为知名的音乐家。此处的假设是：第一，这些most distinguished musicians的确在该校承担实际教学任务，而不是仅仅挂名作招牌。第二，这些知名音乐家不仅精通音乐，而且擅长儿童音乐教学。第三，这些知名音乐家的教学效果的确比普通老师要好。第四，这些知名音乐家的教学费用不太高，大部分父母能承担得起等等。

● 论据(4)说该校的许多毕业生都能成名或成为收入很高的职业音乐家。首先，这里有几个模糊概念。这个many是指多少个孩子？他们占所有在该校学习过的孩子总数的多大比例？这

里的well-known指在什么范围内为人所知？达到了什么样的专业水准？所谓的highly paid
到底有多高？同其他音乐培训学校毕业的孩子相比薪水高出多少？其次，论者要假设这部
分成名、拿高薪的学生是因为这所学校的培养，而不是其他原因，比如：个人努力、家庭
熏陶、父母支持、后来转投其他名师等。再次，最关键的是论者要假设其他音乐培训学校
毕业的孩子的专业成就比这所学校毕业的孩子小，收入也要低一些。否则，谁还上这所学
校呢？

---

74. The president of Grove College has recommended that the college abandon its century-old tradition of all-female education and begin admitting men. Pointing to other all-female colleges that experienced an increase in applications after adopting coeducation, the president argues that coeducation would lead to a significant increase in applications and enrollment. However, the director of the alumnae association opposes the plan. Arguing that all-female education is essential to the very identity of the college, the director cites annual surveys of incoming students in which these students say that the school's all-female status was the primary reason they selected Grove. The director also points to a survey of Grove alumnae in which a majority of respondents strongly favored keeping the college all female.

（参考第147、148、149、156题）

Write a response in which you discuss what questions would need to be answered in order to decide whether the recommendation and the argument on which it is based are reasonable. Be sure to explain how the answers to these questions would help to evaluate the recommendation.

题目整理

论点 The director of the alumnae association opposes the proposal that Grove College should abandon its century-old tradition of all-female education and begin admitting men.

论据 (1) All-female education is essential to the very identity of the college, said the alumnae association director.

(2) The director cites annual surveys of incoming students in which these students say that the school's all-female status was the primary reason they selected Grove.

(3) The director also points to a survey of Grove alumnae in which a majority of respondents strongly favored keeping the college all female.

论证方法

题目中论者主要运用了因果关系论证法和统计数据论证法。

分析提示

● 论者在论据(1)中作了个因果推理，其推理过程是：因为全员女子教育是Grove学院的一个
重要特性，所以不能更改。但问题是：一个大学的特性（identity）是一成不变的吗？任何
教育机构的风格、特性难道不是特定时代背景下的产物？任何教育机构难道不是因为顺应

社会需要才兴盛，不适应社会需要而衰落的吗？无视社会的实际需求，盲目坚持一所大学所谓的传统特性有什么实际意义呢？一所大学的特性固然重要，但这所大学的特性之所以形成，其背后的原因以及大学本身更深层次的话题（比如大学的目的、大学在社会变迁中的角色、大学对传统价值的继承和新社会价值的开拓发展等等）是否更值得考虑？一所大学是更应该坚持其风格、特性这些形式化的东西，还是更应坚持其社会教化、价值传承、推动文明演进等更本质的功能和使命？

● 论者在论据(2)中引用了对每年即将入学的新生的调查数据，声称这些学生认为该校的全员女子教育是他们选择该校的主要原因。问题是：这些调查的方案设计（如调查样本的选择、调查问卷的设计、调查数据的处理、调查结果的核实和验证等等）和实施过程是严格按照科学程序进行的吗？其结论是客观、中立的吗？调查的实施者有没有受行业及其他利益相关方的影响？独立第三方的调查数据有没有拿来作参考？其次，要注意：调查对象是即将入学的新生。这些学生很可能因为已经选择了这所学校，会正面评价这所学校。所以只调查这些学生还不够。那些没有选择这所学校的学生是怎么看这所女子学校的教育特点呢？参考了这些学生的评价后，论者的判断才更可信。

● 论据(3)的问题同论据(2)的几乎一模一样。首先，我们同样要问：这项调查的方案设计（如调查样本的选择、调查问卷的设计、调查数据的处理、调查结果的核实和验证等等）和实施过程是严格按照科学程序进行的吗？其结论是客观、中立的吗？调查的实施者有没有受行业及其他利益相关方的影响？独立第三方的调查数据有没有拿来作参考？其次，论者有没有调查其他人群（比如，曾就读于该校的学生家长、专业教育人士、公司和企业的高管、高等教育研究人员等等）？否则，论者的调查难免片面。

---

75. The following appeared in a letter to the editor of a Batavia newspaper.

"The department of agriculture in Batavia reports that the number of dairy farms throughout the country is now 25 percent greater than it was 10 years ago. During this same time period, however, the price of milk at the local Excello Food Market has increased from $1.50 to over $3.00 per gallon. To prevent farmers from continuing to receive excessive profits on an apparently increased supply of milk, the Batavia government should begin to regulate retail milk prices. Such regulation is necessary to ensure fair prices for consumers."

Write a response in which you discuss what questions would need to be answered in order to decide whether the recommendation is likely to have the predicted result. Be sure to explain how the answers to these questions would help to evaluate the recommendation.

题目整理

论点 The Batavia government should begin to regulate retail milk prices, which is necessary to ensure fair prices for consumers.

论据 (1) The department of agriculture in Batavia reports that the number of dairy farms throughout the country is now 25 percent greater than it was 10 years ago.

(2) During this same time period, however, the price of milk at the local Excello Food Market

has increased from \$1.50 to over \$3.00 per gallon.

(3) Dairy farmers are making excessive profits on an apparently increased supply of milk.

论证方法

题目中论者主要运用了统计数据论证法和列举特征式论证法。

分析提示

● 论据(1)所引数据来自Batavia（印度首都雅加达的旧称）的农业部门，所以数据应该是可靠的。但我们有以下疑问：第一，论者为什么不能提供民间学术机构（non-government academic institutes）或者大学（colleges）、行业协会（industrial associations）的相关数据？把这些数据和政府的官方数据相互参照，更能呈现事实真相。第二，在十年间该国牛奶场的数量增长了25%。这增长速度似乎不慢。但是，这十年间，该市的国内生产总值（gross domestic product）、人口、人均能耗、人均收入（per capita income）、人均消费支出（per capita consumption expenditure）增加了多少？这些都是反映整体经济以及居民消费水平的关键指标。如果这些指标在十年间都至少增长80%以上，那么，该国牛奶场数量25%的增长并不快。第三，25%的增长只是现在和十年前两个时间点的比较。那么，这十年期间牛奶场数量有什么变化？如果一直是稳步上升，其未来趋势也许还会上升；但如果是不断波动，未来的趋势实际上是很难估计的，也许还会下降。第四，即便这个25%的增长是个相当高的增速，但假如新建的牛奶场规模小、经营成本高、产量低呢？如此的话，牛奶场数量的增长未必就会带来大量的牛奶供应。

● 论据(2)引用一个地方市场的数据，指出十年期间，当地的牛奶价格翻了一番。相比牛奶场数量25%的增长，这个翻一倍的价格似乎涨得太快。但问题是：第一，仅仅用一家市场牛奶价格的变化似乎很难说明这个城市牛奶价格的总体水平。很可能这家市场地处黄金地段，那里所有的商品都比其他地方贵50%以上。这就使其缺乏代表性。第二，这十年间，该市的人口、人均收入、人均牛奶消费量、物价水平（也就是通货膨胀水平）等等，分别上涨了多少？如果都是至少25%（比如说人口的增长）、一倍以上或者更多的增长，那么，牛奶价格上涨100%应该是一件很正常的事情。

● 论据(3)是列举特征式论证。论者依据论据(1)(2)体现出来的牛奶市场供应和价格现象，得出结论说奶农们正continuing to receive excessive profits on an apparently increased supply of milk。但论者的判断很可能只是看到了表象。正如前面分析，如果牛奶场数量增加的同时，该市人均牛奶消费量以更快的速度增长、人均收入大幅攀升，物价水平高涨、奶场运营成本（包括人工、运输、牛奶加工成本等）迅速增加，牛奶价格翻倍很可能并没有给奶农带来多少收入（revenues），更不用说超额利润（excessive profits）。

....

76. The following appeared in a newsletter offering advice to investors.

"Over 80 percent of the respondents to a recent survey indicated a desire to reduce their intake of foods containing fats and cholesterol, and today low-fat products abound in many food stores. Since many of the food products currently marketed by Old Dairy Industries are high in fat and cholesterol, the company's sales are likely to diminish greatly and company profits will no doubt decrease. We therefore advise Old Dairy stockholders to sell their shares, and other investors not to purchase stock in this company."

Write a response in which you discuss what questions would need to be answered in order to decide whether the advice and the argument on which it is based are reasonable. Be sure to explain how the answers to these questions would help to evaluate the advice.

题目整理

论点 Old Dairy stockholders should sell their shares, and other investors not to purchase stock in this company.

论据 (1) Over 80 percent of the respondents to a recent survey indicated a desire to reduce their intake of foods containing fats and cholesterol.

(2) Today low-fat products abound in many food stores.

(3) Since many of the food products currently marketed by Old Dairy Industries are high in fat and cholesterol, the company's sales are likely to diminish greatly and company profits will no doubt decrease.

论证方法

题目中论者主要运用了统计数据论证法、列举特征式论证法和因果关系论证法。

分析提示

● 论据(1)在利用统计数据展开论证。问题是：这个调查的方案设计（如调查样本的选择、调查问卷的设计、调查数据的处理、调查结果的核实和验证等等）和实施过程是严格按照科学程序进行的吗？其结论是客观、中立的吗？被调查对象有没有说出他们的真实想法？即便他们果真有a desire to reduce their intake of foods containing fats and cholesterol，他们实际可以做到多少呢？另外，调查的实施者有没有受行业及其他利益相关方的影响？有没有参考独立第三方的调查数据？

● 论据(2)利用列举特征的方式进行论证。low-fat products abound in many food stores这个现象能说明消费者会放弃high-fat-and-cholesterol-content food吗？消费人群是多样化的，人们对食品口味的要求、不同人群的体质和健康水平也是千差万别的。所以，大量出现低脂肪食品并不意味着高脂肪和高胆固醇食品就没有市场空间了。

● 论据(3)是个因果关系论证法。这个因果关系很难成立：首先，即便many of the food products currently marketed by Old Dairy Industries are high in fat and cholesterol，但该公司产品完全可能因为其产品的独特口味、特定的消费群体（比如年轻人，他们一般不像上了年纪的人那样关注食品的脂肪和胆固醇含量）、有效的价格策略保持了较高销售水平。其次，难道Old Dairy Industries只生产高脂肪和高胆固醇的食品？如果它还提供其他的产品和服务（比如，饮料、大型设备、贸易、房地产、通信、金融等），其市场销售及盈利情况都非常不错的话，那么，高脂肪和高胆固醇的食品的市场变化并不会对公司整体销售和盈利状况产生很大的影响。

77. The following recommendation appeared in a memo from the mayor of the town of Hopewell.

"Two years ago, the nearby town of Ocean View built a new municipal golf course and resort hotel. During the past two years, tourism in Ocean View has increased, new businesses have opened there, and Ocean View's tax revenues have risen by 30 percent. Therefore, the best way to improve Hopewell's economy—and generate additional tax revenues—is to build a golf course and resort hotel similar to those in Ocean View."

（参考第169题）

Write a response in which you examine the stated and/or unstated assumptions of the argument. Be sure to explain how the argument depends on these assumptions and what the implications are for the argument if the assumptions prove unwarranted.

题目整理

论点 The best way to improve Hopewell's economy—and generate additional tax revenues—is to build a golf course and resort hotel similar to those in Ocean View.

论据 Two years ago, the nearby town of Ocean View built a new municipal golf course and resort hotel. During the past two years, tourism in Ocean View has increased, new businesses have opened there, and Ocean View's tax revenues have risen by 30 percent.

论证方法

题目中论者只运用了类比论证法。

分析提示

● 论者有纵向类比不当的问题：他假设两年前的情况同样适用于现在。难道这期间没有其他情况出现（比如经济整体下滑、旅游业不景气、频繁发生的灾害性天气、新的时尚运动的出现使高尔夫不再受欢迎等），致使两年前在Ocean View有效的做法如今在Hopewell难以奏效？

● 其次是横向类比不当：论者假设这两个镇完全可比，但两镇的地理位置、地质地貌、风光特色、人文风情、交通通讯、餐饮住宿等等是否完全可比？

● 第三，论者有"在此之后，因此之故"的推理错误：假设先后出现的两个现象之间有因果关系，即，正是因为Two years ago, the nearby town of Ocean View built a new municipal golf course and resort hotel，所以随后就出现During the past two years, tourism in Ocean View has increased, new businesses have opened there, and Ocean View's tax revenues have risen by 30 percent。问题是：没有其他原因导致同样的结果吗？比如，当地的经济形势增长迅速、人们收入增加、休闲娱乐时间充裕、广告商的大规模宣传、旅游环境的改善等等。

● 最后，即便论者的论据都是事实，论者提出的模仿Ocean View以促进Hopewell经济和税收增长的建议依然值得商榷，因为也许还有其他更好的办法，比如：引进新兴电子、软件设计、文化创意、航空物流、转口贸易等等产业。论者总不能假设这些产业全都不适合Hopewell吧？

78. The following appeared in a memo from the vice president of a food distribution company with food storage warehouses in several cities.

"Recently, we signed a contract with the Fly-Away Pest Control Company to provide pest control services at our fast-food warehouse in Palm City, but last month we discovered that over $20,000 worth of food there had been destroyed by pest damage. Meanwhile, the Buzzoff Pest Control Company, which we have used for many years, continued to service our warehouse in Wintervale, and last month only $10,000 worth of the food stored there had been destroyed by pest damage. Even though the price charged by Fly-Away is considerably lower, our best means of saving money is to return to Buzzoff for all our pest control services."

(参考第114、116、117题)

Write a response in which you discuss what specific evidence is needed to evaluate the argument and explain how the evidence would weaken or strengthen the argument.

题目整理

论点　Even though the price charged by Fly-Away is considerably lower, our best means of saving money is to return to Buzzoff for all our pest control services.

论据　(1) Recently, we signed a contract with the Fly-Away Pest Control Company to provide pest control services at our fast-food warehouse in Palm City, but last month we discovered that over $20,000 worth of food there had been destroyed by pest damage.

(2) Meanwhile, the Buzzoff Pest Control Company, which we have used for many years, continued to service our warehouse in Wintervale, and last month only $10,000 worth of the food stored there had been destroyed by pest damage.

论证方法

题目中论者运用了类比论证法和归纳推理论证法。

分析提示

● 是否有其他特殊的原因导致了论据(1)中的结果？比如：上月储存在Palm City仓库那一批次的食品包装出了问题、天气剧烈变化、当地虫害大规模爆发、库房常年使用缺乏维修等。另外，假如储存在Palm City仓库的食品价格较高，即便那里储存的食品遭受虫害的比率和数量同Wintervale仓库的一样或者略低，但就虫害造成的经济损失会高一些，但并不足以说明Fly-Away Pest Control公司所做的灭虫效果差。

● 同理，针对论据(2)，我们也要问：是否有其他不可控的原因导致了"only $10,000 worth of the food stored there had been destroyed by pest damage"这一结果？比如，那里储存的食品具有很强的抗虫性、当地的天气不会爆发虫害、上个月那里出现害虫的数量和频率在一年中属于较轻的月份等。或者，那里储存的食品都是较为便宜的品种，所以即便遭虫害的食品的数量和比率较高，但就损失的货币价值来看，却并不大。这些都需要更多的信息加以佐证。

● 基于对论据(1)(2)的分析，我们可以发现，结论说 "our best means of saving money is to return to Buzzoff for all our pest control services" 中有以下不当推论：其一，论者没有考虑到，因为天气、仓储设施、所储藏食品特点和价格等方面的差异，Palm City 和 Wintervale 两地的食品仓库很可能缺乏可比性。其二，论者很可能有不当归纳推理的问题。即便 Buzzoff 公司在 Wintervale 的灭虫效果较好，难道就能断定该公司在其他城市、其他仓库也能做到同样好吗？如果那些城市和仓库有一些特殊的情况呢？其三，当论者声称把所有灭虫任务都交给 Buzzoff 公司是 our **best means of saving money** 的时候，似乎显得过于武断了。难道没有比 Buzzoff 做得更好的公司？没有其他的防虫、灭虫办法，比如：改进包装、注意灭菌防腐、改善仓储设施等？所有这些，论者都应进一步说明。

79. Since those issues of Newsbeat magazine that featured political news on their front cover were the poorest-selling issues over the past three years, the publisher of Newsbeat has recommended that the magazine curtail its emphasis on politics to focus more exclusively on economics and personal finance. She points to a recent survey of readers of general interest magazines that indicates greater reader interest in economic issues than in political ones. Newsbeat's editor, however, opposes the proposed shift in editorial policy, pointing out that very few magazines offer extensive political coverage anymore.

Write a response in which you discuss what questions would need to be answered in order to decide whether the recommendation and the argument on which it is based are reasonable. Be sure to explain how the answers to these questions would help to evaluate the recommendation.

题目整理

论点 Newsbeat magazine should curtail its emphasis on politics to focus more exclusively on economics and personal finance, said the magazine's publisher.

论据 (1) Those issues of Newsbeat magazine that featured political news on their front cover were the poorest-selling issues over the past three years.

(2) A recent survey of readers of general interest magazines indicates greater reader interest in economic issues than in political ones.

(3) Newsbeat's editor, however, opposes the proposed shift in editorial policy, pointing out that very few magazines offer extensive political coverage anymore.

论证方法

题目中论者运用了列举特征式论证法、统计数据论证法和引用权威论证法。

分析提示

● 论据(1)是个列举特征式论证。论者通过指出 Newsbeat 杂志在过去三年只要每期的封面故事报道了政治类新闻，该期杂志的销量就会下滑这一现象，力图说明该杂志存在报道政治类新闻过多的倾向，暗示正是这种倾向导致这本杂志销量不佳。我们的疑问是：第一，过去三年这本杂志每期在封面故事只要报道了政治新闻就会卖得不好这个结论是谁得出的？是论者自己的观察、该杂志社的统计，还是某个权威的独立第三方研究机构的评价？这个判断是论者全部推论的起点，因而其客观性、可靠性必须要有保证。第二，即便过去三年这本杂志每期的封面故事只要报道了政治新闻，那么那一期的杂志就会卖得不好这个现象属实，我们依然要问：这本杂志"封面故事报道了政治新闻"同"市场销量不佳"这二者之间有因果关系吗？是否是其他原因导致了同一结果？比如，是不是每期这篇政治类封面故事（cover story）的新闻报道和写作质量很差？是不是每次这本杂志封面故事报道的政治新闻同网络和电视上的报道雷同，因此读者觉得没有必要买？或者是不是这本杂志的竞争对手每次关于相同的政治类话题的报道都要比Newsbeat深入？等等这些，都是论者必须回答的问题。

- 论据(2)引用了一项调查。我们的问题是：这项调查的方案设计（如调查样本的选择、调查问卷的设计、调查数据的处理、调查结果的核实和验证等等）和实施过程是否是严格按照科学程序进行的？其结论是客观、中立的吗？调查的实施者没有受行业及其他利益相关方的影响？其次，请大家注意：调查对象是readers of general interest magazines，即"大众类杂志（而非像政治类、军事类、财经类等专门类别）的读者"。那么这些读者代表性如何？他们的阅读兴趣同一些专门类别杂志（如政治、军事、财经、娱乐等）的读者的兴趣一样吗？Newsbeat是属于哪一类别的杂志？大众类还是专门类？如果类别不同，这个调查的参考意义可能十分有限。

- 论据(3)是个引用权威的论证过程。这里的专家（也就是Newsbeat's editor）指出了一个现象：very few magazines offer extensive political coverage anymore. 其字面意思是：现在基本上没有哪本杂志只是报道纯粹的政治话题（而全然忽略其他话题，如经济、理财等）了。其言下之意是：Newsbeat并未忽略财经话题的报道。该论据提到了一个值得论者（也就是the publisher of Newsbeat）考虑的问题：她的建议（Newsbeat magazine should curtail its emphasis on politics to focus more exclusively on economics and personal finance）是否抓到了该杂志面临问题的症结？到底是应该改变Newsbeat这本杂志的报道内容，还是应该提高其报道水平，调整其发行策略，更准确把握其目标读者的阅读兴趣？等等。

80. The following is taken from a memo from the advertising director of the Super Screen Movie Production Company.

"According to a recent report from our marketing department, during the past year, fewer people attended Super Screen-produced movies than in any other year. And yet the percentage of positive reviews by movie reviewers about specific Super Screen movies actually increased during the past year. Clearly, the contents of these reviews are not reaching enough of our prospective viewers. Thus, the problem lies not with the quality of our movies but with the public's lack of awareness that movies of good quality are available. Super Screen should therefore allocate a greater share of its budget next year to reaching the public through advertising."

Write a response in which you discuss what questions would need to be answered in order to decide whether the recommendation and the argument on which it is based are reasonable. Be sure to explain how the answers to these questions would help to evaluate the recommendation.

题目整理

论点 Super Screen should allocate a greater share of its budget next year to reaching the public through advertising.

论据 (1) According to a recent report from our marketing department, during the past year, fewer people attended Super Screen-produced movies than in any other year. And yet the percentage of positive reviews by movie reviewers about specific Super Screen movies actually increased during the past year.

(2) Clearly, the contents of these reviews are not reaching enough of our prospective viewers.

(3) Thus, the problem lies not with the quality of our movies but with the public's lack of awareness that movies of good quality are available.

论证方法

题目中论者运用了列举特征式论证法。论者提到了一个现象，并对这个现象作出自认为合理的解释。

分析提示

● 论据(1)提到了一个似乎矛盾的现象：一方面影评人员对Super Screen电影制片厂去年出品的电影好评多多，另一方面，该厂电影的观众却在减少。我们的疑问首先是那个recent report：该报告来自该电影制片厂的市场部，很可能同这位论者（the advertising director of the Super Screen Movie Production Company）属同一部门。那么，论者提到的这个看似矛盾的现象是否属实？可否提供一项独立第三方做的市场调查来相互佐证？否则，这个作为论者所有推论起点的现象很可能是个伪命题。

● 论据(2)是论者对上述矛盾现象给出的一个解读：Super Screen的电影很好，影评人员给出的评论也属实，但可惜的是，潜在的观众不知道这些影评。该解释似乎很好地解释了论据(1)中提到的现象，但问题是：难道没有其他的合理解读了吗？比如：那些影评是否都客观、公正？那些影评人的观点是否受电影公司的影响？是否观众普遍都不信任影评？如此的话，拍得较差的电影即便有正面的影评也未必能吸引观众。再比如：是否其他的娱乐形式（家庭DVD、网上看电影、戏剧、蹦迪、卡拉OK等等）分流了那些本可以去电影院的观众？还有一种可能：是否都市里高节奏的生活、巨大的工作和生活压力使人们更愿意选择一些简单、方便、个人化的娱乐方式（比如在家看电视、看闲书、郊游远足、玩电子游戏等），从而不再去电影院看电影？等等。

● 结合对论据(1)(2)的分析，可以看出论据(3)的判断过于简单。

● 同理，论者在结论中建议加大广告投入以使公众更加了解他们的电影也显得较为武断。首先，他们的电影是否值得看本身就存有疑问。其次，即便那些电影都很棒，加大广告力度就必然能吸引到观众吗？毕竟，影响人们是否看电影的因素不仅仅只是影片质量，还可能是电影票价、人们的生活方式、其他娱乐形式、去影院看电影的方便和舒适程度等。

81. The following appeared in a business magazine.

"As a result of numerous complaints of dizziness and nausea on the part of consumers of Promofoods tuna, the company requested that eight million cans of its tuna be returned for testing. Promofoods concluded that the canned tuna did not, after all, pose a health risk. This conclusion is based on tests performed on samples of the recalled cans by chemists from Promofoods; the chemists found that of the eight food chemicals most commonly blamed for causing symptoms of dizziness and nausea, five were not found in any of the tested cans. The chemists did find small amounts of the three remaining suspected chemicals but pointed out that these occur naturally in all canned foods."

Write a response in which you discuss what questions would need to be addressed in order to decide whether the conclusion and the argument on which it is based are reasonable. Be sure to explain how the answers to the questions would help to evaluate the conclusion.

题目整理

论点 The canned tuna did not, after all, pose a health risk, according to Promofoods.

论据 (1) Chemists at Promofoods company have done sample tests of the recalled tuna cans.

(2) The chemists found that of the eight food chemicals most commonly blamed for causing symptoms of dizziness and nausea, five were not found in any of the tested cans. The chemists did find small amounts of the three remaining suspected chemicals but pointed out that these occur naturally in all canned foods.

论证方法

题目中论者运用了引用权威论证法和统计数据论证法。

分析提示

- 论据(1)是引用权威（这里的权威是Promofoods公司的化验员）论证，列举了Promofoods公司的检测结果。但自我检查能保证公正、客观吗？为什么不请政府机构或独立第三方来做这些关键的检验？这些抽样化验的方案设计（如样本的选择、调查数据的处理、调查结果的核实和验证等等）和实施过程是否是严格按照科学程序进行的？如何保证试验人员没有在公司的授意下歪曲试验数据？这些论者都没有说明。

- 论据(2)是统计数据论证，但其论证过程给人留下一系列的疑问：论者说能导致头晕目眩症状的八种化学物质，测试中只测出了其中三种少量存在，但论者强调所有罐装食品中都存在这三种化学物质。论者其实是在假设：导致问题的只能是这八种化学物质，它们没问题，则那些罐装金枪鱼就没问题。但首先，假如这些罐装金枪鱼里面存在未知的细菌、病毒或其他化学成分呢？其次，假如那些罐子密封不严，里面的食品变质了呢？再次，那三种监测出来的化学物质在食品中的含量到底是多少？ small amounts 是个非常模糊的表述，small amounts 并不等于就没超过规定剂量。更何况还有其他更特殊的原因？比如，假如这些金枪鱼生存的海域出现了污染，那么即便所有的加工、罐装、储运、卫生监测等过程都没问题，仍然不能保证这些食品的食用安全。

● 最后，论者在题目中的整个推论都是围绕着这些金枪鱼罐头本身找问题。其实，问题就不可能出在其他方面？比如，因为天气、环境的因素，某些人在特定的季节食用某种食物会过敏，出现头晕目眩等症状。

---

82. The following appeared in a memo from the vice president of marketing at Dura-Socks, Inc.

"A recent study of Dura-Socks customers suggests that our company is wasting the money it spends on its patented Endure manufacturing process, which ensures that our socks are strong enough to last for two years. We have always advertised our use of the Endure process, but the new study shows that despite the socks' durability, our customers, on average, actually purchase new Dura-Socks every three months. Furthermore, customers surveyed in our largest market—northeastern United States cities—say that they most value Dura-Socks' stylish appearance and availability in many colors. These findings suggest that we can increase our profits by discontinuing use of the Endure manufacturing process."

（参考第 56、57 题）

Write a response in which you discuss what questions would need to be answered in order to decide whether the recommendation and the argument on which it is based are reasonable. Be sure to explain how the answers to these questions would help to evaluate the recommendation.

题目整理

论点 The company is wasting the money it spends on its patented Endure manufacturing process. Instead，it can increase its profits by discontinuing use of the Endure manufacturing process.

论据 (1) A recent study of Dura-Socks customers suggests that our company is wasting the money it spends on its patented Endure manufacturing process, which ensures that our socks are strong enough to last for two years.

(2) We have always advertised our use of the Endure process, but the new study shows that despite the socks' durability, our customers, on average, actually purchase new Dura-Socks every three months.

(3) Furthermore, customers surveyed in our largest market—northeastern United States cities—say that they most value Dura-Socks' stylish appearance and availability in many colors.

论证方法

题目中论者主要运用了统计数据论证法和归纳推理论证法。

分析提示

● 论据(1)举出了一项研究，该研究是论者整个推论的起点。我们的问题是：这项研究的方案设计（如调查样本的选择、调查数据的处理、调查结果的核实和验证等等）和实施过程是严格按照科学程序进行的吗？其结论是客观、中立的吗？调查的实施者没有受行业及其他利益相关方的影响？等等。

- 在论据(2)中，论者说"Dura-Sock has always advertised its use of the 'Endure' process, but the new study shows that **the average Dura-Sock customer actually purchases new Dura-Socks every three months**"，用以说明这些顾客似乎并不看重该公司袜子的耐穿度。但假如Dura-Sock的消费者每三个月购买一次新的Dura-Socks并非是因为他们讨厌这种袜子耐穿，而是因为他们喜欢每三个月更新一次的Dura-Socks的颜色和款式呢？或者因为Dura-Sock的袜子广受欢迎，人们经常拿它来馈赠亲友呢？

- 论据(3)是个归纳推理：论者以美国东北部城市的消费者喜欢Dura-Socks' stylish appearance and availability in many colors的事实力图说明其他地方的顾客也有一样的消费偏好。但首先，美国东北部城市消费者的消费偏好具有足够的代表性吗？其次，假如顾客喜欢Dura-Socks的样式和多种颜色，并不讨厌这种袜子耐穿呢？难道，顾客看重那些袜子的外观和颜色就必须放弃其耐用性？

- 论者的结论是：Dura-Sock can increase its profits by discontinuing its use of the 'Endure' manufacturing process.论者实际是在假设：Dura-Socks经磨耐穿的工艺妨碍了该公司利润的提高。但这一点论者并未证实。从常识来讲，袜子耐穿是消费者购买的前提。否则，即便它们花色新颖、款式时尚，也未必受顾客的欢迎。如此，论者的结论就很难成立了。

---

83. The following is a letter to the editor of an environmental magazine.

"In 1975 a wildlife census found that there were seven species of amphibians in Xanadu National Park, with abundant numbers of each species. However, in 2002 only four species of amphibians were observed in the park, and the numbers of each species were drastically reduced. There has been a substantial decline in the numbers of amphibians worldwide, and global pollution of water and air is clearly implicated. The decline of amphibians in Xanadu National Park, however, almost certainly has a different cause: in 1975, trout—which are known to eat amphibian eggs—were introduced into the park."

(参考第84题)

Write a response in which you discuss what specific evidence is needed to evaluate the argument and explain how the evidence would weaken or strengthen the argument.

题目整理

论点 The decline of amphibians in Xanadu National Park is due to the introduction of trout into the park in 1975.

论据 (1) In 1975 a wildlife census found that there were seven species of amphibians in Xanadu National Park, with abundant numbers of each species. However, in 2002 only four species of amphibians were observed in the park, and the numbers of each species were drastically reduced.

(2) There has been a substantial decline in the numbers of amphibians worldwide, and global

pollution of water and air is clearly implicated.

(3) In 1975, trout—which are known to eat amphibian eggs—were introduced into Xanadu National Park.

论证方法

题目中论者主要运用了统计数据论证法和因果关系论证法。

分析提示

- 论据(1)引用了不同时期的两项调查进行统计数据论证。但论者需要进一步说明的是：这些调查的方案设计（如调查样本的采集、调查数据的处理、调查结果的核实和验证等等）和实施过程是否是严格按照科学程序进行的？其结论是否是客观、中立的？调查的实施者有没有受行业及其他利益相关方的影响？有没有考虑一些特殊的情形，比如，这些两栖动物是否曾从一地迁徙到另一地，所以在它们的原栖息地很难再发现它们？它们的生活习性是否因为人类对环境的改造而发生了巨大变化，致使用传统的观测手段很难观测到它们？等等。

- 论者在论据(2)中说，在全球范围内两栖类动物的数量也呈现显著下降的趋势，并断定空气和水污染难辞其咎。但论者只是说global pollution of water and air is **clearly** implicated，并未证明a substantial decline in the numbers of amphibians worldwide和global pollution of water and air之间是否存在因果关系。这实际上是个"强词夺理"的逻辑错误。难道没有其他原因导致了同一结果？比如：人类的居住区域不断扩张，侵占了森林、草原、湖泊、河流等这些两栖动物的传统栖息地，人类对昆虫（比如蚊蝇、蝗虫、飞蛾等等）的灭杀破坏了这些两栖动物的食物链，或者自然界出现了捕食这些两栖动物的新物种，等等。

- 论据(3)是个因果关系论证。但论者的推论更像是把先后发生的两件事情当作因果关系，因而是个"在此之后，因此之故"的逻辑错误。论者需要提供证据表明的确是trout的引进，而不是其他的原因导致了Xanadu国家公园两栖动物数量的减少。正如在论据(2)的分析中提到的，人类的居住区域对森林、草原、湖泊、河流等这些两栖动物的传统栖息地的侵占，人类对昆虫（比如蚊蝇、蝗虫、飞蛾等等）的灭杀，自然界中两栖动物的新天敌的出现，甚至是人类对这些两栖动物的捕杀等等，都可以导致同一结果。

84. The following is a letter to the editor of an environmental magazine.

"Two studies of amphibians in Xanadu National Park confirm a significant decline in the numbers of amphibians. In 1975 there were seven species of amphibians in the park, and there were abundant numbers of each species. However, in 2002 only four species of amphibians were observed in the park, and the numbers of each species were drastically reduced. One proposed explanation is that the decline was caused by the introduction of trout into the park's waters, which began in 1975. (Trout are known to eat amphibian eggs.)"

（参考第83题）

Write a response in which you discuss one or more alternative explanations that could rival the proposed explanation and explain how your explanation(s) can plausibly account for the facts presented in the argument.

题目整理

论点 The decline was believed to be caused by the introduction of trout into the park's waters in 1975.

论据 (1) Two studies of amphibians in Xanadu National Park confirm a significant decline in the numbers of amphibians.

(2) In 1975 a wildlife census found that there were seven species of amphibians in Xanadu National Park, with abundant numbers of each species. However, in 2002 only four species of amphibians were observed in the park, and the numbers of each species were drastically reduced.

(3) In 1975, trout—which are known to eat amphibian eggs—were introduced into the waters in Xanadu National Park.

论证方法

题目中论者主要运用了统计数据论证法和因果关系论证法。

分析提示

● 论据(1)试图引用两项研究进行统计数据论证。但论者需要进一步说明的是：这些调查的方案设计（如调查样本的采集、调查数据的处理、调查结果的核实和验证等等）和实施过程是否是严格按照科学程序进行的？其结论是否是客观、中立的？调查的实施者有没有受行业及其他利益相关方的影响？

● 论据(2)对比了两个时期Xanadu国家公园内两栖动物种类和数量的变化。但这些变化是否意味着这些动物正在灭绝？是否是一些特殊情形给人们造成了这些两栖动物正在大量消失的假象？比如说，这些两栖动物是否曾从一地迁徙到另一地，所以在它们的原栖息地很难再发现它们？它们的生活习性是否因为人类对环境的改造而发生了巨大变化（比如从过去的白天活动变成只在远离人迹的地方夜间出来活动），致使用传统的观测手段很难观测到它们？等等。

● 论据(3)是个因果关系论证。但论者的推论更像是把先后发生的两件事情当作因果关系，因而是个"在此之后，因此之故"的逻辑错误。我们完全可以假设有别的原因促使Xanadu国家公园两栖动物数量的减少，而不是论者认定的trout的引进。比如，人类的日常生活和工业活动导致的土壤、空气、水体等环境污染；人类不断扩大的居住区域侵占了森林、草原、湖泊、河流等这些两栖动物传统栖息地；人类对昆虫（比如蚊蝇、蝗虫、飞蛾等等）的灭杀，破坏了这些两栖动物食物链；自然界中这些两栖动物的新天敌的出现；人类捕杀这些两栖动物当作食品或制作工艺品等等，都可以导致同一结果。

85. In a study of the reading habits of Waymarsh citizens conducted by the University of Waymarsh, most respondents said that they preferred literary classics as reading material. However, a second study conducted by the same researchers found that the type of book most frequently checked out of each of the public libraries in Waymarsh was the mystery novel. Therefore, it can be concluded that the respondents in the first study had misrepresented their reading habits.

（参考第87题）

Write a response in which you discuss what specific evidence is needed to evaluate the argument and explain how the evidence would weaken or strengthen the argument.

题目整理

论点 Therefore, it can be concluded that the respondents in the first study had misrepresented their reading habits.

论据 (1) In a study of the reading habits of Waymarsh citizens conducted by the University of Waymarsh, most respondents said that they preferred literary classics as reading material.

(2) However, a second study conducted by the same researchers found that the type of book most frequently checked out of each of the public libraries in Waymarsh was the mystery novel.

论证方法

题目中论者主要运用了统计数据论证法。

分析提示

● 论据(1)(2)分别是两次调查。论者需要进一步说明的是：这些调查的方案设计（如调查对象的选择、调查数据的处理、调查结果的核实和验证等等）和实施过程是否是严格按照科学程序进行的？其结论是否是客观、中立的？调查的实施者有没有受行业及其他利益相关方的影响？

● 论者断言前后两个调查结果的不一致是因为the respondents in the first study had misrepresented their reading habits。这个推论实际上在假设没有其他原因可以导致这一差异，是个"虚假困境"的逻辑错误。因此，论者需进一步说明以下疑问：首先，是否所有的图书都要去图书馆去借？如果Waymarsh的居民愿意自己掏钱购买、收藏文学经典，同时也去图书馆借阅悬疑小说，那么论据(1)(2)就不矛盾。其次，两次调查的对象是否是相同人群？如果第一次调查的人群是大街上随机抽选的人，而第二次调查的对象是经常泡图书馆的人，并且绝大部分是学生，那么结果可能会有很大的不同。大街上人群的背景较为多样化，因而其阅读兴趣较有代表性；而学生这个群体有阅读倾向很正常。第三，是否一些特殊情况干扰了两次调查的结果？比如，一部电影大片或热播电视剧突然让很多人对悬疑小说产生了兴趣；或者图书馆的文学经典不多。最后，是否那些调查对象说出了真实想法？在参与第一次调查的时候，有些人很可能因为心理暗示或者为了显示自己兴趣高雅会声称自己喜欢读文学经典，但等到在图书馆见到悬疑小说时，立刻被好奇心控制了。这些都是值得进一步考虑的可能。

86. The following appeared in a memo at XYZ company.

"When XYZ lays off employees, it pays Delany Personnel Firm to offer those employees assistance in creating résumés and developing interviewing skills, if they so desire. Laid-off employees have benefited greatly from Delany's services: last year those who used Delany found jobs much more quickly than did those who did not. Recently, it has been proposed that we use the less expensive Walsh Personnel Firm in place of Delany. This would be a mistake because eight years ago, when XYZ was using Walsh, only half of the workers we laid off at that time found jobs within a year. Moreover, Delany is clearly superior, as evidenced by its bigger staff and larger number of branch offices. After all, last year Delany's clients took an average of six months to find jobs, whereas Walsh's clients took nine."

（参考第89题）

Write a response in which you discuss what specific evidence is needed to evaluate the argument and explain how the evidence would weaken or strengthen the argument.

题目整理

论点 The proposed shift to using Walsh from Delany would be a mistake.

论据 (1) Laid-off employees have benefited greatly from Delany's services: last year those who used Delany found jobs much more quickly than did those who did not.

(2) Eight years ago, when XYZ was using Walsh, only half of the workers we laid off at that time found jobs within a year.

(3) Moreover, Delany is clearly superior, as evidenced by its bigger staff and larger number of branch offices.

(4) After all, last year Delany's clients took an average of six months to find jobs, whereas Walsh's clients took nine.

论证方法

题目中论者主要运用了列举特征式论证法。论者指出种种现象以支持自己的观点，反驳他人的观点。

分析提示

● 论据(1)列举的前后两个现象未必就是因果关系。论者犯了"在此之后，因此之故"的逻辑错误。首先，论者有证据表明，不是其他原因导致去年选择了Delany人才服务公司的人能更快找到工作呢？比如，当时经济景气、那些选择了Delany人才服务公司的人普遍受过良好的教育、具备熟练的工作技能或者他们对新工作不挑不拣，等等。其次，去年，Delany竞争对手的业绩如何？如果它们普遍都能在短时间内帮助客户找到工作，那么Delany去年的业绩也没什么值得夸耀的。

● 论据(2)提到：Eight years ago, when XYZ was using Walsh, only half of the workers we laid off at that time found jobs within a year. 这其中的道理同论据(1)中推论是一样的：一年之内只有一半被解聘的员工找到工作，也许这跟Walsh无关，比如，当时经济萧条、工作普遍难找、那些人技能和素质较低、对工作较挑剔等。其次，Walsh公司的竞争对手表现如何？如果它们的表现都不如Walsh公司呢？

● 论据(3)提到：Delany is clearly superior, as evidenced by its bigger staff and larger number of branch offices. 但有证据表明，一家公司拥有bigger staff and larger number of branch offices就意味着该公司必然能提供好服务吗？"员工多，分公司多"是否也可以解释为该公司管理无序、员工

效率低下，只能靠粗放式的规模扩张来获得更多利润呢？

- 论据(4)提到：...last year Delany's clients took an average of six months to find jobs, whereas Walsh's clients took nine.但假如后者找到的工作都是很有发展前景、薪水高、待遇好的工作，而前者找到的工作大部分属技术含量低、低薪酬、待遇差的工作呢？

87. In a study of the reading habits of Waymarsh citizens conducted by the University of Waymarsh, most respondents said they preferred literary classics as reading material. However, a second study conducted by the same researchers found that the type of book most frequently checked out of each of the public libraries in Waymarsh was the mystery novel. Therefore, it can be concluded that the respondents in the first study had misrepresented their reading preferences.

（参考第85题）

Write a response in which you examine the stated and/or unstated assumptions of the argument. Be sure to explain how the argument depends on these assumptions and what the implications are for the argument if the assumptions prove unwarranted.

题目整理

论点 Therefore, it can be concluded that the respondents in the first study had misrepresented their reading habits.

论据 (1) In a study of the reading habits of Waymarsh citizens conducted by the University of Waymarsh, most respondents said that they preferred literary classics as reading material.

(2) However, a second study conducted by the same researchers found that the type of book most frequently checked out of each of the public libraries in Waymarsh was the mystery novel.

论证方法

题目中论者主要运用了统计数据论证法。

分析提示

- 论据(1)(2)分别是两次调查。两次调查得出的似乎矛盾的数据是论者全部推论的起点。但论者的推论若要成立，必须假设：这些调查的方案设计（如调查对象的选择、调查数据的处理、调查结果的核实和验证等等）和实施过程严格按照科学程序进行的；其结论是客观、中立、可信的；调查的实施者没有受行业及其他利益相关方的影响，等等。

- 论者断言前后两个调查结果的不一致是因为the respondents in the first study had misrepresented their reading habits。这个推论实际上在假设没有其他原因导致这一差异，是个"虚假困境"的逻辑错误。首先，是否所有的图书都要去图书馆借？假如Waymarsh居民愿意自己掏钱购买、收藏文学经典，同时也去图书馆借阅悬疑小说，那么论据(1)(2)其实并不矛盾。其次，两次调查的对象是否相同人群？如果第一次调查的人群是大街上随机抽选的人，而第二次调查的对象是经常泡图书馆的人，并且绝大部分是学生，那么结果可能会有很大的不同。大街上的人群其背景较为多样化，因而较有代表性；而学生则是较为特殊的群体，表现出特殊的阅读倾向当然很正常。第三，是否一些特殊情况干扰了两次调查的结果？比如，一部电影大片或热播电视剧突然让很多人对悬疑小说产生了兴趣；或者图书馆没有多少文学经典，人们不得不借其他类别的图书。第四，即便是同样的一群人先说喜欢文学经典，而后又跑去借悬疑小说，这依然不能说明什么问题。他们完全可以每天花8个小时看文学经典，花一两个钟头消遣悬疑小说。这有矛盾吗？最后，是否那些调查对象说出了真实想法？在参与第一次调查的时候，人们很可能因为心理暗示或者为了显示自己兴趣高雅而声称自己喜欢读文学经典，但等到在图书馆见到悬疑小说时，立刻被好奇心控制了。这些都是可能出现的情况。

88. The following appeared in a memorandum written by the vice president of Health Naturally, a small but expanding chain of stores selling health food and other health-related products.

"Our previous experience has been that our stores are most profitable in areas where residents are highly concerned with leading healthy lives. We should therefore build one of our new stores in Plainsville, which clearly has many such residents. Plainsville merchants report that sales of running shoes and exercise equipment are at all-time highs. The local health club, which nearly closed five years ago due to lack of business, has more members than ever, and the weight-training and aerobics classes are always full. We can even anticipate a new generation of customers: Plainsville's schoolchildren are required to participate in a program called Fitness for Life, which emphasizes the benefits of regular exercise at an early age."

（参考第9、90题）

Write a response in which you discuss what specific evidence is needed to evaluate the argument and explain how the evidence would weaken or strengthen the argument.

题目整理

论点 Health Naturally should open a store in Plainsville.

论据 (1) Health Naturally's previous experience has been that its stores are most profitable in areas where residents are highly concerned with leading healthy lives, and Plainsville clearly has many such residents.

(2) Plainsville merchants report that sales of running shoes and exercise equipment are at all-time highs.

(3) The local health club, which nearly closed five years ago due to lack of business, has more members than ever, and the weight-training and aerobics classes are always full.

(4) A new generation of customers is coming too: Plainsville's schoolchildren are required to participate in a program called Fitness for Life, which emphasizes the benefits of regular exercise at an early age.

论证方法

　　题目中论者主要运用了归纳推理论证法、引用权威论证法和列举特征式论证法。

分析提示

● 论据(1)运用了归纳推理论证法：即 Health Naturally 在那些居民注重健康生活的地区都赚到了钱，Plainsville 的居民看起来很注重健康，所以，该公司在 Plainsville 开店也会赚到钱。但论者需要提供进一步的证明：论据(2)(3)(4)列举的特点都能够说明 Plainsville 的居民的确注重健康。

● 论据(2)引用 Plainsville 当地商人说法，跑鞋以及运动服的销量达到了最高记录（all-time highs），据此说明当地居民很注重健康生活。但首先，有证据表明这些商人的观察是客观、可信的吗？其次，有没有其他原因促使跑鞋和运动服销量的上升？比如，因为婴儿潮（baby boom）时期出生的孩子成长到了青少年时期，他们普遍喜好运动，所以会购买体育运动服饰；或者因为一项全国或全球体育赛事（the Olympic games or the World Cup soccer for instance）的举行而在短期内引发了该镇居民的体育运动热和购买运动服饰热等等。这些现象都不能说明该地居民都有健康生活的习惯。再次，论据(2)提到的"all-time highs"的销量到底有多大？假如该地的跑鞋和运动服的销量一向很低，比如每年也就是100多件，现在上升两倍，到了300件，这的确是 all-time high，但依然是个非常低的水平，并不足以信。

● 论据(3)提到健康俱乐部会员的增加以及举重和健美操训练班的爆满，并据此认为 Plainsville 的居民都注重健康生活。但首先，这些健康俱乐部以及举重和健美操训练班到底能接收多少会员和学员？假如这些都是 VIP 俱乐部或者场地面积很小的班，吸纳的人员有限，那么所谓的会员增加以及人员爆满就不能说明什么问题。其次，参加这些俱乐部以及训练班的人是不是特定的人群，比如体重超常的人群？如果他们只是一些急于减肥的人，就不能说明所有 Plainsville 的居民都在积极锻炼。

● 论据(4)依然有许多不明确的地方。论者说，该地的学龄儿童要参加 Fitness For Life 项目，这个项目强调 the benefits of regular exercise at an early age。但是，第一，这些孩子在总人口中占多大比例？如果这个比例较低，他们未来的消费需求也不会很大。其次，参加那个项目必然会产生对 Health Naturally 所售产品的需求吗？他们会不会购买其他的替代产品或者 Health Naturally 竞争对手的产品？第三，这些孩子对 Health Naturally 所售产品的需求会不会随着年龄的增长而发生改变？也许到了20多岁时，他们良好的健康状况会使得他们完全放弃对任何所谓健康食品的需求呢？

---

89. The following appeared in a memo at XYZ company.

"When XYZ lays off employees, it pays Delany Personnel Firm to offer those employees assistance in creating résumés and developing interviewing skills, if they so desire. Laid-off employees have benefited greatly from Delany's services: last year those who used Delany found jobs much more quickly than did those who did not. Recently, it has been proposed that we use the less expensive Walsh Personnel Firm in place of Delany. This would be a mistake because eight years ago, when XYZ was using Walsh, only half of the workers we laid off at that time found jobs within a year. Moreover, Delany is clearly superior, as evidenced by its bigger staff and larger number of branch offices. After all, last year Delany's clients took an average of six months to find jobs, whereas Walsh's clients took nine."

（参考第86题）

Write a response in which you examine the stated and/or unstated assumptions of the argument. Be sure to explain how the argument depends on these assumptions and what the implications are for the argument if the assumptions prove unwarranted.

题目整理

论点 The proposed shift to using Walsh from Delany would be a mistake.

论据
(1) Laid-off employees have benefited greatly from Delany's services: last year those who used Delany found jobs much more quickly than did those who did not.

(2) Eight years ago, when XYZ was using Walsh, only half of the workers we laid off at that time found jobs within a year.

(3) Moreover, Delany is clearly superior, as evidenced by its bigger staff and larger number of branch offices.

(4) After all, last year Delany's clients took an average of six months to find jobs, whereas Walsh's clients took nine.

论证方法

题目中论者主要运用了列举特征式论证法。

分析提示

● 论据(1)列举的前后两个现象未必就是因果关系。论者有"在此之后，因此之故"的逻辑错误。首先，论者假设不是其他与Delany无关的原因导致去年选择了Delany人才服务公司的人更快地找到了工作。比如，当时经济景气、那些选择Delany人才服务公司的人普遍受过良好的教育、具备熟练的工作技能或者他们对新工作不挑不拣，等等，这些原因都会使他们快速再就业。其次，论者还假设在去年，Delany的竞争对手的业绩普遍不如Delany好。如果其他公司普遍在更短的时间内帮助客户找到了工作，那么Delany去年的业绩也没什么值得夸耀的。

● 论据(2)提到：Eight years ago, when XYZ was using Walsh, only half of the workers we laid off at that time found jobs within a year. 这其中的道理同论据(1)中推论是一样的：只有一半被解聘的员工在一年之内找到了工作，这也许同Walsh无关？比如，当时经济萧条、工作普遍难找、那些人的技能和素质较低、对工作较挑剔等。其次，Walsh公司的竞争对手表现如何？如果它们的表现都不如Walsh公司呢？

● 论据(3)提到：Delany is clearly superior, as evidenced by its bigger staff and larger number of branch offices. 在此，论者实际在假设：一家公司拥有bigger staff and larger number of branch offices就意味着该公司必然能提供较好的服务。但这个假设显然很不靠谱。"员工多，分公司多"是否也可以解释为该公司管理无序、员工效率低下，只能靠粗放式的规模扩张来获得更多利润呢？

● 论据(4)提到：…last year Delany's clients took an average of six months to find jobs, whereas Walsh's clients took nine. 但假如后者找到的工作都是很有发展前景、薪水高、待遇好的工作，而前者找到的工作大部分属技术含量低、低薪酬、待遇差的工作呢？

---

90. The following appeared in a memorandum written by the vice president of Health Naturally, a small but expanding chain of stores selling health food and other health-related products.

"Our previous experience has been that our stores are most profitable in areas where residents are highly concerned with leading healthy lives. We should therefore build one of our new stores in Plainsville, which clearly has many such residents. Plainsville merchants report that sales of running shoes and exercise equipment are at all-time highs. The local health club, which nearly closed five years ago due to lack of business, has more members than ever, and the weight-training and aerobics classes are always full. We can even anticipate a new generation of customers: Plainsville's schoolchildren are required to participate in a program called Fitness for Life, which emphasizes the benefits of regular exercise at an early age."

（参考第9、88题）

Write a response in which you examine the stated and/or unstated assumptions of the argument. Be sure to explain how the argument depends on these assumptions and what the implications are for the argument if the assumptions prove unwarranted.

题目整理

论点 Health Naturally should open a store in Plainsville.

论据 (1) Health Naturally's previous experience has been that its stores are most profitable in areas where residents are highly concerned with leading healthy lives, and Plainsville clearly has many such residents.

(2) Plainsville merchants report that sales of running shoes and exercise equipment are at all-time highs.

(3) The local health club, which nearly closed five years ago due to lack of business, has more members than ever, and the weight-training and aerobics classes are always full.

(4) A new generation of customers is coming too: Plainsville's schoolchildren are required to participate in a program called Fitness for Life, which emphasizes the benefits of regular exercise at an early age.

论证方法

题目中论者主要运用了归纳推理论证法、引用权威论证法和列举特征式论证法。

分析提示

● 论据(1)运用了归纳推理论证法：即 Health Naturally 在那些居民注重健康生活的地区都赚到了钱，而 Plainsville 的居民看起来很注重健康，所以该公司在 Plainsville 开店也会赚到钱。

这里面的假设是：第一，论据(2)(3)(4)列举的特点都能够说明Plainsville地区的居民确实注重健康生活。其次，没有其他因素导致该地居民（即便他们果真都注重健康生活）不去购买Health Naturally销售的健康食品以及相关产品。我们在下面的分析中会看到，这些假设都是很成问题的。

- 论据(2)引用Plainsville当地商人说法，该地跑鞋以及运动服的销量达到了最高记录（all-time highs），并据此认为这说明当地居民很注重健康生活。这个判断首先要假设这些商人的观察是客观、可信的。其次，还要假设没有其他原因促使跑鞋和运动服销量的上升，比如，因为婴儿潮时期出生的孩子已进入青少年时期，他们普遍喜好运动，所以体育运动服饰的需求增大。或者因为一项全国或全球体育赛事的举行引发了该地区居民的体育运动热和购买运动服饰热等等。这些现象都不能说明该地区的居民都有了健康生活的习惯。再次，论据(2)还要假设销量的"all-time highs"是一种显著的上升。假如该地区的跑鞋和运动服的销量一向很低，比如每年也就是100多件，现在上升两倍，到了300件，这的确是个all-time high，但依然是个非常低的水平，并不足以信。

- 论据(3)提到健康俱乐部会员的增加以及举重和健身操训练班的爆满，并据此认为Plainsville的居民都注重健康生活，这是充满问题的假设。首先，这些健康俱乐部以及举重和健身操训练班到底能接收多少会员和学员？假如这些班吸纳的人员有限，就不能说明会员增加以及人员爆满。其次，论者还要假设，参加这些俱乐部以及训练班的人不是特定的人群，比如体重超常的人群。如果他们只是些急于减肥的人，就不能说明所有Plainsville的居民都在积极锻炼。

- 至于论据(4)，其假设的成分就更大了。该地区学龄儿童要参加Fitness For Life项目，这个项目强调the benefits of regular exercise at an early age。如果这些孩子如论者所说是Health Naturally潜在的消费人群，论者实际在假设：第一，这些孩子在总人口中占较大比例。其次，参加Fitness For Life项目会引发对Health Naturally所售产品的需求。第三，这些孩子对Health Naturally所售产品的需求不会随着年龄的增长而改变。

- 最后，即便论据(2)(3)(4)列举的特点都说明了Plainsville的居民确实注重健康生活，论者的结论要成立依然还要基于以下两个假设：第一，体育锻炼不足以满足人们对健康的需求，人们为了健康的生活还必须购买各种健康食品和相关产品。第二，没有其他竞争对手或者替代产品出现，一旦镇上的居民需要健康食品或相关产品，只能去买Health Naturally的产品。这个假设显然站不住脚。

91. Three years ago, because of flooding at the Western Palean Wildlife Preserve, 100 lions and 100 western gazelles were moved to the East Palean Preserve, an area that is home to most of the same species that are found in the western preserve, though in larger numbers, and to the eastern gazelle, a close relative of the western gazelle. The only difference in climate is that the eastern preserve typically has slightly less rainfall. Unfortunately, after three years in the eastern preserve, the imported western gazelle population has been virtually eliminated. Since the slight reduction in rainfall cannot be the cause of the virtual elimination of western gazelle, their disappearance must have been caused by the larger

number of predators in the eastern preserve.

Write a response in which you discuss what specific evidence is needed to evaluate the argument and explain how the evidence would weaken or strengthen the argument.

题目整理

论点 The virtual elimination of western gazelle must have been caused by the larger number of predators in the eastern preserve.

论据 (1) Three years ago, because of flooding at the Western Palean Wildlife Preserve, 100 lions and 100 western gazelles were moved to the East Palean Preserve, an area that is home to most of the same species that are found in the western preserve, though in larger numbers, and to the eastern gazelle, a close relative of the western gazelle. The only difference in climate is that the eastern preserve typically has slightly less rainfall. Unfortunately, after three years in the eastern preserve, the imported western gazelle population has been virtually eliminated.

(2) The slight reduction in rainfall cannot be the cause of the virtual elimination of western gazelle.

论证方法

题目中论者主要运用了列举特征式论证法。

分析提示

● 针对论据(1)，论者首先要提供进一步的证据来说明三年间东部瞪羚（the eastern gazelle）的数量发生了什么样的变化。因为如果西部瞪羚的数量如论者所言是遭东部保护区内过多的食肉动物（predators）猎食而急剧减少，作为西部瞪羚近亲的东部瞪羚也应该遭受同样的命运。如果只有西部瞪羚的数量急剧减少，到底是什么原因使得东部瞪羚得以存活？但这个关键信息被论者忽略了。

● 论者在论据(2)中排除了降水不足造成西部瞪羚数量减少的可能性，断言是东部保护区内过多的食肉动物造成了西部瞪羚的减少。但这实际上是个"虚假困境"的逻辑错误。因为很可能有这两种原因之外的其他因素造成了这一结果。比如，是否是西部瞪羚身上携带的病菌或寄生虫带给了它们灭顶之灾？是否是东部保护区这三年间气候和环境的变化使得西部瞪羚不适应那里的生存环境？是否是西部瞪羚身上所产生的特殊物质（如毛皮、角、香料等）很有价值，从而遭到人类的捕杀？等等，这些论者也未提及。

● 论者排除降雨是造成西部瞪羚数量减少原因的理由是：the rainfall reduction in the eastern preserve is slight。但slight是个非常模糊的描述。到底少到何种程度并未提及。假如正是降水量导致西部瞪羚赖以生存的一种水草在东部保护区无法生长而连年减少，西部瞪羚数量减少也并非意外。

● 即便迁移到东部保护区的100头狮子促使该区的食肉动物大增，致使这100只西部瞪羚被它们猎食。但随后这100头狮子怎样了呢？一个正常的情形应该是：这些狮子也应该随之大量死亡，因为它们的食物没有了。但论者依然没有提供相关信息。

92. Workers in the small town of Leeville take fewer sick days than workers in the large city of Masonton, 50 miles away. Moreover, relative to population size, the diagnosis of stress-related illness is proportionally much lower in Leeville than in Masonton. According to the Leeville Chamber of Commerce, these facts can be attributed to the health benefits of the relatively relaxed pace of life in Leeville.

（参考第101、103题）

Write a response in which you discuss one or more alternative explanations that could rival the proposed explanation and explain how your explanation(s) can plausibly account for the facts presented in the argument.

题目整理

论点 According to the Leeville Chamber of Commerce, these facts can be attributed to the health benefits of the relatively relaxed pace of life in Leeville.

论据 (1) Workers in the small town of Leeville take fewer sick days than workers in the large city of Masonton, 50 miles away.

(2) Moreover, relative to population size, the diagnosis of stress-related illness is proportionally much lower in Leeville than in Masonton.

论证方法

题目中论者主要运用了列举特征式论证法。

分析提示

● 论者认为是Leeville相对放松的生活节奏造成了论据(1)(2)列举的差别。但这显然只是诸多可能中的一种。至少还有下列四个更为合理的解释：

● 第一个可能的解释：两地不同的经济结构和产业形态造成了差别。一般而言，小城市的经济主要以手工作坊、初级加工制造、农牧业、旅游、零售和服务为主要产业形态。这些经济形态往往没有惨烈的竞争（cut-throat competition），其运作形态大多遵循传统习惯。这些产业从业者的工作和生活方式也就更为个人化和传统化一些，表现为生活节奏较慢。然而大城市却相反。那里的经济主要以大型高端制造业、金融服务业、文化创意、物流配送等等为支柱产业。每个产业里都汇集大量公司，彼此间竞争惨烈，产业参与者的生活节奏不是个人化、传统化的，而是全球化的。其结果必然是日常生活的快节奏和现代化。所以，论者在论据(1)(2)列举的差别反映的只是表象，而深层次的原因在于两地不同的经济结构和产业形态。

● 第二个可能的解释是：两地自然环境和社会环境使然。小城镇的空气和水源污染较轻，人们因为依然遵循传统的宁静而随遇而安（a life philosophy of living as it is）的生活方式，日常生活和工作中的肉体和精神压力自然就小些。而大都市则相反。人们穿梭在充斥着工业废气和汽车尾气的钢筋混凝土楼宇之中，嘴里咀嚼着由淀粉和蛋白质加上各种不知名的添加剂混合而成的快餐（fast food），路上、车上、梦中都在为自己的plans and projects and ambitions 而焦虑，因此两地出现论据(1)(2)列举的差别其实是再正常不过了。

- 第三个可能的解释是：心态（mentality）和观念（mind-set）。在小城镇的人们看来，这个世界的每一天差不多都是相同的。每天的差别只是体现在一页页的日历上，而不是在他们的心里和脸上。人们没有纠结、算计和无尽的渴望。身体不适了，就在家休息，因为那里的人们多是自己雇用自己，即便有用工合同，也多半是非正式的口头君子之约。疯子哪儿都有，但小镇居民普遍不知道什么 stress-related illness。与之相反，都市的人们渴望每天都是新的：新项目、新业绩、新升迁、新工作等。公众面前，每个人的表情和眼神是一样的冷漠、麻木、执著（或者说贪婪）；私底下，内心的纠结、算计和无尽的奢求将他们自我折磨成连自己都不认识的扭曲灵魂。其结果是：生（或者怀疑自己有）莫名其妙的病，经常请假，时常看心理医生，而这些所谓的病因多半是：压力。
- 第四个合理解释是上述三个方面的综合。当然读者也可以有其他独到的解释。

---

93. The following appeared in a memorandum from the manager of WWAC radio station.

"WWAC must change from its current rock-music format because the number of listeners has been declining, even though the population in our listening area has been growing. The population growth has resulted mainly from people moving to our area after their retirement, and we must make listeners of these new residents. But they seem to have limited interest in music: several local stores selling recorded music have recently closed. Therefore, just changing to another kind of music is not going to increase our audience. Instead, we should adopt a news-and-talk format, a form of radio that is increasingly popular in our area."

（参考第 17、109、110 题）

Write a response in which you discuss what questions would need to be answered in order to decide whether the recommendation and the argument on which it is based are reasonable. Be sure to explain how the answers to these questions would help to evaluate the recommendation.

题目整理

论点 WWAC radio station should change to a news-and-talk format.

论据 (1) WWAC must change from its current rock-music format. Its number of listeners has been declining, even though the population in our listening area has been growing. The population growth has resulted mainly from people moving to our area after their retirement, and we must make listeners of these new residents.

(2) But these new comers seem to have limited interest in music: several local stores selling recorded music have recently closed.

(3) News-and-talk format is a form of radio that is increasingly popular in our area.

论证方法

题目中论者主要运用了统计数据论证法、列举特征式论证法和类比论证法。

分析提示

● 首先，论据(1)提到，为了扭转听众人数下降的趋势，WWAC电台必须要改变其现在摇滚乐的风格。这里面显然是假设现行摇滚乐的风格是其听众数量下降的原因。那么问题就是：到底是什么原因导致该广播电台听众人数的下降？论者对此有没有客观、翔实、可信的调查研究？抑或论者只是在对原因作各种主观猜测？另外，论者还提到该广播电台覆盖区域的人口数量在增加，增加的部分主要是迁移来的离退休人员。这实际上是在引用统计数据进行论证。那么，这些增加的人口到底有多少？分别是什么样的职业和教育背景？他们的收入和经济状况、消费水平如何？等等。这些对评估这部分增加人口的广播收听倾向至关重要。

● 论据(2)是列举特征式论证法。论者说该电台本来要推出适合这部分新增人群趣味的音乐风格，但该地区几家录音制品店的倒闭显示这些人对音乐的兴趣不大。对这些模糊而又充满疑问的推论，我们的问题是：到底是什么导致了这几家录音制品店的倒闭？是这些新来的离退休人员拒绝购买，还是其他人群，比如年轻人，有其他获得音乐的方式，比如网上下载音乐，从而导致音像制品销量的下降？或者说是其他原因，比如经济不景气，当地人的总体收入水平、消费能力下降致使这些录音制品销量下滑呢？或者，那里的音像制品店数量是否过多，它们间存在过度竞争，纷纷杀价销售。那样的话，即便那部分新增人群前来购买，依然避免不了部分音像制品店要关张的现象。

● 在论据(3)中，论者说新闻和访谈的节目形式在该地区越来越受人欢迎，建议也采用这种形式。这是在把自己和本地区的其他电台进行类比，或者是在利用人们的从众心理进行推理。但问题是：WWAC电台和其他电台是否具有可比性？其他电台覆盖的人口结构、听众趣味、运营模式是否和WWAC有极大的不同？一旦采用了新闻和访谈的节目样式，是否会赶跑现有的观众？这些都是值得考虑的问题。

---

94. The vice president of human resources at Climpson Industries sent the following recommendation to the company's president.

"A recent national survey found that the majority of workers with access to the Internet at work had used company computers for personal or recreational activities, such as banking or playing games. In an effort to improve our employees' productivity, we should implement electronic monitoring of employees' Internet use from their workstations. Using electronic monitoring software is the best way to reduce the number of hours Climpson employees spend on personal or recreational activities. We predict that installing software to monitor employees' Internet use will allow us to prevent employees from wasting time, thereby increasing productivity and improving overall profits."

(参考第34、58题)

Write a response in which you discuss what questions would need to be answered in order to decide whether the prediction and the argument on which it is based are reasonable. Be sure to explain how the answers to these questions would help to evaluate the prediction.

题目整理

论点 We should implement electronic monitoring of employees' Internet use from their workstations to improve our employees' productivity.

论据 (1) A recent national survey found that the majority of workers with access to the Internet at work had used company computers for personal or recreational activities, such as banking or playing games.

(2) Using electronic monitoring software is the best way to reduce the number of hours Climpson employees spend on personal or recreational activities.

(3) We predict that installing software to monitor employees' Internet use will allow us to prevent employees from wasting time, thereby increasing productivity and improving overall profits.

论证方法

题目中论者主要运用了统计数据论证法和因果关系论证法。

分析提示

● 论据(1)引用的是一项全国调查。对于调查统计，我们首先要问：这项调查的方案设计（如调查样本的选择、调查问卷的设计、调查数据的处理、调查结果的核实和验证等等）和实施过程是否是严格按照科学程序进行的？其结论是否客观、中立？调查的实施者有没有受行业及其他利益相关方的影响？有没有关于同一问题的多个调查（比如来自政府机构的、来自官方和民间科研机构的）相互参照以掌握事实呢？其次，这项全国调查揭示的是全国范围内问题的整体情况，但这些问题是否也出现在 Climpson Industries 公司？即便出现了，问题有多严重？这些都是很大的疑问。

● 论据(2)中，论者在没有提供任何证据的情况下，断言用电子监控软件是防止员工浪费工作时间的最好办法。对这个判断，我们有以下的疑问：首先，在公司电脑上安装软件监控员工上网活动的做法是否合法？是否会侵犯员工的个人隐私？其次，公司员工是否有技术手段去反监控？第三，没有其他更好的办法来防止员工浪费工作时间？比如：教育员工注意自己的时间管理、改善业绩考核的方法、增强他们工作的荣誉感、在公司内部开展更丰富有趣的娱乐活动等也许都是不错的办法。

● 在论据(3)中，论者说对员工上网行为的监控可以 prevent employees from wasting time，进而达到 increasing productivity 和 improving overall profits 的目的。但问题是，首先，在员工的电脑上安装监控软件是否会在公司与员工之间制造不信任感，削弱员工对公司的归属感与忠诚度，造成人浮于事、工作效率降低（这实际会浪费更多的工作时间）？其次，在这样一个人人自危的工作环境里，员工还会关心生产率和公司的利润？第三，购买和安装监控软件以及随后的维护费用是否会很高，增加公司的运营成本？

....

95. The following appeared in a memo from the new vice president of Sartorian, a company that manufactures men's clothing.

"Five years ago, at a time when we had difficulty obtaining reliable supplies of high-quality wool fabric, we discontinued production of our popular alpaca overcoat. Now that we have a new fabric supplier, we should resume production. Given the outcry from our customers when we discontinued this product and the fact that none of our competitors offers a comparable product, we can expect pent-up consumer demand for our alpaca coats. This demand and the overall increase in clothing prices will make Sartorian's alpaca overcoats more profitable than ever before."

（参考第38、96题）

Write a response in which you examine the stated and/or unstated assumptions of the argument. Be sure to explain how the argument depends on these assumptions and what the implications are for the argument if the assumptions prove unwarranted.

题目整理

论点 论者的论点包括一个建议和一项推测。

We should resume production of our alpaca overcoat, which will be more profitable than ever before.

论据 (1) Five years ago, at a time when we had difficulty obtaining reliable supplies of high-quality wool fabric, we discontinued production of our popular alpaca overcoat, and now we have a new fabric supplier.

(2) Given the outcry from our customers when we discontinued this product and the fact that none of our competitors offers a comparable product, we can expect pent-up consumer demand for our alpaca coats.

(3) Considering the overall increase in clothing prices, our charges for alpaca overcoat can also be higher than five years ago.

论证方法

题目中论者主要运用了因果关系论证法和归纳推理论证法。

分析提示

● 论据(1)是个因果关系论证。论者提到，五年前 Sartorian 公司因为得不到可靠的高质量羊毛布料的供应而不得不停产 alpaca overcoat，现在他们有了一种新布料的供应商，于是建议恢复生产。但这里论者有以下假设：首先，要假设这种新布料可以满足恢复生产 alpaca overcoat 的要求。但论者并未讲明新布料就是过去的高质量羊毛布料还是可以替代过去的高质量羊毛布料的新产品。所以用这种新布料是否能生产出当年的 alpaca overcoat 尚存疑问。其次，即便用这种新布料完全可以生产出可与当年的 alpaca overcoat 相媲美的产品，论者还要假设这种布料是恢复生产 alpaca overcoat 的唯一决定因素。但五年间市场情况是否已经全然不同？生产这种新布料做成的 alpaca overcoat 是否需要购进新机器？员工是否需要重新培训？这些都是疑问。

● 论据(2)也是个因果关系论证，但论者列的两个原因都不支持"we can expect pent-up consumer demand for our alpaca coats"的结论。原因很简单，论者的这个推论实际是在假设：五年过去后，消费者依旧会喜欢 alpaca overcoat；其他的竞争对手没有生产与之类似的产品。但这尚是疑问。五年了，流行风尚不知道已经转了多少个轮回，当年的时尚也许早就被消费者淡忘了。论者至少应该提供消费者对 alpaca overcoat 的记忆以及消费倾向的调研报告以资判断。

● 论据(3)是个典型的归纳推理论证：因为五年来服装的整体价格上升了，所以 alpaca overcoat 肯定也能卖上好价钱。但正如在论据(2)分析过的，消费者也许不再喜欢 alpaca overcoat 了。其次，假如消费者仍喜欢 alpaca overcoat，他们也喜欢当前的流行时尚，论者期望的高利润还会出现吗？再次，即使现在 alpaca overcoat 在市场上依然抢手，但如果 Sartorian 公司的竞争对手迅速跟进，并造成市场供应的饱和，论者期望的高利润还是不会出现。

96. The following appeared in a memo from the new vice president of Sartorian, a company that manufactures men's clothing.

"Five years ago, at a time when we had difficulty obtaining reliable supplies of high-quality wool fabric, we discontinued production of our popular alpaca overcoat. Now that we have a new fabric supplier, we should resume production. Given the outcry from our customers when we discontinued this product and the fact that none of our competitors offers a comparable product, we can expect pent-up consumer demand for our alpaca coats. Due to this demand and the overall increase in clothing prices, we can predict that Sartorian's alpaca overcoats will be more profitable than ever before."

（参考第 38、95 题）

Write a response in which you discuss what questions would need to be answered in order to decide whether the prediction and the argument on which it is based are reasonable. Be sure to explain how the answers to these questions would help to evaluate the prediction.

题目整理

论点 论者的论点包括一个建议和一项推测。

We should resume production of our alpaca overcoat, which will be more profitable than ever before.

论据 (1) Five years ago, at a time when we had difficulty obtaining reliable supplies of high-quality wool fabric, we discontinued production of our popular alpaca overcoat, and now we have a new fabric supplier.

(2) Given the outcry from our customers when we discontinued this product and the fact that none of our competitors offers a comparable product, we can expect pent-up consumer demand for our alpaca coats.

(3) Considering the overall increase in clothing prices, our charges for alpaca overcoat can also be higher than five years ago.

论证方法

题目中论者主要运用了因果关系论证法和归纳推理论证法。

分析提示

- 论据(1)是个因果关系论证。论者提到，五年前Sartorian公司因为得不到可靠的高质量羊毛布料的供应而不得不停产alpaca overcoat，现在他们有了一种新布料的供应商，于是建议恢复生产。但问题是，这种新布料就是过去的高质量羊毛布料吗？或者，它是否可以完全替代过去的高质量羊毛布料？其次，即便用这种新布料可以生产出可与当年的alpaca overcoat相媲美的产品，这种新布料是恢复生产alpaca overcoat的唯一决定因素吗？五年间市场情况是否已经全然不同？生产这种新布料做成的alpaca overcoat是否需要购进新机器？员工是否需要重新培训？这些都是极为关键的疑问。

- 论据(2)也是个因果关系论证，但论者列的两个原因都未必支持"we can expect pent-up consumer demand for our alpaca coats"的结论。原因很简单：五年过去后，消费者依旧会喜欢alpaca overcoat吗？其他的竞争对手没有生产与之类似的产品？五年过去了，当年的时尚也许早就被消费者淡忘了。论者至少应该提供消费者对alpaca overcoat的记忆以及消费倾向的调研报告以资判断。

- 论据(3)是个典型的归纳推理：因为五年来服装的整体价格上升了，所以alpaca overcoat肯定也能卖上好价钱。但正如在论据(2)分析过的，消费者也许不再喜欢alpaca overcoat了。其次，假如消费者仍喜欢alpaca overcoat，他们也喜欢当前的流行时尚，论者期望的高利润还会出现吗？再次，即使alpaca overcoat在市场上依旧抢手，但如果Sartorian公司的竞争对手迅速跟进，并造成市场供应的饱和，论者期望的高利润依然不会出现。

---

97. The following appeared in an e-mail sent by the marketing director of the Classical Shakespeare Theater of Bardville.

"Over the past ten years, there has been a 20 percent decline in the size of the average audience at Classical Shakespeare Theater productions. In spite of increased advertising, we are attracting fewer and fewer people to our shows, causing our profits to decrease significantly. We must take action to attract new audience members. The best way to do so is by instituting a 'Shakespeare in the Park' program this summer. Two years ago the nearby Avon Repertory Company started a 'Free Plays in the Park' program, and its profits have increased 10 percent since then. If we start a 'Shakespeare in the Park' program, we can predict that our profits will increase, too."

Write a response in which you discuss what questions would need to be answered in order to decide whether the recommendation is likely to have the predicted result. Be sure to explain how the answers to these questions would help to evaluate the recommendation.

题目整理

论点 Instituting a 'Shakespeare in the Park' program this summer is the best way to attract new audience members.

论据 (1) Over the past ten years, there has been a 20 percent decline in the size of the average audience at Classical Shakespeare Theater productions. In spite of increased advertising, we are attracting fewer and fewer people to our shows, causing our profits to decrease significantly.

(2) Two years ago the nearby Avon Repertory Company started a 'Free Plays in the Park' program, and its profits have increased 10 percent since then. If we start a 'Shakespeare in the Park' program, we can predict that our profits will increase, too.

论证方法

题目中论者主要运用了统计数据论证法和类比论证法。

分析提示

● 论据(1)引用了统计数据来论证。我们的问题是：这些数据如何得来？是论者的推测、观察，还是专业的市场调查机构测算的结果？有没有多个数据用来相互参照？论者有没有出于自己部门利益的考虑，而夸大或歪曲部分数据的可能？这些问题事关论者所谈问题性质的判断，必须要有客观、准确的资料。其次，整个戏剧演出市场在这十年间的变化如何？假如十年来，整个戏剧演出市场萎缩了30%以上，那么，the Classical Shakespeare Theater of Bardville 出现的问题实际上是个正常现象。如果是这样的话，论者就要考虑整个戏剧演出市场是否能够改观、如何影响这个市场、戏剧演出这个行当是否还有前景等更为宏观的问题。因为一家公司实际很难改变一个行业的变化轨迹。但假如整个戏剧演出市场十年来蓬勃发展，营业收入和净利润都翻了数倍，该公司就要考虑是否是自己的营业模式、发展策略等出了问题了。只有在这个前提之下，余下的讨论才有意义。同样道理，论者假如能提供与其具有可比性的另外几家剧院十年来的经营变化，也非常有利于此问题的探讨。

● 论据(2)是个类比论证。论者认为如果模仿两年前邻近一家剧院所做的市场推广措施，也应该能够收到与其类似的效果。但问题是：这两家剧院是否具有可比性？它们的目标观众类似吗？它们所在地方的经济发展水平相仿吗？两地观众的消费能力差别大吗？等等。其次，Avon Repertory Company 两年来实现的10%的利润增长是那个 Free Plays in the Park program 带来的吗？如果这家剧院所在地的其他剧院两年来的利润增长都在10%到20%之间，那么其所实现的10%的利润增长实际上是个很一般的水平，很可能同 Free Plays in the Park program 没有关系。

● 最后，论者在结论中断言，这个夏天实施他建议的 Shakespeare in the Park program this summer 是吸引新观众的最好办法，这等于否定了其他所有的办法。从常识上讲，调整演出剧目、提高演员水平、改进舞台声光布景效果、培育潜在戏剧市场等等，都是可考虑的方案。

....

98. The following is a recommendation from the business manager of Monarch Books.

"Since its opening in Collegeville twenty years ago, Monarch Books has developed a large customer base due to its reader-friendly atmosphere and wide selection of books on all subjects. Last month, Book and Bean, a combination bookstore and coffee shop, announced its intention to open a Collegeville store. Monarch Books should open its own in-store café in the space currently devoted to children's books. Given recent national census data indicating a significant decline in the percentage of the population under age ten, sales of children's books are likely to decline. By replacing its children's books section with a café, Monarch Books can increase profits and ward off competition from Book and Bean."

（参考第7、99题）

Write a response in which you examine the stated and/or unstated assumptions of the argument. Be sure to explain how the argument depends on these assumptions and what the implications are for the argument if the assumptions prove unwarranted.

题目整理

论点 Monarch Books should open its own in-store café in the space currently devoted to children's books.

论据 (1) Since its opening in Collegeville twenty years ago, Monarch Books has developed a large customer base due to its reader-friendly atmosphere and wide selection of books on all subjects. Last month, Book and Bean, a combination bookstore and coffee shop, announced its intention to open a Collegeville store.

(2) Given recent national census data indicating a significant decline in the percentage of the population under age ten, sales of children's books are likely to decline.

(3) By replacing its children's books section with a café, Monarch Books can increase profits and ward off competition from Book and Bean.

论证方法

题目中论者主要运用了类比论证法和因果关系论证法。

分析提示

● 论据(1)是个类比论证。Book and Bean计划要将其独具特色的书店和咖啡馆一体店开到 Collegeville，论者认为也应该在其原本只卖图书的Collegeville店内开上咖啡馆以便同Book and Bean竞争。这里面有以下假设：第一，Book and Bean在Collegeville的开店计划肯定会成功实施。第二，一旦Book and Bean在Collegeville开了店，会对Monarch Books店构成巨大威胁。第三，如果Monarch Books不在书店内开咖啡馆，在同Book and Bean即将开张的书店的竞争中，它肯定落败。

● 论据(2)的成立需要以下假设：首先，总人口中十岁以下的儿童所占百分比的缩小，就必然导致十岁以下儿童的绝对数量的减少。这显然不一定。很可能这个年龄段儿童的绝对数量仍在稳定增加，只是其他年龄段的人口（比如30至40岁之间或者60岁以上的人口）增加过快才造成十岁以下儿童在总人口中所占比例的下降。其次，论者要假设，如果十岁以下儿童的比例和绝对数量都在减少，儿童读物的需求量必然下降。但这也未必。儿童数量降低了，但其购买力不是必然下降。再次，论者还要假设，即便儿童读物的销量下降，这些图书不会因为其价格的上升，反而带来更大的销售额和利润。这也可能不成立。常识告诉我们，图书是越来越贵的。通过做精品图书（或者简单地提高图书价格），销量降少的图书仍然可以带来较多的销售收入。

● 论据(3)需要以下两个假设：第一，如果撤掉儿童图书区，Monarch的一个传统优势（也就是its wide selection of books on all subjects）不会因此而削弱，从而影响读者前来购书的愿望。第二，假如Monarch在书店里开了咖啡馆，各种饮料和食品的气味、可能的纷乱嘈杂不会令一些购书顾客不快。否则，论者期望的increase profits and ward off competition from Book and Bean很难实现。

· ·

99. The following is a recommendation from the business manager of Monarch Books.

"Since its opening in Collegeville twenty years ago, Monarch Books has developed a large customer base due to its reader-friendly atmosphere and wide selection of books on all subjects. Last month, Book and Bean, a combination bookstore and coffee shop, announced its intention to open a Collegeville store. Monarch Books should open its own in-store café in the space currently devoted to children's books. Given recent national census data indicating a significant decline in the percentage of the population under age ten, sales of children's books are likely to decline. By replacing its children's books section with a café, Monarch Books can increase profits and ward off competition from Book and Bean."

（参考第7、98题）

Write a response in which you discuss what specific evidence is needed to evaluate the argument and explain how the evidence would weaken or strengthen the argument.

题目整理

论点 Monarch Books should open its own in-store café in the space currently devoted to children's books.

论据 (1) Since its opening in Collegeville twenty years ago, Monarch Books has developed a large customer base due to its reader-friendly atmosphere and wide selection of books on all subjects. Last month, Book and Bean, a combination bookstore and coffee shop, announced its intention to open a Collegeville store.

(2) Given recent national census data indicating a significant decline in the percentage of the population under age ten, sales of children's books are likely to decline.

(3) By replacing its children's books section with a café, Monarch Books can increase profits and ward off competition from Book and Bean.

论证方法

题目中论者主要运用了类比论证法和因果关系论证法。

分析提示

● 论据(1)是个类比论证。Book and Bean计划要将其独具特色的书店咖啡馆一体店开到Collegeville，论者认为也应该在其原本只卖图书的Collegeville店内开上咖啡馆以便同Book and Bean竞争。论者需要以下三方面的信息：第一，Book and Bean在Collegeville的开店计划最终肯定会成功实施吗？第二，一旦Book and Bean在Collegeville开了店，果真会对Monarch Books店构成巨大威胁？第三，如果Monarch Books不在书店内开咖啡馆，在同Book and Bean即将开张的书店的竞争中，它肯定落败吗？

● 论据(2)是个因果论证。但论者需要对以下的关键信息作进一步的说明：首先，总人口中十岁以下的儿童所占百分比的缩小，是否就必然意味着十岁以下儿童的绝对数量的减少？这显然不一定。很可能这个年龄段儿童的绝对数量仍在稳定增加，只是其他年龄段的人口（比如30至40岁之间或者60岁以上的人口）增加过快才造成十岁以下儿童在总人口中所占比例的下降。其次，即便十岁以下的儿童的比例和绝对数量在减少，儿童读物的需求量就必然下降吗？这也未必。数量降低的儿童购买的童书有可能会更多。再次，即便儿童读物销量出现下降，这些图书会不会因为其价格的上升，反而能带来更大的销售额和利润呢？这极有可能。常识告诉我们，图书是越来越贵的。通过做精品图书（或者简单地提高图书价格），销量降少的图书仍然可以带来较多的销售收入。

● 论据(3)依然是个因果论证。但论者需要解释以下疑问：第一，如果撤掉儿童图书区，Monarch 的一个传统优势（也就是 its wide selection of books on all subjects）会不会因此而削弱，从而影响读者前来购书的愿望？第二，假如 Monarch 在书店里开了咖啡馆，各种饮料和食品的气味、可能的纷乱嘈杂是否会令一些购书顾客不快。如果是这样，论者的推论（By replacing its children's books section with a café, Monarch Books can increase profits and ward off competition from Book and Bean）就很难实现。

---

100. The following was written as a part of an application for a small-business loan by a group of developers in the city of Monroe.

"Jazz music is extremely popular in the city of Monroe: over 100,000 people attended Monroe's annual jazz festival last summer, and the highest-rated radio program in Monroe is 'Jazz Nightly,' which airs every weeknight. Also, a number of well-known jazz musicians own homes in Monroe. Nevertheless, the nearest jazz club is over an hour away. Given the popularity of jazz in Monroe and a recent nationwide study indicating that the typical jazz fan spends close to $1,000 per year on jazz entertainment, a jazz music club in Monroe would be tremendously profitable."

（参考第25、102、164题）

Write a response in which you examine the stated and/or unstated assumptions of the argument. Be sure to explain how the argument depends on these assumptions and what the implications are for the argument if the assumptions prove unwarranted.

题目整理

论点 A jazz music club in Monroe would be tremendously profitable.

论据 (1) Jazz music is extremely popular in the city of Monroe: over 100,000 people attended Monroe's annual jazz festival last summer, and the highest-rated radio program in Monroe is 'Jazz Nightly,' which airs every weeknight. Also, a number of well-known jazz musicians own homes in Monroe.

(2) Nevertheless, the nearest jazz club is over an hour away.

(3) A recent nationwide study indicates that a typical jazz fan spends close to $1,000 per year on jazz entertainment

论证方法

题目中论者运用了列举特征式论证法、诉诸常识法和统计数据论证法。

分析提示

● 论据(1)运用了列举特征式的论证方式，力图说明Jazz is extremely popular in the city of Monroe。但论者的推论需要假设：首先，对"over 100,000 people attended Monroe's annual jazz festival last summer"这个事实，论者要假设10万人次的规模同往年比是个较高的水平。如果往年的参加人数都是15万以上，去年的人数虽说听起来依然壮观，但实际却是下降的趋势。其次，论者要假设每年参与爵士乐音乐节的人绝大多数都来自本地。否则，在Monroe本地成立爵士乐俱乐部难以聚拢人气。其三，对于论者所提"a number of well-known jazz musicians own homes in Monroe"的现象，论者要假设这些音乐家在Monroe拥有住房，完全是因为要在Monroe搞爵士乐，而不是出于其他的考虑。第四，对于"the highest-rated radio program in Monroe is 'Jazz Nightly,' which airs every weeknight"同样说明不了什么。如果所有其他节目都很差呢？所以即便Jazz Nightly在人们的评价中名列第一，也未必说明当地人很喜欢爵士乐。

● 论据(2)是在利用人们的常识展开论证：其他条件相同的情况下，有谁会舍近求远呢？但论者的推论实际上在假设：第一，这家计划中的爵士乐俱乐部具备足够的吸引力，能将本地的爵士乐爱好者留在本地。第二，那些热衷爵士乐的人会因为一个小时的路程放弃附近的爵士乐俱乐部。

● 论据(3)是个统计数据论证。首先，论者要假设：这项研究的方案设计（如调查样本的选择、调查问卷的设计、调查数据的处理、调查结果的核实和验证等等）和实施过程是严格按照科学程序进行的；其结论是客观、中立、可信的；调查的实施者没有受行业及其他利益相关方的影响。其次，他还要假设没有一些特殊因素影响Monroe的爵士乐爱好者的消费习惯。论者提到的调查是一个nationwide study。一个全国的典型指标对一个具体的地方来说，可能没有任何意义。Monroe的消费水平如何、该地区爵士乐爱好者是否愿意为这项娱乐花钱、他们是习惯自我娱乐还是去俱乐部消费，等等这些都会左右他们在音乐方面的消费支出。

101. There is now evidence that the relaxed pace of life in small towns promotes better health and greater longevity than does the hectic pace of life in big cities. Businesses in the small town of Leeville report fewer days of sick leave taken by individual workers than do businesses in the nearby large city of Masonton. Furthermore, Leeville has only one physician for its one thousand residents, but in Masonton the proportion of physicians to residents is five times as high. Finally, the average age of Leeville residents is significantly higher than that of Masonton residents. These findings suggest that people seeking longer and healthier lives should consider moving to small communities.

（参考第92、103题）

Write a response in which you examine the stated and/or unstated assumptions of the argument. Be sure to explain how the argument depends on these assumptions and what the implications are for the argument if the assumptions prove unwarranted.

题目整理

论点 There is now evidence that the relaxed pace of life in small towns promotes better health and greater longevity than does the hectic pace of life in big cities. Therefore, people seeking longer and healthier lives should consider moving to small communities.

论据 (1) Businesses in the small town of Leeville report fewer days of sick leave taken by individual workers than do businesses in the nearby large city of Masonton.

(2) Furthermore, Leeville has only one physician for its one thousand residents, but in Masonton the proportion of physicians to residents is five times as high.

(3) Finally, the average age of Leeville residents is significantly higher than that of Masonton residents.

论证方法

题目中论者主要运用了列举特征式论证法和归纳推理论证法。

分析提示

● 论者整体的论证结构是：首先用论据(1)(2)(3)来展示Leeville小镇上的居民和大都市Masonton的居民三方面的差异，然后假设：第一，假设该三方面的差异足以说明Leeville的居民比Masonton的居民更健康长寿。第二，假设是两个城市不同的生活节奏而不是其他原因造成了这三方面的差异。但这两个假设都不成立。

● 论据(1)(2)(3)未必就能说明Leeville的居民比Masonton的居民更健康长寿。首先，论据(1)提到的Leeville小镇上的公司员工请假次数比邻近大城市Masonton的公司员工少这一现象，这很可能不是因为前者比后者健康，而是因为那里的公司规模较小、管理比较松散。所以，如果公司员工身体偶有不适需要在家休息，他们一般不用很正式地请假。其次，论据(2)所说的Leeville的每千人平均内科医生的数量比Masonton少很多这一现象，也未必能说明前者的居民健康就比后者好。很可能是因为那里的生活设施不方便、交通偏僻、收入较低，因而大夫都不愿意去那里工作。至于论据(3)提到的现象，很可能是那里特殊的人口结构造成的：那里的青壮年都外出工作或生活了，剩下的多是离退休的老年人在那里颐养天年。这完全不是因为那里的人更长寿。

● 造成两地三方面差异的未必是论者所说的生活节奏（the pace of life），完全可能是其他原因，比如：两地不同的经济结构和产业、不同的自然和社会环境和两地居民不同的心态和观念。**关于这一部分的具体分析请参见第92或103道题。**

● 最后，即便论者列举的两个城市三方面的差异确实能说明Leeville的居民普遍比Masonton的居民健康长寿，并且导致差异的原因的确就是两地不同的生活节奏，论者的结论（The relaxed pace of life in small towns promotes better health and greater longevity than does the hectic pace of life in big cities, and therefore, people seeking longer and healthier lives should consider moving to small communities）依然成问题。因为论者仅仅用一大一小两个城市的比较就作出一般性的概括，有以偏概全的嫌疑。

---

102. The following was written as a part of an application for a small-business loan by a group of developers in the city of Monroe.

"Jazz music is extremely popular in the city of Monroe: over 100,000 people attended Monroe's annual jazz festival last summer, and the highest-rated radio program in Monroe is 'Jazz Nightly,' which airs every weeknight. Also, a number of well-known jazz musicians own homes in Monroe. Nevertheless, the nearest jazz club is over an hour away. Given the popularity of jazz in Monroe and a recent nationwide study indicating that the typical jazz fan spends close to $1,000 per year on jazz entertainment, we predict that our new jazz music club in Monroe will be a tremendously profitable enterprise."

（参考第25、100、164题）

Write a response in which you discuss what questions would need to be answered in order to decide whether the prediction and the argument on which it is based are reasonable. Be sure to explain how the answers to these questions would help to evaluate the prediction.

题目整理

论点 Our new jazz music club in Monroe will be a tremendously profitable enterprise.

论据 (1) Jazz music is extremely popular in the city of Monroe: over 100,000 people attended Monroe's annual jazz festival last summer, and the highest-rated radio program in Monroe is 'Jazz Nightly,' which airs every weeknight. Also, a number of well-known jazz musicians own homes in Monroe.

(2) Nevertheless, the nearest jazz club is over an hour away.

(3) A recent nationwide study indicates that a typical jazz fan spends close to $1,000 per year on jazz entertainment

论证方法

题目中论者运用了列举特征式论证法、诉诸常识法和统计数据论证法。

分析提示

● 论据(1)是个列举特征式论证法，论者力图说明Jazz is extremely popular in the city of Monroe。但下列疑问需要回答：首先，论者说有10万多人参加了去年夏天Monroe爵士乐音乐节，这里的over 100,000同往年相比是个什么样的水平？如果往年的参加人数都是15万以上，去年的人数虽说依然壮观，但实际却是下降的趋势。其次，每年参与这个爵士乐音乐节的人是否绝大多数都来自本地？如果那些人多数都是来自外地的话，在Monroe本地成立一个爵士乐俱乐部难以聚拢人气。其三，论者说有许多著名音乐家在Monroe都有家，那么这些音乐家是因为要在Monroe搞爵士乐，还是出于其他的考虑？如果他们住在Monroe仅仅是因为那里风景怡人，则论者推论的说服力就大大减弱了。第四，至于论者说的the highest-rated radio program in Monroe is 'Jazz Nightly,' which airs every weeknight，我们要问的是：是否所有其他节目在听众中的口碑都很差？如此的话，即便Jazz Nightly在人们的评价中名列第一，也未必能说明当地人很喜欢它。

● 论据(2)是在利用人们的常识展开论证：其他条件相同的情况下，有谁会舍近求远呢？但问题是：第一，这家计划中的爵士乐俱乐部具备足够的吸引力将本地的爵士乐爱好者留在本地吗？第二，那些热衷爵士乐的人会因为一个小时的路程就放弃附近的爵士乐俱乐部吗？

● 论据(3)是个统计数据论证。但是，这项研究的方案设计（如调查样本的选择、调查问卷的设计、调查数据的处理、调查结果的核实和验证等等）和实施过程是否是严格按照科学程序进行的？其结论是客观、中立的吗？调查的实施者没有受行业及其他利益相关方的影响？其次，有没有一些特殊因素影响Monroe的爵士乐爱好者的消费习惯？论者说的调查是一个nationwide study。一个全国的典型指标对一个具体的地方来说，可能没有任何意义。Monroe的消费水平如何、该地区的爵士乐爱好者是否愿意为这项娱乐花钱、他们是习惯自我娱乐还是去俱乐部消费，这些都会左右他们在爵士乐方面的消费支出。

---

103. There is now evidence that the relaxed pace of life in small towns promotes better health and greater longevity than does the hectic pace of life in big cities. Businesses in the small town of Leeville report fewer days of sick leave taken by individual workers than do businesses in the nearby large city of Masonton. Furthermore, Leeville has only one physician for its one thousand residents, but in Masonton the proportion of physicians to residents is five times as high. Finally, the average age of Leeville residents is significantly higher than that of Masonton residents. These findings suggest that the relaxed pace of life in Leeville allows residents to live longer, healthier lives.

（参考第92、101题）

Write a response in which you discuss one or more alternative explanations that could rival the proposed explanation and explain how your explanation(s) can plausibly account for the facts presented in the argument.

题目整理

论点 The relaxed pace of life in Leeville allows residents to live longer, healthier lives.

论据 (1) Businesses in the small town of Leeville report fewer days of sick leave taken by individual workers than do businesses in the nearby large city of Masonton.

(2) Furthermore, Leeville has only one physician for its one thousand residents, but in Masonton the proportion of physicians to residents is five times as high.

(3) Finally, the average age of Leeville residents is significantly higher than that of Masonton residents.

论证方法

题目中论者主要运用了列举特征式论证法。

分析提示

● 论者认为是Leeville缓慢的生活节奏造成了论据(1)(2)(3)列举的差别。但这显然只是诸多可能中的一种。至少还有下列四个更为合理的解释：

● 第一个可能的解释：两地不同的经济结构和产业形态造成了差别。因为小城市的经济一般以手工作坊、初级加工制造、农牧业、旅游和零售为主要产业形态。这些经济形态往往没有惨烈的竞争，其运作形态大多遵循传统习惯。因此这些产业从业者的工作和生活节奏就较慢一些。这种经济结构和产业形态带来的结果就是：生病少、健康长寿。然而大城市却相反。那里的经济主要以大型高端制造业、金融服务业、文化创意、电子电气和物流配送等为支柱产业。每个产业里面都汇集大量的公司，之间竞争惨烈，产业参与者的生活是快节奏和现代化，而在生活上常表现为：常生病、生怪病、多挣了钱却短了寿命。所以，论者在论据(1)(2)(3)列举的差别反映的其实是表象，而真正深层次的原因是两地不同的经济结构和产业形态。

● 第二个可能的解释是：两地的自然和社会环境使然。小城镇的空气、水源污染较轻，人们的生活宁静而随遇而安，生活和工作上的压力自然就小些。而大都市则相反，人们穿梭在充斥着工业废气和汽车尾气的钢筋混凝土的楼宇之中，嘴巴里咀嚼着由淀粉和蛋白质加上各种添加剂混合而成的快餐，因此两地出现论据(1)(2)(3)列举的差别是很正常的。

● 第三个可能的解释是：心态和观念。在小城镇的人们看来，这个世界的每一天差不多都是相同的。每天的差别只是体现在一页页的日历上，而不是在他们的心里和脸上。人们没有纠结、算计和无尽的渴望。身体不适了，就在家休息。与之相反，都市的人们渴望每天都是新的：新项目、新业绩、新升迁、新工作等。公众面前，每个人的表情和眼神是一样的冷漠、麻木、执著（或者说贪婪）；私底下，内心的纠结、算计和无尽的奢求将他们自我折磨成连自己都不认识的扭曲灵魂。其结果是：生病，经常请假，或看心理医生，而这些个病因多半是压力。

● 第四个合理解释是上述三个方面的综合。当然读者也可以有自己独到的解释。

---

104. The following appeared in a memo from a vice president of a manufacturing company.

"During the past year, workers at our newly opened factory reported 30 percent more on-the-job accidents than workers at nearby Panoply Industries. Panoply produces products very similar to those produced at our factory, but its work shifts are one hour shorter than ours. Experts say that fatigue and sleep deprivation among workers are significant contributing factors in many on-the-job accidents. Panoply's superior safety record can therefore be attributed to its shorter work shifts, which allow its employees to get adequate amounts of rest."

（参考第32、105、106、167题）

Write a response in which you discuss one or more alternative explanations that could rival the proposed explanation and explain how your explanation(s) can plausibly account for the facts presented in the argument.

题目整理

论点 Panoply's superior safety record can therefore be attributed to its shorter work shifts, which allow its employees to get adequate amounts of rest.

论据 (1) During the past year, workers at our newly opened factory reported 30 percent more on-the-job accidents than workers at nearby Panoply Industries.

(2) Panoply produces products very similar to those produced at our factory, but its work shifts are one hour shorter than ours.

(3) Experts say that fatigue and sleep deprivation among workers are significant contributing factors in many on-the-job accidents.

论证方法

题目中论者主要运用了类比论证法和引用权威论证法。

分析提示

● 论者运用类比和引用权威两种论证方法，作出推论：Panoply Industries公司员工上班时间比论者所在公司员工的上班时间少一个小时，因此该公司生产中发生事故的频率高。论者犯了将同时发生的两件事情解释为因果关系的错误。工作时间长未必就会导致生产中事故的发生，很可能有其他更合理的解释，比如：两家公司生产设备的自动化和人性化程度、员工工作时安全保护措施是否充分、员工是否严格遵守车间安全流程的要求、工厂安全巡检是否严格、员工的工作情绪以及工作压力的大小等等。下面就从其中的三个方面来展开分析：

● 第一，两家公司生产设备的自动化和人性化程度的不同是导致差别的原因。如论者所说，两家公司生产的产品类似，但工作中的事故发生率相差悬殊。但假如Panoply Industries公司采用的生产设备要比论者所在公司的设备先进得多，表现为高度的自动化、人性化和操作的简便化，以及更为细致周到的事故自动纠正和防护能力，那么，差异就很好解释了。有了这样的设备，即便员工偶尔因为疲劳和注意力不集中而出现操作失误，发生事故的几率也会大大降低，更何况Panoply Industries公司还采取了缩短各班次工作时间长度以利于员工休息这样的人性化的管理措施了呢？

● 第二，两家公司对车间生产安全措施的监督和执行的严格程度的不同导致了差异。一般而言，政府和民间机构（比如产业协会或行业协会）对工厂的安全生产流程都有强制性的要求。我们较为熟知的诸如ISO9000等就是具有国际规范的产品生产、产品质量和管理流程的执行标准。企业只要严格实施这些标准，不仅产品质量有保证，生产事故也会大大降低。但事实上，当前发生的很多事故与生产技术没太大关系，问题主要出在对安全生产标准的监督和执行太随意。

● 第三，员工的管理很可能是导致差别的原因。这一点很好理解。现在几乎所有的公司都强调公司架构扁平化（flattened corporate structure）和公司管理的人性化（humanized management）。主要原因是为了要增强公司管理层和员工之间关系的融洽度，使员工工作时能保持积极、饱满、稳定的情绪状态，注意力能高度集中。一个在状态（a worker in a positive and proactive work mood）和一个不在状态的员工，其工作效率是不一样的，因此前者出现生产事故的几率会比后者也要小得多。

105. The following appeared in a memo from the vice president of Butler Manufacturing.

"During the past year, workers at Butler Manufacturing reported 30 percent more on-the-job accidents than workers at nearby Panoply Industries, where the work shifts are one hour shorter than ours. A recent government study reports that fatigue and sleep deprivation among workers are significant contributing factors in many on-the-job accidents. If we shorten each of our work shifts by one hour, we can improve Butler Manufacturing's safety record by ensuring that our employees are adequately rested."

（参考第32、104、106、167题）

Write a response in which you discuss what specific evidence is needed to evaluate the argument and explain how the evidence would weaken or strengthen the argument.

题目整理

论点 If we shorten each of our work shifts by one hour, we can improve Butler Manufacturing's safety record by ensuring that our employees are adequately rested.

论据 (1) During the past year, workers at Butler Manufacturing reported 30 percent more on-the-job accidents than workers at nearby Panoply Industries, where the work shifts are one hour shorter than ours.

(2) A recent government study reports that fatigue and sleep deprivation among workers are significant contributing factors in many on-the-job accidents.

论证方法

题目中论者主要运用了类比论证法和统计数据论证法。

分析提示

● 论据(1)在两家公司间进行了类比论证。论者显然把Panoply Industries公司员工上班时间比Butler Manufacturing公司员工少一个小时解释为该公司生产事故频发的原因。论者在这里犯了将同时发生的两件事情解释为因果关系的逻辑错误。我们需要进一步的资料来证明：首先，Butler公司的工人如实地报告了生产事故的次数。否则，无论是谎报还是瞒报，都会使余下的全部推论变得极不可靠。其次，不是别的因素导致了这一结果。实际上，诸如两家公司生产设备的自动化和人性化程度的不同、员工工作时安全保护措施是否充分、员工是否严格遵守车间安全流程的要求、工厂安全巡检是否严格、员工的工作情绪以及工作压力的大小等都有可能导致两家公司生产事故发生率的差异。

● 论据(2)运用了统计数据论证法。对于这个研究报告的结论，首先，我们需要有资料来证明：这项研究的方案设计（如调查样本的选择、调查问卷的设计、调查数据的处理、调查结果的核实和验证等等）和实施过程是严格按照科学程序进行的；调查的实施者没有受行业及其他利益相关方的影响；有其他的独立第三方（比如行业协会、学术机构等）的相关数据给予佐证等。其次，即便这个官方报告的结论可信，但这个报告得出的结论是否适用Butler公司依然是个问题。

● 在结论中，论者建议 Butler Manufacturing 公司给每个班次都减少一个小时的上班时间，让员工得到充分的休息，以达到减少生产事故的目的。但这个建议若要落实，论者须至少提供两方面的资料：首先，员工是否会将这增加的一个小时的休息时间真正用来休息，而不干别的事情。其次，其他可能导致生产事故的潜在因素是否都消除了。

---

106. The following appeared in a memo from the Board of Directors of Butler Manufacturing.

"During the past year, workers at Butler Manufacturing reported 30 percent more on-the-job accidents than workers at nearby Panoply Industries, where the work shifts are one hour shorter than ours. A recent government study reports that fatigue and sleep deprivation among workers are significant contributing factors in many on-the-job accidents. Therefore, we recommend that Butler Manufacturing shorten each of its work shifts by one hour. Shorter shifts will allow Butler to improve its safety record by ensuring that its employees are adequately rested."

（参考第32、104、105、167题）

Write a response in which you discuss what questions would need to be answered in order to decide whether the recommendation is likely to have the predicted result. Be sure to explain how the answers to these questions would help to evaluate the recommendation.

题目整理

论点 论者的论点包括一项建议和一个预测。

We recommend that Butler Manufacturing shorten each of its work shifts by one hour.

Shorter shifts will allow Butler to improve its safety record by ensuring that its employees are adequately rested.

论据 (1) During the past year, workers at Butler Manufacturing reported 30 percent more on-the-job accidents than workers at nearby Panoply Industries, where the work shifts are one hour shorter than ours.

(2) A recent government study reports that fatigue and sleep deprivation among workers are significant contributing factors in many on-the-job accidents.

论证方法

题目中论者主要运用了类比论证法和统计数据论证法。

分析提示

● 论据(1)在两家公司间进行了类比论证。论者显然把 Panoply Industries 公司员工上班时间比 Butler Manufacturing 公司员工少一个小时解释为该公司生产事故频发的原因。我们的问题是：首先，Butler 公司的工人是否如实地报告了生产事故发生的次数？否则，无论是谎报还是瞒报，都会使余下的全部推论变得极不可靠。其次，是否有别的因素导致了这一结果？实际上，两家公司生产设备的自动化和人性化程度的不同、员工工作时安全保护措施是否充分、员工是否严格遵守车间安全流程的要求、工厂安全巡检是否严格、员工的工作情绪以及工作压力的大小等都可能导致两家公司生产事故发生率的差异。

● 论据(2)属于统计数据论证法。对于这个研究报告的结论，首先，我们的疑问是：这项研究的方案设计（如调查样本的选择、调查问卷的设计、调查数据的处理、调查结果的核实和验证等等）和实施过程是否是严格按照科学程序进行的？调查的实施者有没有受行业及其他利益相关方的影响？有没有独立第三方（比如行业协会、学术机构等）的相关数据与结论对该政府报告的结论予以佐证？等等。其次，即便这个官方报告的结论可信，这个报告得出的结论是否适用Butler公司？这依然是个问题。

● 在结论中，论者建议Butler Manufacturing公司给每个班次都减少一个小时的上班时间，以达到员工得到充分休息、减少班上事故的目的。但问题是：首先，员工是否会将这增加的一个小时的休息时间用来休息，而不干别的事情？其次，其他易引发生产事故的潜在因素是否都消除了？

---

107. The following appeared in a memo from the business manager of a chain of cheese stores located throughout the United States.

"For many years all the stores in our chain have stocked a wide variety of both domestic and imported cheeses. Last year, however, all of the five best-selling cheeses at our newest store were domestic cheddar cheeses from Wisconsin. Furthermore, a recent survey by Cheeses of the World magazine indicates an increasing preference for domestic cheeses among its subscribers. Since our company can reduce expenses by limiting inventory, the best way to improve profits in all of our stores is to discontinue stocking many of our varieties of imported cheese and concentrate primarily on domestic cheeses."

（参考第66、108题）

Write a response in which you examine the stated and/or unstated assumptions of the argument. Be sure to explain how the argument depends on these assumptions and what the implications are for the argument if the assumptions prove unwarranted.

题目整理

论点 The best way to improve profits in all of our stores is to discontinue stocking many of our varieties of imported cheese and concentrate primarily on domestic cheeses.

论据 (1) For many years all the stores in our chain have stocked a wide variety of both domestic and imported cheeses. Last year, however, all of the five best-selling cheeses at our newest store were domestic cheddar cheeses from Wisconsin.

(2) Furthermore, a recent survey by Cheeses of the World magazine indicates an increasing preference for domestic cheeses among its subscribers.

(3) Our company can reduce expenses by limiting inventory.

论证方法

题目中论者主要运用了归纳推理论证法、统计数据论证法和因果关系论证法。

分析提示

● 论据(1)是个归纳推理。论者认为这家新开奶酪店的销售情况能说明其他所有店的销售趋势。该推论需要至少两个假设：首先，论者要假设这家新店具有足够的代表性。但是，该店的地理位置、周边的居民生活习惯、该店采用的一些新店促销活动、去年国际和国内市场奶酪的价格变动所导致的居民对奶酪的消费选择等等，这些都很可能是造成去年该店销售情形的独特原因，使其很难具有代表性。其次，论者所说的这家新店的销售特点是去年的情况。论者的推论若要成立，他还要假设去年的销售特点也是今年及未来几年的销售特点。这同样存在很大疑问。

● 论据(2)引用了一项市场调查。首先，论者要假设：该调查的方案设计（如调查样本的选择、调查问卷的设计、调查数据的处理、调查结果的核实和验证等等）和实施过程是严格按照科学程序进行的；其结论是客观、中立的；调查的实施者没有受行业及其他利益相关方的影响等。其次，此次被调查人是Cheeses of the World杂志的订户。所以，论者还要假设这些订户能代表其他消费者。但这些订户的数量、收入水平、消费习惯等很难具有市场指导意义。

● 论据(3)举出了限制库存的理由：降低成本。但问题是：减少进口奶酪的库存虽说可能会降低这家连锁店的运营成本，但其销售的奶酪品种是否会减少？这家连锁店的传统是储备各式各样的国内外奶酪品种，所以选择的多样性很可能是顾客喜欢这家连锁店的一个重要原因。假如没有了选择的多样性，顾客数量减少，论者期望的盈利状况还会出现吗？

● 结论：提高该企业所有商店的利润有一个最好的方法，即不再储备各种品种的进口奶酪，只储备国产奶酪。这里，论者实际在假设：没有其他更好的提高利润的办法了。但常识告诉我们，提高员工效率、调整营业时间以迎合顾客的特殊需要、调整店面的空间布局、加大广告宣传等都是可以尝试的办法。

108. The following appeared in a memo from the owner of a chain of cheese stores located throughout the United States.

"For many years all the stores in our chain have stocked a wide variety of both domestic and imported cheeses. Last year, however, all of the five best-selling cheeses at our newest store were domestic cheddar cheeses from Wisconsin. Furthermore, a recent survey by Cheeses of the World magazine indicates an increasing preference for domestic cheeses among its subscribers. Since our company can reduce expenses by limiting inventory, the best way to improve profits in all of our stores is to discontinue stocking many of our varieties of imported cheese and concentrate primarily on domestic cheeses."

(参考第66、107题)

Write a response in which you discuss what specific evidence is needed to evaluate the argument and explain how the evidence would weaken or strengthen the argument.

题目整理

论点 The best way to improve profits in all of our stores is to discontinue stocking many of our varieties of imported cheese and concentrate primarily on domestic cheeses.

论据 (1) For many years all the stores in our chain have stocked a wide variety of both domestic and imported cheeses. Last year, however, all of the five best-selling cheeses at our newest store were domestic cheddar cheeses from Wisconsin.

(2) Furthermore, a recent survey by Cheeses of the World magazine indicates an increasing preference for domestic cheeses among its subscribers.

(3) Our company can reduce expenses by limiting inventory.

论证方法

题目中论者主要运用了归纳推理论证法、统计数据论证法和因果关系论证法。

分析提示

● 论据(1)是个归纳推理。论者认为这家新奶酪店的销售情况能说明其他所有店的销售趋势。但下列疑问需要论者作进一步的说明：首先，这家新店具有足够的代表性吗？该店的地理位置、周边的居民生活习惯、该店采用的一些新店促销活动、去年国际和国内市场奶酪的价格变动所导致的居民对奶酪的消费选择等等，这些是否是去年该店销售特点的具体原因？再者，论者说的这家新店的销售特点是去年的情况。今年还会和去年一样吗？未来几年又将如何？这些都是很大的疑问。

● 论据(2)引用了一项市场调查。但首先，该调查的方案设计（如调查样本的选择、调查问卷的设计、调查数据的处理、调查结果的核实和验证等等）和实施过程是严格按照科学程序进行的吗？其结论是客观、中立、可信的吗？调查的实施者没有受行业及其他利益相关方的影响？其次，此次被调查人是Cheeses of the World杂志的订户，但他们能代表所有的消费者吗？这些订户的数量、收入水平、消费习惯等是否因为过于特别而很难具有市场指导意义？

● 论据(3)举出了限制库存的理由：降低成本。但论者需要说明：减少进口奶酪的库存虽说可能降低这家连锁店的运营成本，但其销售的奶酪品种是否会减少？这家连锁店的传统是储备各式各样的国内外奶酪品种，所以选择的多样性很可能是顾客喜欢这家连锁店的一个重要原因。假如没有了选择的多样性，顾客数量减少，论者期望的盈利状况还会出现吗？

● 结论：提高该企业所有商店的利润有一个最好的方法，即不再储备各种品种的进口奶酪，只储备国产奶酪。但是否没有其他更好的提高利润的办法？实际上，提高员工效率、调整营业时间以迎合顾客的特殊需要、调整店面的空间布局、加大广告宣传等都是可以尝试的办法。

109. The following appeared in a memorandum from the general manager of KNOW radio station.

"Several factors indicate that radio station KNOW should shift its programming from rock-and-roll music to a continuous news format. Consider, for example, that the number of people in our listening area over fifty years of age has increased dramatically, while our total number of listeners has declined. Also, music stores in our area report decreased sales of recorded music. Finally, continuous news stations in neighboring cities have been very successful. The switch from rock-and-roll music to 24-hour news will attract older listeners and secure KNOW radio's future."

（参考第17、93、110题）

Write a response in which you examine the stated and/or unstated assumptions of the argument. Be sure to explain how the argument depends on these assumptions and what the implications are for the argument if the assumptions prove unwarranted.

题目整理

论点 题目中论者的论点包括一项建议和一个预测。

(1) Radio station KNOW should shift its programming from rock-and-roll music to a continuous news format.

(2) The switch from rock-and-roll music to 24-hour news will attract older listeners and secure KNOW radio's future.

论据 (1) Several factors indicate that radio station KNOW should shift its programming from rock-and-roll music to a continuous news format. Consider, for example, that the number of people in our listening area over fifty years of age has increased dramatically, while our total number of listeners has declined.

(2) Also, music stores in our area report decreased sales of recorded music.

(3) Finally, continuous news stations in neighboring cities have been very successful.

论证方法

题目中论者主要运用了列举特征式论证法、统计数据论证法和类比论证法。

分析提示

● 论据(1)是个列举特征式论证，其中的"特征"主要是统计数据。论者认为，为了扭转听众人数下降的趋势，KNOW电台应该把现在的摇滚乐节目改为24小时的滚动新闻节目。这里面有以下的假设：首先，论者假设现在的摇滚乐节目是其听众数量下降的原因。然而并没有论证摇滚乐节目是如何使听众人数下降的。另外，论者还提到一个现象：该广播电台覆盖的区域内，50岁以上的人口数量迅速增加，但这家广播电台的听众数量却下降了。论者实际在假设，这家电台覆盖区域内50岁以上的人口数量增加了，其听众人数也应相应增加。同时，结合证据(2)，他还假设这些新增的50多岁的人不喜欢摇滚乐节目，也不购买相关的录音制品。这两个假设难以成立：首先，即便这些50多岁的人成了KNOW电台的忠实听众，但假如其他年龄段的听众大量流失，其听众总人数依然是下降的。其次，即便这些50多岁的人都疯狂地喜欢摇滚乐，他们也未必非得通过收听广播音乐的方式来满足这个爱好。

● 论据(2)依然是个列举特征式论证。论者用该广播电台覆盖区域内录音制品店销量的下降来说明人们对摇滚乐和音乐的兴趣不大。论者是在假设如果人们对摇滚乐和音乐感兴趣，他们一定会去购买相关的录音制品。这个假设显然难以成立。人们完全可以通过一些免费的方式来接触音乐，比如网上下载音乐、翻录和租借录音制品等。

● 论据(3)是个类比论证。论者认为既然邻近一些城市的滚动新闻节目很成功，自己如果效仿也会成功。这里，论者是在假设自己的广播电台和邻近城市的广播电台完全可比。这个推论同样很难成立。各个电台所覆盖区域不同的人口结构、听众趣味、运营模式等，都会决定同一台节目在不同地方受听众欢迎的程度。

● 在结论中，论者乐观地预测：The switch from rock-and-roll music to 24-hour news will attract older listeners and secure KNOW radio's future.这个预测取决于两个假设：其一，那些新增的50多岁的人会有相当一部分人喜欢滚动新闻节目。其次，如果这家KNOW广播电台改节目，过去喜欢摇滚乐的听众不会放弃收听这家电台。但这两个假设都不一定成立。

---

110. The following appeared in a memorandum from the manager of KNOW radio station.

"Several factors indicate that KNOW radio can no longer succeed as a rock-and-roll music station. Consider, for example, that the number of people in our listening area over fifty years of age has increased dramatically, while our total number of listeners has declined. Also, music stores in our area report decreased sales of rock-and-roll music. Finally, continuous news stations in neighboring cities have been very successful. We predict that switching KNOW radio from rock-and-roll music to 24-hour news will allow the station to attract older listeners and make KNOW radio more profitable than ever."

(参考第17、93、109题)

Write a response in which you discuss what questions would need to be answered in order to decide whether the prediction and the argument on which it is based are reasonable. Be sure to explain how the answers to these questions would help to evaluate the prediction.

题目整理

论点 题目中论者的论点包括一项建议和一个预测。

(1) KNOW radio can no longer succeed as a rock-and-roll music station.

(2) We predict that switching KNOW radio from rock-and-roll music to 24-hour news will allow the station to attract older listeners and make KNOW radio more profitable than ever.

论据 (1) Consider, for example, that the number of people in our listening area over fifty years of age has increased dramatically, while our total number of listeners has declined.

(2) Also, music stores in our area report decreased sales of rock-and-roll music.

(3) Finally, continuous news stations in neighboring cities have been very successful.

论证方法

题目中论者主要运用了列举特征式论证法、统计数据论证法和类比论证法。

分析提示

● 论据(1)是个列举特征式论证，其中的"特征"主要是一些统计数据。为了说明KNOW

radio can no longer succeed as a rock-and-roll music station，论者还提到一个现象：该广播电台覆盖的区域内，50岁以上的人口数量迅速增加，但广播电台的听众数量却下降了。问题是，难道这家电台覆盖区域内50岁以上的人口数量的增加必定增加广播听众的人数？即便这些新增的居民中会有一部分人收听广播，但他们非得收听摇滚乐吗？最后，即便这些人中的大多数成了KNOW电台的忠实听众，但假如这家电台其他年龄段的听众大量流失，其听众总人数依然会下降。

● 论据(2)依然是个列举特征式论证。论者用该地区录音制品店销量的下降来说明人们对摇滚乐和对音乐的兴趣不大。我们的疑问是：如果人们对摇滚乐和音乐感兴趣，他们一定会去购买相关的录音制品吗？即便购买相关的录音制品，他们一定要去本地的音乐制品店购买吗？难道不可以邮购和网上订购？难道他们不可以通过免费的方式来满足音乐需求，比如网上下载音乐、翻录和租借录音制品？

● 论据(3)是个类比论证。论者认为既然邻近一些城市的滚动新闻节目很成功，自己如果效仿的话也会成功。问题是：KNOW电台和邻近城市的广播电台完全可比吗？常识告诉我们，各个电台所覆盖区域不同的人口结构、听众趣味、运营模式等，都会决定同一台节目在不同地方受听众欢迎的程度。

● 在结论中，论者乐观地预测：...switching KNOW radio from rock-and-roll music to 24-hour news will allow the station to attract older listeners and make KNOW radio more profitable than ever. 有两个疑问：其一，那些新增的居民中会有相当一部分人喜欢滚动新闻节目吗？其次，如果这家KNOW广播电台改节目，过去喜欢摇滚乐的听众不会就此放弃这家电台，从而使其听众人数继续下降？如此的话，论者的预测就很难成立。

---

111. The following appeared in a memorandum from the owner of Movies Galore, a chain of movie-rental stores.

"In order to stop the recent decline in our profits, we must reduce operating expenses at Movies Galore's ten movie-rental stores. Since we are famous for our special bargains, raising our rental prices is not a viable way to improve profits. Last month our store in downtown Marston significantly decreased its operating expenses by closing at 6:00 P.M. rather than 9:00 P.M. and by reducing its stock by eliminating all movies released more than five years ago. By implementing similar changes in our other stores, Movies Galore can increase profits without jeopardizing our reputation for offering great movies at low prices."

(参考第47、112题)

Write a response in which you examine the stated and/or unstated assumptions of the argument. Be sure to explain how the argument depends on these assumptions and what the implications are for the argument if the assumptions prove unwarranted.

题目整理

论点 By implementing similar changes in our other stores, Movies Galore can increase profits without jeopardizing our reputation for offering great movies at low prices.

论据 (1) Since we are famous for our special bargains, raising our rental prices is not a viable way to improve profits.

(2) Last month our store in downtown Marston significantly decreased its operating expenses by closing at 6:00 P.M. rather than 9:00 P.M. and by reducing its stock by eliminating all movies released more than five years ago.

论证方法

题目中论者主要运用了因果关系论证法和归纳推理论证法。

分析提示

● 论据(1)是个因果关系论证：因为Movies Galore一向以价廉出名，所以提高价格不可取，应缩短营业时间来降低运营成本。这个推论需要以下假设：首先，Movies Galore的竞争对手没有提高租金。假如其他音像出租店都提价了或者其出租价格本来就比Movies Galore高，那么即使Movies Galore的出租价格略涨些，其价格也依然很有竞争力。其次，论者要假设提前下班和减少库存可以大幅度降低运营成本。然而就常识而论，减少三个小时的营业时间充其量也就节省一点水费、电费以及办公费用；而现在的电影一般都是DVD或者VCD的形式，占用的仓储空间并不大，减少库存未必就能降低很多费用。是否有其他办法能削减运营成本？如此：调低员工工资、降低进货价格、注意节约办公用品（如水、电、笔、墨、纸张等）等都是可以考虑的举措。

● 论据(2)是个归纳推理论证法：论者认为在Marston市区店采用的措施，其他店也可以采用。但论者首先要假设，Marston市区店采取的措施是有效的。而论者只是模糊地说"the store in downtown Marston **significantly** decreased its operating expenses"。这个significantly具体是指多少金额、多少降幅？顾客的反应如何？这样做是否给该店的竞争对手留下了空当，从而被他们抢了生意？等等这些论者并未说明。

● 论者在结论中建议将Marston市区店的做法推广到所有的店铺。但Marston市区店的做法是否具备标本意义？其他店是否有一些特殊情况而使得无法将该店的做法照搬过去呢？

● 最后，论者在结论中预测缩短营业时间、减少存货可以increase profits without jeopardizing our reputation for offering great movies at low prices。但这个预测需要以下假设：首先，新政不会导致与初衷相悖的后果，比如老电影库存的减少让有些顾客不再光顾。其次，营业时间的缩短不会令部分顾客在他们最方便的时间（比如晚6点以后8点之前）租不到想要的电影。否则，论者的期望也许会落空。

112. The following appeared in a memorandum from the owner of Movies Galore, a chain of movie-rental stores.

"In order to reverse the recent decline in our profits, we must reduce operating expenses at Movies Galore's ten movie-rental stores. Since we are famous for our special bargains, raising our rental prices is not a viable way to improve profits. Last month our store in downtown Marston significantly decreased its operating expenses by closing at 6:00 p.m. rather than 9:00 p.m. and by reducing its stock by eliminating all movies released more than five years ago.

Therefore, in order to increase profits without jeopardizing our reputation for offering great movies at low prices, we recommend implementing similar changes in our other nine Movies Galore stores."

（参考第47、111题）

Write a response in which you discuss what questions would need to be answered in order to decide whether the recommendation and the argument on which it is based are reasonable. Be sure to explain how the answers to these questions would help to evaluate the recommendation.

题目整理

论点 To increase profits without jeopardizing our reputation for offering great movies at low prices, we recommend implementing similar changes in our other nine Movies Galore stores.

论据 (1) In order to reverse the recent decline in our profits, we must reduce operating expenses at Movies Galore's ten movie-rental stores. Since we are famous for our special bargains, raising our rental prices is not a viable way to improve profits.

(2) Last month our store in downtown Marston significantly decreased its operating expenses by closing at 6:00 p.m. rather than 9:00 p.m. and by reducing its stock by eliminating all movies released more than five years ago.

论证方法

题目中论者主要运用了因果关系论证法和归纳推理论证法。

分析提示

- 论据(1)是个因果关系论证：因为Movies Galore一向以价廉出名，所以提高价格不可取，应缩短营业时间来降低运营成本。这里面有以下疑问：首先，Movies Galore的竞争对手有没有提高租金？假如其他音像出租店都提了价，或者其出租价格本来就比Movies Galore高，那么即使Movies Galore的出租价格略涨些，其价格也依然很有竞争力。其次，提前下班和减少库存是否可以大幅度降低运营成本？就常识而论，减少三个小时的营业时间充其量也就节省一点水费、电费以及其他很少的办公费用；而现在的电影一般都是DVD或者VCD的形式，占用的仓储空间并不大，减少库存未必就能降低很多费用。再次，难道没有其他的办法了？诸如调低员工工资、降低进货价格、注意节约办公用品等？

- 论据(2)是个归纳推理论证法：论者认为在Marston市区店采用的措施其他店也可以采用。但是Marston市区店采取的措施有效吗？论者只是模糊地说"the store in downtown Marston **significantly** decreased its operating expenses"。但这个significantly具体是指多少金额、多少降幅？顾客的反应如何？这样做是否给该店的竞争对手留下了空当，从而被他们抢了生意？等等这些论者并未说明。

- 论者在结论中建议将Marston市区店的做法推广到所有的店铺。但Marston市区店的做法是否具备标本意义？其他店是否有特殊情况而使得无法将该店的做法照搬过去？

- 论者建议推广Marston市区店经验的目的在于提高利润。但这个推广行为会不会导致一些与初衷相悖的后果？假如老电影库存的减少让有些顾客不再光顾那里了？营业时间的减少是否会令部分顾客在他们最方便的时间（比如晚6点以后8点之前）无法租到他们想要的电影呢？如果是那样，论者的期望也许就不会实现。

---

113. The following is a recommendation from the personnel director to the president of Acme Publishing Company.

"Many other companies have recently stated that having their employees take the Easy Read Speed-Reading Course has greatly improved productivity. One graduate of the course was able to read a 500-page report in only two hours; another graduate rose from an assistant manager to vice president of the company in under a year. Obviously, the faster you can read, the more information you can absorb in a single workday. Moreover, Easy Read would cost Acme only $500 per employee—a small price to pay when you consider the benefits. Included in this fee is a three-week seminar in Spruce City and a lifelong subscription to the Easy Read newsletter. Clearly, to improve productivity, Acme should require all of our employees to take the Easy Read course."

（参考第126、127、161题）

Write a response in which you discuss what questions would need to be answered in order to decide whether the advice and the argument on which it is based are reasonable. Be sure to explain how the answers to these questions would help to evaluate the advice.

题目整理

论点　To improve productivity, Acme should require all of our employees to take the Easy Read course.

论据　(1) Many other companies have recently stated that having their employees take the Easy Read Speed-Reading Course has greatly improved productivity. One graduate of the course was able to read a 500-page report in only two hours; another graduate rose from an assistant manager to vice president of the company in under a year.

(2) Obviously, the faster you can read, the more information you can absorb in a single workday.

(3) Moreover, Easy Read would cost Acme only $500 per employee—a small price to pay when you consider the benefits.

(4) Included in this fee is a three-week seminar in Spruce City and a lifelong subscription to the Easy Read newsletter.

论证方法

题目中论者主要运用了归纳推理论证法和诉诸常识法。

分析提示

- 论据(1)举了许多公司作例子，运用的是不完全归纳法，属于归纳推理论证。但问题是：首先，那些公司所说的事情是真实可信的吗？是否经过核实？其次，即便上述事情可信，那些公司具有普遍的代表性吗？论者所说的many other companies中的many到底是多少家？

10家、20家还是50家？最后，论者在这里还有横向类比不当的嫌疑。别的公司适用，自己公司也适用吗？自己公司的情况和他们具有可比性吗？

- 论据(2)(3)(4)都是在利用常识展开论证。论据(2)所说的"一个人读的越快，吸收的信息量就越大"乍听起来似乎有道理，但经不起推敲。如果一个人阅读很快，但相关基础知识欠缺、逻辑思维混乱、批判性思考能力差、不善于把书本信息同实际经验相互参照印证，他是不可能真正从阅读中吸收多少有用信息的。

- 论据(3)说"Easy Read would cost Acme only \$500 per employee—a small price to pay when you consider the benefits"。言下之意是，这笔投入很划算。但问题是：第一，论据(1)提到的benefits都是听来的，其真实性并未证实。第二，假如这个Easy Read培训课程不仅不能取得预期效果，反而耽误了员工的工作时间，其成本代价还会是一笔简单的\$500 per employee的投入吗？第三，到底这家Acme Publishing Company有多少员工？假如其员工上千的话，都接受培训意味着50万美元的开支。这还会是论者所说的a small price吗？

- 论者在论据(4)中说，培训课程每个员工500美元的报价中还包括a three-week seminar in Spruce City and a lifelong subscription to the Easy Read newsletter。这听起来很诱人，但那要看对谁。公司员工也许会喜欢，但公司老板呢？员工们三个星期不干活对公司意味着什么？哪个老板会养闲人？这个培训课程从长期来看，也许有利于该公司增强其人力资本的储备。但对这些远期的潜在收益，公司老板未必真的很关心。毕竟，这些员工随时有可能离职。今天对他们进行培训，明天他们就可能是竞争对手的人力资本了。

---

114. The following appeared in a memo from the vice president of a food distribution company with food storage warehouses in several cities.

"Recently, we signed a contract with the Fly-Away Pest Control Company to provide pest control services at our warehouse in Palm City, but last month we discovered that over \$20,000 worth of food there had been destroyed by pest damage. Meanwhile, the Buzzoff Pest Control Company, which we have used for many years in Palm City, continued to service our warehouse in Wintervale, and last month only \$10,000 worth of the food stored there had been destroyed by pest damage. Even though the price charged by Fly-Away is considerably lower, our best means of saving money is to return to Buzzoff for all our pest control services."

（参考第78、116、117题）

Write a response in which you discuss what questions would need to be answered in order to decide whether the recommendation and the argument on which it is based are reasonable. Be sure to explain how the answers to these questions would help to evaluate the recommendation.

题目整理

论点 Even though the price charged by Fly-Away is considerably lower, our best means of saving money is to return to Buzzoff for all our pest control services.

论据 (1) Recently, we signed a contract with the Fly-Away Pest Control Company to provide pest control services at our warehouse in Palm City, but last month we discovered that over $20,000 worth of food there had been destroyed by pest damage.

(2) Meanwhile, the Buzzoff Pest Control Company, which we have used for many years in Palm City, continued to service our warehouse in Wintervale, and last month only $10,000 worth of the food stored there had been destroyed by pest damage.

论证方法

题目中论者运用了类比论证法和归纳推理论证法。

分析提示

● 是否有其他特殊的原因导致了论据(1)中的结果？比如：上月储存在Palm City仓库那一批次的食品包装出了问题、天气剧烈变化、当地虫害大规模爆发、库房常年使用缺乏维修等。另外，假如储存在Palm City仓库的食品价格较高，即便那里储存的食品遭受虫害的比率和数量同Wintervale仓库的一样或者略低，但就虫害造成的经济损失会高一些，但并不足以说明Fly-Away Pest Control公司的灭虫效果差。

● 同理，针对论据(2)，我们也要问：是否有其他不可控的原因导致了"last month only $10,000 worth of the food stored there had been destroyed by pest damage"这一结果？比如，那里储存的食品具有很强的抗虫性、当地的天气不会招虫害的爆发、上个月那里出现害虫的数量和频率在一年中属于较轻的月份等。或者，那里储存的食品都是较为便宜的品种，所以即便遭虫害的食品的数量和比率较高，就损失的货币价值来看，却并不大。

● 基于对论据(1)(2)的分析，我们可以发现，结论说"our best means of saving money is to return to Buzzoff for all our pest control services"中有以下不当推论：其一，论者没有考虑到，因为天气、仓储设施、所储藏食品特点和价格等方面的差异，Palm City和Wintervale两地的食品仓库很可能缺乏可比性。其二，论者很可能有不当归纳推理的问题。即便Buzzoff公司在Wintervale的灭虫效果较好，难道就能断定该公司在其他城市、其他仓库也能做到同样好吗？如果那些城市和仓库有一些特殊的情况呢？其三，当论者声称把所有灭虫任务都交给Buzzoff公司是our **best means of saving money** 的时候，似乎显得过于武断了。难道没有比Buzzoff做得更好的公司？没有其他的防虫、灭虫办法，比如：改进包装、注意灭菌防腐、改善仓储设施等？

---

115. The following appeared in a memo from a vice president of a large, highly diversified company.

"Ten years ago our company had two new office buildings constructed as regional headquarters for two different regions. The buildings were erected by two different construction companies—Alpha and Zeta. Even though the two buildings had identical floor plans, the building constructed by Zeta cost 30 percent more to build, and its expenses for maintenance last year were twice those of the building constructed by Alpha. Furthermore, the energy consumption of the Zeta building has been higher than that of the Alpha building every year since its construction. Such data, plus the fact that Alpha has a stable workforce with little employee turnover, indicate that we should use Alpha rather than Zeta for our contemplated new building project."

（参考第69、70题）

Write a response in which you examine the stated and/or unstated assumptions of the argument. Be sure to explain how the argument depends on these assumptions and what the implications are for the argument if the assumptions prove unwarranted.

 题目整理

 论点 We should use Alpha rather than Zeta for our contemplated new building project.

论据 (1) Ten years ago our company had two new office buildings constructed as regional headquarters for two different regions. The buildings were erected by two different construction companies—Alpha and Zeta. Even though the two buildings had identical floor plans, the building constructed by Zeta cost 30 percent more to build, and its expenses for maintenance last year were twice those of the building constructed by Alpha.

(2) Furthermore, the energy consumption of the Zeta building has been higher than that of the Alpha building every year since its construction.

(3) Alpha has a stable workforce with little employee turnover.

论证方法

题目中论者主要运用了归纳推理论证法。

分析提示

● 论据(1)说十年前Alpha公司承建的大楼的建筑成本比当时Zeta公司承建的大楼要低30%，尽管这两幢大楼的平面结构图完全一样。去年Alpha所建这幢大楼的维护成本只是Zeta公司所建的相同大楼的一半。在这里，论者要假设：第一，没有其他与Alpha公司及其所建工程无关的因素导致了这幢Alpha大楼较低的建筑成本和维护成本。一些特殊因素，比如，Alpha大楼所在地区较低的人工成本、该地区日照充足（因而不用花钱做楼宇的外墙保温处理）、该地区良好的环境条件（比如没有工业污染、没有沙尘暴、天气不是太潮湿、四季气候稳定等）、这幢大楼使用者比较爱护这幢楼的内外设施、这幢大楼良好的物业管理等，都会导致差异。第二，论者要假设，去年一年两幢大楼不同的维护成本可以代表过去十年间的维护成本的差异。假如在过去十年间，这两幢大楼的维护成本每年都是上下波动的呢？假如十年平均下来，Zeta大楼的年维护费用比Alpha大楼的低呢？论者仅选取一年的数据进行比较，有歪曲数据的嫌疑。

● 论据(2)说，Alpha大楼的能耗自建成以来都比Zeta大楼低。在此，论者需要假设：是否是其他一些与Alpha公司及其所建工程无关的因素导致这幢Alpha大楼能耗较低？比如，Alpha大楼所在地区一年四季大多天气晴朗、日照充足、温度适宜，这样的话，Alpha大楼根本不需要制冷或制热的空调系统，能耗自然就低。相反，Zeta大楼所在城市因为四季以及早晚温差大、天气经常剧烈变化，必须高度依赖空调，其能耗自然就高。另外，其他的因素，诸如两个大楼不同的物业管理水平、人们的节能意识、两个大楼不同的使用率（比如Alpha大楼的使用面积只有一半，而Zeta大楼全部面积常年都投入使用）、两地不同的用电成本等。

- 论据(3)说Alpha公司的员工队伍稳定，基本没有人员流动。论者意在说明Alpha公司较好的人事管理和员工队伍素质。但论者同样要假设不是其他的原因，比如Alpha公司缺乏良好的个人绩效考评机制、平均主义的分配方式、或者员工年龄偏大等，使那里的员工不愿离去。或者因为Alpha公司养了一大批低能懒散的员工，这些员工难以找到工作，所以不愿离开这家可以偷懒的公司。如此的话，Alpha公司稳定的员工队伍同其人事管理水平和员工队伍素质实际上没什么关系。

- 最后，即便论者所说的论据都有道理，但用十年前的事情来说明现在的情况显然不太合适。因为他要假设，这十年来两家公司没有发生此消彼长的变化。

---

116. The following appeared in a memo from the vice president of a food distribution company with food storage warehouses in several cities.

"Recently, we signed a contract with the Fly-Away Pest Control Company to provide pest control services at our warehouse in Palm City, but last month we discovered that over $20,000 worth of food there had been destroyed by pest damage. Meanwhile, the Buzzoff Pest Control Company, which we have used for many years in Palm City, continued to service our warehouse in Wintervale, and last month only $10,000 worth of the food stored there had been destroyed by pest damage. This difference in pest damage is best explained by the negligence of Fly-Away."

（参考第78、114、117题）

Write a response in which you discuss one or more alternative explanations that could rival the proposed explanation and explain how your explanation(s) can plausibly account for the facts presented in the argument.

题目整理

论点 The difference in pest damage is best explained by the negligence of Fly-Away.

论据 (1) Recently, we signed a contract with the Fly-Away Pest Control Company to provide pest control services at our warehouse in Palm City, but last month we discovered that over $20,000 worth of food there had been destroyed by pest damage.

(2) Meanwhile, the Buzzoff Pest Control Company, which we have used for many years in Palm City, continued to service our warehouse in Wintervale, and last month only $10,000 worth of the food stored there had been destroyed by pest damage.

论证方法

题目中论者主要运用了类比论证法。

分析提示

- 对于论据(1)中的结果"over $20,000 worth of food there had been destroyed by pest damage"，至少可以有以下不同的原因，比如：上月储存在Palm City仓库那一批次的食品包装出了问题、那里的天气出现剧烈变化、当地虫害大规模爆发、库房常年使用缺乏维修等。另外，假如储存在Palm City仓库的食品价格较高，即便那里储存的食品遭受虫害的比率和数量同

Wintervale 仓库的一样或者略低，但就虫害所造成的经济损失依然会高一些，尽管这并不足以说明 Fly-Away Pest Control 公司的灭虫效果差。这也是一种解释。

● 同理，针对论据(2)中的结果 "last month only \$10,000 worth of the food stored there had been destroyed by pest damage"，同样可以有以下不同的原因，比如：那里储存的食品具有很强的抗虫性、当地的天气不会爆发虫害、上个月那里出现害虫的数量和频率在一年中属于较轻的月份等。而且，假如那里储存的食品都是较为便宜的品种，即便遭虫害的食品的数量和比率较高，但如果仅仅从货币价值来看，损失不会太大。

● 基于对论据(1)(2)的分析，我们可以发现，因为天气、仓储设施、所储藏食品的特点和价格等因素，Palm City 和 Wintervale 两地的食品仓库很可能缺乏可比性。因而，论者的结论 "the difference in pest damage is best explained by the negligence of Fly-Away" 显得过于武断。

---

117. The following appeared in a memo from the vice president of a food distribution company with food storage warehouses in several cities.

"Recently, we signed a contract with the Fly-Away Pest Control Company to provide pest control services at our warehouse in Palm City, but last month we discovered that over \$20,000 worth of food there had been destroyed by pest damage. Meanwhile, the Buzzoff Pest Control Company, which we have used for many years in Palm City, continued to service our warehouse in Wintervale, and last month only \$10,000 worth of the food stored there had been destroyed by pest damage. Even though the price charged by Fly-Away is considerably lower, our best means of saving money is to return to Buzzoff for all our pest control services."

（参考第78、114、116题）

Write a response in which you examine the stated and/or unstated assumptions of the argument. Be sure to explain how the argument depends on these assumptions and what the implications are for the argument if the assumptions prove unwarranted.

题目整理

论点 Even though the price charged by Fly-Away is considerably lower, our best means of saving money is to return to Buzzoff for all our pest control services.

论据 (1) Recently, we signed a contract with the Fly-Away Pest Control Company to provide pest control services at our warehouse in Palm City, but last month we discovered that over \$20,000 worth of food there had been destroyed by pest damage.

(2) Meanwhile, the Buzzoff Pest Control Company, which we have used for many years in Palm City, continued to service our warehouse in Wintervale, and last month only \$10,000 worth of the food stored there had been destroyed by pest damage.

论证方法

题目中论者运用了类比论证法和归纳推理论证法。

分析提示

● 论据(1)显示由Fly-Away公司负责虫害控制的仓库出现了较大的损失。在此，论者要假设没有特殊的原因导致价值两万多的食品遭受虫灾。诸如上月储存在Palm City仓库那一批次的食品包装出了问题、天气剧烈变化、当地虫害大规模爆发、库房常年使用缺乏维修等，这些特殊因素造成了灾害，并不能充分说明Fly-Away Pest Control公司防虫技术差。另外，假如储存在Palm City仓库的食品价格较高，即便那里储存的食品遭受虫害的比率和数量同Wintervale仓库的一样或者略低，但就虫害所造成的经济损失会高一些，但这同样不足以说明Fly-Away Pest Control公司的灭虫效果差。

● 同理，针对论据(2)，论者也要假设没有其他不可控的原因导致上月遭受虫灾的食品价值只有一万。比如，那里储存的食品具有很强的抗虫性、当地的天气不会爆发虫害、上个月那里出现害虫的数量和频率在一年中属于较轻的月份等，这些都有可能是原因。还有一种可能是，假如那里储存的食品都较为便宜，所以即便遭虫害的食品的数量和比率较高，损失并不会很大。但这同样不能说明Bussoff公司的灭虫能力更强。

● 基于对论据(1)(2)的分析，我们可以发现，结论说"our best means of saving money is to return to Buzzoff for all our pest control services"中有以下不当推论：其一，论者没有考虑到，因为天气、仓储设施、所储藏食品特点和价格等方面的差异，Palm City和Wintervale两地的食品仓库很可能缺乏可比性。其二，论者很可能有归纳推理不当的问题。即便Buzzoff Company在Wintervale的灭虫效果较好，难道就能断定该公司在其他城市、其他仓库也能做到同样好吗？如果那些城市和仓库有特殊情况呢？其三，当论者声称把所有灭虫任务都交给Buzzoff公司是our **best means of saving money** 的时候，他要假设：第一，没有比Buzzoff做得更好的公司了。第二，没有其他的防虫和灭虫的办法。但从常识上讲，改进食品包装、注意灭菌防腐、改善仓储设施等，都是常见的有效防虫办法。

---

118. The following appeared as part of an article in a business magazine.

"A recent study rating 300 male and female advertising executives according to the average number of hours they sleep per night showed an association between the amount of sleep the executives need and the success of their firms. Of the advertising firms studied, those whose executives reported needing no more than six hours of sleep per night had higher profit margins and faster growth. On the basis of this study, we recommend that businesses hire only people who need less than six hours of sleep per night."

（参考第14题）

Write a response in which you discuss what questions would need to be answered in order to decide whether the recommendation and the argument on which it is based are reasonable. Be sure to explain how the answers to these questions would help to evaluate the recommendation.

题目整理

论点 We recommend that businesses hire only people who need less than six hours of sleep per night.

论据 (1) A recent study rating 300 male and female advertising executives according to the average number of hours they sleep per night showed an association between the amount of sleep the executives need and the success of their firms.

(2) Of the advertising firms studied, those whose executives reported needing no more than six hours of sleep per night had higher profit margins and faster growth.

论证方法

题目中论者主要运用了统计数据论证法、因果关系论证法和归纳推理论证法。

分析提示

● 论据(1)是统计数据论证法。我们的疑问是：这300名参加调研的人员具有代表性吗？对他们的遴选是否严格按照抽样调查的操作程序进行的？其中男女比例的分配是否合理、是否能反映这个行业男女的真实比例？实施这项研究的机构是否中立、客观？该研究者有没有受到行业及其他利益相关方的干扰和影响？等等。

● 论据(2)看似一个因果关系论证。论者认为那些广告公司的管理人员每晚不足6个小时的睡眠时间是他们所在公司 had higher profit margins and faster growth 的原因。首先，论者很可能犯了把同时出现的两件事情当作彼此有因果关系的错误。论者引用的 recent study 实际已经讲得很清楚：在 the amount of sleep the executives need 和 the success of their firms 之间仅仅是有某种关联性。即二者有关联性，而不是因果关系。其次，即便可以在 the amount of sleep the executives need 和 the success of their firms 之间作因果关系推论，难道就没有其他的原因导致了同样的结果？比如：是否是这些睡眠较少的经理人所在的行业出现了繁荣气象，业务繁多，不得不加班加点做业务，因此没有足够的睡眠时间，而公司的盈利水平因为整个行业的繁荣而迅速增长？也就是说，不是因为他们的睡眠时间少而是因为行业的景气给他们公司带来了高额利润？再比如，是否是因为这些高盈利的广告公司普遍都有严格的管理制度？在管理的高压之下，这些经理人不得不拼命工作，一再压缩自己的睡眠时间。这样的话，这些广告公司的高盈利实际上不是这些经理人睡眠少的结果，而是高度严格的管理制度给公司带来利润的增长。

● 在结论中，论者把只在广告行业内做的研究结论进行推广，断定任何公司要想盈利，都应该聘请睡眠时间少的人员。这实际上是把一个尚有疑问的结论简单归纳推广。问题是，这个结论果真会放之四海而皆准吗？

119. Evidence suggests that academic honor codes, which call for students to agree not to cheat in their academic endeavors and to notify a faculty member if they suspect that others have cheated, are far more successful than any other methods at deterring cheating among students at colleges and universities. Several years ago, Groveton College adopted such a code and discontinued its old-fashioned system in which teachers closely monitored students. Under the old system, teachers reported an average of thirty cases of cheating per year. In the first year the honor code was in place, students reported twenty-one cases of cheating; five years later, this figure had dropped to fourteen. Moreover, in a recent survey, a majority of Groveton students

said that they would be less likely to cheat with an honor code in place than without.

（参考第22、120、138题）

Write a response in which you discuss one or more alternative explanations that could rival the proposed explanation and explain how your explanation(s) can plausibly account for the facts presented in the argument.

题目整理

论点 Evidence suggests that academic honor codes, which call for students to agree not to cheat in their academic endeavors and to notify a faculty member if they suspect that others have cheated, are far more successful than are other methods at deterring cheating among students at colleges and universities.

论据 (1) Several years ago, Groveton College adopted such a code and discontinued its old-fashioned system in which teachers closely monitored students. Under the old system, teachers reported an average of thirty cases of cheating per year. In the first year the honor code was in place, students reported twenty-one cases of cheating; five years later, this figure had dropped to fourteen.

(2) Moreover, in a recent survey, a majority of Groveton students said that they would be less likely to cheat with an honor code in place than without.

论证方法

题目中论者主要运用了统计数据论证法和归纳推理论证法。

分析提示

- 首先，在论据(1)中论者提到，过去由老师来监考的情况下，每年大概有30起学生作弊事件；而在现在无人监考情况下，第一年学生们报告的作弊事件有21起，五年后，该数字降为14。论者把这一变化归因于新的honor code制度。但是，对这一结果，至少还可以有另外两种解释：解释一，之前学生作弊事件多是因为老师监管较严，只要发现作弊就上报，所以作弊人次多。而新制度强调学生自律和相互监督，结果学生自我监管较松，相互包庇，对他人作弊多数选择隐瞒不报，故报告的作弊人次逐年减少。解释二，过去强调老师监考，老师承担了全部的监督责任。他们尽职尽责，学生作弊经常被揭出。然而新制度强调学生自我约束，向老师汇报其他学生作弊的情况。如此一来，老师的监督责任弱化了。甚至可能出现即便有同学向他们反映其他学生作弊行为，这些老师却不及时向学校通报的情形。这样的话，新制度下学生的作弊发生率自然就在统计上表现为下降。

- 在论据(2)的调查中，论者说多数的Groveton students said that they would be less likely to cheat with an honor code in place than without。论者显然认为这个调查结果说明新的honor code制度增强了学生的自尊和道德自律，使他们主动放弃作弊。但是，这个调查结果完全可以有另外一个解释：这些学生并没有回答他们的真实想法；他们因为看到新制度对他们有利而故意说谎，目的在于希望这个宽松的制度能延续下去。

- 在结论中，论者用多年前只发生在Groveton大学的案例作为证据，得出结论说"academic honor codes are far more successful than any other methods at deterring cheating among students at colleges and universities"。这是一个归纳推理的论证过程，但是因为论者只举了一个例证，他的归纳推论很可能是以偏概全。

....

120. Several years ago, Groveton College adopted an honor code, which calls for students to agree not to cheat in their academic endeavors and to notify a faculty member if they suspect that others have cheated. Groveton's honor code replaced a system in which teachers closely monitored students. Under that system, teachers reported an average of thirty cases of cheating per year. The honor code has proven far more successful: in the first year it was in place, students reported twenty-one cases of cheating; five years later, this figure had dropped to fourteen. Moreover, in a recent survey, a majority of Groveton students said that they would be less likely to cheat with an honor code in place than without. Such evidence suggests that all colleges and universities should adopt honor codes similar to Groveton's. This change is sure to result in a dramatic decline in cheating among college students.

（参考第22、119、138题）

Write a response in which you discuss what questions would need to be answered in order to decide whether the recommendation is likely to have the predicted result. Be sure to explain how the answers to these questions would help to evaluate the recommendation.

题目整理

论点 All colleges and universities should adopt honor codes similar to Groveton's. This change is sure to result in a dramatic decline in cheating among college students.

论据 (1) Several years ago, Groveton College adopted an honor code, which calls for students to agree not to cheat in their academic endeavors and to notify a faculty member if they suspect that others have cheated. Groveton's honor code replaced a system in which teachers closely monitored students. Under that system, teachers reported an average of thirty cases of cheating per year. The honor code has proven far more successful: in the first year it was in place, students reported twenty-one cases of cheating; five years later, this figure had dropped to fourteen.

(2) Moreover, in a recent survey, a majority of Groveton students said that they would be less likely to cheat with an honor code in place than without.

论证方法

题目中论者主要运用了统计数据论证法和类比论证法。

分析提示

● 首先，在论据(1)中，论者提到过去由老师来监考的情况下，每年大概有30起学生作弊事件；而在现在无人监考情况下，第一年学生们报告的作弊事件有21起，五年后，该数字降为14。那么，我们要问：之前学生作弊事件多是否同老师监管较严、只要发现作弊就上报有关？而新制度下学生作弊事件减少是否同学生自我监管较松、隐瞒不报有关？而且，论者并没有提到过去和现在该校学生人数的变化。假如过去学生人数较多，30个作弊事件仅占学生的较低比例；而现在虽然学生作弊的绝对数量下降，但由于学生人数总量的下降，实际上学生作弊的比例上升了呢？更何况，论者只提到新的honor code实施后第一年和第五年的情形，并没有提及中间三年学生作弊的情况。假如这中间几年学生作弊的事件总量又重新上升了呢？还能说这个新政是有效的吗？

● 在论据(2)的调查中，论者说多数的Groveton students said that they would be less likely to cheat with an honor code in place than without。我们要问：这里的majority到底是多少被调查学生中的majority？如果只有20个学生参与了抽样调查，即便他们中的18个人都表示新的honor code让他们不再作弊了，相对于该校可能几万的学生来说，会因为样本过小而说明不了什么问题。而且，这些学生说出了他们的真实想法了吗？他们有没有可能因为新制度对他们有利而故意隐瞒事实真相？这项调查是由谁来做的？是否客观、中立？这些都是很重要的问题。

● 在结论(2)中，论者建议"All colleges and universities should adopt honor codes similar to Groveton's"。这实际是类比论证：在一地有效的办法，在其他地方也会有效。但论者并没有提供其他高校的学生作弊情况。假如其他学校的学生作弊本来就很少，还有效仿的必要吗？即便其他学校也有严重的学生作弊现象，但原因和Groveton College的一样吗？这个尚存疑问的honor code在那里就必然有效吗？这些都没有答案。

---

121. The following appeared in a memo from the director of a large group of hospitals.

"In a controlled laboratory study of liquid hand soaps, a concentrated solution of extra strength UltraClean hand soap produced a 40 percent greater reduction in harmful bacteria than did the liquid hand soaps currently used in our hospitals. During our recent test of regular-strength UltraClean with doctors, nurses, and visitors at our hospital in Worktown, the hospital reported significantly fewer cases of patient infection (a 20 percent reduction) than did any of the other hospitals in our group. Therefore, to prevent serious patient infections, we should supply UltraClean at all hand-washing stations, including those used by visitors, throughout our hospital system."

（参考第62、122、124题）

Write a response in which you examine the stated and/or unstated assumptions of the argument. Be sure to explain how the argument depends on these assumptions and what the implications are for the argument if the assumptions prove unwarranted.

题目整理

论点 To prevent serious patient infections, we should supply UltraClean at all hand-washing stations, including those used by visitors, throughout our hospital system.

论据 (1) In a controlled laboratory study of liquid hand soaps, a concentrated solution of extra strength UltraClean hand soap produced a 40 percent greater reduction in harmful bacteria than did the liquid hand soaps currently used in our hospitals.

(2) During our recent test of regular-strength UltraClean with doctors, nurses, and visitors at our hospital in Worktown, the hospital reported significantly fewer cases of patient infection (a 20 percent reduction) than did any of the other hospitals in our group.

论证方法

题目中论者主要运用了统计数据论证法和归纳推理论证法。

分析提示

● 论据(1)(2)运用的都是统计数据论证法。针对论据(1)，论者需要假设：这个实验的方案设计（如试验样本的选择、数据的处理、研究结果的核实和验证等）和实施过程是严格按照科学程序进行的；其结论是客观、中立的；试验的实施者没有受行业及其他利益相关方的影响等。其次，要注意，这次实验室研究用的是超强浓缩的UltraClean溶液（a concentrated solution of extra strength UltraClean）。一般而言，即使这种溶液的杀菌、消毒效果一般，其浓缩液体的使用效果也会比相同成分普通浓度的溶液要好。问题是：其他品牌的浓缩洗手液同该品牌的普通浓度的洗手液相比，其杀菌效果如何？假如浓缩洗手液至少比普通浓度的洗手液效果要好70%以上的话，论者说的UltraClean浓缩洗手液除菌效果比其他洗手液强40%的优势也就不稀奇了。

● 论据(2)说普通型（regular-strength）UltraClean在Worktown医院收到较好的使用效果，病人的感染发病率降低了20%。但论者必须假设不是其他原因导致了这一结果，比如：是否Worktown特殊的气候致使试验期间感染病例较少？是否Worktown地区的公共卫生状况较好，人们的健康水平整体较好呢？是否是Worktown那家医院的严格卫生管理降低了病人的感染率？是否是Worktown地区独特的人口结构（比如青壮年居多，而老人和儿童比较少）使那里的居民一般不会感染上病毒？等等。

---

122. The following appeared in a memo from the director of a large group of hospitals.

"In a controlled laboratory study of liquid hand soaps, a concentrated solution of extra strength UltraClean hand soap produced a 40 percent greater reduction in harmful bacteria than did the liquid hand soaps currently used in our hospitals. During our recent test of regular-strength UltraClean with doctors, nurses, and visitors at our hospital in Worktown, the hospital reported significantly fewer cases of patient infection (a 20 percent reduction) than did any of the other hospitals in our group. The explanation for the 20 percent reduction in patient infections is the use of UltraClean soap."

（参考第62、121、124题）

Write a response in which you discuss one or more alternative explanations that could rival the proposed explanation and explain how your explanation(s) can plausibly account for the facts presented in the argument.

题目整理

论点 The explanation for the 20 percent reduction in patient infections is the use of UltraClean soap.

论据 (1) In a controlled laboratory study of liquid hand soaps, a concentrated solution of extra strength UltraClean hand soap produced a 40 percent greater reduction in harmful bacteria than did the liquid hand soaps currently used in our hospitals.

(2) During our recent test of regular-strength UltraClean with doctors, nurses, and visitors at our hospital in Worktown, the hospital reported significantly fewer cases of patient infection (a 20 percent reduction) than did any of the other hospitals in our group.

论证方法

题目中论者主要运用了统计数据论证法和归纳推理论证法。

分析提示

● 论据(1)(2)运用的都是统计数据论证法。论据(1)说，对超强浓缩的UltraClean溶液（a concentrated solution of extra strength UltraClean），实验室研究表明，它要比论者所在医院目前使用的洗手液要多杀死40%的有害细菌。言下之意，这种超强浓缩的UltraClean溶液效果很好。但我们完全可以从另一个不同的角度来解释这种差别：即使某种溶液的杀菌、消毒效果一般，其浓缩液体的使用效果也会比相同成分普通浓度的溶液好。一个简单的检验方法是，将一些其他品牌的浓缩洗手液同该品牌的普通浓度的洗手液相比，看其杀菌效果有何差别。假如浓缩液至少比普通浓度的洗手液效果要好70%以上的话，论者说的UltraClean超强浓缩洗手液除菌效果比其他洗手液强40%的优势也就不稀奇了。

● 论据(2)说普通型UltraClean在Worktown医院收到较好的使用效果，病人的感染发病率降低了20%。但很可能有其他原因可以解释这一结果，比如：是否Worktown特殊的气候致使试验期间感染病例较少？是否Worktown地区的公共卫生状况较好，人们的健康水平整体较好呢？是否是Worktown医院的严格卫生管理降低了病人的感染率？是否是Worktown地区独特的人口结构（比如青壮年居多，而老人和儿童比较少）使那里的居民一般不会感染上病毒？等等。

● 结论中，论者主要依据UltraClean洗手液在Worktown医院的良好表现，建议将UltraClean推广到所有医院。这里论者运用归纳推理：既然同样的东西在一地有效，那它在别的地方应同样有效。但论者必须假设：其他地方以及那里的医院没有一些特殊的情况使这种推广收不到预期效果，比如：各地医院的卫生管理水平、各地公共卫生状况、地理环境和气候、人们的生活习惯以及对洗手液的消费偏好、各地不同的人口结构等。

123. The following appeared in a health newsletter.

"A ten-year nationwide study of the effectiveness of wearing a helmet while bicycling indicates that ten years ago, approximately 35 percent of all bicyclists reported wearing helmets, whereas today that number is nearly 80 percent. Another study, however, suggests that during the same ten-year period, the number of accidents caused by bicycling has increased 200 percent. These results demonstrate that bicyclists feel safer because they are wearing helmets, and they take more risks as a result. Thus, there is clearly a call for the government to strive to reduce the number of serious injuries from bicycle accidents by launching an education program that concentrates on the factors other than helmet use that are necessary for bicycle safety."

（参考第41、125题）

Write a response in which you discuss what questions would need to be answered in order to decide whether the recommendation and the argument on which it is based are reasonable. Be sure to explain how the answers to these questions would help to evaluate the recommendation.

题目整理

论点 There is clearly a call for the government to strive to reduce the number of serious injuries from bicycle accidents by launching an education program that concentrates on the factors other than helmet use that are necessary for bicycle safety.

论据 (1) A ten-year nationwide study of the effectiveness of wearing a helmet while bicycling indicates that ten years ago, approximately 35 percent of all bicyclists reported wearing helmets, whereas today that number is nearly 80 percent.

(2) Another study, however, suggests that during the same ten-year period, the number of accidents caused by bicycling has increased 200 percent.

论证方法

题目中论者主要运用了统计数据论证法。

分析提示

- 论据(1)(2)举了两项研究进行统计数据论证。但是，这些调查的方案设计（如调查样本的选择、调查数据的处理、调查结果的核实和验证等）和实施过程是严格按照科学程序进行的吗？其结论是客观、中立的吗？调查的实施者没有受行业及其他利益相关方的影响？

- 论据(1)(2)这两项研究揭示了一个违背常理的结果：十年来，骑自行车戴安全帽的人增多了，然而自行车事故却增长了两倍。论者的解释是，因为骑自行车的人戴了安全帽，就感觉自己很安全，所以就会骑车冒险。但至少下列疑问需要回答：首先，现在的安全帽和过去的安全帽一样安全可靠吗？其次，戴安全帽足以避免绝大多数事故吗？第三，有没有其他的因素导致了同样的结果，比如：现在的自行车设计的行车速度较快、自行车数量的急剧增加、没有足够的自行车专用车道、机动车数量的急剧增加、行人和机动车不守交规、交通管理力量严重欠缺、人口的大量增加以及道路拥堵程度的上升等？

- 论者在结论中建议加强自行车安全教育，并且将教育的重点放在其他因素，而不仅仅强调戴安全帽。但这个建议会引发以下的疑问：自行车安全教育会引起大家的重视吗？政府会常年坚持实施这种教育吗？未来自行车还会是人们的主要交通工具吗？是否骑车人一旦注意骑车安全就可以避免交通事故？等等。另外，论者认为可以不必强调安全帽的重要性，这一点似乎也与人们的常识相悖。

124. The following appeared in a memo from the director of a large group of hospitals.

"In a controlled laboratory study of liquid hand soaps, a concentrated solution of extra strength UltraClean hand soap produced a 40 percent greater reduction in harmful bacteria than did the liquid hand soaps currently used in our hospitals. During our recent test of regular-strength UltraClean with doctors, nurses, and visitors at our hospital in Worktown, the hospital reported significantly fewer cases of patient infection (a 20 percent reduction) than did any of the other hospitals in our group. Therefore, to prevent serious patient infections, we should supply UltraClean at all hand-washing stations, including those used by visitors, throughout our hospital system."

（参考第62、121、122题）

Write a response in which you discuss what specific evidence is needed to evaluate the argument and explain how the evidence would weaken or strengthen the argument.

题目整理

论点 To prevent serious patient infections, we should supply UltraClean at all hand-washing stations, including those used by visitors, throughout our hospital system.

论据 (1) In a controlled laboratory study of liquid hand soaps, a concentrated solution of extra strength UltraClean hand soap produced a 40 percent greater reduction in harmful bacteria than did the liquid hand soaps currently used in our hospitals.

(2) During our recent test of regular-strength UltraClean with doctors, nurses, and visitors at our hospital in Worktown, the hospital reported significantly fewer cases of patient infection (a 20 percent reduction) than did any of the other hospitals in our group.

论证方法

题目中论者主要运用了统计数据论证法和归纳推理论证法。

分析提示

● 论据(1)(2)运用的都是统计数据论证法。针对论据(1)，论者需要提供证据说明：这个实验的方案设计（如试验样本的选择、数据的处理、研究结果的核实和验证等）和实施过程是严格按照科学程序进行的；其结论是客观、中立的；试验的实施者没有受行业及其他利益相关方的影响等。其次，要注意，这次实验室研究用的是超强浓缩的UltraClean溶液。一般而言，即使这种溶液的杀菌、消毒效果一般，其浓缩液体的使用效果也会比相同成分普通浓度的溶液要好。问题是：其他品牌的浓缩洗手液同该品牌的普通浓度的洗手液相比，其杀菌效果如何？假如浓缩洗手液至少比普通浓度的洗手液效果要好70%以上的话，论者说的UltraClean浓缩洗手液除菌效果比其他洗手液强40%的优势也就不稀奇了。

● 论据(2)说普通型UltraClean在Worktown医院收到较好的使用效果，病人的感染发病率降低了20%。但论者是否有证据表明不是其他原因导致了这一结果，比如：是否Worktown特殊的气候致使试验期间感染病例较少？是否Worktown地区的公共卫生状况较好，人们的健康水平整体较好呢？是否Worktown医院的严格卫生管理降低了病人的感染率？是否是Worktown地区独特的人口结构（比如青壮年居多，而老人和儿童比较少）使那里的居民一般不会感染上病毒？等等。

● 结论中，论者主要依据UltraClean洗手液在Worktown医院的良好表现，建议将UltraClean推广到所有医院。这里论者运用归纳推理：既然同样的东西在一地有效，那它在别的地方应同样有效。但是，其他地方以及那里的医院有没有一些特殊的情况使这种推广收不到预期效果呢？比如：各地医院的卫生管理水平、各地公共卫生状况、地理环境和气候、人们的生活习惯以及对洗手液的消费偏好、各地不同的人口结构等。对这些，论者同样需提供进一步的论证。

125. The following appeared in a health newsletter.

"A ten-year nationwide study of the effectiveness of wearing a helmet while bicycling indicates that ten years ago, approximately 35 percent of all bicyclists reported wearing helmets, whereas today that number is nearly 80 percent. Another study, however, suggests that during the same ten-year period, the number of accidents caused by bicycling has increased 200 percent. These results demonstrate that bicyclists feel safer because they are wearing helmets, and they take more risks as a result. Thus there is clearly a call for the government to strive to reduce the number of serious injuries from bicycle accidents by launching an education program that concentrates on the factors other than helmet use that are necessary for bicycle safety."

(参考第41、123题)

Write a response in which you discuss what specific evidence is needed to evaluate the argument and explain how the evidence would weaken or strengthen the argument.

题目整理

论点 There is clearly a call for the government to strive to reduce the number of serious injuries from bicycle accidents by launching an education program that concentrates on the factors other than helmet use that are necessary for bicycle safety.

论据 (1) A ten-year nationwide study of the effectiveness of wearing a helmet while bicycling indicates that ten years ago, approximately 35 percent of all bicyclists reported wearing helmets, whereas today that number is nearly 80 percent.

(2) Another study, however, suggests that during the same ten-year period, the number of accidents caused by bicycling has increased 200 percent.

论证方法

题目中论者主要运用了统计数据论证法。

分析提示

● 论据(1)(2)是统计数据论证。先提出疑问：这些调查的方案设计（如调查样本的选择、调查数据的处理、调查结果的核实和验证等）和实施过程是严格按照科学程序进行的吗？其结论是客观、中立的吗？调查的实施者没有受行业及其他利益相关方的影响？

● 论据(1)(2)这两项研究揭示了一个违背常理的结果：十年来，骑自行车戴安全帽的人增多了，然而事故却增长了两倍。论者的解释是，因为骑自行车的人戴了安全帽，就感觉自己很安全，所以就会骑车冒险。但下列问题需要证明：首先，现在的安全帽和过去的安全帽一样安全可靠吗？其次，戴安全帽足以避免绝大多数自行车事故吗？第三，有没有其他因素导致了同样的结果，比如：现在的自行车设计的行车速度较快、自行车数量的急剧增加、没有足够的自行车专用车道、机动车数量的急剧增加、行人和机动车不守交规、交通管理力量严重欠缺、人口的大量增加以及道路拥堵程度的上升？

● 论者在结论中建议加强自行车安全教育，并且将教育的重点放在其他因素，而不是只强调戴安全帽。但论者可否证明：自行车安全教育会引起大家的重视吗？政府会常年坚持进行这种教育吗？未来自行车还会是人们的主要交通工具吗？骑车人一旦注意骑车安全是否就可以避免交通事故？等等。另外，论者认为可以不必强调安全帽的重要性，这一点也与人们的常识相悖。

---

126. The following is a recommendation from the personnel director to the president of Acme Publishing Company.

"Many other companies have recently stated that having their employees take the Easy Read Speed-Reading Course has greatly improved productivity. One graduate of the course was able to read a 500-page report in only two hours; another graduate rose from an assistant manager to vice president of the company in under a year. Obviously, the faster you can read, the more information you can absorb in a single workday. Moreover, Easy Read would cost Acme only $500 per employee—a small price to pay when you consider the benefits. Included in this fee is a three-week seminar in Spruce City and a lifelong subscription to the Easy Read newsletter. Clearly, Acme would benefit greatly by requiring all of our employees to take the Easy Read course."

（参考第 113、127、161 题）

Write a response in which you discuss what specific evidence is needed to evaluate the argument and explain how the evidence would weaken or strengthen the argument.

题目整理

论点 Acme would benefit greatly by requiring all of our employees to take the Easy Read course.

论据 (1) Many other companies have recently stated that having their employees take the Easy Read Speed-Reading Course has greatly improved productivity. One graduate of the course was able to read a 500-page report in only two hours; another graduate rose from an assistant manager to vice president of the company in under a year.

(2) Obviously, the faster you can read, the more information you can absorb in a single workday.

(3) Moreover, Easy Read would cost Acme only $500 per employee—a small price to pay when you consider the benefits.

(4) Included in this fee is a three-week seminar in Spruce City and a lifelong subscription to the Easy Read newsletter.

论证方法

题目中论者主要运用了归纳推理论证法和诉诸常识法。

分析提示

● 论据(1)举了许多公司作例子，运用的是不完全归纳法，属于归纳推理论证。但下列疑问论者需提供证据加以说明：首先，那些公司说的事情真实可信吗？经过核实了吗？其次，即便上述事情可信，那些公司具有代表性吗？论者说的 many other companies 中的 many 到底是多少家？10家、20家还是50家？many 是个很模糊的数量描述。最后，论者在这里还有横向类比不当的嫌疑。别的公司适用的，自己的公司也一定适用？自己公司的情况和他们具有可比性吗？

● 论据(2)(3)(4)都是运用常识展开论证。论据(2)所说的"一个人读的越快，吸收的信息量就越大"听起来似乎有道理，但经不起推敲。如果一个人阅读速度很快，但其相关基础知识欠缺、逻辑思维混乱、批判性思考能力差、不善于把书本信息同实际经验相互参照印证，他是不可能真正从阅读中吸收有用信息的。

● 论据(3)说"Easy Read would cost Acme only \$500 per employee—a small price to pay when you consider the benefits"。言下之意是，这笔投入很划算。但下列几个方面论者需进一步说明：第一，论据(1)提到的 benefits 都是听来的，其真实性并未证实。第二，假如这个 Easy Read 培训课程不能取得预期效果，还耽误了员工的工作时间，其成本代价还会是一笔简单的 \$500 per employee 的投入吗？第三，这家 Acme Publishing Company 有多少员工？假如员工上千的话，都接受培训意味着50万美元的开支。这还会是论者所说的 a small price 吗？

● 论者在论据(4)中说，培训课程 \$500 per employee 的报价中还包括 a three-week seminar in Spruce City and a lifelong subscription to the Easy Read newsletter。对于该公司的员工而言，这听起来很诱人。但公司老板也会这样看吗？员工们三个星期不干活对公司意味着什么？哪个老板会养闲人？这个培训课程从长期来看也许有利于该公司增强其人力资本的储备。但对这些远期的潜在收益，公司老板未必关心。毕竟，这些员工随时都有可能离职；今天对他们进行培训，明天他们就可能是竞争对手的人力资本了。

---

127. The following is a recommendation from the personnel director to the president of Acme Publishing Company.

"Many other companies have recently stated that having their employees take the Easy Read Speed-Reading Course has greatly improved productivity. One graduate of the course was able to read a 500-page report in only two hours; another graduate rose from an assistant manager to vice president of the company in under a year. Obviously, the faster you can read, the more information you can absorb in a single workday. Moreover, Easy Read would cost Acme only \$500 per employee—a small price to pay when you consider the benefits. Included in this fee is a three-week seminar in Spruce City and a lifelong subscription to the Easy Read newsletter. Clearly, to improve overall productivity, Acme should require all of our employees to take the Easy Read course."

（参考第113、126、161题）

Write a response in which you discuss what questions would need to be answered in order to decide whether the recommendation and the argument on which it is based are reasonable. Be sure to explain how the answers to these questions would help to evaluate the recommendation.

题目整理

论点 To improve overall productivity, Acme should require all of our employees to take the Easy Read course.

论据 (1) Many other companies have recently stated that having their employees take the Easy Read Speed-Reading Course has greatly improved productivity. One graduate of the course was able to read a 500-page report in only two hours; another graduate rose from an assistant manager to vice president of the company in under a year.

(2) Obviously, the faster you can read, the more information you can absorb in a single workday.

(3) Moreover, Easy Read would cost Acme only $500 per employee—a small price to pay when you consider the benefits.

(4) Included in this fee is a three-week seminar in Spruce City and a lifelong subscription to the Easy Read newsletter.

论证方法

题目中论者主要运用了归纳推理论证法和诉诸常识法。

分析提示

● 论据(1)举了许多公司作例子，运用的是不完全归纳法，属于归纳推理论证。但首先，那些公司所说的事情真实可信吗？经过核实了吗？其次，即便上述事情可信，那些公司有代表性吗？论者所说的many other companies中的many到底是多少家？ 10家、20家还是50家？many是个很模糊的数量描述。最后，论者在这里还有横向类比不当的嫌疑。别的公司适用的，自己的公司也一定适用？自己公司的情况和他们具有可比性吗？

● 论据(2)(3)(4)都是在运用常识展开论证。论据(2)所说的"一个人读的越快，吸收的信息量就越大"听起来似乎有道理，但经不起推敲。如果一个人阅读速度很快，但其相关基础知识欠缺、逻辑思维混乱、批判性思考能力差、不善于把书本信息同实际经验相互参照印证，他是不可能真正从阅读中吸收有用信息的。

● 论据(3)说"Easy Read would cost Acme only $500 per employee—a small price to pay when you consider the benefits"。言下之意是这笔投入很划算。但是，第一，论据(1)提到的benefits都是听来的，其真实性并未证实。第二，假如这个Easy Read培训课程不能取得预期效果，反而耽误了员工的工作时间，其成本代价还会是一笔简单的$500 per employee的投入吗？第三，这家Acme Publishing Company有多少员工呢？假如员工上千的话，都接受培训意味着50万美元的开支。这还会是论者所说的a small price吗？

● 论者在论据(4)中说，培训课程$500 per employee的报价中还包括a three-week seminar in Spruce City and a lifelong subscription to the Easy Read newsletter。对于该公司的员工而言，这听起来很诱人。但公司老板也会这样看吗？员工们三个星期不干活对公司意味着什么？

哪个老板会养闲人？这个培训课程从长期来看也许有利于该公司增强其人力资本的储备。但对这些远期的潜在收益，公司老板未必关心。毕竟，这些员工随时都可能离职；今天对他们进行培训，明天他们就可能是竞争对手的人力资本了。

··

128. The following appeared in a letter from the owner of the Sunnyside Towers apartment complex to its manager.

"One month ago, all the showerheads in the first three buildings of the Sunnyside Towers complex were modified to restrict maximum water flow to one-third of what it used to be. Although actual readings of water usage before and after the adjustment are not yet available, the change will obviously result in a considerable savings for Sunnyside Corporation, since the corporation must pay for water each month. Except for a few complaints about low water pressure, no problems with showers have been reported since the adjustment. Clearly, modifying showerheads to restrict water flow throughout all twelve buildings in the Sunnyside Towers complex will increase our profits further."

（参考第35、52、129题）

Write a response in which you discuss what specific evidence is needed to evaluate the argument and explain how the evidence would weaken or strengthen the argument.

题目整理

论点 Modifying showerheads to restrict water flow throughout all twelve buildings in the Sunnyside Towers complex will increase our profits further.

论据 (1) One month ago, all the showerheads in the first three buildings of the Sunnyside Towers complex were modified to restrict maximum water flow to one-third of what it used to be.

(2) Although actual readings of water usage before and after the adjustment are not yet available, the change will obviously result in a considerable savings for Sunnyside Corporation, since the corporation must pay for water each month.

(3) Except for a few complaints about low water pressure, no problems with showers have been reported since the adjustment.

论证方法

题目中论者主要运用了归纳推理论证法、因果关系论证法和列举特征式论证法。

分析提示

● 论据(1)是归纳推理。论者认为如果在这三座公寓楼采用的节水省钱的办法有效的话，将其推广到其他公寓楼会同样有效。但是，这三座楼有代表性吗？里面居住的人数、居住习惯、对洗浴水流的要求能代表所有12座公寓楼的情况吗？再者，这项试验是在一个月前实施的，那么，这一个月期间公寓住户的情况是否能代表全年的情况？这一个月是不是一年中的淡季？对这些问题，论者需提供进一步的解释。

● 论据(2)进行了因果推理：因为the corporation must pay for water each month，所以the change will obviously result in a considerable savings for Sunnyside Corporation。但下列疑问需要论者提供进一步的佐证：首先，如论者所说actual readings of water usage before and after the adjustment are not yet available，所以我们并不知道减小洗浴龙头的水流是否真的节水了。假如住户在洗浴时，因为水流小而洗更长的时间呢？用水量岂不一样多甚至更多？再者，当地的水价是多少？如果该公寓所在的城市靠近河流，取水非常方便，因而水价极低呢？最后，到底水费开支占该公司的总开支中多大比例？如果本来水费只占较小比例，a considerable savings for Sunnyside Corporation也就很难成立了。

● 论据(3)是列举特征式论证。论者认为住户很少投诉，因此就不存在什么问题。但住户没有反映问题不等于没问题。

● 最后，在结论中论者认为如果将这项节水措施推而广之的话，会获得更多的利润。但问题是：其他公寓的住户会接受这个水流小的龙头吗？他们会因为不适应这样的水龙头而搬走吗？或者，因为水龙头出水小，他们在使用过程中就频繁地调整水龙头阀门，致使水龙头破损呢？所有这些，都需要更多的佐证。

---

129. The following appeared in a letter from the owner of the Sunnyside Towers apartment complex to its manager.

"Last week, all the showerheads in the first three buildings of the Sunnyside Towers complex were modified to restrict maximum water flow to one-third of what it used to be. Although actual readings of water usage before and after the adjustment are not yet available, the change will obviously result in a considerable savings for Sunnyside Corporation, since the corporation must pay for water each month. Except for a few complaints about low water pressure, no problems with showers have been reported since the adjustment. Clearly, modifying showerheads to restrict water flow throughout all twelve buildings in the Sunnyside Towers complex will increase our profits further."

（参考第35、52、128题）

Write a response in which you examine the stated and/or unstated assumptions of the argument. Be sure to explain how the argument depends on these assumptions and what the implications are for the argument if the assumptions prove unwarranted.

题目整理

论点 Modifying showerheads to restrict water flow throughout all twelve buildings in the Sunnyside Towers complex will increase our profits further.

论据 (1) Last week, all the showerheads in the first three buildings of the Sunnyside Towers complex were modified to restrict maximum water flow to one-third of what it used to be.

(2) Although actual readings of water usage before and after the adjustment are not yet available, the change will obviously result in a considerable savings for Sunnyside Corporation, since the corporation must pay for water each month.

(3) Except for a few complaints about low water pressure, no problems with showers have been reported since the adjustment.

论证方法

题目中论者主要运用了归纳推理论证法、因果关系论证法和列举特征式论证法。

分析提示

● 论据(1)是归纳推理。论者认为如果在这三座公寓楼采用的节水省钱的办法有效的话，将其推广到其他公寓楼会同样有效。但论者需要以下假设以使其推论成立：第一，这三座楼要有代表性，里面居住的人数、居住习惯、对洗浴水流的要求要能代表所有12座公寓楼的情况。第二，这项试验是在一周前实施的，论者要假设，这一周期间公寓住户的情况要能代表其全年的情况。但问题是，该公寓住户全年用水量都是稳定的吗？上一周是不是一年中用水最少的时间段？

● 论据(2)进行了因果推理：因为the corporation must pay for water each month，所以the change will obviously result in a considerable savings for Sunnyside Corporation。但该推论需要以下假设：第一，如论者所说actual readings of water usage before and after the adjustment are not yet available，所以我们并不知道减小洗浴龙头的水流是否真的节水了。所以，论者要假设，没有其他会让这些住户的用水量增加的情形出现。假如住户在洗浴时，因为水流小而洗更长的时间呢？用水岂不一样多甚至更多？第二，当地水价较高，或者水费是Sunnyside Towers一项大的支出。如果该公寓所在的城市靠近河流，取水非常方便，因而水价极低呢；并且，水费本来只占该公司总开支的较小比例，a considerable savings for Sunnyside Corporation也就很难成立了。

● 论据(3)是列举特征式论证。论者认为住户很少投诉，因此就不存在什么问题。但住户没有反映问题不等于没问题。

● 最后，在结论中论者认为如果将这项节水措施推而广之的话，会获得更多的利润。但论者要假设：其他公寓的住户会接受这个水流小的水龙头；他们不会因为不适应这样的水龙头而搬走；他们也不会因为水龙头出水小，就在使用过程中胡乱调整水龙头阀门，致使水龙头破损。

---

130. The following memorandum is from the business manager of Happy Pancake House restaurants.

"Butter has now been replaced by margarine in Happy Pancake House restaurants throughout the southwestern United States. Only about 2 percent of customers have filed a formal complaint, indicating that an average of 98 people out of 100 are happy with the change. Furthermore, many servers have reported that a number of customers who ask for butter do not complain when they are given margarine instead. Clearly, either these customers cannot distinguish butter from margarine or they use the term 'butter' to refer to either butter or margarine. Thus, to avoid the expense of purchasing butter, the Happy Pancake House should extend this cost-saving change to its restaurants throughout the rest of the country."

（参考第15、51、131、133题）

Write a response in which you examine the stated and/or unstated assumptions of the argument. Be sure to explain how the argument depends on these assumptions and what the implications are for the argument if the assumptions prove unwarranted.

题目整理

论点 To avoid the expense of purchasing butter, the Happy Pancake House should extend this cost-saving change to its restaurants throughout the rest of the country.

论据 (1) Butter has now been replaced by margarine in Happy Pancake House restaurants throughout the southwestern United States. Only about 2 percent of customers have filed a formal complaint, indicating that an average of 98 people out of 100 are happy with the change.

(2) Furthermore, many servers have reported that a number of customers who ask for butter do not complain when they are given margarine instead.

(3) Clearly, either these customers cannot distinguish butter from margarine or they use the term 'butter' to refer to either butter or margarine.

论证方法

题目中论者主要运用了统计数据论证法和引用权威论证法。

分析提示

● 论据(1)试图在告诉我们一项调查。针对这项调查，论者首先需要以下假设：这些调查的方案设计（如调查样本的选择、调查数据的处理、调查结果的核实和验证等）和实施过程是严格按照科学程序进行的；其结论是客观、中立、可信的；调查的实施者没有受行业及其他利益相关方的影响；等等。其次，论者说只有2%的顾客投诉，剩下98%顾客的反应都被他解释成满意。这显然有问题，论者的逻辑是"非此即彼"，一个"虚假困境"。论者实际在否认这么一种可能，即，绝大部分顾客都非常不满意，但许多人不愿向店家投诉，只是心里决定下次不再来这里消费了。如此的话，虽说表面上只有2%的顾客投诉，但实际上大部分顾客已经怨声载道。

● 论据(2)是个引用权威的论证手法。论者引用服务员的话：a number of customers who ask for butter do not complain when they are given margarine instead. 在此，论者要假设：首先，这里的服务员全都汇报了真实情况。但这个假设很成问题。因为如果每位顾客的任何合情合理的要求都必须满足的话，这意味着他们的工作量将会增加很多。因此，这些服务员因为劳累或者工作态度的问题，很可能对顾客的要求推脱延迟，并且掩盖事实说顾客对得到的是butter还是margarine抱无所谓态度。其次，即便服务员反映的情况属实，论者还要假设顾客表达了他们的真实想法。顾客没投诉并不表示他们没有不满。

● 论据(3)是论者编造的又一个"虚假困境"。很少有人不会区分butter和margarine，而顾客用butter来随便指称butter或margarine更是牵强。更大的可能是这些顾客不愿为了一点儿butter破坏了就餐时的心情。

● 在结论中，论者建议把人造黄油代替天然黄油的办法推广到国内的其他连锁店。这里隐含着一个归纳推理：在一地看似有效的做法，在另外一地也会有效。但实施这项推广活动需要以下假设：别处的顾客也会那么温和地表达他们的不满；那些地方没有特别激烈的竞争，顾客们如有不满不会选择其他的餐馆；别处的消费者不会因为传统饮食习惯，根本就不能接受人造黄油等。

131. The following memorandum is from the business manager of Happy Pancake House restaurants.

"Butter has now been replaced by margarine in Happy Pancake House restaurants throughout the southwestern United States. Only about 2 percent of customers have complained, indicating that an average of 98 people out of 100 are happy with the change. Furthermore, many servers have reported that a number of customers who ask for butter do not complain when they are given margarine instead. Clearly, either these customers cannot distinguish butter from margarine or they use the term 'butter' to refer to either butter or margarine. Thus, we predict that Happy Pancake House will be able to increase profits dramatically if we extend this cost-saving change to all our restaurants in the southeast and northeast as well."

（参考第15、51、130、133题）

Write a response in which you discuss what questions would need to be answered in order to decide whether the prediction and the argument on which it is based are reasonable. Be sure to explain how the answers to these questions would help to evaluate the prediction.

题目整理

论点 Happy Pancake House will be able to increase profits dramatically if we extend this cost-saving change to all our restaurants in the southeast and northeast as well.

论据 (1) Butter has now been replaced by margarine in Happy Pancake House restaurants throughout the southwestern United States. Only about 2 percent of customers have complained, indicating that an average of 98 people out of 100 are happy with the change.

(2) Furthermore, many servers have reported that a number of customers who ask for butter do not complain when they are given margarine instead.

(3) Clearly, either these customers cannot distinguish butter from margarine or they use the term 'butter' to refer to either butter or margarine.

论证方法

题目中论者主要运用了统计数据论证法和引用权威论证法。

分析提示

● 论据(1)试图在告诉我们一项调查。针对这项调查，我们的问题是：这些调查的方案设计（如调查样本的选择、调查数据的处理、调查结果的核实和验证等）和实施过程是否是严格按照科学程序进行的？其结论是客观、中立的吗？调查的实施者没有受行业及其他利益相关方的影响？有没有参考独立第三方提供的数据？等等。其次，论者说只有2%的顾客投诉，剩下98%顾客的反应都被他解释成满意。这显然有问题，论者的逻辑是"非此即彼"，一个"虚假困境"。论者实际上否认了这么一种可能，即，绝大部分客人都非常不满意，但许多人不愿向店家投诉，只是心里决定下次不再来这里消费了。这样的话，虽说表面上只有2%的顾客投诉，但实际上大部分顾客都已经怨声载道。再者，即便这些没有投诉的98%顾客并非人人心里都很不满，其中的一部分人也许不太在意butter和margarine的区别，但至少不能把他们都说成是"happy with the change"。这种"非此即彼"的逻辑很难自圆其说。

● 论据(2)是个引用权威的论证手法。论者引用服务员的话：a number of customers who ask for butter do not complain when they are given margarine instead. 对此，我们同样要问：首先，这里的服务员有没有汇报真实情况？如果每位顾客的任何合情合理的要求都必须满足的话，这意味着他们的工作量将会增加很多。因此，这些服务员因为劳累或者工作态度的问题，很可能对顾客的要求推脱延迟，并且掩盖事实说顾客对得到是butter还是margarine抱无所谓态度。其次，即便服务员反映的情况属实，但顾客到底有没有表达他们的真实想法？顾客没投诉并不表示他们没有不满。

● 论据(3)是论者编造的又一个"虚假困境"。很少有人不会区分butter和margarine，而顾客用butter来随便指称butter或margarine更是牵强。更大的可能是这些顾客不愿为了一点儿butter破坏了就餐时的心情。

● 在结论中，论者建议把人造黄油代替天然黄油的办法推广到东南部和东北部的连锁店。这里隐含着一个归纳推理：在一地看似有效的做法，在另外一地也会有效。但问题是，别处的顾客也会那么温和地表达他们的不满吗？那些地方的竞争是否特别激烈，顾客们如有不满就会选择其他餐馆？或者，那里的消费者因为传统习惯，根本就不能接受人造黄油？这些问题论者都要回答。

....

132. The following appeared in a letter to the school board in the town of Centerville.

"All students should be required to take the driver's education course at Centerville High School. In the past two years, several accidents in and around Centerville have involved teenage drivers. Since a number of parents in Centerville have complained that they are too busy to teach their teenagers to drive, some other instruction is necessary to ensure that these teenagers are safe drivers. Although there are two driving schools in Centerville, parents on a tight budget cannot afford to pay for driving instruction. Therefore an effective and mandatory program sponsored by the high school is the only solution to this serious problem."

（参考第134、136题）

Write a response in which you examine the stated and/or unstated assumptions of the argument. Be sure to explain how the argument depends on these assumptions and what the implications are for the argument if the assumptions prove unwarranted.

题目整理

论点 All students should be required to take the driver's education course at Centerville High School. An effective and mandatory program sponsored by the high school is the only solution to this serious problem.

论据 (1) In the past two years, several accidents in and around Centerville have involved teenage drivers.

(2) Since a number of parents in Centerville have complained that they are too busy to teach their teenagers to drive, some other instruction is necessary to ensure that these teenagers are safe drivers.

(3) Although there are two driving schools in Centerville, parents on a tight budget cannot afford to pay for driving instruction.

论证方法

题目中论者主要运用了统计数据论证法和因果关系论证法。

分析提示

- 论据(1)是统计数据论证法。这里面有一系列的假设：首先，论者假设那些交通事故都很严重，否则，论者不会在结论里将学生驾车安全问题定性为serious problem。但问题是，除了用一个模糊的several来描述外，论者并没有告诉我们在过去两年间到底发生了多少起涉及青少年驾车的交通事故，以及这些事故所造成的人员伤亡情况。如果其间仅仅发生两三起没有大伤亡的事故，学生驾车的问题好像并不是太严重。其次，从前后逻辑关系看，论者认定这些交通事故的主要责任都在这些青少年，但并未提供有效论证。再次，即使那些交通事故的责任在学生，造成事故的具体原因是什么？是他们交通知识和驾驶技术不够，还是别的原因？论者强调这些学生需要上驾驶课程，显然是认为学生缺乏交通知识和驾驶技术。如果是其他原因，比如：该地人流和车流过密、道路过窄、交通标志不明、交通指挥疏导不力、交通执法不严等，论者的逻辑就很成问题了。

- 论据(2)(3)都是因果关系论证。论据(2)依据"a number of parents in Centerville have complained that they are too busy to teach their teenagers to drive"，排除了由家长来教学生驾车的可能性。论据(3)依据"parents on a tight budget cannot afford to pay for driving instruction"，排除了学生去驾校学习驾驶的可能性。然后，论者得出结论"An effective and mandatory (driving) program sponsored by the high school is **the only solution** to this serious problem"。论者显然认为，除了跟父母学、在驾校学以及上学校的驾驶课程之外，没有其他可以解决问题的方式了。这似乎很牵强。实际上，诸如：学生的亲戚和朋友教授驾驶技术、地方政府出资建一所针对青少年的驾驶培训学校、政府为在驾校学习驾驶的学生提供补贴、学校提供校车接送学生上学和放学、所有在Centerville的学校联合开通学生交通专线等，都是可以考虑的解决办法。

- 最后，在结论中，论者强调"the driver's education course at Centerville High School"必须是强制性的（mandatory）。论者同样要假设：第一，如果不免费的话，这个强制性的驾驶课程不太贵，学生家长都能承受。第二，这个强制性的课程不会遭到部分有条件自己教孩子学开车的家长的反对。第三，这个学校发起的学习驾驶计划最终能减少由学生驾车引起的交通事故等。

133. The following memorandum is from the business manager of Happy Pancake House restaurants.

"Butter has now been replaced by margarine in Happy Pancake House restaurants throughout the southwestern United States. Only about 2 percent of customers have complained, indicating that an average of 98 people out of 100 are happy with the change. Furthermore, many servers have reported that a number of customers who ask for butter do not complain when they are given margarine instead. Clearly, either these customers cannot distinguish butter from margarine or they use the term 'butter' to refer to either butter or margarine. Thus, to avoid the expense of purchasing butter and to increase profitability, the Happy Pancake House should extend this cost-saving change to its restaurants in the southeast and northeast as well."

（参考第 15、51、130、131 题）

Write a response in which you discuss what specific evidence is needed to evaluate the argument and explain how the evidence would weaken or strengthen the argument.

题目整理

论点 To avoid the expense of purchasing butter and to increase profitability, the Happy Pancake House should extend this cost-saving change to its restaurants in the southeast and northeast as well.

论据 (1) Butter has now been replaced by margarine in Happy Pancake House restaurants throughout the southwestern United States. Only about 2 percent of customers have complained, indicating that an average of 98 people out of 100 are happy with the change.

(2) Furthermore, many servers have reported that a number of customers who ask for butter do not complain when they are given margarine instead.

(3) Clearly, either these customers cannot distinguish butter from margarine or they use the term 'butter' to refer to either butter or margarine.

论证方法

题目中论者主要运用了统计数据论证法和引用权威论证法。

分析提示

● 论据(1)试图在告诉我们一项调查。首先，针对这项调查，我们需要的进一步的证据是：这些调查的方案设计（如调查样本的选择、调查数据的处理、调查结果的核实和验证等）和实施过程是否是严格按照科学程序进行的？其结论的客观性、中立性是否有保证？调查的实施者没有受行业及其他利益相关方的影响？有没有参考独立第三方提供的数据？等等。其次，论者说只有2%的顾客投诉，剩下98%顾客的反应都被他解释成满意。这显然有问题，论者的逻辑是"非此即彼"。论者实际上否认了这么一种可能，即，绝大部分顾客都非常不满意，但许多人不愿向店家投诉，只是心里决定下次不再来这里消费了。这样的话，虽说表面上只有2%的顾客投诉，但实际上大部分顾客都已经怨声载道。论者没有论述以上这种可能性。再者，即便这些没有投诉的98%顾客并非人人心里都很不满，其中的一部分人也许不太在意butter和margarine的区别，但至少不能把他们都说成是"happy with the change"。论者这种"非此即彼"的逻辑很难自圆其说。

- 论据(2)是个引用权威的论证手法。论者引用服务员的话：a number of customers who ask for butter do not complain when they are given margarine instead. 首先，论者有无证据表明服务员汇报的情况属实？如果每位顾客任何合情合理的要求服务员都必须满足的话，这意味着他们的工作量将会增加很多。因此，这些服务员因为劳累或者工作态度的问题，很可能推脱顾客的要求，并且掩盖事实说顾客不在意得到的是butter还是margarine。其次，即便服务员反映的情况属实，但顾客到底有没有表达他们的真实想法？顾客没投诉并不表示他们没有不满。

- 论据(3)是论者编造的又一个"虚假困境"。很少有人不会区分butter和margarine，而顾客用butter来随便指称butter或margarine，这种说法很牵强。很有可能是这些顾客不愿为了一点儿butter破坏了就餐时的心情。论者需要进一步弄清楚顾客的真实心态。

- 在结论中，论者建议把人造黄油代替天然黄油的办法推广到东南部和东北部的连锁店。这里隐含着一个归纳推理：在一地看似有效的做法，在另外一地也会有效。但问题是，别处的顾客也会那么温和地表达他们的不满吗？那些地方的竞争是否特别激烈，顾客们如有不满就会选择其他餐馆？或者，那里的消费者因为传统习惯，根本就不能接受人造黄油呢？没有关于这些问题的更多佐证，论者想提高利润的目的恐怕难以实现。

134. The following appeared in a letter to the school board in the town of Centerville.

"All students should be required to take the driver's education course at Centerville High School. In the past two years, several accidents in and around Centerville have involved teenage drivers. Since a number of parents in Centerville have complained that they are too busy to teach their teenagers to drive, some other instruction is necessary to ensure that these teenagers are safe drivers. Although there are two driving schools in Centerville, parents on a tight budget cannot afford to pay for driving instruction. Therefore an effective and mandatory program sponsored by the high school is the only solution to this serious problem."

（参考第132、136题）

Write a response in which you discuss what specific evidence is needed to evaluate the argument and explain how the evidence would weaken or strengthen the argument.

题目整理

论点 All students should be required to take the driver's education course at Centerville High School. An effective and mandatory program sponsored by the high school is the only solution to this serious problem.

论据 (1) In the past two years, several accidents in and around Centerville have involved teenage drivers.

(2) Since a number of parents in Centerville have complained that they are too busy to teach their teenagers to drive, some other instruction is necessary to ensure that these teenagers are safe drivers.

(3) Although there are two driving schools in Centerville, parents on a tight budget cannot afford to pay for driving instruction.

论证方法

题目中论者主要运用了统计数据论证法和因果关系论证法。

分析提示

● 论据(1)是统计数据论证法。但论者还需提供更多的细节以支持其推论：首先，论者在结论里将学生驾车安全问题定性为serious problem。但在论据(1)中，除了用一个模糊的several来描述外，论者并没有告诉我们在过去两年间到底发生了多少起涉及青少年驾车的交通事故，以及这些事故所造成的人员伤亡情况。如果其间仅仅发生两三起没有大伤亡的事故，学生驾车的问题好像并不是太严重。其次，从前后逻辑关系看，论者认定这些交通事故的主要责任都在这些青少年，但并未提供有效论证。再次，即使那些交通事故的责任在学生，造成事故的具体原因是什么？是他们交通知识和驾驶技术不够，还是别的原因？论者强调这些学生需要上驾驶课程，显然是认为学生缺乏交通知识和驾驶技术。其他因素，比如：该地人流和车流过密、道路过窄、交通标志不明、交通指挥疏导不力、交通执法不严等，显然都可能导致相同的结果。对此，论者没有提供更多的论证。

● 论据(2)(3)都是因果关系论证。论据(2)依据"a number of parents in Centerville have complained that they are too busy to teach their teenagers to drive"，排除了由家长来教学生驾车的可能性。论据(3)依据"parents on a tight budget cannot afford to pay for driving instruction"，排除了学生去驾校学习驾驶的可能性。然后，论者得出结论"An effective and mandatory (driving) program sponsored by the high school is **the only solution** to this serious problem"。但问题是，除了跟父母学、在驾校学以及上学校的驾驶课程之外，没有其他解决问题的方式了吗？论证的推论极为牵强。实际上，诸如：学生的亲戚和朋友教授驾驶技术、地方政府出资建一所针对少年的驾驶培训学校、政府为在驾校学习驾驶的学生提供补贴、学校提供校车接送学生上学和放学、所有在Centerville的学校联合开通学生交通专线等，都是可以考虑的解决方法。

● 最后，在结论中，论者强调"the driver's education course at Centerville High School"必须是强制性的。但问题是：首先，如果不免费的话，这个强制性的驾驶课程会不会太贵，部分学生家长承受不起怎么办？其次，这个强制性的课程会不会遭到一些有条件自己教孩子学开车的家长的反对？再次，这个学校发起的学习驾驶计划最终能否减少由学生驾车引起的交通事故？等等这些都需要更多的资料佐证。

135. The data from a survey of high school math and science teachers show that in the district of Sanlee many of these teachers reported assigning daily homework, whereas in the district of Marlee, most science and math teachers reported assigning homework no more than

two or three days per week. Despite receiving less frequent homework assignments, Marlee students earn better grades overall and are less likely to be required to repeat a year of school than are students in Sanlee. These results call into question the usefulness of frequent homework assignments. Most likely the Marlee students have more time to concentrate on individual assignments than do the Sanlee students who have homework every day. Therefore teachers in our high schools should assign homework no more than twice a week.

（参考第137、140题）

Write a response in which you discuss what specific evidence is needed to evaluate the argument and explain how the evidence would weaken or strengthen the argument.

题目整理

论点 Teachers in our high schools should assign homework no more than twice a week.

论据 (1) The data from a survey of high school math and science teachers show that in the district of Sanlee many of these teachers reported assigning daily homework, whereas in the district of Marlee, most science and math teachers reported assigning homework no more than two or three days per week.

(2) Despite receiving less frequent homework assignments, Marlee students earn better grades overall and are less likely to be required to repeat a year of school than are students in Sanlee. These results call into question the usefulness of frequent homework assignments.

(3) Most likely the Marlee students have more time to concentrate on individual assignments than do the Sanlee students who have homework every day.

论证方法

题目中论者主要运用了统计数据论证法、因果关系论证法和归纳推理论证法。

分析提示

● 论据(1)是统计数据论证，论者引用一项对高中数学及自然老师的调查。对下列疑问，论者需要提供进一步的材料加以说明：这项调查的方案设计（如调查样本的选择、调查问卷的设计、调查数据的处理、调查结果的核实和验证等）和实施过程是否是严格按照科学程序进行的？参与调查的老师都如实回答问题了吗？其结论客观、中立吗？调查的实施者有没有受行业及其他利益相关方的影响？

● 论据(2)是因果关系论证。论者展示了 Sanlee 和 Marlee 两个区学生成绩的差异。结合论据(1)提供的两个区的高中数学及自然老师在给学生布置家庭作业这件事上的不同做法，论者得出结论说是老师布置家庭作业做法上的不同造成了两个区学生成绩的差异。这个推论一个明显的特点是：把一前一后出现的两个现象理解成因果关系。这是一个"在此之后，因此之故"逻辑错误。为准确判断论者的推理过程，以下几个疑问需要证据：第一，两个地区数学和自然两类课程老师的做法是否可以代表所有老师的做法？两个区其他课程的老师也都像这两个科目的老师这样布置家庭作业吗？如果不是，这两个科目老师的做法有代表性吗？第二，这两个地区学生学习成绩的差异是否可能是由其他因素引起的？比如，Sanlee 的学生成绩差是因为该区的教育设施落后、经济欠发达、学生基础较弱、老师的整体教学水平有待提高等；而Marlee的学生成绩好很可能是因为学生家庭教育配合得比较好、学生基础好、老师教学水平高等。第三，论者说Marlee区的学生普遍成绩较好，学生留级的现象也比Sanlee区的学生少。但出现这个差异是否是因为这两个区对学生实施了不同评分和升学政策了呢？假如Marlee区的学校鼓励给学生高分，一般不对学生作留级处理，以此来树立学生的自信心，而Sanlee区的学校的做法却恰恰相反，这样的话，论者的结论就有问题。

● 论据(3)提到了两个区的数学和自然老师在布置家庭作业这件事情上不同做法的影响，即：the Marlee students have more time to concentrate on individual assignments than do the Sanlee students who have homework every day. 言下之意是，Marlee区的学生没有家庭作业的负担，个人活动时间就很充裕，而Sanlee区的学生每天有家庭作业。但结果却是，家庭作业少的学生成绩好，家庭作业多的学生成绩差。这很可能只是个假象。假如Marlee区的学生尽管没有家庭作业，他们主动把自由活动的时间用来学习；而Sanlee区的学生因为厌倦做家庭作业，多数采取了敷衍应付的学习态度了呢？这样的话，导致两个区学生成绩差异的并不是家庭作业的多少，而是学习态度。

● 结论中的建议"Teachers in our high schools should assign homework no more than twice a week"是要将不多布置家庭作业的做法推广到所有高中的学科。这有以偏概全的逻辑错误。

---

136. The following appeared in a letter to the school board in the town of Centerville.

"All students should be required to take the driver's education course at Centerville High School. In the past two years, several accidents in and around Centerville have involved teenage drivers. Since a number of parents in Centerville have complained that they are too busy to teach their teenagers to drive, some other instruction is necessary to ensure that these teenagers are safe drivers. Although there are two driving schools in Centerville, parents on a tight budget cannot afford to pay for driving instruction. Therefore an effective and mandatory program sponsored by the high school is the only solution to this serious problem."

（参考第132、134题）

Write a response in which you discuss what questions would need to be answered in order to decide whether the recommendation and the argument on which it is based are reasonable. Be sure to explain how the answers to these questions would help to evaluate the recommendation.

题目整理

论点 All students should be required to take the driver's education course at Centerville High School. An effective and mandatory program sponsored by the high school is the only solution to this serious problem.

论据 (1) In the past two years, several accidents in and around Centerville have involved teenage drivers.

(2) Since a number of parents in Centerville have complained that they are too busy to teach their teenagers to drive, some other instruction is necessary to ensure that these teenagers are safe drivers.

(3) Although there are two driving schools in Centerville, parents on a tight budget cannot afford to pay for driving instruction.

论证方法

题目中论者主要运用了统计数据论证法和因果关系论证法。

分析提示

● 论据(1)是统计数据论证法。但首先，Centerville High School学生驾驶的问题是否很严重？论者在结论里将学生驾车安全问题定性为serious problem。但在论据(1)中，除了用一个模糊的several来描述外，论者并没有告诉我们在过去两年间到底发生了多少起涉及青少年驾驶的交通事故，以及这些事故造成的人员伤亡情况。如果其间仅仅发生两三起没有大伤亡的事故，学生驾车的问题好像并不是太严重。其次，谁是那些交通事故的主要责任人？从前后逻辑关系看，论者似乎认为这些交通事故的主要责任都在这些青少年，但并未提供有效论证。再次，即使那些交通事故的责任在学生，造成事故的具体原因是什么？是他们缺乏交通知识和驾驶技术，还是别的原因？论者强调这些学生需要上驾驶课程，显然是认定学生缺乏交通知识和驾驶技术。但其他因素，比如：该地人流和车流过密、道路过窄、交通标志不明、交通指挥疏导不力、交通执法不严等，显然都可能导致相同的结果。对此，论者没有提供更多佐证加以说明。

● 论据(2)(3)都是因果关系论证。论据(2)依据"a number of parents in Centerville have complained that they are too busy to teach their teenagers to drive"，排除了由家长来教学生驾车的可能性。论据(3)依据"parents on a tight budget cannot afford to pay for driving instruction"，排除了学生去驾校学习驾驶的可能性。然后，论者得出结论"An effective and mandatory (driving) program sponsored by the high school is the only solution to this serious problem"。但问题是，除了跟父母学、在驾校学以及上学校的驾驶课程之外，没有其他解决问题的方式？论证的推论极为牵强。实际上，诸如：学生的亲戚和朋友教授驾驶技术、地方政府出资建一所针对青少年的驾驶培训学校、政府为学生在驾校学习驾驶提供补贴、学校提供校车接送学生上学和放学、所有在Centerville的学校联合开通学生交通专线等等，都是可以考虑的解决方法。

● 最后，在结论中，论者强调"the driver's education course at Centerville High School"必须是强制性的。判断该建议是否可行论者需回答：首先，如果不免费的话，这个强制性的驾驶课程如果太贵，部分学生家长承受不起怎么办？其次，这个强制性的课程会不会遭到一些有条件自己教孩子学开车的家长的反对？再次，这个学校发起的学习驾驶计划最终能否减少由学生驾车引起的交通事故？

137. While the Department of Education in the state of Attra recommends that high school students be assigned homework every day, the data from a recent statewide survey of high school math and science teachers give us reason to question the usefulness of daily homework. In the district of Sanlee, 86 percent of the teachers reported assigning homework three to five times a week, whereas in the district of Marlee, less than 25 percent of the teachers reported assigning

homework three to five times a week. Yet the students in Marlee earn better grades overall and are less likely to be required to repeat a year of school than are the students in Sanlee. Therefore, all teachers in our high schools should assign homework no more than twice a week.

（参考第135、140题）

Write a response in which you examine the stated and/or unstated assumptions of the argument. Be sure to explain how the argument depends on these assumptions and what the implications are for the argument if the assumptions prove unwarranted.

题目整理

论点 The usefulness of daily homework assignments to high school students is questionable, and therefore, all teachers in our high schools should assign homework no more than twice a week.

论据 (1) While the Department of Education in the state of Attra recommends that high school students be assigned homework every day, the data from a recent statewide survey of high school math and science teachers give us reason to question the usefulness of daily homework. In the district of Sanlee, 86 percent of the teachers reported assigning homework three to five times a week, whereas in the district of Marlee, less than 25 percent of the teachers reported assigning homework three to five times a week.

(2) Yet the students in Marlee earn better grades overall and are less likely to be required to repeat a year of school than are the students in Sanlee.

论证方法

题目中论者主要运用了统计数据论证法、因果关系论证法和归纳推理论证法。

分析提示

● 论据(1)是统计数据论证，论者引用的是一项对高中数学及自然老师的调查，这项调查是论者全部推论的起点和基础。在推论中，论者需要以下假设：第一，这项调查的方案设计（如调查样本的选择、调查问卷的设计、调查数据的处理、调查结果的核实和验证等）和实施过程是严格按照科学程序进行的。第二，参与调查的老师都如实回答了问题。第三，该调查的结论客观、中立，调查的实施者没有受行业及其他利益相关方的影响。

● 论据(2)是因果关系论证。论者展示了Sanlee和Marlee两个区学生成绩的差异。结合论据(1)提供的两个区的高中数学及自然老师在给学生布置家庭作业这件事上的不同做法，论者显然认为是老师布置家庭作业做法上的不同造成了两个区学生成绩的差异。这个推论一个明显的特点是：把一前一后出现的两个现象理解成因果关系，犯了"在此之后，因此之故"的逻辑错误。同时，论者还需要有以下几个假设：第一，假设Marlee和Sanlee两个地区数学和自然课程老师的做法可以代表所有老师的做法。问题是，两个区其他课程的老师也都像这两个科目的老师这样布置家庭作业吗？如果不是，这两个科目老师的做法岂不缺乏代表性？第二，假设这两个地区学生学习成绩的差异不是由其他因素引起的。但这个假设很难成立。比如，Sanlee的学生成绩差是因为该区的教育设施落后、经济欠发达、学生基础较薄弱、老师的整体教学水平有待提高等；而Marlee的学生成绩好很可能是因为学生家庭教育配合得比较好、学生基础好、老师教学水平高等。第三，论者说Marlee区的学生普遍成绩较好，学生留级的现象也比Sanlee区的学生少。但这个差异是否是因为这两个区对学生实施了不同评分和升学政策而产生的？假如Marlee区的学校鼓励给学生打高分，一般不对学生作留级处理，以此来树立学生的自信心，而Sanlee区的学校的做法却恰恰相反，这样的话，论者的结论就很有疑问了。

● 结论中的建议 "all teachers in our high schools should assign homework no more than twice a week" 是要将少布置家庭作业的做法推广到所有高中的学科。这有以偏概全的逻辑错误。

138. The following appeared as an editorial in the student newspaper of Groveton College.

"To combat the recently reported dramatic rise in cheating among college students, colleges and universities should adopt honor codes similar to Groveton's, which calls for students to agree not to cheat in their academic endeavors and to notify a faculty member if they suspect that others have cheated. Groveton's honor code replaced an old-fashioned system in which teachers closely monitored students. Under that system, teachers reported an average of thirty cases of cheating per year. The honor code has proven far more successful: in the first year it was in place, students reported twenty-one cases of cheating; five years later, this figure had dropped to fourteen. Moreover, in a recent survey conducted by the Groveton honor council, a majority of students said that they would be less likely to cheat with an honor code in place than without."

（参考第22、119、120题）

Write a response in which you discuss what specific evidence is needed to evaluate the argument and explain how the evidence would weaken or strengthen the argument.

题目整理

论点 To combat the recently reported dramatic rise in cheating among college students, colleges and universities should adopt honor codes similar to Groveton's.

论据 (1) Groveton's honor code calls for students to agree not to cheat in their academic endeavors and to notify a faculty member if they suspect that others have cheated. Groveton's honor code replaced an old-fashioned system in which teachers closely monitored students. Under that system, teachers reported an average of thirty cases of cheating per year. The honor code has proven far more successful: in the first year it was in place, students reported twenty-one cases of cheating; five years later, this figure had dropped to fourteen.

(2) Moreover, in a recent survey conducted by the Groveton honor council, a majority of students said that they would be less likely to cheat with an honor code in place than without.

论证方法

题目中论者主要运用了统计数据论证法和类比论证法。

分析提示

● 首先，在论据(1)中论者提到，过去由老师来监考的情况下，每年大概有30起学生作弊事件；而在新的honor code制度之下，第一年学生们报告的作弊事件有21起，五年后，该数字降为14，学生们作弊现象少了。论者把这一变化归因于honor code制度。但是，论者可否证明不是别的因素在发挥作用？比如：之前学生作弊事件多是否同老师监管较严、只要发现作弊就上报有关？而新办法下学生作弊事件减少是否同学生自我监管较松、隐瞒不报有关？而且，论者并没有提到过去和现在该校的学生人数。假如过去学生人数较多，30个作弊事件占学生人数的比例很低；现在虽然学生作弊的绝对数量下降了，但由于学生总量的下降，而实际上学生作弊的比例上升呢？更何况，论者只提到新的honor code实施后第一年和第五年的情形，并没有提中间三年学生作弊的情况。假如这中间几年学生作弊的事件总量又上升了呢？我们还能说这个新政有效吗？

- 论据(2)说的调查是Groveton honor council做的。首先，这项调查的方案设计（如调查样本的选择、调查问卷的设计、调查数据的处理、调查结果的核实和验证等）和实施过程是否是严格按照科学程序进行的？其结论客观吗？Groveton honor council能够秉持中立吗？它有没有受到既得利益者的影响？为什么不让独立第三方来调查？这些需要论者进一步的说明。其次，论者说"students said that they would be less likely to cheat with an honor code in place than without"。这里的majority到底是多少？如果只有20个学生参与了抽样调查，即便其中18个人都表示新的honor code让他们不再作弊了，相对于该校可能几万的学生来说，也会因为样本过小而说明不了什么问题。而且，这些学生说了他们的真实想法了吗？有没有可能因为新政对他们有利而故意隐瞒自己的态度？这些都需要更多的佐证。

- 在结论中，论者建议"colleges and universities should adopt honor codes similar to Groveton's"。这实际在作类比论证：在一地有效的办法，在其他地方也会有效。但论者并没有提供其他高校的学生作弊情况。假如其他一些学校的学生作弊本来就很少，还有效仿的必要吗？即便其他学校也有严重的学生作弊现象，但原因和Groveton College的一样吗？这个尚存疑问的honor code在那里就必然有效吗？

··

139. The following appeared in a memo from a budget planner for the city of Grandview.

"Our citizens are well aware of the fact that while the Grandview Symphony Orchestra was struggling to succeed, our city government promised annual funding to help support its programs. Last year, however, private contributions to the symphony increased by 200 percent, and attendance at the symphony's concerts-in-the-park series doubled. The symphony has also announced an increase in ticket prices for next year. Such developments indicate that the symphony can now succeed without funding from city government and we can eliminate that expense from next year's budget. Therefore, we recommend that the city of Grandview eliminate its funding for the Grandview Symphony from next year's budget. By doing so, we can prevent a city budget deficit without threatening the success of the symphony."

（参考第61、141、143、162题）

Write a response in which you discuss what questions would need to be answered in order to decide whether the recommendation is likely to have the predicted result. Be sure to explain how the answers to these questions would help to evaluate the recommendation.

题目整理

论点 论者的论点包含一个建议和一项预测。

(1) Such developments indicate that the symphony can now succeed without funding from city government and we can eliminate that expense from next year's budget. Therefore, we recommend that the city of Grandview eliminate its funding for the Grandview Symphony from next year's budget.

(2) By doing so, we can prevent a city budget deficit without threatening the success of the symphony.

论据 (1) Last year, however, private contributions to the symphony increased by 200 percent, and attendance at the symphony's concerts-in-the-park series doubled.

(2) The symphony has also announced an increase in ticket prices for next year.

论证方法

题目中论者主要运用了统计数据论证法、类比论证法和因果关系论证法。

分析提示

● 论据(1)列举了两个重要数据。但问题是：第一，论者说：Last year, however, private contributions to the symphony increased by 200 percent. 那么一年前，这个交响乐团得到了多少私人赞助？如果数量很少，那么200 percent的增长说明不了问题。其二，公园音乐会的上座率也存在类似问题：如果之前的基数很低，提高一倍说明不了什么问题。再者，这些公园音乐会收费吗？收多少？这些公园音乐会是否能有效带动这个交响乐团在音乐厅里演出的上座率？这些通常具有音乐普及和教育性质的公园音乐会能否使公众对交响乐曲产生兴趣并成为实际的欣赏者和消费者？其三，论者说的那些数据都是去年的情况。去年的情形能说明今年和未来的状况吗？假如今后境况变得更差了呢？论者有纵向类比错误。

● 论据(2)是个因果关系论证。论者认为既然The Symphony has also announced an increase in ticket prices for next year，那么他们的收入就不成问题了。但是，其一，乐团只是宣布下一年的票价上浮计划而已。这个计划对今年的票房收入没影响，并且该计划可否实施尚不得而知。其二，即便下一年提票价，能提多少？其三，提高票价之后，音乐会的上座率会下降吗？可否维持现状或者稳定上升？第四，乐团运营的其他费用，比如：付给乐团成员的工资、设备和道具的成本、演出场地的租金、宣传和交通费用等等，会上升吗？如果这些费用上涨较多，提高票价并不能带来多少净收入。第五，其他交响乐团是否会对该乐团构成竞争？其他的音乐形态，比如摇滚、戏剧、电影是否会分流一部分观众和听众？等等。

● 在结论(2)中，论者预测By doing so, we **can prevent a city budget deficit** without threatening the success of the symphony。言下之意，资助这家交响乐团是the city of Grandview出现财政赤字的原因。这似乎有张冠李戴的嫌疑。一个地方政府的开支有许许多多的项目。常理上讲，一家乐团不会花费太多，对它的资助无论如何也造成不了财政赤字。

140. While the Department of Education in the state of Attra suggests that high school students be assigned homework every day, the data from a recent statewide survey of high school math and science teachers give us reason to question the usefulness of daily homework. In the district of Sanlee, 86 percent of the teachers reported assigning homework three to five times a week, whereas in the district of Marlee, less than 25 percent of the teachers reported assigning homework three to five times a week. Yet the students in Marlee earn better grades overall and are less likely to be required to repeat a year of school than are the students in Sanlee. Therefore, we recommend that all teachers in our high schools should assign homework no more than twice a week.

（参考第135、137题）

Write a response in which you discuss what questions would need to be answered in order to decide whether the recommendation and the argument on which it is based are reasonable. Be sure to explain how the answers to these questions would help to evaluate the recommendation.

题目整理

论点 The usefulness of daily homework assignments to high school students is questionable, and we recommend that all teachers in our high schools should assign homework no more than twice a week.

论据 (1) While the Department of Education in the state of Attra suggests that high school students be assigned homework every day, the data from a recent statewide survey of high school math and science teachers give us reason to question the usefulness of daily homework. In the district of Sanlee, 86 percent of the teachers reported assigning homework three to five times a week, whereas in the district of Marlee, less than 25 percent of the teachers reported assigning homework three to five times a week.

(2) Yet the students in Marlee earn better grades overall and are less likely to be required to repeat a year of school than are the students in Sanlee.

论证方法

题目中论者主要运用了统计数据论证法、因果关系论证法和归纳推理论证法。

分析提示

● 论据(1)是统计数据论证，论者引用的是一项对高中数学及自然老师的调查，这项调查是论者全部推论的起点和基础。但问题是：第一，这项调查的方案设计（如调查样本的选择、调查问卷的设计、调查数据的处理、调查结果的核实和验证等）和实施过程是严格按照科学程序进行的吗？第二，参与调查的老师是否都如实回答了问题？第三，该调查的结论客观、中立吗？调查的实施者有没有受行业及其他利益相关方的影响？

● 论据(2)是因果关系论证。论者展示了Sanlee和Marlee两个区学生成绩的差异。结合论据(1)提供的两个区的高中数学及自然老师在给学生布置家庭作业这件事上的不同做法，论者显然认为是老师布置家庭作业做法上的不同造成了两个区学生成绩的差异。这个推论把一前一后出现的两个**现象**理解成因果关系，犯了"在此之后，因此之故"的逻辑错误。同时，论者的推论还有以下疑问：第一，Marlee和Sanlee这两个地区数学和自然课程老师的做法可以代表所有老师的做法吗？这两个区其他课程的老师也都像这两个科目的老师这样布置家庭作业吗？如果不是，这两个科目老师的做法岂不缺乏代表性？第二，这两个地区学生学习成绩的差异不是由其他因素引起的？比如，Sanlee的学生成绩差是因为该区的教育设施落后、经济欠发达、学生基础较薄弱、老师的整体教学水平有待提高等；而Marlee的学生成绩好很可能是因为学生家庭教育配合得比较好、学生基础好、老师教学水平高等。第三，论者说Marlee区的学生普遍成绩较好，学生留级的现象也比Sanlee区的学生少。但这个差异是否是因为这两个区对学生实施了不同评分和升学政策而产生的？假如Marlee区的学校鼓励给学生打高分，一般不对学生作留级处理，以此来树立学生的自信心，而Sanlee区的学校的做法却恰恰相反，这样的话，论者的结论就很有疑问了。

● 结论中的建议"all teachers in our high schools should assign homework no more than twice a week"是要将少布置家庭作业的做法推广到所有高中的学科。但这里有以偏概全的逻辑错误。其他学校难道不会因为一些具体的原因，比如学科性质、老师的态度、学生的态度等，而无法实施论者的建议？

141. The following appeared in a memo to the board of the Grandview Symphony.

"The city of Grandview has provided annual funding for the Grandview Symphony since the symphony's inception ten years ago. Last year the symphony hired an internationally known conductor, who has been able to attract high-profile guest musicians to perform with the symphony. Since then, private contributions to the symphony have doubled and attendance at the symphony's concerts-in-the-park series has reached new highs. Now that the Grandview Symphony is an established success, it can raise ticket prices. Increased revenue from larger audiences and higher ticket prices will enable the symphony to succeed without funding from the city government."

（参考第61、139、143、162题）

Write a response in which you discuss what specific evidence is needed to evaluate the argument and explain how the evidence would weaken or strengthen the argument.

题目整理

论点 Increased revenue from larger audiences and higher ticket prices will enable the symphony to succeed without funding from the city government.

论据 (1) Last year the symphony hired an internationally known conductor, who has been able to attract high-profile guest musicians to perform with the symphony.

(2) Since then, private contributions to the symphony have doubled and attendance at the symphony's concerts-in-the-park series has reached new highs.

(3) Now that the Grandview Symphony is an established success, it can raise ticket prices.

论证方法

题目中论者主要运用了列举特征式论证法、统计数据论证法和类比论证法。

分析提示

● 论者的整体论证框架是个列举特征式论证。论据(1)(2)(3)都是论者列举的用以证明Grandview Symphony已经获得成功而无需财政支持的现象（Signs）。论据(1)说该乐团已经聘请了一位国际知名指挥，这位指挥可以吸引知名的客席音乐家来这家乐团演出。但以下疑问需要论者作进一步的解释：第一，名指挥要价往往很高。聘请这位国际知名的指挥花了多少钱？是否会使本已靠财政补贴度日的乐团更加捉襟见肘？第二，有了名指挥就必然可以招徕知名音乐家吗？著名指挥的名望应该是诸多吸引音乐家参演因素中的一个，而不是全部。第三，即便有些知名音乐家应这位指挥之邀，同意和Grandview Symphony合作，他们也未必每次都能参加该乐团的演出。毕竟，他们只是客席音乐家（guest musicians），并不是该乐团的签约音乐家。

● 论据(2)运用的是统计数据论证，论者提到了两个重要数据。但问题是：第一，论者说private contributions to the symphony have doubled。那么一年前，这个交响乐团得到了多少私人赞助？如果数量很少（比如仅仅两三万美元），那么"从去年以来赞助翻一番"说明不了什么问题。其二，公园音乐会的上座率也存在类似问题：如果之前的基数很低，所谓的new highs并不会非常多。再者，公园音乐会收费吗？收多少？这些公园音乐会是否能有效带动这个交响乐团在音乐厅里演出的上座率？这些通常具有音乐普及和教育性质的公园音乐会能否使公众对交响乐曲产生兴趣并成为实际的欣赏者和消费者？其三，论者说的那些数据是去年的情况。去年的情况能说明今年和未来的情况吗？假如今后境况变得更差了呢？这里论者犯有纵向类比的错误。

● 论据(3)是个因果关系论证。论者认为既然the Grandview Symphony is an established success，那么他们就可以提价，该乐团今后的收入就不成问题了。首先，论者这里面有一个循环论证的谬误。该乐团的运作是否已经取得成功本来是个待定的问题，但论者却断定其已经成功，并以之为前提，建议该乐团提高演出票价。除此之外，还有以下问题需要论者的进一步证明：其一，乐团只是有可能提高票价而已。这个计划对今年的票房收入没有影响，并且该计划最终可否实施尚不得而知。其二，即便下一年提了票价，又能提多少？其三，提高票价之后，音乐会的上座率会下降吗？可否维持现在的上座率或者保持稳定上升？第四，乐团运营的其他费用，比如付给乐团成员的工资、设备和道具的成本、演出场地的租金、宣传和交通费用等会上升吗？如果这些费用上涨较多，提高票价并不能带来多少净收入。第五，其他交响乐团是否会对该乐团构成竞争？或者其他的音乐形态，比如摇滚、戏剧、电影是否会分流一部分观众和听众？

....

142. Hospital statistics regarding people who go to the emergency room after roller-skating accidents indicate the need for more protective equipment. Within that group of people, 75 percent of those who had accidents in streets or parking lots had not been wearing any protective

clothing (helmets, knee pads, etc.) or any light-reflecting material (clip-on lights, glow-in-the-dark wrist pads, etc.). Clearly, the statistics indicate that by investing in high-quality protective gear and reflective equipment, roller skaters will greatly reduce their risk of being severely injured in an accident.

Write a response in which you examine the stated and/or unstated assumptions of the argument. Be sure to explain how the argument depends on these assumptions and what the implications are for the argument if the assumptions prove unwarranted.

题目整理

论点 By investing in high-quality protective gear and reflective equipment, roller skaters will greatly reduce their risk of being severely injured in an accident.

论据 (1) Hospital statistics regarding people who go to the emergency room after roller-skating accidents indicate the need for more protective equipment.

(2) Within that group of people, 75 percent of those who had accidents in streets or parking lots had not been wearing any protective clothing (helmets, knee pads, etc.) or any light-reflecting material (clip-on lights, glow-in-the-dark wrist pads, etc.).

论证方法

题目中论者主要运用了统计数据论证法和因果关系论证法。

分析提示

● 论据(1)讲得很明白：所有的统计数据都来自医院，数据源就是医院的急诊室病例。那么论者要假设：第一，获取这些统计数据的调查方案设计（如调查样本的选择、调查数据的处理、调查结果的核实和验证等）和实施过程是严格按照科学程序进行的；其结论是客观、中立的；调查的实施者没有受行业及其他利益相关方（如药厂、急救设备制造商等）的影响。第二，医院急诊室的接诊和病例处理情况具有代表性。

● 论据(2)指出了两个同时出现的现象：在大街上和停车场玩轮滑的受伤者中，大多数（75%）都没佩戴防护设备，并且论者认为后者是前者的原因。但论者显然把同时发生的两件事情看作因果关系。他认定没有其他原因会导致同一结果。诸如大街上和停车场内密集的人流和车流、年轻的轮滑者喜欢惊险刺激的轮滑动作、没有经过轮滑培训、玩轮滑时特定的天气和灯光条件等都很可能是真正的原因。

● 最后，论者在结论中建议轮滑者 investing in high-quality protective gear and reflective equipment 以避免重伤，这其中同样有若干假设：第一，他假设多数轮滑受伤者的伤势都很严重。第二，他假设那些 high-quality protective gear and reflective equipment 可以避免严重的伤势。第三，他要假设一般防护设备的保护效果要比他所说的 high-quality protective gear and reflective equipment 差很多。第四，他还要假设没有其他手段可以实现同样的防护目的。

143. The following appeared in a memo from a budget planner for the city of Grandview.

"When the Grandview Symphony was established ten years ago, the city of Grandview agreed to provide the symphony with annual funding until the symphony became self-sustaining. Two years ago, the symphony hired an internationally known conductor, who has been able to attract high-profile guest musicians to perform with the symphony. Since then, private contributions to the symphony have tripled and attendance at the symphony's outdoor summer concert series has reached record highs. Now that the symphony has succeeded in finding an audience, the city can eliminate its funding of the symphony."

（参考第61、139、141、162题）

Write a response in which you examine the stated and/or unstated assumptions of the argument. Be sure to explain how the argument depends on these assumptions and what the implications are for the argument if the assumptions prove unwarranted.

题目整理

论点 The city can eliminate its funding of the symphony.

论据
(1) When the Grandview Symphony was established ten years ago, the city of Grandview agreed to provide the symphony with annual funding until the symphony became self-sustaining. Two years ago, the symphony hired an internationally known conductor, who has been able to attract high-profile guest musicians to perform with the symphony.

(2) Since then, private contributions to the symphony have tripled and attendance at the symphony's outdoor summer concert series has reached record highs.

(3) The symphony has succeeded in finding an audience.

论证方法

题目中论者主要运用了列举特征式论证法、统计数据论证法和类比论证法。

分析提示

● 论者的整体论证框架是个列举特征式论证。论据(1)(2)(3)都是论者列举的用以证明 Grandview Symphony已经获得成功而无需财政支持的现象。论据(1)说该乐团已经聘请了一位国际知名指挥，这位指挥可以吸引一流的客席音乐家来这家乐团演出。但这其中至少有以下几个假设：第一，名指挥要价往往很高。所以，论者要假设聘请这位国际知名指挥并没有花太多的钱，或者至少这笔费用可以得到当地政府的补贴。否则，这岂不会使本已靠财政补贴度日的乐团捉襟见肘？第二，论者要假设，有了名指挥就必然可以招徕知名音乐家。但是，著名指挥的名望只是诸多吸引音乐家参演因素中的一个，而不是全部。第三，即便有些知名音乐家应这位指挥之邀，同意和Grandview Symphony合作，论者还要假设他们的加盟可以长期稳定地提高该乐团的演出水平。但这个假设也许靠不住。毕竟，这些音乐家只是客席音乐家，并不是该乐团的签约音乐家，因而可能不会长期待在这家乐团。

● 论据(2)运用的是统计数据论证，但这个推论同样需要以下假设：第一，论者说private contributions to the symphony have tripled。那么论者要假设，两年前交响乐团得到了数目很大的私人赞助。如果数目很少，三倍的增长没什么意义。其二，夏季室外音乐会的上座率也存在类似问题：如果之前观众人数很少，record highs说明不了问题。再者，这些室外音乐会收费吗？收多少？这些室外音乐会是否能有效带动这个交响乐团在音乐厅里演出的上座率？这些通常具有音乐普及和教育性质的室外音乐会能否使公众对交响乐曲产生兴趣并成为实际的欣赏者和消费者？其三，论者说的那些数据都是两年来的情况。但两年前的情形能说明今年和未来的情况吗？假如今后的境况变得更差了呢？论者这里有纵向类比的错误。

● 论据(3)是个因果关系论证。论者认为既然The symphony has succeeded in finding an audience，那么该乐团的收入应该不成问题了。首先，论者这里有一个循环论证的谬误。该乐团之所以要聘请国际知名指挥、吸引一流音乐家的加盟，目的就是希望能增加该乐团的听众人数。这本来是个待定的问题，但论者却断定该目标已经成功（succeeded in finding an audience）。难道论者所指的听众就是那些参加夏日室外音乐会的听众？即便未来该乐团的听众能持续增加，它还会面临一系列的问题：其一，演出票价如何定？低了不行，高了，听众人数又会减少。其二，乐团运营的费用，比如付给乐团成员的工资、设备和道具的成本、演出场地的租金、宣传和交通费用等会上升吗？如果这些费用上涨过快，即便该乐团的票房收入增加，其净收入也未必会增加多少。第三，其他交响乐团是否会对Grandview Symphony乐团构成很强的竞争？或者，其他的音乐形态，比如摇滚、戏剧、电影是否会分流一部分观众和听众？等等这些，论者都要假设会朝着有利于该乐团的方向发展。

144. The citizens of Forsythe have adopted more healthful lifestyles. Their responses to a recent survey show that in their eating habits they conform more closely to government nutritional recommendations than they did ten years ago. Furthermore, there has been a fourfold increase in sales of food products containing kiran, a substance that a scientific study has shown reduces cholesterol. This trend is also evident in reduced sales of sulia, a food that few of the healthiest citizens regularly eat.

（参考第53、151题）

Write a response in which you examine the stated and/or unstated assumptions of the argument. Be sure to explain how the argument depends on these assumptions and what the implications are for the argument if the assumptions prove unwarranted.

题目整理

论点 The citizens of Forsythe have adopted more healthful lifestyles.

论据 (1) Their responses to a recent survey show that in their eating habits they conform more closely to government nutritional recommendations than they did ten years ago.

(2) Furthermore, there has been a fourfold increase in sales of food products containing kiran, a substance that a scientific study has shown reduces cholesterol.

(3) This trend is also evident in reduced sales of sulia, a food that few of the healthiest citizens regularly eat.

论证方法

题目中论者主要运用了统计数据论证法、列举特征式论证法和归纳推理论证法。

分析提示

● 论据(1)引用一项调查展开论证。对此，论者要假设：这个调查的方案设计（如调查样本的选择、调查数据的处理、调查结果的核实和验证等）和实施过程是严格按照科学程序进行的；调查对象没有因为从众心理或者担心别人的嘲笑而故意夸大他们"健康饮食习惯"；该调查的实施者没有受行业及其他利益相关方的影响；其结论是客观、中立的等等。

● 论据(2)是个列举特征式论证。但论者的推论若要成立，则要假设其所说的现象（a fourfold increase in sales of food products containing kiran, a substance that a scientific study has shown reduces cholesterol）是该地居民意识到 kiran 有利于健康，因而经常吃富含 kiran 的食品。假如当地居民因为生活水平下降，他们不得不消费某些特定食品，如玉米、大豆、荞麦，而这些食品中含较多的 kiran 呢？或者这些居民偏爱的某些食品含有较高的 kiran 含量？再者，论者说的含有 kiran 的食品销量上涨了四倍是源于大部分的 Forsythe 居民还是小部分人？如果是后者，那么就缺乏代表性。还有，从上下文来看，含 kiran 的食品销量上涨了四倍是在 10 年间实现的。那么，其他含有较高营养成分（比如 Vitamin、Calcium、Unsaturated fatty acid 等）的食品在这 10 年间的销量增长情况如何？如果普遍都上涨了四倍甚至更高，那么，含有 kiran 的食品销量上涨了四倍并不能说明什么问题。最后，kiran 对身体有益只是科学研究过程中的一个说法。这个说法是否被科学家验证过依然是个未知数。

● 论据(3)也是列举特征式论证，也有同样问题：论者说 sulia 是"最健康的市民"不吃的一种食品。其中假设的逻辑是："最健康的市民"不吃的食品就是不利于健康的食品。这个逻辑显然很成问题。首先，青壮年一般都是最健康的群体。假如青壮年普遍喜欢吃肉而不喜欢吃蔬菜，那么，蔬菜就是不利于健康的食品吗？另外，是否有其他原因导致 Forsythe 居民的 sulia 消费量减少了呢，比如当地气候的变化、耕地的减少等使得 sulia 的种植（假如它是一种作物）变得越来越困难了，或者因为进口和运输的问题，这种 sulia 运不进来，因此 sulia 在当地的消费量自然减少了呢？

● 最后，论者的全部推论实际是个归纳推理：论者用 Forsythe 居民的饮食习惯的变化这一事实来说明他们的生活习惯变得更健康了。这实际是在假设饮食习惯完全能代表生活习惯。但健康的生活习惯仅仅就是食用健康食品吗？该地居民的运动习惯如何？文艺娱乐习惯怎样？他们的生活节奏是否很快、压力是否很大？他们对生活环境的要求如何？居民间的关系是否融洽？社会心态是否宽容？等等这些内容论者并未提及。

145. The following appeared in a memo to the board of directors of a company that specializes in the delivery of heating oil.

"Most homes in the northeastern United States, where winters are typically cold, have traditionally used oil as their major fuel for heating. Last heating season, that region experienced 90 days with below-normal temperatures, and climate forecasters predict that this weather pattern will continue for several more years. Furthermore, many new homes are being built in the region in response to recent population growth. Because of these trends, we can safely predict that this region will experience an increased demand for heating oil during the next five years."

（参考第60、146、150、154、155题）

Write a response in which you discuss what questions would need to be answered in order to decide whether the prediction and the argument on which it is based are reasonable. Be sure to explain how the answers to these questions would help to evaluate the prediction.

题目整理

论点 Because of these trends, we can safely predict that this region will experience an increased demand for heating oil during the next five years.

论据 (1) Most homes in the northeastern United States, where winters are typically cold, have traditionally used oil as their major fuel for heating.

(2) Last heating season, that region experienced 90 days with below-normal temperatures, and climate forecasters predict that this weather pattern will continue for several more years.

(3) Furthermore, many new homes are being built in the region in response to recent population growth.

论证方法

题目中论者主要运用了统计数据论证法、类比论证法、引用权威论证法和列举特征式论证法。

分析提示

● 论据(1)是个类比论证，其中的推理过程是：既然美国东北部的家庭传统上都用燃油采暖，那么他们现在和将来很可能还会如此。但是，传统的习惯不会改变吗？油价的频繁波动是否会迫使这些家庭调整采暖习惯以降低生活成本？电采暖是否会以其清洁、成本低廉的优势慢慢取代传统的燃油采暖？在其他地区和城市生活的年轻人是否会把那里不同的采暖方式（如电采暖、地热采暖、管道采暖等）带到这个地区，从而改变本地居民的采暖习惯？

● 论据(2)是一个引用统计数据论证的过程。问题是：首先，90天的低温期是不是个较长的时间段？如果常年的低温期都保持在100天或者更长，那么上个采暖季的90天低温期也就不算什么了。其次，论者说的低温期应该是一个低于平均值较多的温度。但到底有多低？仅仅模糊地说below-normal temperatures，很难有说服力。第三，论者引用了权威（climate forecasters）来支持其观点。但这些天气预报员即便是真正的专家，他们的预测有多可靠？

- 论据(3)运用了列举特征式论证法：既然人口增加了、建的房子多了，对燃油的需求自然就会上升。但问题是，第一，这些增加的人口多数都要买房？假如他们都租房住呢？或者，他们只是流动人口，冬季的时候都要离开此地？第二，难道那些新建的房屋都会采用燃油采暖，而不是其他的采暖方式？

- 即便论者的上述论据(1)(2)(3)都有道理，论者"this region will experience an increased demand for heating oil during the next five years"的预测依然存在疑问。过去的事情未必能说明将来。科技在进步，人们的生活习惯都在改变；即便是气候，五年之间也会有很多难以预料的情况发生。谁能保证，该地区居民的燃油使用率不会大幅度提高，即便他们将来依旧使用燃油采暖，但对燃油的需求量却会大幅下降呢？

---

146. The following appeared in a memo to the board of directors of a company that specializes in the delivery of heating oil.

"Most homes in the northeastern United States, where winters are typically cold, have traditionally used oil as their major fuel for heating. Last heating season, that region experienced 90 days with below-normal temperatures, and climate forecasters predict that this weather pattern will continue for several more years. Furthermore, many new homes are being built in the region in response to recent population growth. Because of these trends, we can safely predict that this region will experience an increased demand for heating oil during the next five years."

（参考第60、145、150、154、155题）

Write a response in which you discuss what specific evidence is needed to evaluate the argument and explain how the evidence would weaken or strengthen the argument.

题目整理

论点 Because of these trends, we can safely predict that this region will experience an increased demand for heating oil during the next five years.

论据 (1) Most homes in the northeastern United States, where winters are typically cold, have traditionally used oil as their major fuel for heating.

(2) Last heating season, that region experienced 90 days with below-normal temperatures, and climate forecasters predict that this weather pattern will continue for several more years.

(3) Furthermore, many new homes are being built in the region in response to recent population growth.

论证方法

题目中论者主要运用了统计数据论证法、类比论证法、引用权威论证法和列举特征式论证法。

分析提示

- 论据(1)是个类比论证，其中的推理过程是：既然美国东北部的家庭传统上都用燃油采暖，那么他们现在和将来很可能还会如此。但是，传统的习惯不会改变吗？油价的频繁波动是否会迫使这些家庭调整采暖习惯以降低生活成本呢？电采暖是否会以其清洁、成本低廉的优势慢慢取代传统的燃油采暖？在其他地区和城市生活的年轻人是否会把那里不同的采暖方式（如电采暖、地热采暖、管道采暖等）带到这个地区，从而改变本地居民的采暖习惯？等等这些都需要进一步的说明。

● 论据(2)是一个引用统计数据论证的过程。问题是：首先，90天的低温期是不是个较长的时间段？论者并未提供往年的低温期时间跨度。如果常年的低温期都维持在100天或者更长，那么上个采暖季的90天低温期也就不算什么了。其次，论者说的低温期应该是一个低于平均值较多的温度。但到底有多低？只是模糊地说below-normal temperatures，很难有说服力。第三，论者引用了权威（climate forecasters）来支持其观点。但这些天气预报员即便是真正的专家，他们的预测有多可靠呢？

● 论据(3)使用的是列举特征式论证法：既然人口增加了、建的房子多了，对燃油的需求自然就会上升。这里至少两个问题需要佐证：第一，这些增加的人口多数都要买房？假如他们都租房住呢？或者他们是流动人口，冬季的时候都要离此地？第二，难道那些新建的房屋都会采用燃油采暖，而不是其他的采暖方式？

● 即便论者的上述论据(1)(2)(3)都有道理，论者"this region will experience an increased demand for heating oil during the next five years"的预测依然存在疑问。过去的事情未必能说明将来。科技在进步，人们的生活习惯都在改变；即便是气候，五年之间也会有很多难以预料的情况发生。谁能保证，该地区居民的燃油使用率不会大幅度提高，即便他们将来依旧使用燃油采暖，但对燃油的需求量却会大幅下降呢？

---

147. The following recommendation was made by the president and administrative staff of Grove College, a private institution, to the college's governing committee.

"We recommend that Grove College preserve its century-old tradition of all-female education rather than admit men into its programs. It is true that a majority of faculty members voted in favor of coeducation, arguing that it would encourage more students to apply to Grove. But 80 percent of the students responding to a survey conducted by the student government wanted the school to remain all female, and over half of the alumnae who answered a separate survey also opposed coeducation. Keeping the college all female will improve morale among students and convince alumnae to keep supporting the college financially."

（参考第74、148、149、156题）

Write a response in which you discuss what specific evidence is needed to evaluate the argument and explain how the evidence would weaken or strengthen the argument.

题目整理

论点 We recommend that Grove College preserve its century-old tradition of all-female education rather than admit men into its programs.

论据 (1) 80 percent of the students responding to a survey conducted by the student government wanted the school to remain all female, and over half of the alumnae who answered a separate survey also opposed coeducation.

(2) Keeping the college all female will improve morale among students and convince alumnae to keep supporting the college financially.

论证方法

题目中论者主要运用了统计数据论证法和因果关系论证法。

分析提示

● 论者在论据(1)中引用了两项调查的数据,是典型的统计数据论证法。首先,论者需要提供更多的证据来说明:这些调查的方案设计(如调查样本的选择、调查问卷的设计、调查数据的处理、调查结果的核实和验证等)和实施过程都是严格按照科学程序进行的;其结论是客观、中立的;调查的实施者没有受特殊立场或相关既得利益者的影响;独立第三方的相关调查数据也同时作为参考,等等。其次,要注意:这两项调查的调查对象都缺乏代表性。前者的调查对象是该校的学生,而调查的实施方是该校的学生会(student government)。这些在校生很可能更愿意对本校作出正面评价。所以只对这些学生进行调查有自说自话的嫌疑。那些没有选择这所学校的学生是怎么看这所女子学校的教育特点呢?而第二个调查的调查对象是该校的校友(alumnae)。同前一个调查一样,这些校友因为对自己的母校怀有感情,他们的评价很可能也不是客观的。论者为什么不调查其他人群(比如,该校学生的家长、专业教育人士、公司和企业的高管、高等教育研究人员等)?参考了多方人士的评价后,论者的判断才会更客观。

● 论据(2)是个因果关系论证。论者认为,因为保持该校传统有两项好处,即improve morale among students和convince alumnae to keep supporting the college financially,所以这个传统应该保留。但有下列疑问需要论者作出说明:第一,对这两方面的"好处(merits)",论者并未提供有效的证明。所以,难以取信于人。第二,论者为何不提延续该校女校的传统之缺点(demerits)?诸如,招生面狭窄、不利于学生身心成长、不利于学生适应未来社会角色等等,这些都是很容易想到的女校的缺点。第三,论者为何不提男女同校教育的好处?更丰富的生源、正常的学生身心成长、健全的社会角色的适应、将来更为庞大的校友圈、更为充裕的校友捐献、更大的学校影响力等等,这些好处,论者为何避而不谈?

● 最后,提出要保留Grove College百年女校传统建议的是该校的president and administrative staff。那么,这些人特殊的身份和职务是否会影响他们建议的客观性和中立性?教育专家、学生家长、工商企业人士、政府教育机构等各界人士有什么意见?这方面的相关资料同样很重要。

148. The following recommendation was made by the president and administrative staff of Grove College, a private institution, to the college's governing committee.

"We recommend that Grove College preserve its century-old tradition of all-female education rather than admit men into its programs. It is true that a majority of faculty members voted in favor of coeducation, arguing that it would encourage more students to apply to Grove. But 80 percent of the students responding to a survey conducted by the student government wanted the school to remain all female, and over half of the alumnae who answered a separate survey also opposed coeducation. Keeping the college all female will improve morale among students and convince alumnae to keep supporting the college financially."

（参考第74、147、149、156题）

Write a response in which you examine the stated and/or unstated assumptions of the argument. Be sure to explain how the argument depends on these assumptions and what the implications are for the argument if the assumptions prove unwarranted.

题目整理

论点 We recommend that Grove College preserve its century-old tradition of all-female education rather than admit men into its programs.

论据 (1) 80 percent of the students responding to a survey conducted by the student government wanted the school to remain all female, and over half of the alumnae who answered a separate survey also opposed coeducation.

(2) Keeping the college all female will improve morale among students and convince alumnae to keep supporting the college financially.

论证方法

题目中论者主要运用了统计数据论证法和因果关系论证法。

分析提示

● 论者在论据(1)中引用了两项调查的数据。首先，论者需要以下假设：这些调查的方案设计（如调查样本的选择、调查问卷的设计、调查数据的处理、调查结果的核实和验证等）和实施过程都是严格按照科学程序进行的；其结论是客观、中立的；调查的实施者没有受特殊立场或相关既得利益者的影响；独立第三方的相关调查数据也同时作为参考，等等。其次，要注意：这两项调查的调查对象都缺乏代表性。所以，论者要假设这些调查对象的特性不会干扰调查结果的可信度。前者的调查对象是该校的学生，而调查的实施方是该校的学生会。这些在校生很可能更愿意对本校作出正面评价。所以只对这些学生进行调查有自说自话的嫌疑。那些没有选择这所学校的学生是怎么看这所女子学校的教育特点呢？而后一个调查的对象是该校的校友。同前一个调查一样，这些校友因为对自己的母校怀有感情，他们的评价很可能也不是客观的。论者为什么调查其他人群（比如，该校学生的家长、专业教育人士、公司和企业的高管、高等教育研究人员等）？参考了多方人士的评价后，论者的判断才会更客观。

● 论据(2)是个因果关系论证。论者认为，因为保持该校传统有两项好处，即improve morale among students和convince alumnae to keep supporting the college financially，所以这个传统应该保留。但论者至少需要以下假设：第一，这两方面的好处是真实可信的。但论者并未对此提供有效的证明。第二，延续女校的传统不会产生一些弊病（defects）。但是，诸如招生面狭窄、不利于学生身心成长、不利于学生适应未来社会角色等，这些都是很容易想到的女校的缺点。第三，男女同校教育不具备女校的很多优点。但是，更丰富的生源、学生正常的身心成长、健全的社会角色的适应、多样化的教学内容、将来更为庞大的校友圈、更为充裕的校友捐资、更大的学校影响力等等，这些好处，都是很有可能实现的。

● 最后，建议要保留Grove College百年女校的传统的是该校的president and administrative staff。那么，论者还要假设，这些人的身份和职务不会影响他们建议的客观性和中立性。但实际上，教育专家、学生家长、工商企业人士、政府教育机构等各界人士的意见至少也具有同样重要的参考价值。

---

149. The following recommendation was made by the president and administrative staff of Grove College, a private institution, to the college's governing committee.

"We recommend that Grove College preserve its century-old tradition of all-female education rather than admit men into its programs. It is true that a majority of faculty members voted in favor of coeducation, arguing that it would encourage more students to apply to Grove. But 80 percent of the students responding to a survey conducted by the student government wanted the school to remain all female, and over half of the alumnae who answered a separate survey also opposed coeducation. Keeping the college all female will improve morale among students and convince alumnae to keep supporting the college financially."

（参考第74、147、148、156题）

Write a response in which you discuss what questions would need to be answered in order to decide whether the recommendation is likely to have the predicted result. Be sure to explain how the answers to these questions would help to evaluate the recommendation.

题目整理

论点 We recommend that Grove College preserve its century-old tradition of all-female education rather than admit men into its programs.

论据 (1) 80 percent of the students responding to a survey conducted by the student government wanted the school to remain all female, and over half of the alumnae who answered a separate survey also opposed coeducation.

(2) Keeping the college all female will improve morale among students and convince alumnae to keep supporting the college financially.

论证方法

题目中论者主要运用了统计数据论证法和因果关系论证法。

分析提示

● 论者在论据(1)中引用了两项调查的数据。但问题是：首先，这些调查的方案设计（如调查样本的选择、调查问卷的设计、调查数据的处理、调查结果的核实和验证等）和实施过程是否都是严格按照科学程序进行的？其结论是否客观、中立？调查的实施者没有受特殊立场或相关既得利益者的影响？独立第三方的相关调查数据有没有拿来作参考？等等。其次，要注意：这两项调查的调查对象都缺乏代表性。前者的调查对象是该校的学生，而调查的实施方是该校的学生会。这些在校生很可能更愿意对本校作出正面评价。所以，只对这些学生进行调查有自说自话的嫌疑。那些没选择这所学校的学生是怎么看这所女子学校的教育特点呢？而后一个调查的对象是该校的校友。同前一个调查一样，这些校友因为对自己的母校怀有感情，他们的评价很可能也不是客观的。论者为什么不调查其他人群（比如，该校学生的家长、专业教育人士、公司和企业的高管、高等教育研究人员等等）？参考了多方人士的评价后，论者的判断才会更客观。

● 论据(2)是个因果关系论证。论者认为，因为保留该校传统有两项好处，即improve morale among students 和 convince alumnae to keep supporting the college financially，所以这个传统应该保留。但是，第一，对这两项"好处"，论者并未提供有效的证明。所以难以取信于人。第二，论者为什么不提延续该校女校的传统之缺点？诸如，招生面狭窄、不利于学生身心成长、不利于学生适应未来社会角色等等，这些都是很容易想到的女校的缺点。第三，论者为什么不提男女同校教育的好处？更丰富的生源、学生正常的身心成长、健全的社会角色的适应、多样化的教学内容、将来更为庞大的校友圈、更为充裕的校友捐资、更大的学校影响力等等，这些好处，论者为何避而不谈？

● 最后，建议要保留Grove College百年女校的传统的是该校的president and administrative staff。那么，这些人的身份和职务是否会影响他们建议的客观性和中立性？教育专家、学生家长、工商企业人士、政府教育机构等各界人士的意见是什么？

---

150. The following appeared in a letter from a firm providing investment advice to a client.

"Homes in the northeastern United States, where winters are typically cold, have traditionally used oil as their major fuel for heating. Last year that region experienced 90 days with below-average temperatures, and climate forecasters at Waymarsh University predict that this weather pattern will continue for several more years. Furthermorc, many new homes have been built in this region during the past year. Because these developments will certainly result in an increased demand for heating oil, we recommend investment in Consolidated Industries, one of whose major business operations is the retail sale of home heating oil."

（参考第60、145、146、154、155题）

Write a response in which you discuss what questions would need to be answered in order to decide whether the recommendation and the argument on which it is based are reasonable. Be sure to explain how the answers to these questions would help to evaluate the recommendation.

题目整理

论点 该题目的论点包括一项预测和一个建议。

These developments will certainly result in an increased demand for heating oil, and we recommend investment in Consolidated Industries, one of whose major business operations is the retail sale of home heating oil.

论据 (1) Homes in the northeastern United States, where winters are typically cold, have traditionally used oil as their major fuel for heating.

(2) Last year that region experienced 90 days with below-average temperatures, and climate forecasters at Waymarsh University predict that this weather pattern will continue for several more years.

(3) Furthermore, many new homes have been built in this region during the past year.

论证方法

● 题目中论者主要运用了统计数据论证法、类比论证法、引用权威论证法和列举特征式论证法。

分析提示

● 论据(1)是个类比论证，其中的推理过程是：既然美国东北部的家庭传统上都用燃油采暖，那么他们现在和将来也会如此。但问题是：传统的习惯不会改变吗？油价的频繁波动是否会迫使这些家庭调整采暖习惯以降低生活成本？电采暖是否会以其清洁、成本低廉的优势而慢慢取代传统的燃油采暖？在其他地区和城市生活的年轻人是否会把那里不同的采暖方式（如电采暖、地热采暖、管道采暖等）带到这个地区，从而改变本地居民的采暖习惯？

● 论据(2)是一个引用统计数据论证的过程。但问题是：首先，90天的低温期是个较长的时间段吗？论者并未提供历史数据用来比较。如果常年的低温期都是100或者更长，那么上个采暖季的90天低温期也就不算什么了。其次，论者说的低温期到底是个什么样的温度水平？他也没有提供可以用来比较的历史数据。只是模糊地说below-average temperatures，很难有说服力。第三，论者引用了权威（climate forecasters at Waymarsh University）来支持其观点。但这些专家的预测到底有多可靠？

● 论据(3)运用列举特征式论证法：建的房子多了，对燃油的需求自然就会上升。但是，第一，这些新建的房屋都会采用燃油采暖，而不是其他的采暖方式（如太阳能）吗？会不会有一些新的建筑科技（比如出色的墙体保暖技术）可以使新的房屋根本不需要额外的采暖了呢？第二，去年建了许多房屋，今后还会建很多房屋吗？

● 即便论者上述论据(1)(2)(3)都有道理，论者"These developments will certainly result in an increased demand for heating oil"的预测和投资Consolidated Industries公司的建议依然有以下疑问：第一，该地区居民的燃油使用率会不会大幅度提高，即便他们将来依旧使用燃油采暖，但对燃油的需求量却下降了？第二，Consolidated Industries公司肯定会因该地区居民的燃油采暖而受益颇多，从而带来其销售和利润的上升吗？它的运营成本会上升得更快吗？它会在与其对手的竞争中获胜吗？等等这些都是关键的疑问。

151. Benton City residents have adopted healthier lifestyles. A recent survey of city residents shows that the eating habits of city residents conform more closely to government nutritional recommendations than they did ten years ago. During those ten years, local sales of food products containing kiran, a substance that a scientific study has shown reduces cholesterol,

have increased fourfold, while sales of sulia, a food rarely eaten by the healthiest residents, have declined dramatically. Because of these positive changes in the eating habits of Benton City residents, we predict that the obesity rate in the city will soon be well below the national average.

（参考第53、144题）

Write a response in which you discuss what questions would need to be answered in order to decide whether the prediction and the argument on which it is based are reasonable. Be sure to explain how the answers to these questions would help to evaluate the prediction.

题目整理

论点 The obesity rate in the city will soon be well below the national average.

论据 (1) A recent survey of city residents shows that the eating habits of city residents conform more closely to government nutritional recommendations than they did ten years ago.

(2) During those ten years, local sales of food products containing kiran, a substance that a scientific study has shown reduces cholesterol, have increased fourfold.

(3) Sales of sulia, a food rarely eaten by the healthiest residents, have over the same period declined dramatically.

论证方法

题目中论者主要运用了统计数据论证法和列举特征式论证法。

分析提示

● 论据(1)引用一项调查展开论证。首先，这个调查的方案设计（如调查样本的选择、调查数据的处理、调查结果的核实和验证等）和实施过程是严格按照科学程序进行的吗？那些调查对象有没有因为从众心理或者担心别人的嘲笑而故意夸大他们的"健康饮食习惯"？其结论是客观、中立的吗？调查的实施者没有受行业及其他利益相关方的影响？这些，论者都未加说明。

● 论据(2)是个列举特征式论证。但论者说的这一现象是该地居民意识到kiran有利于健康，因而多食富含kiran的食品？假如因为生活水平下降，他们不得不消费某些特定食品，如玉米、大豆、荞麦，而这些食品中含较多的kiran呢？或者说这些居民偏爱的某些食品含有较高的kiran含量？再者，论者说的含有kiran的食品销量涨了四倍是Benton City大多数居民的购买行为造成的，还是小部分人的购买行为造成的？如果是后者，那么就缺乏代表性。从上下文来看，10年来含kiran的食品销量涨了四倍。那么，其他含有较高营养成分（比如Vitamin、Calcium、Unsaturated fatty acid等等）的食品在这10年间的销量增长情况如何？如果普遍都涨了四倍甚至更高，那么，含有kiran的食品销量上涨了四倍并不能说明什么问题。最后，kiran对身体有益只是科学研究过程中的一个说法。这个说法是否被科学家验证过依然是个未知数。

● 论据(3)也是列举特征式论证，也有同样问题：论者说sulia是"最健康的市民"不吃的一种食品。但问题是"最健康的市民"不吃的食品就是不利于健康的食品吗？首先，从常识来讲，青壮年是最健康的群体。假如青壮年普遍喜欢吃肉而不喜欢吃蔬菜，那么，蔬菜就是不利于健康的食品吗？另外，是否有其他原因致使Benton City居民的sulia消费量减少了呢，比如当地气候的变化、耕地的减少使得sulia的种植（假如它是一种作物的话）变得越来越困难了，或者因为进口和运输的问题，sulia运不进来，因此sulia在当地的消费量自然减少了呢？

● 最后，论者依据论据(1)(2)(3)得出结论：The obesity rate in the city will soon be well below the national average。这个结论是个充满风险的逻辑跳跃。首先，饮食习惯和一个人肥胖与否完全是两个概念。一个人有良好的饮食习惯，但这个人的体重完全可能超标。其次，论者只是说Benton City的居民在过去10年间的饮食习惯有了进步，但并没有说其他地方居民的饮食习惯有了什么样的变化。假如其他地方居民的饮食习惯都比Benton City居民的进步大，Benton City的居民仍然会在一些健康指标，比如肥胖症人群的比例，落后于全国的平均水平。

---

152. The following appeared in a memo to the board of directors of Bargain Brand Cereals.

"One year ago we introduced our first product, Bargain Brand breakfast cereal. Our very low prices quickly drew many customers away from the top-selling cereal companies. Although the companies producing the top brands have since tried to compete with us by lowering their prices and although several plan to introduce their own budget brands, not once have we needed to raise our prices to continue making a profit. Given our success in selling cereal, we recommend that Bargain Brand now expand its business and begin marketing other low-priced food products as quickly as possible."

（参考第153题）

Write a response in which you discuss what questions would need to be answered in order to decide whether the recommendation and the argument on which it is based are reasonable. Be sure to explain how the answers to these questions would help to evaluate the recommendation.

题目整理

论点 Given our success in selling cereal, we recommend that Bargain Brand now expand its business and begin marketing other low-priced food products as quickly as possible.

论据 (1) One year ago we introduced our first product, Bargain Brand breakfast cereal. Our very low prices quickly drew many customers away from the top-selling cereal companies.

(2) Although the companies producing the top brands have since tried to compete with us by lowering their prices and although several plan to introduce their own budget brands, not once have we needed to raise our prices to continue making a profit.

论证方法

题目中论者主要运用了类比论证法。论者认为既然一年前某种产品的市场策略获得了成功，现在把它运用在其他产品上也可以成功。

分析提示

● 论据(1)说Bargain Brand Cereals公司一年前开始做谷物早餐（breakfast cereal），其低价位策

略使其迅速获得成功。但问题是：第一，论者说的 many customers 中的 many 到底指多少？如果谷物类早餐市场的全部市场容量不过就是一两千份，即便是其80%的市场份额也不会有太大的利润。第二，有没有其他原因，而不是论者说的低价，促使 Bargain Brand Cereals 迅速占领市场？比如，因为谷物类早餐市场的规模相对小，很多公司都不大重视；当前的市场参与者经营得不是很精细，出现了一定的市场空白，而恰恰是这个市场空白造就了 Bargain Brand Cereals 的成功等。

● 论据(2)提到，尽管其他知名早餐品牌也在大力降价，有几家正在计划引入廉价的经济型早餐，Bargain Brand Cereals 却一直可以维持低价策略并保持盈利。这里有以下的疑问：第一，是否其他知名早餐品牌的经营重点不是谷物类早餐，因此他们不愿意和 Bargain Brand Cereals 进行你死我活的价格战（price war）？在他们眼里，只要能占据一定的市场份额、有一点盈利可以冲抵基本运营成本就行了。他们的经营重点是中午和晚上的正餐，所以不愿意在早餐上拼死降价。第二，是否 Bargain Brand Cereals 真正的竞争对手仍在筹划当中，尚未与它开始实质的竞争？虽然如论者所说，several plan to introduce their own budget brands，但毕竟 Bargain Brand Cereals 开业才一年。再过半年或者一年之后，等到这些新的市场竞争者进入之后，也许 Bargain Brand Cereals 的好日子就结束了。第三，论者只是说 Bargain Brand Cereals "not once have we needed to raise our prices to continue making a profit"，但并未说该公司的利润空间在价格一降再降之后，已经变得很小。如果该公司的利润空间很小，那就意味着如果再有新的竞争对手实施更大幅度的降价，很可能 Bargain Brand Cereals 也撑不住了。

● 结论中，论者建议 Bargain Brand Cereals 将其在经济型谷物早餐上的策略复制到其他产品上。这显然是个类比推论。但问题是：其他的食品同谷物类早餐具有可比性吗？它们的原材料价格、加工制作工艺、所需要的人工和佐料的投入以及市场的竞争格局等等，还会使该公司的低价策略奏效吗？

153. The following appeared in a memo to the board of directors of Bargain Brand Cereals.

"One year ago we introduced our first product, Bargain Brand breakfast cereal. Our very low prices quickly drew many customers away from the top-selling cereal companies. Although the companies producing the top brands have since tried to compete with us by lowering their prices and although several plan to introduce their own budget brands, not once have we needed to raise our prices to continue making a profit. Given our success in selling cereal, we recommend that Bargain Brand now expand its business and begin marketing other low-priced food products as quickly as possible."

（参考第152题）

Write a response in which you examine the stated and/or unstated assumptions of the argument. Be sure to explain how the argument depends on these assumptions and what the implications are for the argument if the assumptions prove unwarranted.

题目整理

论点 Given our success in selling cereal, we recommend that Bargain Brand now expand its business and begin marketing other low-priced food products as quickly as possible.

论据 (1) One year ago we introduced our first product, Bargain Brand breakfast cereal. Our very low prices quickly drew many customers away from the top-selling cereal companies.

(2) Although the companies producing the top brands have since tried to compete with us by lowering their prices and although several plan to introduce their own budget brands, not once have we needed to raise our prices to continue making a profit.

论证方法

题目中论者主要运用了类比论证法。

分析提示

● 论据(1)说Bargain Brand Cereals公司一年前开始做谷物早餐，其低价位策略使其迅速获得成功。但论者需要至少以下假设：第一，这个breakfast cereal市场具有足够的规模。论者说的many customers中的many到底指多少？如果谷物类早餐市场的全部市场容量不过就是一两千份，即便是其80%的市场份额也不会有太大的利润，因此很难说得上是真正的商业模式的成功。第二，不是论者认为的低价策略，而是其他促使Bargain Brand Cereals迅速占领市场。假如，因为谷物早餐的市场规模小，很多公司都不大重视；当前的市场参与者经营得不是很精细，出现了一定的市场空白。而恰恰是这个市场空白造就了Bargain Brand Cereals的成功。因此很难说是低价策略在发挥作用。

● 论据(2)提到，尽管其他的知名早餐品牌也在大力降价，有几家对手正在计划引入廉价的经济型早餐，Bargain Brand Cereals却一直可以维持低价策略并保持盈利。这个推论同样需要以下假设：第一，没有低价策略以外的原因促成了Bargain Brand Cereals的成功。是否其他知名早餐品牌的经营重点并不在谷物类早餐上，因此他们不愿意和Bargain Brand Cereals进行你死我活的价格战？也许在他们眼里，只要能占据一定的市场份额、获得一些盈利可以冲抵基本运营成本就行了。他们的经营重点是中午和晚上的正餐，所以不愿意在早餐上拼死降价。第二，论者要假设未来不会产生强硬的竞争对手。是否Bargain Brand Cereals真正的竞争对手仍在筹划当中，尚未开始实质的竞争？虽然如论者所说several plan to introduce their own budget brands，但毕竟Bargain Brand Cereals开业才一年。再过半年或者一年之后，等到新的市场竞争者进入之后，也许Bargain Brand Cereals的好日子就结束了。第三，论者要假设其低价策略是可持续的。论者只是说Bargain Brand Cereals "not once have we needed to raise our prices to continue making a profit"，但并未说该公司的利润空间在价格一降再降之后，是否已经变得很小。如果该公司的利润空间很小，那就意味着如果再有新的竞争对手实施更大幅度的降价，很可能Bargain Brand Cereals也撑不住了。

● 结论中，论者建议Bargain Brand Cereals将其在经济型谷物早餐上的策略复制到其他产品上。这是个类比推论。他实际在假设其他的食品同谷物类早餐具有可比性。但是，谷物类早餐和其他食品在原材料价格、加工制作工艺、所需要的人工和佐料的投入以及市场的竞争格局等方面的差异，还会使该公司的低价策略奏效吗？

154. The following appeared in a letter from a firm providing investment advice to a client.

"Homes in the northeastern United States, where winters are typically cold, have traditionally used oil as their major fuel for heating. Last year that region experienced twenty days with below-average temperatures, and local weather forecasters throughout the region predict that this weather pattern will continue for several more years. Furthermore, many new homes have been built in this region during the past year. Based on these developments, we predict a large increase in the demand for heating oil. Therefore, we recommend investment in Consolidated Industries, one of whose major business operations is the retail sale of home heating oil."

（参考第60、145、146、150、155题）

Write a response in which you discuss what questions would need to be answered in order to decide whether the recommendation and the argument on which it is based are reasonable. Be sure to explain how the answers to these questions would help to evaluate the recommendation.

题目整理

论点 该题目的论点包括一项预测和一个建议。

(1) Based on these developments, we predict a large increase in the demand for heating oil.

(2) Therefore, we recommend investment in Consolidated Industries, one of whose major business operations is the retail sale of home heating oil.

论据 (1) Homes in the northeastern United States, where winters are typically cold, have traditionally used oil as their major fuel for heating.

(2) Last year that region experienced twenty days with below-average temperatures, and local weather forecasters throughout the region predict that this weather pattern will continue for several more years.

(3) Furthermore, many new homes have been built in this region during the past year.

论证方法

题目中论者运用了统计数据论证法、类比论证法、引用权威论证法和列举特征式论证法。

分析提示

● 论据(1)是个类比论证，其中的推理过程是：既然美国东北部的家庭传统上都用燃油采暖，那么他们现在和将来也会如此。但问题是：传统的习惯不会改变吗？油价的频繁波动是否会迫使这些家庭调整采暖习惯以降低生活成本？电采暖是否会以其清洁、成本低廉的优势而慢慢取代传统的燃油采暖？在其他地区和城市生活的年轻人是否会把那里不同的采暖方式（如电采暖、地热采暖、管道采暖等）带到这个地区，从而改变本地居民的采暖习惯？

● 论据(2)是一个引用统计数据论证的过程。问题是：首先，20天的低温期是个较长的时间段吗？论者并未提供历史数据用来比较。如果常年的低温期都是50或者更长，那么上个采暖季的20天低温期也就不算什么了。其次，论者说的低温期到底是个什么样的温度水平？他也没有提供可以用来比较的历史数据。只是模糊地说 below-average temperatures，很难有说服力。第三，论者引用了权威（local weather forecasters）来支持其观点。但这些专家的预测到底有多可靠？

- 论据(3)运用列举特征式论证法：建的房子多了，对燃油的需求自然就会上升。但是，第一，这些新建的房屋都会采用燃油采暖，而不是其他的采暖方式（如太阳能）吗？会不会有一些新的建筑科技（比如出色的墙体保暖技术），可以使新的房屋根本不需要额外的采暖了呢？第二，去年一年建了很多房屋。今后还会保持该趋势吗？

- 即便论者上述论据(1)(2)(3)都有道理，论者"a large increase in the demand for heating oil"的预测和投资 Consolidated Industries 公司的建议依然有以下疑问：第一，该地区居民的燃油的使用率会不会大幅度提高，即便他们依旧使用燃油采暖，但对燃油的需求量却下降了？第二，Consolidated Industries 公司肯定会因该地区居民的燃油采暖而受益颇多，从而带来其销售和利润的上升吗？它的运营成本会上升得更快吗？它会在与其对手的竞争中占据优势吗？等等这些疑问都需要回答。

155. The following appeared in a letter from a firm providing investment advice to a client.

"Homes in the northeastern United States, where winters are typically cold, have traditionally used oil as their major fuel for heating. Last year that region experienced twenty days with below-average temperatures, and local weather forecasters throughout the region predict that this weather pattern will continue for several more years. Furthermore, many new homes have been built in this region during the past year. Because of these developments, we predict an increased demand for heating oil and recommend investment in Consolidated Industries, one of whose major business operations is the retail sale of home heating oil."

（参考第60、145、146、150、154题）

Write a response in which you discuss what specific evidence is needed to evaluate the argument and explain how the evidence would weaken or strengthen the argument.

题目整理

论点 该题目的论点包括一项预测和一个建议。

Because of these developments, we predict an increased demand for heating oil and recommend investment in Consolidated Industries, one of whose major business operations is the retail sale of home heating oil.

论据 (1) Homes in the northeastern United States, where winters are typically cold, have traditionally used oil as their major fuel for heating.

(2) Last year that region experienced twenty days with below-average temperatures, and local weather forecasters throughout the region predict that this weather pattern will continue for several more years.

(3) Furthermore, many new homes have been built in this region during the past year.

论证方法

题目中论者运用了统计数据论证法、类比论证法、引用权威论证法和列举特征式论证法。

分析提示

● 论据(1)是个类比论证，其中的推理过程是：既然美国东北部的家庭传统上都用燃油采暖，那么他们现在和将来也会如此。但下列疑问需要进一步的证证：传统的习惯不会改变吗？油价的频繁波动是否会迫使这些家庭调整采暖习惯以降低生活成本？电采暖是否会以其清洁、成本低廉的优势而慢慢取代传统的燃油采暖？在其他地区和城市生活的年轻人是否会把那里不同的采暖方式（如电采暖、地热采暖、管道采暖等）带到这个地区，从而改变本地居民的采暖习惯？等等。

● 论据(2)是一个引用统计数据论证的过程。但是，首先，20天的低温期是个较长的时间段吗？论者并未提供历史数据用来比较。如果常年的低温期都是50或者更长，那么上个采暖季的20天低温期也就不算什么了。其次，论者说的低温期到底是个什么样的温度水平？他也没有提供可以用来比较的历史数据。只模糊地说below-average temperatures，很难有说服力。第三，论者引用了权威（local weather forecasters）来支持其观点。但这些专家的预测到底有多可靠？

● 论据(3)运用列举特征式论证法：建的房子多了，对燃油的需求自然就会上升。但论者是否有进一步的证据表明：第一，这些新建的房屋都会采用燃油采暖，而不是其他的采暖方式（如太阳能）吗？会不会有一些新的建筑科技（比如出色的墙体保暖技术），可以使新的房屋根本不需要额外的采暖了呢？第二，去年一年建了很多房屋，今后还会保持这种趋势吗？

● 即便论者上述论据(1)(2)(3)都有道理，论者 "an increased demand for heating oil" 的预测和投资 Consolidated Industries 公司的建议依然有以下疑问：第一，该地区居民的燃油使用效率会不会大幅度提高，即便他们依然使用燃油采暖，但对燃油的需求量却下降了？第二，Consolidated Industries 公司肯定会因该地区居民的燃油采暖而受益颇多，从而带来其销售和利润的上升？它的运营成本会上升得更快吗？它会在与其对手的竞争中占据优势吗？等等这些也需要更多的佐证。

. . . .

156. The following recommendation was made by the president and administrative staff of Grove College, a private institution, to the college's governing committee.

"Recently, there have been discussions about ending Grove College's century-old tradition of all-female education by admitting male students into our programs. At a recent faculty meeting, a majority of faculty members voted in favor of coeducation, arguing that it would encourage more students to apply to Grove. However, Grove students, both past and present, are against the idea of coeducation. Eighty percent of the students responding to a survey conducted by the student government wanted the school to remain all female, and over half of the alumnae who answered a separate survey also opposed coeducation. Therefore, we recommend maintaining Grove College's tradition of all-female education. We predict that keeping the college all-female will improve morale among students and convince alumnae to keep supporting the college financially."

（参考第74、147、148、149题）

Write a response in which you discuss what questions would need to be answered in order to decide whether the recommendation is likely to have the predicted result. Be sure to explain how the answers to these questions would help to evaluate the recommendation.

题目整理

论点 该论者的论点包括一个建议和一项预测。

(1) We recommend maintaining Grove College's tradition of all-female education.

(2) We predict that keeping the college all-female will improve morale among students and convince alumnae to keep supporting the college financially.

论据 Grove students, both past and present, are against the idea of coeducation. Eighty percent of the students responding to a survey conducted by the student government wanted the school to remain all female, and over half of the alumnae who answered a separate survey also opposed coeducation.

论证方法

题目中论者主要运用了统计数据论证法。

分析提示

● 论者在论据中引用了两项调查的相关数据，是典型的统计数据论证法。但问题是：首先，这些调查的方案设计（如调查样本的选择、调查问卷的设计、调查数据的处理、调查结果的核实和验证等）和实施过程是否都是严格按照科学程序进行的？其结论是否客观、中立？调查的实施者没有受特殊立场或相关既得利益者的影响？独立第三方的相关调查数据有没有拿来作参考？等等。其次，要注意：这两项调查的调查对象都缺乏代表性。前者的调查对象是该校的学生，而调查的实施方是该校的学生会。这些在校生很可能更愿意正面评价这所学校。所以只对这些学生进行调查有自说自话的嫌疑。那些没选择这所学校的学生是怎么看这所女子学校的教育特点呢？而后一个调查的对象是该校的校友。同前一个调查一样，这些校友因为对自己的母校怀有感情，他们的评价很可能也不是客观的。论者为什么不调查其他人群（比如，该校学生的家长、专业教育人士、公司和企业的高管、高等教育研究人员等）？参考了多方人士的评价后，论者的判断才会更客观。

● 在结论中，论者认为，如果保留该校传统会有两项好处，即improve morale among students 和convince alumnae to keep supporting the college financially。但是，第一，对这两项"好处"，论者并未提供有效的证明。所以，难以取信于人。第二，论者为什么不提延续女校的传统之缺点？诸如，招生面狭窄、不利于学生身心成长、不利于学生适应未来社会角色等等，这些都是很容易想到的女校的缺点。第三，论者为何不提男女同校教育的好处呢？更丰富的生源、学生正常的身心成长、健全的社会角色的适应、多样化教学内容、将来更为庞大的校友圈、更为充裕的校友捐资、更大的学校影响力等等，这些好处，论者为什么避而不谈？

● 最后，建议要保留Grove College百年女校的传统的是该校的president and administrative staff。那么，这些人的身份和职务是否会影响他们建议的客观性和中立性？教育专家、学生家长、工商业人士、政府教育机构等各界人士的意见是什么？

---

157. The following appeared in a memo from the marketing director of Top Dog Pet Stores.

"Five years ago Fish Emporium started advertising in the magazine Exotic Pets Monthly. Their stores saw sales increase by 15 percent after their ads began appearing in the magazine. The three Fish Emporium stores in Gulf City saw an even greater increase than that. Because Top Dog Pet Stores is based in Gulf City, it seems clear that we should start placing our own ads in Exotic Pets Monthly. If we do so, we will be sure to reverse the recent trend of declining sales and start making a profit again."

（参考第158题）

Write a response in which you examine the stated and/or unstated assumptions of the argument. Be sure to explain how the argument depends on these assumptions and what the implications are for the argument if the assumptions prove unwarranted.

题目整理

论点 该题目的论点包括一项预测和一个建议。

(1) We should start placing our own ads in Exotic Pets Monthly.

(2) If we do so, we will be sure to reverse the recent trend of declining sales and start making a profit again.

论据 (1) Five years ago Fish Emporium started advertising in the magazine Exotic Pets Monthly. Their stores saw sales increase by 15 percent after their ads began appearing in the magazine. The three Fish Emporium stores in Gulf City saw an even greater increase than that.

(2) Because Top Dog Pet Stores is based in Gulf City, it seems clear that we should start placing our own ads in Exotic Pets Monthly.

论证方法

题目中论者主要运用了因果关系论证法和类比论证法。

分析提示

● 论据(1)是个因果关系论证。五年前，Fish Emporium在Exotic Pets Monthly杂志上开始做广告，随后其销量上升了15%。论者首先就假设，前者就是后者的原因。这显然是把先后发生的两件事情看作因果关系，犯有"在此之后，因此之故"的逻辑错误。其次，论者要假设没有其他原因导致同样的结果。Fish Emporium投放了广告之后出现的销售额的上升完全可能是整体经济的改善带来的，如人们收入的提高、新的鱼类品种的引进、老龄化社会的到来（老年人更愿意养一些花鸟鱼虫）、经济出现通货膨胀导致人们对一些宠物的投机和爆炒。第三，论者还要假设，Fish Emporium 的店面数目要足够多，至少不止 Gulf City 的三家。如果其店面数总共也就六七家，那么，其总体 15% 的销售增长多半是 Gulf City 那三家带来的。那样的话，其销量的增长是因为投放了广告这样的推论就很可疑了。

- 论据 (2) 是个类比论证法。论者的推论是：既然 Fish Emporium 在 Exotic Pets Monthly 杂志上投放广告实现了销量的增长，Top Dog Pet 如果效仿，结果也会不错。显然，这个推论要假设 Top Dog Pet 和 Fish Emporium 二者具有可比性。但问题是：第一，观赏鱼的市场规律和宠物狗的是一样的吗？第二，现在的宠物市场和五年前相比不会有巨大的变化？第三，Exotic Pets Monthly 这本杂志的读者群也都喜欢宠物狗吗？第四，有没有其他读者群更大的关于宠物狗的杂志，或者说其他更为直接有效的广告媒介可供选择，比如像电视、广播上的宠物狗节目和互联网上的一些宠物狗网站？

- 论者在结论中预测，一旦在 Exotic Pets Monthly 投放了广告，Top Dog Pet 一定会 reverse the recent trend of declining sales and start making a profit again。这个预测显然要假设：Top Dog Pet 近来销量下降的原因是市场宣传不够、广告投放不足。但是，其一，这个假设的原因未经证明。其二，论者否定了是别的原因导致了 Top Dog Pet 销量的下滑。

---

158. The following appeared in a memo from the marketing director of Top Dog Pet Stores.

"Five years ago, Fish Emporium started advertising in the magazine Exotic Pets Monthly. Their stores saw sales increase by 15 percent. The three Fish Emporium stores in Gulf City saw an even greater increase than that. Because Top Dog has some of its largest stores in Gulf City, it seems clear that we should start placing our own ads in Exotic Pets Monthly. If we do so, we will be sure to reverse the recent trend of declining sales and start making a profit again."

（参考第 157 题）

Write a response in which you discuss what specific evidence is needed to evaluate the argument and explain how the evidence would weaken or strengthen the argument.

题目整理

论点 该题目的论点包括一项预测和一个建议。

(1) We should start placing our own ads in Exotic Pets Monthly.

(2) If we do so, we will be sure to reverse the recent trend of declining sales and start making a profit again.

论据 (1) Five years ago, Fish Emporium started advertising in the magazine Exotic Pets Monthly. Their stores saw sales increase by 15 percent. The three Fish Emporium stores in Gulf City saw an even greater increase than that.

(2) Because Top Dog has some of its largest stores in Gulf City, it seems clear that we should start placing our own ads in Exotic Pets Monthly.

论证方法

题目中论者主要运用了因果关系论证法和类比论证法。

分析提示

● 论据(1)是个因果关系论证。五年前, Fish Emporium 在 Exotic Pets Monthly 杂志上开始做广告, 随后其销量上升了15%。在这里, 论者显然假设前者就是后者的原因。这是把先后发生的两件事情看作因果关系, 犯有"在此之后, 因此之故"的逻辑错误。问题是, 有没有其他原因导致同样的结果? Fish Emporium 投放了广告之后出现的销售额的上升完全可能是整体经济的改善带来的, 如人们收入的提高、新的观赏鱼品种的引进、老龄化社会的到来(老年人更愿意养一些花鸟鱼虫等)、经济出现通货膨胀导致人们对一些宠物的投机和爆炒。其次, Fish Emporium 总共有多少家店面? 如果店面总共也就六七家, 其15%的销售增长多半是Gulf City 那三家店作出的贡献。那么, 其销量的增长是因为投放了广告这样的推论就很可疑了, 很可能是Gulf City 特殊的情况导致了增长。这些都需要进一步的证据加以说明。

● 论据(2)是个类比论证法。论者的推论是: 既然Fish Emporium 在 Exotic Pets Monthly 杂志上投放广告实现了销量的增长, Top Dog Pet 如果效仿, 结果也会不错。但问题是, 第一, Top Dog Pet 和 Fish Emporium 二者具有可比性吗? 观赏鱼的市场规律和宠物狗的是一样的吗? 第二, 现在的宠物市场和五年前相比不会有巨大的变化? 第三, Exotic Pets Monthly 这本杂志的读者群也都喜欢宠物狗? 第四, 有没有其他更为专业、读者群更大的关于宠物狗的杂志, 或者其他更为直接有效的广告媒介可供选择, 比如像电视、广播上的宠物狗节目和互联网上的一些宠物狗网站? 这些都需要更多的佐证。

● 论者在结论中预测, 一旦在 Exotic Pets Monthly 投放了广告, Top Dog Pet 一定会 reverse the recent trend of declining sales and start making a profit again。这个预测显然要假设: Top Dog Pet 近来销量下降的原因是市场宣传不够、广告投放不足。但是, 其一, 这个假设的原因未经证明。其二, 论者并没有证明不是别的原因导致了 Top Dog Pet 销量的下滑。

---

159. The following appeared in a letter to the editor of the Balmer Island Gazette.

"The population on Balmer Island increases to 100,000 during the summer months. To reduce the number of accidents involving mopeds and pedestrians, the town council of Balmer Island plans to limit the number of mopeds rented by each of the island's six moped rental companies from 50 per day to 30 per day during the summer season. Last year, the neighboring island of Torseau enforced similar limits on moped rentals and saw a 50 percent reduction in moped accidents. We predict that putting these limits into effect on Balmer Island will result in the same reduction in moped accidents."

(参考第5、173题)

Write a response in which you discuss what questions would need to be answered in order to decide whether the prediction and the argument on which it is based are reasonable. Be sure to explain how the answers to these questions would help to evaluate the prediction.

题目整理

论点 Putting the limits on moped rentals into effect on Balmer Island will result in 50 percent reduction in moped accidents.

论据 (1) The population on Balmer Island increases to 100,000 during the summer months. To reduce the number of accidents involving mopeds and pedestrians, the town council of Balmer Island plans to limit the number of mopeds rented by each of the island's six moped rental companies from 50 per day to 30 per day during the summer season.

(2) Last year, the neighboring island of Torseau enforced similar limits on moped rentals and saw a 50 percent reduction in moped accidents.

论证方法

题目中论者主要运用了纵向和横向类比的论证法。

分析提示

● 首先在论据(2)中，论者把去年发生在邻岛 Torseau 的事情同本岛今年的情形进行简单类比。问题是：去年的事情今年是否同样可行？别的地方的做法，本地是否行得通？两个岛屿的具体情况，比如人口密度、交通工具、交通设施、道路状况、交通警察的力量配备、交通执法水平、人口素质等等是否都具有可比性？

● 其次，论者只是说"Last year, the neighboring island of Torseau enforced similar limits on moped rentals and saw a 50 percent reduction in moped accidents"，但并没有提供这个"similar limits"的具体细节。我们要问的问题是：去年 Torseau 岛的政策是如何实施的？是简单地限制 moped 的数量，还是同时实施了配套措施，比如对 moped 驾驶者进行交通法规的教育、对行人的教育和管理、改善交通标志、加强天气预报及路况预警等等？对这些，论者都语焉不详。

● 论者在整个论证过程中始终暗含着：moped 驾驶者以及过多的 moped 引发了频繁的交通事故。但这一点论者并未证明。于是我们不得不问：难道没别的原因，比如，夏季该岛上骤然增加的人口（尤其是流动人口）、本地交通标志不足、交警配备不够、交通管理低效、甚至是夏季闷热的天气等，导致了交通事故？

● 再有，论者建议的限制 moped 的措施仅限于夏季的几个月；但其想要达到的目标却是 a 50 percent reduction in moped accidents。这看起来像是个降低交通事故的全年目标。那么问题是：夏季 Balmer 岛上涉及 moped 的交通事故占该岛全年涉及 moped 的交通事故多大比例？如果该岛上发生涉及 moped 的交通事故绝大部分都发生在冬、春、秋三季，那么即便是对岛上的 moped 实施更大比例的限制，恐怕也很难实现全年降低 50% 的目标。

● 最后，论者限制 moped 的建议是否会使岛上因为交通工具的不足而使拥堵状况更严重，因而带来更多的交通事故？岛上现有的公共交通设施能否满足限制 moped 之后激增的交通需求？等等这些都是很大的问题。

160. The following appeared in a recommendation from the President of the Amburg Chamber of Commerce.

"Last October, the city of Belleville installed high-intensity lighting in its central business district, and vandalism there declined almost immediately. The city of Amburg, on the other hand, recently instituted police patrols on bicycles in its business district. However, the rate of vandalism here remains constant. Since high-intensity lighting is clearly the most effective way to combat crime, we recommend using the money that is currently being spent on bicycle patrols to install such lighting throughout Amburg. If we install this high-intensity lighting, we will significantly reduce crime rates in Amburg."

（参考第172题）

Write a response in which you discuss what questions would need to be answered in order to decide whether the recommendation is likely to have the predicted result. Be sure to explain how the answers to these questions would help to evaluate the recommendation.

题目整理

论点 论者的论点包括一个建议和一项预测。

(1) Since high-intensity lighting is clearly the most effective way to combat crime, we recommend using the money that is currently being spent on bicycle patrols to install such lighting throughout Amburg.

(2) If we install this high-intensity lighting, we will significantly reduce crime rates in Amburg.

论据 (1) Last October, the city of Belleville installed high-intensity lighting in its central business district, and vandalism there declined almost immediately.

(2) The city of Amburg, on the other hand, recently instituted police patrols on bicycles in its business district. However, the rate of vandalism here remains constant.

论证方法

题目中论者主要运用了因果关系论证法、类比论证法和归纳推理论证法。

分析提示

● 论据(1)是因果关系论证。但论者列举的前后两个现象high-intensity lighting和decline in vandalism there之间未必就是因果关系。很可能是别的原因导致了同样的结果，比如：是10月份寒冷的天气让那些爱搞破坏的人不愿到外面闲逛了？是不是中央商业区的人流增加了，更有利于监督vandalism行为？是不是较好的照明条件改善了那里的视觉环境，从而也改善了人们的情绪，人们的举止更文明得体，破坏行为也因此减少呢？

● 论据(2)也是因果关系论证，论者也犯有"在此之后，因此之故"的逻辑错误：police patrols和continuously constant vandalism之间很可能没有因果关系。真正的问题也许不是police patrols无效，而是另有原因。比如，因为那些警察骑自行车很难追击那些搞破坏的人，因而没有震慑力。或者，因为经济不景气，失业率上升，人们内心普遍怀有不满和愤懑。

● 论者在结论(1)中断言Belleville市的强力照明（high-intensity lighting）是打击犯罪的最有效办法，建议Amburg把花在自行车巡逻上的钱用在全城安装强力照明。这个推论至少有以下问题：第一，除了谈及强力照明和警察自行车巡逻两种对付破坏公共设施行为的办法以外，论者并未列举其他办法进行比较。他凭什么断定强力照明是最有效的办法？第二，即便强力照明在Belleville有效，但也仅仅是对付破坏公共设施行为有效而已。论者将这种办法推广到所有的犯罪行为，这是个错误的归纳推理，有以偏概全的嫌疑。第三，论者建议Amburg效法Belleville的做法，这很可能是一种不当的类比论证。这两个城市未必有可比性。第四，论者建议Amburg把花在自行车巡逻上的钱用在Amburg全城安装强力照明。但问题是，这笔钱够在全城安装这种强力照明设备吗？

● 最后，在结论(2)中，论者预测：一旦Amburg实施了Belleville的做法，就会大量减少Amburg市的犯罪率。这里面显然有个假设：破坏行为在Amburg的全部犯罪案例中占相当高的比例和相当大的数量。但这一点论者并未证明。

------

161. The following is a recommendation from the personnel director to the president of Acme Publishing Company.

"Many other companies have recently stated that having their employees take the Easy Read Speed-Reading Course has greatly improved productivity. One graduate of the course was able to read a 500-page report in only two hours; another graduate rose from an assistant manager to vice president of the company in under a year. Obviously, the faster you can read, the more information you can absorb in a single workday. Moreover, Easy Read would cost Acme only $500 per employee—a small price to pay when you consider the benefits. Included in this fee is a three-week seminar in Spruce City and a lifelong subscription to the Easy Read newsletter. Clearly, Acme would benefit greatly by requiring all of our employees to take the Easy Read course."

(参考第113、126、127题)

Write a response in which you examine the stated and/or unstated assumptions of the argument. Be sure to explain how the argument depends on these assumptions and what the implications are for the argument if the assumptions prove unwarranted.

题目整理

论点 Acme would benefit greatly by requiring all of our employees to take the Easy Read course.

论据 (1) Many other companies have recently stated that having their employees take the Easy Read Speed-Reading Course has greatly improved productivity. One graduate of the course was able to read a 500-page report in only two hours; another graduate rose from an assistant manager to vice president of the company in under a year.

(2) Obviously, the faster you can read, the more information you can absorb in a single workday.

(3) Moreover, Easy Read would cost Acme only $500 per employee—a small price to pay when you consider the benefits.

(4) Included in this fee is a three-week seminar in Spruce City and a lifelong subscription to the Easy Read newsletter.

论证方法

题目中论者主要运用了归纳推理论证法和诉诸常识法。

分析提示

- 论据(1)举了许多公司作例子，运用的是不完全归纳法，属于归纳推理论证。论者首先要假设，那些公司所说的事情是真实可信的。再者，即便上述事情可信，论者还要假设那些公司具有代表性。但论者说的many other companies中的many到底是多少家？10家、20家还是50家？many是个很模糊的数量描述。最后，论者在这里还有横向类比不当的嫌疑。别的公司适用的，自己的公司也适用吗？自己公司的情况和他们具有可比性吗？

- 论据(2)(3)(4)都是在运用常识展开论证。论据(2)所说的"一个人读的越快，吸收的信息量就越大"听起来似乎有道理，但经不起推敲。因为论者是在假设阅读速度是决定一个人获取信息的唯一因素。常识告诉我们，如果一个人阅读速度很快，但其相关基础知识欠缺、逻辑思维混乱、批判性思维能力差、不善于把书本信息同实际经验相结合，他是不可能真正从阅读中吸收多少有用信息的。

- 论据(3)说Easy Read would cost Acme only $500 per employee—a small price to pay when you consider the benefits。言下之意是这笔投入很划算。但是，第一，论者要假设论据(1)提到的benefits都是切实可靠的。但这些benefits都是听别的公司转述的，其真实性未经证实。第二，论者还要假设只要参与这个课程，都能收到明显的效果。假如这个Easy Read培训课程不能取得预期效果，反而耽误了员工的工作时间，其成本代价还会是一笔简单的$500 per employee的投入吗？第三，论者需要假设这家Acme Publishing Company的员工队伍不太庞大。假如其员工上千的话，都接受培训意味着50万美元的开支。这还会是论者说的a small price吗？

- 论者在论据(4)中说，培训课程$500 pcr employee的报价中还包括a three-week seminar in Spruce City and a lifelong subscription to the Easy Read newsletter，认为这是该课程吸引人的地方之一。但这个看法显然是要假设公司的老板也站在员工的立场上来看待这个课程。试想，员工们三个星期不干活对公司意味着什么？哪个老板会养闲人？这个培训课程从长期来看也许有利于该公司增强其人力资本的储备。但对这些远期的潜在收益，公司老板未必关心。毕竟，这些员工随时都有可能离职。今天对他们进行培训，明天他们就可能是竞争对手的人力资本了。

---

162. The following appeared in a memo from a budget planner for the city of Grandview.

"It is time for the city of Grandview to stop funding the Grandview Symphony Orchestra. It is true that the symphony struggled financially for many years, but last year private contributions to the symphony increased by 200 percent and attendance at the symphony's concerts-in-the-park series doubled. In addition, the symphony has just announced an increase in ticket prices for next year. For these reasons, we recommend that the city eliminate funding for the Grandview

Symphony Orchestra from next year's budget. We predict that the symphony will flourish in the years to come even without funding from the city."

（参考第61、139、141、143题）

Write a response in which you discuss what questions would need to be answered in order to decide whether the recommendation is likely to have the predicted result. Be sure to explain how the answers to these questions would help to evaluate the recommendation.

题目整理

论点 论者的论点包含一个建议和一项预测。

    (1) We recommend that the city eliminate funding for the Grandview Symphony Orchestra from next year's budget.

    (2) We predict that the symphony will flourish in the years to come even without funding from the city.

论据 (1) Last year private contributions to the symphony increased by 200 percent and attendance at the symphony's concerts-in-the-park series doubled.

    (2) In addition, the symphony has just announced an increase in ticket prices for next year.

论证方法

题目中论者主要运用了统计数据论证法、类比论证法和因果关系论证法。

分析提示

● 论据(1)列举了两个重要数据。但问题是：第一，论者说"Last year private contributions to the symphony increased by 200 percent"。那么，一年前这个交响乐团收到的私人赞助是多少？如果数量很少，那么200 percent的增长就没什么意义。其二，公园里音乐会的上座率也存在类似问题：如果之前的观众数量很少，提高一倍说明不了什么问题。再者，这些公园音乐会收费吗？收多少？公园音乐会是否能有效带动这个交响乐团在音乐厅里演出的上座率？这些通常具有音乐普及和教育性质的公园音乐会能否使公众对交响乐曲产生兴趣并成为实际的欣赏者和消费者？其三，论者所说的那些数据都是去年的情况。去年的情况能说明今年和未来的情况吗？假如今后情况变得更差了呢？论者这里犯了纵向类比错误。

● 论据(2)是个因果关系论证。论者认为既然"the symphony has just announced an increase in ticket prices for next year"，那么他们的收入应该不成问题了。但是，其一，乐团只是宣布下一年的票价上浮计划而已。这个计划对今年的票房收入没有影响，并且该计划是否实施尚不得而知。其二，即便下一年提了票价，能提多少呢？其三，提高票价之后，音乐会的上座率会下降吗？可否维持现状或者稳定上升？

● 在结论(2)中，论者预测"the symphony will flourish in the years to come even without funding from the city"。这个预测显得过于乐观。因为即便论据(1)(2)所说的都属实，如果有其他不利的情况出现，这家乐团依然会出现运营困难。比如：未来付给乐团成员的工资、设备和道具的成本、演出场地的租金、宣传和交通费用等等，会上涨吗？如果这些费用上涨较多的话，即便该乐团的演出票价上浮，也许依然不能带来多少净收入。又比如，其他的交响乐团是否会对Grandview Symphony Orchestra构成竞争？或者，其他的音乐形态，比如摇滚、戏剧、电影是否会分流一部分观众和听众？等等这些都是难以预料的情况。

163. The following memo appeared in the newsletter of the West Meria Public Health Council.

"An innovative treatment has come to our attention that promises to significantly reduce absenteeism in our schools and workplaces. A study reports that in nearby East Meria, where consumption of the plant beneficia is very high, people visit the doctor only once or twice per year for the treatment of colds. Clearly, eating a substantial amount of beneficia can prevent colds. Since colds are the reason most frequently given for absences from school and work, we recommend the daily use of nutritional supplements derived from beneficia. We predict this will dramatically reduce absenteeism in our schools and workplaces."

（参考第36、166题）

Write a response in which you discuss what questions would need to be answered in order to decide whether the recommendation is likely to have the predicted result. Be sure to explain how the answers to these questions would help to evaluate the recommendation.

题目整理

论点 An innovative treatment has come to our attention that promises to significantly reduce absenteeism in our schools and workplaces.

论据 (1) A study reports that in nearby East Meria, where consumption of the plant beneficia is very high, people visit the doctor only once or twice per year for the treatment of colds. Clearly, eating a substantial amount of beneficia can prevent colds.

(2) Since colds are the reason most frequently given for absences from school and work, we recommend the daily use of nutritional supplements derived from beneficia.

(3) We predict this will dramatically reduce absenteeism in our schools and workplaces.

论证方法

题目中论者主要运用了统计数据论证法、类比论证法和因果关系论证法。

分析提示

● 论据(1)提到了一项研究报告，属于统计数据论证。我们的疑问是：首先，这些调查的方案设计（如调查样本的选择、调查数据的处理、调查结果的核实和验证等）和实施过程是否是严格按照科学程序进行的？其结论是否客观、中立？调查的实施者有没有受行业及其他利益相关方的影响？等等。其次，论者提到，在East Meria人们经常吃plant beneficia，那里的人们感冒少。这两者只是同时发生的两个现象，但论者断定前者是后者的原因。这个推论很不可靠。难道不可能是其他因素使East Meria的居民很少感冒？比如，那里的人们更注重锻炼？那的自然环境更健康？等等。再次，即便吃了beneficia可以预防感冒，但论者说的eating a substantial amount of beneficia到底指吃多少？天天吃？顿顿吃？怎么吃？这里的substantial amount是个非常模糊的数量界定。

- 论据(2)是个因果关系论证。论者的推论过程是：因为beneficia在East Meria可以预防和治疗感冒，而感冒是West Meria的人们旷课和旷工最为经常的理由，所以，论者建议the daily use of nutritional supplements derived from beneficia。首先，论者在此处用了类比论证。既然beneficia在East Meria有效，那么它在West Meria也应该一样有效。但问题是，这两个地方具有可比性吗？这两个地方的人口结构、地理环境、气候、人们的生活和饮食习惯等等，都相同吗？其次，West Meria的人们是否把感冒当作旷工和旷课的借口？再次，即便吃beneficia可以防治感冒，论者推荐食用的nutritional supplements derived from beneficia会和直接吃beneficia一样管用吗？其推荐的使用剂量（daily use）合适吗？会不会有副作用？

- 在论据(3)中，论者预测daily use of nutritional supplements derived from beneficia会dramatically reduce absenteeism in our schools and workplaces。问题是，即便这个nutritional supplements有效，即便West Meria的人们旷工和旷课的确多数都是感冒所致，但谁能保证未来不会有其他的原因导致那里的人重新又频繁感冒呢？比如：新感冒病毒的产生、气候的变化等。

---

164. The following was written by a group of developers in the city of Monroe.

"A jazz music club in Monroe would be a tremendously profitable enterprise. At present, the nearest jazz club is over 60 miles away from Monroe; thus, our proposed club, the C Note, would have the local market all to itself. In addition, there is ample evidence of the popularity of jazz in Monroe: over 100,000 people attended Monroe's jazz festival last summer, several well-known jazz musicians live in Monroe, and the highest-rated radio program in Monroe is 'Jazz Nightly.' Finally, a nationwide study indicates that the typical jazz fan spends close to $1,000 per year on jazz entertainment. We therefore predict that the C Note cannot help but make money."

（参考第25、100、102题）

Write a response in which you discuss what questions would need to be answered in order to decide whether the prediction and the argument on which it is based are reasonable. Be sure to explain how the answers to these questions would help to evaluate the prediction.

题目整理

论点 A jazz music club in Monroe would be a tremendously profitable enterprise, and the C Note cannot help but make money.

论据 (1) There is ample evidence of the popularity of jazz in Monroe: over 100,000 people attended Monroe's jazz festival last summer, several well-known jazz musicians live in Monroe, and the highest-rated radio program in Monroe is 'Jazz Nightly.'

(2) At present, the nearest jazz club is over 60 miles away from Monroe; thus, our proposed club, the C Note, would have the local market all to itself.

(3) A nationwide study indicates that the typical jazz fan spends close to $1,000 per year on jazz entertainment.

论证方法

题目中论者运用了诉诸常识法、列举特征式论证法和统计数据论证法。

分析提示

● 论据(1)是个列举特征式论证法，论者力图说明爵士乐在Monroe很受大家的欢迎。但下列疑问需要回答：首先，论者说去年夏天有10万多人参加了每年一次的Monroe爵士乐音乐节，这里的"over 100,000"同往年比是个什么样的水平？如果往年参加的人数都是15万人以上，去年的人数虽说听起来颇为壮观，但实际却是下降的。其次，每年参与这个爵士乐音乐节的人是否绝大多数都来自本地？如果那些人多数都是来自外地的话，在Monroe本地发起成立一个爵士乐俱乐部难以聚拢人气。其三，论者说一些著名的爵士乐音乐人住在Monroe，这些音乐家在Monroe拥有住房，是因为要在Monroe搞爵士乐，还是出于其他的考虑？如果他们住在Monroe仅仅是因为那里风景怡人，则论者推论的说服力就大大减弱了。第四，至于论者说的"the highest-rated radio program in Monroe is 'Jazz Nightly' "，我们要问的是：是否其他节目的口碑都很差？如此的话，即便Jazz Nightly在人们的评价中位居第一，也未必说明当地人真正喜欢它。

● 论据(2)运用人们的常识展开论证：其他条件相同的情况下，有谁会舍近求远？但问题是：第一，这家计划中的爵士乐俱乐部具备足够的吸引力，能将本地的爵士乐爱好者留在本地吗？第二，那些热衷爵士乐的人会因为仅仅60多英里的路程就放弃附近的爵士乐俱乐部吗？

● 论据(3)是个统计数据论证。但是，这项研究的方案设计（如调查样本的选择、调查问卷的设计、调查数据的处理、调查结果的核实和验证等）和实施过程是否是严格按照科学程序进行的？其结论是客观、中立的吗？调查的实施者没有受行业及其他利益相关方的影响吗？其次，有没有一些特殊因素影响Monroe这个地方的爵士乐爱好者的消费习惯？论者说的调查是一个nationwide study。一个全国的典型指标对某个地方来说，可能没有任何意义。Monroe当地的消费水平如何、该地区的爵士乐爱好者是否愿意为这项娱乐花钱、他们是习惯自我娱乐还是去俱乐部消费，这些都会左右他们在爵士乐方面的消费支出。

● 最后，即使上述三个证据都是真实的，论者的结论"A jazz music club in Monroe would be a tremendously profitable enterprise, and the C Note cannot help but make money"。有证据表明凡是做流行的行当就必定能赚到钱吗？要开这家爵士乐俱乐部的话，其经营者的管理能力如何？资金是问题吗？会有很多竞争对手吗？其他的娱乐项目会分流爵士乐爱好者吗，这些都是很大的问题。

· ·

165. Humans arrived in the Kaliko Islands about 7,000 years ago, and within 3,000 years most of the large mammal species that had lived in the forests of the Kaliko Islands were extinct. Previous archaeological findings have suggested that early humans generally relied on both fishing and hunting for food; since archaeologists have discovered numerous sites in the

Kaliko Islands where the bones of fish were discarded, it is likely that the humans also hunted the mammals. Furthermore, researchers have uncovered simple tools, such as stone knives, that could be used for hunting. The only clear explanation is that humans caused the extinction of the various mammal species through excessive hunting.

（参考第54题）

Write a response in which you discuss one or more alternative explanations that could rival the proposed explanation and explain how your explanation(s) can plausibly account for the facts presented in the argument.

题目整理

论点 Humans caused the extinction of the various mammal species through excessive hunting.

论据 (1) Humans arrived in the Kaliko Islands about 7,000 years ago, and within 3,000 years most of the large mammal species that had lived in the forests of the Kaliko Islands were extinct.

(2) Previous archaeological findings have suggested that early humans generally relied on both fishing and hunting for food; since archaeologists have discovered numerous sites in the Kaliko Islands where the bones of fish were discarded, it is likely that the humans also hunted the mammals.

(3) Furthermore, researchers have uncovered simple tools, such as stone knives, that could be used for hunting.

论证方法

题目中论者运用了因果关系论证法、诉诸常识法和列举特征式论证法。

分析提示

● 关于Kaliko群岛上大型哺乳动物消失的原因，可以有许多种猜想。这些猜想只要逻辑上能自圆其说，并且和题目中已经确认的考古发现相吻合就可以。所以，除了题目中提供的说法以外，还可以有以下猜测：早期人类毁坏了哺乳动物生存和栖息的森林、夺取了它们赖以为继的食物、带给它们传染病、驯养了一些专门捕猎哺乳动物的家畜等，这些都可以提供解释。下面，我们仅就第一种情形展开叙述。具体如下：

● 人类在距今7000年前到达Kaliko群岛之后，发现那个地方很棒。不仅森林葱郁，野果飘香，飞禽走兽繁盛，而且，周边的海里鱼虾富饶。人类的先祖就住了下来。

● 当时，这些岛上还生活着其他大型哺乳动物。这些大型哺乳动物全都以岛上的几种嫩芽和野果为食，性情温顺。他们不攻击这些新来的人类，因为那些浑身长满长毛的家伙好像更喜欢吃麋鹿、兔子、田鼠等动物的肉。至于草根野果之类，人类只是偶尔吃点，完全不会给哺乳动物造成饥荒。所以，人类和大型哺乳动物在最初的几百年内和平共处。

● 但渐渐地，那些大型哺乳动物发现这些浑身长毛、直立行走的家伙们变得越来越聪明了。他们会做石刀、石斧、梭镖和弓箭之类的玩意儿，还会挖陷阱。这些样子古怪的工具给他们带来了更多吃的东西，他们群体的数量增加得更快了。那些哺乳动物开始发现树上最大最甜的果子不时被手脚利索的人类摘走。但他们不生气，因为野果太丰富了。

- 这些哺乳动物真正的灾难在一个风雨交加、雷鸣电闪的夜晚悄然到来了。
- 闪电击中了一棵枯死的大树。树着了，烧煳了人类挂在枯树干上的几大块鹿肉。鹿肉很快被从火中抢了出来。这群人类的头儿万分惋惜地看着这几块烧焦的肉。扔了怪可惜，他决定先尝一口。他咬了一小口，又一大口，然后狂吃，再然后众人争抢。这烤煳的肉太好吃了！他们决定要让这堆火一直烧下去。
- 第二天，这些人类多了一项工作：砍树，取柴。于是，这堆火一直烧着。
- 再后来的事情就简单了：人类的数量更多了，烤肉烤鱼也总是有的；只是，岛上的树被砍得越来越少了。那些大型哺乳动物发现野果不够吃了。他们恨那些爱吃肉的人类，但已经无力同数量庞大的人类对抗。在人类登上Kaliko群岛大约3000年的时候，这些大型哺乳动物迁移到别的岛上去了。
- 这些哺乳动物一走了之，全然不为后来的考古学家着想。这些喜欢挖挖泥巴、敲敲石头的家伙们至今还在寻找这些大型哺乳动物的踪迹，一直没有定论。偶尔，一些业余人士（听说还包括一些准备考GRE的）也来凑凑热闹，但提供的多是版本各异的猜想而已。

166. The following memo appeared in the newsletter of the West Meria Public Health Council.

"An innovative treatment has come to our attention that promises to significantly reduce absenteeism in our schools and workplaces. A study reports that in nearby East Meria, where fish consumption is very high, people visit the doctor only once or twice per year for the treatment of colds. This shows that eating a substantial amount of fish can clearly prevent colds. Furthermore, since colds are the reason most frequently given for absences from school and work, attendance levels will improve. Therefore, we recommend the daily use of a nutritional supplement derived from fish oil as a good way to prevent colds and lower absenteeism."

（参考第36、163题）

Write a response in which you discuss what questions would need to be answered in order to decide whether the recommendation and the argument on which it is based are reasonable. Be sure to explain how the answers to these questions would help to evaluate the recommendation.

题目整理

论点 We recommend the daily use of a nutritional supplement derived from fish oil as a good way to prevent colds and lower absenteeism.

论据 (1) A study reports that in nearby East Meria, where fish consumption is very high, people visit the doctor only once or twice per year for the treatment of colds. This shows that eating a substantial amount of fish can clearly prevent colds.

(2) Furthermore, since colds are the reason most frequently given for absences from school and work, attendance levels will improve.

论证方法

题目中论者主要运用了统计数据论证法、类比论证法和因果关系论证法。

分析提示

● 论据(1)提到了一项研究报告，属于统计数据论证。首先，我们的疑问是：这项调查的方案设计（如调查样本的选择、调查数据的处理、调查结果的核实和验证等）和实施过程是否是严格按照科学程序进行的？其结论是否客观、中立？调查的实施者有没有受行业及其他利益相关方的影响？等等。其次，论者提到在East Meria人经常吃鱼，那里的人很少感冒。这两者只是同时发生的两个现象，但论者断定前者是后者的原因。难道不可能是其他因素使East Meria的居民很少感冒？比如，那里的人们更注重锻炼？那里的环境更健康？或者特殊的人口结构（比如青壮年人口比例高，老人和儿童比例少）？等等。再次，论者只是说East Meria的居民很少因为感冒去医院看病，那么，这是否是因为那里的人一般得了感冒不去看医生，而是自己想办法处理？如果是这样的话，很可能那里的人们并不少得感冒，他们只是得了感冒不去医院看病而已。更或者，即使East Meria的居民很少因为感冒去医院，他们是否因为其他的病经常去看医生，而且那些病恰恰是和吃鱼多有关？第四，即便吃鱼可以减少感冒，但论者说的eating a substantial amount of fish到底指吃多少？天天吃？顿顿吃？怎么吃？这里的substantial amount是个非常模糊的数量界定。

● 论据(2)是个因果关系论证。论者的推论过程是：因为吃鱼在East Meria似乎可以防治感冒，而感冒又是West Meria的人们旷课和旷工最为经常的理由，所以，如果West Meria的人们多吃鱼的话，会有attendance levels will improve的结果。首先，论者在这里进行了一个类比论证。既然吃鱼在East Meria有效，那么，它在West Meria也应该一样有效。但问题是，这两个地方具有可比性吗？这两个地方的人口结构、地理环境、气候条件、人们的生活和饮食习惯等都相同？其次，West Meria的人们是否把感冒当作旷工和旷课的借口？

● 最后，在结论中，论者认为recommend the daily use of a nutritional supplement derived from fish oil as a good way to prevent colds and lower absenteeism。但问题是，即便吃鱼可以降低得感冒的几率，论者推荐食用的nutritional supplements derived from fish oil会和直接吃鱼一样管用吗？其推荐的使用剂量合适吗？会不会产生其他的副作用？

---

167. The following appeared in a memo from a vice president of Alta Manufacturing.

"During the past year, Alta Manufacturing had thirty percent more on-the-job accidents than nearby Panoply Industries, where the work shifts are one hour shorter than ours. Experts believe that a significant contributing factor in many accidents is fatigue caused by sleep deprivation among workers. Therefore, to reduce the number of on-the-job accidents at Alta, we recommend shortening each of our three work shifts by one hour. If we do this, our employees will get adequate amounts of sleep."

（参考第32、104、105、106题）

Write a response in which you discuss what questions would need to be answered in order to decide whether the recommendation and the argument on which it is based are reasonable. Be sure to explain how the answers to these questions would help to evaluate the recommendation.

题目整理

论点 论者的论点包括一项建议和一个预测。

(1) To reduce the number of on-the-job accidents at Alta, we recommend shortening each of our three work shifts by one hour.

(2) If we do this, our employees will get adequate amounts of sleep.

论据 (1) During the past year, Alta Manufacturing had thirty percent more on-the-job accidents than nearby Panoply Industries, where the work shifts are one hour shorter than ours.

(2) Experts believe that a significant contributing factor in many accidents is fatigue caused by sleep deprivation among workers.

论证方法

题目中论者主要运用了类比论证法和引用权威论证法。

分析提示

● 论据(1)将两家公司进行类比论证。论者把Panoply公司每天总工时比Alta 公司少一个小时这一现象解释为 "During the past year, Alta Manufacturing had thirty percent more on-the-job accidents than nearby Panoply Industries" 的原因。问题是：首先，Alta公司的工人是否如实报告了岗位事故发生的次数？否则，无论是谎报还是瞒报，都会使接下来的推论变得不可信。其次，是否有别的因素导致了这一结果？实际上，诸如两家公司生产设备的自动化和人性化程度的不同、员工工作时安全保护措施是否充分、员工是否严格遵守车间安全流程要求、工厂安全巡检是否严格、员工的工作情绪以及工作压力的大小等都可能导致两家公司岗位事故发生率的差异。

● 论据(2)属于引用权威论证法。对于专家及其看法，我们的疑问是：首先，这些专家是否了解Alta公司所在的行业、该公司车间的设备性能、操作流程等具体情况？他们的学术及专业水准如何？他们的观点有没有受行业及其他利益相关方的影响？其次，这些专家的判断 "a significant contributing factor in many accidents is fatigue caused by sleep deprivation among workers" 是个泛泛的判断。many accidents 是否涵盖了Alta公司所在行业的行业特性和生产流程特点了呢？这个一般性的结论是否适用Alta公司？这些都是问题。

● 在结论中，论者建议Alta公司减少每个班次一个小时的上班时间，让员工得到充分休息，减少岗位事故。但问题是：首先，员工是否会将这增加的一个小时的休息时间用来休息，而不干别的事情？其次，是否同时消除了其他易引发岗位事故的潜在因素？

168. The following is a letter that recently appeared in the Oak City Gazette, a local newspaper.

"The primary function of the Committee for a Better Oak City is to advise the city government on how to make the best use of the city's limited budget. However, at some of our recent meetings we failed to make important decisions because of the foolish objections raised by committee members who are not even residents of Oak City. People who work in Oak City but who live elsewhere cannot fully understand the business and politics of the city. After all, only Oak City residents pay city taxes, and therefore only residents understand how that money could best be used to improve the city. We recommend, then, that the Committee for a Better Oak City vote to restrict its membership to city residents only. We predict that, without the interference of non-residents, the committee will be able to make Oak City a better place in which to live and work."

Write a response in which you discuss what questions would need to be answered in order to decide whether the recommendation is likely to have the predicted result. Be sure to explain how the answers to these questions would help to evaluate the recommendation.

题目整理

论点 论者的论点包括一项建议和一个预测。

(1) We recommend, then, that the Committee for a Better Oak City vote to restrict its membership to city residents only.

(2) We predict that, without the interference of non-residents, the committee will be able to make Oak City a better place in which to live and work.

论据 (1) The primary function of the Committee for a Better Oak City is to advise the city government on how to make the best use of the city's limited budget. However, at some of our recent meetings we failed to make important decisions because of the foolish objections raised by committee members who are not even residents of Oak City.

(2) People who work in Oak City but who live elsewhere cannot fully understand the business and politics of the city. After all, only Oak City residents pay city taxes, and therefore only residents understand how that money could best be used to improve the city.

论证方法

题目中论者主要运用了列举特征式论证法和因果关系论证法。

分析提示

● 论据(1)是个列举特征式论证。因为几位非本地委员的反对使得Committee for a Better Oak City在最近的几次会议上无法达成若干重大决议，试者试图列举这些事件来表明这些非本地委员不了解Oak City的实际情况，是在干扰该委员会的工作。这个推论有以下问题：第一，论者说这些非本地委员的反对意见foolish。但何以见得这些意见就是foolish的？判断标准是什么？论者并未证明。所以，论者在这里有人身攻击的嫌疑。第二，论者所说的这些非本地委员的罪状是他们在几次会议上阻止了Committee for a Better Oak City通过重大决议。那么，他们反对什么决议？如果他们反对那些不能很好地利用该市有限的财政预算的决议呢？第三，这些非本地的委员提出了反对意见后，本地委员持什么态度？如果绝大多数本地委员赞同那些反对意见呢？如此的话，还能说这些非本地委员不了解Oak City、在干扰Committee for a Better Oak City的工作吗？

● 论据(2)是个因果关系论证。论者的推论是：Oak City 的本地居民才纳税。一个人只有纳了税才会理解如何花钱会使他所在的城市变得更好。那些非本地的委员们不纳税，因此他们不了解本市的商业和政治。这里的问题是：论者的逻辑前提"一个人只有纳了税才会理解如何花钱会使他所在的城市变得更好"显然讲不通。一个人对一个城市的财政预算如何支出、钱该如何花才能把这个城市建设得更美好的知识，同这个人对这座城市的了解和感情、这个人的专业知识以及他对这个城市的未来定位的理解等有密切关系，而同他是否是该城市的居民好像没有必然联系。

● 最后，论者预测，如果不让非 Oak City 本地居民加入，Committee for a Better Oak City 会使 Oak City 成为宜居的城市。这很可能过于武断。实际上对于任何城市来说，假如它要成为具有广泛魅力的城市，往往都要听取非本地居民和专家的意见和建议。这一方面是因为本地人由于过于习惯他们所在的城市，对本市的优缺点、特色以及未来发展方向感觉迟钝了；另一方面，这也是因为如果一个城市是开放的，它必定或多或少要被外来的文化所影响，在时间的长河中，既保持其传统的魅力，又不停地自我更新。所以，多听听非本地居民的意见才有可能使Oak City 变得更好。

···

169. The following appeared in a memo from the mayor of Brindleburg to the city council.

"Two years ago, the town of Seaside Vista opened a new municipal golf course and resort hotel. Since then, the Seaside Vista Tourism Board has reported a 20% increase in visitors. In addition, local banks reported a steep rise in the number of new business loan applications they received this year. The amount of tax money collected by Seaside Vista has also increased, allowing the town to announce plans to improve Seaside Vista's roads and bridges. We recommend building a similar golf course and resort hotel in Brindleburg. We predict that this project will generate additional tax revenue that the city can use to fund much-needed public improvements."

(参考第77题)

Write a response in which you discuss what questions would need to be answered in order to decide whether the recommendation is likely to have the predicted result. Be sure to explain how the answers to these questions would help to evaluate the recommendation.

题目整理

论点 论者的论点包括一项建议和一个预测。

(1) We recommend building a similar golf course and resort hotel in Brindleburg.

(2) We predict that this project will generate additional tax revenue that the city can use to fund much-needed public improvements.

论据 Two years ago, the town of Seaside Vista opened a new municipal golf course and resort hotel. Since then, the Seaside Vista Tourism Board has reported a 20% increase in visitors. In addition, local banks reported a steep rise in the number of new business loan applications they received this year. The amount of tax money collected by Seaside Vista has also increased, allowing the town to announce plans to improve Seaside Vista's roads and bridges.

论证方法

题目中论者只运用了类比论证法。

分析提示

- 论者首先有纵向类比不当的问题：他假设两年前的事情同样适用于现在。难道这期间没有其他情况出现（比如经济整体下滑、旅游业不景气、频繁发生的灾害性天气使多数人暂缓出行、新的时尚运动的出现使高尔夫不再受欢迎等），使得两年前在 Seaside Vista 的有效做法如今在 Brindleburg 难以奏效？

- 其次是横向类比不当：论者假设这两个城市完全可比，发生在 Seaside Vista 的事情也会发生在 Brindleburg。但这两个地方的地理位置、地质地貌、人文风情、交通、通讯、餐饮住宿等等完全可比吗？

- 第三，论者有"在此之后，因此之故"的推理错误：假设先后出现的两个现象之间有因果关系，即，正是因为两年前 Seaside Vista 开了高尔夫球场和度假宾馆，所以当地旅游业、地方银行贷款和地方财政收入等都出现了喜人的变化。问题是：没有其他原因导致同样的结果吗？比如，当地经济形势增长迅速、人们收入的增加和休闲娱乐时间的充裕、广告商的大规模宣传、旅游环境的改善等等。

- 最后，即便论者的论据都是事实，论者提出的模仿 Seaside Vista 以促进 Brindleburg 经济和税收增长的建议依然值得商榷，因为也许还有其他更好的办法，比如：引进新兴电子、软件设计、文化创意、航空物流、转口贸易等等产业。

170. The following appeared in a memo from the vice president of a company that builds shopping malls around the country.

"The surface of a section of Route 101, paved just two years ago by Good Intentions Roadways, is now badly cracked with a number of dangerous potholes. In another part of the state, a section of Route 40, paved by Appian Roadways more than four years ago, is still in good condition. In a demonstration of their continuing commitment to quality, Appian Roadways recently purchased state-of-the-art paving machinery and hired a new quality-control manager. Therefore, I recommend hiring Appian Roadways to construct the access roads for all our new shopping malls. I predict that our Appian access roads will not have to be repaired for at least four years."

Write a response in which you discuss what questions would need to be answered in order to decide whether the recommendation is likely to have the predicted result. Be sure to explain how the answers to these questions would help to evaluate the recommendation.

题目整理

论点 论者的论点包括一项建议和一个预测。

(1) I recommend hiring Appian Roadways to construct the access roads for all our new shopping malls.

(2) I predict that our Appian access roads will not have to be repaired for at least four years.

论据 (1) The surface of a section of Route 101, paved just two years ago by Good Intentions Roadways, is now badly cracked with a number of dangerous potholes. In another part of the state, a section of Route 40, paved by Appian Roadways more than four years ago, is still in good condition.

(2) In a demonstration of their continuing commitment to quality, Appian Roadways recently purchased state-of-the-art paving machinery and hired a new quality-control manager.

论证方法

题目中论者主要运用了归纳推理论证法、列举特征式论证法和类比论证法。

分析提示

● 论据(1)比较两个筑路公司所铺的一段道路，进行归纳推理论证。然后，将归纳结果加以比较。问题是：其一，选取的两家公司的那段路能说明问题吗？它们有代表性吗？假如恰好选取了 Good Intentions Roadways 所铺的一段较差的路和 Appian Roadways 所铺的一段较好的路呢？或者前者的那段路后来遭受了较为严重的超负荷使用，而后者却是一段使用较少的路面呢？其二，这两家筑路公司的整体施工质量难道只能通过这两段路面来鉴别？其他方面，比如用户的评价、权威机构的质量认证、连续多年的工程施工记录等，都可以衡量它们的施工质量。但论者没有提供这些方面的情况。

● 论据(2)属于列举特征式论证。论者力图用 "Appian Roadways recently purchased state-of-the-art paving machinery and hired a new quality-control manager" 来说明 Appian Roadways 公司对施工质量的追求。但是，这些现象很可能说明 Appian Roadways 公司过去多年来一直在使用落后的设备，并且负责工程质量的经理频繁更换，一直不能有效监督工程质量。其次，论者为什么不说 Good Intentions Roadways 最近做了什么？假如该公司最近也在淘汰旧的机器设备，将其整体设备的完好率从过去的85%提高到95%呢？假如该公司的质量控制人员都在这家公司干了30年以上，并且领取的是全行业最高的薪酬呢？

● 最后，在结论中论者预测，由 Appian Roadways 公司来铺设 the access roads for all our new shopping malls，会有 our Appian access roads will not have to be repaired for at least four years 这样良好的结果。这是个类比论证：论者将这家公司所铺的一段40号公路的使用寿命同即将铺的通路（access roads）进行类比。但显然这两类道路很难具有可比性。一类是公路，另一类是供行人使用的通路。两者对设计、人流、车流、硬度、耐磨度等等各项要求都会有很大的不同。

171. The following appeared as a letter to the editor from the owner of a skate shop in Central Plaza.

"Two years ago the city voted to prohibit skateboarding in Central Plaza. They claimed that skateboard users were responsible for the litter and vandalism that were keeping other visitors from coming to the plaza. In the past two years, however, there has only been a small increase in the number of visitors to Central Plaza, and litter and vandalism are still problematic. Skateboarding is permitted in Monroe Park, however, and there is no problem with litter or vandalism there. In order to restore Central Plaza to its former glory, then, we recommend that the city lift its prohibition on skateboarding in the plaza."

（参考第3题）

Write a response in which you discuss what questions would need to be answered in order to decide whether the recommendation and the argument on which it is based are reasonable. Be sure to explain how the answers to these questions would help to evaluate the recommendation.

题目整理

论点 In order to restore Central Plaza to its former glory, then, we recommend that the city lift its prohibition on skateboarding in the plaza.

论据 (1) Two years ago the city voted to prohibit skateboarding in Central Plaza. They claimed that skateboard users were responsible for the litter and vandalism that were keeping other visitors from coming to the plaza. In the past two years, however, there has only been a small increase in the number of visitors to Central Plaza, and litter and vandalism are still problematic.

(2) Skateboarding is permitted in Monroe Park, however, and there is no problem with litter or vandalism there.

论证方法

题目中论者主要运用了统计数据论证法、列举特征式论证法和类比论证法。

分析提示

● 论据(1)和论据(2)分别列举了Centra Plaza和Monroe Park两个地方对玩滑板车的不同政策导致的不同结果，并进行了对比。论者在这里分别运用了列举特征式论证法和类比论证法。在论据(1)中，论者还描述了过去两年间Central Plaza的客流和乱扔垃圾及破坏公共设施行为的变化，因此，属于统计数据论证。首先，针对论者所说的 "In the past two years, there has only been a small increase in the number of visitors to Central Plaza, and litter and vandalism are still problematic"，我们的问题是：这些数据是如何得到的？是专业的市场调查公司的统计、媒体的报道还是论者的观察？其客观、中立性是否有保证？论者作为the owner of a skate shop in Central Plaza的身份是否会影响他立场的独立性？这些数据中的一些模糊的表述（比如a small increase和problematic）该如何界定？

- 假设论者提供的信息完全真实，综合论据(1)(2)，可以得出结论：玩滑板车与乱扔垃圾和破坏公共设施行为没有必然的联系，因为自从Central Plaza禁止在大楼内玩滑板车，Monroe Park允许玩滑板车以来，两地乱扔垃圾和破坏公共设施行为前后没有变化。我们的疑问是：第一，滑板车运动对Monroe Park的客流有什么影响？论者并未提供相关数据，因而也无法把它同Central Plaza的情况作比较。第二，两个地方乱扔垃圾和破坏公共设施的情况不同，是否有别的原因？比如说，这两个地方不同的物业和管理水平。因为Central Plaza的物业和管理水平较差，所以即便禁止玩滑板车，客流和乱扔垃圾及破坏公共设施的现象依然未见显著改观；而Monroe Park因为有较好的物业和管理水平，即便允许玩滑板车，那里很少有乱扔垃圾及破坏公共设施的现象。

- 最后，论者在结论中的建议"In order to restore Central Plaza to its former glory, then, we recommend that the city lift its prohibition on skateboarding in the plaza"似乎并未抓住问题的关键。因为即便滑板车运动如他所说未必是导致Central Plaza客流不多、乱扔垃圾和破坏公共设施现象盛行的原因；恢复滑板车运动也未必就能增加客流、减少乱扔垃圾和破坏公共设施现象。除了加强Central Plaza的物业和管理水平以外，其他因素可能也要考虑：比如，经济周期的影响、通货膨胀对人们消费意愿的压抑、周边其他商业中心对其顾客的分流、Central Plaza内商家的经营水平等。

---

172. The following appeared in a recommendation from the president of Amburg's Chamber of Commerce.

"Last October the city of Belleville installed high-intensity lighting in its central business district, and vandalism there declined within a month. The city of Amburg has recently begun police patrols on bicycles in its business district, but the rate of vandalism there remains constant. We should install high-intensity lighting throughout Amburg, then, because doing so is a more effective way to combat crime. By reducing crime in this way, we can revitalize the declining neighborhoods in our city."

（参考第160题）

Write a rcsponse in which you discuss what specific evidence is needed to evaluate the argument and explain how the evidence would weaken or strengthen the argument.

题目整理

论点 该论者的论点包括一个建议和一项预测。

(1) We should install high-intensity lighting throughout Amburg.

(2) By reducing crime in this way, we can revitalize the declining neighborhoods in our city.

论据 (1) Last October the city of Belleville installed high-intensity lighting in its central business district, and vandalism there declined within a month.

(2) The city of Amburg has recently begun police patrols on bicycles in its business district, but the rate of vandalism there remains constant.

(3) Installing high-intensity lighting is a more effective way to combat crime.

论证方法

题目中论者主要运用了因果关系论证法、类比论证法和归纳推理论证法。

分析提示

- 论据(1)是因果关系论证。但论者列举的前后两个现象high-intensity lighting和decline in vandalism there之间未必就是因果关系。论者有"在此之后，因此之故"的逻辑错误。论者需提供更多的资料证明不是别的原因导致了同样的结果，比如：是10月份寒冷的天气让那些爱搞破坏的人不愿到外面闲逛了？是不是中央商务区的人流增加了，更有利于监督破坏行为？是不是良好的照明条件改善了那里的视觉环境，从而也改善了人们的情绪，人们举止更文明得体，破坏行为也因此减少了呢？

- 论据(2)也是因果关系论证，论者也有"在此之后，因此之故"的逻辑错误：police patrols和continuously constant vandalism之间很可能没有因果关系。真正的问题也许不是police patrols无效，而是另有原因。比如，因为那些警察骑自行车很难追击那些搞破坏的人，因而没有震慑力。或者，因为经济不景气，失业率上升，人们内心普遍怀有不满。

- 论者在结论(3)中断言"Installing high-intensity lighting is a more effective way to combat crime"。这个结论至少有以下问题：第一，论者并未考虑Amburg和Belleville两地的差异。也许是这些差异使得强力照明（high-intensity lighting）在Belleville更加有效。所以，论者建议Amburg效法Belleville的做法很可能是不当的类比论证。第二，即便强力照明在Belleville有效，但只是对付破坏公共设施的行为有效。论者将这种办法推广到所有的犯罪行为，是个错误的归纳推理，有以偏概全的嫌疑。

- 最后，在结论(2)中，论者预测：一旦Amburg实施了Belleville的做法，就会revitalize the declining neighborhoods in our city。这里面显然有个假设：破坏公共设施的行为是导致Amburg出现declining neighborhoods的唯一原因。但这一点论者并未证明。

173. The following appeared in a letter to the editor of the Balmer Island Gazette.

"The population on Balmer Island doubles during the summer months. During the summer, then, the town council of Balmer Island should decrease the maximum number of moped rentals allowed at each of the island's six moped and bicycle rental companies from 50 per day to 30 per day. This will significantly reduce the number of summertime accidents involving mopeds and pedestrians. The neighboring island of Torseau actually saw a 50 percent reduction in moped accidents last year when Torseau's town council enforced similar limits on moped rentals. To help reduce moped accidents, therefore, we should also enforce these limitations during the summer months."

（参考第5、159题）

Write a response in which you examine the stated and/or unstated assumptions of the argument. Be sure to explain how the argument depends on these assumptions and what the implications are for the argument if the assumptions prove unwarranted.

题目整理

论点 To help reduce moped accidents, therefore, we should also enforce these limitations during the summer months.

论据 (1) The population on Balmer Island doubles during the summer months. During the summer, then, the town council of Balmer Island should decrease the maximum number of moped rentals allowed at each of the island's six moped and bicycle rental companies from 50 per day to 30 per day. This will significantly reduce the number of summertime accidents involving mopeds and pedestrians.

(2) The neighboring island of Torseau actually saw a 50 percent reduction in moped accidents last year when Torseau's town council enforced similar limits on moped rentals.

论证方法

题目中论者主要运用了纵向和横向的类比论证法。

分析提示

● 首先在论据(2)中，论者把去年发生在邻岛Torseau的事情同本岛今年的情形进行类比。论者假设这两个地方在时间和空间上具有可比性。但这个假设存在诸多疑问。去年的事情今年是否同样可行？别的地方的做法，本地是否行得通？两个岛屿的具体情况，比如人口密度、交通工具、交通设施、道路状况、交通警察的力量配备、交通执法水平、人口素质等等是否都具有可比性？

● 论者在论据(1)中说，限制moped出租的数量will significantly reduce the number of summertime accidents **involving mopeds and pedestrians**。论者显然是在假设：过多的moped以及行人是引发交通事故的主要原因。但这一点论者并未证明。难道没别的原因会导致同样的结果？比如，夏季该岛上骤然增加的人口，尤其是流动人口？本地交通标志不足、交警配备不够？交通管理低效、甚至是夏季天气闷热，人们交通警觉意识下降等等？

● 最后，论者在结论中建议："To help reduce moped accidents, therefore, we should also enforce these limitations during the summer months"。这里面的假设是，夏季moped的交通事故占全年moped的交通事故的较大比例。但这一点未经证明。如果该岛上moped的交通事故绝大部分都发生在冬、春、秋三季，那么，即便在夏季限制岛上的moped出租，全年的moped交通事故不见得会减少。

174. A recent sales study indicates that consumption of seafood dishes in Bay City restaurants has increased by 30 percent during the past five years. Yet there are no currently operating city restaurants whose specialty is seafood. Moreover, the majority of families in Bay City are two-income families, and a nationwide study has shown that such families eat significantly fewer home-cooked meals than they did a decade ago but at the same time express more concern about healthful eating. Therefore, the new Captain Seafood restaurant that specializes in seafood should be quite popular and profitable.

（参考第39题）

Write a response in which you discuss what questions would need to be addressed in order to decide whether the conclusion and the argument on which it is based are reasonable. Be sure to explain how the answers to the questions would help to evaluate the conclusion.

题目整理

论点 The new Captain Seafood restaurant that specializes in seafood should be quite popular and profitable.

论据 (1) A recent sales study indicates that consumption of seafood dishes in Bay City restaurants has increased by 30 percent during the past five years.

(2) Yet there are no currently operating city restaurants whose specialty is seafood.

(3) Moreover, the majority of families in Bay City are two-income families, and a nationwide study has shown that such families eat significantly fewer home-cooked meals than they did a decade ago but at the same time express more concern about healthful eating.

论证方法

题目中论者主要运用了统计数据论证法和因果关系论证法。

分析提示

● 论据(1)运用统计数据进行论证。但问题是：这些调查的方案设计（如调查样本的选择、调查数据的处理、调查结果的核实和验证等）和实施过程是否是严格按照科学程序进行的？其结论是客观、中立的吗？调查的实施者有没有受行业及其他利益相关方的影响？其次，即使这些数据是可信的，但假如五年前 consumption of seafood dishes in Bay City restaurants 是个很低的水平，30% 的上升又有什么意义呢？再者，过去五年，当地餐馆其他菜品的销量如何？假如其他菜品的销量五年间都至少增长 150%，那么 30% 的增长实际上是个微不足道的变化。

● 在论据(2)中，论者作了个因果关系论证：因为 Bay City 存在专营海鲜菜肴的市场空白，所以开一家海鲜餐馆肯定赚钱。但是，我们需要搞明白为什么会出现这个市场空白。如果是因为一些不可控的因素，比如新鲜海产品的供应非常困难、运输和储存海产品的成本非常高、加工海鲜产品需要的佐料奇缺、当地的气候条件不适合经常食用海鲜等等，所谓的市场空白也就不存在了。

● 论据(3)同样利用统计数据进行论证。但首先，普遍情况未必可以代表个案，一个全国范围内的调查对 Bay City 来说可能毫无意义。其次，即使那些双职工家庭 eat significantly fewer home-cooked meals than they did a decade ago，论者有证据可以证明他们都会去吃本地餐馆的海鲜吗？而且，当论者说，那些双职工家庭 eat significantly fewer home-cooked meals than they did a decade ago but **at the same time express more concern about healthful eating** 时，他是在假设未来 Captain Seafood restaurant 提供的海鲜食品在这些双职工家庭眼里会是 healthy food，但这一点论者并未证明。

附　录

附录1:
改句子练习答案

(1) This insult was the last straw. I decided to leave Marcia, and I spent the next few hours preparing for the trip.

分析: the last straw属陈词滥调; 第二个句子太啰唆。可改为:

This insult was *unbearable*, so I decided to leave Marcia, spending the next few hours preparing for the trip.

(2) Sam's new book illustrates the ludicrous intractability of a particular mind-set.

分析: ludicrous, intractability, mind-set属于抽象的生僻词。可改为: Sam's new book illustrates *a funny man habitually deaf to whatever advice.*

(3) Scott Daniel was a fine basketball player. I believe he was the best to play in the league in the last 20 years. He was really fine.

分析: 只是fine, really fine, 但没有具体细节, 没有说服力。可改为: Scott Daniel was a fine basketball player. *Over the past 20 years, he had won 18 times the most valuable player in NBA league. Insiders widely considered him the only competitor of Michael Jordan, the basketball king, in the history of this game.*

(4) *Vis-à-vis* our *tête-à-tête*, I must say the rendezvous filled me with ennui.

分析: *Vis-à-vis* (*adv.* in company, together), *tête-à-tête* (*adv.* in private), rendezvous (*n.* a place for a meeting; such a meeting at a certain place), ennui(*n.* boredom) 使整个句子过于文雅。可改为:

To be frank, the meeting was boring.

(5) In the following weeks at school, I worked frantically. Every day I became busier and busier.

分析：I became busier and busier 太不具体。可改为：

In the following weeks at school, I worked frantically. *Every day l found less time under my control, and I couldn't go to bed until 2:00 a. m, but had to rise at 5 o'clock.*

(6) As we entered the restaurant, Nick stated that the chicken there was good but the service was bad.

分析：entered, stated 偏于正式；good, bad 过于模糊。可改为：As we went into the restaurant, Nick *said* that the chicken there was *passable* but the service *spoiled all your taste.*

(7) In the final analysis, there are few rugged individualists in this day and age who are really down to earth in expressing nothing but the truth about the seamy side of life. Perhaps in the near future...

分析：这是个极糟糕的句子。不明白作者到底想说什么，但部分同学很是偏爱。其主要问题是：堆砌词藻（in the final analysis, in this day and age, expressing noting but, perhaps, in the near future），乱用词（rugged, down to earth, express, seamy side of life），句式僵硬（There be..., It's...这样的句型要少用，结构太僵硬），致使表意不清。可改为：

Today, few favor only darkness in life.

(8) We will never know everything about the atom, but some of the recent discoveries have been fascinating.

分析：前半句是毫无意义的铺陈，后半句啰唆、用词空泛（fascinating），而且没把内容讲明白。像 recent 这样模糊的时间用语尽量少用。可改为：

Physicists made some key discoveries last week.

(9) Graduate school can be a procrustean bed.

分析：a procrustean bed是在卖弄学问。可改为：

Graduate school is like McDonald's ice-cream machine: you pay a one-dollar coin and get one sweet cone, always the same.

(10) Pestering on the part of mendicants should be interdicted.

分析：on the part of是多余的表达；interdict是生僻词。另外，一般情况下，主动语态比被动语态表意清楚、直接。可改为：

Local governments should manage to stop beggars' pestering.

附录2:
常见的关系副词列表

accordingly	finally	likewise	still
afterwards	further	meanwhile	subsequently
also	furthermore	moreover	then
anyway	hence	namely	thereafter
besides	however	nevertheless	thereby
certainly	incidentally	next	therefore
consequently	indeed	nonetheless	thus
conversely	instead	now	undoubtedly
earlier	later	similarly	

另外,有些短语,比如:as a result, by this means, for this reason, for example, for instance, in addition, in the same way, in contrast, in this manner, in fact, in particular,on the other hand等,它们在复合句中的用法以及在句中的位置同上面列表中的关系副词在通常情况下都是一样的。例如:

Some senators oppose legislation restricting free trade; **in addition**, they assail proposals to increase corporate taxes.

在这个例句中,短语in addition的前后分别使用了分号和逗号将两个相对独立的句子分开,从而使整个句子变成了标准的复合句。

附录3:
标点符号用法练习

下面用法不当的标点符号该如何改?

(1) The sun was already low in the sky, it would soon be dark. 应改为:

    A. The sun was already low in the sky, **and**/so it would soon be dark.

    B. The sun was already low in the sky; it would soon be dark.

    C. The sun was already low in the sky; **therefore**, it would soon be dark. 或者 The sun was already low in the sky; it, **therefore**, would soon be dark.

    D. The sun was already low in the sky. It would soon be dark.

(2) On the morning of June 28, 1969, the weather finally cleared, **but** the climbers, wearied by their efforts of the previous days, could not attempt the summit. 应改为:

On the morning of June 28, 1969, the weather finally cleared; **but** the climbers, wearied by their efforts of the previous days, could not attempt the summit.

因为该句已经有逗号,所以but前面就用分号,而不是通常情况下的逗号。

(3) Most working people get at least one raise a year, **nevertheless**, inflation often leaves them with no increase in buying power. 应改为:

    A. Most working people get at least one raise a year; **nevertheless**, inflation often leaves them with no increase in buying power.

    B. Most working people get at least one raise a year. **Nevertheless**, inflation often leaves them with no increase in buying power.

当关系副词位于后一个句子句首时,该关系副词前面可以是分号或句号,而不是逗号。但要注意:

◆ 当前后两个句子很短时,可以用连词直接连接这两个句子而不再加上逗号。例如:

Many students are called **but** few came to class.

◆ 关系副词thus, then, still, otherwise, hence可直接放在后一个句子之首而不再带逗号。例如:

The rise of the dollar against foreign currencies drives up the price of our exports; thus we lose customers abroad.

◆ 关系副词therefore, nevertheless, nonetheless, instead, thus, then, still, otherwise, hence可直接放在后一个句子的谓语动词之前而不带任何标点符号。例如:

The hole in the ozone layer is steadily growing; we must **therefore** stop sending fluorocarbons into the atmosphere.

◆ 当复合句由相当于关系副词的词组连接时,该词组在句中的位置和标点符号同一般的关系副词相同。例如:

Many young Englishmen condemned the English war against France in the 1790s; **in the same manner**, many young Americans condemned the American war against North

Vietnam in the 1960s. 或者 Many young Englishmen condemned the English war against France in the 1790s; many young Americans, **in the same manner**, condemned the American war against North Vietnam in the 1960s.

附录4：
三篇范文文后问题参考答案

❶ 文章中有两个纵向类比、三个横向类比、一处比喻性类比、两处定义法论证、一处反证，请将这些论证方法找出来。

　　答 请参阅下面文章中的标注与说明。

❷ 文章在哪些地方对他人的不同观点进行了反驳？

　　答 文章在第七至第九三个自然段，分别对他人的不同意见进行了反驳，以加强自己的观点和立场的可信度与说服力。

❸ 全篇的逻辑结构是怎样的？

　　答 全篇是个归纳推理。全文以儿童为例，依据互联网上的部分内容不适合儿童，推出结论：应对互联网上的黄色内容加以控制。

Censorship or Common Sense

A 5-year-old is not ready to confront the world. This should be obvious, but it doesn't seem that way to many free-speech advocates.

The objections are coming from some usual sources: the American Civil Liberties Union, for example, and Web publishers. They are angry that some libraries around the country have installed software on their computers to block out Internet material that's unsuitable for children.

Traditionally, the library has been a safe place for children. And librarians have long been the guardians of public virtue. While they have been firm supporters of the First Amendment, they haven't generally interpreted it to mean that they should acquire large holdings of published pornography and make such materials available to children.

> 纵向类比：在这一自然段中，作者运用了纵向类比，将librarians过去的做法同现在的做法进行类比。认为他们现在应该像过去一样是guardians of public virtue。

Librarians have always acquired books according to their own discrimination and their sense of what is appropriate to their neighborhoods. They generally refuse to buy, among other things, pornography. This isn't censorship; it's common sense.

If a library were to have a section of pornographic books, would we want these to be printed in large, colorfully illustrated, lightweight volumes, shelved near the floor where they were easily available to children? Probably not. But we have gone to a great deal of trouble to insure that computers are user-friendly, with brightly colored graphics and easily accessible information.

> 横向类比：这里，作者将图书馆对少儿不宜的读物的做法同人们现在对互联网上不健康内容的做法进行了横向类比。

Material on the Internet is not only uncensored but also unedited. Adults can be expected to make their own evaluations of what they find. Children, who lack experience and knowledge, cannot.

The debate over the filtering of the Internet is a bit like the debate over grants given out by the National Endowment for the arts. It's all tangled up in false cries of censorship. Censorship is a legal term; it refers to government action prohibiting material from being circulated. This is very different from a situation in which a museum or an arts panel decides not to use public money to finance an exhibition or an artist.

> 定义法：这里，作者对什么是censorship进行了定义。
>
> 横向类比：在本自然段，作者横向类比了两种行为：控制互联网上儿童不宜的内容同博物馆支持艺术家的展览。

Commendably, our society defends freedom of speech with great vigor. But there is a difference between allowing everything to be said and allowing everyone to hear it. We should know this by now, having seen the effects that exposure to television and movie violence has on children.

> 定义法：这里，作者对freedom of speech意味着什么进行了定义。
>
> 横向类比：这里，作者将互联网上儿童不宜的内容对孩子的不良影响同电影、电视中的暴力行为对孩子的影响进行了横向类比。

The A. C. L. U. and the American Library Association say that the use of filtering software in computers is censorship because it blocks access to constitutionally protected speech. But these cries are baffling and unfounded. The only control libraries are asserting is over a small portion of the audience, not over the material itself. Moreover, this control has a powerful historical precedent: parental guidance is even older than the Constitution.

> 反证法：这里，作者认为控制互联网上儿童不宜的内容只是不让这部分内容被孩子看到，而非取消这些内容，并以此来说明对自己指责的荒谬性。
>
> 纵向类比：这里，作者将当前控制互联网上儿童不宜的内容的行为同父母对孩子的教育引导进行了纵向类比。

The protection of children should be instinctive. A man may have the right to stand on the street and spew

> 比喻式类比：这里，作者将放任互联网上儿童不宜的内容比喻为恶汉骂街。

obscenities at passers-by, but he would be ordered to leave a kindergarten classroom.

It is absurd to pretend that adults and children are the same audience, and it is shameful to protect the child pornographer instead of the child.

New York Times, October 19, 1998

Passage II

❶ 文章的第二自然段至倒数第二自然段的逻辑思路是怎样的？

㉄ 由第一自然段末尾的 ...they should declare the causes... 和最后一个自然段的WE，therefore...，我们可以看出：文章全篇是个因果关系推理。文章的第二自然段到倒数第二自然段的作用就是在论证为什么这个因果关系是成立的。具而言之，有以下的逻辑思路：

在第二自然段，作者由常识推出人的四大权利（equality，life，liberty and the pursuit of happiness）；随后在第三自然段，作者依据这四大权利对政府进行定义：政府的设立是为了满足上述四大权利，并且政府是在经过民众的同意之后才获得了它的权力。紧接着，在第四自然段，作者轻松地进行了演绎推理：只要政府的行为有悖于上述四大权利，民众即有权利废除或变更政府。然后，从第五自然段到倒数第二自然段，作者运用列举特征的论证方法全力论证了一点：大英帝国在北美十三州的种种行径说明了其在北美的殖民地政府完全背离了上述的四大权利。那么，一个自然而然的演绎推理就是：北美十三州有权废除殖民地政府，宣布独立。(具体请参阅下面文章中的标注与说明。)

❷ 文章在哪些地方对北美十三州宣布独立的行为进行了辩护？

㈡ 作者利用第四自然段的后半部分，即Prudence，indeed，will dictate that...for their future Security，对北美民众的独立进行了辩护。

然后，在倒数第二、第三自然段又进行了辩护。

The Declaration of Independence

The Declaration of Independence was approved by Continental Congress on July 2, 1776, and published two days later.

When in the Course of human Events, it becomes necessary for one People to dissolve the Political Bands which have connected them with another, and to assume among the Powers of the Earth, the separate and equal Station to which the Laws of Nature and of Nature's God entitle them, a decent Respect to the Opinions of Mankind requires that they should declare the causes which impel them to the Separation.

诉诸常识法：推出演绎推理的第一个大前提。

WE hold these Truths to be self-evident, that all Men are created equal, that they are endowed by their Creator with certain unalienable Rights, that among these are Life, Liberty and the Pursuit of Happiness.

定义法：利用上述前提对政府进行定义。

That to secure these Rights, Governments are instituted among Men, deriving their just Powers from the Consent of the Governed.

That whenever any Form of Government becomes destructive of these Ends, it is the Right of the People to alter or to abolish it, and to institute new Government, laying its Foundation on such Principles, and organizing its Powers in such Form, as to them shall seem most likely to effect their Safety and Happiness. Prudence, indeed, will dictate that Governments long established should not be changed for light and transient Causes; and accordingly all Experience hath shown, that Mankind are more disposed to suffer, while Evils are sufferable, than to right themselves by abolishing the Forms to which they are accustomed. But when a long Train of Abuses and Usurpations, pursuing invariably

归纳推理论证法：根据上述政府的定义，推出民众相对于政府的权力。

the same Object, evinces a Design to reduce them under absolute Despotism, it is their Right, it is their Duty, to throw off such Government, and to provide new Guards for their future Security.

列举特征式论证法：自该段以下至倒数第二段，主要运用列举特征的论证方式论证：英帝国在北美十三州的所作所为完全符合上述演绎推理。北美十三州的民众有权力废除同英帝国的关系而宣布独立。

Such has been the patient Sufferance of these Colonies; and such is now the Necessity which constrains them to alter their former Systems of Government. The History of the present King of Great Britain is a History of repeated Injuries and Usurpations, all having in direct Object the

Establishment of an absolute Tyranny over these States. To prove this, let Facts be submitted to a candid World.

HE has refused his Assent to Laws, the most wholesome and necessary for the public Good.

HE has forbidden his Governors to pass Laws of immediate and pressing Importance, unless suspended in their Operation till his Assent should be obtained; and when so suspended, he has utterly neglected to attend to them.

HE has refused to pass other Laws for the Accommodation of large Districts of People, unless those People would relinquish the Right of Representation in the Legislature, a Right inestimable to them, and formidable to Tyrants only.

HE has called together Legislative Bodies at Places unusual, uncomfortable, and distant from the Depository of their public Records, for the sole Purpose of fatiguing them into Compliance with his Measures.

HE has dissolved Representative Houses repeatedly, for opposing with manly Firmness his Invasions on the Rights of the People.

HE has refused for a long Time, after such Dissolutions, to cause others to be elected; whereby the Legislative Powers, incapable of the Annihilation, have returned to the People at large for their exercise; the State remaining in the mean time exposed to all the Dangers of Invasion from without, and the Convulsions within.

HE has endeavored to prevent the Population of these States; for that Purpose obstructing the Laws for Naturalization of Foreigners; refusing to pass others to encourage their Migrations hither, and raising the Conditions of new Appropriations of Lands.

HE has obstructed the Administration of Justice, by refusing his Assent to Laws for establishing Judiciary Powers.

HE has made Judges dependent on his Will alone, for the Tenure of their Offices, and the Amount and Payment of their Salaries.

HE has erected a Multitude of new Offices, and sent hither Swarms of Officers to harass our People, and eat out their Substance.

HE has kept among us, in Times of Peace, Standing Armies, without the consent of our Legislatures.

HE has affected to render the Military independent of and superior to the Civil Power.

HE has combined with others to subject us to a Jurisdiction foreign to our Constitution, and unacknowledged by our Laws; giving his Assent to their Acts of pretended Legislation:

FOR quartering large Bodies of Armed Troops among us:

FOR protecting them, by a mock Trial, from Punishment for any Murders which they should commit on the Inhabitants of these States:

FOR cutting off our Trade with all Parts of the World:

FOR imposing Taxes on us without our Consent:

FOR depriving us, in many Cases, of the Benefits of Trial by Jury:

FOR transporting us beyond Seas to be tried for pretended Offences:

FOR abolishing the free System of English Laws in a neighboring Province, establishing therein an arbitrary Government, and enlarging its Boundaries, so as to render it at once an Example and fit Instrument for introducing the same absolute Rules into these Colonies:

FOR taking away our Charters, abolishing our most valuable Laws, and altering fundamentally the Forms of our Governments:

FOR suspending our own Legislatures, and declaring themselves invested with Power to legislate for us in all Cases whatsoever.

HE has abdicated Government here, by declaring us out of his Protection and waging War against us.

HE has plundered our Seas, ravaged our Coasts, burnt our Towns, and destroyed the Lives of our People.

HE is, at this Time, transporting large Armies of foreign Mercenaries to complete the Works of Death, Desolation, and Tyranny, already begun with circumstances of Cruelty and Perfidy, scarcely paralleled in the most barbarous Ages, and totally unworthy the Head of a civilized Nation.

HE has constrained our fellow Citizens taken Captive on the high Seas to bear Arms against their Country, to become the Executioners of their Friends and Brethren, or to fall themselves by their Hands.

HE has excited domestic Insurrections amongst us, and has endeavored to bring on the Inhabitants of our Frontiers, the merciless Indian Savages, whose known Rule of Warfare, is an undistinguished Destruction, of all Ages, Sexes and Conditions.

IN every stage of these Oppressions we have Petitioned for Redress in the most humble Terms: Our repeated Petitions have been answered only by repeated Injury. A Prince, whose Character is thus marked by every act which may define a Tyrant, is unfit to be the Ruler of a free People.

NOR have we been wanting in Attentions to our British Brethren. We have warned them from Time to Time of Attempts by their Legislature to extend an unwarrantable Jurisdiction over us. We have reminded them of the Circumstances of our Emigration and Settlement here. We have appealed to their native Justice and Magnanimity, and we have conjured them by the Ties of our common Kindred to disavow these Usurpations, which would inevitably interrupt our Connections and Correspondence. They too have been deaf to the Voice of Justice and of Consanguinity. We must, therefore, acquiesce in the Necessity, which denounces our Separation, and hold them, as we hold the rest of Mankind, Enemies in War, in Peace, Friends.

WE, therefore, the Representatives of the UNITED STATES OF AMERICA, in GENERAL CONGRESS, Assembled, appealing to the Supreme Judge of the World for the Rectitude of our Intentions, do, in the Name, and by Authority of the good People of these Colonies, solemnly Publish and Declare, That these United Colonies are, and of Right ought to be, FREE AND INDEPENDENT STATES; that they are absolved from all Allegiance to the British Crown, and that all political Connection between them and the State of Great Britain, is and ought to be totally dissolved; and that as FREE AND INDEPENDENT STATES, they have full Power to levy War, conclude Peace, contract Alliances, establish Commerce, and to do all other Acts and Things which INDEPENDENT STATES may of right do. And for the support of this Declaration, with a firm Reliance on the Protection of divine Providence, we mutually pledge to each other our Lives, our Fortunes, and our sacred Honor.

Passage Ⅲ

1. 文章的第二至第三自然段运用了什么样的论证方法?

   (答) 请参阅下面文章中的标注与说明。

2. 文章的第四至第八自然段运用了什么样的论证方法?

   (答) 在第四自然段提出一系列问题之后,作者在第五至第八自然段主要运用了因果关系论证法。具体请参阅下面文章中的标注与说明。

Skeptical View of Russia's Economy

By Mark Medish

It was John Maynard Keynes who observed that Russia's economy provided ample evidence to support con-tradictory theories. In this respect, things in Russia today are not much different from the 1920s.

Recent business headlines from Russia point to a flourishing scene, with galloping bond issuances, surging equities and big oil mergers. Macroeconomic performance is also strong. The federal budget is in surplus; inflation is in single digits; the current account is surging; and central bank reserves exceed $ 60 billion. Real annual gross domestic product growth is about 4 percent. Gone are the days of Russia's International Monetary Fund tutelage. The 1998 financial collapse is a distant memory.

> 列举特征式论证法:本段采用了列举特征论证。
>
> 统计数据论证法:本段还引用数据进行论证。

Yet President Vladimir Putin's recent address to parliament on the state of the country was downbeat. He told his countrymen that Russia's "economic foundation, although it has become considerably sounder, is nevertheless unreliable and very weak." Mr. Putin's strength is his candour.

> 引用权威论证法和诉诸常识法:作者引用俄罗斯前总统普京对该国经济形势的评价。这是引用权威论证。同时,作者认为普京的评价是可信的,因为普京诚实。这是在利用常识进行论证。

What does he know that investors do not? Could Russia be heading towards another crash or a serious slowdown, as some analysts are now suggesting?

A possible answer is that Mr. Putin and his advisers are convinced that real trouble appreciation, caused by capital inflows fuelled mostly by the oil and gas sector, is a potential risk. Left unchecked, it would undermine the economy's new-found dynamism and competitiveness. Over-reliance on oil revenues will also damp the reformist zeal that is the key to long-run growth.

> 普京低调评价俄罗斯经济的原因之一。

The deeper reason for his gloominess may be that Mr. Putin distinguishes between headline news and what

> 普京低调评价俄罗斯经济的原因之二。

is happening below the surface. Perhaps the impending parliamentary elections in December and the presidential ballot next March have sharpened his sensitivity to the realities facing the vast majority of Russia's people.

As Mr. Putin noted in his speech, a quarter of Russians survive on incomes below subsistence, as officially defined. Clearly, abundant natural resource wealth is not a sufficient condition for durable, equitable national prosperity. Without a strategic approach to reform, Russia's growth spurt will

原因之二的原因。

dissipate and windfall profits will once more retreat offshore.

普京低调评价俄罗斯经济的原因之三。

Opinion polls favour Mr. Putin for a second term. But whether he will be able to refocus his economic program is an open question. Several crucial tests will determine whether Mr. Putin's legacy is that of a moderniser.

The first test is diversification. Russia must master its hydrocarbons, or they will master Russia. It needs to upgrade, diversify and privatise its pipelines to boost export capacity. The emerging government strategy to develop new exit routes to the Barents Sea and the Far East bodes well.

At the same time Russia must diversify its productive base away from energy and defence towards higher value-added civilian manufacturing, services and the "new economy." Another test, therefore, is whether the authorities find the wisdom to promote small and medium-sized enterprises. Some gains have been made in tax reform, but generally the state is overbearing through its regulation.

The third test is banking reform. Here the shadow of 1998 is long. Will Mr. Putin be able to break the liquidity bottleneck by nurturing a network of financial institutions that actually mediate credit to the real economy? Without this, domestic investment in Russia will remain the domain of industrial heavyweights and oligarchs.

Fourth, Russia needs better infrastructure. The new Russian economy is being hampered by the crumbling Soviet legacy. Again, banks and capital markets should be the conduit for investment.

Finally, a second Putin term will be judged by what it does for social services, including education, pensions, and health. Mr. Putin made clear that Russia is undergoing unprecedented demographic woes in terms of morbidity and life expectancy. An economy can only be as strong as its people.

The international community could do much to help, by ensuring speedier accession to the World Trade Organization, predicated on deeper liberalization and market-oriented structural reforms. But ultimately meeting the challenge will require powerful leadership from Mr. Putin-provided the beleaguered Russian population gives him the opportunity in the forthcoming ballot cycle.

www.cnn.com

附录5：
文章修改注意事项

以下是大家在修改自己的文章或给别人改文章的过程中，应密切关注的要点：

◆ 文章的第一个意群段（往往是文章前一两个自然段）是否给出了一个反映文章中心思想的主题句？如果没有，读者在读完文章后，是否能很容易地总结出文章的中心思想？文章的正文部分是否充分展开或论证了文章的中心思想？文章的部分段落是否谈了一些与文章中心思想无关的内容，因而需要删去或改写？

◆ 你的文章思路是否很清晰？读者在看完文章后，是否能很轻松地总结出你的文章要点？

◆ 你的文章中是否有部分要点让人理解起来有困难？你文章里的各要点之间有没有自相矛盾的地方？

◆ 文章各意群段之间、各自然段之间、各要点之间是否联系紧凑、过渡自然？

◆ 文章的开头是否有趣、短、能提领全文？文章的结尾是否有趣、短、耐人寻味？

◆ 文章的遣词造句是否让人感觉不正式？语言是否过于夸张、空洞？观点是否过于绝对、偏激？

◆ 语法的问题更多是个习惯和态度的问题，而不是知识性的问题。所以，文章要经常改，以纠正其中的语法错误。出现频率较高的语法错误包括：句子不完整——缺少主、谓、宾等句子成分；分号、逗号和单/双引号的用法不正确；句子中出现人称和数量不一致；冠词（a，an，the）用法不当；当然，还有拼写错误。对于这些地方，请给予高度关注。

附录6:
新版ISSUE题库的压缩

根据ISSUE题目的特点,将新版ISSUE题库的149道题中的128道题进行了分组。共计33组。需注意的是,个别题目被分到多个组里。因为这些题目涉及的内容具有广泛的相关性,同多方面的内容有联系。

每道题目前面的数字是该题在本书上篇第五章中的编号。

第1组:

① As people rely more and more on technology to solve problems, the ability of humans to think for themselves will surely deteriorate.

㉖ The luxuries and conveniences of contemporary life prevent people from developing into truly strong and independent individuals.

㉞ The human mind will always be superior to machines because machines are only tools of human minds.

第2组:

② To understand the most important characteristics of a society, one must study its major cities.

⑤ **Claim:** Governments must ensure that their major cities receive the financial support they need in order to thrive.

Reason: It is primarily in cities that a nation's cultural traditions are preserved and generated.

⑰ It is primarily in cities that a nation's cultural traditions are generated and preserved.

第3组:

③ Educational institutions have a responsibility to dissuade students from pursuing fields of study in which they are unlikely to succeed.

⑬ Universities should require every student to take a variety of courses outside the student's field of study.

⑮ Educational institutions should actively encourage their students to choose fields of study that will prepare them for lucrative careers.

⑳ Some people believe that college students should consider only their own talents and interests when choosing a field of study. Others believe that college students should base their choice of a field of study on the availability of jobs in that field.

㉜ College students should base their choice of a field of study on the availability of jobs in that field.

㉟ Educational institutions should dissuade students from pursuing fields of study in which they are unlikely to succeed.

㊴ College students should be encouraged to pursue subjects that interest them rather than the courses that seem most likely to lead to jobs.

46 Universities should require every student to take a variety of courses outside the student's field of study.

98 Educational institutions should actively encourage their students to choose fields of study in which jobs are plentiful.

129 College students should base their choice of a field of study on the availability of jobs in that field.

135 Educational institutions should actively encourage their students to choose fields of study that will prepare them for lucrative careers.

136 Educational institutions should actively encourage their students to choose fields of study in which jobs are plentiful.

137 Educational institutions have a responsibility to dissuade students from pursuing fields of study in which they are unlikely to succeed.

140 Some people believe that universities should require every student to take a variety of courses outside the student's field of study. Others believe that universities should not force students to take any courses other than those that will help prepare them for jobs in their chosen fields.

第4组:

6 A nation should require all of its students to study the same national curriculum until they enter college.

14 A nation should require all of its students to study the same national curriculum until they enter college.

96 A nation should require all of its students to study the same national curriculum until they enter college.

116 A nation should require all of its students to study the same national curriculum until they enter college.

第5组:

7 Some people believe that government funding of the arts is necessary to ensure that the arts can flourish and be available to all people. Others believe that government funding of the arts threatens the integrity of the arts.

80 Nations should suspend government funding for the arts when significant numbers of their citizens are hungry or unemployed.

88 **Claim:** Nations should suspend government funding for the arts when significant numbers of their citizens are hungry or unemployed.
Reason: It is inappropriate—and, perhaps, even cruel—to use public resources to fund the arts when people's basic needs are not being met.

第6组:

8 **Claim**: In any field—business, politics, education, government—those in power should step down

after five years.

Reason: The surest path to success for any enterprise is revitalization through new leadership.

⑪ In any profession—business, politics, education, government—those in power should step down after five years.

⑭⑨ In any field—business, politics, education, government—those in power should be required to step down after five years.

第7组:

⑧ **Claim:** In any field—business, politics, education, government—those in power should step down after five years.

Reason: The surest path to success for any enterprise is revitalization through new leadership.

⑯ Some people believe that in order to be effective, political leaders must yield to public opinion and abandon principle for the sake of compromise. Others believe that the most essential quality of an effective leader is the ability to remain consistently committed to particular principles and objectives.

⑥② Leaders are created by the demands that are placed on them.

⑥⑨ Some people believe it is often necessary, even desirable, for political leaders to withhold information from the public. Others believe that the public has a right to be fully informed.

⑨④ The effectiveness of a country's leaders is best measured by examining the well-being of that country's citizens.

⑫③ The best way for a society to prepare its young people for leadership in government, industry, or other fields is by instilling in them a sense of cooperation, not competition.

⑫⑧ Some people argue that successful leaders in government, industry, or other fields must be highly competitive. Other people claim that in order to be successful, a leader must be willing and able to cooperate with others.

⑭⑦ The effectiveness of a country's leaders is best measured by examining the well-being of that country's citizens.

第8组:

⑩ Nations should pass laws to preserve any remaining wilderness areas in their natural state, even if these areas could be developed for economic gain.

③① Society should make efforts to save endangered species only if the potential extinction of those species is the result of human activities.

⑥③ There is little justification for society to make extraordinary efforts—especially at a great cost in money and jobs—to save endangered animal or plant species.

⑥⑦ Some people believe that society should try to save every plant and animal species, despite the expense to humans in effort, time, and financial well-being. Others believe that society need not make extraordinary efforts, especially at a great cost in money and jobs, to save endangered species.

⑲ When old buildings stand on ground that modern planners feel could be better used for modern purposes, modern development should be given precedence over the preservation of historic buildings.

㉕ Some people claim that a nation's government should preserve its wilderness areas in their natural state. Others argue that these areas should be developed for potential economic gain.

⑭ Nations should pass laws to preserve any remaining wilderness areas in their natural state.

第9组：

⑪ People's behavior is largely determined by forces not of their own making.

⑨ People's behavior is largely determined by forces not of their own making.

第10组：

⑫ Governments should offer a free university education to any student who has been admitted to a university but who cannot afford the tuition.

㉕ Governments should offer college and university education free of charge to all students.

第11组：

⑬ Universities should require every student to take a variety of courses outside the student's field of study.

㊻ Universities should require every student to take a variety of courses outside the student's field of study.

⑦⓪ **Claim:** Universities should require every student to take a variety of courses outside the student's major field of study.

Reason: Acquiring knowledge of various academic disciplines is the best way to become truly educated.

⑩② Universities should require every student to take a variety of courses outside the student's field of study.

⑪② Requiring university students to take a variety of courses outside their major fields of study is the best way to ensure that students become truly educated.

第12组：

⑰ Formal education tends to restrain our minds and spirits rather than set them free.

㊷ Students should always question what they are taught instead of accepting it passively.

㊽ Educators should teach facts only after their students have studied the ideas, trends, and concepts that help explain those facts.

⑥⑧ Some people believe that the purpose of education is to free the mind and the spirit. Others believe that formal education tends to restrain our minds and spirits rather than set them free.

⑧⑦ **Claim**: Any piece of information referred to as a fact should be mistrusted, since it may well be proven false in the future.

Reason: Much of the information that people assume is factual actually turns out to be inaccurate.

92 Educators should base their assessment of students' learning not on students' grasp of facts but on the ability to explain the ideas, trends, and concepts that those facts illustrate.

第13组：

18 The well-being of a society is enhanced when many of its people question authority.

50 Government officials should rely on their own judgment rather than unquestioningly carry out the will of the people they serve.

86 Some people believe that government officials must carry out the will of the people they serve. Others believe that officials should base their decisions on their own judgment.

115 Government officials should rely on their own judgment rather than unquestioningly carry out the will of the people whom they serve.

第14组：

22 **Claim**: The best way to understand the character of a society is to examine the character of the men and women that the society chooses as its heroes or its role models.

Reason: Heroes and role models reveal a society's highest ideals.

24 The best way to teach is to praise positive actions and ignore negative ones.

29 The best way to teach—whether as an educator, employer, or parent—is to praise positive actions and ignore negative ones.

52 The best way to teach is to praise positive actions and ignore negative ones.

70 **Claim**: Universities should require every student to take a variety of courses outside the student's major field of study.

Reason: Acquiring knowledge of various academic disciplines is the best way to become truly educated.

77 The most effective way to understand contemporary culture is to analyze the trends of its youth.

112 Requiring university students to take a variety of courses outside their major fields of study is the best way to ensure that students become truly educated.

122 The best way to understand the character of a society is to examine the character of the men and women that the society chooses as its heroes or its role models.

123 The best way for a society to prepare its young people for leadership in government, industry, or other fields is by instilling in them a sense of cooperation, not competition.

第15组：

22 **Claim**: The best way to understand the character of a society is to examine the character of the men and women that the society chooses as its heroes or its role models.

Reason: Heroes and role models reveal a society's highest ideals.

44 **Claim**: It is no longer possible for a society to regard any living man or woman as a hero.

Reason: The reputation of anyone who is subjected to media scrutiny will eventually be diminished.

75 In this age of intensive media coverage, it is no longer possible for a society to regard any living man or woman as a hero.

84 It is no longer possible for a society to regard any living man or woman as a hero.

122 The best way to understand the character of a society is to examine the character of the men and women that the society chooses as its heroes or its role models.

第16组：

23 Governments should place few, if any, restrictions on scientific research and development.

36 Governments should not fund any scientific research whose consequences are unclear.

72 Governments should not fund any scientific research whose consequences are unclear.

第17组：

27 In any field of inquiry, the beginner is more likely than the expert to make important contributions.

108 Critical judgment of work in any given field has little value unless it comes from someone who is an expert in that field.

110 Critical judgment of work in any given field has little value unless it comes from someone who is an expert in that field.

139 **Claim:** Major policy decisions should always be left to politicians and other government experts.

Reason: Politicians and other government experts are more informed and thus have better judgment and perspective than do members of the general public.

第18组：

28 The surest indicator of a great nation is represented not by the achievements of its rulers, artists, or scientists, but by the general welfare of its people.

85 Some people believe that in order to thrive, a society must put its own overall success before the well-being of its individual citizens. Others believe that the well-being of a society can only be measured by the general welfare of all its people.

113 **Claim**: The surest indicator of a great nation is not the achievements of its rulers, artists, or scientists.

Reason: The surest indicator of a great nation is actually the welfare of all its people.

120 **Claim**: The surest indicator of a great nation must be the achievements of its rulers, artists, or scientists.

Reason: Great achievements by a nation's rulers, artists, or scientists will ensure a good life for the majority of that nation's people.

121 Some people claim that you can tell whether a nation is great by looking at the achievements of its rulers, artists, or scientists. Others argue that the surest indicator of a great nation is, in fact, the general welfare of all its people.

127 The surest indicator of a great nation is not the achievements of its rulers, artists, or scientists, but

the general well-being of all its people.

(145) The general welfare of a nation's people is a better indication of that nation's greatness than are the achievements of its rulers, artists, or scientists.

第19组：

(30) Teachers' salaries should be based on their students' academic performance.

(83) Teachers' salaries should be based on the academic performance of their students.

第20组：

(33) As we acquire more knowledge, things do not become more comprehensible, but more complex and mysterious.

(57) The main benefit of the study of history is to dispel the illusion that people living now are significantly different from people who lived in earlier times.

(74) Knowing about the past cannot help people to make important decisions today.

(109) Some people believe that scientific discoveries have given us a much better understanding of the world around us. Others believe that science has revealed to us that the world is infinitely more complex than we ever realized.

(133) **Claim**: Knowing about the past cannot help people to make important decisions today.

Reason: The world today is significantly more complex than it was even in the relatively recent past.

(134) **Claim**: Knowing about the past cannot help people to make important decisions today.

Reason: We are not able to make connections between current events and past events until we have some distance from both.

第21组：

(34) In any situation, progress requires discussion among people who have contrasting points of view.

(49) **Claim**: We can usually learn much more from people whose views we share than from those whose views contradict our own.

Reason: Disagreement can cause stress and inhibit learning.

(76) We can usually learn much more from people whose views we share than from people whose views contradict our own.

(118) We can learn much more from people whose views we share than from people whose views contradict our own.

第22组：

(37) Society should identify those children who have special talents and provide training for them at an early age to develop their talents.

(40) **Claim**: When planning courses, educators should take into account the interests and suggestions of their students.

Reason: Students are more motivated to learn when they are interested in what they are studying.

47 Educators should find out what students want included in the curriculum and then offer it to them.

58 Learning is primarily a matter of personal discipline; students cannot be motivated by school or college alone.

90 Educators should take students' interests into account when planning the content of the courses they teach.

142 **Claim**: Colleges and universities should specify all required courses and eliminate elective courses in order to provide clear guidance for students.

Reason: College students—like people in general—prefer to follow directions rather than make their own decisions.

第23组:

38 It is primarily through our identification with social groups that we define ourselves.

78 People's attitudes are determined more by their immediate situation or surroundings than by society as a whole.

第24组:

43 The increasingly rapid of life today causes more problems than it solves.

91 The primary goal of technological advancement should be to increase people's efficiency so that they have more leisure time.

第25组:

45 Competition for high grades seriously limits the quality of learning at all levels of education.

138 Some people believe that competition for high grades motivates students to excel in the classroom. Others believe that such competition seriously limits the quality of real learning.

第26组:

51 Young people should be encouraged to pursue long-term, realistic goals rather than seek immediate fame and recognition.

71 Young people should be encouraged to pursue long-term, realistic goals rather than seek immediate fame and recognition.

第27组:

53 If a goal is worthy, then any means taken to attain it are justifiable.

144 True success can be measured primarily in terms of the goals one sets for oneself.

第28组:

56 Many important discoveries or creations are accidental: it is usually while seeking the answer to one question that we come across the answer to another.

59 Scientists and other researchers should focus their research on areas that are likely to benefit the

greatest number of people.

131 **Claim**: Researchers should not limit their investigations to only those areas in which they expect to discover something that has an immediate, practical application.

Reason: It is impossible to predict the outcome of a line of research with any certainty.

第29组：

79 **Claim**: The best test of an argument is its ability to convince someone with an opposing viewpoint.

Reason: Only by being forced to defend an idea against the doubts and contrasting views of others does one really discover the value of that idea.

146 The best test of an argument is the argument's ability to convince someone with an opposing viewpoint.

第30组：

81 All parents should be required to volunteer time to their children's schools.

95 All parents should be required to volunteer time to their children's schools.

第31组：

82 Colleges and universities should require their students to spend at least one semester studying in a foreign country.

97 Colleges and universities should require their students to spend at least one semester studying in a foreign country.

100 Colleges and universities should require their students to spend at least one semester studying in a foreign country.

124 All college and university students would benefit from spending at least one semester studying in a foreign country.

第32组：

104 To be an effective leader, a public official must maintain the highest ethical and moral standards.

107 To be an effective leader, a public official must maintain the highest ethical and moral standards.

第33组：

105 **Claim**: Imagination is a more valuable asset than experience.

Reason: People who lack experience are free to imagine what is possible without the constraints of established habits and attitudes.

106 In most professions and academic fields, imagination is more important than knowledge.

126 In most professions and academic fields, imagination is more important than knowledge.

下面是余下的20道没有编成组的题目。为方便大家随时整理这些题目，也将它们一并附在这里。

4 Scandals are useful because they focus our attention on problems in ways that no speaker or reformer ever could.

9 In any field of endeavor, it is impossible to make a significant contribution without first being strongly influenced by past achievements within that field.

19 Governments should focus on solving the immediate problems of today rather than on trying to solve the anticipated problems of the future.

21 Laws should be flexible enough to take account of various circumstances, times, and places.

41 The greatness of individuals can be decided only by those who live after them, not by their contemporaries.

54 In order to become well-rounded individuals, all college students should be required to take courses in which they read poetry, novels, mythology, and other types of imaginative literature.

55 In order for any work of art—for example, a film, a novel, a poem, or a song—to have merit, it must be understandable to most people.

60 Politicians should pursue common ground and reasonable consensus rather than elusive ideals.

61 People should undertake risky action only after they have carefully considered its consequences.

65 Every individual in a society has a responsibility to obey just laws and to disobey and resist unjust laws.

66 People who are the most deeply committed to an idea or policy are also the most critical of it.

73 Colleges and universities should require all faculty to spend time working outside the academic world in professions relevant to the courses they teach.

89 Claim: Many problems of modern society cannot be solved by laws and the legal system.
Reason: Laws cannot change what is in people's hearts or minds.

93 Unfortunately, in contemporary society, creating an appealing image has become more important than the reality or truth behind that image.

101 Although innovations such as video, computers, and the Internet seem to offer schools improved methods for instructing students, these technologies all too often distract from real learning.

103 The best ideas arise from a passionate interest in commonplace things.

130 Some people believe that corporations have a responsibility to promote the well-being of the societies and environments in which they operate. Others believe that the only responsibility of corporations, provided they operate within the law, is to make as much money as possible.

132 Some people believe that our ever-increasing use of technology significantly reduces our opportunities for human interaction. Other people believe that technology provides us with new and better ways to communicate and connect with one another.

141 It is more harmful to compromise one's own beliefs than to adhere to them.

143 No field of study can advance significantly unless it incorporates knowledge and experience from outside that field.

附录7:

新GRE作文评分标准及ETS提供的 ISSUE和ARGUMENT范文

注 ① 本附录所有内容除必要的编辑变动外,均来自美国ETS官方网站(网址: http://www.ets.org/gre)

② 除Issue范文的Sample IV和Argument范文的Sample IV外,其余的范文都是旧版GRE写作的范文,因而都没有写作指引(Instructions)。

Scoring Guide and Samples of GRE Issue Writing

1. Scoring Guide of GRE Issue Writing

Score 6

In addressing the specific task directions, a 6 response presents a cogent, well-articulated analysis of the issue and conveys meaning skillfully.

A typical response in this category:

- articulates a clear and insightful position on the issue in accordance with the assigned task;
- develops the position fully with compelling reasons and/or persuasive examples;
- sustains a well-focused, well-organized analysis, connecting ideas logically;
- conveys ideas fluently and precisely, using effective vocabulary and sentence variety;
- demonstrates facility with the conventions of standard written English (i.e., grammar, usage and mechanics), but may have minor errors.

Score 5

In addressing the specific task directions, a 5 response presents a generally thoughtful, well-developed analysis of the issue and conveys meaning clearly.

A typical response in this category:

- presents a clear and well-considered position on the issue in accordance with the assigned task;
- develops the position with logically sound reasons and/or well-chosen examples;
- is focused and generally well organized, connecting ideas appropriately;
- conveys ideas clearly and well, using appropriate vocabulary and sentence variety;
- demonstrates facility with the conventions of standard written English, but may have minor errors.

Score 4

In addressing the specific task directions, a 4 response presents a competent analysis of the issue and conveys meaning with acceptable clarity.

A typical response in this category:

- presents a clear position on the issue in accordance with the assigned task;
- develops the position with relevant reasons and/or examples;
- is adequately focused and organized;
- demonstrates sufficient control of language to express ideas with reasonable clarity;
- generally demonstrates control of the conventions of standard written English, but may have some errors.

Score 3

A 3 response demonstrates some competence in addressing the specific task directions, in analyzing the issue and in conveying meaning, but is obviously flawed.

A typical response in this category exhibits ONE OR MORE of the following characteristics:

- is vague or limited in addressing the specific task directions and in presenting or developing a position on the issue;
- is weak in the use of relevant reasons or examples or relies largely on unsupported claims;
- is poorly focused and/or poorly organized;
- has problems in language and sentence structure that result in a lack of clarity;
- contains occasional major errors or frequent minor errors in grammar, usage or mechanics that can interfere with meaning.

Score 2

A 2 response largely disregards the specific task directions and/or demonstrates serious weaknesses in analytical writing.

A typical response in this category exhibits ONE OR MORE of the following characteristics:

- is unclear or seriously limited in addressing the specific task directions and in presenting or developing a position on the issue;
- provides few, if any, relevant reasons or examples in support of its claims;
- is unfocused and/or disorganized;
- has serious problems in language and sentence structure that frequently interfere with meaning;
- contains serious errors in grammar, usage or mechanics that frequently obscure meaning.

Score 1

A 1 response demonstrates fundamental deficiencies in analytical writing.

A typical response in this category exhibits ONE OR MORE of the following characteristics:

- provides little or no evidence of understanding the issue;

- provides little or no evidence of the ability to develop an organized response;
- has severe problems in language and sentence structure that persistently interfere with meaning;
- contains pervasive errors in grammar, usage or mechanics that result in incoherence.

• •

Score 0

A typical response in this category is off topic (i.e., provides no evidence of an attempt to address the assigned topic), is in a foreign language, merely copies the topic, consists of only keystroke characters or is illegible or nonverbal.

• •

总结以上ISSUE作文评分标准，我们可以得出以下结论：
- 论点必须深刻、独到，并能分析ISSUE问题的复杂性；
- 论证要集中（即，不跑题）、充分、可信；
- 文章逻辑清楚、结构完整；
- 文字表达流畅、准确，遣词造句富于变化，语言规范。

下面的ETS例文，尤其是那些5分和6分作文中，大家要注意结合每篇文章后面改卷人员的评语来体会文章的要点。

注意，并非那些5分和6分作文的方方面面都值得模仿。比如，部分篇章的开头和结尾段的写作过于冗长，中间正文的结构和节奏过于呆板、沉重。这些方面，大家还是要多参考本书的要求。

另外，下面这些例文是考生写的文章，里面仍然有一些拼写、用词以及标点符号等方面的错误。但显然，只要文章的分析、论证和组织结构出色，偶尔出现这些小的错误并不妨碍作文得高分。

2. Samples of GRE Issue Writing

Sample I

In our time, specialists of all kinds are highly overrated. We need more generalists—people who can provide broad perspectives.

Score 6 Essay:

In this era of rapid social and technological change leading to increasing life complexity and psychological displacement, both positive and negative effects among persons in Western society call for a balance in which there are both specialists and generalists.

Specialists are necessary in order to allow society as a whole to properly and usefully assimilate the masses of new information and knowledge that have come out of research and have been widely disseminated through mass global media. As the head of Pharmacology at my university once said (and

I paraphrase): "I can only research what I do because there are so many who have come before me to whom I can turn for basic knowledge. It is only because of each of the narrowly focused individuals at each step that a full and true understanding of the complexities of life can be had. Each person can only hold enough knowledge to add one small rung to the ladder, but together we can climb to the moon." This illustrates the point that our societies level of knowledge and technology is at a stage in which there simply must be specialists in order for our society to take advantage of the information available to us.

Simply put, without specialists, our society would find itself bogged down in the Sargasso sea of information overload. While it was fine for early physicists to learn and understand the few laws and ideas that existed during their times, now, no one individual can possibly digest and assimilate all of the knowledge in any given area.

On the other hand, over specialization means narrow foci in which people can lose the larger picture.No one can hope to understand the human body by only inspecting one's own toe-nails. What we learn from a narrow focus may be internally logically coherent but may be irrelevant or fallacious within the framework of a broader perspective. Further, if we inspect only our toe-nails, we may conclude that the whole body is hard and white. Useful conclusions and thus perhaps useful inventions must come by sharing among specialists. Simply throwing out various discoveries means we have a pile of useless discoveries, it is only when one can make with them a mosaic that we can see that they may form a picture.

Not only may over-specialization be dangerous in terms of the truth, purity and cohesion of knowledge, but it can also serve to drown moral or universal issues. Generalists and only generalists can see a broad enough picture to realize and introduce to the world the problems of the environment. With specialization, each person focuses on their research and their goals. Thus, industrialization, expansion, and new technologies are driven ahead. Meanwhile no individual can see the wholistic view of our global existence in which true advancement may mean stifling individual specialists for the greater good of all.

Finally, over-specialization in a people's daily lives and jobs has meant personal and psychological compartmentalization. People are forced into pigeon holes early in life (at least by university) and must conciously attempt to consume external forms of stimuli and information in order not to be lost in their small and isolated universe. Not only does this make for narrowly focused and generally poorly-educated individuals, but it guarantees a sense of loss of community, often followed by a feeling of psychological displacement and personal dissatisfaction.

Without generalists, society becomes inward-looking and eventually inefficient. Without a society that recognizes the importance of broad-mindedness and fora for sharing generalities, individuals become isolated. Thus, while our form of society necessitates specialists, generalists are equally important. Specialists drive us forward in a series of thrusts while generalists make sure we are still on the jousting field and know what the stakes are.

Essay Readers' Commentary:

This is an outstanding analysis of the issue—insightful, well reasoned, and highly effective in its use of language. The introductory paragraph announces the writer's position on the issue and provides the context within which the writer will develop that position: "In this era of rapid social and technological change leading to increasing life complexity and psychological displacement..."

The argument itself has two parts. The first part presents a compelling case for specialization, primarily in the field of medicine. The second part presents an equally compelling, well-organized case against overspecialization based on three main reasons:

—logical (narrowly trained specialists often fail to understand the whole)

—moral (usually generalists understand what is needed for "the greater good")

—personal (specializing/pigeonholing too early can be psychologically damaging)

The argument's careful line of reasoning is further strengthened by the skillful use of expert testimony (quotation from a prominent medical researcher) and vivid metaphor (to inspect only one's toenails is to ignore the whole body).

It is not only the reasoning that distinguishes this response. The language is precise and often figurative ("bogged down in a Sargasso sea of information overload," "a pile of useless discoveries," and "specialists drive us forward in a series of thrusts, while generalists make sure we are still on the jousting field"). The reader is constantly guided through the argument by transitional phrases and ideas that help organize the ideas and move the argument forward. This is an exceptionally fine response to the topic.

Score 5 Essay:

Specialists are not overrated today. More generalists may be needed, but not to overshadow the specialists. Generalists can provide a great deal of information on many topics of interest with a broad range of ideas. People who look at the overall view of things can help with some of the large problems our society faces today. But specialists are necessary to gain a better understanding of more in depth methods to solve problems or fixing things.

One good example of why specialists are not overrated is in the medical field. Doctors are necessary for people to live healthy lives. When a person is sick, he may go to a general practitioner to find out the cause of his problems. Usually, this kind of "generalized" doctor can help most ailments with simple and effective treatments. Sometimes, though, a sickness may go beyond a family doctor's knowledge or the prescribed treatments don't work the way they should. When a sickness progresses or becomes diagnosed as a disease that requires more care than a family doctor can provide, he may be referred to a specialist. For instance, a person with constant breathing problems that require hospitalization may be suggested to visit an asthma specialist. Since a family doctor has a great deal of knowledge of medicine, he can decide when his methods are not effective and the patient needs to see someone who knows more about the specific problem; someone who knows how it begins, progresses, and specified treatments. This is an excellent example of how a generalied person may not be equipped enough to handle something as well as a specialized one can.

Another example of a specialist who is needed instead of a generalist involves teaching. In grammar school, children learn all the basic principles of reading, writing, and arithematic. But as children get older and progress in school, they gain a better understanding of the language and mathematical processes. As the years in school increase, they need to learn more and more specifics and details about various subjects. They start out by learning basic math concepts such as addition, subtraction, division, and multiplication. A few years later, they are ready to begin algebraic concepts, geometry, and calculus. They are also ready to learn more advanced vocabulary, the principles of how all life is composed and how it functions. One teacher or professor can not provide as much in depth discussion on all of these topics as well as one who has learned the specifics and studied mainly to know everything that is currently known about one of these subjects. Generalized teachers are required to begin molding students at a very early age so they can get ready for the future ahead of them in gaining more facts about the basic subjects and finding out new facts on the old ones.

These are only two examples of why specialists are not highly overrated and more generalists are not necessary to the point of overshadowing them. Generalists are needed to give the public a broad understanding of some things. But, specialists are important to help maintain the status, health, and safety of our society. Specialists are very necessary.

Essay Readers' Commentary:

This writer presents a well-developed analysis of the complexities of the issue by discussing the need for both the generalist and the specialist.

The argument is rooted in two extended examples, both well chosen. The first (paragraph 2) begins with a discussion of the necessity for medical generalists (the general practitioner) as well as specialists and moves into an example within the example (breathing problems and the need for an asthma specialist). This extension from the general to the specific characterizes the example in the next paragraph as well. There, the discussion centers on education from elementary to high school, from basic arithmetic to calculus.

The smooth development is aided by the use of appropriate transitions: "but," "usually," and "for instance," among others. The essay ends by revisiting the writer's thesis.

While the writer handles language and syntax well, several lapses in clarity keep this otherwise well-argued response out of the 6 category. The problems vary from the lack of a pronoun referent ("When a sickness progresses or becomes diagnosed,...he may be referred to a specialist") to an error in parallel structure ("how it begins, progresses and specified treatments"), to loose syntax and imprecise language ("Generalized teachers are required to begin molding students at a very early age so they can get ready for the future ahead of them in gaining more facts about the basic subjects.")

Score 4 Essay:

Specialists are just what their name says: people who specialize in one part of a very general scheme of things. A person can't know everything there is to know about everything. This is why specialists are helpful. You can take one general concept and divide it up three ways and have three fully developed different concepts instead of one general concept that no one really knows about. Isn't it better to really know something well, than to know everything half-way.

Take a special ed teacher compared to a general ed teacher. The general ed teacher knows how to deal with most students. She knows how to teach a subject to a student that is on a normal level. But what would happen to the child in the back of the room with dyslexia? She would be so lost in that general ed classroom that she would not only not learn, but be frustrated and quite possibly, have low self-esteem and hate school. If there is a special ed teacher there who specializes in children with learning disabilities, she can teach the general ed teacher how to cope with this student as well as modify the curriculum so that the student can learn along with the others. The special ed teacher can also take that child for a few hours each day and work with her on her reading difficulty one-on-one, which a general ed teacher never would have time to do.

A general ed teacher can't know what a special ed teacher knows and a special ed teacher can't know what a general ed teacher knows. But the two of them working together and specializing in their own things can really get a lot more accomplished. The special ed teacher is also trained to work on the child's self-esteem, which has a big part in how successful this child will be. Every child in the United States of America has the right to an equal education. How can a child with a learning disability receive the same equal education as a general ed student if there was no specialist there to help both teacher and child?

Another thing to consider is how a committee is supposed to work together. Each person has a special task to accomplish and when these people all come together, with their tasks finished, every aspect of the community's work is completely covered. Nothing is left undone. In this case there are many different specialists to meet the general goal of the committee.

When you take into account that a specialist contributes only a small part of the generalist aspect, it seems ridiculous to say that specialists are overrated. The generalists looks to the specialists any time they need help or clarification on their broad aspect. Specialists and generalists are part of the same system, so if a specialist is overrated, then so is a generalist.

Essay Readers' Commentary:

This is an adequate analysis of the issue. After a somewhat confusing attempt to define "specialists" in the introductory paragraph, the writer presents a pertinent example (the special education teacher) to illustrate the importance of specialists. The example dominates the response and contributes positively to the overall score of 4.

The second example, how a committee works, is less persuasive. However, it does seem to help clarify the writer's definition of "general" as an umbrella term meaning the total collection of what specialists know about a topic.

Although the writer's views about the relationship between "generalist" and "specialist" are unusual, they do become clear in the conclusion of the essay. Yet, these ideas are not developed in sufficient depth or with enough logical control to earn a score higher than 4.

The writing is generally error free. There are few problems in sentence structure, grammar, and usage, although the phrasing is at times imprecise and wordy. Overall, this response displays clearly adequate control of the elements of written English.

Score 3 Essay:

To quote the saying, "Jack of all trades, master of none," would be my position on the statement. I feel specialists in all areas of knowledge lead to a higher standard of living for everyone. Specializing in different areas allows us to use each others talents to the highest level and maximize potential. As an example, if a person required brain surgery, would they rather have a brain surgeon or a general practitioner doing the work? Clearly a specialist would do the better job and give the patient a chance at a better life.

A university education starts by laying the groundwork for general knowledge but then narrows down to a specific field. General knowledge and a broad prospective are important, but if there was no focus on specific areas, our overall knowledge as a population would be seriously lessened.

Another example of specialists not being overated would be international trade. Not every nation can provide for themselves. They need to get products and ideas from other parts of the world because they are better at providing them. This allows for a growing economy if two different nations can provide each other with two different products. If one country can produce oranges better than another, it should trade the oranges for the fish that it can not produce. If generalizing was the normal thing to do and both countries tried to produce all kinds of products, the countries would probably survive, but not have the standard of living they presently have.

Essay Readers' Commentary:

The writer's position is clear: specialists are important and necessary. However, the position is not adequately supported with reasons or logical examples.

Paragraph 1 presents an appropriate example of the brain surgeon versus the general practitioner. However, the example of an increasingly narrow university education in paragraph 2, contains only two sentences and is seriously undeveloped. It does little to advance the writer's position.

Paragraph 3 offers yet another example, the most developed of all. Unfortunately, this example is not clearly logical. The writer tries to argue that the "specialist" country (one that is a better producer of oranges) is superior to the "generalist" country (presumably one that produces oranges as well as other products). This generalist country, the writer tells us, would be inferior to the other. This conclusion does not emerge logically from the writer's argument, and it seems to be at odds with everyday reality.

Although language is used with some imprecision throughout the essay, the writer's meaning is not obscured. The main reasons for the score of 3 are the lack of sufficient development and inappropriate use of examples.

Score 2 Essay:

In the situation of health I feel that specialists are very important. For example if a person has heart problems, choose a heart specialist over a genral medicine Dr. However if a person is having a wide range of syptoms, perhaps choose a Dr. with a wide range of experience might be more helpful.

It also depends on the type of problem you are having. For example I would not suggest taking a troubled child to a theorpist who specializes in marriage problems. In some cases have a specialists helps to insure that you are getting the best possibly treatment. On the other hand dealing with a person who has a wide range of experience may be able to find different ways of dealing with a particular problem.

Since the quotation did not state exactly what type of specialist we are dealing with it is also hard to determine the importance of having a specialist is. For example the could be health or problems with a car, or basically anything else. I feel that this information should not have been left out. I guess the bottom line is that I feel sometimes a specialist is very important.

Essay Readers' Commentary:

This is a seriously flawed analysis of the issue. The response argues in favor of specialists, but neither the reasons nor the examples are persuasive. The example of not taking "a troubled child to see a therapist who specializes in marriage problems" is both simplistic and off the mark since it differentiates between two specialists, not between a generalist and a specialist.

The sentences are so poorly formed and phrased that the argument is at times hard to follow. Nevertheless, this is not a 1 essay: the writer presents a position on the issue, develops that position with some very weak analysis, and communicates some ideas clearly

Score 1 Essay:

I disagree with the statement about specialists, we need specialists who take individual areas and specialize. A generalists can pinpoint a problem. He or she cannot determine the magnitude of the problem. A specialist can find the root of the problem. When he or she has years working in that specific field. For example, when i got sick i went to a doctor. He did blood work, x-ray, talk to me, ect. He prescribed me a medicine. I got worst. So i decided to go another doctor. Now, i am doing great. A specialist knows the facts right away. Otherwise, it will take longer or not at all.

> **Essay Readers' Commentary:**
>
> This response presents a fundamentally deficient discussion of the issue.
>
> The first sentence states the writer's position in support of specialists, but that position is not followed by a coherent argument. Some of the ideas seem contradictory (e.g., "generalists can pinpoint a problem") and the example is confusing. If the essay explained that the first (unsuccessful) doctor was a generalist and the second (successful) doctor was a specialist, the example would be useful. However, as written, the example is unclear and even misleading. The concluding statement only adds to the confusion.
>
> Since most of the sentences are short and choppy, the ideas they try to communicate are also choppy. The writer needs to provide transitional phrases and ideas to bring logical cohesion to this response. Also, basic errors in usage and grammar are pervasive, but it is primarily the lack of a coherent argument that makes this response a 1.

Sample II

> It is unfortunate that today's educators place so much emphasis on finding out what students want to include in the curriculum and then giving it to them. It is the educators' duty to determine the curriculum and the students' duty to study what is presented to them.

Score 6 Essay:

The statement above conceals intesting connotations far above curriculum development. Issues of classroom control and development of scholarly talents arc at stake, not simply a debate over which books are acceptable or over revisionist histories.

The statement itself is a bit misleading in that in my experience, student control over curriculum hardly existed. Each year, there were certain course offerings made available, and students were to choose from those offerings, of course bearing in mind requirements for graduation set forth by the administration. On a classroom level, the immediate, initial material may have been somewhat directed by the students, but this was a part of the process allowed by the teacher/professor in order to gain the interest and attention of the students. However, too much of any one thing becomes problematic; letting students set the curriculum, as with letting students choose and design their own major in college, serves ultimately to dilute the quality of the educational experience unless a single advisor can devote significant amounts of time to the individual student. This amount of time, or even the expense to the student of this individual attention, seem to indicate that resources would be better allocated elsewhere.

Of course, any school in which the students decide "what goes" is bound to have problems controlling students. Once the educators, be they administrators or teachers, are under the control of students, even a democratic situation would be like holding royalty accountable to the mob. Presently, students hear for hours that they should not forget to use a condom in the heat of the moment, and educators think the message gets through, while half the kids can't even remember to bring a pencil to class. Students go to school not to simply learn the Pythagorean theorem, but to learn direction and receive guidance. This cannot occur when students are in charge, and standards, already hard to find in America's contemporary public schools, will become unenforceable. If students dictate and administrators do, students will never learn academic responsibility, and if they can't be held accountable for homework, what other responsibilities will they avoid when they get older?

But in another sense, teachers and students do exist in a partnership of sorts. Teachers are there to satisfy the needs of the student, and the student, while perhaps not being the most experienced/ knowledgeable person on what his/her needs actually are (versus wants), at least should be afforded some say. In addition, we must remember what the purpose of education is, and that there are different levels of education.

In high school, the focus is not so much on learning actual material. The focus is on developing study habits, and on social interaction. The best secondary schools promote an environment in which individual creativity and pacing can be developed, where students are taught to think on their own, and learn to debate and argue in a scholarly way, through writing and other formal methods of discourse. Group collaboration and interpersonal skills are developed and honed. The actual details of what is studied and tested is of less importance. Whether a student reads Maya Angelou, or Yeats, or Euripides essentially is beside the point as long as a student's mind is cultivated, not just their ability to record and recite. What is important is that secondary students develop and grow in the hands of the professionals.

The secondary educational experience is designed to prepare a student for college. It is in college where the individual learns to examine the world and how it works, and the individual's place in it.

As for duty, it is the educators' duty not simply to determine the curriculum, but to present it effectively. They cannot half-heartedly paint it on the blackboard, they must enliven it and actually teach. Hard work must be lauded, while freeloaders are punished. These are the duties of teachers, and the duty of the students is not just to learn or study, but to grow. An independent mind is what students need, and that mind has to be in a position to want and be able to question beyond the material presented, not simply to question its legitimacy. That distinction, though subtle, is the difference between letting the students follow a self-destructive course of premature self-determination on the one hand, and permitting on the other hand the fostering of great talents through a cooperative, mentoring relationship.

Essay Readers' Commentary:

This is an insightful, well-articulated discussion of curricular responsibility and the larger issue of academic responsibility. After a brief introduction examining assumptions implied by the topic, the writer skillfully develops the position that letting students dictate the curriculum could dilute the educational experience. Allowing students to determine the curriculum, the writer claims, will deny them the guidance and direction they need to learn academic responsibility.

The argument is strengthened by the discussion of how teachers and students can work in partnership to satisfy the needs of students. The argument is further advanced with concrete examples from high school courses showing how teachers provide guidance for students through group collaboration, development of interpersonal skills, and preparation for college. The examples are varied (from condom use to reading Angelou, Yeats, or Euripedes) and used effectively to further support the writer's position.

In the conclusion, the writer thoughtfully discusses how educators should not only determine the curriculum but present it in an enlivened and appropriate manner. The final sentence, contrasting a "self-destructive course of premature self-determination" and "a cooperative, mentoring relationship," ties the ideas together.

The response is clearly organized, although the writer does not rely on conventional phrases (such as "first," "second," etc.) to signal the organizational structure. Instead, the organization and focus progress through the line of reasoning that moves fluently and coherently from one paragraph to the next.

Language use is generally precise and effective (e.g., "holding royalty accountable to the mob"), and sentence structure is well controlled (e.g., "hard work must be lauded, while freeloaders are punished"). The few errors are minor, the kind that can easily be made—and forgiven—under testing conditions.

This outstanding response received a score of 6.

Score 5 Essay:

As an elementary educator, I believe this stance is extremist. Educators and the public must come to a middle road. The high road and the low road are intimated in this statement. I believe the high road on this topic (from whence should curriculum come) represents a nouveau approach. Ask the students what they want to learn and study for the year; then meander, research and branch off of their interests. The low road on this topic (directly endorsed by this statement) is old fashioned and outdated. The assumptions behind this view include a magical ability by teachers to infuse reams of information, data and knowledge into students' brains that then become internalized and applied by the students.

In a complex and frightening society, we must look to the middle road. We must infuse the best of the high and the low roads. Current research has had a lot to say on curriculum development. Overreaching arguments defend the quality of students' self-directed learning. However, in order to prepare our students for this society, we must have developed the backbone and anchor for curriculum. Content and performance standards (i.e. curricula) need to be developed by the district's educators as a map for teachers. When educators provide students with choices WITHIN the map of curriculum, students relish in the freedom and take ownership for their learning.

Were we to provide students the ultimate authority in curriculum development, we would be doing an injustice not only to our students but to society as a whole. There are specific skills and abilities that need to be developed and taught—regardless of students' (or for that matter, teachers') interest. In my profession as an elementary educator and as a parent, I value the abilities to read, write and be mathematically proficient. Those students not mastering those critical skills are at a disadvantage. We see those students become destructive or depressed. I have observed students struggling with the basics become outcasts in their own little worlds. Very young outcasts grow into adult outcasts.

I do NOT think it is unfortunate that today's educators emphasize students' interests. It IS our duty, however, to provide the parameters for their education. We can not simply state that educators determine curriculum and students follow. This is just not reality in the classrooms. When standards and curricular maps have been developed, teachers of today's children have the responsibility (yes, the duty!) to bring life to those maps. One crucial and successful way, is to provide students variety and choices within the context of "what needs to be covered." The educator who brings curricula to life for her students and gives her students the responsibility to make choices helps to prepare our children for thriving—not just surviving.

Essay Readers' Commentary:

This response presents a well-developed analysis of the issue and displays strong control of the elements of writing. The writer argues in favor of a "middle road" position on the issue by analyzing the pros and cons of both teacher-determined and student-driven curricula. The argument is clear and well focused, supported with first-hand experience and the results of educational research.

The writer endorses a curriculum that emphasizes strong basic skills (reading, writing, and math) and reminds the reader that the teachers' ultimate responsibility should be to bring curricula to life in order to "prepare our children for thriving—not just surviving."

The careful choice of words and carefully structured paragraphs help unify the structure of the argument. Overall, this response displays a strong command of analytical writing skills and thus received a score of 5.

Score 4 Essay:

The above quotation a concrete example of a major problem in our society today. While probably stated with good intentions, the quotation misses the mark on the path education needs to follow. As our society changes, so do our educational needs, and thus our educational curriculum needs to change also.

I find fault with the quotation on two fronts. First, the quotation does not acknowledge that curriculum must change. It seems to say the educator should decide when to change the curriculum. This does not lead to optimal learning conditions, ask anyone who studied high school history out of outdated textbooks. One can also infer some students won't be taught up-to-date information in a wide variety of areas. This can become ideologically dangerous. What happens when students are not given full teachings of such vital movements as the Equal Rights Amendment or the Constitution of their country? An unenlightened society is a grave society with little hope. Curriculum must change, and should not be left to input from a single voice.

The second argument answers who should make curriculum adjustments. Obviously the educator still plays a large role in this matter. The students also need to be part of the decision process. The two groups need a give and take relationship when deciding topics for the classroom. If the students could benefit from learning material that is presently not taught in the classroom, it should be entered. Sex education and AIDS education classes needed to be part of the curriculum to inform young people. Those classes were added and have worked well.

A third party that has a role in curriculum development is private business, including research labs, goods and service providers, and financial businesses. By hiring employees with certain capabilities they have indirectly influenced curriculum for years. As time passes they will have more input by demanding subpar schools raise the level of student test scores in certain areas, either by stating so or by not hiring unqualified students.

The quotation echoes of a time when school learning consisted of the three "R" s and little else. For better or worse our society is much more complex now than then. For our schools to keep pace with our society we need to adjust our curriclum to what it should be, what we want it to be, and what it needs to be.

Essay Readers' Commentary:

This writer presents a competent discussion of the issue. The essay's argument—that curriculum should be determined by many voices, including that of private business—is clearly expressed and adequately developed. The writer supports this position with relevant reasons, including an analysis of the need for private business to become involved in education. Examples are clearly relevant (e.g., sex education and AIDS education are cited as examples of how schools are offering new classes to meet the contemporary needs), and the writer uses details to help develop and illustrate important points. While the essay presents several ideas that are thought provoking—e.g., "An unenlightened society is a grave society with little hope"—those ideas are not expressed precisely or persuasively enough to merit a score of 5.

The conclusion is appropriate; it reinforces the main idea of the essay, that schools need to keep pace with society and adjust curricula to meet the needs of both students and employers.

The essay consistently displays adequate control over the conventions of academic writing. Sentence structure is generally adequate, although many of the sentences would benefit from restructuring and the use of transitions to more effectively communicate the writer's ideas.

For all of these reasons—competent analysis and adequate control of the elements of writing—this essay received a score of 4.

Score 3 Essay:

In today's society, there is too much emphasis placed on students desires rather than their needs. The students of today should have to study what is presented to them, rather than what is desired by them. Students are searching for the easy way out, and educators' are supplying them with that. Students should not only be presented with mandatory curriculum, but the educators should strive to insure that each individual student truly gains from their education, rather than just breezing through it.

It is vital to the continued success and expansion of the United States, that the young people be challenged in their curriculum and be encouraged to succeed in all that they do. The educators should determine a more strenuous curriculum, and enforce it at an earlier age. Thus, the young people of today will expect to be challenged, rather than avoiding it. Students have the easy way out, and they are not truly giving all that they can. There is so much potential that is just waiting to flourish, but it is the educators' responsibility to tap into that potential.

In conclusion, it is the educators responsibility to enforce curriculum and than raquesting it. Students should be challenged and expect curriculum that will eventually lead them to a path of success.

Essay Readers' Commentary:

This brief response is flawed by its generalities, repetition, and limited development. The central thesis—that it is the burden of educators to teach what they believe is necessary and that our educational system should not allow students to "breeze through" the educational system—is not adequately supported. The middle of the essay merely repeats much of what was said in the introduction. The writer discusses the concepts of students' potential and educators' responsibilities in only the most general terms.

The two-sentence conclusion simply repeats earlier discussion and does not sufficiently tie together and comment upon the earlier discussion. To earn a score of 4, this response would need to provide specific reasons and examples that more adequately develop its main points.

Also, the phrasing is often vague ("giving all that they can" and "path of success"), and the syntax is at times poorly controlled ("young people of today will expect to be challenged, rather than avoiding it.") Still, the problems are not severe or frequent. For all of these reasons, this response received a 3.

Score 2 Essay:

There are many school violences in each school. Those are big problems to our govenment and social. School violences effect the studying of students. This is very serious, even some students are nervious to go school. In fact, the government must give students a clean place to study. Teachers should help students know it is a duty to study. So, everyone should face those big problems.

Do we know what are students' ideas? Do the educators try to know? Most educators hope the govenment can give students more and help them more. These are people's hope. But it is so unfortunate that students can't have a good place to study. Also, teachers have to teach the students. Not that students can know what to study by themself. In the compus, there are many guys sell the drugs and acohol to younger students. Why those guys can go into the school? That is also the main problem.

When we were little, we didn't know what is correct and what is wrong. So we lose ourself easily. At the same time, we need much care from parents and teachers. So our teachers and parents play the important roles and they own must do better. Because some students learn some bad habits from their teachers and parents.

If we want to resolve all the problems, we must face the problems and find out the reasons, then try to resolve them. We also must care about all students. If we can help them, tring to do our best. Then, the problems will become less and less.

Essay Readers' Commentary:

This is a seriously flawed response to the topic. The writer begins by discussing school violence and the need for a good place to study, parental and teacher influence, and resolution of school problems. The issue of who should determine the curriculum, teachers or students, is implied but not addressed directly. In fact, teacher-directed learning seems to be a small point in a series of concerns related to school violence. The development of a position on the issue is unfocused and disorganized. Even the example, drug selling, relates to school violence and not to curricular responsibility. Had the writer not included references to teachers helping students know what to study, the essay would have received a score of 1 instead of a 2.

Also, problems with correct use of tense, diction, word order, sentence structure, and subject-verb agreement interfere with meaning, reinforcing the paper's low score.

Score 1 Essay:

Today some educators place much emphasis on what students want, there is a conflict about what is the educator's duty for what educatee should get.

Normally, the college or university in our country, students just study what they are tought, it is the professor's duty to dermine what should appear in the classroom. Nowday china has taken the polices of opening reforming,every thing chang vastly. Students can't get the job position from goverment authority but must look for the work chance by themself, so students have taken great care to what they learn int the college and what kind of knowlege does the job market need. If our high education institute ignore this chang and keep the tranditional teaching method, it will seem as wast student's time and money and the colleges will lost their student.

It may be the best way for the developing country to reform their high education system, especially with those majors that closely connected with market or industry application. We must give our student most upcoming technology or skill to meet the need of outdoor of our college, the information from students may be the best reference for the educator to determine what they should take to the classroom.

Essay Readers' Commentary:

This response displays little ability to develop and organize a coherent discussion of the issue.

The writer takes the position that China needs to reform its traditional approach to curriculum by becoming more student-centered and technologically current. However, the discussion is generally confusing and barely addresses the central issue presented in the topic.

Of the three paragraphs, the one-sentence introduction is simply a variation of the topic statement. The middle paragraph does not advance an opinion in a coherent manner, and the final paragraph shifts the focus to the need for technology in the curriculum.

The errors (comma splices, misspellings, verb problems, etc.) are numerous and intrusive.

This response would need considerable rewriting in order to earn a higher score than 1.

Sample III

The best ideas arise from a passionate interest in commonplace things.

Score 6 Essay:

Even the most brilliant thinkers, from Socrates to Satre, live lives in time. A childhood, an adolescence, an adulthood; these are common to me and you as well as the greatest writers. Furthermore, many of the great thinkers we esteem in our Western culture lived somewhat unevetful lives. What distinguished their life from say a common laborer was their work. Therefore, what provided the grist for their work? One might say that they were brilliant and this alone was sufficient to distinguish their lives from the masses. Intellect alone can not devise situations or thoughts from no where; there must be a basis and that basis is most common, if not always, observation of the common, of the quotidian. Critics of this idea may argue that these thinkers were products of fine educations and were well schooled in the classics. This, they may point to, is the real basis for their knowledge. I would argue that although it may be a benefit to study classics and be well schooled in diverse disciplines, these pursuits merely refine and hone an ability each and every person has, the ability to study human nature. Where best to study human nature than in the day to day routine each one of us can witness in him or herself or those around us.

I propose that the two best disciplines to understand this power of the commonplace and its ability to cause a groundswell of thought are philosophy and literature. Every school of philosophy, from the Greeks to our day, share a common mission or intent and that is to understand and explain human existence, with all of its concommitant features. Generally speaking, the Greek philosophers, epitomized in Aristotle, attempted to set down rules for human behavior founded on logic. These rules applied not only to the rare forms of human behavior but largely focused on the more mundane motions of daily life. Many of Aristotle's rules were based on his observations of others as well as himself. Contrast this venture with the existentialists of our century who attempted to look behind the real motivations of human behavior as well understand man's relation to the Universe. To do this, what did these philosophers do? They studied those around them; they submerged themselves in the commonplace, in cities with hordes of annonymous people. While the existentialists, as well those philosophers before, exploited their uncommon eduation and intellect, the basis for their movement was ordinary human behavior and existence.

Finally, literature is similar to philosophy in that it seeks to explain and understand human behavior and therefore rooted in the commonplace. Nevertheless, its relative strength over philosophy is literature's ability to emotionally and spiritually move the reader through the use of contrived situations and fictional characters. It can do this when even the central theme of a piece maybe love between a man and a woman (e.g. commonplace). Literature also distinguishes itself from philosophy in that the breadth of the fiction may be huge. The plot and the detail can be quite ordinary or fanatastic. However, this does not mean that the central themes of all literature, whether ordinary or fantastic, deal with human beings and the problems they find in the world, something which we all share.

In conclusion, I hope it has been shown that a passionate desire to understand and explain human behavior, the significance of our existence and deal constructively with the challanges of life are the centerpieces of at least in two of the most influential areas in human thought. What is more commonplace than the existence of man.

Essay Readers' Commentary:

This is a well-focused and insightful analysis of the issue. Beginning with the observation that the greatest thinkers "live lives in time," the writer reasons that the great thinkers develop their ideas through observation of common occurrences and everyday reality. One of the strengths of this response is the way in which it thoughtfully considers the opposing claim: that great thinkers are primarily the product of fine education, and that, being "well schooled in the classics," they are far removed from everyday life. The writer notes that, while it "may be a benefit to study classics," it is nevertheless true that being "well schooled in diverse disciplines" will simply "refine and hone an ability to study human nature" in its everyday manifestations. This observation is indicative of the writer's sophisticated grasp of the complexities of the issue.

The writer goes on to demonstrate the intellectual "power of the commonplace" by skillfully developing two compelling examples from academic life: philosophy and literature. Aristotle is cited as a philosopher who studied the "more mundane motions of daily life." Similarly, the writer explains, twentieth-century existentialists, in attempting to understand man's relation to the universe, found inspiration in the commonplace.

Another strength in this essay is the way it introduces an idea and then builds on that idea as the argument unfolds. For instance, in a discussion of the existentialists in the second paragraph, the writer expands on an earlier point about "thinkers" in general: the existentialists may have "exploited their uncommon education and intellect," but the "basis for their movement was ordinary human behavior and existence." It is logical connections such as these that make for a coherent and well-focused discussion.

The writer uses language fluently and controls sophisticated syntax throughout the essay: "I would argue that although it may be a benefit to study classics and be well schooled in diverse disciplines, these pursuits merely refine and hone an ability each and every person has, the ability to study human nature."

This is not a flawless paper: word choice, for example, is not always precise. But the essay's cogent analysis, effective organization, and sophisticated sentence structure merit a solid score of 6.

Score 5 Essay:

I can agree with the statement above that, "The best ideas arise from a passionate interest in commonplace things." The statement is an accurate description of how many people form great ideas from ordinary things in life. Sports are all great ideas that are made from commonplace things. What makes sports some of the best ideas is not what they began as but what they evolved into.

All athletic competitions began from commonplace things being brought together for the purpose of entertainment, excercise, and social interaction. Many of the sports people enjoy today are the results of someone's idea creating a new dimension of our lifestyle out of an ordinary object. Baseball, basketball, and track especially show that the idea of creating something wonderful out of ordinary objects is true.

Who would have thought that a stick and a ball would spawn into a national pastime, a generational tie between father and son, a national bond between all races, and a multibillion dollar industry. Baseball began when someone decided to throw a ball at someone with a stick and that person with the stick would then try to hit the ball. What a simple concept and what a wonderful consequence.

Today the simple game of baseball is played all over the world. It is a sport that crosses international divides of religion, race, and politics. This one simple game, a bat hitting a ball, can bring the whole world together. But baseball is just one sport that shows the ablitiy to bridge cultural gaps.

When Mr. Naismith nailed a peachbasket to a post and threw a ball into it he had no idea that millions of people would be playing his game today. Mr. Naismith invented the game of basketball, which most everyone has played at some point in his or her life. Throwing a ball into a basket. What could be more simple or commonplace than a ball and a peach basket?

Today, basketball is the new American pastime. It replaced baseball because it is cheaper than baseball and it can be played by only one person. This interest in balls and new uses for them, as we can see in both baseball and basketball, brought about a huge social phenomena of excercise and new social interaction that would bring people together rather than divide them.

It doesn't take a ball to create a sport from a commonplace item. Track and field has no balls used in it, unless you consider the shotput a ball. The whole sport of track and field is made of simple ideas: running, jumping, and throwing. Simple but yet it is one of the most watched events worldwide as evidenced by the recent Olympic Games. For example, team relay races consist of four people running around an oval track passing a baton to each other. A baton that is the only object you need to have a relay race, a baton is definetly a commonplace thing. Yet this event has such stars as Carl Lewis who is known world wide.

Sports and how they were created is the epitome of the idea that "the best ideas arise form a passionate interest in commonplace things." What might have seemed boring at the time of hitting a ball, or throwing a ball into a net, or passing a baton are all now events that millions take part in and even more watch. What makes these ideas great is that they all bring people from different backgrounds together, wether they intended to or not.

Essay Readers' Commentary:

This response presents a thoughtful, if not especially well-developed, discussion of the issue. Drawing examples from the world of sports, the writer notes that most sports begin with a simple idea. Baseball, for example, "began when someone decided to throw a ball at someone with a stick and that person with the stick would then try to hit the ball." From this simple idea came a sport that is played and enjoyed all over the world. Instead of focusing solely on the universal appeal of sports, however, the paper introduces the idea that sports cross "international divides of religion, race, and politics." This is a perceptive idea, but it is not effectively supported or sustained.

Throughout the response, ideas are expressed clearly and word choice is accurate. Sentences are at times well formed and varied: "Today the simple game of baseball is played all over the world. It is a sport that crosses international divides of religion, race, and politics. This one simple game, a bat hitting a ball, can bring the whole world together." On the whole, however, this is a 5 essay; it lacks the insightful, well-articulated analysis necessary for a score of 6.

Score 4 Essay:

While the best ideas do indeed arise from mankind's interest in the commonplace, one must realize that the "commonplace ideas" of our current society continue to evolve at such a rapid rate that we entered the Twenty-First Century on a wave of thought, ideas, and creation that would surely baffle our forefathers.

Simply put, Thomas Jefferson, a brilliant, and progressive thinker, was motivated to create certain societal services that he felt necessary for his time. Historians report that Mr. Jefferson witnessed a fire which destroyed a man's home. The victim was left with nothing. Mr. Jefferson, thinking it most unfortunate that a man should lose all his worldly posessions, developed a system of homeowners insurance. Of course today, we have taken insurance to a new and all-encompassing level. President Roosevelt adored nature and found great solace while visiting Yosemite in Wyoming. Among his many accomplishments, Rooselvelt, our twenty-sixth President, is perhaps best known for his creation of a National Parks Protection program.

Over time, the basic needs of mankind have been met due to interests in the commonplace mixed with a progressive trait in man to make things simpler, faster, less expensive, and more gratifying.

Today, our "simple thoughts" turn to ideas such as space stations, the technological superhighway, and electric vehicles. Sadly, we must also repair much of the fallout from some of our "commonplace" inspired ideas. For example, evolved transportation has a price as we work to restore our environment.

If we are inspired by the simple motivations, dreams, and tasks of everyday life then we must make a commitment to development our muse. Perhaps, the best way to move ahead is to step back; to re-examine and learn from the art, science, history, love and war of our founding fathers. Perhaps simple is best. After all, that's where all the best ideas are born.

Essay Readers' Commentary:

This writer presents a competent discussion of the issue. The opening paragraph introduces two ideas that serve as the primary focus of the paper: that the best ideas are the result of an interest in commonplace things; and that our ideas are evolving at a rate of rapidity that would "surely baffle our forefathers." These two ideas are adequately developed in the course of the paper, but not with enough logical development or complexity to merit a score of 5.

The second paragraph, which considers the way in which ideas arise from an interest in commonplace things, is the most thoroughly developed section of the response. The examples are relevant: Thomas Jefferson, who used everyday observations to come up with the idea of homeowners insurance, and Theodore Roosevelt, whose passionate interest in nature led him to develop the National Parks Protection program.

The essay's other area of focus—the rapid rate at which our ideas change—is discussed in the third paragraph. Some good ideas emerge, but, unfortunately, they are not well developed.

Although the response is organized with an introduction, three supporting paragraphs, and a conclusion, the organization would be stronger if the ideas in one paragraph or section were more clearly connected to the points made in the next section.

While there are some errors, they are not severe enough to interfere with meaning. In general, the writer expresses ideas adequately, although at times the wording seems almost haphazard and therefore a bit confusing: "to re-examine and learn from the art, science, history, love and war of our founding fathers." For reasons of adequate content and adequate presentation of ideas, this response received a score of 4.

Score 3 Essay:

The best ideas arise from a passionate interest in commonplace things. This is something I learned from everyday experiences. I always found that the things I decorated my life with abundantly, were the things I treasured most. It could be a memory, a possesion, or just a view. It's hard to create a whole picture without first looking at the pieces within it. My whole life of school and studies have brought me to college and have sparked my interest in applying to a graduate program. Never before did I realize how these little efforts would create this dream. In my field of dietetics many would be amazed to find that the food we eat could kill us or help us from disease.

There are many times where I'll be looking at the beautiful view, and I just have to go out and enjoy it. I do this by walking, gardening, or just lying in the grass. The feeling of the warm sun makes me dream. I know I'm not the only one who tends to overlook the basic things, like the tree outside that you used to climb, or the food you eat to give you energy and growth. We just have to take the time from our busy schedules to stop and smell the roses. Everyone's life is different, with our own experinces and thoughts to motivate us, and no matter who we are, some of the simplest things can bring great achievements in our lives.

Essay Readers' Commentary:

This is a limited response because it does not adequately analyze the issue. The discussion is primarily concerned with the writer's own personal enjoyment of commonplace things. As such it never fully engages the topic's central issue—the quality of the ideas that come from those commonplace things. Early in the response, the writer makes the following observation: "I always found that the things I decorated my life with abundantly, were the things I treasured most." This is typical of the simplistic analysis that characterizes this response.

At the end of the first paragraph, the writer does make some hesitant steps toward a discussion of the ideas that might come from these everyday experiences, mentioning that "in my field of dietetics many would be amazed to find that the food we eat could kill us or help us from disease." This insight is not adequately developed, however, and, in the second paragraph, the writer returns to a discussion of the idea that one must enjoy the little things in life. In short, the paper is limited in its development, revealing only a partial understanding of the topic's assertion.

In general, the there is control of standard written English language and sentence structure. This response received the score of 3 because its analysis is simplistic, and its development is limited.

Score 2 Essay:

In reading such a passage as the one given to me as an assignment I can't help but think of an analogy that entered my mind. It is my enduring interest in the field of multimedia. I say this because of the ideas in which I cultivate as an artist of many media materials such as paints, film, computer animated software, etc. Being an expressionist I take in my surroundings and personal experiences from commonplaces and things and tell a story from my perspective using the various tools whether it be computer aided or hand drawn. My ideas come from people or things because it tells a story. The story can be abstract, little, big, or even strange. To record stories like these may spark ideas that may come to me in a domino effect. It's beautiful I shared this with you to conclude that sometimes even common things such as a pencil and an empty page can spelllout your fate and unlimited possibilities when you have a passion or an interest that drives your hunger for innovation.

Essay Readers' Commentary:

This response is seriously flawed in its analysis of the issue. The writer attempts to address the topic by focusing on his or her interest in "multimedia" art. Yet, while isolated words and phrases from the topic appear throughout, the paper never clearly states a position on the issue. For example, in a discussion of multimedia art, the writer makes the following observation: "Being an expressionist I take in my surroundings and personal experiences from commonplaces and things and tell a story from my perspective using the various tools whether it be computer aided or hand drawn." The discussion circles around the issue, without ever really engaging it.

The response is also marked by serious flaws in language use: inaccurate word choice ("ideas in which I cultivate as an artist"), unclear pronoun reference ("My ideas come from people or things because it tells a story"), and, in general, a debilitating lack of clarity and precision. These errors frequently interfere with meaning, a characteristic of many responses scored 2.

Score 1 Essay:

The best ideas arise from a passionate interest in commonplace things because they are from places in the heart. These iseas draw you to learn more about them. The idea or ideas have become passionate to you by either personal experience or by observation. It catches your attention and causes you to examine why or how the occurance /idea exsists. Instientively the desire to know more about the idea pushes you into futher research of the subject. The idea can be something you don't understand to be acceptable or unacceptable. The drive to understand leads to passion and that passion drives you to develope a great idea.

Essay Readers' Commentary:

This response is fundamentally flawed because it does not present an organized, coherent response to the topic. Sentences and fragments are strung together with little, if any, underlying logic. The writer's position seems to be that the more passionate we are about an idea, the more we will pursue it. This idea is repeated but is not really developed or clearly explained.

The errors are so pervasive and fundamental that they seriously interfere with meaning. This response requires considerable revisions to receive a score higher than 1.

Sample IV

As people rely more and more on technology to solve problems, the ability of humans to think for themselves will surely deteriorate.

Discuss the extent to which you agree or disagree with the statement and explain your reasoning for the position you take. In developing and supporting your position, you should consider ways in which the statement might or might not hold true and explain how these considerations shape your position.

Score 6 Essay:

The statement linking technology negatively with free thinking plays on recent human experience over the past century. Surely there has been no time in history where the lived lives of people have changed more dramatically. A quick reflection on a typical day reveals how technology has revolutionized the world. Most people commute to work in an automobile that runs on an internal combustion engine. During the workday, chances are high that the employee will interact with a computer that processes information on silicon bridges that are .09 microns wide. Upon leaving home, family members will be reached through wireless networks that utilize satellites orbiting the earth.

Each of these common occurrences could have been inconceivable at the turn of the 19th century.

The statement attempts to bridge these dramatic changes to a reduction in the ability for humans to think for themselves. The assumption is that an increased reliance on technology negates the need for people to think creatively to solve previous quandaries. Looking back at the introduction, one could argue that without a car, computer, or mobile phone, the hypothetical worker would need to find alternate methods of transport, information processing and communication. Technology short circuits this thinking by making the problems obsolete.

However, this reliance on technology does not necessarily preclude the creativity that marks the human species. The prior examples reveal that technology allows for convenience. The car, computer and phone all release additional time for people to live more efficiently. This efficiency does not preclude the need for humans to think for themselves. In fact, technology frees humanity to not only tackle new problems, but may itself create new issues that did not exist without technology. For example, the proliferation of automobiles has introduced a need for fuel conservation on a global scale. With increasing energy demands from emerging markets, global warming becomes a concern inconceivable to the horse-and-buggy generation. Likewise dependence on oil has created nation-states that are not dependent on taxation, allowing ruling parties to oppress minority groups such as women. Solutions to these complex problems require the unfettered imaginations of maverick scientists and politicians.

In contrast to the statement, we can even see how technology frees the human imagination. Consider how the digital revolution and the advent of the internet has allowed for an unprecedented exchange of ideas. WebMD, a popular internet portal for medical information, permits patients to self research symptoms for a more informed doctor visit. This exercise opens pathways of thinking that were previously closed off to the medical layman. With increased interdisciplinary interactions, inspiration can arrive from the most surprising corners. Jeffrey Sachs, one of the architects of the UN Millenium Development Goals, based his ideas on emergency care triage techniques. The unlikely marriage of economics and medicine has healed tense, hyperinflation environments from South America to Eastern Europe.

This last example provides the most hope in how technology actually provides hope to the future of humanity. By increasing our reliance on technology, impossible goals can now be achieved. Consider how the late 20th century witnessed the complete elimination of smallpox. This disease had ravaged the human race since prehistorical days, and yet with the technology of vaccines, free thinking humans dared to imagine a world free of smallpox. Using technology, battle plans were drawn out, and smallpox was systematically targeted and eradicated.

Technology will always mark the human experience, from the discovery of fire to the implementation of nanotechnology. Given the history of the human race, there will be no limit to the number of problems, both new and old, for us to tackle. There is no need to retreat to a Luddite attitude to new things, but rather embrace a hopeful posture to the possibilities that technology provides for new avenues of human imagination.

Essay Readers' Commentary:

The author of this essay stakes out a clear and insightful position on the issue and follows the specific instructions by presenting reasons to support that position. The essay cogently argues that technology does not decrease our ability to think for ourselves, but merely provides "additional time for people to live more efficiently." In fact, the problems that have developed alongside the growth of technology (pollution, political unrest in oil-producing nations) actually call for more creative thinking, not less.

In further examples, the essay shows how technology allows for the linking of ideas that may never have been connected in the past (like medicine and economic models), pushing people to think in new ways. Examples are persuasive and fully developed; reasoning is logically sound and well supported.

Ideas in the essay are connected logically, with effective transitions used both between paragraphs ("However" or "In contrast to the statement") and within paragraphs. Sentence structure is varied and complex and the essay clearly demonstrates facility with the "conventions of standard written English (i.e., grammar, usage and mechanics)," with only minor errors appearing. Thus, this essay meets all the requirements for receiving a top score, a 6.

Score 5 Essay:

Surely many of us have expressed the following sentiment, or some variation on it, during our daily commutes to work: "People are getting so stupid these days!" Surrounded as we are by striding and strident automatons with cell phones glued to their ears, PDA's gripped in their palms, and omniscient, omnipresent CNN gleaming in their eyeballs, it's tempting to believe that technology has isolated and infantilized us, essentially transforming us into dependent, conformist morons best equipped to sideswip one another in our SUV's.

Furthermore, hanging around with the younger, pre-commute generation, whom tech-savviness seems to have rendered lethal, is even less reassuring. With "Teen People" style trends shooting through the air from tiger-striped PDA to zebra-striped PDA, and with the latest starlet gossip zipping from juicy Blackberry to teeny, turbo-charged cell phone, technology seems to support young people's worst tendencies to follow the crowd. Indeed, they have seemingly evolved into intergalactic conformity police. After all, today's tech-aided teens are, courtesy of authentic, hands-on video games, literally trained to kill; courtesy of chat and instant text messaging, they have their own language; they even have tiny cameras to efficiently photodocument your fashion blunders! Is this adolescence, or paparazzi terrorist training camp?

With all this evidence, it's easy to believe that tech trends and the incorporation of technological wizardry into our everyday lives have served mostly to enforce conformity, promote dependence, heighten comsumerism and materialism, and generally create a culture that values self-absorption and personal entitlement over cooperation and collaboration. However, I argue that we are merely in the inchoate stages of learning to live with technology while still loving one another. After all, even given the examples provided earlier in this essay, it seems clear that technology hasn't impaired our thinking and problem-solving capacities. Certainly it has incapacitated our behavior and manners; certainly our values have taken a severe blow. However, we are inarguably more efficient in our badness these days. We're effective worker bees of ineffectiveness!

If T\technology has so increased our senses of self-efficacy that we can become veritable agents of the awful, virtual CEO's of selfishness, certainly it can be beneficial. Harnessed correctly, technology can improve our ability to think and act for ourselves. The first challenge is to figure out how to provide technology users with some direly-needed direction.

Essay Readers' Commentary:

The language of this essay clearly illustrates both its strengths and weaknesses. The flowery and sometimes uncannily keen descriptions are often used to powerful effect, but at other times this descriptive language results in errors in syntax. See, for example, the problems of parallelism in the second-to-last sentence of paragraph 2 ("After all, today's tech-aided teens ...").

There is consistent evidence of facility with syntax and complex vocabulary ("Surrounded as we are by striding and strident automatons with cell phones glued to their ears, PDA's gripped in their palms, and omniscient, omnipresent CNN gleaming in their eyeballs, it's tempting to believe..."). However, such lucid prose is often countered by an over-reliance on abstractions and tangential reasoning. For example, what does the fact that video games "literally train [teens] to kill" have to do with the use or deterioration of thinking abilities?

Because this essay takes a complex approach to the issue (arguing, in effect, that technology neither enhances nor reduces our ability to think for ourselves, but can do one or the other, depending on the user) and because the author makes use of "appropriate vocabulary and sentence variety," a score of 5 is appropriate.

Score 4 Essay:

In all actuality, I think it is more probable that our bodies will surely deteriorate long before our minds do in any significant amount. Who can't say that technology has made us lazier, but that's the key word, lazy, not stupid. The ever increasing amount of technology that we incorporate into our daily lives makes people think and learn every day, possibly more than ever before. Our abilities to think, learn, philosophize, etc. may even reach limits never dreamed of before by average people. Using technology to solve problems will continue to help us realize our potential as a human race.

If you think about it, using technology to solve more complicating problems gives humans a chance to expand their thinking and learning, opening up whole new worlds for many people. Many of these people are glad for the chance to expand their horizons by learning more, going to new places, and trying new things. If it wasn't for the invention of new technological devices, I wouldn't be sitting at this computer trying to philosophize about technology. It would be extremely hard for children in much poorer countries to learn and think for themselves with out the invention of the internet. Think what an impact the printing press, a technologically superior mackine at the time, had on the ability of the human race to learn and think.

Right now we are seeing a golden age of technology, using it all the time during our every day lives. When we get up there's instant coffee and the microwave and all these great things that help us get ready for our day. But we aren't allowing our minds to deteriorate by using them, we are only making things easier for ourselves and saving time for other important things in our days. Going off to school or work in our cars instead of a horse and buggy. Think of the brain power and genius that was used to come up with that single invention that has changed the way we move across this globe.

Using technology to solve our continually more complicated problems as a human race is definately a good thing. Our ability to think for ourselves isn't deteriorating, it's continuing to grow, moving on to higher though functions and more ingenious ideas. The ability to use what technology we have is an example.

Essay Readers' Commentary:

This essay meets all the criteria of a level-4 essay. The writer develops a clear position ("Using technology to solve our problems will continue to help us realize our potential as a human race"). The position is then developed with relevant reasons ("using technology to solve more complicated problems gives humans a chance to expand their thinking and learning" and "we are seeing a golden age of technology").

Point 1, "using technology," is supported with the simple but relevant notion that technology allows us access to information and abilities to which we would not normally have access. Similarly, point 2, the "golden age," is supported by the basic description of our technologically saturated social condition. Though the overall development and organization of the essay does suffer from an occasional misdirection (see paragraph 3's abrupt progression from coffee pots to the benefits of technology to cars), the essay as a whole flows smoothly and logically from one idea to the next.

It is useful to compare this essay to the level-3 essay presented next. Though both essays entail some surface-level discussion and often fail to probe deeply into the issue, this writer does take the analysis a step further. In paragraph 2, the distinction between this essay and the next one (the level-3 response) can most clearly be seen. To support the notion that advances in technology actually help increase thinking ability, the writer draws a clever parallel between the promise of modern, sophisticated technology (computer) and the actual "impact" of equally "promising" and pervasive technologies of the past (printing press).

Like the analysis, the language in this essay clearly meets the requirements for a score of 4. The writer displays sufficient control of language and the conventions of standard written English. The preponderance of mistakes are of a cosmetic nature ("trying to solve more complicating problems.") There is a sentence fragment ("Going off...") along with a comma splice ("Our ability...isn't deteriorating, it's continuing to grow...") in paragraph 3. However, these errors are minor and do not interfere with the clarity of the ideas being presented.

Score 3 Essay:

There is no current proof that advancing technology will deteriorate the ability of humans to think. On the contrary, advancements in technology had advanced our vast knowledge in many fields, opening opportunities for further understanding and achievement. For example, the problem of dibilitating illnesses and diseases such as alzheimer's disease is slowing being solved by the technological advancements in stem cell research. The future ability of growing new brain cells and the possibility to reverse the onset of alzheimer's is now becoming a reality. This shows our initiative as humans to better our health demonstrates greater ability of humans to think.

One aspect where the ability of humans may initially be seen as an example of deteriorating minds is the use of internet and cell phones. In the past humans had to seek out information in many different enviroments and aspects of life. Now humans can sit in a chair and type anything into a computer and get an answer. Our reliance on this type of technology can be detrimental if not regulated and regularily substituted for other information sources such as human interactions and hands on learning. I think if humans understand that we should not have such a reliance on computer technology, that we as a species will advance further by utilizing the opportunity of computer technology as well as the other sources of information outside of a computer. Supplementing our knowledge with internet access is surely a way for technology to solve problems while continually advancing the human race.

Essay Readers' Commentary:

This essay never moves beyond a superficial discussion of the issue. The writer attempts to develop two points: that advancements in technology have progressed our knowledge in many fields and that supplementing rather than relying on technology is "surely a way for technology to solve problems while continually advancing the human race." Each point, then, is developed with relevant but insufficient evidence. In discussing the potential of technology to advance knowledge in many fields (a broad subject, rife with possible examples), the writer uses only one limited and very brief example from a specific field (medicine and stem-cell research).

Development of the second point is hindered by a lack of specificity and organization. The writer creates what might be best described as an outline. The writer cites a need for regulation/supplementation and warns of the detriment of over-reliance upon technology. However, the explanation of both the problem and solution is vague and limited ("Our reliance...can be detrimental. If humans understand that we should not have such a reliance...we will advance further"). There is neither explanation of consequences nor clarification of what is meant by "supplementing." This second paragraph is a series of generalizations that are loosely connected and lack a much-needed grounding.

In the essay, there are some minor language errors and a few more serious flaws (e.g., "The future ability of growing new brain cells" or "One aspect where the ability of humans may initially be seen as an example of deteriorating minds"). Despite the accumulation of such flaws, the writer's meaning is generally clear. Thus, this essay earns a score of 3.

Score 2 Essay:

In recent centuries, humans have developed the technology very rapidly, and you may accept some merit of it, and you may see a distortion in society occured by it. To be lazy for human in some meaning is one of the fashion issues in thesedays. There are many symptoms and resons of it. However, I can not agree with the statement that the technology make humans to be reluctant to thinkng thoroughly.

Of course, you can see the phenomena of human laziness along with developed technology in some place. However, they would happen in specific condition, not general. What makes human to be laze of thinking is not merely technology, but the the tendency of human that they treat them as a magic stick and a black box. Not understanding the aims and theory of them couses the disapproval problems.

The most important thing to use the thechnology, regardless the new or old, is to comprehend the fundamental idea of them, and to adapt suit tech to tasks in need. Even if you recognize a method as a all-mighty and it is extremely over-spec to your needs, you can not see the result you want. In this procedure, humans have to consider as long as possible to acquire adequate functions. Therefore, humans can not escape from using their brain.

In addition, the technology as it is do not vain automatically, the is created by humans. Thus, the more developed tech and the more you want a convenient life, the more you think and emmit your creativity to breakthrough some banal method sarcastically.

Consequently, if you are not passive to the new tech, but offensive to it, you would not lose your ability to think deeply. Furthermore, you may improve the ability by adopting it.

Essay Readers' Commentary:

The language of this essay is what most clearly links it to the score of 2. Amidst sporadic moments of clarity, this essay is marred by serious errors in grammar, usage and mechanics that often interfere with meaning. It is unclear what the writer means when he/she states, "To be lazy for human in some meaning is one of the fashion issues in these days," or "to adapt suit tech to tasks in need."

Despite such severe flaws, the writer has made an obvious attempt to respond to the prompt ("I can not agree with the statement that the technology make humans to be reluctant to thinking thoroughly") as well as an unclear attempt to support such an assertion ("Not understanding the aims and theory of them [technology] causes the disapproval problems" and "The most important thing to use the technology ... is to comprehend the fundamental idea of them"). On the whole, the essay displays a seriously flawed but not fundamentally deficient attempt to develop and support its claims.

(**Note:** In this specific case, the analysis is tied directly to the language. As the language falters, so too does the analysis.)

Score 1 Essay:

Humans have invented machines but they have forgot it and have started everything technically so clearly their thinking process is deterioating.

> **Essay Readers' Commentary:**
>
> The essay is clearly on topic, as evidenced by the writer's usage of the more significant terms from the prompt: "technically" (technologically), "humans," "thinking" (think) and "deteriorating" (deteriorate). Such usage is the only clear evidence of understanding. Meaning aside, the brevity of the essay (one sentence) clearly indicates the writer's inability to develop a response that follows the specific instructions given ("Discuss the extent to which you agree or disagree with the statement above and explain your reasoning for the position you take").
>
> The language, too, is clearly level 1, as the sentence fails to achieve coherence. The coherent phrases in this one-sentence response are those tied to the prompt: "Humans have invented machines" and "their thinking process is deteriorating." Otherwise, the point being made is unclear.

Scoring Guide and Samples of GRE Argument Writing

1. Scoring Guide of GRE Argument Writing

Score 6

In addressing the specific task directions, a 6 response presents a cogent, well-articulated examination of the argument and conveys meaning skillfully.

A typical response in this category:

- clearly identifies aspects of the argument relevant to the assigned task and examines them insightfully;
- develops ideas cogently, organizes them logically and connects them with clear transitions;
- provides compelling and thorough support for its main points;
- conveys ideas fluently and precisely, using effective vocabulary and sentence variety;
- demonstrates facility with the conventions of standard written English (i.e., grammar, usage and mechanics), but may have minor errors.

Score 5

In addressing the specific task directions, a 5 response presents a generally thoughtful, well-developed examination of the argument and conveys meaning clearly.

A typical response in this category:

- clearly identifies aspects of the argument relevant to the assigned task and examines them in a generally perceptive way;
- develops ideas clearly, organizes them logically and connects them with appropriate transitions;

- offers generally thoughtful and thorough support for its main points;
- conveys ideas clearly and well, using appropriate vocabulary and sentence variety;
- demonstrates facility with the conventions of standard written English, but may have minor errors.

Score 4

In addressing the specific task directions, a 4 response presents a competent examination of the argument and conveys meaning with acceptable clarity.

A typical response in this category:
- identifies and examines aspects of the argument relevant to the assigned task, but may also discuss some extraneous points;
- develops and organizes ideas satisfactorily, but may not connect them with transitions;
- supports its main points adequately, but may be uneven in its support;
- demonstrates sufficient control of language to convey ideas with reasonable clarity;
- generally demonstrates control of the conventions of standard written English, but may have some errors.

Score 3

A 3 response demonstrates some competence in addressing the specific task directions, in examining the argument and in conveying meaning, but is obviously flawed.

A typical response in this category exhibits ONE OR MORE of the following characteristics:
- does not identify or examine most of the aspects of the argument relevant to the assigned task, although some relevant examination of the argument is present;

mainly discusses tangential or irrelevant matters, or reasons poorly;
- is limited in the logical development and organization of ideas;
- offers support of little relevance and value for its main points;
- has problems in language and sentence structure that result in a lack of clarity;
- contains occasional major errors or frequent minor errors in grammar, usage or mechanics that can interfere with meaning.

Score 2

A 2 response largely disregards the specific task directions and/or demonstrates serious weaknesses in analytical writing.

A typical response in this category exhibits ONE OR MORE of the following characteristics:
- does not present an examination based on logical analysis, but may instead present the writer's own views on the subject; does not follow the directions for the assigned task;

- does not develop ideas, or is poorly organized and illogical;
- provides little, if any, relevant or reasonable support for its main points;
- has serious problems in language and sentence structure that frequently interfere with meaning;
- contains serious errors in grammar, usage or mechanics that frequently obscure meaning.

···

Score 1

A 1 response demonstrates fundamental deficiencies in analytical writing.

A typical response in this category exhibits ONE OR MORE of the following characteristics:

- provides little or no evidence of understanding the argument;
- is extremely brief and/or disorganized, providing little evidence of an organized response;
- has severe problems in language and sentence structure that persistently interfere with meaning;
- contains pervasive errors in grammar, usage or mechanics that result in incoherence.

···

Score 0

A typical response in this category is off topic (i.e., provides no evidence of an attempt to respond to the assigned topic), is in a foreign language, merely copies the topic, consists of only keystroke characters, or is illegible or nonverbal.

···

总结以上ARGUMENT作文评分标准，可以得出以下结论：
- 文章必须能准确识别题目中突出的推理/论证谬误和漏洞；
- 必须对这些推理/论证的谬误和漏洞展开充分的说明和分析；
- 文章逻辑要清楚、转折和过渡要自然紧凑、结构完整；
- 文字表达流畅、准确，遣词造句富于变化，语言规范。

下面的ETS例文，尤其是那些5分和6分作文中，大家要注意结合每篇文章后面改卷人员的评语来体会文章的要点。

注意，并非那些5分和6分作文的方方面面都值得模仿。比如，部分篇章的开头和结尾段的写作过于冗长，中间正文的结构和节奏过于呆板、沉重。这些方面，大家还是要多参考本书的要求。

同ISSUE作文一样，下面这些例文是考生写的文章，里面仍然有一些拼写、用词以及标点符号等方面的错误。但显然，只要文章的分析、论证和组织结构出色，偶尔出现这些小的错误并不妨碍作文得高分。

2. Samples of GRE Argument Writing

Sample I

Hospital statistics regarding people who go to the emergency room after roller-skating accidents indicate the need for more protective equipment. Within this group of people, 75 percent of those who had accidents in streets or parking lots were not wearing any protective clothing (helmets, knee pads, etc.) or any light-reflecting material (clip-on lights, glow-in-the-dark wrist pads, etc.). Clearly, these statistics indicate that by investing in high-quality protective gear and reflective equipment, roller skaters will greatly reduce their risk of being severely injured in an accident.

Score 6 Essay:

The notion that protective gear reduces the injuries suffered in accidents seems at first glance to be an obvious conclusion. After all, it is the intent of these products to either provent accidents from occuring in the first place or to reduce the injuries suffered by the wearer should an accident occur. However, the conclusion that investing in high quality protective gear greatly reduces the risk of being severely injured in an accident may mask other (and potentially more significant) causes of injuries and may inspire people to over invest financially and psychologically in protective gear.

First of all, as mentioned in the argument, there are two distinct kinds of gear-preventative gear (such as light reflecting material) and protective gear (such as helmets). Preventative gear is intended to warn others, presumably for the most part motorists, of the presence of the roller skater. It works only if the "other" is a responsible and caring individual who will afford the skater the necessary space and attention. Protective gear is intended to reduce the effect of any accident, whether it is caused by another, the skater or some force of nature. Protective gear does little, if anything, to prevent accidents but is presumed to reduce the injuries that occur in an accident. The statistics on injuries suffered by skaters would be more interesting if the skaters were grouped into those wearing no gear at all, those wearing protective gear only, those wearing preventative gear only and those wearing both. These statistics could provide skaters with a clearer understanding of which kinds of gear are more beneficial.

The argument above is weakened by the fact that it does not take into account the inherent differences between skaters who wear gear and those who do not. If is at least likely that those who wear gear may be generally more responsible and/or safety conscious individuals. The skaters who wear gear may be less likely to cause accidents through careless or dangerous behavior. It may, in fact, be their natural caution and responsibility that keeps them out of the emergency room rather than the gear itself. Also, the statistic above is based entirely on those who are skating in streets and parking lots which are relatively dangerous places to skate in the first place. People who are generally more safety conscious (and therefore more likely to wear gear) may choose to skate in safer areas such as parks or back yards.

The statistic also goes not differentiate between severity of injuries. The conclusion that safety gear prevents severe injuries suggests that it is presumed that people come to the emergency room only with severe injuries. This is certainly not the case. Also, given that skating is a recreational activity that may be primarily engaged in during evenings and weekends (when doctors' offices are closed), skater with less severe injuries may be especially likely to come to the emergency room for treatment.

Finally, there is absolutely no evidence provided that high quality (and presumably more expensive) gear is any more beneficial than other kinds of gear. For example, a simple white t-shirt may provide the same preventative benefit as a higher quality, more expensive, shirt designed only for skating. Before skaters are encouraged to invest heavily in gear, a more complete understanding of the benefit provided by individual pieces of gear would be helpful.

The argument for safety gear based on emergency room statistics could provide important information and potentially saves lives. Before conclusions about the amount and kinds of investments that should be made in gear are reached, however, a more complete understanding of the benefits are needed. After all, a false confidence in ineffective gear could be just as dangerous as no gear at all.

Essay Readers' Commentary:

This outstanding response demonstrates the writer's insightful analytical skills. The introduction, which notes that adopting the topic's fallacious reasoning could "inspire people to over invest financially and psychologically in protective gear," is followed by a comprehensive examination of each of the argument's root flaws. Specifically, the writer exposes several points that undermine the argument:

—that preventive and protective gear are not the same

—that skaters who wear gear may be less prone to accidents because they are, by nature, more responsible and cautious

—that the statistics do not differentiate by the severity of the injuries

—that gear may not need to be high-quality to be beneficial

The discussion is smoothly and logically organized, and each point is thoroughly and cogently developed. In addition, the writing is succinct, economical, and generally error-free. Sentences are varied and complex, and diction is expressive and precise.

In sum, this response exemplifies the very top of the 6 range described in the scoring guide. If the writer had been less eloquent or provided fewer reasons to refute the argument, the paper could still have received a 6.

Score 5 Essay:

The argument presented is limited but useful. It indicates a possible relationship between a high percentage of accidents and a lack of protective equipment. The statistics cited compel a further investigation of the usefulness of protective gear in preventing or mitigating roller-skating related injuries. However, the conclusion that protective gear and reflective equipment would "greatly reduce. risk of being severely injured" is premature. Data is lacking with reference to the total population of skaters and the relative levels of experience, skill and physical coordination of that population. It is entirely possible that further research would indicate that most serious injury is averted by the skater's ability to react quickly and skillfully in emergency situations.

Another area of investigation necessary before conclusions can be reached is identification of the types of injuries that occur and the various causes of those injuries. The article fails to identify the most prevalent types of roller-skating related injuries. It also fails to correlate the absence of protective gear and reflective equipment to those injuries. For example, if the majority of injuries are skin abrasions and closed-head injuries, then a case can be made for the usefulness of protective clothing mentioned. Likewise, if injuries are caused by collision with vehicles (e.g. bicycles, cars) or pedestrians, then light-reflective equipment might mitigate the occurences. However, if the primary types of injuries are soft-tissue injuries such as torn ligaments and muscles, back injuries and the like, then a greater case could be made for training and experience as preventative measures.

Essay Readers' Commentary:

This strong response gets right to the work of critiquing the argument, observing that it "indicates a possible relationship" but that its conclusion "is premature." It raises three central questions that, if answered, might undermine the soundness of the argument:

—What are the characteristics of the total population of skaters?

—What is the usefulness of protective or reflective gear in preventing or mitigating rollerskating-related injuries?

—What are the types of injuries sustained and their causes?

The writer develops each of these questions by considering possible answers that would either strengthen or weaken the argument. The paper does not analyze the argument as insightfully or develop the critique as fully as required for a 6 paper, but the clear organization, strong control of language, and substantial degree of development warrant more than a score of 4.

Score 4 Essay:

Although the argument stated above discusses the importance of safety equipment as significant part of avoiding injury, the statistics quoted are vague and inconclusive. Simply because 75 percent of the people involved in roller-skating accidents are not wearing the stated equipment does not automatically implicate the lack of equipment as the cause of injury. The term "accidents" may imply a great variety of injuries. The types of injuries one could incur by not wearing the types of equipment stated above are minor head injuries; skin abrasions or possibly bone fracture of a select few areas such as knees, elbows, hands, etc. (which are in fact most vulnerable to this sport); and/or injuries due to practising the sport during low light times of the day. During any physically demanding activity or sport people are subjected to a wide variety of injuries which cannot be avoided with protective clothing or light-reflective materials. These injuries include inner trauma (e.g., heart-attack); exhaustion; strained muscles, ligaments, or tendons; etc. Perhaps the numbers and percentages of people injured during roller-skating, even without protective equipment, would decrease greatly if people participating in the sport had proper training, good physical health, warm-up properly before beginning (stretching), as well as take other measures to prevent possible injury, such as common-sense, by refraining from performing the activity after proper lighting has ceased and knowing your personal limitations as an individual and athlete. The statistics used in the above reasoning are lacking in proper direction considering their assertions and therefore must be further examined and modified so that proper conclusions can be reached.

> **Essay Readers' Commentary:**
>
> This adequate response targets the argument's vague and inconclusive "statistics." The essay identifies and critiques the illogical reasoning that results from the misguided use of the argument's statistics:
>
> —that non-use of equipment may be "automatically" assumed to be the cause of injury
>
> —that "accidents" may refer to minor injuries
>
> —that injuries may result from other causes—skating in the dark, failure to train or warm-up properly, failure to recognize one's physical limitations
>
> The writer competently grasps the weaknesses of the argument. The ideas are clear and connected, but the response lacks transitional phrases. Development, too, is only adequate.
>
> Control of language is better than adequate. The writer achieves both control and clarity and ably conforms to the conventions of written English. Overall, though, this 4 response lacks the more thorough development that would warrant a score of 5.

Score 3 Essay:

The arguement is well presented and supported, but not completely well reasoned. It is clear and concisely written. The content is logically and smoothly presented. Statistics cited are used to develop support for the recommendation, that roller skaters who invest in protective gear and reflective equipment can reduce their risk of severe, accidental injuries. Examples of the types of protective equipment are described for the reader. Unfortunately, the author of the argement fails to note that merely by purchasing gear and reflective equipment that the skater will be protected. This is, of course, falacious if the skater fails to use the equipment, or uses it incorrectly or inappropriately. It is also an unnecessary assumption that a skater need purchase high-quality gear for the same degree of effectiveness to be achieved. The argument could be improved by taking these issues into consideration, and making recommendations for education and safety awareness to skaters.

> **Essay Readers' Commentary:**
>
> The first half of this generally well-written but limited response merely describes the argument. The second half of the paper identifies two assumptions of the argument:
>
> —that people who purchase protective gear will use the gear
>
> —that high-quality gear is more effective than other gear
>
> These points are sufficient to constitute some analysis and thus warrant a score of 3. However, neither of these analytic points is developed sufficiently to merit a score of 4.

Score 2 Essay:

To reduce the accidents from roller skating we should consider about it causes and effects concurrently to find the best solution. Basically the roller-skating players are children, they had less experiences to protect themselves from any kind of dangerous. Therefore, it should be a responsible of adult to take care them. Adult should recommend their child to wear any protective clothing, set the rules and look after them while they are playing.

In the past roller-skating is limited in the skate yard but when it became popular people normally play it on the street way) Therefore the number of accidents from roller-skating is increased. The skate manufacturer should have a responsibility in producing a protective clothing. They should promote and sell them together with skates. The government or state should set the regulation of playing skate on the street way like they did with the bicycle.

To prevent this kind of accident is the best solution but it needs a coorperation among us to have a concious mind to beware and realize its dangerous.

Score 1 Essay:

the protective equipment do help to reduce the risk of being severly injuryed in an accident since there are 75% Of those who had accidents in streets or parking lots were not wearing any protectivel clothing. such as hemlets, kenn pads, etc. or any light-reflecting materials such as clip-on lights, glow-in-the-dark wrist pads ets. if they do have protective eqipment that only a quarter accident may happen, also that can greatly reduce their risk ofbeing severly injuryed in an accident, that can save some lives and a lot of energy and money for the treatment. the protective equipment do help to reduce the risk of being severly injuryed in an accident since there are 75% Of those who had accidents in streets or parking lots were not wearing any protectivel clothing. such as hemlets, kenn pads, etc. or any light-reflecting materials such as clip-on lights, glow-in-the-dark wrist pads ets. if they do have protective eqipment that only a quarter accident may happen, also that can greatly reduce their risk ofbeing severly injuryed in an accident, that can save some lives and a lot of energy and money for the treatment. the protective equipment do help to reduce the risk of being severly injuryed in an accident since there are 75% Of those who had accidents in streets or parking lots were not wearing any protectivel clothing. such as hemlets, kenn pads, etc. or any light-reflecting materials such as clip-on lights, glow-in-the-dark wrist pads ets. if they do have protective eqipment that only a quarter accident may happen, also that can greatly reduce their risk ofbeing severly injuryed in an accident, that can save some lives and a lot of energy and money for the treatment.

Essay Readers' Commentary:

This fundamentally deficient response uncritically accepts the reasoning of the topic: "the protective equipment do help to reduce the risk of being severely injured in an accident." There is no evidence, though, that the writer is able to understand or analyze the argument; what follows, except for a few additional words, merely copies the topic. This two-sentence response is repeated—verbatim—two more times.

Language and usage are equally problematic. The few words that have been added, in combination with the words of the topic, results in incoherence. In sum, this essay fits all of the scoring guide descriptors for a 1.

Sample II

The University of Claria is generally considered one of the best universities in the world because of its instructors' reputation, which is based primarily on the extensive research and publishing record of certain faculty members. In addition, several faculty members are internationally renowned as leaders in their fields. For example, many of the faculty from the English department are regularly invited to teach at universities in other countries. Furthermore, two recent graduates of the physics department have gone on to become candidates for the Nobel Prize in Physics. And 75 percent of the students are able to find employment after graduating. Therefore, because of the reputation of its faculty, the University of Claria should be the obvious choice for anyone seeking a quality education.

Score 6 Essay:

While the University of Claria appears to have an excellent reputation based on the accomplishments and reputations of its faculty, one would also wish to consider other issues before deciding upon this particular institution for undergraduate or graduate training. The Physics and English departments are internationally known, but these are only two of the areas in which one might study. Other departments are not listed; is this because no others are worth mentioning, or because no other departments bothered to turn in their accomplishments and kudos to the publicity office?

The assumption is that because English and Physics have excellent brains in the faculty offices, their teaching skills and their abilities to pass on knowledge and the love of learning to their students are equally laudable. Unfortunately, this is often not the case. A prospective student would certainly be advised to investigate thoroughly the teaching talents and attitudes of the professors, the library and research facilities, the physical plant of the departments in which he or she was planning to study, as well as the living arrangements on or off campus, and the facilities available for leisure activities and entertainment.

This evaluation of the University of Claria is too brief, and too general. Nothing is mentioned about the quality of overall education; it only praises the accomplishments of a few recent graduates and professors. More important than invitations to teach elsewhere, which might have been engineered by their own departmental heads in an attempt to remove them from the campus for a semester or two, is the relationship between teacher and student. Are the teaching faculty approachable? Are they helpful? Have they an interest in passing on their knowledge? Are they working for the future benefit of the student or to get another year closer to retirement? How enthusiastic are the students about the courses being taught and the faculty members who teach those classes? Are there sufficient classes available for the number of students? Are the campus buildings accessible; how is the University handling all those cars? Is the University a pleasant, encouraging, interesting, challenging place to attend school? What are its attitudes about education, students, student ideas and innovations, faculty suggestions for improvement?

What about that 75% employment record? Were those students employed in the field of their choice, or are they flipping burgers and emptying wastebaskets while they search for something they are trained to do. A more specific statement about the employability of students from this University is needed in order to make the argument forceful.

The paragraph given merely scratches the surface of what must be said about this University in order to entice students and to convince them that this is the best place to obtain a quality education. Much more work is needed by the public relations department before this can be made into a four-color brochure and handed out to prospective students.

Essay Readers' Commentary:

The writer of this outstanding response acknowledges that the University of Claria may "appear" to have a sterling reputation, but cogently argues that such a reputation is perhaps unwarranted in light of the thin and misleading information provided. The paper's insightful critique targets several instances of unsound reasoning in the argument:

—that the argument identifies academic achievements in only two departments;

—that publications and research prove little about the quality of teaching at Claria; and

—that the student employment statistic lacks specificity and may be entirely bogus.

The writer probes each questionable assumption and offers alternative explanations, pointing out, for instance, that invitations for faculty to teach elsewhere may have been purposely arranged in order to temporarily remove them from campus and that the employed students may be "flipping burgers and emptying wastebaskets."

In addition, the response perceptively analyzes many features — omitted by the argument — that could more convincingly make the case that Claria is "the obvious choice." The writer suggests that the search for a quality education would, at least, need to investigate the teaching strengths of the faculty; ideally one would also ask about research facilities, the university's physical plant, availability of classes, even parking arrangements!

Although the fourth paragraph ("What about that 75% employment record?") interrupts this discussion, the response is, on the whole, logically and effectively organized. Each paragraph develops the central premise: that the argument is uncompelling because it fails to use more valid indices of educational quality.

The writing is succinct, graceful, and virtually error-free, distinguished by impressive diction ("kudos," "laudable," "engineered," "entice"), as well as syntactic sophistication. For all of these reasons, the response earns a 6.

Score 5 Essay:

While it is true that the facts presented in the above passage contribute to the idea that the University of Claria is a fine university, it can hardly be concluded from the propaganda that the University of Claria is the best university for every applicant. For example, it appears, based on the passage, that the University of Claria is largely a research-oriented university. No where in the passage, however, is the quality of the education discussed. The faculty/student ratio is not discussed. It is largely possible that while many of the faculty are teaching at universities in other countries, the students at U. Claria are left being taught by graduate students or non-doctoral instructors.

Secondly, the passage states that 75 percent of graduates from U. Claria find jobs. One wonders where these graduates obtained their jobs. It is possible that very few graduates are able to find work in their fields of major. The number of graduates who enroll in graduate school is also not disclosed. One would expect a large number of graduates from a research-oriented university to pursue research careers. These students would undoubedtly require a graduate school education, rather than simply a Bachelor's level degree. By stating that 75 percent of graduates find employment, the reader is left to wonder why these students entered the workforce, rather than graduate school, since graduates with Bachelor's level degrees often do not land research-oriented jobs.

Lastly, the socioeconomic status of the institution is not disclosed. Perhaps the University of Claria is an expensive school located in the heart of a large metropolitain city. Certain prospective applicants to the university may not be able to afford such a costly school, nor may the like the idea of living in a crowded metropolis. The fact that the argument leaves our the socioeconomic status of the school leads the reader to believe that the school perhaps has something to hide; perhaps its socioeconomic situation is not something it is proud of. In addition to the "sales pitch" passage, above, the argument should include facts that a diverse group of students may find useful, such as the cost of education and the quality of its teaching program. Only after evaluating all the facts might a student strongly agree that the University of Claria is one of the best universities in the world.

Essay Readers' Commentary:

After dismissing the argument's unsupported conclusion about the University of Claria, this strong response thoughtfully critiques the argument's presumptive line of reasoning. The response targets a root flaw in the argument's logic: that the data provided fail to constitute meaningful evidence of educational quality. The writer notes the lack of essential statistics—e.g., the faculty/student ratio—and argues quite effectively that invitations for faculty to teach in other countries may not be a reliable index of educational merit.

Paragraphs 2 and 3 address additional flaws in the argument:

—whether the 75% of employed graduates found work related to their majors;

—whether, in a research-oriented institution like Claria, it might not be expected that most graduates would go on to graduate school;

and

—whether Claria might not be affordable to all applicants or might be located in an area that some would find undesirable.

The analysis is clear, sensible, and logically organized, but development is neither as uniform nor as full as is required for a score of 6. Nor is the response as precise as a 6. In the final paragraph, for instance, references to Claria's cost are vaguely described as "the socioeconomic status of the institution."

The response exhibits generally good control of language, but awkward phrasing and inflated language sometimes result in a lack of clarity (e.g., "left being taught," "fields of major," "Bachelor's level degree"). Overall, this response merits a score of 5. It presents a well-developed and effectively written critique, but lacks the cogency, development, and insightfulness of a 6.

Score 4 Essay:

The argument states that anyone who is looking for a quality education should choose The Universtiy of Claria based on the instructors they have to offer. The argument assumes that students can learn better from faculty members who are internationally renowned and who have been invited to universities in other countries to teach. The proof of their argument rests on the fact that two recent graduates have been candidates for the Nobel Prize in Physics, and that 75 percent of their graduates find employment upon graduation.

According to the argument, strong faculty members help determine the quality of education that a student will recieve at a particular institution. The passage does not clearly state whether or not the faculty members that were included in the research were actually instructors. Neither does it offer any examples of the variables and procedures of the research. Assuming that the faculty members are actually instructors, their assumption would be a fair, for the students in the English and Physics departments. However, these examples are vague and would not allow a fair determination.

This argument does compare the findings with other universities which may compete. It assumes that a 75 percent graduate employment rate is one of the best employment rates of all schools, and that it is the only school whose graduates have been nominated for a Nobel Prize. It also doesn't say whether or not the graduates nominated actually won the Nobel Prize, and in fact, a candidate from another university may have done better.

The argument is not strong enough to be convincing to the reader. It needs to have more background information as to the type of research conducted to make the assumption, and it needs to have more examples of the strength of the faculty members and graduates. Finally, it needs to have comparisons with other universities and their competing credentials.

Essay Readers' Commentary:

While the first paragraph of this adequate response merely summarizes the argument, the remainder of the essay identifies and analyzes several significant flaws in the argument. The second paragraph intelligently questions whether the "renowned" faculty members actually teach; if so, the writer notes, the claim that Claria offers "a quality education" would still only be true for some departments. This is a relevant critique, but thinly developed and described with less clarity than is required for a score of 5.

The third paragraph continues to critique the argument's faulty logic. The writer points out that the employment statistic is deceptive since it hasn't been compared to rates at other universities, and that the argument never establishes that the "two recent graduates" won the Nobel Prize. These are apt criticisms, but minimally developed.

Organization is clear and logical, even better than adequate. The writer generally exhibits sufficient control, but awkward sentences and unclear pronoun referents ("their assumption would be a fair," "it needs to have comparisons with other universities and their competing credentials") demonstrate only adequate fluency. For these reasons, the paper deserves a score of 4.

Score 3 Essay:

Any university which is generally considered as one of the best universities in the world may not necessarily the best in all fields of studics. Also quality eduction doesn't mean that there is a lot of research. Quality eduction may be one that fulfill requirement of the country. Some of the developing country even don't have enough food or other basic requirement, so in those countries quality education is one that can fulfill a typical people requirement.

Another point is that 75% of the students are able to find employment after graduating. It is not necessarily avery high employment rate. If there are other universities, and 80% or more students from those universities are able to find employment after graduating and also there might not be extensive research then those ones might be the first choice for anyone seeking quality education.

Also reputation of the universities is based upon the extensive resrarch and publishing record of CERTAIN faculty members, and it doesn't mean that the other faculty members are also eqally capable.

So it is clear that reputation of its certain faculty, doesn't cause univ. of claria obivious choice for anyone seeking quality education. We know because 75% of students employed is maybe not high employment rate. Other universities may have 80% more students are able to find employment after graduating and also might be first choice.

Also, reputation of university might is based on the research and publishing record of certain faculty members, and it doesn't mean that other faculty are equally capable. Also quality education doesn't mean that there is alot of research. Quality eucation may be one that fulfill tequirment of the country. I think students who are considering universities to go to school should look at record and research record of all faculty and their departments, and what field of study they want. They should find out emplyment rates and reputation of university. They should also find out about student housing and money for students. Then they can make good choice.

Essay Readers' Commentary:

There is some competent reasoning in this limited response. However, tangential analysis, thin development, and an accumulation of both major and minor language errors mark it as obviously flawed.

The first sentence disputes the argument's claim, pointing out that Claria may not be the best "in all fields of studies." The rest of the paragraph, however, fails to add to or develop this critique. Indeed, the final sentence of the paragraph ("quality education is one that can fulfill a typical people requirement") is barely coherent.

Despite this weak beginning, the response goes on to offer two sensible reasons to question the assertion that Claria is the "obvious choice":

—The 75% employment rate may not be very high; other universities

may exceed this rate.

—All of Claria's faculty may not be equally capable.

There is a discernible organizational plan in this response, with an introductory paragraph, two analytical observations, and a concluding paragraph that offers a definitive rejection of the argument, repeats the main points, and goes on to offer advice. The writing, however, is less than competent. There are errors in grammar, usage, and mechanics that limit the writer's ability to convey meaning clearly. For this reason, and because the analysis is only thinly developed, the essay earns a score of 3.

Score 2 Essay:

I found this article moderately reasoned. One of the reasons I did not find this article well reasoned is due to the fact that there was no concrete evidence given to support some of the article's claims. For instance, the English department at the University might actually be as internationally renowned as mentioned but due to the lack of names, it makes the claims harder to believe. The abscence of names makes the members of the university, in the mind of the reader, seem like fictitious characters. Also, due to the notariety of the Nobel Peace Prize, it would have been beneficial to the article if the writer would have at least given the particular field the two anonymous winners received their prize, which once again puts doubt in the mind of the reader regarding the validity of the article or moreso the information the article contains. In essence the article had the potential to be very well-reasoned but due to the lack of more concrete information, the article was less believable.

> **Essay Readers' Commentary:**
>
> The first sentence of this seriously flawed response expresses some praise for the argument reasoning, leading the reader to expect an uncritical acceptance of the argument. Instead, the following sentences are apparently aimed at challenging the argument. What follows, though, is neither an agreement with the argument nor a logical critique.
>
> Rather than analyzing the unfounded claims, the essay complains about the lack of "concrete evidence." In particular, the writer believes that Claria's assertions would be more believable if the article included both the names of the "internationally renowned" faculty and the fields in which the two Claria graduates won Nobel Prizes. However, these are only superficial criticisms; there are glaring flaws in the argument, but the writer misses these. In addition, the second criticism is unfounded; the Nobel Prize category (physics) is mentioned in the argument, and the former Claria students are described only as "candidates," not as winners.
>
> There are grammatical errors (e.g., "the particular field the two anonymous winners received their prize") and imprecise word choices. For the most part, though, the writer's meaning is clear. The response merits only a 2 because it fails to logically analyze the argument.

Score 1 Essay:

Is true that University of Claria is generally consider one of the best university in world. Because instructors reputations. Because research and publishing record. Because teach in other countries. Because win Nobel prizes. Because find employment after graduating. But other school good just as Claria. Can be little money. Can be good teachers too.

> **Essay Readers' Commentary:**
>
> This fundamentally deficient response appears to recognize that the argument consists of a statement supported by reasons. However, there is no evidence of an ability to understand and analyze the argument. There is also no evidence of an ability to develop an organized response.
>
> In addition, there are severe and persistent errors in language and sentence structure. In the few instances where the language appears controlled, the phrasing is borrowed directly from the argument topic. For all these reasons, this response requires a score of 1.

Sample III

The following is taken from a memo from the advertising director of the Silver Screen Movie Production Company.

"According to a recent report from our marketing department, fewer people attended movies produced by Silver Screen during the past year than in any other year. And yet the percentage of generally favorable comments by movie reviewers about specific Silver Screen movies actually increased during this period. Clearly, the contents of these reviews are not reaching enough of our prospective viewers; so the problem lies not with the quality of our movies but with the public's lack of awareness that movies of good quality are available. Silver Screen should therefore spend more of its budget next year on reaching the public through advertising and less on producing new movies."

Score 6 Essay:

The argument presented above is relatively sound, however, the author fails to recognize all the elements necessary to evaluate his situation. The idea that more money be invested in advertising may be a helpful one, but perhaps not because people are unaware of the current reviews. To clarify, it may be necessary to advertise more in order to increase sales, however that could be due to many circumstances such as a decrease in the public's overall attendance, an increase in the cost of movies, or a lack of trust in the opinions of the reviewers.

The advertising director first needs to determine the relative proportion of movie goers that choose to see Silver Screen films. That will help him to understand his market share. If the population in general is attending less, then he may still be out-profiting his competitors, despite his individual sales decrease. In fact, his relative sales could be increasing. Determining where he stands in his market will help him to create and implement an action plan.

Another important thing to consider is the relative cost of attending movies to the current standard of living. If the standard of living is decreasing, it may contribute to an overall decrease in attendance. In that case, advertising could be very helpful, in that a clever campaign could emphasize the low cost of movies as compared to many other leisure activities. This could offset financial anxieties of potential customers.

Finally, it is important to remember that people rarely trust movie reviewers. For that reason, it is important that the films appeal to the populus, and not critics alone. The best advertisement in many cases is word of mouth. No matter what critics say, people tend to take the opinions of friends more seriously. This supports continual funding to produce quality movies that will appeal to the average person.

There is no reason that silver screen should not spend more on advertisement, however, there is reason to continue to invest in diverse, quality films. Furthermore, the company must consider carefully what it chooses to emphasize in its advertisement.

Essay Readers' Commentary:

Although the response begins by stating that the argument "is relatively sound," it immediately goes on to develop a critique. The response identifies three major flaws in the argument and provides a careful and thorough analysis. The main points discussed are that

—the fall-off in attendance might be industry wide

—the general state of the economy might have affected movie

attendance

—movie goers "rarely trust movie reviewers"

Each of these points is developed; together they are presented within the context of a larger idea: that while spending more money on advertising may be helpful, the company should "continue to invest in diverse, quality films."

This is a smoothly written, well-developed analysis in which syntactic variety and the excellent use of transitions make for a virtually seamless response. This paper clearly merits a score of 6.

Score 5 Essay:

The advertising director of Silver Screen should lose his job. It is clear that his analysis of the decrease in attendance in the past year was incomplete. A better qualified individual might have explored the issue further by doing several different things. First of all, surveys of the general population could provide a clue to the decreased viewership. They may find that people aren't as willing to pay the high prices anymore. A survey may also reveal that people are aware of Silver Screen, but opt not to see the films. An inspection of the nature of the films made by Silver Screen could also hint to the root of the problem. If Silver Screen produces a lot of the same type of movie, then the problem may be that they don't produce enough to appeal to the diverse interests of the population. For instance, if their movies typically contain excessive violence and foul language, parents won't take their children to these films. That is a significant portion of the potential viewing population lost.

The ad director mentions that reviewers liked specific films and gave more favorable reviews than in the past. But he neglects to mention the specific numbers- critics may have raved about 2 movies and turned their thumbs down the 10 others. If that's the case, it's no wonder that viewership has declined.

Spending more on advertising, and less on production, as the ad director suggests, could drive the company out of business. If the media builds a lot of hype over a new release that was poorly produced, people are more likely to be disappointed, and skeptical about future productions. This is certainly not in the company's best interests. What is in the company's best interest is a broader scope of the problem, and different approaches to solving it.

Essay Readers' Commentary:

This strong response begins with an attack on the advertising director of Silver Screen but quickly shifts to identifying major flaws in the argument. The main points of the critique are that

—the real reasons for a decline in viewership have not yet been identified;

—Silver Screen may not produce different kinds of movies to appeal to diverse interests;

—the number of favorably reviewed movies may actually have been very low; and

—spending money to produce a possibly poor movie could hurt rather than help the company.

Although more points are made here than are made in the sample 6 response on this topic, each of the points made in the 6 paper is developed. That is not the case here. In this response, each point is supported (by perhaps an additional sentence), but it is not further developed. The paper is smoothly organized with few but appropriate transitions. The writing is strong with some variety in syntax. For these reasons, this response earns a score of 5.

Score 4 Essay:

Although the reasoning in this arguement is logical, the writer failed to consider other reasons for the disparity between the percentage of people attending the company's movie and the percentage of favorable reviews. Perhaps the fault lies with the reviewers and not the production company; the public may not trust the critics' reviews. Another possibility for the attendance drop is that the general public does not find the subject matter of the movies enticing. If that were the case, spending less on producing new movies in an effort to re-direct funds to advertising could backfire by further limiting the types of movies available to the potential audience. Maybe the general public is simply not impressed with the critically-acclaimed qualities of the movies (such as eloquent screenplays, artful cinematography, and realistic acting) and and would prefer seeing flashy special effects and big-name stars. The possible reasons for the attendance decline are numerous; even aspects not directly related to the movie industry (such as the improving quality of television programming and the increasing popularity of home computer use) may play large roles. The company's management would be wise to consider and study the entire realm of possibilities before making drastic changes in its budget based on one statistical discovery.

Essay Readers' Commentary:

This response identifies and analyzes some important flaws in the argument. Although the number of points mentioned is the same as that in the sample 5 paper, this response remains at the 4 score level because the points of the critique are only minimally developed or supported.

The essay identifies four points:

—the public might not trust critics

—the movies' subject matter might not be appealing

—the public might prefer seeing special effects or big-name stars rather than good cinematography or realistic acting

—perhaps improvement in TV programming or increased use of home computers has kept people away from movie theaters

Ideas in the response are conveyed well and clearly; the use of language is generally strong. But the paper's "bare-bones" analysis gives it a list-like quality, It is therefore merely adequate and merits a score of 4.

Score 3 Essay:

This argument states the problem but the conclusion is not compatible to the rest of the statement.

Silver Screen recognized that fewer people attended movies in the studied year. I would recommend that they find out if this was happening with the entire movie market. It might of have been a poor year for movies for all movie companies.

Silver Screen recognized that of the movies that they did, they received favorable reviews. It should be concluded that they are doing well with the movies that they are making. Obviously, they are on track with the consumer in what they are producing.

I understand the conclusion that more people need to be exposed to the movies available for viewing. The last statement focuses on the fact that advertising needs to be increased, but does it by cutting production costs. This is wrong, instead of continuing what is working the company plans on focusing on advertising while taking away from producing. The consumers like the movies they make. If Silver Screen focuses their funds with advertising, producing funds will suffer. It will not matter how much advertising is done, if it is a poorly produced movie, nobody will want to go? Eventually, Silver Screen will get the reputation of producing bad movies. There has to be some compromise which doesn't hurt producing costs.

Essay Readers' Commentary:

This response is flawed. It makes two points, the first of which is undeveloped (paragraph 2) and the second of which (the remainder of the essay) is mainly discussion rather than analysis, although some meager analysis is present. The author also offers a questionable assumption of his or her own in stating in paragraph 4 that "the consumers like the movies they make." Overall, there is nothing incisive or convincing in this paper. It is loosely organized and not well developed.

The response is clear; what errors there are never interfere with a reader's understanding, but there are frequent minor errors in language, syntax, and punctuation.

For all of these reasons, the response is clearly limited and deserves a score of 3.

Score 2 Essay:

Americans are spending millions of their hard earned dollars to see the latest theatrical productions, and we here at Silver Screen want to exploit our share of that profit. Surveys have proven that our movies are better than ever, but yet our attendance is lower than ever. This finding screams one shortcoming: advertisement.

Try to think of the last movie you remember. The movie which probably leaps into everyone's mind is Independence Day. Why? Certainly not because of the actual film, but because of all the 'hype' which the movie received. Furthermore, this grand production paid off big for the production company.

Does anyone that you know drive by the theatre just to see what is playing and then pick a film based on the catchiness of the title? No Viewers buy tickets for movies which they have seen effectively advertised on television and radio.

Not only must Silver Screen advertise more, but we must advertise when it really counts: Monday Night Football, the evening news, awards shows, etc.

Everyone has heard the saying, "you must spend money to make money", and it is proven true in this industry.

From a completely economical standpoint, the ad is actually more important than the film itself. Consumers are compelled by the preview and buy a ticket. I am not suggesting that we compromise the integrity of our films, but I cannot overstate the importance of this decision.

Therefore, I submit that the Silver Screen Production Company attempt to secure 30% of the fiscal budget for advertisement. It will be the best money you have ever spent.

Essay Readers' Commentary:

The writer of this seriously flawed response has adopted the position that she or he works for Silver Screen and that it is her or his job to present in expanded form the fallacious reasoning of the argument. In so doing, the writer turns the argument task into an issue-like discussion. The writer presents no analysis of the argument.

The paper is characterized by a series of undeveloped paragraphs, yet there is some variety in syntax and there is adequate control of both language and the elements of writing. However, even though the writing may be typical of a 4 score level, the absence of any kind of critique requires a score of 2.

Score 1 Essay:

The author make a conclusion that Silver Screen should spend more of its budget next year on reaching the public through advertising and less on producing new movies. Becase the author think the public is lack of awareness that movies quality are available. Althogh the percentage of generally favorable comments by movie reviews actually increased during this period, it is the opnion of the movie reviews which not stand for the reviews of the most people. So these fact is not sufficient provide the conclusion. Furthermore the author think we need let more prospective viewer have the same opnion of the movie viewer. It is not unreasonable that it will decrease his inference. So I don't think it is a good conclusion for Silver Screen to spend more money on advertise instead of improve the quality of movie.

Essay Readers' Commentary:

This fundamentally flawed response is characterized by three essential deficiencies:

—It provides little evidence of the ability to understand and analyze the argument.

—It provides little evidence of the ability to develop an organized response.

—It contains a pervasive pattern of errors in grammar and usage that results in incoherence.

Where the language makes sense and looks controlled, the writer has relied on the language and phrasing of the argument topic. Where the writer has relied on her or his own knowledge and command of language and syntax, we see serious and fundamental deficiencies. Thus, this response requires a score of 1.

Sample IV

In surveys Mason City residents rank water sports (swimming, boating and fishing) among their favorite recreational activities. The Mason River flowing through the city is rarely used for these pursuits, however, and the city park department devotes little of its budget to maintaining riverside recreational facilities. For years there have been complaints from residents about the quality of the river's water and the river's smell. In response, the state has recently announced plans to clean up Mason River. Use of the river for water sports is therefore sure to increase. The city government should for that reason devote more money in this year's budget to riverside recreational facilities.

Write a response in which you examine the stated and/or unstated assumptions of the argument. Be sure to explain how the argument depends on the assumptions and what the implications are if the assumptions prove unwarranted.

Score 6 Essay:

While it may be true that the Mason City government ought to devote more money to riverside recreational facilities, this author's argument does not make a cogent case for increased resources based on river use. It is easy to understand why city residents would want a cleaner river, but this argument is rife with holes and assumptions, and thus, not strong enough to lead to increased funding.

Citing surveys of city residents, the author reports city resident's love of water sports. It is not clear, however, the scope and validity of that survey. For example, the survey could have asked residents if they prefer using the river for water sports or would like to see a hydroelectric dam built, which may have swayed residents toward river sports. The sample may not have been representative of city residents, asking only those residents who live upon the river. The survey may have been 10 pages long, with 2 questions dedicated to river sports. We just do not know. Unless the survey is fully representative, valid, and reliable, it can not be used to effectively back the author's argument.

Additionally, the author implies that residents do not use the river for swimming, boating, and fishing, despite their professed interest, because the water is polluted and smelly. While a polluted, smelly river would likely cut down on river sports, a concrete connection between the resident's lack of river use and the river's current state is not effectively made. Though there have been complaints, we do not know if there have been numerous complaints from a wide range of people, or perhaps from one or two individuals who made numerous complaints. To strengthen his/her argument, the author would benefit from implementing a normed survey asking a wide range of residents why they do not currently use the river.

Building upon the implication that residents do not use the river due to the quality of the river's water and the smell, the author suggests that a river clean up will result in increased river usage. If the river's water quality and smell result from problems which can be cleaned, this may be true. For example, if the decreased water quality and aroma is caused by pollution by factories along the river, this conceivably could be remedied. But if the quality and aroma results from the natural mineral deposits in the water or surrounding rock, this may not be true. There are some bodies of water which emit a strong smell of sulphur due to the geography of the area. This is not something likely to be affected by a clean-up. Consequently, a river clean up may have no impact upon river usage. Regardless of whether the river's quality is able to be improved or not, the author does not effectively show a connection between water quality and river usage.

A clean, beautiful, safe river often adds to a city's property values, leads to increased tourism and revenue from those who come to take advantage of the river, and a better overall quality of life for residents. For these reasons, city government may decide to invest in improving riverside recreational facilities. However, this author's argument is not likely significantly persuade the city government to allocate increased funding.

Essay Readers' Commentary:

This insightful response identifies important assumptions and thoroughly examines their implications. The proposal to spend more on riverside recreational facilities rests on three questionable assumptions, namely:

- that the survey provides a reliable basis for budget planning
- that the river's pollution and odor are the only reasons for its limited recreational use
- that efforts to clean the water and remove the odor will be successful

By showing that each assumption is highly suspect, this essay demonstrates the weakness of the entire argument. For example, paragraph 2 points out that the survey might not have used a representative sample, might have offered limited choices, and might have contained very few questions on water sports.

Paragraph 3 examines the tenuous connection between complaints and limited use of the river for recreation. Complaints about water quality and odor may be coming from only a few people and, even if such complaints are numerous, other completely different factors may be much more significant in reducing river usage. Finally, paragraph 4 explains that certain geologic features may prevent effective river clean-up. Details such as these provide compelling support.

In addition, careful organization ensures that each new point builds upon the previous ones. For example, note the clear transitions at the beginning of paragraphs 3 and 4, as well as the logical sequence of sentences within paragraphs (specifically paragraph 4).

Although this essay does contain minor errors, it still conveys ideas fluently. Note the effective word choices (e.g., "rife with...assumptions" and "may have swayed residents"). In addition, sentences are not merely varied; they also display skillful embedding of subordinate elements. For example, note the sustained parallelism in the first sentence of the concluding paragraph.

Since this response offers cogent examination of the argument and conveys meaning skillfully, it earns a score of 6.

Score 5 Essay:

The author of this proposal to increase the budget for Mason City riverside recreational facilities offers an interesting argument but to move forward on the proposal would definitely require more information and thought. While the correlations stated are logical and probable, there may be hidden factors that prevent the City from diverting resources to this project.

For example, consider the survey rankings among Mason City residents. The thought is that such high regard for water sports will translate into usage. But, survey responses can hardly be used as indicators of actual behavior. Many surveys conducted after the winter holidays reveal people who list exercise and weight loss as a top priority. Yet every profession does not equal a new gym membership. Even the wording of the survey results remain ambiguous and vague. While water sports may be among the residents' favorite activities, this allows for many other favorites. What remains unknown is the priorities of the general public. Do they favor these water sports above a softball field or soccer field? Are they willing to sacrifice the municipal golf course for better riverside facilities? Indeed the survey hardly provides enough information to discern future use of improved facilities.

Closely linked to the surveys is the bold assumption that a cleaner river will result in increased usage. While it is not illogical to expect some increase, at what level will people begin to use the river? The answer to this question requires a survey to find out the reasons our residents use or do not use the river. Is river water quality the primary limiting factor to usage or the lack of docks and piers? Are people more interested in water sports than the recreational activities that they are already engaged in? These questions will help the city government forecast how much river usage will increase and to assign a proportional increase to the budget.

Likewise, the author is optimistic regarding the state promise to clean the river. We need to hear the source of the voices and consider any ulterior motives. Is this a campaign year and the plans a campaign promise from the state representative? What is the timeline for the clean-up effort? Will the state fully fund this project? We can imagine the misuse of funds in renovating the riverside facilities only to watch the new buildings fall into dilapidation while the state drags the river clean-up.

Last, the author does not consider where these additional funds will be diverted from. The current budget situation must be assessed to determine if this increase can be afforded. In a sense, the City may not be willing to draw money away from other key projects from road improvements to schools and education. The author naively assumes that the money can simply appear without forethought on where it will come from.

Examining all the various angles and factors involved with improving riverside recreational facilities, the argument does not justify increasing the budget. While the proposal does highlight a possibility, more information is required to warrant any action.

Essay Readers' Commentary:

Each paragraph in the body of this perceptive essay identifies and examines an unstated assumption that is crucial to the argument. The major assumptions discussed are:

- that a survey can accurately predict behavior
- that cleaning the river will, in itself, increase recreational usage
- that state plans to clean the river will actually be realized
- that Mason City can afford to spend more on riverside recreational facilities

Support within each paragraph is both thoughtful and thorough. For example, paragraph 2 points out vagueness in the wording of the survey: Even if water sports rank *among* the favorite recreational activities of Mason City residents, other sports may still be much more popular. Thus, if the first assumption proves unwarranted, the argument to fund riverside facilities—rather than soccer fields or golf courses—becomes much weaker. Paragraph 4 considers several reasons why river clean-up plans may not be successful (the plans may be nothing more than campaign promises or funding may not be adequate). Thus, the weakness of the third assumption undermines the argument that river recreation will increase and riverside improvements will be needed at all.

Instead of dismissing each assumption in isolation, this response places them in a logical order and considers their connections. Note the appropriate transitions between and within paragraphs, clarifying the links among the assumptions (e.g., "Closely linked to the surveys..." or "The answer to this question requires...").

Along with strong development, this response also displays facility with language. Minor errors in punctuation are present, but word choices are apt and sentences suitably varied in pattern and length. The response uses a number of rhetorical questions, but the implied answers are always clear enough to support the points being made.

Thus, the response satisfies all requirements for a score of 5, but its development is not thorough or compelling enough for a 6.

Score 4 Essay:

The problem with the arguement is the assumption that if the Mason River were cleaned up, that people would use it for water sports and recreation. This is not necessarily true, as people may rank water sports among their favorite recreational activities, but that does not mean that those same people have the financial ability, time or equipment to pursue those interests.

However, even if the writer of the arguement is correct in assuming that the Mason River will be used more by the city's residents, the arguement does not say why the recreational facilities need more money. If recreational facilities already exist along the Mason River, why should the city allot more money to fund them? If the recreational facilities already in existence will be used more in the coming years, then they will be making more money for themselves, eliminating the need for the city government to devote more money to them.

According to the arguement, the reason people are not using the Mason River for water sports is because of the smell and the quality of water, not because the recreational facilities are unacceptable.

If the city government alloted more money to the recreational facilities, then the budget is being cut from some other important city project. Also, if the assumptions proved unwarranted, and more people did not use the river for recreation, then much money has been wasted, not only the money for the recreational facilities, but also the money that was used to clean up the river to attract more people in the first place.

Essay Readers' Commentary:

This competent response identifies two unstated assumptions:

- that cleaning up the Mason River will lead to increased recreational use
- that existing facilities along the river need more funding

Paragraph 1 offers reasons why the first assumption is questionable (e.g., residents may not have the necessary time or money for water sports). Similarly, paragraphs 2 and 3 explain that riverside recreational facilities may already be adequate and may, in fact, produce additional income if usage increases. Thus, the response is adequately developed and satisfactorily organized to show how the argument depends on questionable assumptions.

However, this essay does not rise to a score of 5 because it fails to consider several other unstated assumptions (e.g., that the survey is reliable or that the efforts to clean the river will be successful). Furthermore, the final paragraph makes some extraneous, unsupported assertions of its own. Mason City may actually have a budget surplus so that cuts to other projects will not be necessary, and cleaning the river may provide other real benefits even if it is not used more for water sports.

This response is generally free of errors in grammar and usage and displays sufficient control of language to support a score of 4.

Score 3 Essay:

Surveys are created to speak for the people; however, surveys do not always speak for the whole community. A survey completed by Mason City residents concluded that the residents enjoy water sports as a form of recreation. If that is so evident, why has the river not been used? The blame can not be soley be placed on the city park department. The city park department can only do as much as they observe. The real issue is not the residents use of the river, but their desire for a more pleasant smell and a more pleasant sight. If the city government cleans the river, it might take years for the smell to go away. If the budget is changed to accomodate the clean up of the Mason River, other problems will arise. The residents will then begin to complain about other issues in their city that will be ignored because of the great emphasis being placed on Mason River. If more money is taken out of the budget to clean the river an assumption can be made. This assumption is that the budget for another part of cit maintenance or building will be tapped into to. In addition, to the budget being used to clean up Mason River, it will also be allocated in increasing riverside recreational facilites. The government is trying to appease its residents, and one can warrant that the role of the government is to please the people. There are many assumptions being made; however, the government can not make the assumption that people want the river to be cleaned so that they can use it for recreational water activities. The government has to realize the long term effects that their decision will have on the monetary value of their budget.

Essay Readers' Commentary:

Even though much of this essay is tangential, it offers some relevant examination of the argument's assumptions. The early sentences mention a questionable assumption (that the survey results are reliable) but do not explain how the survey might have been flawed. Then the response drifts to irrelevant matters—a defense of the city park department, a prediction of budget problems and the problem of pleasing city residents.

Some statements even introduce unwarranted assumptions that are not part of the original argument (e.g., "The residents will then begin to complain about other issues" and "This assumption is that the budget for another part of city maintenance or building will be tapped into"). Near the end, the response does correctly note that city government should not assume that residents want to use the river for recreation. Hence, the proposal to increase funding for riverside recreational facilities may not be justified.

In summary, the language in this response is reasonably clear, but its examination of unstated assumptions remains limited and therefore earns a score of 3.

Score 2 Essay:

This statement looks like logical, but there are some wrong sentences in it which is not logical.

First, this statement mentions raking water sports as their favorite recreational activities at the first sentence. However, it seems to have a ralation between the first sentence and the setence which mentions that increase the quality of the river's water and the river's smell. This is a wrong cause and result to solve the problem.

Second, as a reponse to the complaints from residents, the state plan to clean up the river. As a result, the state expects that water sports will increase. When you look at two sentences, the result is not appropriate for the cause.

Third, the last statement is the conclusion. However, even though residents rank water sports, the city government might devote the budget to another issue. This statement is also a wrong cause and result.

In summary, the statement is not logical because there are some errors in it. The supporting setences are not strong enough to support this issue.

Essay Readers' Commentary:

Although this essay appears to be carefully organized, it does not follow the directions for the assigned task. In his/her vague references to causal fallacies, the writer attempts logical analysis but never refers to any unstated assumptions. Furthermore, several errors in grammar and sentence structure interfere with meaning (e.g., "This statement looks like logical, but there are some wrong sentences in it which is not logical").

Because this response "does not follow the directions for the assigned task" and contains errors in sentence structure and logical development, it earns a score of 2.

Score 1 Essay:

The statement assumes that everyone in Mason City enjoys some sort of recreational activity, which may not be necessarily true. They statement also assumes that if the state cleans up the river, the use of the river for water sports will definitely increase.

Essay Readers' Commentary:

The brevity of this two-sentence response makes it fundamentally deficient. Sentence 1 states an assumption that is actually not present in the argument, and sentence 2 correctly states an assumption but provides no discussion of its implications. Although the response may begin to address the assigned task, it offers no development. As such, it is clearly "extremely brief ... providing little evidence of an organized response" and should earn a score of 1.

附录8:
与ISSUE题目相关的泛读材料

新版ISSUE题库数目庞大,题目涉及的内容颇为繁杂。部分题目涉及的内容/话题不仅让人感觉陌生,而且还较为抽象。但正如前面所讲,凭我们的常识就可以对付所有的ISSUE题目。写作的关键在于学会如何展开对题目的分析,而这一点在"1+5"写作模型部分已详细讲过。

但是,新版ISSUE题库中的149道题目还有这样的特点:它们涉及的内容具有相当高的集中度。比如,传统和现代、历史和现实、理性/理智和情感、科技和社会(人性/伦理)、竞争与合作、知识的本质、教育的目的等内容都直接或间接地体现在相当数量的题目之中。这里所选的14个话题(共计15篇文章)是与所有ISSUE题目相关度最高的主题。阅读这些文章会有利于我们展开思路、熟悉复杂和抽象概念的表达方式、找到使用地道英语写作的感觉。

当然,我们不可能将所有与ISSUE题目内容相关的文章都放到这里,而且也没必要。对于类似于批评和表扬哪个更有利于实现教育的目的、学生应如何计划自己的将来这些话题,大家只要稍加思索即有心得,没必要在这里增加大家的复习工作量。这里所选的文章意在突出一些话题哲学思辨的特点,因而可能会让一些同学感觉第一遍读起来有些困难。但只要多一点耐心,绝大多数同学读起来应该毫无问题。

最后强调一点:这些文章只适合读,不适合背;只适合启发思路,不宜照搬(尤其不要整段照搬到考场作文之中)。切记切记!

1. The Value of History

What's in History?

By Michael J. Ring

Having served as the capital of the Confederate States of America, the city of Richmond, Virginia has seen its share of triumph, tragedy, strife, and bloodshed. As such it holds an important place in the annals of American history. Unfortunately, the parks and battlefields dotting the regional landscape do not seem to hold much of a place at all in locals' and visitors' minds.

This summer I spent a few short hours in Richmond and had an opportunity to see a couple of the historic sites around the city. Apparently I was one of a very select few people to have this desire. In fact, in an hour spent at Cold Harbor National Battlefield, a friend and I were the only visitors.

Admittedly, the battlefields around Richmond are not as famous or as historically significant as turning points like Gettysburg and Vicksburg. Still, Richmond and its suburbs are nearly one million strong, and between natives and visitors somebody should show just a little more interest in its history.

Of course, I didn't have to go to Virginia to see history ignored. Boston, after all, is a city of the greatest historical importance where many natives and tourists alike show more interest in Filene's Basement than the Old North Church. When was the last time that you walked the Freedom Trail?

As we enter the Third American Century, Americans know all too little about the first two. As a nation, we don't visit historical sites, don't learn our nation's stories, and don't recognize the people and places that shaped this nation.

So why is all this important? Humanists love to expound upon the importance of history as a reflection of our culture and our mind. But on more practical terms, there are very important reasons for studying history. And as we approach new challenges as a nation, our lack of appreciation for history has stopped being just a nuisance and annoyance to crabby history buffs such as myself. Indeed, our ignorance will harm our nation's ability to solve national and world problems in our next century.

First off, Americans' habitual ignorance of the political process and our lack of awareness and respect for our history are intertwined. Those who know history can more fully appreciate the powers available in our political process. Americans who whine about their votes not counting would be wise to study an election such as 1960where contests were decided by mere fractions of percentage points. Great political achievements such as the economic protections of the New Deal and the civil rights legislation of the 1960s were made possible only by a bloc of voters committed to those programs. The pundits of political doom can be proven wrong by a committed electorate—Harry S. Truman is testament to that.

Beside a greater appreciation for our political process, an understanding of history offers us policy lessons as well. Many of the challenges facing our nation today were also examined in similar situations in the past.

Take, for example, the sentiment among the political right that international political bodies are harmful to United States sovereignty. Organizations such as the United Nations are favorite targets of conservative Republican wrath. I suggest those political isolationists who favor a smaller role for America on the world stage need only look back some eighty years, to the aftermath of the First World War. The United States, fearful of losing its sovereignty, chose not to join the League of Nations. Without the world s most powerful nation, the League was hapless to halt German and Japanese military aggression and expansion, and the rest is history.

Of course, it is not only conservatives who need to hit the history books in order to deduce a solution to one of today's problems. Many liberals defend bilingual education as the best way to incorporate immigrant children into the American educational system. But time and again in social history, through various immigrant groups, immersion in English proves to be the ticket to American prosperity. The sooner an immigrant group can grasp full command of English, the more quickly the group will enjoy success in American society.

Of course, we do not have the room in these pages to explore fully the issues in these summaries, nor can we discuss other historical situations from which we can learn answers to today's problems. But hopefully we can see the value of history's lessons for today's problems, and decide that in looking to the future, we should also take a glance at the past.

(Readers can find the original at http://tech.mit.edu/V119/N31/col31ring2.31c.html)

2. The Meaning of Life

What Our Life Should Be Like?

By M. Fethullah Gulen

Are all of life's hardships worth enduring? The answer depends on what our goal is in living. In fact, understanding life's purpose is a slow and absorbing process. We sense its mystery while reflecting upon our existence and humanity. Therefore, our concept of life evolves gradually throughout our lives.

The purpose of our creation is obvious: to reach our utmost goals of belief, knowledge, and spirituality; to reflect on the universe and humanity, and thus prove our value as human beings. Fulfilling this ideal is possible only through systematic thinking and systematic behavior. Thought will provoke action, and thereby start a "prosperous cycle." This cycle will produce more complex cycles, generating between the heart's spirituality and the brain's knowledge, and thereby develop ever-more complex ideas and produce larger projects.

Carrying out such a process calls for strong belief, consciousness, and understanding. People with these characteristics can realize and analyze the unreflective lifestyles of others. Such people think, do what they believe to be right, and then reflect upon their behavior, thereby continually deepening their thoughts and acquiring new ideas. They believe that only those who reflect deeply are productive, and that the pain and suffering they endure makes their belief stronger and more acceptable.

They live a life of reflection by observing their souls within and the world without every day, sometimes reading it like a book or embroidering their minds with the wisdom they acquire. They believe that the universe was created to be "read" and understood, and that the purpose of our lives must be nothing but that.

On its own, existence of our lives is the very bounty that leads us to a prosperous path of bounties. Given this, we should appreciate its value. Since we were created, as was a whole universe of bounties, we must use these gifts and benefit from them.

To reach this goal, we must use our willpower, a voice heard by the universe around us, and develop our abilities and skills to their furthest extent, thus proving ourselves to be willful beings. Our duty is to reflect upon our place in life, our responsibilities, and our relationship with this vast universe. We should use our inner thoughts to explore the hidden side of the surrounding world. As we do so, we will begin to feel a deeper sense of our selves, see things differently, witness that events are not what they seem, and realize that events are trying to communicate something to us.

I believe that this should be life's real purpose. We are the most important living creation in this universe. In fact, we are more like its soul and essence from which the rest of the universe develops. Given this, we should reflect upon and observe it so that we may realize and fulfill the purpose of our creation. Our duty is to hunt for insights and divine joys in our hearts and souls, for only this way of life can move us beyond the frustrating endeavors of a totally materialistic and painful life.

What makes this painful life worth living is the joy we feel while moving along the path and receiving the gifts we are given. Those who walk this path are constantly delighted with various insights. They run enthusiastically toward their final goal like a river flowing to the sea.

We do not believe that happiness comes from temporary outer sources. True happiness comes from within. Our inner world is a realm of divine insights, and our consciousness is a follower of these insights. As we beckon and wait all our lives for the slightest glimpse, our souls sing in utter pleasure.

(Readers can find the original at http://www.mlife.org/content/view/54/69/)

3. Intellect vs. Emotion

Which One, Intellect or Emotion, is More Important?

By O. C. Hampton

In looking around us and into the general structure of the universe, the most palpable and obvious departments we can discover therein are the final ones of male and female. The origin of these may be traced to the no less palpable principles of wisdom and love, a duality observable in all the dispensations of Divine Providence, and for aught we know to the contrary, a duality constituting the Infinite mind itself.

This matter of duality receives amongst mankind the several names of positive and negative, active and passive, male and female, love and wisdom, differentiating all things into a constant duality without any exception. Intellect and emotion in man are merely finite manifestations of the dual principles of wisdom and love, transmuted to the sublime offices of reason and religion in man. The first is necessary to develop, define, explain, to illustrate the character as well as necessity of discipline, self-government, church government, organization, order and regulations, necessary to the existence of it self-perpetuating community. The second is necessary to the development of the religions sentiment, together with all the Pentecostal gifts, inspirations, ministrations from the spirit world, prophecies, tongues, healings of disease, together with all sympathy for human sufferings, going out of one's self to do good to others. Unless these principles of wisdom and love are equally and normally developed in the individual—his or her efforts to attain to spiritual perfection must necessarily be abortive.

An individual all composed of intellect is a monster who needs regenerating to ever become normal. One who is all emotion is in the same degree abnormal, and needs reconstructing quite as well. The golden mean between these extremes is a well-balanced mind, under the influence of a thoughtful, serene and unostentatious wisdom, and at the same time so thoroughly imbued with love, good-will and sympathy toward others as to develop a high standard of social benevolence to all and without partiality.

I often feel a solid concern, that I accordingly labor earnestly to resolve in myself this happy normal medium in order to become as useful and highly beneficial to society as possible. Intellect relates to all matters within the domain of reason. Emotion relates to all those indescribably grand and important matters within the domain of religion and inspiration, often transcending the bounds of reason, but never necessarily contradicting her suggestion. Intellect enables us to search into all truth that can be discovered by logical research, experiment and analysis.

Emotion presents to its the beauty of holiness, the peace of righteousness, love to each other, sympathy and tenderness toward the suffering, the glory and perfect splendor of purity, and often opens up a vista of sublimity and glory far-reaching even into the serenest recesses of heaven itself. And yet intellect and emotion are so perfectly correlated that one is in every way and under all circumstances necessary to the other, in the highest and most harmonious development of which humanity is capable.

If one is so far overborne by the other that spontaneity in the direction of either is forestalled or annihilated, the abnormal results of mental and spiritual disaster and sorrow are sure to follow, and persistently continue until the normal equilibrium is restored.

I found in my earlier experiences great need to strenuously watch and regulate these powers of intellect and emotion, and cultivate them with regard to something like a consistent balance. I found my emotions sometimes so far in the ascendant that I was in great danger of turning fool on my own hands and going into ecstasies beyond all bounds of consistency or propriety. At other times my intellect would become so positive and persistently concentrated upon some abstruse study or question, that I could not relinquish my grasp of it.

I remember once of being so persistently beset with a problem in algebra that I could scarcely keep it out of my mind for a moment, even while at religious worship. Hereupon I shut my algebra and did not open it again for more than two years. By this means in similar cases I restored my normal condition of mind and gradually disciplined myself into a condition equally removed from both intellectual and emotional extremes.

We must be thoughtful upon this matter of healthy development of mind, or we may have to regret having spent a useless life among the Arctic icebergs of an intellectual North Pole, or in traversing an equatorial Sahara of emotional enthusiasm, neither of which will confer much happiness upon the individual, and still less blessing and benefit to the community.

(The piece is excerpted from *The Shaker Manifesto*, Vol. X, No. 10, October, 1880.)

4. Purpose of Education

Toward Good Thinking On Essential Questions

By Howard Gardner

As one concerned with pre-college education, I'm gratified by the attention paid to this topic over the last two decades. At the same time I have to signal my uneasiness that so much of the discussion centers on means: Should we have charters, vouchers, teachers' unions, national tests etc. I think it is essential that we step back, at least periodically, and ask about the ends or aims of education.

My own answer can be stated succinctly. A dozen or more years of education should yield students who can think well about the essential questions of human life: Who are we, where do we come from, what's the world made of, what have humans achieved and what can we achieve, how does one lead a good life? Many people, institutions and experiences can contribute to formulating these questions and the answers. The distinct contribution of formal education is to equip students with the ways of thinking, the scholarly disciplines that have been constructed over the years to allow individuals to think well and deeply about these questions and some viable answers.

In speaking of disciplines, I have something specific in mind. Disciplines did not always exist; they are human-created methods and structures for approaching long-standing puzzles. Historians evaluate documents and testimony to reconstruct plausible accounts of past events. Scientists generate hypotheses about how the world works, collect data relevant to those hypotheses, analyze the data objectively and then revise or endorse the original hypotheses or theories. The arts are also disciplines: they involve clear procedures for production (how does one write a fugue, stage a ballet, render a portrait) and for interpreting the productions of others. For those inclined to dismiss the disciplines, imagine a world without such mental furniture.

By a convenient pun, the attainment of disciplines requires discipline. This is because our natural, common-sense ways of making sense of the world are non- or even anti-disciplinary. Only through years of asking questions and following well-honed strategies can we replace common-sense accounts (e. g., human beings have always existed, the best portraits are photographs) with more nuanced and grounded disciplinary accounts.

The disciplines are arguably the most important human inventions of the last two millenniums. Yet their importance tends to be obscured, especially in the rhetoric-filled discourse of education. Instead, we hear a lot about facts, skills, tests and subject matter. None of these terms should be dismissed, but they attain fresh significance when they are considered in a disciplinary context.

First, skills. I know no one who opposes the acquisition of basic skills: reading, writing, and arithmetic. One cannot even enter the disciplinary worlds unless one has mastered the three R's. Basic skills are the means for acquiring the disciplines, just as the disciplines (and ultimately interdisciplinary amalgams) provide the means for thinking well about important issues.

Next, facts. You cannot think well about a topic or question unless you have information, data, and facts. However, that information should be acquired not for its own sake but as a means of finding a better answer to a consequential question. Facts can only be well used if they relate to one another in a meaningful way: otherwise, they are simply "inert knowledge." Facts need the connective tissue of disciplines, or they are undisciplined, rote information.

Subject matter is typically collapsed with disciplines, but it is important to honor a distinction. One can have lots of facts in a subject without having any disciplinary understanding. Too often a person is considered a master because she or he has taken a certain number of courses, often called Carnegie units. A person understands to the extent that he or she can apply knowledge appropriately in a new situation. Only an individual in possession of disciplinary moves can do this.

Which brings us to tests, or assessments. There may be some who oppose assessments, but I am not in their ranks. Not in the least! At the same time, I reject as inadequate most of the short-answer instruments currently being adopted at the state level. These instruments may probe factual or subject-matter knowledge, but they typically fall short of probing disciplinary mastery and understanding. In life no one presents us with four choices, the last of which reads "none of the above."

I favor instruments that actually determine whether a person can think in a disciplined way. So rather than ask students to name nine Civil War battles, I would ask them to assess two historical accounts based on the same primary documents (or create their own). Rather than asking students to recall a chemical formula, I would provide them with data from an experiment and ask them to extract the regularities (and perhaps indicate which other data need to be collected next). Rather than asking students to memorize authors or lines from a poem, I would ask them to edit or complete an unfinished poem.

Every educational philosophy reflects a certain knowledge base and a certain value system. My educational regimen builds on findings from cognitive science. These findings indicate that, when young, individuals develop intuitive theories that are very powerful and difficult to eradicate. While some are on the mark, most are remote from the disciplines. Only a concerted effort over years to establish disciplinary ways of thinking can eradicate or educate the unschooled mind. My own belief is that this goal is best achieved by focusing in depth on certain important topics; not only does one come to understand those topics well, but in the process one gains incipient mastery for what it is like to use the methods of a discipline.

This incipient mastery can be built upon for the rest of one's life. I am idealistic enough to believe that once individuals have genuinely understood a theory like evolution, a historical period like the Holocaust, a work of art like "The Marriage of Figaro," they will insist on commensurate understanding of other topics in the future.

Pursuing this line of reasoning, I find myself out of sympathy with a preordained canon. One can acquire disciplinary ways of thinking from a variety of topics, and it simply does not matter that much which ones happen to be used. It is more important, in my view, to use examples that are valued by the community and that come alive for students than to insist that everyone read the same play or master the same theorem or learn the same topics in science. I don't care that much if one can name the planets; one can always request that information from a Palm Pilot. I care mightily that half of the American population (and perhaps some of our recent Presidents) can't distinguish astronomical from astrological ways of thinking and that two-thirds of Americans don't see the disciplinary difference between evolutionary and creationist accounts of the origins of human beings.

In putting forth these views, I find myself at odds with much of the program put forth by E. D. Hirsch Jr. Perhaps it is possible to reconcile our work to some extent—for example, by emphasizing his "Core Knowledge" in early grades and my disciplinary focus for the later grades. I have admiration for his democratic vision, his belief in public education and his sponsoring of programs in our schools. Still I think it is valuable to put forth these quite different educational visions: one focusing on questions and on ways of thinking, the other on factual answers and on shared knowledge. The value is in part epistemological, different views of the mind's use; in part cultural, different views of an educated society.

(This piece was originally published in *New York Times*, 1999.)

What Do Tests Test?

By Howard Gardner

A few years ago I sat in on a discussion in Chicago where local political and educational leaders crowed over rising scores on a standardized test for public school children. I broke in to ask some questions: Was it not true that whenever a new version of a test was adopted, scores quickly dropped? And wasn't it the case that scores recovered over the next few years as students and teachers became accustomed to the test?

The group conceded that this was indeed the pattern. The city's test had been administered a dozen times by then. It was obvious that students were not learning important skills; they were learning how to take a certain kind of test. The testing tail was wagging the academic dog.

The Chicago story could be replayed across the country. Most states have adopted new academic standards, and many are beginning to ratchet up standardized testing, too. Kentucky introduced new exams eight years ago that are far more demanding than the Chicago ones, but has rescinded them under pressure from parents and teachers because the scores at some schools have remained stubbornly low. Virginia and Massachusetts have had disappointing yearly results with their new testing.

Early next year, fourth graders in New York State will have to take a new reading and writing test that differs considerably from the previous format. Rather than the old multiple-choice approach, two-thirds of the new three-day exam involves writing critiques and personal essays. The aim is to promote analytical writing skills as well as reading proficiency.

But already a number of teachers are reportedly afraid that they'll be judged by the performance of ill-prepared students, and parents have expressed concern that their children's scores will be considered in applications for gifted programs and selective middle schools.

Should such new tests be embraced as a necessary medicine or are they yet another useless exercise in the perennial struggle to improve public education? It is a mistake to polarize the debate: there are good and poor ways of conducting tests. It makes more sense to ask what we are trying to achieve and then to make decisions accordingly. With any proposed test, I always ask four questions.

Does it focus on something indisputably important?

Does it test the desired skill directly, or does it use other methods as an index of the student's proficiency (for example, testing students' "writing ability" by asking them to choose the best-written of four sample passages)?

Are teachers prepared to help students acquire the required skills, and do they have the necessary resources?

Could students who do well on one test do well on a different sort of exam that presumably tests the same skill?

The New York test seems to do well on the first two criteria. No one doubts the importance of being able to write analytically about what one has read or to compose a personal essay. It is a significant advance to ask students to write freely, rather than simply to edit or critique a passage.

As for preparedness, however, legitimate questions have been raised about whether New York fourth graders have the background to fill in blank pages under timed conditions and whether teachers know how to prepare children from families that do not stress reading and writing.

This brings us to the fourth and most crucial question. Whenever a new exam is introduced, there is a temptation on the part of teachers to "teach the test." It might now seem far better to teach students how to write a personal essay than to ask them multiple-choice questions about a passage. Yet it is possible even with essay tests to teach students to do well through mimicry rather than through real writing skills.

Here's how this might work in New York. Teachers could instruct students that a personal essay must have three paragraphs, each with a different topic sentence; that the first paragraph must begin with an opinion; that the second paragraph must include two vivid images, and so on. Undoubtedly, fourth graders could learn to write such an essay.

But what would happen if they were then asked to write a letter or a response to a newspaper article? Would they do any better than children who hadn't been taught the essay-writing techniques? Educators and parents should value the development of knowledge and skills that go beyond a single test. High performance should be an incidental result of strong general preparation.

Soon most states, including New York, will be mandating so-called high-stakes tests in many subjects at several grade levels. We must proceed cautiously before we place students minds and hearts at risk with tests of dubious quality whose meaning can be over-interpreted and whose consequences can be devastating.

Yes we need rigorous academic standards, but we must also give youngsters models when it comes to developing the most crucial skills: love of learning, respect for peers and good citizenship. That is what they need most to pass the test of life.

(This piece was originally published in *New York Times*, 1998.)

5. Books, Experiences & Knowledge

Can We Trust Our Knowledge?

By Woods Lee

During the great golden age of philosophy, in the seventeenth and eighteenth centuries, problems about the nature of human knowledge divided philosophers into two schools; and despite changing idioms and increased understanding of the methods of science, the division to a large degree persists.

On the one hand, the empiricists, whose leading thinkers were John Locke, George Berkeley, and David Hume, held that all our ideas come from experience and that no proposition about any matter of fact can be known to be true independently of experience. On the other hand, the rationalists, whose most important representatives were Rene Descartes, Baruch Spinoza, and Gottfried Leibniz, maintained that there are "innate ideas," and that certain general propositions can be known to be true in advance of, or in the absence of, empirical verification.

In their competition, the empiricists seem to have gained an upper hand. After all, except our knowledge of the self in our heart and of the God in Paradise, hardly can we find adequately convincing evidence for any other knowledge based on the so-called innate ideas instead of experiences.

But even though all human knowledge comes really indeed from experiences, the true troublesome issue is: Is all this knowledge reliable?

One convenient proof for the reliability of sciences is that so many scientific laws have proved workable very well. In fact, we are using all these scientific laws any time and anywhere.

However, no matter how thoroughly we have tested a scientific law—better, let's say "hypothesis"—there is always the possibility that new evidence will show up to prove it false.

For instance, around the close of the nineteenth century, many physicists seemed virtually certain that Newtonian mechanics was absolutely correct. A wide variety of its consequences had been tested under many different circumstances, and Newton's laws stoop up extremely well. But early in the twentieth century it became clear that we now call "classical physics" would have to undergo major revisions, and a profound scientific revolution ensued. Modern physics, which included quantum mechanics and relativity theory, was the result. We can never be sure that any hypothesis we currently accept as correct will not have to be abandoned or modified at some time in the future as a result of new evidence.

"But sciences do have made many predictions, and most of which finally turn out to be accurate," someone might rebut.

For all we know now, nevertheless, every scientific prediction about future may go wrong. By this, we mean not merely that science is fallible, that it will sometimes err in its predictions, but also that nature (or the whole universe), as the object of all scientific researches, might at any moment (for all we can know) become irregular on such a wide scale that any kind of scientific prediction of future occurrences would be utterly impossible.

To some degree, it is somewhat unreasonable to demand all scientific predictions must be correct. The best we can hope for scientific conclusions is that they are probable.

But when we ask that they be probable, in this sense, we are only asking that they be based upon the best possible evidence. The scientist has fashioned his hypotheses in the light of all available information, and he has tested them experimentally on many occasions under a wide variety of circumstances. He has summoned all of the available evidence, and he has brought it to bear on the problem at hand. Such scientific predictions are obviously probable; hence, they are rationally credible.

Therefore, what sciences offer us is never certainty but probability, at varied degree of course. If so, what advantages do sciences have over such practices as astrology, crystal gazing, and blind guessing?

At this time, here come some philosophers, Karl Raimund Popper for example, who claim that prediction of the future is no part of the business of science. Accordingly, the function of scientific investigation is to find powerful general hypotheses that adequately explain all known facts that have occurred so far.

As long as such a generalization succeeds in explaining the new facts that come along, it is retained; if it fails to explain new facts, it must be modified or rejected. The sole purpose of scientific experimentation is to try to find weaknesses in such hypotheses—that is to criticize them or try to refute them.

Such a philosophy is telling us a cold idea: All scientific conclusions are potentially wrong.

In this case, should we still hold our belief in sciences and our knowledge?

6. Scientific Advancement vs. Human Society

Will Computers Be Smarter Than Human Mind ?

By Raymond Kurzweil

Computers today exceed human intelligence in a broad variety of intelligent yet narrow domains such as playing chess, diagnosing certain medical conditions, buying and selling stocks, and guiding cruise missiles. Yet human intelligence overall remains far more supple and flexible.

One reason for this disparity in capabilities is that our most advanced computers are still simpler than the human brain—currently about a million times simpler. But this disparity will not remain the case as we go through the early part of the next century.

Computers doubled in speed every three years at the beginning of the twentieth century, every two years in the 1950s and 1960s, and are now doubling in speed every twelve months. This trend will continue, with computers achieving the memory capacity and computing speed of the human brain by around the year 2020.

Achieving the basic complexity and capacity of the human brain will not automatically result in computers matching the flexibility of human intelligence. The organization and content of these resources—the software of intelligence—is equally important. One approach to emulating the brain's software is through reverse engineering—scanning a human brain (which will be achievable early in the next century) and essentially copying its neural circuitry in a neural computer (a computer designed to simulate a massive number of human neurons) of sufficient capacity.

Once a computer achieves a human level of intelligence, it will necessarily roar past it. Since their inception, computers have significantly exceeded human mental dexterity in their ability to remember and process information. A computer can remember billions or even trillions of facts perfectly, while we are hard pressed to remember a handful of phone numbers. A computer can quickly search a database with billions of records in fractions of a second. Computers can readily share their knowledge bases. The combination of human-level intelligence in a machine with a computer's inherent superiority in the speed, accuracy, and sharing ability of its memory will be formidable.

A common reaction to the proposition that computers will seriously compete with human intelligence is to dismiss this specter based primarily on an examination of contemporary capability. After all, when I interact with my personal computer, its intelligence seems limited and brittle, if it appears intelligent at all.

But the state of the art in computer technology is anything but static. Computer capabilities are emerging today that were considered impossible one or two decades ago. Examples include the ability to transcribe accurately normal continuous human speech, to understand and respond intelligently to natural language, to recognize patterns in medical procedures such as electrocardiograms and blood tests with an accuracy rivaling that of human physicians, and, of course, to play chess at a world-championship level. In the next decade, we will see translating telephones that provide real-time speech translation from one human language to another, intelligent computerized personal assistants that can converse and rapidly search and understand the world's knowledge bases, and a profusion of other machines with increasingly broad and flexible intelligence.

In the second decade of the next century, it will become increasingly difficult to draw any clear distinction between the capabilities of human and machine intelligence. The advantages of computer intelligence in terms of speed, accuracy, and capacity will be clear. The advantages of human intelligence, on the other hand, will become increasingly difficult to distinguish.

Also keep in mind that the progression of computer intelligence will sneak up on us. As just one example, consider Gary Kasparov's confidence in 1990 that a computer would never come close to defeating him. After all, he had played the best computers, and their chess-playing ability—compared to his—was pathetic. But computer chess playing made steady progress, gaining forty-five rating points each year. In 1997, a computer sailed past Kasparov, at least in chess.

Evolution has been seen as a billion-year drama that led inexorably to its grandest creation: human intelligence. The emergence in the early twenty-first century of a new form of intelligence on Earth that can compete with, and ultimately significantly exceed, human intelligence will be a development of greater importance than any of the events that have shaped human history. It will be no less important than the creation of the intelligence that created it, and will have profound implications for all aspects of human endeavor, including the nature of work, human learning, government, warfare, the arts, and our concept of ourselves.

This specter is not yet here. But with the emergence of computers that truly rival and exceed the human brain in complexity will come a corresponding ability of machines to understand and respond to abstractions and subtleties. Human beings appear to be complex in part because of our competing internal goals. Values and emotions represent goals that often conflict with each other, and are an unavoidable by-product of the levels of abstraction that we deal with as human beings. As computers achieve a comparable—and greater—level of complexity, and as they are increasingly derived at least in part from models of human intelligence, they, too, will necessarily utilize goals with implicit values and emotions, although not necessarily the same values and emotions that humans exhibit.

A variety of philosophical issues will emerge. Are computers thinking, or are they just calculating? Conversely, are human beings thinking, or are they just calculating? The human brain presumably follows the laws of physics, so it must be a machine, albeit a very complex one. Is there an inherent difference between human thinking and machine thinking? To pose the question another way, once computers are as complex as the human brain, and can match the human brain in subtlety and complexity of thought, are we to consider them conscious?

For example, if a person scans his brain through a noninvasive scanning technology of the twenty-first century (such as an advanced magnetic resonance imaging), and downloads his mind to his personal computer, is the "person" who emerges in the machine the same consciousness as the person who was scanned? That "person" may convincingly implore you that "he" grew up in Brooklyn, went to college in Massachusetts, walked into a scanner here, and woke up in the machine there. The original person who was scanned, on the other hand, will acknowledge that the person in the machine does indeed appear to share his history, knowledge, memory, and personality, but is otherwise an impostor, a different person.

Even if we limit our discussion to computers that are not directly derived from a particular human brain, they will increasingly appear to have their own personalities, evidencing reactions that we can only label as emotions and articulating their own goals and purposes. They will appear to have their own free will. They will claim to have spiritual experiences. And people—those still using carbon-based neurons or otherwise—will believe them.

One often reads predictions of the next several decades discussing a variety of demographic, economic, and political trends that largely ignore the revolutionary impact of machines with their own opinions and agendas. Yet we need to reflect on the implications of the gradual, yet inevitable, emergence of true competition to the full range of human thought in order to comprehend the world that lies ahead.

(The story was originally published in *The Age of Spiritual Machines*©, 1999.)

7. Technological Development vs. Humanity

A New Concept of Progress

By Ravi Batra

In common parlance, the term "progress" is associated with technical and scientific advancement, or anything which enhances the comforts of life. Humanity is said to have made tremendous progress today because life seems so much more comfortable these days than it was a few centuries ago.

People today can travel fast by automobile and airplanes, whereas only in the last century they were traveling by horse-drawn buggies and bullock carts. If we go back to ancient times, people had to travel on foot.

Thus progress is commonly understood as an increase in living comforts through scientific inventions, which have eased our lives not only physically but also intellectually. The invention of paper has helped spread the ideas of scholars. People can now engage their minds reading novels and other literature. Thus, scientific discoveries may be credited with tremendous advance that humanity has made in the physical and intellectual realm.

However, all this may not be progress.

To be sure, science has resulted in a great change in the mode of living, but most scientific discoveries have also created problems non-existent before. Faster travel today has increased the risk of accident; industrialization has resulted in environmental pollution and cancer and other diseases unheard of in the past; modern medicine quickly cures the malady but generates side-effects requiring further treatment. Even in the intellectual sphere, there is much available to keep the mind occupied, but people today suffer from emotional problems and neuroses that did not afflict them before.

Can you think of any invention, which while reducing life's boredom has not added to life's danger at the same time? If dishwashers wash our dishes, air conditioners cool our rooms, laundry machines clean our clothes, automobiles do our walking and so on, life certainly appears blissful relative to what our forefathers had to endure in a science-less world. But then they did not have to contend with electric shocks, fatal accidents, air, water, land and noise pollution, noxious automobile fumes, urban congestion, super-selfishness, crime and so on.

While the concept of progress in the material sphere is at best dubious, things are no better in the intellectual sphere.

People in ancient times were intellectually backward, but they did not suffer from emotional stress and neuroses. One who is less scholarly is also less prone to mental disturbances, whereas an intellectual is highly vulnerable in this regard. He creates unnecessary problems in his own web of imagination, and experiences sleepless nights. Hence in the intellectual sphere also progress is unlikely, if not impossible, because the feeling of increased pleasure is likely to be balanced by one of increasing pain.

The barometer of progress in the ultimate analysis must be mental pleasure that is really nothing but a mental vibration expressed through the relaxation of the nerves.

A person who has won an argument over another is usually very happy and sometimes delirious with joy. But after a while, he will experience a corresponding amount of pain in some other aspect of his mind. The reason is that human mind has a certain finite mass and volume. Purely intellectual study and analysis fail to enhance this mass; all they do is to increase the activity and play of ideas within a given intellectual arena. With a greater number of thoughts crisscrossing a given mental area, the result inevitably is an increased clash in the mind. Hence occur the mental breakdowns; hence the neuroses, hence the growing need for psychiatrists in intellectually developed societies.

Is then progress possible at all? The answer is yes.

Human existence has three aspects—physical, mental and spiritual. While the first two are not amenable to progress, the third is. Increased happiness in that sphere is not neutralized by increased misery.

While physical and intellectual activities deal with the limited, spirituality is concerned with the unlimited. Hence the goal in the spiritual arena is not the finite but the infinite. Therefore, the feeling of pleasure resulting from spiritual activity is not accompanied by pain, or happiness by misery.

This then is true progress.

In the spiritual experience there is no negative movement; every effort there is a forward march unaccompanied by any deleterious side-effect.

Spiritual activities include meditation and selfless living. Without providing help to the needy, the forward movement to the infinite is impossible.

And since the mind's goal is infinitude, the spiritual life results in an expansion in the volume as well as the mass of the mind. As a result, the mental conflict declines and the nerves get relaxation. The person becomes broad-minded. He or she seeks to serve others, to share in their pains. A community that respects the selfless beings and attempts to emulate them also then experiences increased happiness without corresponding pain.

That is when true progress occurs in the entire society. The degree of selflessness, therefore, is the true gauge of society's progress, not its material development, nor its intellectual attainment.

While real progress is unlikely in the material and mental sphere, human beings should by no means abandon scientific and intellectual pursuits. But scientific advances should be "spiritualized"; that is to say, they should be accompanied by spiritual practices at the same time. For such practices enable us to gain increasing mastery over our body and mind. All detrimental effects of scientific and intellectual developments on the human organism can thus be brought under control.

During the past century, thousands of remarkable inventions and new theories have almost totally transformed our way of life. But spiritually, we have stagnated and even moved backwards. Consequently, battles and wars have been deadlier in the current century than ever before. Rising greed, crime, drugs and environmental pollution threaten to overwhelm the delicate thread of life on our finite planet.

The moral is that change in the physical and mental spheres, without spiritual advance, is ultimately self-destructive.

(This article was first published in *New Renaissance Magazine*, Vol. 2 No. 1.)

8. Technological Advancement vs. Social Ethics

With Cloning of a Sheep, Ethical Ground Shifts

By Gina Kolata

When a scientist whose goal is to turn animals into drug factories announced on Saturday in Britain that his team had cloned a sheep, the last practical barrier in reproductive technology was breached, experts say, and with a speed that few if any scientists anticipated.

Now these experts say the public must come to grips with issues as grand as the possibility of making carbon copies of humans and as mundane, but important, as what will happen to the genetic diversity of livestock if breeders start to clone animals.

For starters, quipped Dr. Ursula Goodenough, a cell biologist at Washington University in St. Louis, with cloning, "there'd be no need for men."

But on a more serious note, Dr. Stanley Hauerwas, a divinity professor at Duke University, said that those who wanted to clone "are going to sell it with wonderful benefits" for medicine and animal husbandry. But he said he saw "a kind of drive behind this for us to be our own creators."

Dr. Kevin FitzGerald, a Jesuit priest and a geneticist at Loyola University in Maywood, Ill., cautioned that people might not understand clones. While a clone would be an identical, but much younger, twin of the adult, people are more than just the sum of their genes. A clone of a human being, he said, would have a different environment than the person whose DNA it carried and so would have to be a different person. It would even have to have a different soul, he added.

In an interview, Wilmut, a 52-year-old embryologist at the Roslin Institute in Edinburgh who led the epoch-making sheep-cloning, said he wanted to create new animals that could be used for medical research, and he dismissed the notion of cloning humans. "There is no reason in principle why you couldn't do it," he said. But he added, "All of us would find that offensive."

Yet others said that might be too glib. "It is so typical for scientists to say they are not thinking about the implications of their work," said Dr. Lee Silver, a biology professor at Princeton University. Perhaps, he added, "the only way they can validate what they are doing is to say they are just doing it in sheep."

Few experts think that sheep or other farm animals would be the only animals to be cloned. While cloning people is illegal in Britain and several other countries, John Robertson, a law professor at the University of Texas at Austin who studies reproductive rights and bioethics, said there were no laws against it in the United States.

If such a law was passed, Silver said, doctors could set up clinics elsewhere to offer cloning. "There's no way to stop it," Silver said. "Borders don't matter."

Dr. Ronald Munson, an ethicist at the University of Missouri at St. Louis, said the cloning itself was relatively simple. "This technology is not, in principle, controllable," he said. "It doesn't require the sort of vast machines that you need for atom-smashing. These are relatively standard labs. That's the amazing thing about all this biotechnology. It's fundamentally quite simple."

One immediate implication of cloning, Silver said, would be for genetic engineering:custom-tailoring genes. Currently, scientists are unable to take a gene and simply add it to cells. The process of adding genes is so inefficient that researchers typically have to add genes to a million cells to find one that takes them up and uses them properly. That makes it very difficult to add genes to an embryo—or a person—to correct a genetic disease or genetically enhance a person, Silver said. But now, "it all becomes feasible," he said.

After adding genes to cells in the laboratory, scientists could fish out the one cell in a million with the right changes and use it to clone an animal—or a person. "All of a sudden, genetic engineering is much, much easier," Silver said.

Wilmut is hoping that the genes for pharmacologically useful proteins could be added to sheep mammary cells and that the best cells could be used for cloning. The adult cloned sheep would produce the proteins in their milk, where they could be easily harvested.

Because cloning had been considered so far-fetched, scientists had discouraged ethicists from dwelling on its implications, said Dr. Daniel Callahan, a founder of the Hastings Center, one of the first ethics centers.

In the early 1970s, "there was an enormous amount of discussion about cloning,"Callahan said, and ethicists mulled over the frightening implications. But scientists dismissed these discussions as idle speculation about impossible things, Callahan recalled, and urged ethicists not to dwell on the topic.

"A lot of scientists got upset," Callahan said. "They said that this is exactly the sort of thing that brings science into bad repute and you people should stop talking about it."

In the meantime, however, cloning had captured the popular imagination. In his 1970 book, "Future Shock," Alvin Toffler speculated that "cloning would make it possible for people to see themselves anew, to fill the world with twins of themselves."

Woody Allen's 1973 movie "Sleeper" involved a futuristic world whose leader had left behind his nose for cloning purposes. Allen played a character charged with cloning to bring the leader back. A later movie, "The Boys From Brazil," released in 1978, involved a Nazi scheme to clone multiple Hitlers. That same year, a science writer, David Rorvik, published a book, "In His Image: The Cloning of a Man," that purported to be the true story of a wealthy man who had secretly had himself cloned but was found to be a hoax.

But gradually, the notion disappeared from sight, kept alive only in the animal husbandry industry, where companies saw a huge market for cloned animals and where the troubling ethical implications of cloning could be swept aside.

Now these questions are back to haunt ethicists and theologians.

Clones of animals, FitzGerald said, might sound appealing—scientists could clone the buttery Kobe beef cattle or the meatiest pigs, for example. But these cloned creatures would also share an identical susceptibly to disease, he cautioned. An entire cloned herd could be wiped out overnight if the right virus swept through it.

FitzGerald wondered if people would actually try to clone themselves. "Because we have all this technology and we have this ability," he said, "we can spin off these fantasies. But that doesn't mean we'd do it. It would be going against everything we desire for the human race."

Others are less sure. Robertson can envision times when cloning might be understandable. Take the case of a couple whose baby was dying and who wanted, literally, to replace the child. Robertson does not think that would be so reprehensible.

Cloning might also be attractive to infertile couples who want children and who "want to be sure that whatever offspring they have has good genes," Robertson said.

Of course, there are legal issues, Robertson said, like the issue of consent. "Would the person being cloned have an intellectual property right or basic human right to control their DNA?" he asked. If the person did, and consented to the cloning, would cloning be procreation, as it is now understood?

Robertson thinks not. After all, he said, "replication is not procreation."

(This piece was first published in *New York Times*, 1997.)

9. Personality vs. Behavior

What's Personality Got to Do With It?

By Carol Ritberger

People always want to learn more about themselves just as they do with the outside world. But first, take a quick glance at the following questions to see whether they usually pop up in you mind day by day even without your clear awareness of them.

1）Do you rely on your logic to make decisions, or do you make decisions because they feel right?

2）Do you prefer to stick with a daily routine rather than put yourself in unfamiliar situations?

3）Do you suppress your own feelings and tend to put other people's emotional needs before your own?

4）Do you find that you consistently answer a question with a question?

5）Do you seem to march to your own drummer and have a difficult time getting on the same wavelength with other people?

While you are unique in who you are, how you answered these questions tells much about your personality and why you do the things you do.

Many people think that personality is just something that we develop as a result of our experiences and conditioning. However it is really much, much more.

It is the very core of who you are, and its inherent neurological blueprint that determines the way you think, why you make the choices and decisions you do, and why you are attracted to some people and not to others.

When you think about your personality, think of it as your automatic pilot that guides the outward direction you will take in life and which helps you stay on course. As your automatic pilot, it monitors your progress and makes course adjustments whenever necessary so you do not find yourself in untenable situations. Your personality is what helps you function, survive and learn from your experiences. It is responsible for establishing the boundaries by which you live your life, and forms the expectations that you have of yourself and others.

When life compliments your boundaries, you feel in control, you move forward with a sense of confidence, you make choices that empower you, and your ability to cope with life's challenges is greatly enhanced. However, whenever you move outside of these personality boundaries you find yourself feeling compromised, immobilized by fear and doubt, your outlook on life becomes negative and you experience stress and distress on all levels: physically, emotionally, mentally and spiritually.

The Personality Color Connection

I am often asked, "Why do I use color to describe the different personality types?" I use it because color itself is non-threatening, and I have found that it is better to use neutral words to describe the differences in people rather than labeling them with words that are negative and offensive. Besides that, color is a universal language that we can all relate to, and one that we use to express how we are feeling. For example.. I am red with anger, or I am having a blue day, or I am green with envy.

There are four colors that I use to describe the four different personality types: Red, Orange, Yellow and Green. Each of these four colors has its own their own unique observable and predictable pattern of behavior which reveals the personality type long before a word is spoken. Here are the four different personality colors, and as I briefly describe each of these four colors, don't be surprised if you find yourself relating to one of them more than to the others.

The Red Personality

Reds are logical, practical and down-to-earth and do not display their emotions easily. They are conservative and traditional and would rather stay with what is tried and true rather than having to change. Reds are the backbone of society and believe that rules are important, and should be followed. Reds do not like surprises, so their lives tend to be very well organized and planned. Because of their high need for structure, they are controlling both of their environment and people, and are seen by others as being domineering. Reds are punctual and become irritated when other people waste their time. Reds are natural leaders and are driven by the need for power and control.

The Orange Personality

This emotionally driven personality needs to be liked and accepted. They are caregivers and emotional nurturers and tend to put the emotional needs of others before their own. They are worriers, and will worry about anything and everything, and in fact, many times may not even know what they are worrying about. Oranges are loyal, sensitive, considerate, polite and cooperative people and seek to create environments that are conflict free. They are team players and will not make a decision until they have discussed it with the people who will be affected by the outcome. Family and family activities are important to them and the quality of their relationships with others directly affects how they feel about themselves.

The Yellow Personality

Yellows are self-confident personalities who will challenge anything and everything: authority, rules, and established ways of thinking. Their primary purpose in life is to solve problems and find better ways of doing things. They are perpetually curious and who want to know how things work, understand why they don't work, and identify what needs to be done to make them work better. Yellows are conceptual deep thinkers. They enjoy getting lost in their heads as a way of exploring new ideas and looking for innovative ways to make a difference. They are the true visionaries who like to think out-of-the-box. Yellows will avoid relationships or situations that are emotionally complex or ones whose outcome is anything less than a win-win for all involved.

The Green Personality

Greens live in a world of intangibles where hopes, dreams and emotions are most important. They have rich, vivid imaginations and thrive in environments that encourage the use of their creative abilities and talents. This personality marches to its own drummer and finds it difficult to get on the same wavelength with any personality other than its own. Their greatest gift is their highly developed intuition which allows them to sense what others are feeling and to find the hidden meanings behind others actions and words. Greens love to learn about themselves and are always looking for ways that can help them better understand how to express their feelings and can teach them how to create relationships that are free of expectations and conditions.

Undoubtedly, the more you know your personality, the better you can steer your sail in life. Here are just a few of the benefits you will experience from learning more about who you are:

Discover your natural talents and personality strengths.

Make decisions based on your fulfilling your needs rather than the needs of others.

Create relationships that are mutually beneficial and emotionally satisfying.

Learn how to set healthy boundaries.

Express your needs, wants and desires in a way that others will hear them.

Harness the differences in people and turn them into positives rather than seeing them as negatives.

Turn your inner potential into an outer reality.

(This article is excerpted from the author's book *What Color is Your Personality*, Hay House, Inc., December 1999.)

10. Competition vs. Cooperation

Can Competition Bring in Fairness?

By Benjamin R. Tucker

The supposition that competition means war rests upon old notions and false phrases that have been long current, but are rapidly passing into the limbo of exploded fallacies.

Competition means war only when it is in some way restricted, either in scope or intensity, that is, when it is not perfectly free competition; for then its benefits are won by one class at the expense of another, instead of by all at the expense of nature's forces. When universal and unrestricted, competition means the most perfect peace and the truest cooperation; for then it becomes simply a test of forces resulting in their most advantageous utilization.

As soon as the demand for labor begins to exceed the supply, making it an easy matter for every one to get work at wages equal to his product, it is for the interest of all (including his immediate competitors) that the best man should win; which is another way of saying that, where freedom prevails, competition and cooperation are identical.

What the person who goes out into the work-a-day world will see there depends very much upon the power of his mental vision. If that is strong enough to enable him to see that the evils around him are caused by a prohibition of competition in certain directions, it is not unlikely that he will be filled with a "wish to foster competition". Such, however, will not be the case with a man who so misapprehends competition as to suppose that monopoly is its soul.

Instead of its soul, it is its antithesis. Whatever the reason for which men strive for wealth, as a general thing they get it, not by competition, but by the application of force to the suppression of certain kinds of competition, in other words, by governmental institution and protection of monopoly.

Inasmuch as the monopolist is the victor, it is true that to deny him the spoils of victory is to sheathe the sword of monopoly. But you do not thereby sheathe the sword of competition (if you insist on calling it a sword), because competition yields no spoils to the victor, but only wages to the laborer.

When my some people say that all monopolies are "resultants of a competition as free as nature could make it," he makes competition inclusive of the struggle between invasive forces, whereas he ought to know that free competition, in the economic sense of the phrase, implies the suppression of invasive forces, leaving a free field for the exercise of those that are non-invasive.

If a man were to declare that, when the benefits of labor cease to be won by one class at the expense of another and when they are shared by all at the expense of nature's forces, labor loses its raison d'etre and dies, his sanity would not long remain unquestioned; but the folly of such an utterance is not lessened an iota by the substitution of the word competition for the word labor. As long as the gastric juice continues to insist upon its rights, I fancy that neither labor nor competition will lack a raison d'etre, even though the laborer or competitor should find himself under the necessity of wresting his "spoils" from the bosom of his mother earth instead of from the pocket of his brother man.

In Mrs. Glass's recipe for cooking a hare, the first thing was to catch the hare. So in Mr. Horn's recipe for the solution of economic forms in ethical concepts, the first thing is to get the concepts. Now, the concepts of mutual confidence and good-fellowship are not to be obtained by preaching, otherwise the church militant would long ago have become the church triumphant; or, by force, otherwise progress would have gone hand in hand with authority instead of with liberty; but only by unrestricted freedom.

That is, by competition, the necessary condition of confidence, fellowship, and cooperation, which can never come as long as monopoly—the economic expression of hostility and mastership—continues to exist.

(This piece is excerpted from the book *Individual Liberty: Selections From the Writings of Benjamin R. Tucker*, Kraus Reprint Co., Millwood, NY, 1973.)

11. Idealism vs. Realism

Is Idealism Good for Society?

By Dave Pollard

My recent review of the 1929-1939 Great Depression opened my eyes to the dangers of idealism, which manifested itself in ideologies that aggravated and prolonged the misery of millions.

I grew up in the 1960s, and I saw idealism as a force for good—ending the War in Vietnam, opposing the neoconservative excesses, creating some community-based models for living, and making a living, that we would be wise to study closely as the world charges towards a series of complex crises that none of the prevailing political orthodoxies has the faintest idea how to cope with.

Not surprisingly, I became an idealist. Maybe I always was.

So idealism in the 1930s impeded desperately needed change, and helped prolong the Depression and propel the world into the global war; but idealism in the 1960s helped bring about needed change, and brought an end to the regime of a deranged ideologue (Nixon) and an end to war.

So, is idealism a good thing or a bad thing, in general and specifically in today's context?

Just to be clear, I'm referring to idealism in the common "dictionary" sense of thinking about and aspiring to achieve things in ideal terms, not the narrower meaning of the word in philosophic and religious taxonomy. In its extreme form, idealism becomes utopianism, a belief in striving for an impossibly perfect society, and a fierce, uncompromising, intolerant belief in a specific ideology or code of beliefs as superior to all others. Its opposite, depending on your point of view, is either pragmatism or realism. Pragmatism, a belief in incremental, practical, readily achievable change, has the advantages of often being consensus-driven and more easily achievable, but carries the risks of "end justifies the means" rationalization. Realism (again, referring to the term's use in common parlance not its technical meaning) is, of course, in the eyes of the beholder, and can serve as anything from a sturdy defense of the status quo ("you can't change it, it's been going on for ten thousand years") to an excuse for defeatism, resignation, even suicide.

A lot of the world's most inspiring and enlightening books are ideological—they imagine, and assert as possible, something "better" than what exists today. They stretch our minds and force us to challenge the myths of our current culture, the myths that, as long as everything appears to be going reasonable well, entrench us in our thinking, reinforce our narrow frames, make us like everybody else. Ideologies carry with them implicit moral codes of what is "right" and "good", how we humans should behave. They become our frames, the lenses through which we "see" the world and which make us (at least unless and until the next compelling ideology shatters that frame) blind to other ideologies. Even pragmatism (though not the end-justifies-the-means variety) can be viewed as an ideology—an ideology that is opposed to any "idealistic", "extreme" ideologies.

Are non-human creatures idealistic, ideological? My answer would be that they are not—not because they are not capable of such intellectualization (many creatures evidently have rich imaginations), but because they don't need them. If that's the case, why would the human species have evolved idealism? What need does idealism serve that it would be selected for in the evolution of our species? Wouldn't our society be more peaceful, more content, if we all thought the status quo ideal, or didn't think of ideals at all?

My theory is that idealism is a stress reaction, the intellectualization of an intuitive acknowledgement that something is very wrong and needs to be changed, much like the instinctive reactions of mice, when they find themselves in conditions of overcrowding, to hoard, to attack each other, to create hierarchy, and hence to reduce their numbers quickly to sustainable levels. If the status quo were "ideal", there would be no purpose for idealism. I would guess that at some point thirty thousand years ago, with much of the large game on which humans had lived a leisurely life suddenly extinct, and with the sudden onset of the final ten thousand year expansion of glaciation of the last ice age, life became something much less than ideal, and some people idealized a less vulnerable world of agriculture and settlement, and set about creating it. They did so, I would suggest, because they had to—there was no other choice except to perish.

We now live (despite the efforts to deny it by those at the top of the hierarchy that agriculture and settlement necessitated) in another time in which life is, and will certainly be for our children and grandchildren, once again much less than ideal. We now have some very limited knowledge that agriculture and settlement, and subsequent human innovations and technologies, each designed ideally to make life better and to solve immediate problems that had to be solved, have in fact created as many new problems to be solved as they have solved themselves. So we are now living in a complex human society with millions of ideologies, each "imagined" to direct us to solve perceived urgent and threatening problems. And because there are now so many of us living so closely together, these ideologies conflict violently with each other. We have devised political systems that allow us to vote, somewhat democratically, for the ideology that we think has the best chance of working, but these systems are increasingly breaking down as many grow impatient and overthrow or subvert the democratic vote in favor of their own personal, selfish ideology, or opt out of the process as they perceive their ideology to be unrepresented by any of the people at the top of the social hierarchy.

As we now see everywhere, idealization and ideology have ceased being evolutionary advantages that allow us to imagine and collectively institute adaptations that can improve our quality of life. As human society has grown larger and more complex, its adaptability has waned proportionately; and idealization and ideology are now mostly just wishful thinking and noise, imaginings that make us unhappy, angry, impatient, and ultimately violent yet offer no real hope of being realized.

This is why I believe there is such growing interest in rediscovering community, a "political" unit that is much smaller and less complex and hence more adaptable, where idealism is realizable and therefore still has value. Pioneers have always recognized this. The great challenge today is that there is no place left to go where our large, massively complex and dysfunctional global political cultures do not hold sway. We can run but we cannot hide.

John Gray is an idealist who essentially espouses reducing the degree to which idealism and ideology drive our actions and behaviors. He argues that it is too late to achieve idealistic changes in our society—human society is now too vast, interdependent and complex to be "saved", and we will have to leave it up to nature to correct our excesses. Despite this belief, or perhaps because of it, he urges us to refocus our lives on things we can "realistically" change: Our own impact on the Earth and on our communities, physical and virtual, and our own awareness and understanding of joy in and belonging to these communities. He suggests we do this for our own sake and for the sake of those we love and care about, rather than because he thinks this will spread virally to create a new and enlightened human consciousness. Our role, he is saying, is simply to be models, for those around enough to learn from and be inspired by, and to be aware of and happy with life's astonishing joys. This does not mean denying our ideals, but rather putting them in their place, and not being consumed by them.

I was ready to realize this and, while I am still and will always be an idealist (we are what we are) I am trying to learn to inflict my idealism less on others and on myself; and instead be real, do what I can, and what I love, and what makes a difference in important small ways. I want to be a model, not a preacher.

Our only choice, ultimately, is the choice between which of the three masters to follow: (1) The organisms that make up our bodies, which make most decisions on "our" behalf for us, and which evolved our minds for their collective well-being; (2) Our culture and society, which is trying to make us sacrifice ourselves for the benefit of all the human mice in this horrifically overcrowded and violence-ridden laboratory; and (3) Gaia, the Earth-organism that is quietly telling us what our place is as part of all life on Earth, and how to behave accordingly. We have no choice but to obey the first master, and we are brought up to follow and even lay down our lives for the second, where our idealism holds sway. There are those who believe, of course, that Gaia, a life-world self-organized for its own collective benefit, is also an ideal and an ideological construct. There is no arguing with such people, since their argument is circular and hermetically sealed inside their own frame of understanding. I don't believe Gaia is an ideal or ideology, any more than the Earth revolving around the sun (once such a heretical idea, so threatening to prevailing ideology, that merely espousing it could get you killed) is. Gaia simply is. You can observe it at work, and see how it makes sense, and made sense for billions of years before we arrived on the planet, and will make sense long after we're gone. It is an adaptation that works.

I also don't believe that following Gaia is spiritual—she (I use the female term endearingly and metaphorically) meets none of the definitions of spiritualism: she is not immaterial (on the contrary!), she is not deific or supernatural (merely natural), she is not religious (tied to a single set of values, though she does not even care about values) or even sacred (in the sense of demanding worship or idolizing). She is physical. She is connected and connecting. She is all of us, all of life on Earth. She just is. When the sun goes nova and obliterates all life on Earth, she will be no more.

I choose to follow Gaia, the third master, because I no longer believe the second master works or can be made to work. It is broken beyond repair. And Gaia is different from the other two masters in that she does not make demands of us, all she asks of us is that we pay attention, listen, and learn. And if we don't, she will cut us a lot of slack in our youthful folly, and only correct our excesses when it is the consensus of all the life on Earth that it is time to do so.

No idealist, she.

(Readers can find the original of the piece, slightly altered in editing, at http://howtosavetheworld.
ca/2006/05/18/is-idealism-good-for-society/)

12. Economic Development vs. Environmental Proverty

Environment Degradation and Poverty

While international environmental concerns are often expressed in broad terms such a desertification or climatic change, the environmental problems of concern to vulnerable groups in marginal areas are generally quite localized in nature, revolving around immediate issues, such as the degradation of a particular rangeland or soil erosion on farmland or the progressive shortening of fallow.

These affect the poor because they are directly related to household food security.

Degradation of the resource base generally translates into decreases in production or income and thus in the availability of food. Declining soil fertility leads to lower crop yields while rangeland depletion reduces plantation harvest, and any deterioration in water quality adversely affects the fish catch.

Degradation of common property resources pulls labor away from directly productive activities towards gathering—simply collecting non-wood and minor forest products—and probably diminishes opportunities for deriving income from this source.

Linkages with food security can also be less direct. Shortages of biomass may result in a transition to lower-nutrition foods that require less fuel for cooking.

In addition, recurrent drought or natural calamities also directly result in progressive loss of food security prospects.

In their quest for food security, the rural poor have sometimes little choice but to overuse the limited resources available to them. The resulting environmental degradation imposes further constraints on their livelihood in what has been called a "downward spiral" or "vicious circle."

They are often forced to make trade-offs between immediate household food requirements and environmental sustainability both in production and consumption.

Their negligible man-made capital assets, ill-defined or non-existent property rights, limited access to financial services and other markets, inadequate safety nets in time of stress or disaster, and lack of participation in decision-making can result in their adopting "short time horizons," which favor immediate imperatives over longer-term objectives.

This can result in coping strategies that rely on the drawing down of the capital available to them—mainly in the form of natural resources. It also makes them more vulnerable to environmental degradation, including degradation wrought by others than the poor themselves.

The poor may be both agents and victims of environmental degradation, especially in marginal areas, where the resource base is ill-suited to agriculture.

But it cannot be assumed that the poor have an intrinsic propensity to degrade environmental resources. On the contrary, many poor traditional communities demonstrate an admirable environmental ethic and have developed complex resource management regimes. There is little evidence that the rural poor, when offered an appropriate environment—including secure tenure and access to markets—pursue resource-degrading strategies.

Thus, while poverty may be an underlying cause of environmental degradation, it is more accurately seen as a proximate cause influenced by a complex of policy and institutional factors. The very same processes that lead to and perpetuate poverty constrain the poor in their decision-making with regard to natural resource management.

Affluence and poverty affect the environment in different ways: poverty eradication would not erase environmental degradation but change the nature of environmental problems facing society.

(This piece is excerpted from the *Rural Poverty Report 2001* issued by the International Fund for Agricultural Development, an agency of the United Nations.)

13. School Education us. Family Education

Six Types of School-Family-Community Involvement

By Forest Tsui

Research indicates that family involvement in schools increases student achievement (Henderson& Berla, 1994; Ballen & Moles, 1994; Epstein, 1995). The benefits of parent and family involvement include higher test scores and grades, better attendance, more completion of homework, more positive attitudes and behavior, higher graduation rates, and greater enrollment in higher education.

A literature review of school-family partnerships indicates that benefits are apparent not only for younger children but all students through high school. Although parent involvement typically is strongest at the primary level, continued involvement through the middle grades and at the secondary school level is important in encouraging and guiding children's development and achievement.

When schools regard their relationship with families as a partnership in which school and home share responsibility for children's learning, the result is an increase in the levels and types of parent involvement as well as the support that families demonstrate for the school. When this partnership is extended to include the larger community, the benefits are greater yet. Perhaps most important is that when responsibility for children's learning is shared by the school, home, and community, children have more opportunities for meaningful, engaged learning. Students are able to see the connection between the curriculum in the school and the skills that are required in the real world.

According to a survey by the U. S. Department of Education in 2001, 92% of nation-wide educators identified strengthening family members' roles in student learning as an issue that should receive the highest priority for public education policy.

A Gallup Poll in 1997 also shows that the amount of parent involvement is the number one factor people cited as the reason why some schools are better than others.

Experts in school-family partnership think there are at least six important types of cooperation between families, schools, and other community organizations.

They include：

Parenting

Families must provide for the health and safety of children, and maintain a home environment that encourages learning and good behavior in school. Schools provide training and information to help families understand their children's development and how to support the changes they undergo.

Communicating

Schools must reach out to families with information about school programs and student progress. This includes the traditional phone calls, report cards, and parent conferences, as well as new information on topics such as school choice and making the transition from elementary school to higher grades. Communication must be in forms that families find understandable and useful, for example, schools can use translators to reach parents who don't speak English well and it must be two-way, with educators paying attention to the concerns and needs of families.

Volunteering

Parents can make significant contributions to the environment and functions of a school. Schools can get the most out of this process by creating flexible schedules, so more parents can participate, and by working to match the talents and interests of parents to the needs of students, teachers, and administrators.

Learning at home

With the guidance and support of teachers, family members can supervise and assist their children at home with homework assignments and other school-related activities.

Decision-making

Schools can give parents meaningful roles in the school decision-making process, and provide parents with training and information so they can make the most of those opportunities. This opportunity should be open to all segments of the community, not just people who have the most time and energy to spend on school affairs.

Collaboration with community

Schools can help families gain access to support services offered by other agencies, such as healthcare, cultural events, tutoring services, and after-school child-care programs. They also can help families and community groups provide services to the community, such as recycling programs and food pantries.

14. Man vs. Morality

Why Be Moral?

By Joel Feinberg

Of all human ethical issues, this is "the ultimate question": "Why should I do what morality requires if can better serve my own interests otherwise?"

This is a question that arises naturally, if not frequently, in everyone's experience.

Suppose you find a wallet containing $ 5,000 in cash. Surely the morally right thing to do (at least according to the prevailing moral code) would be to return the wallet with the money to its owner. But would this truly be the most reasonable course of action?

Think of what you have to gain: an expression of gratitude, some small satisfaction at having done your duty (mixed with nagging doubts that you are a fool), and maybe a small reward. Now compare these benefits with what you have to lose—namely, the $ 5,000 itself. It would seem that the losses involved in doing your "duty" (if that's what it is) far outweigh the gains. (Perhaps the example might be still more convincing if the money belonged not to a private person but to a great corporation or the federal government.)

Looking at the matter in this way, wouldn't you be a fool to return the money? Isn't it unreasonable, indeed profoundly, contrary to reason, voluntarily to choose a loss in preference to a gain for oneself? And yet this is what morality seems continually to require of us: that we put the interests of other people ahead of our own.

How, then, can it be reasonable to be moral?

One line of reply to this challenge immediately suggests itself. Not to return the property of others is tantamount to stealing it. If other people were ever to find out that you are, in effect, a thief, their opinion of you would drop drastically and your reputation might never fully recover. Moreover, if the authorities were to make this discovery about you, the consequences might be still worse. Even if no one ever found you out, you might become just a bit bolder in the face of subsequent temptations, until your very success finally would betray you, and you would be found out. The idea that it can ever pay to do what morally wrong, in short, is always a miscalculation.

Glaucon and Adeimantus, two characters in Plato's *Republic*, are not satisfied with this kind of answer.

That there are advantages in having the reputation of being moral and upright (or "just" as you put it) is perfectly evident; what they wish to learn from Socrates is whether there are corresponding advantages in really being, as opposed to merely seeming, morally upright. If it is reasonable to be honest only because dishonesty doesn't pay, then, it would seem, it is reasonable to be honest only when dishonesty doesn't pay; the ideally wise man would then be he who is able to have the "best of both worlds" by seeming, but not really being, moral.

Socrates' answer to the challenge of Glaucon and Adeimantus is long and detailed. He stresses that **the elements of unjust man's soul are necessarily discordant just as the elements of a sick man's body are out harmony; so the question whether injustice can ever pay is as "ridiculous" as the question whether it can be more conducive to happiness to be sick than to be healthy.**

So, at least in Socrates' eyes, there is a necessary and invariant connection between duty and self-interest. Many other great moralists have also found unthinkable the notion that a person ever truly profits in the long run from being immoral.

Whatever else morality may be, these writers argue, it must be something reasonable. And surely, they go on, it cannot be reasonable for a person deliberately to act contrary to his or her own interest.

Hence, it follows that the dictates of morality (assumed to be reasonable) never require sacrifice of self-interest. Some critics of this tradition have suggested that the main reason why it has seemed unreasonable for a person act contrary to his or her won interest is the assumption that normal people are incapable of so acting, and that traditional moral philosophers, Socrates included, have tacitly assumed that truth of psychological egoism.

But if people can be motivated to do their duties for duty's sake, quite apart from calculations of self-interest, as Immanuel Kant argued, then the question "Why be moral?" does not arise in its usual form.

Therefore, we seems to be able to conclude that, a person's commitment to the supremacy of morality over self-interest (or the opposite) is "beyond reason, neither rational nor irrational," and yet is of the very most fundamental significance, amounting in effect to the decision to "be a certain sort of person."

In this sense, the ultimate question (as the existentialists might have put it) is whether one can "authentically"—that is in a manner true to oneself—choose to have one sort of character rather than the other.

In one word, morality is in the end an issue of self-option.

(This slightly edited piece is excerpted from *Reason & Responsibility* edited by Joel Feinberg, 6th edition, Wadsworth Publishing Co., Belmont California, 1985).

参考书目

谷约.妙手著文章.北京：世界知识出版社，1999

汪福祥.英语写作技巧新编.北京：外文出版社，1997

Joel Feinberg. 1985. Reason and responsibility. California: Wadsworth Publishing Company

John Chaffee, Christine Mcmahon and Barbara Stout. 2002. Critical thinking and thoughtful writing: a rhetoric with reading. Indianapolis: Houghton Mifflin Company

Larry W. Burton, Daniel McDonald. 2001. The language of argument. 10th ed. Pearson Longman

后 记

当我在键盘上敲进本书最后一个字符的时候，连续数月奋战带来的身心疲惫在刹那间全都消失了。掠过心头的，是一丝欣慰。

现在，那些欧美发达国家正为所谓的后现代社会问题而挠头，而我们却还在思考着怎样才能更快而平稳地进入现代化社会，这就是差距。

而今天正在为游学西方拼搏的人们就是搭建在这段差距之上的钢轨和枕木。借助他们，中国也许能更顺利地跃过现代化进程中的坎坷和鸿沟。

实际上，国人东渡扶桑、负笈欧美的冲动与这个国家曲折的近代化和现代化的进程是相伴始终的。甚至可以说，正是前者推动了后者。从19世纪上半叶至今，这个过程绵延不断，已逾百年。这也许就是文化的薪火传承；这也许就是一个古老文明不屈的努力吧。

在此，我要向所有为振兴中国而努力拼搏的人们表示敬意。为自己能够给他们提供些微帮助而感到的欣悦，看来也不算过分。最有资格对本书的质量作出评价的，当然是读者。我的电子信箱是：forestlandll@yahoo.com.cn。来信虽然未必一一回复，但必当恭敬拜读。

平日里，参加GMAT的考生时常问我该怎样复习和准备GMAT中的作文（Analytical Writing Assessment）。当时，我多半是语焉不详。现在问题简单了：在我专门为GMAT写作而撰写的参考书出版之前，现在这本书就是不错的备考资料。GMAT写作同样包括ISSUE写作和ARGUMENT写作两项任务。除了各自的作文题库不同外，GRE写作和GMAT写作完全可以按照相同的路数来准备。因此，本书的理论部分完全适用于GMAT写作的复习和准备。

从某种意义上讲，生命的唯一价值就在于对希望的追寻。

祝愿所有为希望而奔波的人们，一路走好。

李建林

2004年3月5日于北京竹茗园

再版后记

两个纪念日使2011年注定成为不凡之年——辛亥革命100周年和中国共产党成立90周年。

无论从什么维度来看，这两件事都堪称大事件。它们结束了中国巍巍乎两千余年封建王朝的历史，也改写了整个中华民族命运的轨迹。尽管直到今天，学界对于辛亥革命的意义仍有持续的探讨，但如果从国人外争民族独立与解放、内求宪政与民主共和的角度来看，这两起事件所承载的历史使命其实是一脉相承的。

而且，观察这种历史承继性还有一个有趣的角度，这就是中国的海外留学生在其间所发挥的巨大影响与作用。

国人纪念辛亥革命100周年，当然要缅怀伟大的民主主义革命先行者孙中山先生。中山先生最早用来汇聚革命志士的政党则是同盟会。正是在这个组织里，跃动着一大批海外学子的身影。史载，在同盟会成立之初的1905年和1906年，共有963人参加该组织，其中863人是游学日本的中国留学生，所占比例近90%。而在1911年4月27日那场被称为辛亥革命预演的广州黄花岗起义中，原本温文尔雅的旅日学生慷慨赴死、奋力冲杀。在倒下的黄花岗七十二烈士中，留日学生就有八名。如此牺牲令中山先生痛心不已，扼腕感喟"吾党精华，付之一炬"！

十年后，在浙江嘉兴南湖的游船上的13位中共一大代表中，有8人皆是归国留学生，占六成多。而中共创始人陈独秀和李大钊（二人均未赴会）早年也都曾留学日本。

如果从1847年19岁的容闳赴美求学算起，国人越洋游学的历史已有164年，恰与中国的近现代史同步。起初每年不过几十上百人，且多是官派；到后来，自费游学者渐多。1894—1895甲午海战的惨败强烈刺痛了国人，东瀛遂成学习的样板，然后有了留日高潮。在20世纪头十年中，留日学生总数达5万人以上。正是这些人成了同盟会及后来的辛亥革命的先锋和中坚。

实际上，自1840年鸦片战争以来，中国所发生的历次重大历史变革都少不了留学生的影响、参与和领导。从这个意义上讲，整个中国近现代史完全可由期间国人的海外留学史来演绎。

而始于上世纪90年代并绵延至今的新一代留学潮却将国人的海外游学推到前所未有的规模。

从1872到1978的百余年间，国人游学海外者总计约13万；及至2007年，这一数字已达121万；而如今的中国留学海外者的数量仍然每年都在增长。

回首国人百年留学史，紧随每一次大规模的海外求学潮的，都是一次次深刻的社会变革。海涛翻滚，风云际会，下一个中国大变革何时到来？又会以怎样的形式？带来什么样的结果呢？

历史不能假设，也无法猜测。唯有拭目以待！

是为本次修订版之后记。

李建林
2011年5月于北京通州寓所